Books by Walter Johnson

THE BATTLE AGAINST ISOLATION

WILLIAM ALLEN WHITE'S AMERICA

THE UNITED STATES: EXPERIMENT IN DEMOCRACY
(with Avery Craven)

HOW WE DRAFTED ADLAI STEVENSON

1600 PENNSYLVANIA AVENUE: PRESIDENTS AND THE PEOPLE, 1929–1959

THE FULBRIGHT PROGRAM: A HISTORY
(with Francis J. Colligan)

Edited by Walter Johnson

SELECTED LETTERS OF WILLIAM ALLEN WHITE

ROOSEVELT AND THE RUSSIANS: THE YALTA CONFERENCE
By Edward R. Stettinius, Jr.

TURBULENT ERA: A DIPLOMATIC RECORD OF FORTY YEARS, 1904–1945
By Joseph C. Grew

THE PAPERS OF ADLAI E. STEVENSON
Volume I: Beginnings of Education, 1900–1941
Volume II: Washington to Springfield, 1941–1948
Volume III: Governor of Illinois, 1949–1953
Volume IV: "Let's Talk Sense to the American People," 1952–1955
Volume V: Visit to Asia, the Middle East, and Europe — March–August 1953
Volume VI: Toward a New America, 1955–1957

The Papers of Adlai E. Stevenson

The Papers of

Adlai E. Stevenson

VOLUME VI

Toward a New America

1955-1957

LITTLE, BROWN and COMPANY · Boston · Toronto

FIRST EDITION

T 04/76

The editors gratefully acknowledge the permission of the following authors, publishers, individuals, and institutions to reprint selected materials as noted:

Archibald S. Alexander, Frank Altschul, Eugenie Anderson, Mary Anderson,
Warwick Anderson, Wayne N. Aspinall, The Associated Press, Brooks Atkinson,
Lauren Bacall, Mary Bancroft, Clarence A. Berdahl, Richard Bolling, Stimson Bullitt,
Everett Case, CBS News, the *Chicago Sun-Times, The Christian Century,* Benjamin
V. Cohen, Grace Shepard Coleman, Alistair Cooke, Norman Cousins, Mary Creighton,
Jonathan Daniels, Kenneth S. Davis, Edison Warner Dick, Charles C. Diggs, Jr.,
Irving Dilliard, Doubleday & Company, Inc., Melvyn and Helen Gahagan Douglas,
James E. Doyle, Roxane Eberlein, James T. Farrell, Lloyd K. Garrison, Harry D.
Gideonse, Richard P. Graebel, Herb Graffis, Leon Green, Harper & Row, Seymour
Harris, Brooks Hays, John Hersey, Mary Hochschild, John Horne, Kermit Hunter,
Homer A. Jack, Gerald W. Johnson, Barry D. Karl, George F. Kennan, Jean Kerr,
Ernst Krenek, The Laymen's League, *Life* magazine, Ada MacLeish, Macmillan Pub-
lishing Company, Inc., T. S. Matthews, Earl Mazo, Michael Monroney, Wayne Morse,
The New Republic, the *New York Times,* Louis Nizer, William O'Brian, H. Talbot
Pearson, James Reston, Tommy Reston, Harriet Welling Richards, James Rowe,
Harrison E. Salisbury, Dore Schary, Arthur Schlesinger, Jr., Eric Sevareid, Adele
Dunlap Smith, John Sparkman, Speech Communication Association, Leland Stowe,
Syracuse University Press, Niccolo Tucci, University of Iowa Libraries, University of
Tennessee Library, Jacob J. Weinstein, Theodore White, G. Mennen Williams, Paul
Ziffren, for all items from their publications and writings as detailed in the footnotes.

Cowles Communications, Inc., for permission to reprint the article "Why I Raised the
H-Bomb Question" by Adlai E. Stevenson from *Look* magazine, Volume 21, number 3,
February 5, 1957. Copyright © 1957 by Cowles Magazines, Inc.

Harper & Row, Publishers, for selections from *The New America* by Adlai E.
Stevenson. Copyright © 1957 by Adlai Ewing Stevenson.

Library of Congress Cataloging in Publication Data

Stevenson, Adlai Ewing, 1900-1965.
    The papers of Adlai E. Stevenson.

    Includes bibliographical references.
    CONTENTS: v. 1. Beginnings of education, 1900-1941.
—v. 2. Washington to Springfield, 1941-1948.—
v. 3. Governor of Illinois, 1949-1953. [etc.]
    1. United States—Politics and government—20th
century—Collected works 2. Stevenson, Adlai Ewing,
1900-1965, I. Johnson, Walter, 1915-   ed.
E742.5.S747   973.921'092'4   73-175478
ISBN 0-316-46731-6   (v. 6)

*Published simultaneously in Canada
by Little, Brown & Company (Canada) Limited*

PRINTED IN THE UNITED STATES OF AMERICA

Foreword

After reading the typewritten manuscript of Kenneth S. Davis, *A Prophet in His Own Country: The Triumphs and Defeats of Adlai E. Stevenson,* Stevenson wrote Davis on March 19, 1957, "While I think the book brings it out, the essence of the campaign of '56 was *Truth* — as I saw it. We owe the people the truth about their affairs or they can't make intelligent decisions; and the Reps [Republicans] have not told them the truth, the whole truth, rather they have lulled them to sleep etc. etc."[1]

The central issue of the 1956 campaign, Stevenson explained in a speech at Harrisburg, Pennsylvania, on September 13, 1956, was

> whether America wants to stay on dead center, mired in complacency and cynicism; or whether it wants once more now to move forward — to meet our human needs, to make our abundance serve all of us and to make the world safer — in short, to build a New America.
>
> The Republicans pose the issues of this campaign in terms of slogans — "peace, prosperity, progress."
>
> I pose these issues in terms of facts — the grim facts of America's unmet human needs, the facts of a revolutionary world in the hydrogen age.
>
> Here are some facts:
>
> In four years — four years of wealth and abundance — our government has let the shortage of schoolrooms and teachers get worse.

[1] This handwritten letter is in the possession of Mr. Davis. Stevenson also made many comments in the margins of the manuscript itself, but this has unfortunately been destroyed.

[*vii*]

It has done almost nothing to stop the slum cancer which today infects 10 million American dwellings. And juvenile delinquency, which breeds in slums and poor schools, has increased at a frightening rate.

We have done nothing to help the lot of the poor and of our older people, most of whom must now subsist in a penury that gets worse as the cost of living climbs to the highest point in our history.

We have done precious little to aid the fight against cancer, arthritis, mental disease and other crippling and killing diseases, or to make up the shortage of doctors and nurses.

We have watched higher costs and lower prices close on the hapless, helpless farmer whose only offense is that he has done his job too well.

And the small businessman is now backed to the wall.

Instead of turning our natural resources — our rivers, lands and forests — to the public good, we have seen them raided for private profit.

And the facts of our progress toward peace are even more sobering. The Soviets have advanced, while we have fallen back, not only in the competition for strength of arms, but even in the education of engineers and scientists. Millions of people have moved more toward the false promises of Communism than the true faith in freedom. And today there is doubt in the world about whether America really believes in the freedom which is our birthright and the peace which is our greatest hope.[2]

Throughout his campaign, Stevenson warned that complacency contained the seeds of decay, not of growth. And he added that complacency was "at war with our national genius."[3] He also warned that the New America "is not made up of small decisions."[4]

In May, 1957, Stevenson wrote in his "Author's Note" to the volume of his 1956 speeches and program papers:

These issues did not die with the 1956 election. On the contrary, today they are more alive than ever, and sooner or later the American people and their leaders will have to come to grips with them. For each of these issues demands a decision.

These decisions can be delayed a little but they cannot be evaded forever. The issues were not born of a political campaign — they grew out of the changing character of our own country, and the even more rapid changes in the world beyond our borders. They are the facts of life of the new America.

[2] Adlai E. Stevenson, *The New America*, edited by Seymour E. Harris, John Bartlow Martin, and Arthur Schlesinger, Jr. (New York: Harper, 1957), p. 11.
[3] Ibid., p. 228.
[4] Ibid., p. 150.

One of my keenest disappointments in the 1956 campaign was its failure to evoke any real debate of issues. In the climate of opinion which then prevailed, it was easy — and politically astute — for my opponents to brush them aside. Yet the illumination of problems, needs and dangers, and alternatives for dealing with them are the very purpose of a campaign, especially for the Presidency.[5]

In an interview on June 26, 1956, Stevenson was asked: "What is the basic purpose of most of your speeches — to win votes, to inform, to stimulate the intellect?"

He replied: "To win votes is first, of course; that's the object of most political speaking. But how do you do that? You can win votes through demagogy, but that is intolerable and should never be resorted to. You can win votes by appealing to passions, and that may work some of the time, but it never succeeds in the long run, and the people who resort to such means soon find that out. Then there are appeals to self-interest; these are not necessarily demagogy — appeals to fear, lust, cupidity, self-interest. The best way to win votes, though, is through reason — facts and reason will bring people around. People are educable on the issues; you can, I believe, induce conviction by reason. If I didn't believe that I couldn't believe in the democratic process. So my basic purpose is to inform."

In the same interview he was asked: "Why do your speeches mean so much to you? Why do you spend so much time on them?"

He replied: "For two reasons. You owe it to the people to communicate as well as you can, if you are to fulfill your responsibility to democracy. I think a candidate should work on his own speeches because that is the best way to acquire the information and understanding of the issues of the campaign; it is a learning, synthesizing process. Second is the personal satisfaction I derive from working on a speech. Now the price may be too high; that's what I'm told. Some people think that I sacrifice too much time which ought to be devoted to public relations, to seeing people, meeting and talking with them. I'm not sure these days that what a candidate says in his speeches determines how the election goes to any large degree. There are too many other factors that intervene."[6]

In his attempt to fulfill his responsibility to a democratic society, Stevenson raised issues which the Eisenhower Administration either ignored or handled in an inadequate manner. He advocated the suspension of nuclear testing in the atmosphere, reduction of tensions with the

[5] Ibid., p. xi.

[6] Interview with Stevenson by Russel Windes, Jr., and James A. Robinson. See their article, "Public Address in the Career of Adlai E. Stevenson," *Quarterly Journal of Speech,* Vol. XLII, No. 3 (October, 1956), pp. 225–233.

Soviet Union, the end of the draft, increased assistance to underdeveloped societies through the United Nations in order to remove economic development from the Cold War, substantial federal assistance to education and to the poor; and he stressed the need to eliminate the slums. He spoke of the pressing necessity of improved race relations, of the desirability of increased medical service to the public, of the obligation to provide additional assistance to the aged; and he decried the destruction of natural resources for private profit. He was the first presidential candidate to raise the issue of the quality of life in America.[7] And he challenged Americans to demonstrate by deeds that they actually believed in freedom.

He told the American Society of Newspaper Editors on April 21, 1956:

> We have drifted and stumbled long enough. It is time to restore the true image of America, once so well known and well loved, which gave birth to the Declaration of Independence and the Four Freedoms — a nation marked, not by smugness, but by generosity; not by meanness, but by magnanimity; not by stale conservatism and a weary reliance on dollars and arms, but by broad vision and moral and social passion.
>
> It is time to regain the initiative; to release the warm, creative energies of this mighty land; it is time to resume the onward progress of mankind in pursuit of peace and freedom.

During and after the 1956 campaign, Stevenson was dismayed at the failure of most newspapers and radio and television commentators to probe in any significant depth the challenging issues facing American life. They did not help, he believed, to illuminate the problems confronting a democratic society. Instead, they contributed to the already dangerous complacency permeating American society.

Nor, in his opinion, had the congressional leadership of the Democratic party assisted in clarifying the issues of the 1950's. In control of both houses of Congress in 1955 and 1956, this leadership had not furnished the national Democratic party with a substantial record of achievement. Instead, that leadership had followed a policy of collaboration with the Eisenhower Administration. After his defeat in 1956, Stevenson became a prime force in the founding and the activities of the Democratic Advisory Council. With the establishment of the council, the national party had an effective instrument to issue policy statements unparalleled for a party out of power in the executive branch of government.

[7] See Arthur Schlesinger, Jr., "Adlai E. Stevenson," an essay accompanying the Arnold Michaelis recording *Adlai,* Columbia Record D-25-793 (1968).

Stevenson announced at the first meeting of the Democratic Advisory Council on January 3, 1957, that it was the purpose of the council "to advance Democratic programs and principles throughout the country." He observed from his own experience: "We can't be an effective opposition party just every four years for a couple of months." And he stated: "The Democratic party is not just a Congressional party, it is a National Party. Opposed as it is by the great publicity resources of the government, by most of the press and the money of the country, it needs all the vitality, interest and energy it can mobilize."

In this volume — as in the previous volumes of *The Papers of Adlai E. Stevenson* — Stevenson's own words are presented in letters, postcards, press conferences, and speeches. These volumes are a documentary biography of Adlai E. Stevenson and, at the same time, a documentary history in his own words of the extraordinary, and often bewildering, changes that remolded the United States and the world during his lifetime from 1900 to 1965.

In selecting the materials from Stevenson's papers to be published in these volumes, the editors decided to emphasize the documents that helped answer such questions as: How did he educate himself? How did he become the man he became? What were the key influences in his life? How did he understand his times? How did he articulate the problems of his times?

Because of the large volume of mail Stevenson received it was impossible for him to acknowledge or properly respond to it without the help of his secretaries and law partners. Stevenson authorized them to draft letters over his name, to be signed by his personal secretary, Carol Evans, without going over his desk. Phyllis Gustafson signed when Miss Evans was absent. Although he dictated and signed an impressive number of letters himself, he once told Carol Evans that he did not think his signature was important or added anything to a letter. Letters of great importance frequently went first to one of his law partners, depending on the nature of the matter, and were brought by them to Stevenson's attention.

When letters were written over Stevenson's name by an aide, the author's initials with those of his secretary were typed in the left-hand margin of the carbon copy for identification. For example, if on a carbon copy of a letter the initials WWW/AH are found in the left-hand margin, this indicates that it was dictated by W. Willard Wirtz and typed by his secretary, Arlene Huff. If Mr. Wirtz deemed it unnecessary to clear the letter with Stevenson before it went out, the letter was signed by Carol Evans. If the letter was considered important enough to be read by Stevenson before mailing, it was usually presented to him first

in draft form, then typed in final form and signed by Miss Evans or by
Stevenson himself.

When Stevenson dictated a letter, his initials with those of the secretary were placed on the left-hand margin of the carbon copy. Some of
these letters were then returned to his desk for one reason or another
(he sometimes added a postscript by hand; or he might redraft the
letter), and were signed by him. The others were signed, usually, by
Carol Evans.

Stevenson and his law partners and the principal aides generally
followed these procedures during the 1956 campaign. Stevenson established his headquarters for the 1956 general election in Washington,
D.C., where a large correspondence section was formed to acknowledge
the enormous amount of mail he received as a presidential candidate.
He also kept open his law office in Chicago, where mail was received
and handled by Miss Evans and a small group of helpers. Much of the
mail from his Chicago law office and his home at Libertyville was forwarded to the Washington headquarters for acknowledgment. The
Washington headquarters acquired a "signature wheel" for affixing
Stevenson's signature to letters written by authorized members of the
campaign staff. In Chicago, Miss Evans continued to sign his name to
letters written for him there.

Because the collection of Stevenson's papers consists mainly of
carbon copies, it is impossible to know whether he or one of his authorized associates signed them. It is, of course, possible to determine
whether he was actually their author. But whether he composed and
signed them personally or not, the letters and memoranda are considered to be his because he authorized them to be done in his behalf.

When we have made deletions from letters, speeches, or other
papers, we indicate this by ellipses. We have provided editorial comment on any item where it was necessary for clarity or continuity.

The editors had a large collection of papers available for Volume VI.
This volume is, therefore, much more selective than Volumes I, II, III
and IV. Stevenson provided in his will that material about his governorship be deposited in the Illinois State Historical Library and the re-
mainder be deposited in the Princeton University Library. Stevenson's
most important correspondence was at his home in Libertyville when he
died. The editors selected some of the material for this volume from the
material at Libertyville before the collection was divided between the
two depositories. Some items are still in the possession of Adlai E.
Stevenson III.

The editors of these volumes searched widely for handwritten documents. Stevenson enjoyed writing by hand — he must have, since he

wrote so many letters and postcards. Some people, particularly before Stevenson became governor of Illinois, failed to save them. Many people were most cooperative, placing all their Stevenson items at our disposal. Some preferred to send us only selections from their collections. A few refused to send us any material at all.[8]

After reading the typescript of this volume, W. Willard Wirtz, formerly Stevenson's law partner and Secretary of the Department of Labor under President Kennedy and President Johnson, wrote the editors about the personal letters included in this volume:

> A few of us know how much the Governor said beyond what he actually meant, or believed. He played a game, in conversation and on paper. Some of it was just manners. Friendliness. And this included a good deal of exaggeration. Some more of it was part of trying ideas on for size even when he knew they didn't fit, often for the purpose of getting the other side of the idea (which appealed to him more) developed. He was short, in both respects, on discretion. There was also a common element of complaining, going considerably beyond what he felt. And he over-personalized, especially in the first person.
>
> Perhaps this is all part of what his "papers" are supposed to reveal. But I shudder a little about the extent to which strangers are going to misinterpret.

Some letters, which would cause unnecessary anguish to people still living, the editors have not included in these volumes, or they have made appropriate deletions within such letters. These deletions are indicated by ellipses.

Over the years Stevenson wrote many letters to Mrs. Edison Dick and her family. Some were dictated and transcribed on the typewriter, and some were handwritten. Mrs. Dick submitted extracts to the editors from handwritten letters she received from Governor Stevenson. She has indicated with ellipses material that was deleted by her. The originals of all the handwritten letters are in her possession.

The location of other handwritten letters, postcards or originals of typewritten letters is given in the footnote references. Since the majority of the papers in Volume VI are in the Princeton University Library (some in the distribution, probably inadvertently, went to the Illinois State Historical Library in Springfield), the editors identify the location of only those papers that are *not* in the Princeton collection. Papers at the Illinois State Historical Library will be identified as A.E.S., I.S.H.L.

---

[8] Katie Louchheim wrote: "These were [some of] the women who owned a share in Adlai's destiny." *By the Political Sea* (Garden City, New York: Doubleday, 1970), p. 108.

Most of Stevenson's letters were signed with his full name; those signed "AD" or "ADLAI" were to close personal or political friends. Because we have had to work, in most cases, with carbon copies, it is impossible to know how these letters and memoranda were signed. Hence, signatures have been omitted from such items. Whenever we have located the original letter, and he signed it otherwise than with his full name, we have included the signature.

When he wrote by hand, Stevenson had several idiosyncrasies. He spelled "it's" without the apostrophe; he used "thru" for "through," etc. We have left them as he wrote them and have not added a *sic*.

When references in a letter were not clear, the editors wrote to the recipient of the letter (or to his heirs) to seek clarification. The responses — many of them reflected in the footnotes — have been extremely valuable and added a dimension that would not have been possible to achieve unless these volumes were edited shortly after Governor Stevenson's death.

The editors generally have not included letters written to Stevenson. Publishing letters written by people still alive or recently deceased requires obtaining formal permission — a time-consuming task. Instead, the editors have summarized the contents of an incoming letter where it was necessary to make Stevenson's reply understandable.

Adlai E. Stevenson, as those who knew him well realize, corrected copies of his speeches up to the minute or second of delivery. Moreover, many of these last-minute-corrected speeches the editors have been unable to locate in the depositories. Stevenson sometimes gave these to reporters and they apparently were not returned to him. The editors decided, therefore, to rely on the texts of Stevenson's speeches that he himself approved for publication in *The New America,* edited by Seymour E. Harris, John Bartlow Martin, and Arthur Schlesinger, Jr. (New York: Harper, 1957). We are aware that these editors occasionally pruned the texts of speeches to avoid repetition. But without the copies of the finally corrected speeches, we felt that the speeches as published in *The New America* (the text of which Stevenson approved) were to be relied upon rather than a press release of the speech or a carbon copy. Whenever speeches are used that are not included in this publication, the editors indicate whether the text was taken from a press release, carbon copy, or some other source.

Under the legal agreement between Walter Johnson and Adlai Stevenson III, Borden Stevenson, and John Fell Stevenson, Adlai III agreed to read each volume before publication. In the event of disagreement as to the inclusion of any item of his father's papers, the matter was to be referred to Judge Carl McGowan for final — and irrevocable — decision. Adlai III objected to nothing included in this volume.

Contents

	Foreword	*vii*
One.	*The Quest for the 1956 Democratic Nomination*	*1*
Two.	*The 1956 Campaign*	*197*
Three.	*Titular Head of the Democratic Party — Again*	*371*
	Acknowledgments	*545*
	Index	*547*

Illustrations

(*between pages 238 and 239*)

Stevenson's home in Libertyville

Declaring his candidacy for the Democratic nomination at November, 1955, press conference

Greeting the 1956 Democratic Convention after his nomination

With vice presidential nominee Senator Estes Kefauver

Campaign stop, 1956

With Adlai III, Nancy, John Fell, and Mr. and Mrs. Ernest Ives at Libertyville, 1956

Campaign train in Michigan

Campaign speech at Toledo, Ohio

California motorcade

Campaign train in Pennsylvania

(*between pages 494 and 495*)

With supporters in Long Beach, California

Campaign rally in California

Bill Blair, Marietta Tree, Arthur M. Schlesinger, Jr., and campaign manager Jim Finnegan

Campaigning at Fayette County Courthouse in Kentucky, October, 1956

With Eleanor Roosevelt after his October, 1956, speech at Madison Square Garden, New York

Campaign motorcade in Lexington, Kentucky

With John Fell in Providence, Rhode Island

1956 photo used extensively on campaign posters

Part One

The Quest for the 1956 Democratic Nomination

O n November 15, 1955, Adlai E. Stevenson announced, in a prepared statement issued in Chicago: "I shall be a candidate for the Democratic nomination for President next year, which I suspect is hardly a surprise." Later in his statement, he said, "The task of the Democratic party is to make 'prosperity and peace' not just a political slogan but an active search for a better America and a better world."[1]

The next day Stevenson revealed at a press conference that he would enter the Minnesota primary to be held on March 20, but he added that this was the only firm decision he had made about primaries. Stevenson also announced that James A. Finnegan, former president of the Philadelphia City Council, was to be his campaign manager. Hyman B. Raskin, former deputy chairman of the Democratic National Committee and law partner of Stephen A. Mitchell, would be assistant campaign manager. Harry Ashmore, editor of the Arkansas Gazette, and Roger Tubby would be Stevenson's special assistants.

Mr. Tubby, formerly assistant press secretary for President Truman, became Stevenson's press secretary, assisted by C. K. McClatchy, of the Sacramento Bee. Mrs. Edison Dick and Barry Bingham were cochairmen of the National Stevenson for President Committee, of which Archibald Alexander was executive director. Stevenson's law partners, W. Willard Wirtz, Newton N. Minow, and William McCormick Blair, Jr., and his secretary, Miss Carol Evans, comprised part of his personal staff.

On December 16, 1955, Senator Estes Kefauver announced his candidacy for the Democratic nomination, and this made a grueling primary campaign inevitable.

[1] For the complete text of the statement, see The Papers of Adlai E. Stevenson, Vol. IV, pp. 591–592.

Richard Spencer, an old Chicago friend of Stevenson, wrote on November 9, 1955, that regardless of personal considerations Stevenson had to run and added that it was "not your lot to rest content until you have grappled with the greatest challenge an individual can be called upon to face."

To Richard Spencer[2]

November 16, 1955

My dear Dick:

I find you have been having some correspondence with my office, and now I have your letter of November 9. I am touched and grateful, and it reminds me of a long past in which your loyalty and encouragement emerge conspicuously. I have "gone and done it," not with any weary sense merely of doing my duty nor with any great exhilaration, but with a comfortable feeling that it is right and that it has fallen to my lot in my generation to do all I can to preserve the dialogue that makes democracy work and that could even make it better. Moreover, with experience I am less anxious and harrassed than I used to be — indeed, I have concluded that I can't do everything with perfection and there are some things I can't even do at all.

With affectionate regards, I am

Cordially,

During his governorship, Stevenson had known Mrs. Bernice Van der Vries, of Winnetka, Illinois, a Republican who served in the state House of Representatives for twenty-two years.

To Bernice T. Van der Vries[3]

November 16, 1955

Dear Bernice:

I saw in the paper the other day that you are retiring. This means something more to me than that — you are retiring!

I carried away from Springfield many happy memories and some enlarged and some shrunken esteems. There was no larger one than mine for you, and, as a citizen, I really hate to see you relinquish that formidable assignment which you ennobled so cheerfully and so gracefully.

Warmest wishes.

Cordially,

[2] A copy is in the Adlai E. Stevenson collection, Illinois State Historical Library (A.E.S., I.S.H.L.).

[3] A copy is in A.E.S., I.S.H.L.

Mrs. Ralph Hines and Mrs. John Alden Carpenter — Stevenson's former sister-in-law and mother-in-law, respectively — expressed their concern that the former Mrs. Stevenson might issue a statement antagonistic to him.

To Mrs. Ralph Hines

November 16, 1955

Dear Betty:

I have thought and talked a little about what we discussed. Our view is as follows: If you or your mother are asked, reply at once. If you are not interrogated, we think it better not to volunteer anything for the present because it would certainly cause the newspapers (and, as you know, they will virtually all be hostile) to ask Ellen for a statement and she will have the last word. If she does say something critical or unfriendly, then we feel that you and your mother should promptly issue a statement expressing gratification as citizens with my candidacy and pledging your support.

I hope you will agree that this is best, but whatever you do is okay with me. As to your generosity, I would suggest that you just send it along in a check to me or to William McCormick Blair, Jr. and we will add it to the other funds coming in for the pre-convention campaign expenses. . . .

You are awfully good to me to think of all this and I am grateful.

Best love,

Stevenson, who had delivered an address at the University of Virginia on November 11, met with former Secretary of State Dean Acheson in Washington before returning to Chicago.

To Dean Acheson

November 16, 1955

My dear Dean:

Thank you so much for the material from Paul[4] via you! And thanks also for that delightful and enlightening luncheon. It is hard to drink and eat so well and listen attentively too, but I contrived all three — thanks to you.

---

[4] Paul H. Nitze, president of the Foreign Service Educational Foundation in Washington, who had been chairman of the Policy Planning Staff of the Department of State when Acheson was Secretary of State.

I only wish there were more opportunities to talk with you. I get a lot of information and suggestions on foreign affairs, but not enough from Acheson!

Yours,

To Yousuf Karsh[5]

November 21, 1955

My dear friend:

So many thanks for your letter. I think of the enclosed proofs I like the one from the earlier sittings, which I have marked, the best. I have been sending around for years such frightful pictures in response to countless requests that some of these would be a delight for me as well as the recipients. If they are not too expensive, please let me know how much a few hundred of these, in dull finish, might cost. You were good to think of giving them to me and they would be welcome but I am afraid you would never be able to give me as many as I shall need.

I will remember you to Mrs. [Ernest L.] Ives, who has now gone to North Carolina, and she, like myself, will look forward to seeing you again — and soon, I hope!

Cordially yours,

Andrew Cordier, executive assistant to the Secretary-General of the United Nations, wrote Stevenson that members of the staff and of delegations who were part of the Church House Group at the time of the Preparatory Commission of the United Nations in London during the fall of 1945 were to have a tenth anniversary reunion.

To Andrew W. Cordier[6]

November 21, 1955

Dear Andy:

How I wish I could join you "Church Housers" on Friday! Your letter brought back a flood of memories of those stirring, hopeful days ten years ago in the chill and fog of post-war London.[7]

I can see it all — Church House, our meeting room, the faces round

[5] The noted Ottawa photographer of celebrities, who took the portrait photograph that Stevenson used for years.

[6] A copy is in A.E.S., I.S.H.L.

[7] See *The Papers of Adlai E. Stevenson*, Vol. II.

the green table, the laughter, the solemnity, the anxiety, yes, and the cocktail parties! And I can remember, too, my nervousness among all those experienced diplomats who turned out to be such dear and helpful friends; and also moments of gaiety, like the time Andre Gromyko found a picture of the dancing girls from San Francisco at his place and solemnly announced: "Gentlemen — this — was — not — on the — agenda — at San Francisco"!

I wish I might be with you to live again one of the happiest, most fruitful intervals of my life among some friends whom I long to see again — and before we get much older and can no longer recognize each other!

Please give them all my affectionate regards and regrets.

Cordially,

Stevenson spoke at the University of Texas on September 28, 1955, and then he and the speaker of the House of Representatives, Sam Rayburn, visited Senator Lyndon B. Johnson at his ranch. At a press conference, which Johnson dominated, Stevenson, with a broad smile on his face, finally said: "I'd like to come back to Texas and either talk or listen — whatever they'll permit me to do."[8]

To Lyndon B. Johnson

November 21, 1955

Dear Lyn:

Ever so many thanks for your letter and the picture. Evidently you Texans can look into the sun with a sharper eye than I can!

I enjoyed our telephone talk and I understand your position, of course.[9] But one thing you must promise me: If you ever find out why writers write what they do about us without asking us, let me know. My guess is that it wouldn't be any fun to ask and it certainly would take some effort, and then there would always be the unhappy prospect of truth and no intrigue!

More of that another time, however. Meanwhile — rest! — the wars are all ahead.

Cordially yours,

[8] See Alfred Steinberg, *Sam Johnson's Boy: A Close-Up of the President from Texas* (New York: Macmillan, 1968), pp. 421–422.
[9] Senator Johnson did not support Stevenson's quest for the nomination.

Senator Richard Russell of Georgia wrote Stevenson on November 16, 1955, that his announcement and plans assured him the nomination.[10] If the party adopted a "reasonable platform," Russell added, a unified Democratic party would elect him President.

To Richard B. Russell[11]

November 22, 1955

Dear Dick:

So many thanks for your good letter. It arrived with one from my friend and college classmate, Bill Stevenson, President of Oberlin College. He tells me they are frantically eager to have you come to the Oberlin Mock Democratic Convention on May 4 and 5 next year to speak. I have heard it said that this is the oldest and best and liveliest of these college conventions in the country. Moreover, this is but the second time in the history of this splendid college that the student body has voted Democratic. We dare not lose [let] these youngsters get away from us, and I hope you can find your way out there for some fun in May.

I should like very much to have a talk with you but I don't know when it will be unless by chance you are coming this way for some reason. If you are, by all means let me know. . . .

Cordially,

P.S. I have just recalled that I am going to be at Alicia Patterson Guggenheim's[12] place a few miles east of Kingsland, Georgia from Saturday, November 26, to Monday the 28th, writing a speech and shooting quail. . . .

Mrs. Daisy Borden Harriman was Democratic National Committeewoman from the District of Columbia for many years, and also served as Ambassador to Norway 1933–1940. She was married to a second cousin of W. Averell Harriman. On November 14, 1955, she wrote Stevenson saying that she was sorry that she had to resign from the Citizens for Stevenson Committee because her family felt she should be "neutral." At a Democratic National Committee dinner on November 19, 1955, Stevenson, in the midst of criticizing the Eisenhower Administra-

[10] Senator Russell had withheld a public statement in support of Stevenson until the closing weeks of the 1952 campaign. See *The Papers of Adlai E. Stevenson,* Vol. IV, p. 89.

[11] A copy is in A.E.S., I.S.H.L.

[12] Publisher of *Newsday* and a longtime friend of Stevenson's.

tion, stated: "I agree that it is a time for catching our breath; I agree that moderation is the spirit of the times. But we best take care lest we confuse moderation with mediocrity, or settle for half answers to hard problems. . . . Moderation, yes. Stagnation, no!"[13] *The next day Governor G. Mennen Williams of Michigan criticized Stevenson's policy of "moderation" and Governor Averell Harriman of New York declared that there "is no such word as 'moderation' or 'middle-of-the-road' in the Democratic vocabulary." In June, 1956, Harriman announced his candidacy for the Democratic nomination.*

To Daisy Borden Harriman[14]

November 23, 1955

My dear Mrs. Harriman:

I was enchanted by your letter and touched, pleased and gratified. How sweet of you to write me and how nice of you to think that way. Nothing has been more distasteful to me of late than my apparent conflict with Averell whom I have genuinely loved. I wish it were not so and I have been confused about what to do about it. That you think I am doing the right thing, therefore, comforts me all the more.

With affectionate regards —

Yours,

Lady Mary Spears, Ellen Stevenson's aunt, wrote from England and expressed the hope that the former Mrs. Stevenson would not create difficulties.

To Lady Mary Spears

November 23, 1955

My dear Mary:

Thanks for your letter. I have no news from Ellen but I think you are quite right to "play along," as I am sure that in her state if anything can be done at all it is through friendliness and persuasion rather than hostility and shame.

I am asking Carol [Evans] to enclose the copy of my speech on the 19th. The dinner was a great success and my problem now seems to be less one of taking the lead for the nomination and more one of keeping it. Isn't it wonderful how a new crisis can develop every day in politics?

Affectionately,

[13] The speech is reprinted in Adlai E. Stevenson, *What I Think* (New York: Harper, 1956), pp. 105–113.
[14] A copy is in A.E.S., I.S.H.L.

Senator Estes Kefauver wrote Stevenson that it was "good seeing you" at the Democratic National Committee meeting, commended him on his speech, and asked for a copy of it.

To Estes Kefauver

November 25, 1955

Dear Estes:

So many thanks for your gracious note. I wish we could have had more of an opportunity to talk together. But you know what these meetings are like!

Enclosed is a copy of my speech, although I confess I am at a loss to know why you should want it!

Cordially,

After spending the Thanksgiving holiday at the plantation of Alicia Patterson, Stevenson traveled to Miami to deliver a speech. While there he sent his editor at Harper & Brothers the introduction for his forthcoming book, What I Think.

To John Fischer[15]

November 30, 1955

Dear Jack:

Enclosed are two copies of this wretched introduction — at last! I have not had a chance to read over this last edition, which is being typed up in Miami in the midst of extreme turmoil. I shall try to read through it in a day or so for any further corrections; and I will be at home in Libertyville on Saturday and Sunday (telephone 2-4466). If you want to telephone me with any suggested changes I would certainly welcome them.

Also, I shall be in New York on the 7th and 8th, leaving on the 9th, and could squeeze in a conference with you or Cass[16] if necessary.

Writing in fits and starts — not to mention thinking in fits — is about as unsatisfactory a way to produce anything as I can contrive, and I am good at contriving unsatisfactory ways of working. So I have little pride about the enclosure and great confidence, as you know, in your taste and judgment.

I also enclose a dedication.

Hastily,

ADLAI

---

[15] The original is in the possession of the State Historical Society of Wisconsin.
[16] Cass Canfield, chairman of the board of Harper & Brothers.

P.S. You will note that this Introduction is dated Thanksgiving Day, November 24, on which evening actually I gave it some more or less concluding licks; but I wonder if you would think it better if it were dated some time prior to the announcement of my candidacy — say, October 15th.

A.E.S.

Archibald MacLeish, Boylston Professor of Rhetoric and Oratory at Harvard University, had served as a speechwriter during Stevenson's 1952 campaign and continued to send him drafts for speeches.

To Archibald MacLeish[17]

[no date]

Dear Archie —

I've just read it — beautiful, superb! — and much too good for this weeks encounter with the AFL–CIO convention I think — good in the sober, thoughtful, literary sense. I'll save it — for Calif. in Feb. I think.

Blessings & thanks!

AES

Seymour E. Harris, professor of economics at Harvard University, frequently sent Stevenson material for speeches.

To Seymour E. Harris[18]

December 6, 1955

Dear Seymour:

I was delighted to have your letter and also your comments on the labor speech. I have worked it up over the weekend, and I hope it will suffice, though it doesn't much resemble what I started with.

I am delighted to hear that you have my son John Fell,[19] and I am going to see to it now that he doesn't neglect this opportunity! But don't spare the rod.

I think your suggestion about the backgrounds of the 200 most important appointees is good. I believe George Ball's[20] office has already

[17] This handwritten postcard is in the MacLeish collection, Library of Congress. It is postmarked December 6, 1955.

[18] A copy is in A.E.S., I.S.H.L.

[19] John Fell Stevenson was an undergraduate at Harvard, enrolled in one of Mr. Harris's courses.

[20] A former law partner of Stevenson's who was active in both the 1952 and 1956 campaigns.

done some work on this, but I am taking the liberty of passing your letter along to Clayton Fritchey[21] with the thought that maybe the National Committee office could give it some consideration.

Warm regards, and my everlasting thanks for all your kindness, encouragement — and labor!

Cordially,

To Clayton Fritchey[22]

December 6, 1955

Dear Clayton:

Note the attached letter from Seymour Harris. I think his suggestion has merit. I believe we are going to have more and more trouble, due to the press, in making the business control of government proposition stick or amount to much in a time of manifest prosperity for most people.

I should welcome your reaction as to the possibility of subsidizing his project, at your convenience.

Cordially,

Herbert Agar, a former editor of the Louisville Courier-Journal *and author of many books about the United States including* The Price of Union *(Boston: Houghton Mifflin, 1950), had contributed material for Stevenson's 1952 campaign speeches. Mr. Agar, who lived in England, was a director of the publishing firm of Rupert Hart-Davis, Ltd., which was negotiating for the British rights to* What I Think.

To Herbert Agar[23]

December 12, 1955

Dear Herbert:

In the confusion hereabouts I suspect I neglected to answer your letter from the South of France some time ago. Meanwhile, I corresponded with Rupert [Hart-Davis], and I believe we have an understanding about the book if you *really* want to publish it at all.

The Introduction I finished between shooting quail and exhorting the multitudes during a few days of whistle-stopping through Florida and

---

[21] Deputy chairman of the Democratic National Committee and editor of *Democratic Digest.*
[22] A copy is in A.E.S., I.S.H.L.
[23] A copy is in A.E.S., I.S.H.L.

Arkansas last week, and no doubt Cass Canfield or Jack Fis[ch]er have sent along a copy to you.

I have an anxious feeling that you and Rupert may be publishing this with meager prospects of commercial advantage. If that is the case, please don't hesitate to abandon the project on my account.

After three months of almost incessant travel and travail I have now come to rest here in Chicago, and shall remain stationary, I hope, for at least a month or six weeks before I resume my weary journey. During this interval I want to reflect a little on the substance of the campaign and the means whereby I can say some of the things that need saying in these times. This in turn reminds me that there is no more perceptive, sensitive and eloquent observer of America than Herbert Agar. So if you are moved to pass along your estimate of our land as you see it and what it has of promise for America and the world, it would be awfully, awfully welcome.

With most affectionate greetings to dear Barbie[24] and to you, I am

Yours ever,

To Mrs. Ernest L. Ives[25]

December 12, 1955

Dear Buffie:

I have your letters and I am ever so grateful, and also comforted by the news about Tim and Adrienne.[26] But Christmas without you and Ernest for the first time in many years will be difficult and a little dreary, but I am sure I can make do with Adlai and Nancy[27] for a part of the time and John Fell. So, please don't worry in the least. As to the presents, well, I am just going to relax and not make the same effort that we have in the past. If you can think of anything I can send you and Ernest it would be helpful *to be told*. I have, of course, some ties I bought in Italy, if that device is not too threadbare. I should have hung onto my zebra and sent you that![28]

. . . As for New Year's, come by all means *if you want to,* but that is not a difficult interval for me as you know. The real problem is the Christmas presents. I don't see much prospect of coming to Carolina in

[24] Mrs. Agar.
[25] The original is in the Elizabeth Stevenson Ives collection, Illinois State Historical Library (E.S.I., I.S.H.L.).
[26] Mrs. Ives's son and daughter-in-law, Mr. and Mrs. Timothy R. Ives.
[27] Mr. and Mrs. Adlai E. Stevenson III.
[28] Mrs. Ives cannot positively explain this allusion. She adds, however, "My recollection is that the zebra skin I have in this house [the Stevenson family home in Bloomington, Illinois] came from Adlai." Letter to C. Eric Sears, January 13, 1975.

January. I think perhaps I will just settle down here unless I decide to go off somewhere for some sun. I plan to go to California by way of Denver, etc. etc. the first of February for a big affair at Fresno on my birthday. I might even come back by way of the Jenkins ranch[29] for a bit and touch base in the Southwest. I think I have to be in Connecticut on February 25 for a speech; but all of the spring and winter schedule is still uncertain.

The news from the children is good and I will prod Nancy about her wedding presents. She has had to virtually redecorate and rebuild their three room apartment by hand and I suppose has been diverted, but she seems to find time to write me long and comforting letters. . . .

I am fine and happy to see an end to this awful three months of almost incessant travel and work. Florida, Oklahoma and Arkansas are okay, and New York far better than I ever thought possible. On the whole things are better than they should be, and how to keep them this way is the problem. I think we will go ahead with Don Laughlin[30] in Bloomington and probably try to get individuals in other major downstate towns to constitute an "Executive Committee" of the Illinois Committee.[31] Jane[32] seems to think that Dr. Karl Meyer[33] would be the best for State Chairman if he can be persuaded to do it. I have a strong feeling I will need a lot of help from Ernest in the Illinois picture when you return in the spring, and perhaps he should be designated in some official way as a member of the Executive Committee or something. If you or he have any ideas, let me know. As to the book,[34] I will speak to [Roger] Tubby, but I doubt if he has any views or even knows about it. Adlai, incidentally, thought the second part better than the first. I run into it everywhere and all good.

My love to Tim and Adrienne —

Affectionately,
ADLAI

P.S. I should be glad to see Billy Graham. Governor Clement of Tennessee has spoken to me about him frequently.

29 Rancho de la Osa, owned by Stevenson's friend Dick Jenkins, located about sixty miles south of Tucson, Arizona.

30 An old friend from Stevenson's home town.

31 The Illinois branch of the National Stevenson for President Committee.

32 Mrs. Edison Dick, cochairman of the National Stevenson for President Committee.

33 Head of the Cook County Hospital and a prominent Chicago Democrat.

34 Elizabeth Stevenson Ives and Hildegarde Dolson, My Brother Adlai (New York: William Morrow, 1956).

To Gerald W. Johnson[35]

December 13, 1955

Dear Gerald:

Thanks for that note of November 26. . . . One of the troubles with my situation, as you know, is that having been in the forefront so long the hazard of exhausting the advantages of novelty, not to mention content, is constant. I propose now to withdraw from the platform for six weeks and content myself with an occasional statement — if I can think of something suitable to say!

How I wish I were blessed with your tongue and pen — even, indeed, your mind!

Yours,

Mr. and Mrs. Lloyd K. Garrison, Stevenson's close personal friends and active supporters in the 1952 campaign, held a party in New York for potential contributors to the 1956 campaign. The movie of Stevenson's 1953 trip through Asia, the Middle East, and Europe was shown.

To Mr. and Mrs. Lloyd K. Garrison

December 13, 1955

My beloved Garrisons:

It was a great evening — for the Irish, the Scotch, the English, the Jews, and even Negroes, domestic and foreign! If anyone had as good a time as I did he must have been disorderly. But what an effort for you! I pray that you will not let your acquaintance with Stevenson get too exhausting.

Anyway, thanks, and thanks again, for a multitude of things, and gayest wishes for the holidays.

Affectionately,

To John E. Cassidy[36]

December 13, 1955

Dear John:

While in Florida recently, various blessings befell me — delegates, sail fish, and Jackie Hart! That enchantress implanted an unexpected kiss on my right cheek, to the accompaniment of photographers' flash

[35] Columnist for the *New Republic* and formerly with the Baltimore *Sun*.
[36] A member of the law firm of Cassidy, Sloan and Crutcher of Peoria, Illinois. A copy is in A.E.S., I.S.H.L.

bulbs and gubernatorial confusion. Later I sat by her at lunch and discovered that she was soon to be your daughter-in-law. I assume, of course, that you made the selection for your son, and congratulate you again for your extraordinary judgment and power of persuasion!

Yours,

On November 30, 1955, veteran CBS newscaster Eric Sevareid attempted to analyze the "political Stevenson." Among the characteristics mentioned were Stevenson's so-called indecisiveness, his attitude about public office, his wit and humor, and his anxiety about the quality of American life and about America's position in the world. Sevareid recounted an episode in Springfield when Stevenson was governor, noting that "when he makes up his mind he is extremely decisive," and that to Stevenson public office was first and last a public trust; that good administration was inseparable from good morals.

Ending his broadcast, Sevareid quoted Gerald Johnson: "To keep him in the ring, demolishing the sawdust-stuffed guards produced to reassure and the pasteboard dragons to terrify us is, a highly desirable public service."

To Eric Sevareid[37]

December 13, 1955

Dear Eric:

I have been traveling of late and somewhere in the clouds I read Sevareid Newsmakers CBS Radio, November 30, 1955. I almost wept — on several counts: your charity, and the reminder of those days in Springfield when I felt so useful, even adequate.

I am afraid, my dear friend, you understand me too well. That you can write of me as you do is gratifying, but I worry if it can last! I am so glad you picked up that wonderful line of Gerald Johnson. Surely the current disrepute of humor and self-deprecation must be wrong. Your summarization of my anxieties about America and its *quality* was the tonic I needed for some more utterances along that line. I keep thinking of great, jagged mountains melting into an even, molten mass. Is that what we are doing — in a high-powered two-tone automobile?

I was distressed that you could not get to Arkansas. There was a chance there for some relaxation. I wish you could come to Libertyville for a night during the next month or six weeks, when I shall be alone, with blood pressure normal.

Cordially and gratefully,

[37] A copy is in A.E.S., I.S.H.L.

On October 2, 1955, Adlai E. Stevenson was received "upon affirmation of faith in Jesus Christ into full membership" in the First Presbyterian Church of Lake Forest, Illinois.[38] This soon became public knowledge and Stevenson received hundreds of irate letters, many from Unitarians who feared he had deserted religious liberalism and some from people who felt he was insincere and had acted from political motivation. On October 28, 1955, Stevenson wrote the Reverend Kenneth Walker, of the Unitarian Church in Bloomington, Illinois, of which he was a member: "The story about the church business is not complicated. While in Springfield there was no Unitarian Church and I attended the Presbyterian Church, and became a devoted admirer of Dick Graebel, the minister whom I believe you know. Somewhat at his instigation, when I returned to Lake Forest, there again being no Unitarian Church, I attended the Presbyterian Church from time to time where my old friend Bob Andrus is the pastor. Feeling the want of some church identification thereabouts, I concluded to formalize my membership. Meanwhile, I shall continue to go, when circumstances permit, to the Unitarian Church . . . and I consider myself no less a Unitarian than before. I hope there is nothing wrong with this. My understanding was that Unitarians have no objection to membership or association with other churches. . . . Moreover, as you also know, my father's family have been Presbyterians for generations. I had not thought this would cause any anxiety, and my Presbyterian friends seem to have none. . . ."

On October 25, 1955, Stevenson wrote to the Reverend Robert G. Andrus: ". . . Forgive this plaintive note. . . . Unitarians are adding more & more letters to the 300 a day I have to cope with. I PRAY, literally, that no more will be said. . . ." A few days later he wrote Andrus: "I'm not sure about what I've done, but the volume of this corres[pondence]. is mounting and if you could suggest a reply to this person it would be so helpful."[39]

After Newsweek, December 12, 1955, published a brief story, Stevenson on December 15 met with Mr. Andrus and Mr. Walker, together with the Reverend Jack Mendelsohn of All Souls Unitarian Church in Indianapolis (he had formerly been at Rockford, Illinois), and the Reverend Richard Paul Graebel of the First Presbyterian Church of Springfield, Illinois. The four ministers drafted a letter to Stevenson stating that he could belong to both churches without "inconsistency." They added: "While we understand that you respect theologians, we

[38] Stevenson had been weighing this decision for some time. See The Papers of Adlai E. Stevenson, Vol. IV, pp. 443–444.
[39] Both of these handwritten letters are in the possession of Mr. Andrus.

know that doctrinal rigidity has never limited the comfort you find in Christian faith, worship and fellowship." His membership in the Presbyterian Church, they wrote, "was accepted with the understanding that you would maintain your lifelong affiliation with the Unitarian Church of Bloomington, your home town. Descended from active Unitarians on your mother's side and equally active Presbyterians, including many ministers, on your father's side, we understand perfectly that you have found a local church home without forsaking a lifelong commitment, and that you have also united your parental religious endowments."[40]

To the Reverend Frederick May Eliot[41]

December 16, 1955

Dear Dr. Eliot:

Kenneth Walker was kind enough to show me your kind telegram. Your confidence is heartening in view of the commotion what seemed to me a harmless action seems to have provoked. I guess I was awfully naive, but the temperamental reaction of some of my Unitarian friends has both surprised and disturbed me.

For your information I enclose a copy of a letter which may be of interest and also informative. I hope it is not necessary to advertise this incident any more. Also, I have every intention of continuing to attend the new Unitarian fellowship on the North Shore when circumstances permit. My "circumstances" are not very permissive lately!

With my utmost esteem and gratitude, I am

Cordially yours,

Stevenson prepared the following form letters, which were sent to those who objected to what he had done.

Dear ———:

I am sorry that you feel so badly about my going to a Presbyterian church occasionally, which I have done for many years when Unitarian churches were not handy. Nor as a liberal Unitarian do I see anything wrong with joining forthrightly and helping to support a liberal Presby-

[40] The *Christian Century*, in its December 21, 1955, issue, published an understanding editorial and concluded: "We trust that Mr. Stevenson will find all the spiritual help he has sought in his new church fellowship, and we are confident that church and public will respect the reticence with which he has surrounded his act."

[41] President of the American Unitarian Association.

terian church. I didn't know I was changing, but perhaps we never do. Horrors!

I enclose a copy of a letter which some minister friends sent me in December, and I have had reassuring and understanding support from Dr. Eliot and all the people in Boston and at Meadville Theological Seminary. I can't for the life of me understand the deluge of embittered mail from Unitarians that I always thought were liberal in their attitudes towards Christian worship.

Cordially yours,

Dear ———:

Your letter interested me and I am afraid, like so many, you are somewhat misinformed about the Unitarian denomination of the Protestant Church. My great grandfather was a Presbyterian minister; so was my uncle; and so is my first cousin. My father's family have been Presbyterians since long before our Republic was founded, but I have found myself much in sympathy with the views of the Unitarian Church of which my mother was a member. It may interest you to know more about them and I enclose a little pamphlet which you will find informative.

With kind thanks for your thought of me and your interest, I am

Sincerely yours,

To Mrs. Ernest L. Ives[42]

December 16, 1955

Dear Buffie:

Your letter to Mary Lou[43] brought tears to her eyes, what with all the thoughtfulness. And as for me, I must know whence comes that quotation. I think it so good I might want to use it on my Christmas card next year — "Everything we call a trial," etc.

I came home last night to find the tree up, decorated, lighted, and the house garlanded and lovely after a visitation by four self-starting angels — Ellen Smith, Betty Welles, Marian Sudler and Rosalind Oates.[44] So now all I have to worry about is the Christmas presents, and I'm not going to do much worrying.

---

42 The original is in E.S.I., I.S.H.L.
43 Stevenson's housekeeper at Libertyville.
44 Stevenson's old friends and Lake Forest neighbors Mrs. Hermon D. Smith, Mrs. Edward H. Welles, Mrs. Carroll Sudler, and Mrs. James F. Oates, Jr.

The McGowans[45] are going to come for Christmas dinner, and the children will be home not long afterward, I suspect, so all is well.

I hope and pray that it is with you, too. Your letter sounded cheerful — and so am I!

Much love to you all.

ADLAI

Joseph S. Clark, Jr., mayor of Philadelphia, who had assisted Stevenson in preparing his Miami speech, was planning to run in the primary for the U.S. Senate.

To Joseph S. Clark, Jr.[46]

December 16, 1955

Dear Joe:

I have not yet properly thanked you for getting me to Miami and arming me. The latter you probably regretted, in view of my awful performance there. I thought the speech good, including the revisions!, but the delivery awful. For that I have only the appalling lights to blame and a certain irritation I seem to have developed about excessive attention from the flash bulbs and the electronic tortures of our life.

Anyway, you were more than good to me, and I marvel at your industry and productivity. What's more, you can write, and I can't say that about many of our companions on the barricades.

Your time must be drawing near and I hope all is unwinding smoothly. If there is anything I can possibly do, I am sure you will let me know.

Yours,

P.S. And thanks again for that very welcome and tangible encouragement!

---

[45] Mr. and Mrs. Carl McGowan. Mr. McGowan had been Stevenson's assistant in Springfield during his governorship.
[46] A copy is in A.E.S., I.S.H.L.

To Herbert H. Lehman[47]

December 17, 1955

Dear Herbert:

I have come to rest, or rather to a halt, at last and find your letter of December 1. As you have probably heard from Julius,[48] the immigration hearing was postponed. . . .[49]

My appearance before the AFL–CIO was most gratifying. The speech seemed appropriate, and their reception was as warm as anything I have experienced in some time. Likewise I had the personal satisfaction of feeling that I had not made just perfunctory political obeisances to labor. I wonder sometimes if you get as much satisfaction out of even slightly unorthodox political behavior as I do. I am sure you must. There is no other way to account for your apparent good health and equilibrium.

The luncheon meeting of the Stevenson for President group yielded almost as much money as I spent in the entire campaign running for Governor in 1948. Perhaps it was therefore abnormally heartening to a barefoot boy from the prairies. I did not like what I heard about Averell [Harriman]'s state of mind. When I called him on the phone he was most cordial, but I was told that he has been rather bitter to some of his visitors. I had so hoped all this might be avoided, and I am going to have to ask you to instruct me in that regard if you can.

I went from New York to Arkansas, where the news was all good. The Senators[50] joined me and also Sparkman,[51] Long[52] the Governor,[53] and all of the political leaders of the state.

There is much to report, but the newspapers are more comprehensive — and also better written, I fear!

With affectionate regards to you and Mrs. Lehman, and renewed expressions of my gratitude for your encouragement and confidence — and, Merry Christmas!

Yours,

P.S. I have just heard this moment about your speech at the National Press Club today. You were more than good to me — as ever![54]

47 Democratic senator from New York. A copy is in A.E.S., I.S.H.L.
48 Julius Edelstein, Senator Lehman's assistant.
49 Stevenson planned to testify regarding the need for reforming the U.S. immigration laws.
50 J. W. Fulbright and John McClellan.
51 Senator John Sparkman, of Alabama.
52 Senator Russell Long, of Louisiana.
53 Orval Faubus.
54 Senator Lehman presented a Stephen S. Wise Award to Elmer Davis at a meeting at the National Press Club in Washington, D.C., on December 16, 1955, and in his accompanying remarks praised Stevenson.

Emmett Till, a black youth from Chicago, was visiting relatives on a farm near Greenwood, Mississippi, when he allegedly whistled at a white woman. Shortly afterward, he was kidnapped by a group of white men, and his body was found in a nearby river. The white woman's husband and his half-brother were tried and found not guilty of the murder and on November 9, 1955, a grand jury refused to indict them for kidnapping. Arthur M. Schlesinger, Jr., professor of history at Harvard University, wrote Stevenson about the Till murder and enclosed a letter from James Wechsler of the New York Post.

To Arthur M. Schlesinger, Jr.

December 19, 1955

Dear Arthur:

I return Mr. Wechsler's letter herewith. No one can approve of the Till case, and anyone can say so, and say it over and over again. I believe Governor [Hugh] White and many prominent people in Mississippi have done just that. I hardly know what Mr. Wechsler would want me to do, unless it was just to shout, which helps things very little even if it pleases some Negro leaders and evidently my very much esteemed friends at the *Post*. But I am concerned with the deliberate disenfranchisement of Negroes in Mississippi. I said something about this in New York at the labor meeting, and if you did not see it I should like to send you a copy. I have also asked Roy Wilkins[55] for some legal research as to the limits of federal interference in state election procedures.

Moreover, I have talked with some of the Mississippi leaders, including the very excellent Congressman Smith,[56] from Greenville. I doubt if he approves of what happened in the Till case any more than you or Mr. Wechsler, and I think from all I hear things are going to be different in the new killing case, where there was a witness.[57]

I am in the usual disorder, aggravated by Christmas, the children, and all of the year-end and holiday problems, with my sister absent. But

[55] Executive secretary of the National Association for the Advancement of Colored People.

[56] Frank E. Smith, author of *Congressman from Mississippi* (New York: Pantheon Books, 1964).

[57] Stevenson apparently refers to another Mississippi murder case, in which Elmer Kimbell, a white patron of a service station, shot a black attendant, Clinton Melton, alleging self-defense, although the local sheriff said that Melton apparently had no gun. At the trial, held in March, 1956, in the same courtroom that had been the scene of the Till murder trial, the owner of the service station testified that he had witnessed the shooting, which followed a threat by the defendant to kill Melton, and that the victim had been unarmed. The all-white jury nevertheless acquitted Kimbell. See the New York *Times*, December 9, 1955; March 13 and 14, 1956.

things around my office, now a "headquarters," begin to assume some comforting shapes and [Bill] Blair, [James] Finnegan, et al., have contrived to provide me with almost three weeks with only an occasional utterance!

With affectionate Christmas wishes to you and Marian and the children,

Cordially,

To Mrs. Eugene Meyer[58]

December 19, 1955

My dear dear Agnes —

I'm shamelessly negligent; I've neglected your precious letters and have more to report than time to report it. Actually it has been a ghastly 3 months and more, and with all this experience with relentless pressure I sometimes wonder how I can deliberately face what's to come. Duty? Can any impersonal, honest sense be so compelling? Vanity? I had thought not, having experienced the honor once before and having dealt with it as well or better than I shall ever be able to again. Yet, vanity it must be. And having long denounced, inwardly and certainly, the presumption, arrogance and insensitivity of anyone who would SEEK a Presidential nomination, here I am doing just that!

So I feel in a way that all the exertions of the past 3 months is but inexorable retribution and that I am doomed to pay and pay for my apostasy.

But for now, for a few delicious days, I shall, pray God, be mostly in the country with my children, or two of them at least. And *today* I've spent at home "doing the Christmas," and what a horror that has become! But I should tell you with your family! At all events my sister has carried the burden in part in years past but this year she stayed down in N.C. [North Carolina] to be with her son and it fell to my lot to do the sordid business. But lest you feel too sorry for me, dear Agnes, let me hastily report that I believe in angels!; indeed 4 visited my home the other day while I was in Chicago and I returned to find a tree, decorated, lit, wreaths on the doors and the living room garlanded! (verb?) And I even had a charming volunteer here half the afternoon deftly wrapping presents for office, family, neighbors — including one for you!

And of *that* I must say a word. I had thought to send you my most precious possession because you have been so kind and good to me and

[58] Lecturer and writer on the problems of education and wife of the owner of the Washington *Post*. This handwritten letter is in the Agnes Meyer files, Princeton University Library.

because I love you dearly. It is a 17 or 18th century oval Russian ikon on mother of pearl set in a rectangular silver frame 4 or 5 inches long. I bought it from a hungry aristocrat in the "thieves market" in Moscow 30 years ago when I was an adventuring young man.[59] But after wrapping it, I've unwrapped it, because I decided not to send it to you! it seemed a little too formidable; might look in bad taste. Do you understand, or am I wrong? I concluded instead to send you the reverse — a gay, laughing, fat little billiken Eskimo carved by an Eskimo from a walrus tooth and given to me in Alaska. He'll make you smile confortably; and I hope sometimes you'll hold him in your left hand and think of me, if you've nothing better to do! Anyway, smiling at my fat little smiling man is better than contemplating the exquisite, sad countenance of an ancient blessed Mary peeling off her mother of pearl background. And being gay and light hearted gets to be awfully important when there are so many grim, preoccupied people about — Or is it diffent about you!

But last night there *was* gaiety here. I had my whole office staff out — 45 — for a buffet supper. They arrived with charming, touching surprises for me, including a huge grab bag from which I had to pull every manner of object, each accompanied by an amusing verse. There were presentations with speeches and it was a spirited and happy evening that pleased them, I pray — because it almost killed me!

12/20
And now I've read your blessed, beautiful letter of the 17th, dear Agnes. Yes; perhaps, as you say, the answer to the anxiety indicated above is that I AM "reconciled with myself," and *you* HAVE had much to do with it; your confidence in me, my directions and, if you please, my self confidence. . . .

I would love to go to Wash[ington] & see you; Nassau, where I've never been, makes me dream and sigh. And, who knows, maybe something will come to pass. . . . My present plan — tentative — is to stay here and work until late Jan. and then go west with stops en route reaching Fresno on 2/5 where a large fiesta of the Calif. Democratic Clubs takes place, I speak, and my birthday as a native son of Calif is duly celebrated. From there in some devious way — by Oregon Washington & Salt Lake — I get back East in time to speak at Hartford to the New England Democrats on 2/25. Then the primaries *start!*

It seems incredible that we take this means of preparing a man for a

[59] For Stevenson's trip to Russia in 1926, see *The Papers of Adlai E. Stevenson*, Vol. I, pp. 167–169; Kenneth S. Davis, *A Prophet in His Own Country: The Triumphs and Defeats of Adlai E. Stevenson* (Garden City, New York: Doubleday, 1957), pp. 153–159.

Presidential campaign, not to mention that method of preparing a man for the Presidency! It always reminds me of Grandfather [Stevenson]'s story of the political meeting in Ky. after the Civil war when all of the candidates pointed to their wounds and physical misfortunes as reasons for popular support, until finally one candidate rose and allowed as how he had not fought for the Blue or the Grey, but that if physical infirmity was a qualification for public office in Graves County, Ky. well he was "the rupturedest SOB in the whole damn state!"

So, I guess I have to show my physical stamina and, incidentally, exhibit some intellectual and possibly even moral, vigor for the next solid year.

But to return to your letters, which I love and want and need, (except your fluency and vibrant style fills me with envy!) I have three things to say that I must record before my time and your patience have fled.

1. The advisory committee of women. I am glad to hear that progress is being made in the assembly of names. But I had thought of it as, say, 10 or 12 of the best names we could get: "best" in the sense of the largest public impact among women; and not a great big collection of names, altho they would *all* be valuable for local use by the Stevenson-for-Pres. cttees. Actually the purpose was more political — to identify women with my campaign — than actually advisory, wasn't it? You mention a meeting here in Chicago. Couldn't I ask them for suggestions about campaign positions in various fields — which you would secretly draft for me! A big group with some idea that they are going to be sitting at my right hand may be hard to organize & get started in the first place, and in the second it might in fact be quite a problem for me!

2. I was disturbed by what you said about joining the Presbyterian church in Lake Forest, not just because *you* said it, but because it must reflect a broader cynicism. Tho I can't even hope to explain it to everyone, I can to you. It has caused me grave embar[r]assment; I did it to fulfill a gnawing need since I returned here from Spfd. and because of, I suppose, incessant pressure from the local Pres. minister and the Spfd. Pres minister whom I love like few other people in my life. It was done all in great secrecy to avoid the very reaction you indicate; and then a fool member of the Session "talked" and the minister fumbled. But my first allegiance continues with the Unitarians, and, pray God, you will *not* be afflicted with prearranged "pictures of me going in and out of church from now on," any more than in the past. I will try to tell you all about religion in my life which came late and emphatically and has been a solace and strength I had not known.

3. I wanted to talk to you about Israel. Because I agree that we

should go further than the Tri Partite declaration[60] — and said so a long time ago — I suggested a possible way (at Va) of making a security pact effective. If you never know who's guilty of aggression a security treaty could quickly lose its vitality. But I can't go further now, except to say that some temperance in talking to Am[erican]. Jews and in their thinking — the Zionists — is the imperative of any progress in my judgment. There will have to be give as well as take, and there will have to be tranquity [tranquillity?] on the border and on the air waves for awhile first. Frankly I don't think the Am. Jews have been helping much in that direction lately. I was one of the 10 members of the U S deleg. to the UN in 1947 which *literally* created Israel[61] & I feel no deeper international involvement & I dont, *confidentially, like* the shouting that has been going on lately aided & abetted by some Dem. senators — Kefauver included — at $500 per shout. I quietly asserted that it should be the policy of this govt. not to permit any change in the status quo by force — and the more noisy Zionists have been denouncing me as a traitor ever since, and, frankly, I'm getting damn well fed up with it. Reason has all but been smothered in clamor lately and thats a dangerous thing for Israel *and the U S.* Moreover I'm about the only leading Democrat left with whom the Arabs will still talk in confidence and that is worth, or could be worth, far more to the people who genuinely want Israel to succeed, which means with her neighbors, than some more shouting.

But enough — I'm just back from Goshen Ind. with my son.[62] It has been about the worst of our misfortunes. He will be alright in time — or almost alright — but who knows what the death of two of his dearest friends beside him in the front seat will mean and do inwardly.

———

[60] On May 25, 1950, Britain, France, and the United States had pledged to uphold the armistice lines between Israel and her Arab neighbors that had resulted from United Nations mediation in the fighting of 1948–1949. However, unlimited migration into Israel was seen by both Israelis and Arabs as a threat to these boundaries, exacerbating existing tension between the two sides. For Stevenson's firsthand observation of the problems of Arab-Israeli relations and the vexing Palestine question, see *The Papers of Adlai E. Stevenson*, Vol. V.

[61] For Stevenson's role in the formation and early sessions of the United Nations, see *The Papers of Adlai E. Stevenson*, Vol. II.

[62] John Fell Stevenson had been injured in an automobile accident, described in the editorial introduction to the next document.

Fri AM

Now Im at the office & have your dear telephone message.[63] Thank you, and m[a]y God reward and bless you for all you've done for me, dear Agnes, — among all your beneficiaries!

Merry Christmas — in dreadful haste,

ADLAI

In December, 1955, John Fell Stevenson and three of his classmates from Harvard University were driving home for the holidays. On December 21, near Goshen, Indiana, a truck passed another truck and smashed head-on into the car John Fell was driving. (The truck driver was indicted for reckless driving and involuntary homicide.) Two of the boys, William S. North III and William C. Boyden, Jr. — intimates of John Fell since childhood — were killed. The third suffered minor injuries. John Fell suffered a shattered kneecap, lost a number of teeth, and was badly cut and bruised. Stevenson flew to Goshen and returned with his son to Passavant Hospital in Chicago.

President Eisenhower wired on December 21, 1955: "Distressed to read on the ticker that your son, John, has been seriously injured. I send you my most prayerful hopes that he will soon recover."

To Dwight D. Eisenhower[64]

December 27, 1955

Dear Mr. President —

I am deeply grateful for your most thoughtful and kind message about John Fell; and he was at first incredulous and then profoundly impressed and grateful too!

He is mending rapidly now after a successful operation on his leg and will no doubt be himself in time. Our greatest concern is that the parents of his friends will be given the strength to live through and beyond this tragedy.

I hope, sir, that your splendid recovery[65] is not tempting you to too great exertion at this trying time of the year for you.

With renewed thanks — in which John Fell joins with all the emphasis a cracked jaw permits!

Sincerely and respectfully yours,

[63] Mrs. Meyer spoke by telephone to Stevenson daily during the period of John Fell's recuperation, as did Mrs. Franklin D. Roosevelt.

[64] This handwritten letter is in the Dwight D. Eisenhower Library, Abilene, Kansas.

[65] President Eisenhower had suffered a heart attack on September 24, but had begun to resume official activities in mid-October.

Hollywood producer Dore Schary wrote about Stevenson's speech in Chicago on November 19 at the Democratic National Committee dinner: "The words you said were rich and an abundant harvest — perhaps too abundant — because you were forced to hurry your delivery and as a result some of the sock points were too rapidly winged away into the ether. Please, Guv, a little slower on the pace. Allow the audience to absorb as you go along." He added that former President Harry S. Truman had received an enthusiastic reception at a fund-raising dinner in Los Angeles for the Truman Library and that Truman's support for Stevenson's candidacy was a necessity.

To Dore Schary[66]

December 30, 1955

Dear Dore:

I am 'way behind in my correspondence generally, not to mention my correspondence with Dore Schary. The trouble with that guy is that he says something and you can't just "answer" his letters.

So, let me just say that I am full of gratitude for those letters and also for your Christmas thought of me. I am sure you are exactly right about the pace of my speeches. I have, I confess, a hopeless addiction. I always attempt to get too much in a speech, and of course I shall have to write less if I am going to talk slower.

I was delighted to hear your report of President Truman's reception. Certainly he will live long in the hearts of Americans who respect courage. As to his "support," my guess is that he will really try to create the public impression of neutrality, and, in his *own* way, be neutral. He tells me that he feels he can be more effective in keeping harmony and unity in the party if he does not espouse any individual candidate and thus sacrifice his position as conciliator. After the convention I have no doubt the problem will be not what he will do but how he will do it.

I hope all is well with you and your family and that you will give them my best wishes. I am happy to report that John Fell is mending rapidly now and that his father is about ready to relax.

Happy New Year!

Yours,

P.S. I had the most affectionate telephone call from H.S.T. about John Fell the other day.

[66] A copy is in A.E.S., I.S.H.L.

To Mrs. Franklin D. Roosevelt[67]

December 30, 1955

My dear Mrs. Roosevelt:

So many thanks for your note. I am hastily forwarding some more copies of "the prayer."[68] Let me know if you want still more. We will have plenty left over.

I have visited Frank's[69] splendid farm, and indeed he presented me with a splendid Suffolk ram more than a year ago in, I suppose, an heroic effort to improve the sheep population of Illinois! Well, the ram has increased it but I can't guarantee that he has improved it. I hope on another trip to New York I will have a chance to see Frank, but I think he should be cautious about getting identified with me politically until the New York situation has evolved a little further.

Do tell Elliott[70] to let me know when he is passing this way some time. I have never known him as I have the other boys. My son Borden roomed with his son at college, as you may know.

John Fell is mending rapidly in body, but the spirit will be slower I fear. The outpouring of sympathy and concern from around the country has surprised me. I enclose a copy of the message I have been sending about in an effort to keep abreast of the mail.

With affection and gratitude,

Faithfully yours,

Mrs. Eugene Meyer made suggestions on December 28, 1955, about Stevenson's campaign, sent him material to read, and was helping to organize a Women's Committee for him.

[67] The original is in the Franklin D. Roosevelt Library, Hyde Park, New York.

[68] The "prayer" Stevenson had on his Christmas cards was attributed to an unknown Confederate soldier:

> I asked God for strength, that I might achieve,
> I was made weak, that I might learn humbly to obey . . .
> I asked for health, that I might do greater things,
> I was given infirmity, that I might do better things . . .
> I asked for riches, that I might be happy,
> I was given poverty that I might be wise . . .
> I asked for power, that I might have the praise of men,
> I was given weakness, that I might feel the need of God . . .
> I asked for all things, that I might enjoy life,
> I was given life, that I might enjoy all things . . .
> I got nothing that I asked for — but everything I had hoped for,
> Almost despite myself, my unspoken prayers were answered.
> I am among all men, most richly blessed.

[69] Franklin D. Roosevelt, Jr.

[70] Her son, Elliott Roosevelt.

To Mrs. Eugene Meyer[71]

[no date]

I didn't know that the best things come in envelopes! Thanks for two wonderful tonics — at the end of the year and the beginning. You are good, great, gentle and wise and you have told me what I had not wholly understood — Being who and what I am I cannot do otherwise. But where will come the strength and patience to do it well? My beloved John Fell I brought home tonight in a cast and sparkling with some fine false teeth. I am the luckiest happiest living mortal this very night & to that I've just added your New Year letter. I wish I could have proposed a toast at your birthday — to love that lifts & stirs and makes no demands — AES

What happens to time? Is there ever enough to think, to write, to read?

To Harry S. Truman

January 3, 1956

Dear Mr. President:

I have recently heard that you plan to travel abroad this spring and summer. This news reminds me of the reaction I have felt of late to the expansion of the direct missionary work of the Russians in Asia and the unhappy fact that there is concurrently virtual silence in the Western world. In part this is due to the fact that there is virtually no one in the present administration who can do much to counteract, from an exalted public relations and propaganda point of view, the positive effect of such Soviet courtship, not to mention the negative effect of such blunders as Dulles' Goa statement and the everlasting military emphasis.[72]

[71] This handwritten postcard is in the Agnes Meyer files, Princeton University Library.

[72] The Secretary of State, in December, 1955, referred to Goa, an enclave on the west coast of India that Portugal had held since 1510, as a "Portuguese province." This raised a storm of protest in India, which was disputing Portugal's claim to the territory at that moment. Critics charged that despite Dulles's declaration of the neutral position of the United States in the dispute, his phrase appeared to favor Portugal's claims and carried overtones of colonialism that would tend to drive India further into alignment with the Communist bloc. As A. M. Rosenthal explained, "To say a territory is a province carries the implication that it is a part of the motherland and so not a matter for international dispute." He added that the press of India, Singapore, Burma and Ceylon were denouncing the statement as "one of the greatest diplomatic blunders of modern history." See "Goa Issue a Windfall for Russians in India," New York *Times*, December 11, 1955, sec. 4, p. 5. (India later invaded Goa in December, 1961, in violation of the United Nations charter, and the occupied territory, together with two other former Portuguese holdings, became a Union territory in March, 1962.)

From these reflections I have moved on to the idea that you are perhaps the only other American who could do something of this kind effectively. I wonder, therefore, if you could be persuaded to travel through South and East Asia on your return. I should think the administration would have to publicly welcome such a possibility. Even the press would have a hard time discrediting your stature and esteem abroad.

The country would be quickly reminded that the advantages of the mission of Wendell Willkie with the blessing of President Roosevelt were enormous.[73] Your symbolic value would be far greater. And I should also think the administration would want to provide staff and help. After all, from their point of view politically, regardless of the advantages to the country, such a project would have great merit as tangible bi-partisanship.

You will detect here both impetuosity and spontaneity — but also, I hope, an idea that is animated by anxious concern for the deterioration of our country's image in a decisive area.

Respectfully,

P.S. It suddenly occurred to me that all this may have been considered by you long since. If so, forgive me for bothering you!

Homer A. Jack, the minister of the Unitarian church in Evanston, Illinois, sent Stevenson a copy of the sermon he planned to deliver on January 8, 1956, concerning Stevenson's joining the Presbyterian Church. It was supportive of the action and concluded: "In any case, this freedom of choice in religion includes the freedom of a presidential candidate, even a President, to choose to leave a denomination, or the freedom to choose to join several denominations."

To the Reverend Homer A. Jack

January 3, 1956

Dear Homer:

I am touched by your letter and your understanding of what I have done, perhaps carelessly. I had, I confess, never anticipated the violent

---

[73] Wendell L. Willkie, the Republican candidate for President in 1940, traveled in 1941 and 1942 to Britain, the Near East, Russia and China as President Roosevelt's personal representative. "His purposes, he said, were to demonstrate American unity, to 'accomplish certain things for the President,' and to find out 'about the war and how it can be won.'" James MacGregor Burns, *Roosevelt: The Soldier of Freedom* (New York: Harcourt Brace Jovanovich, 1970), p. 275. See also Wendell L. Willkie, *One World* (New York: Simon & Schuster, 1943).

reaction of some Unitarians. I have been identified with the Unitarian Church by inheritance since birth, and by conviction since maturity because I thought they were liberals in religion as well as elsewhere. Indeed, I find that, among many, worshiping God and identifying with a convenient Protestant church community is some sort of treacherous, faithless act. What has stung me most of all is the impression from many letters that politics somehow motivated formalizing my connection with the Presbyterian Church in Lake Forest, which I have attended off and on for more than twenty years.

I suppose I should have been a little more thoughtful and perceptive about the consequences and should have resisted the incessant blandishments of Bob Andrus and my old and beloved friend, Dick Graebel, of the Presbyterian church in Springfield, but it seemed only the natural thing to do as I have been in and out of this church for a long time and most of my closest friends in Lake Forest go there.

Actually, I go more often, when time permits, to the new Unitarian fellowship, at Highwood, and I am very hopeful that its sphere of influence is going to enlarge.

I suppose you saw the enclosed statement that some of my ministerial friends put together. I am not sure that Kenneth Walker had his heart in it, but Jack Mendelsohn certainly did, and I gather he had your views about the non-exclusive character of genuine Unitarianism.

I wish so much I could come on Sunday. It happens, most unfortunately, that I have to wheel my son onto an airplane at Midway to Boston which leaves at 11:45 that morning. I should not feel right about it if I were not there myself to see him off on some sort of an improvised stretcher. Hence, I cannot possibly make the service. I hope you will understand and forgive me and accept my profound thanks for what you are doing.

Cordially,

H. Talbot Pearson, executive director of the Unitarian Laymen's League, wrote expressing the hope that John Fell would soon recover, and said of the furor caused by Stevenson's joining the Presbyterian Church: "It is safe to say your Unitarian friends here have a proper appreciation of your promptings in the matter, but we may need to appoint a special public relations officer to deal with the mail bag."

To H. Talbot Pearson[74]

[no date]

Thank you so much for your kind & understanding letter of 12/28. I'm distressed that I've caused you such inconvenience — nor did I know that it was so difficult for a Protestant to practice Christianity!

I too have had a lot of letters — mostly Unitarian protests, but enclosed is one today that warmed my heart & may interest you. We here have adopted the practice of acknowledging letters and enclosing a copy of the statement of the 4 ministers in explanation. If your office would care to do that I would be glad to send a lot of mimeograph copies.

You were so kind to think of John Fell — he is mending rapidly now.

AES

On December 16, 1955, Stevenson sent a letter he had just received, criticizing him for not being sufficiently pro-Israel, to Senator Hubert Humphrey. Humphrey replied that the United States should stand by Israel. On the other hand, Humphrey stated that our economic assistance to the Arab states was insufficient and that the United States had not pressed sufficiently for a settlement of the Arab refugee problem. Stevenson's article for Look, *"No Peace for Israel," August 11, 1953, was considered by some supporters of Israel to be too objective.*[75]

To Hubert H. Humphrey

January 4, 1956

Dear Hubert:

I guess *we* don't disagree at all on Israel, but I am afraid that many Zionists in this country disagree with *us*, in that they seem to positively resent any sympathetic, helpful and friendly, expressions about the Arabs and their problems. As the lady who wrote to us said: "We want no 'neutrals.'"

You may recall that I was a member of the U.S. Delegation to the General Assembly in 1947. It was our delegation — ten of us — in effect, that created Israel, so I have had a long, intimate, and sympathetic feeling for our little friend. I wish I could say the same for some

[74] This handwritten letter is in the possession of the Laymen's League of the Unitarian-Universalist Association, Boston, Massachusetts. It was probably written in early January, 1956.

[75] This article is reprinted in *The Papers of Adlai E. Stevenson,* Vol. V.

of the extremists who think to befriend her by making more difficult the reconciliation with her neighbors, which is her best hope for survival and success. I have tried to be a temperate and restraining influence among the Zionists, which I think does them and their objective a service even if it does me a disservice with them.

So many thanks for enclosing your speeches. I am everlastingly amazed at your productivity and versatility — and vitality!

Affectionate regards to you and Muriel.[76]

Yours,

Former Vice President Henry A. Wallace wrote Stevenson and mentioned that he had delivered a speech on the farm problem in Des Moines, Iowa, on November 15, 1955. He wrote: "If I can be of help to you in a quiet, non-political way which will not embarrass either you or me, do not hesitate to call on me." He added that he intended to vote for President Eisenhower. In a letter to Barry Bingham on December 10 about the Stevenson for President Committee, Wallace stated that he was not in politics. He added: "Dozens of times I have said that I thought the Stevenson campaign speeches were the best political speeches made by any candidate in this Century, not excepting Roosevelt."

To Henry A. Wallace[77]

January 6, 1956

Dear Mr. Wallace:

So many thanks for your letter of December 10. I am mortified that it has not come to my attention long before this, but somehow my organization has not been built up as rapidly as the volume of mail. I am sure you will understand and forgive me.

I was much touched and gratified by your charitable comments and good will. I remember so well not only the meetings to which you refer in Washington long ago, but also those meetings of the BEW which I attended on behalf of Col. Knox.[78] It seems another age, doesn't it?

Do send me, if you will, the copy of your Iowa speech on November 15. I saw only a brief account of it in the Chicago papers at the time.

With best wishes and my gratitude for your encouragement, I am

Cordially yours,

[76] Mrs. Humphrey.

[77] A copy is in A.E.S., I.S.H.L.

[78] Stevenson represented Secretary of the Navy Frank Knox at meetings of the Board of Economic Warfare in Washington during World War II. See *The Papers of Adlai E. Stevenson*, Vol. II.

To Benjamin H. Swig[79]

January 6, 1956

Dear Ben:

I had thought I had imposed upon you not enough but more than enough and that I would not be obliged to do so again. However, it has been suggested by some of my more active supporters in California, including your friend Pat Brown,[80] that you would be the ideal Finance Chairman for the pre-convention campaign in California.

I know this is a frightening assignment and I am loathe to ask you to do it, but it may not be too hard as I doubt if the requirements will be shocking, and I am sure you will get a lot of help in view of the extensive support my candidacy seems to have evoked down there.

I am sending a copy of this note to Pat so that he will know that I have approached you; and I hardly need add that I earnestly hope you will see fit to give him a hand.

With warmest wishes and my apologies again, I am

Cordially yours,

Stevenson sent the following telegram to his old friend Carl Sandburg on the poet's seventy-eighth birthday.

To Carl Sandburg

January 6, 1956

MY WARMEST GREETINGS ON THE BIRTHDAY OF ILLINOIS' MOST ELOQUENT SON. MAY YOUR STURDY VOICE SING OF AMERICA FOR MANY YEARS TO COME.

To Harry S. Truman

January 10, 1956

Dear Mr. President:

I have just read now the proof sheets of installment 28 of the Memoirs. I know you will understand my wanting to comment, in all friendliness, about several of the things you say there about the 1952 campaign.[81]

Your criticisms are candid, and this permits me to take pleasure and

---

[79] Owner of the Fairmont Hotel in San Francisco and a close friend of Stevenson.
[80] Edmund G. Brown, attorney general of the State of California.
[81] Mr. Truman's memoirs were being serialized in *Life* magazine and in newspapers. For the installment to which Stevenson refers, see the New York *Times*, February 22, 1956, p. 20; see also Harry S. Truman, *Memoirs*, Vol. II: *Years of Trial and Hope, 1946–1952* (Garden City, New York: Doubleday, 1956), pp. 491–500; *The Papers of Adlai E. Stevenson*, Vol. IV, particularly pp. 90–91.

satisfaction, too, from your kind and indeed charitable comments regarding our general accomplishments in 1952.

Regarding the "mistakes," I have no thought except to remove any element of misunderstanding which might in any way have contributed to your feeling about them.

I think you will agree, with respect to my decision to have a personal friend[82] made Chairman of the National Committee, that if this was a mistake it was one that the great majority of Presidential candidates have traditionally made.

I set up my headquarters in Springfield because I was Governor of Illinois. It was my capital, and my continuing responsibility was there throughout the campaign. I could not in good conscience have done differently about this.

The reference to "the mess in Washington" was, as you very fairly indicate, an inadvertence. I should perhaps note that this reference was in a letter, not in an interview. Either in dictation or in transcription the quotes were left out of my reference to what the man who had written to me said.

You refer to my "alienating many influential Democratic political leaders at the outset," and thus sacrificing perhaps millions of votes. I know, of course, that Governor [Allan] Shivers of Texas and Governor [Robert F.] Kennon of Louisiana were alienated by my position on tidelands oil.[83] There was a basic principle involved there, one for which you had stood with vigor. Governor [James F.] Byrnes of South Carolina and Senator [Pat] McCarran of Nevada also appear to have opposed my candidacy. And I am suggesting only that while needless alienation of Democratic support would seem to me the appropriate subject of criticism, the loss of support due to a candidate's stand on matters of principle should not.

Of the "poor coordination between Washington and Springfield" I can only say that I was frankly unaware of it at the time, that I know from subsequent knowledge that what you say is true, that I regret it and cannot wholly blame it on what were the inordinate pressures of the moment.

I am afraid that we do remember differently the conversations and events reflected by your suggestion that "when it seemed to me too late, Stevenson asked me to get into the campaign." We talked about that, as I recall it, only on the occasion of my visit with you in your office in Washington on August 12 when you graciously agreed to make six or

[82] Stephen A. Mitchell.
[83] See Stevenson's speech on this issue at New Orleans, October 10, 1952, in *The Papers of Adlai E. Stevenson*, Vol. IV, pp. 150–158.

seven speeches toward the end of the campaign in major centers in the East and Middle West. You expressed a desire, as I recall, to conclude in St. Louis. You also informed me of a Labor Day commitment, I believe, and a dam dedication together with a speech in California. But your reference to a later and belated request from me to change what I had thought were our arrangements made on August 12 to cover the whole campaign comes now as a surprise to me. I repeat, though, that I was grateful indeed for all you did.

If you are right that I went "on the defensive in Cleveland and other cities on the question of so-called Communists in Government," I can only say that my words served my intentions very poorly. I could not ignore, but had to correct, the distortions of fact and the even uglier innuendos about my own position on this issue. As I reread these speeches now they seem to me bluntly forthright on the subject of the Republican campaign smear and slander on the Communist issue. I have spoken in public not once but a score of times my heartfelt belief that you saw this issue clearly and did more than anyone else in the world to fight communism.

Finally, let me say again that while you may be right that if I had accepted "in good faith" your proposal on January 20 (not 30)[84] to run for the nomination I would have received at least three million more votes, I don't see how I could have done it — even if I had wanted to, because I had already asked the people of Illinois to re-elect me Governor and it was too late to withdraw my petition.

Well! I feel better! And I hope you do too. I know you will realize that this letter is not animated by vexation, but by the hope that giving you my understanding of these things may diminish a little your own feeling about them.

I know there were mistakes. I know, too, that you will share with me the consolation I got the other day from an advertisement headline: "Everybody Has 20-20 Hindsight."

You know, from what I have already said elsewhere, about my admiration for your extraordinary workmanship in compiling these memoirs. That feeling is unchanged.[85]

Respectfully yours,

P.S. I assume you have seen the enclosed admirable review from the London Times Literary Supplement.

---

[84] Actually January 22, 1952. See Davis, *A Prophet in His Own Country*, pp. 387–389; *The Papers of Adlai E. Stevenson*, Vol. III, p. 490.

[85] Mr. Truman replied on January 16, 1956, that he was glad that Stevenson understood his statements and actions of 1952. He added that while at a meeting in Minnesota, he had heard some favorable comments on Stevenson's Presidential candidacy.

Vanessa Brown (in private life Mrs. Mark Sandrich), an actress and radio commentator living in California, was concerned with promoting wider popular understanding of political issues through the use of public communications. She wrote Stevenson suggesting that he appear on a television program that would show him at home after dinner with members of his family.

To Vanessa Brown

January 10, 1956

Dear Vanessa:

I am mortified that I have not acknowledged your nice letter before this. But my life has become uncommonly burdened of late and it has only now emerged from a neglected heap.

While I agree with you that the little details about one's life seem to be a useful means of popularizing a person, I am sure you will agree with me that it is also almost intolerably distasteful to be so perpetually exposed. The newspaper diagrams of President Eisenhower's insides not long ago seem to me to have exceeded the tolerances.

However, I have no doubt that the public relations gentlemen will humanize me and expose me to the point of regurgitation — at least by me! — if they can. Just this morning I looked up in the commutation train and a flash bulb went off in my eyes and the newspaper photographer remarked: "Just wanted to show you riding with the common people, Guv." I had thought I had been riding with the common people all my life, but I guess we have to prove it every few minutes.

However, I am wandering, and you have a good idea. I shall bear it in mind; and you also have a good idea about the periodic television show. The difficulties are twofold: (1) money; because they will only take newsworthy things unless you buy the time, as you know; and (2) there is such a thing as becoming old hat and losing one's freshness and scarcity value. The latter consideration, I am told, is especially important in my case in view of the fact that I will have difficulty at best of performing at the level of expectation which my beloved eggheads have established.

It was nice of you to write me. It would be still nicer if you were to come to see me when you pass through Chicago as you must from time to time.

With my warm regards and happy recollections of our meeting in New York what seems like a long time ago, I am

Cordially yours,

Senator Lehman replied to Stevenson's letter of December 17, 1955, that every effort had to be made to maintain relations on as cordial a basis as possible with Governor Averell Harriman. Otherwise, it would be difficult to mobilize all efforts for the election itself.

To Herbert H. Lehman

January 10, 1956

Dear Herbert:

I emphatically agree with you about the importance of not aggravating the situation in New York. I have done everything within reason to restrain my friends, and I think they have been obedient on the whole. However, lately I detect a feeling that there is not enough mutuality. I hope you will keep me informed and not hesitate to suggest anything I should do at any time. The important thing is the election and not the nominee. This is the trouble with primaries and choosing up sides all across the country. I am afraid they always leave ugly feelings and diluted energies at best.

With warmest good wishes to you and Mrs. Lehman, I am

Cordially,

Al Weeks, of Bellingham, Washington, was chairman of a meeting to honor Mrs. Franklin D. Roosevelt.

To Al Weeks[86]

January 10, 1956

I AM GLAD THAT THE DEMOCRATS OF YOUR SECOND CONGRESSIONAL DISTRICT ARE HONORING MRS. ELEANOR ROOSEVELT, A GREAT AND GRACIOUS LADY WHOSE LIFETIME OF DEVOTED SERVICE TO HER FELLOW MAN IS BOTH AN EXAMPLE AND AN INSPIRATION TO ALL OF US. IN HONORING HER YOUR COMMITTEE IS HONORING ITSELF AND THE CAUSE WHICH IT SERVES. WARMEST REGARDS TO ALL OF YOU.

To Mrs. Eugene Meyer[87]

[no date]

Agnes dear —

You are not only a remarkable woman, you are an heroic Christian — "There is no freedom except through loving and the being loved which

[86] This telegram is in the Franklin D. Roosevelt Library, Hyde Park, New York.

[87] This handwritten letter is in the Agnes Meyer files, Princeton University Library. It is postmarked January 11, 1956.

results from unselfish giving of one's whole soul." I know this. I really know it; my mother, sister, ministers galore have told it to me. I've, what's more, discovered it for myself. But somehow I needed awfully to be told it again just now, when the pressures are rising, the irritability point closer & closer, self pity, self love, weariness, anxiety and all the garden varieties of difficulties rising up about me, now that John Fell has gone back to college and, with a thud, I've dropped back in my old, earthy world.

But why do I pick out just that sentence from your last blessed lesson! Don't worry — Im getting more self confidence (or is it "don't give a damn"?) and I *will* bring my two sides together *in public*, as you say, more & more as I relax & enjoy it!

And now Goldie Myerson[88] & a bunch of Zionists are at the gate and I must leap from you and charity, beauty, love, understanding, to the statesman role! Can I? "Yes, you can," she said. (But can I keep awake is another question).

Love, in great haste.

AES

The Reverend Richard Paul Graebel wrote Stevenson that denomina-tionalism was the "last refuge of the scoundrel who has lost his Christian faith." He suggested that Stevenson deliver a talk entitled "This Nation, Under God" to the American people of all denominations and no denominations and "lift this thing to a higher level."

To the Reverend Richard Paul Graebel

January 12, 1956

Dear Dick:

I have read your superb letter. My, how I wish there were more Graebels in the Protestant pulpits — Unitarian, Presbyterian and what not!

I think you will like the enclosed copy of a letter from a gentleman who is unknown to me. I have had splendid support and encouragement from the Unitarian hierarchy in Boston. I wish I could say the same for all of my "liberal" Unitarian brethren.

What you have suggested about a discussion on the theme "This Nation, Under God" strikes a vibrant chord. I have been thinking of the same thing. Moreover, I have had a letter from a Unitarian minister who

---

[88] Minister of Labor in the Israeli government. Later in 1956, she had her name changed to Golda Meir.

has preached a sermon about me, suggesting something of the same kind, but how, where, when can I ever contrive to prepare what would have to be a ringing declaration of faith in religion rather than in denominationalism. I rather wish I could drop the whole wretched campaign and concentrate on this for a bit, but I can't even find time to handle my correspondence let alone write anything. How fortunate Lincoln is to have you in Lincoln's church![89]

Yours,

P.S. Do you think *you* could do some part time drafting of a speech along this line? I think you have doubtless seen what I wrote a year or so ago for a program called "This I Believe."[90] If you haven't, Carol [Evans] will send it to you.

To Herbert Agar

January 18, 1956

Dear Herbert:

When I wrote you a few weeks ago I gave you fair warning that I would be asking for help, and here I am! Please be utterly frank with me if the following is not within your current resources of time and energy.

After declining for a number of years, I am committed to speak to the American Society of Newspaper Editors at their spring meeting on April 21. I think you know the setting and atmosphere of this meeting and the reverberating possibilities of what is said there. The audience, while personally friendly, will be professionally critical, I assume, yet susceptible to the impression of a thoughtful, imaginative speech. I had rather thought to make this speech one of my three or four major "efforts" during the primary campaign, which extends from February through June.

While I have not been able to think much about this occasion, I have for a long time wanted to do something that might be called "The Image of America." What that is I am sure you know better than I, but I think of the impression which our country creates in the minds of people all over the world and how that impression is made up of countless incidents of American life and behavior, some of them trivial and apparently meaningless in themselves, some of them gross and ghastly, like [Secretary of State] Dulles' late performance, and all of them

---

[89] The Lincoln family pew, still to be seen in the First Presbyterian Church in Springfield, Illinois, is reserved for the use of the governor of the state and his family or honored guests on special occasions.

[90] See Stevenson, *What I Think*, pp. 151–152.

strangely powerful when viewed in the aggregate. I want to bring out the point that we deface the vision of America in the minds of people around the world too often, sometimes by lack of understanding of our point of view, sometimes heedlessly, and of late more often for reasons of domestic politics and political gain, real or fancied, at a disproportionate price in prestige abroad.

You will recall, I know, that I talked of this a little in the lectures at Harvard, which you published.[91] It is a theme which I know has preoccupied you for years and about which you have convictions based on uncommon experience here and abroad. If you felt you could find time to draft something for me along this line it would be infinitely helpful.

I leave in a few days for Arizona, California, Oregon, Washington and Utah on an exhausting primary campaign tour that causes me to wonder how I happened ever to attempt this twice. I begin to understand why women have a second baby! At all events, I see painfully little time ahead for the sort of careful thought and preparation which such a speech at such a time and before such an audience requires. Confidently, hopefully and gratefully I turn to you.

With affectionate greetings to Barbie[92] and my best always to you, I am

Yours,

Harry S. Truman replied to Stevenson's letter of January 3, 1956, that he was reluctant to take a trip overseas since the opposition party was in control of the White House. He suggested that former Ambassador Chester Bowles would be ideal. Truman added that John Foster Dulles's actions and statements had lost the United States almost all of its friends. In an interview with James Shepley, "How Dulles Averted War," Life, January 16, 1956, Dulles stated: "You have to take chances for peace, just as you must take chances in war. Some say we were brought to the verge of war. Of course we were brought to the verge of war. The ability to get to the verge of war without getting into the war is the necessary art. If you cannot master it, you inevitably get into wars. If you try to run away from it, if you are scared to go to the brink, you are lost."

Truman mentioned in his letter that Mrs. Truman was reading My Brother Adlai, *but that she had the flu and had not completed the book.*

[91] The British edition of *Call to Greatness* was published by Rupert Hart-Davis, Ltd.

[92] Mrs. Agar.

To Harry S. Truman

January 20, 1956

Dear Mr. President:

I understand perfectly your reluctance. I had not thought of any direct approach but rather dropping the suggestion that they approach you to undertake this mission in the Nation's interest. Of course I suppose this would be tantamount to the acknowledgement of the unhappy state to which they have brought opinion with respect to America in Asia and they would therefore be the more reluctant to do it, especially after Dulles' latest extravaganza. Certainly I would not expect to make any positive gestures. I agree, also, about Chester, but that would be quite a different level from what I had in mind.

You are ahead of me as to my sister's book. I read some of the manuscript but I have not had a chance to see the book yet. And now I must leave for the West on this weary primary journey. Somehow the expenditure of all the time and money in internal competition disconcerts me a little.

I am sorry to hear of Mrs. Truman's illness and I trust that she is mending rapidly.

Cordially,

p.s. You left some indelible impressions in the Twin Cities — all good, and heartening to our plans!

To Mrs. Eugene Meyer[93]

January 22, 1956

My dear Agnes —

So you think it will keep me "bouncing" over this appalling trail if I think of your adventures in 1943! I wish it were so; indeed I wish I had your energy of mind & spirit & body as of now, let alone 1943! But I'll not forget the challenge dear Agnes, and I'll try to have fun. What's more I really might have a little fun what with a couple of "time outs" for writing etc in Phoenix and Rancho Santa Fe — but it would be even more fun in Nassau. And I pray that you too will have some fun; and if, as I suspect, thoughtful writing is *fun* for you, then why not, my dear Agnes, disembody a bit and write me some of your ideas in speech form — denouncing the Reps., their spirit and narrow, material visi[o]n — extolling the virtues of — well you'll know what to say!! In short, I'm in search of a good ghost, and I love a dear gallant lady who just might have some ghost in her in her beloved, turbulent and teeming

---

[93] This handwritten letter is in the Agnes Meyer files, Princeton University Library.

soul. Don't ask me what to write, to talk about, because thats what I'm asking myself eve[r]y day.

There's so much to talk about; I wonder, for example, if the full implications of the Dulles story and the Pres' statement that he didnt know what he said have been considered.[94] Sometimes I get a little frightened — and when I do I feel very lonesome because no one else does or seems to & I suspect I must get things all out of proportion.

I'm off tomorrow on the first leg of this horrible schedule — to have fun!! Farewell; I *will* think of you and bless you time & again, because I believe what you tell me & that does a lot for my id or ego, or whatever self esteem and a hungry heart is!

Love — (in horrid haste)

ADLAI

1/22/56   P.S. How do you think my campaign's going? Honestly! I get a little worried, altho we're begin[nin]g to get some mon[e]y & therefor[e] some staff, there is so much to do I get a little faint now and then. Blessings & prayers.   A

———

Lord — How you can write!!

Senator Humphrey wrote Stevenson that it was unwise to underestimate Senator Estes Kefauver in the Minnesota primary. It was possible, he warned, that Republicans would vote in the Democratic primary to administer a blow to Stevenson, Governor Orville Freeman, and himself.

To Hubert H. Humphrey

January 30, 1956

Dear Hubert:

You were thoughtful to send me your statement about the Minnesota Primary. I can't agree more about making sure that we don't underestimate Kefauver and I am counting on you — most of all — to make sure this doesn't happen!

Sincerely,

[94] See James Shepley, "How Dulles Averted War," *Life*, January 16, 1956.

On January 31, 1956, Stevenson opened his campaign for California's convention votes. He delivered the following speech at the Oakland Municipal Auditorium on February 1.[95]

Thank you for the lovely birthday cake that you were good enough to present to me while I was having that splendid dinner. The birthday cake, I notice, is not on my agenda and I can't quite understand why it isn't if I am so emaciated after two days' campaigning in California. Anyway, there will be some left over — I think — if you want to come forward when we conclude the ceremony.

I have had the good fortune in my lifetime to see, I believe, most of the corners of the earth and many of its most beautiful sights, and I know nothing finer than what I saw this morning when I flew into Alameda across the hills and there set before me San Francisco Bay and the Golden Gate. It was a wonderful sight and it never ceases to fascinate me — to exhilarate me — to exalt a sometimes feeble spirit.

But you know, the wonderful thing about Alameda County which I have discovered tonight for the first time, is that it is just as beautiful indoors as it is outdoors and I am grateful to everyone of you for coming here not only on my behalf, but I believe on behalf of that which I should like to feel that I represent — the Democratic Party.

I have even enjoyed having a box luncheon with you in spite of the fact that there were five cameras photographing my larynx (laughter). And you have been so good to me already in my visit to California that you have shaken off my right arm — which is a very painless exercise to an unemployed politician (laughter).

I don't feel altogether a stranger here. The fact of the matter is that I flew to the South Pacific during the war some 14 years ago from the Alameda Naval Air Station.[96] I thought just this evening as I was coming here, that perhaps if it hadn't been for that trip I might never have been in politics and might never have come back to Alameda under circumstances such as this — because there and in the following years in the mud of Liri Valley in Italy and on those burning atolls I saw something of the sacrifice, something of the cost in treasure and in blood of the preservation of those things that we hold dearest. So I concluded that if one freely gave his life and his health in war that he might as well give a little of his time in peace, which is as good a reason for going into politics as any I know.

95 The text is based on a mimeograph copy of the speech. Typographical errors have been corrected by the editors.

96 For Stevenson's tour of the Pacific theater with Secretary of the Navy Frank Knox in 1943, see *The Papers of Adlai E. Stevenson*, Vol. II, pp. 70ff.

I'm told that this audience comprises all segments of the community here — there might even be some people here representative of organized labor (applause). Well, Pat,[97] evidently you didn't mislead me for once. I'm one of those people who don't believe that organized labor is a menace to society (applause). And what's more, I am convinced that the union of the two great segments of the labor movement in this country will make not for less, but for more responsibility and influence in our common life, that labor's problems are solved only as the nation's problems are solved, that fifteen million people will flourish in the labor movement only as a much larger number of people flourish in the United States, and that conversely, a nation cannot long be healthy if any segment of it is unhealthy, if, for example, the farmer who constitutes some 13% of us is unhealthy. I can't even be sure that this great influence in our life is all going to vote Democratic but I'm praying (applause).

I'm told once more that there may be people here from the University of California (applause), even from Mills College (laughter) and probably from other surrounding educational institutions. Well, I was right on all counts. May I say to you that I don't feel uncomfortable with you either (laughter). I'm one of those who don't even believe that students are dangerous or that all professors are subversive (applause).

I know that we live in an era marked, scarred, if I may say so, among other things, by a new form of anti-intellectualism, but to those of you who have likewise been afflicted with these epithets, I say, — Eggheads of the world arise (laughter-applause). I was even going to add that you have nothing to lose but your yolks (laughter).

I was much amused by what a very distinguished scholar wrote to me not long ago commenting on these matters, these perplexities of our contemporary life which have concerned so many of us. And he said: "Since when were education and ideas disqualifications for public office in the United States?" (applause). What's more, I don't feel an alien here for other reasons. Long ago — before, I suspect, most of you were born, I resided in Berkeley, California (applause) and I should like to point out to some of my Republican friends that that town seems to have flourished in spite of my having lived there (laughter). But the most phenomenal thing that people witness when they fly over the mountains into Alameda and the East Bay area is the incredible growth of this community of Alameda and of Contra Costa Counties and, for that matter, of California — the second largest state in our union — which stands now in excess of thirteen million people living here on the rim of the Pacific. I wonder what you are going to do to insure the

[97] Attorney General Edmund G. Brown.

allegiance to the Democratic party of all these new areas? Anyway, it's going to be up to you, to you who are here tonight, and your counterparts throughout the country, and to what you throughout the State can do to insure that they are not misled.

I thought too that perhaps undoubtedly the most significant fact of our present day world is, of course, the cold war, this contest between a new imperialism, if you please, a new tyranny certainly, and what we have come to respect as western civilization. But next to this most significant contemporary fact is the fact of growth, the incredible, the remarkable expansion and the growing pains that go with it, the deficiency of schools, of school teachers, of highways, of hospitals, of all the social services, the problem of jobs, of providing in an expanding society expanding employment opportunities for the rapidly expanding labor force. More people nowadays are living longer. Automation is going to increase our leisure hours. A great migration is taking place from the farm to the city. We have found for the first time almost, I suppose, in history, the phenomena of mass education, of mass communication, standardization, conformity — even mass manipulation. All of these are characteristics of contemporary society about which I think we have thought all too little.

There are other problems, too, vast problems that tax our imagination, tax all of our resources of intellect, like the proper integration of minorities into our society, the proper integration of the less fortunate in this expanding society. This is a larger part, if you please, of our national life and if something isn't done now, when will it be done? It's not likely that it will be done when the struggle for a living and the contest between various segments of the community gets tougher. Not only are there vast material advantages in building deeper and broader stability into our economy by increasing our purchasing power — by expanding the participation of these groups — but there is also a vast problem of social morality in a society which has never been modest about declaring its fidelity to democracy and to equality among all.

Now these problems of growth that surround you here in California perhaps more perceptibly than almost anywhere else, are by no means isolated here. They are by no means characteristic only of California. You can see them all over the world. I've seen it in the steaming ports of West Africa, I've seen it in the teeming Indian villages — with a rising revolution of expectancy throughout the whole civilized world. And all down the great Pacific base of which California is an integral part. You see it too, and here lies the great opportunity for the sustenance of California and our nation's growth in the enlarging opportunities of commerce and for development in Asia.

[47]

Now, it's these problems, these problems of the world and these future problems of America that we should be thinking about in these contemporary times. These are the vast problems that are going to afflict us and confront us most certainly only tomorrow. I wonder if just the repetition of the old cliches of 20 years ago, of 10 years ago, are any longer good enough? I wonder if it's good enough just to tell an audience what it wants to hear just because it has heard it before?

It has been too long a habit and a custom of political speaking in our country — it's all too easy to talk about the things that made a liberal a liberal a few years ago. What we have to do now is to face the facts that most of these problems are almost obsolete as we are confronted with infinitely greater, newer problems taxing our imagination and our resources that are so much more perplexing than those we have dealt with in the past (applause).

I hope I don't sound partisan when I ask you what the Republicans can do with these problems of the future? My impression is that they are only now beginning to deal with the problems of the past. And I wonder if they are dealing with them this year because it's an election year (applause). But I suppose we must be thankful for every small thing and that imitation after all is the sincerest form of flattery (applause); so for my part, I'm very grateful that my Republican friends have at last decided to adopt all of the Democratic program. But it's not good enough.

You can't conduct foreign policy on the basis of alternate hot and cold declarations, on the basis of slogans like "unleashing Chiang Kai-shek," like "massive retaliation" and like "liberation" of the satellites and all of this nonsense that has gone on for years. You can't even conduct foreign diplomacy in this dangerous world from a news stand (applause). And you certainly can't conduct it with conflicting statements by the President and the Secretary of State, let alone when the conflicts are aided and abetted by those part time Secretaries of State, Senator [William] Knowland and Vice President [Richard M.] Nixon of California.

But I must not detain you too long. I was told to speak here only briefly and then to sit down and eat my birthday cake. But I must say a word about this Democratic side of our affair. The Republicans have failed to guarantee a fair share of our national income for the farmers; they have failed to halt the steady deterioration of our public educational facilities; they have largely nullified the conservation policies that have prevailed for almost a half a century (applause). They have talked a good game on highways and produced nothing, that is, until yesterday, when the President announced that he had abandoned the Republican program and adopted the Democratic program. And they have played, I suggest, fast and loose with all individual rights — individual rights of Americans — in the name of internal security (applause).

You mustn't get excited, this is just a primary campaign, not an election (laughter). They have jettisoned or curtailed the Federal programs intended to halt the urban blight that threatened so many of our cities. And these failures have confronted us with a variety of national problems all of them important, many of them urgent. Indeed, they have resulted in the presentation, as I have said, to Congress of a new legislative program in the year 1956, all of which was previously recommended by the Democrats and denounced by the Republicans. These matters are important, they deserve discussion, they deserve action, but I suggest that they are also symptoms of a larger failure, the failure to understand the spirit of America and the challenge of our generation.

We live in a perilous time. We live also in a time of danger and a time of hope and we are offered on the one hand, complacency to blind us to the one and deny us the other. The Republican bookkeeper tells us we cannot afford to maintain our military strength and the Republican politicians tell us we don't need to. If we complain that something seems to be missing from our daily lives, that our schools are not good enough and our highways are not good enough and that the cities are overcrowded and the old people frustrated and the psychiatrists overworked — if we mention these things — the mighty Republican chorus tells us, never mind, we have never had it so good. Well, maybe not, but I suggest that there has never been a time when Americans were satisfied with what they had. We are people who have lived by our faith in greater tomorrows, in the march of our national history; we have learned that there can be no turning back and no standing still.

Growth is the very order of our existence in America, we could survive, I think, almost anything except stagnation. Government has an inescapable role in this process: it can stimulate progress or retard it, and here I think we find the essential difference in the concept of the two parties. As a contemporary American philosopher put it, in the philosophy of the Democratic party, "Government is an art to be practiced," while in the Republican philosophy, "It is a status to be enjoyed." The Democrat goes into power firm in the conviction that there is much to be gained; the Republican goes into power with the equally firm conviction that there is much to lose.

On every front we have seen these truths illustrated in the past three years. Human needs have been reluctantly recognized, greedily met, usually under the pressure of political expediency as we have seen so conspicuously already in this campaign year of 1956.

The coming automation of industry is viewed more with alarm than as an opportunity to produce more goods with less human effort.

The revolution in agriculture which has produced food and fibre in excess of our current needs is regarded as a threat to our bank balance rather than an opportunity to raise living standards at home and abroad. Sometimes it appears that our leaders are actually frightened by our nation's strength and its vast richness and they seem to take counsel of those who would hoard what we have and stare out apprehensively through shuttered windows at an angry and envious world. But the way of the miser, I submit, was never the way of Uncle Sam.

It would be foolhardy, I believe, to dissipate our wealth and our power, but it would be fatal to dissipate our potential. We have never had the strength nor the desire to subjugate the world but we do have the resources to sustain our position of world leadership and to demonstrate that man can be secure and prosperous and free too (applause). You know the men, the hardy men your forefathers, who led the rolling tide of westward migration to these shores brought with them a saying that stands as well today. "We don't claim we're better than anybody else but we insist we're just as good" (applause).

In so many ways this golden State of California symbolizes our nation's best, its present and also its limitless future. Here was the end point, here was the terminus of those who followed the sun and who wrote so much of our history. Here your daily growth creates great problems and also monumental opportunities. Here you share your broad oceans with the nations of Asia on its far perimeter, the old nations. They too grapple uncertainly with new problems that may shake the future of all the world for good or for evil. Here you are eternally reminded by the breadth of your terrain and the bounty of your national endowment that we are just getting started in this young giant of a country of ours and that the means are at hand to shape a future beyond a dream of even the '49ers.

But I have neglected to say to you why I am here tonight. I said a great deal — probably more than I intended — but I suppose I should confess that I am here seeking the Presidency of the United States (applause). I'm glad you approve (laughter). I did not say that I am qualified for the Presidency of the United States and if anyone says to you that he is, will you tell him that he lacks the first qualification which is humility (applause).

But I do say to you that I am available (laughter). I do say to you that there are others like yourself who have urged me again to seek an office that beggars human ambition and that exceeds human capacity. And I shall do so gladly and I hope in good spirit, I hope with wisdom and certainly with an everlasting and patient concern for what lies in the heart of all we undertake in public life in America — and that is, the welfare of the United States and all of its citizens.

I heard this afternoon a story I'll share with you that illustrates my position. It was told to me by a distinguished fellow citizen. He said that some years ago before the war, some German scholars wanted to recruit a highly competent archaeologist to do some work in the hot lands of the Middle East and they inserted in scholarly journals an advertisement: "Wanted — a holder of a graduate degree in archaeology. He must be not over 35 years of age because the work is very arduous and finally he must be able to speak and decipher both classic Hebrew and classic Greek."

Well, the very following morning an applicant appeared at the door. He was an old man bent over with age, hobbling on a stick, and they said: "Why have you come?" And he said: "I have come in response to your advertisement." And they said: "Well, are you under 35?" "No, I'm at least twice that." "Well, have you a graduate degree in archaeology?" "I ain't never been to school at all." "Well, you speak classic Hebrew and Greek?" "Don't speak English very well." "Well, why have you come?" "I just come to tell you you can count on me" (laughter).

Well, I have just come here tonight to tell you you can count on me if you want to. Thank you (applause).

On February 2, 1956, Stevenson received a telegram in San Francisco from Franklin H. Williams, the West Coast secretary of the National Association for the Advancement of Colored People, stating that thousands of West Coast citizens were concerned about his position on civil rights. Stevenson was asked to state his position on a Fair Employment Practices Commission; the amendment proposed by Representative Adam Clayton Powell that would forbid federal funds for segregated schools; a nonsegregation amendment to federally financed housing; and, the need of strengthening the Civil Rights section of the Department of Justice. Stevenson replied by telegram.[98]

To Franklin H. Williams

February 4, 1956

In response to your telegram I am forwarding the following references to the record which I believe set forth my position on the issues about which you inquired. As Governor of Illinois I twice recommended

---

[98] The text is taken from a mimeograph copy of a press release.

and vigorously supported fair employment practices legislation; reorganized and strengthened the Commission on Human Relations; and ordered desegregation in the Illinois National Guard. Schools in East St. Louis and Alton were desegregated for the first time during my term. I used the National Guard to restore order in the Cicero riots.

Speaking before the American Municipal Association in Miami on November 30, 1955, I said this in regard to government action in the housing field: "Interwoven in this picture of inadequate income for adequate housing are the ugly complications of racial and national differences. The latest arrivals huddle in center city, and urban ghettoes are passed on from generation to generation of newcomers. For many of these, barriers of prejudice become confining walls as real as the towering buildings that hem them in, and even those whose incomes make it possible for them to escape often find they are barred from the parade, for prejudice extends not only to those who might be their neighbors, but to those who control rental and credit policies. Here, certainly, is a condition that demands the best that is in us — by law, by the activity of human relations agencies, by good will in the business community, by Christian decency."

In December, 1955, before the convention of the AFL–CIO in New York, I said: "I want to talk with you about what I think these hopes and aspirations (of the merged labor unions) are, and about what seems to me to be our proper course in pursuing them. They are, to begin with, I suggest, the hopes and aspirations not just of labor, not just of any single group in America, but to all Americans, without regard to race or religion or national origins. All colors your convention motto says, and all creeds. I hope with all my heart that there will be in this united labor movement no compromise with this essential, basic principle. There has been too much preaching and not enough practicing of what true equality of opportunity really means." I also said in the AFL–CIO address: "And while I adverted to this subject of voting, let me say that like you, too, and every democracy-loving person in America, Republican or Democrat, I've been shocked and shamed by the recent reports of bloody violence and gross intimidation to prevent people from exercising their right, indeed, their duty to vote in one section of our country."

On anti-segregation provisions in school aid legislation, I said this in an address before the National Education Association in Chicago on July 6, 1955: "While this program will by no means meet the whole construction need, it would be a long American step in the right direction. And I hope that what is good for all will not be lost to all by any linking together of the school aid and desegregation issues which would delay realization of our hopes and expectations on either of these vital fronts. In the long run segregation and discrimination, like other obsolete heritages, will yield quickest to the general advance of education."

On January 20, 1956, in a letter to Mr. Cecil Newman of the Minneapolis Spokesman,[99] which was released to the press, I made this comment on the Powell Amendment: "I hardly think such an amendment necessary. The Supreme Court has declared that no child may be barred from attending any public school on the basis of race. Any school which accepts public funds is a public school. It follows, therefore, that acceptance of Federal funds by a school district brings its schools under the jurisdiction of the Court. There are further reasons, too, why I think such an amendment undesirable as a matter of policy and unnecessary as a matter of law. The process of merging the old dual school systems often results in additional expense. A postponement of Federal aid may well delay, therefore, the process of transition which is already in progress in many areas where segregation was formerly required by law."

In commenting on the State of the Union Message recommendation of President Eisenhower that a special commission be created to study possible violations of the civil rights provisions of the Constitution I said in January that such a study seemed unnecessary. Where such violations have occurred, I pointed out, the Department of Justice already has adequate investigative machinery to establish the facts and full authority to take appropriate action."

In regard to the position of the Federal Administration in general and the Department of Justice in particular in the enforcement of the civil rights section of the Constitution, I have said: "I cannot foretell what a president would or would not do in hypothetical circumstances. But I do know that it is the president's duty under the Constitution to take care that laws be faithfully executed."

Stevenson delivered the following speech to the California Democratic Council state convention in Fresno, California, on February 4, 1956.[100]

Everyone likes to come to California. Indeed, from the growth out here, it looks as though everyone East of the Rockies *had* come to California, and come to stay. And I am no exception; I like to come here too, and not just to see glamorous California, but because I was born

---

99 A Negro-owned newspaper established in 1934.

100 The text is based on a mimeograph copy of a press release. Typographical errors have been corrected by the editors.

here, and I like to see what you're doing. The trouble is that each time I come you have done so much with it I can't recognize the old place!

Some fifty years ago my parents did not take Horace Greeley's advice to "Go West, young man" and took me *from* California *to* Illinois. But perhaps it is just as well they took me back to Illinois because at least the Presidential competition is tougher here in California, where, I am told, at least one Vice President, one Senator and one Governor are ready to save civilization — especially from one another.

And mention of the Presidency brings me back to Fresno and to you, because you Californians will have a great deal to do with America's decision in 1956 and in the years to come.

Perhaps the hardest question a candidate for President faces is: Why are you a candidate? It is not merely modesty — or the effort to conceal the lack of it — that makes it difficult to say why one seeks an office so freighted with mankind's destiny. I doubt if any thoughtful person would dare to say that he is wholly qualified to fill it. (And certainly I'm sure that all who respect our system and understand our times, would agree that such a responsibility is not a prize to be won in a popularity contest among good fellows; nor in an endurance contest to determine who can cover the most ground, shake the most hands and utter the safest ambiguities.)

And so I shall not attempt to answer the question, and simply say that I think the important thing in our system is to continue and improve the dialogue between the two great parties in order to give our sovereign, the people, educated, understanding choices between men and measures. I have the profound conviction that there are certain things our party, and our people, must say and do. It is in the hope that I can help them say and do these things that I gladly give myself to the battle again, knowing full well its burdens and brutalities, win or lose. During the primary I hope we can keep in mind that our great objective should not be just the choice of a leader, but the triumph next November of our common cause, our concepts and convictions about America and our time on earth.

You may properly ask, too, how I would conduct myself in the campaign. Well, to that I can only reply that I have been your leader before and you must be familiar with the merchandise. It has aged a bit, but it has not changed, in spite of all the stories I hear about the new Stevenson which is shortly to be unveiled. Indeed, I am cheered by the unanimity of disagreement about what this new model is to be.

I shall try in these coming months to fool no one, including myself — not with slogans or false promises or easy answers to hard problems.

The American people are entitled to know what is inside a candidate, as well as outside.

What's more, the reports you have heard about my new found solemnity remind me of a favorite Lincoln story: Two ladies in a railway coach were conversing. "I think," one said, that "Jefferson (Davis) will succeed." "Why do you think so," the other asked. "Because, Jefferson is a praying man." "But so," the other insisted, "is Abraham a praying man." "Yes," the troubled lady concluded, "but the Lord will think Abraham is joking." Carl Sandburg adds that Lincoln "said it was the best story about himself he had 'ever read in the newspapers' . . . and that he loved it."

I must frankly add to what I've said about myself that it is quite possible that I would not be the best candidate for you, if winning is the first objective of any political race, because I have an allergy for hollow promises. But I am told that promises pay, that they are indispensable to victory, and that keeping them is far less important than making them.

Well, I don't agree. And even if extravagant promises won a lot of votes for the Republicans last time, within two years the people gave the Congress back to the Democrats, and this time they will finish the job. One reason will be that the hucksters' arts of salesmanship, misbranding and exaggeration have enveloped the government and its communication with the people as never before. Truth has been trespassed too much of late by those who should serve her best — the people's servants. And I say to you frankly that I don't intend to take positions in this campaign which would reduce my effectiveness as President — regardless of the cost in votes.

For this campaign must deal with the great issues of our time — of war and peace; of our strength and our commitments; of the social revolution in the underdeveloped world and the new Communist challenge; of disarmament; of individual freedom and equal opportunity for all Americans; of monopoly and single interest government; of saving our natural resources from the greedy; and so on. We can meet these problems and all the myriad demands on the home front only as we are honest, forthright and responsible. To exploit them for cheap political ends is to cheat the people of their democratic birthright — their right to honest understanding of their problems. Let's leave those deceptive techniques to those who value the people's credulity less than we Democrats, for we *are* the people.

So, I am sorry if I cannot go as far as one or another of my friends would like on one or another of these issues. For I think that anyone who would occupy the most awesome office on earth must preserve its responsibility and perspective, and be able to *do* things rather than just talk about them. It seems to me that the right answers to most of today's hard problems do not lie at the extremes. But restraint and responsibility in tone and emphasis do not mean dilution or half measures. They mean, as St. Paul said to the Corinthians: "And every man that striveth for the mastery is temperate in all things."

The best example of intemperance we have lately witnessed is, I think, the Secretary of State's recent magazine advertising of his peculiar talent for rattling the saber and brandishing the atomic bomb — thereby scaring the daylights out of friends and neutrals the world around. If the Eisenhower administration has to do more bragging, it would be better to boast about resolute marches to the brink of peace than the brink of war.

We have heard a constant drumbeat from the Republican politicians and press that we are prosperous and at peace and all is well. We saw this sedative propaganda reach the apex of foolishness after the summit meeting only a few months ago.[101] But it is hard to find any area of the world where our situation has not deteriorated in late years. While we have reduced our strength we have enlarged our commitments. While we brag about massive retaliation and atomic intimidation, Russia talks of peace, of trade, of friendship, of economic development and the things the sensitive, suspicious, hungry Asians want to hear.

In this age everyone knows that we have the awesome power of atomic intimidation and that there are extremities, God forbid, in which we might be compelled to use it. But what is demanded of the powerful is a high sense of responsibility. The most effective deterrent is the unity and the strength of ourselves and our friends — the unity to act when necessary and the strength to take action suited to the aggression. This is far more than a question of power politics; it is a question of moral responsibility and accountability.

I agree that politics should stop at the water's edge, but surely that should not prevent us from trying to pull Mr. [John Foster] Dulles back to dry ground.

I have been reassured, as you have, by the more temperate, forthright and realistic statements coming out of Washington this week since the arrival of Prime Minister [Anthony] Eden. I only hope that they won't be diluted by the usual conflicting statement to appease the right-wing Republicans. After three years of practice I hope they have learned

---

[101] President Eisenhower and the British and French prime ministers had met with Soviet leaders and officials at Geneva in July, 1955.

down there that you really can't ride two elephants going in opposite directions at the same time.

And another thing; the sudden Soviet pressure for a treaty of friendship implying that any agreement on Germany depends on the United States accepting this treaty calls for careful consideration.[102] We must not appear to the free peoples of the world either to reject offers of friendship, or to submit to blackmail. Such a treaty offers two dangers — a false sense of security among us and our friends, without any concrete guarantee for German unity.

I wish the Secretary of State well in his great difficulties. For the fact is, of course, that the problems of the world today surpass any mortal's power or wisdom and can be dealt with only by a concert of our moral and mental resources sustained by an electorate that is fully informed and not anesthetized with slogans and sales talk.

As for the claim that there are no issues here at home, we are reminded that *for twenty years the Republican party fought — except in election years — the whole of what they derisively still call the "New Deal" — social security, public housing, minimum wages, farm income supports, a flexible fiscal policy, resource development, federal aid to education, medical care, etc. That our Republican friends are now accepting all of these things makes us grateful. After all, imitation is the sincerest form of flattery. But the basic issue is: who means what he says about these domestic issues and who doesn't?* Who is going to do anything about putting these agreed principles into effect, and who isn't?

On the farm problem: Which are we to take seriously — an election year Republican promise, or three years of Republican performance during which all their 1952 campaign promises were broken and the farmer's share of the national income dropped by $4 billions?

What about schools? Which are we to take seriously? An election year

---

[102] Soviet Premier Nikolai Bulganin proposed, on January 25, 1956, a twenty-year treaty of friendship and cooperation between the United States and the U.S.S.R. President Eisenhower, advised by Secretary of State Dulles, refused the offer on January 28, on grounds that such a bilateral treaty would be incompatible with America's commitments to our allies and membership in the United Nations. Bulganin, in a note dated February 1, 1956, called on the President to reconsider his decision, saying that Russia would be willing to make similar treaties with Britain, France and other nations, and suggesting rather bluntly that several key issues such as German reunification could not be discussed without such a treaty as a prerequisite. For the text of this note, see the New York *Times*, February 3, 1956. The Soviet proposals were widely regarded in the West as a propaganda maneuver designed to make an offer which the United States could not accept, while to refuse it would put the United States in the apparent position of rejecting an opportunity of "liquidating the so-called Iron Curtain," in Bulganin's words. The President in early March pledged further study, but he said that his basic position remained unchanged.

Republican proposal that we build half the new schools we need, or three years of Republican performance consisting of one conference?[103] (And who knows more about the school problem than California, where the school teacher shortage is already some 14,000, where enrollment will increase by nearly one million in the next eight years.)

Behind today's glowing phrases about conservation and development of our natural resources are three years of performance marked by the nullification of policies that have prevailed for almost half a century. And it is interesting to note that here in California, which has suffered so dreadfully this winter, there were no floods in the area where the Central Valley Project had built its dams. It was only where persistent controversy over the details of how to control and use your water resources that the terrible floods wrought their havoc.

They have talked piously of the housing shortage — while they junked or slashed the programs intended to halt the urban blight that threatens our cities.

They have played politics with the individual rights of Americans in the name of internal security. Yet there is nothing more sacred than a man's reputation and nothing more solemn than the government's duty to protect it.

In short, we are confronted with a variety of national problems — all of them important, many of them urgent. And President Eisenhower has blandly and proudly presented a new legislative program, largely designed to reverse the policies so loudly proclaimed three years ago when the Republicans took over.

It looks as though our Republican friends had not so much pursued Democratic policies as been pursued by them! And in these days the typical Republican document proclaims that America has no problems — and then goes on to propose Democratic solutions for them!

Why is this? Well, 1956 is an election year, and intimate personal experience and Republican history reminds me of what Disraeli said of the government of Robert Peel: "The right honorable gentleman uses two languages; one during his hour of courtship, another for his years of possession." Well, this is courtship year!

These matters, as I say, are important. They deserve discussion and

---

[103] For the four-day White House Conference on Education, held in November, 1955, see Dwight D. Eisenhower, *Mandate for Change* (Garden City, New York: Doubleday, 1963), p. 500. The President later blamed the Democratic-controlled Congress for refusing to authorize school funds he had requested, especially in the case of the 1956 bill for construction funds which was rejected after Representative Adam Clayton Powell had succeeded in amending it so as to deny such funds to any state which failed to comply with the Supreme Court's 1954 ruling on school desegregation. Ibid., pp. 499–500, 552.

action. But I suggest that they are also symptoms of infinitely larger issues — the problem of growth which, next to the cold war, is the most significant fact of modern society — its remarkable expansion and the resulting growing pains.

There are two ways of looking at America, at its future, and at the role of government in meeting — yes, and in shaping — that future.

One of these ways is to look at today (with frequent side glances at yesterday) — to think in terms of hanging on to what we have and staying where we are.

And if we complain that something seems to be missing from our daily lives — if we are anxious, fearful, insecure, if our cities are over-crowded, the juvenile courts overburdened, the older people frustrated, and the psychiatrists overworked, if millions of us have not enjoyed the vaunted prosperity we hear so much about — if we mention these things a Republican chorus tells us, never mind, after all, we've never had it so good.

But I would speak for a different view of America. We live in a time of danger and a time of great hope. Whoever offers us complacency blinds us to the one and denies us the other.

I suggest that there has never been a time when Americans were wholly satisfied. We are a people who have lived by our faith in greater tomorrows. In the march of our history we have learned that there can be no turning back, and no standing still. Growth is the very order of our existence in America. We could survive, I think, almost anything except stagnation.

Government has an inescapable role in this process. It can stimulate progress or retard it. More than this, it is today through our agencies of government that we are choosing between the often divergent paths of material and of spiritual growth.

The historic Republican concern — which has its very real point, and its equally important danger — is that government not "interfere" in people's lives. And so, even in its present election year enlightenment, the Republican administration moves grudgingly, offering at best half answers to hard problems. It reluctantly recognizes people's immediate needs but not our hopes or our plans, neither our concerns about the future nor our dreams, our physical necessities but none of our yearning for spiritual growth.

On every front we have seen these truths illustrated in the last three years. Human needs have been haltingly recognized and even more slowly met — usually under the pressures of political expediency.

But the fact remains, and has remained from the time of the Book of Proverbs and long before — that no nation can survive which will not look ahead, which dares not dream. Unless we can conceive a further future for ourselves, a second journey, we shall remain what we have sometimes seemed to be in recent years — a nation concerned not with its own destiny but only with its fear of the destiny of its adversary.

A people which gives up the vision and settles for the thing we have come to call "security" is a nation sick and in mortal danger, for security as an end and aim is a sick man's vain delusion. Security in the true sense of that word is never gained as an end in itself. Nations are secure when they are alive, and alive when they are moving toward their proper ends, the ends they dream of. We were secure when we had the West to open; a continent to achieve; the Golden Gate to win; when we measured every choice against that high endeavor.

The problems which keep us tossing on our beds at night are problems not of death but of life. It is not loss or lack which challenges our genius as a people, but wealth and plenty.

Shall we use our strength to stand still? Shall we use it to build walls around ourselves, imitating our enemies in the delusive hope that thus we can overcome them? Or shall we take this God's plenty and set ourselves a second labor on this continent and beyond it in the world? Shall we conceive and build for ourselves a new civilization such as men have never seen — a new wealth of freedom and of life — using the material means we have acquired, the leisure we have won, the amelioration of sickness and suffering and the lengthening of the span of life we have been given? Shall we conceive for ourselves a world truly and creatively at peace in which the Republic shall be secure in the only true security — the security of life and hope? Shall we imagine a nation of enlarged and richer lives in which the great fruitful labors shall go forward — a society dedicated to its proper end and vigorous with a hope and purpose no tyranny can destroy?

We have the means. Have we the vision?

And this is the great question we are now called upon to solve. The journey to which we were committed in the early days of the Republic has been completed. The new continent has been explored. The rim of the Pacific — golden California — is settled — and then some! The problem of food has been solved — and then some! Industry has provided our necessities — and then some! A vast and complex system of commerce has been perfected. Our standard of living has been fixed above any present level of comparison. Our science is successful. Our skills are fabulous. We know the how of more know-how than any society in history.

But this is not the end. It was not for these successes only that we set out, three centuries and more ago, from the tidal rivers of Virginia and the Massachusetts rocks. Our triumphs have been spectacular, but each one as we have achieved it has left us questions still to answer.

Today's challenges are more than yesterday's; tomorrow's may be harder still. I do not know. But I do know that we cannot fail to solve our problems as they arise so long as we maintain faith in ourselves, not in dictators or symbols or images, but in each other — and in something higher, stronger and wiser. We may look to our public men for leadership — but we must not forget that our ultimate reliance resides here, with people like you, in meetings like this which bring together men and women who have insisted upon their right and recognized their obligation to participate in the processes of a people's party and a people's government. Your commitment, in the end, is no different from mine — to devote your energies to the furtherance of the ideals you believe to be right.

The future demands of us no departure from principle, no restrictive new political doctrine. It simply demands that we continue with good heart to adapt to an age of change the marvelous, flexible instrument of government which is our heritage — and that we never lose sight of the better tomorrows — that we make our faith a living thing.

This, I say, is the way — the only way — we can pursue our highest destiny in an age that may, in Toynbee's phrase, see the tribes of mankind become the family of man.

The following four letters were written while Stevenson was at Rancho Santa Fe, California.

Alicia Patterson and Adlai Stevenson had been friends since about 1925 or 1926. In July, 1926, Stevenson went on a trip to Russia and Miss Patterson married and moved to London and later to New York. He did not see her again until he went to New York in 1946 as a delegate to the General Assembly of the United Nations, when they renewed their friendship. Until her death in 1963 Miss Patterson was publisher of the Long Island, New York, daily newspaper Newsday *and, in private life, Mrs. Harry Guggenheim.*

To Alicia Patterson

February 8, 1956

My dear Alicia:

So many thanks for your birthday note. How I wish I had been with you and Janet[104] on that gay evening instead of plowing through the

---

[104] Janet Chase Hauck, a childhood friend of Miss Patterson's from Chicago and wife of a New York City artist. Like Miss Patterson, she had known Stevenson since her early teens.

East Bay, or whatever Bay or Valley I was plowing through just then.

Your report on the lunch with De Sapio[105] was most interesting and it confirms what we had been repeatedly told about their cynical plans to trip me, if possible, and pounce on the carrion. I don't care very much about that, but I am anxious to avoid obscuring my image and that is exceedingly difficult in the type of campaign I have been expected to do here: six or eight talks a day to enormous groups, all wildly enthusiastic, and with a constantly hostile and critical press, and a party element more interested in extremism on the racial issue, Israel, etc. than on winning elections. This element seems to be quite powerful in the Democratic party here and puts temperate behavior in the posture of reaction very quickly; but I shall try not to forget "To thine ownself be true."

On to Oregon!

Devotedly,

To Mrs. Eugene Meyer[106]

February 8, 1956

My dear Agnes:

I have arrived at Rancho Santa Fe at last, after as rugged an ordeal as I can recall. I find your letters awaiting me, but I have so far had no opportunity to read more than your charitable remarks about the Fresno speech. Here among the intense young liberals it missed the mark. Evidently what they want to hear about is civil rights, minorities, Israel, and little else, and certainly no "vague futures." However, the general response I am told from home was flattering, and your letter serves to reassure me more than anything that has happened. Estes [Kefauver], after his fashion, told the Negro leaders in private that he would shut off all aid to any segregated school, etc. etc. When it leaked and the press interrogated him he promptly denied it. This state, as you know, is a bewildering array of diverse interests, and the Democratic party has little leadership and organization, but my following seems to be large and some of the more sober people realize that to win in November you have to carry more than the minority groups and the Democratic regulars.

I am more tired than I should be, but find a peculiar resilience that I hope endures a few more months of this ordeal. But I do not enjoy it, and what makes me uncomfortable and depressed is the rapid sequence of total surprises with no preparation or previous indoctrination. I have

---

[105] Carmine De Sapio, Democratic committeeman from New York.
[106] The original is in the Agnes Meyer files, Princeton University Library.

never enjoyed slapstick politics or extemporaneous speaking, and that seems to be all that is contemplated. The result, of course, is that the image comes out confused and the misquotations are at least as numerous as the accuracies. It is an awkward posture for me to be in when I am trying to be the "responsible" candidate and most of the pressures are either for irresponsibility or banality.

Another time I shall have better preparation and better understanding of this strange and wonderful state and its strange and not so wonderful politics.

I am so thankful for your wire about the Powell Amendment.[107] It illustrates my problem. I have no thoughtful advice on this sort of thing in spite of the fact that Harry Ashmore has been travelling with me continuously. My staff troubles are by no means resolved.

Visions of beaches dancing in the sun and blue sea dazzle my weary head. Have a good time; and I shall write again when I have an opportunity to examine your longer letter.

Affectionately,
Adlai

P.S. I have neglected the most important thing of all: I am sending a note to Eugene [Meyer] to thank him for running that speech in full, which must have caused not a little trouble, if I know anything about newspaper makeup.

Stevenson had known Helen Kirkpatrick since before her marriage to Robbins Milbank, when she was a foreign correspondent for the Chicago Daily News. He stayed with the Milbanks in Burlingame during his tour of California.

To Mr. and Mrs. Robbins Milbank[108]

February 8, 1956

My dear Milbanks:

Bless you and thank you for the one tranquil and tolerable day I have had in my beloved and beautiful native state.

I am afraid this past week is the best example I have seen of how *not* to prepare for a primary campaign. Southern California has been an ordeal without precedent since I stopped running for Governor, but the

---

[107] Mrs. Meyer supported Stevenson's position on the Powell amendment but recommended that he call a meeting with leaders of the National Association for the Advancement of Colored People.

[108] The original is in the possession of Mrs. Milbank.

crowds have been vast and enthusiastic while the words have been more weary and confused and ill-considered than ever. The minority group pressures and intensities are worse, if anything, than in the North, all of which I was unprepared for.

But I hope I haven't done much positive harm to Adlai's cause!

You were so good to us at Burlingame and I wish I could come back and settle in that guest house for a quiet week.

All of the best to you both,

Yours,
ADLAI

To Paul Ziffren[109]

February 8, 1956

Dear Paul:

And now it is on to Oregon — before I have had an opportunity to catch my breath and reflect on the experiences of this animated week in California. But one thing that was not obscured in the confusion was your constant support and encouragement. I have a better understanding now of the infinite difficulties of party organization and administration in Southern California, and my respect for your dexterity and talent has mounted daily.

So many thanks, and my best to that engaging Mickey.[110]

Cordially,
ADLAI

In Los Angeles on February 7, 1956, Stevenson had reiterated his opposition to the Powell amendment and he also stated that he would not enforce desegregation of public schools by the use of federal troops. He pleaded for understanding and patience. Asked to set a date for the completion of school integration, he suggested January 1, 1963, the hundredth anniversary of the Emancipation Proclamation. There were groans from the audience.[111] Eric Sevareid said over the Columbia Broadcasting System on February 14, 1956: "It is safe enough for a Northern governor, like Harriman of New York, to demand federal force to compel integration in the old South, and to support the Powell amendment. . . . But this happens to be one of those rare situations in

[109] Democratic National Committeeman from California. The original is in the possession of Mr. Ziffren.

[110] Mrs. Ziffren.

[111] See Stuart Gerry Brown, *Conscience in Politics: Adlai E. Stevenson in the 1950's* (Syracuse, New York: Syracuse University Press, 1961), pp. 89–111, for a discussion of the civil rights issue in the 1956 campaign.

[64]

which the moderate position requires more courage than the extreme positions. . . . The only impressive call to calmness and common sense has come from Mr. Adlai Stevenson, though this has already cost him dear, politically, among some Negro and some labor groups."[112]

Robert Roth wrote in the Philadelphia Bulletin, February 12, 1956: "Adlai E. Stevenson . . . is waging a primary campaign that has veteran politicians shaking their heads." In California, Roth observed that party leaders admired Stevenson's "courage, his eloquence and his dedicated approach to the problems of government, and they were impressed by the large crowds that turned out for him. But they were dismayed by his insistence on campaigning in his own way and his refusal to play the game according to what they consider the time tested rules for success. They fear that his scholarly speeches sprinkled with allusions to Toynbee and St. Paul may be over the heads of most listeners nor are they pleased when their candidate takes strong positions on controversial and sometimes unpopular issues when he could just as easily take no position at all."

Roth added: "He has invariably reserved the right to speak as he pleased with regard to how he felt on any issue at any time and without regard to the political effect of what he might say. . . . To campaign that way takes character, courage and integrity. It excites the admiration and wins the acclaim of many of the thoughtful. Whether it wins elections or not is another matter."

After a week of speechmaking and meetings in California, Stevenson campaigned in Oregon, Washington, and Utah. He issued the following statement on integration in Portland, Oregon, on February 12.[113]

Recent newspaper reports about my views on civil rights cause me to say, first of all, that I am surprised that anything I could say on that subject would still be news. My attitude has not changed since I first had a part in integrating Negroes in the Naval service fifteen years ago and my views have been reflected in my subsequent public record.

I believe deeply that it is the first obligation of every citizen of this Republic to work for the full realization of the goals stated in our original charter — freedom and equality for all Americans.

Freedom, as I understand it, means that a man may advance to the limit of his natural endowment without hindrance because of his race or religion.

112 Senator Richard Neuberger read this broadcast and other statements supporting Stevenson's position into the *Congressional Record*, February 17, 1956, pp. 2411–2414.
113 The text is taken from a mimeograph copy of a release prepared for the press.

Equality, as I understand it, means that each citizen shall be judged on his own merits. And particularly it means that every citizen shall be guaranteed equal treatment under law.

In the course of more than 150 years the letter and spirit of these objectives have been spelled out by the Supreme Court. Steadily the legal base of our civil liberties has been broadened until today the court requires full equality of treatment in virtually every public activity supported by public funds. The latest interpretation applies directly to the public schools.

The question then is not what we are trying to accomplish but how we should go about it.

The Supreme Court itself has clearly recognized that we cannot by the stroke of a pen reverse customs and traditions that are older than the Republic. Instead of establishing a fixed time limit for compliance with its decrees it has established the test of good faith as the measurement of progress in the cases before the District Courts.

We have already seen heartening results in the short time since the court's decision. In more than half the seventeen states which required or permitted segregation, the process of integrating the public schools has been completed or well begun. In the others, as the court has recognized, the transition will require more time. True integration requires more than the mere presence of children of two races in the same classroom; it requires a change in the hearts and minds of men. No child can be properly educated in a hostile atmosphere.

In the five or six states where public opinion does not yet sustain the court's decision we are faced with one of the ultimate tests of democracy and of our Federal system. There we are attempting to secure and protect the declared rights of local minorities in the face of the adverse views of controlling local majorities.

This condition imposes special burdens on all of us and even heavier burdens on public officials. I can think of no greater disservice to our country than to exploit for political ends the tensions that have followed in the wake of the Supreme Court decision.

Our purpose must be to attain unity, harmony and civilized relations, not to set section against section or race against race. And as a practical matter we must recognize that punitive action by the Federal government may actually delay the process of integration in education.

We will not, for example, reduce race prejudice by denying to areas afflicted with it the means of improving the educational standards of all their people.

Certainly we will not improve the present condition for future prospects of any Negro citizen by coercive Federal action that will arm the extremists and disarm the men of good will in the South who, with courage and patience, have already accomplished so much.

I suggest no slowing down of the effort to bring to reality the American concept of full equality for all our citizens. We must proceed, as the court has said, with all reasonable speed. But we must recognize that it is reason alone that will determine our rate of continued progress and guard against a reversal of the trend that has made the last three decades the period of greatest advancement for our Negro citizens on all fronts.

I had hoped the action of the court and the notable record of compliance that still far outweighs the instances of overt resistance would remove this issue from the political arena and make possible its orderly resolution without the emotional coloration of a Presidential contest. I still consider this not only possible but essential.

Mrs. Franklin D. Roosevelt declared in Chicago on February 14, 1956: "The confusion and misunderstanding that has arisen concerning Adlai Stevenson's position on civil rights seems to me difficult to understand. No one of the candidates has a clearer record, beginning with his participation in the integration of the Negro into the Navy and continuing through his actions in Illinois." Mrs. Roosevelt continued: "He has never quibbled in any speech as to his stand on civil rights. His answer to the question in Los Angeles as to whether he would use federal troops to enforce desegregation in the South was entirely correct." Later she observed: "I have stated that I would like an amendment passed to the Federal Aid to Education Bill, but if the passage of an amendment endangers the passage of the bill I would be for the passage of the bill." Mrs. Roosevelt concluded: "I know that Mr. Stevenson sees this question in its broadest context. I know that he believes we must be a nation with equality and justice for all our citizens and I trust in his integrity and in his judgment as to the best methods to be employed."

When Stevenson read this statement he wired Mrs. Roosevelt from Seattle.

To Mrs. Franklin D. Roosevelt[114]

February 14, 1956

HAVE JUST RECEIVED HERE A COPY OF YOUR WONDERFUL STATEMENT SUPPORTING MY STAND ON CIVIL RIGHTS. THIS OF COURSE

114 This telegram is in the Franklin D. Roosevelt Library, Hyde Park, New York.

WILL BE HELPFUL IN THE CAMPAIGN, BUT IT IS MOST VALUABLE
TO ME PERSONALLY AS EVIDENCE OF YOUR UNDERSTANDING.

ADLAI

*At Salt Lake City on February 17, 1956, Stevenson commented on
Vice President Nixon's statement that a "Republican" Chief Justice
handed down the 1954 desegregation decision.*[115]

. . . Mr. Nixon, the Republican party all-purpose politician, gave one
of his all-purpose speeches in New York in honor, if you please, of
Lincoln's Birthday. I was reminded that two years ago the Republican
National Committee sent Senator [Joseph] McCarthy across the country to lecture on "Twenty Years of Treason," also in honor of the man
who first used the phrase "with malice toward none." But we Democrats
should, I suppose, be grateful to the Vice President that he did it so
early in the season. He cured us quickly of any illusions we may have
entertained that the campaign in this fateful year might be conducted
by both parties on a level that would serve to develop the issues and the
real differences between the two parties. Instead, the Vice President
made it quite clear that he would proceed in the months ahead, as he
has in the years behind, according to his own familiar standards of
political morality.

And there is even greater irony in the fact that he spoke in celebration
of the memory of Abraham Lincoln when he sought to exploit the
critical and sensitive issues of our race relations for political ends.

The party of Lincoln could lay claim to the gratitude of our Negro
citizens. But the party of Nixon cannot — when he callously violates the
cherished independence of the Supreme Court by making a great point
before a partisan audience that its historic desegregation decision was
handed down by a *Republican* Chief Justice, and goes on to applaud
what "we," the Republicans, have done.

Some part of the whirlwind sown by cynical words is already visible.
People who oppose the Court's decision are now citing the Vice President's words as proof of what they have charged — that the order to
desegregate the public schools is political in character.

The charge is, of course, without foundation. Warren is no more a
Republican Chief Justice than the seven members who were appointed
under previous administrations are *Democratic* Justices. These nine men
jointly performed their duty according to their consciences and their

[115] The text is taken from a mimeograph copy of a press release.

convictions as Judges and as the interpreters of our Constitution when they reaffirmed the principle of genuine equality for all our citizens, and set forth means of attaining the desegregation of the public schools by orderly, legal means that take into account the ancient customs, prejudices and difficulties that obstruct the path to that goal. That was a judicial act, an American act. And I say it is deeply disturbing to find a high public official, the Vice President of the United States himself, treating it as a partisan act.

There is a rising tension in the South — which has already produced incidents of violence and terror and mob rule, and a variety of more subtle forms of intimidation intended to deprive Negro citizens of their rights. But it is not enough just to cry out in emotional protest against these things. Our purpose must be to find an answer to the problem, and I suggest that an answer will never be found by cynical politicians who seek to gain votes by pitting angry men against each other.

It is significant, I think, that the White House has declined comment on the Vice President's New York speech — and I hope that this will not be another of those cases in which Mr. Nixon receives a Presidential blessing after the fact for his hatchet work. . . .

While back at Libertyville preparing for a speaking tour in Connecticut, New York and Minnesota, Stevenson had Senator and Mrs. Herbert H. Lehman to lunch.

To Herbert H. Lehman

February 20, 1956

Dear Herbert:

On the way home after dropping you and Mrs. Lehman at the station, I thought of a thousand things I wanted to talk about, and I hope that somehow I can contrive another opportunity before too long.

Your patience and understanding of my attitude about the civil rights matter was comforting and prompts me to send along the enclosed statement, which I was not sure you had seen. Please do not bother to acknowledge — and for Heaven's sake, come again, stay longer, and bring Edith![116]

With affection to you both, and so many thanks for your all too brief visit.

Cordially yours,

[116] Mrs. Lehman.

To Mrs. Eugene Meyer[117]

February 20, 1956

My dear Agnes:

I returned yesterday after my long and weary journey to confront an enormous pile of accumulated mail — and a relentless schedule that gives me but a brief breathing spell.

Your wonderful letters are here and I am lifted again. Somehow you seem to know *what* I need to hear, *when* I need to hear it. Just what sort of mysterious transmission this is I cannot understand, nor will I attempt to. It's too good to disturb!

The journey was too long and the schedule too full. I think the staff have learned something, but it's almost impossible to deal with the local people. You know the problem, I am sure. I think I am storing up experiences however, for a political essay on "How *Not* To Choose a President."

I will be on the lookout for John Hayes' analysis of the television appearances.[118] We have a man on our staff doing that now, named [William Parmenter] Wilson. I know nothing of his background, but he seems a bright, modest and thoughtful lad who should profit from Mr. Hayes' report and not be allergic to the comments of others. I shall tell him that he could talk to Mr. Hayes either here or there, and I have no doubt that he will do so.

. . . The [Washington] *Post* editorial on the segregation business gave me heart. I am much disturbed by what I have found out, especially on this trip to California. There are many racial discriminations right in California, especially in housing and the new developments that are springing up everywhere, and also, of course, in the labor unions. But the intensity, cultivated by ministers, labor leaders, and politicians, is all directed to the South, and as intemperately as any place I have visited, I fear. I have had, of course, very bad reactions from New York, and Herbert Lehman was here yesterday for luncheon, more pained than indignant, and of course anxious to be helpful. But ultimately we have to face the fact that the ultimate sanction, force, will solve nothing. Meanwhile, I suppose my problem is largely one of attitude and the necessity for mingling more passion with my reason. It's this sort of thing when talking to sensible people, especially leaders, that always seems to me so unnecessary, but I am wrong — again! I suppose the

[117] The original is in the Agnes Meyer files, Princeton University Library. The postscript is handwritten.

[118] Mrs. Meyer had written that Mr. Hayes, of the Washington *Post,* was studying films of Stevenson's 1952 campaign and would send him recommendations.

proper approach is to feel passionately, pray fervently, and act reasonably.

I have a letter from Eugene, which likewise has given me a great lift.[119] There was much bad reaction to the Fresno speech, because I did not denounce Republican sins and warm over the New Deal from A to Izzard as per the expected prescription. Your letter, therefore, was more of a solace, and I have even taken the liberty of sending copies to some of my critics, anonymously of course.

I was delighted that you found Buffie [Ives] *simpatico*. I am sure that there was much mutuality in that, and that the transmission belt was working fine. I haven't seen her for months and months, and I hope she is getting calmed down. She was quite weary and agitated in the autumn.

I am noting Sunday, April 22,[120] on the schedule right now, and I have no reason to think it won't work, unless those wretched schedulers have killed me by that time. The next day I have to speak in Pennsylvania.

What would you think about my talking to the editors about "The Image of America," a take-off point for a discussion of economic and propaganda war with the Russians, Chinese, et al. Or is it a little too thin? Don't worry about this, but if ideas occur to you that would be helpful both to the editors and to myself, they would be really welcome.[121]

I hear the photographs[122] are in the office in town, and tomorrow I shall have an unveiling!

With affection, and earnest hope that you and Eugene are soaking up all the good things of the Bahamas — and I don't mean liquid!

Cordially,

ADLAI

P.S. . . . I *love* the pictures, especially the one with your left hand raised. So many thanks.

And now your letter — almost the *most* useful I've had!! How to lift the New Deal social ideas from the status of "programs" to rights. I shall use it at the Univ[ersity] of Minn[esota]. next week. Bless you — again!

[119] Mr. Meyer had written that the Washington *Post* had printed in full Stevenson's speech at Fresno, California, and had featured it because it was on a "new level."

[120] Stevenson was scheduled to speak to the American Society of Newspaper Editors in Washington, D.C., on April 21, 1956, and Mrs. Meyer had asked him to have dinner with her and some friends the following day.

[121] Stevenson's final choice of topic was defense and foreign policy. In his speech he advanced a controversial proposal to suspend testing of the hydrogen bomb. This speech is reprinted in this volume, pp. 110–121.

[122] The editors have been unable to discover what photographs Stevenson refers to.

Actress Lauren Bacall, the wife of actor Humphrey Bogart, wrote Stevenson on February 10, 1956, that he had seemed disturbed when he talked with her in Los Angeles about the Fresno speech, and she urged him not to lose heart. She said that he must say what he believed, and added: "I know you are a man of enormous conscience — but surely omission of certain phrases will not infringe on your being yourself."

To Mrs. Humphrey Bogart[123]

February 20, 1956

My dear Betty:

I am back from my long journey through the West and find your good letter and also the equipment for my splendid pencil, which has not only colored some pages, but provoked some admiring glances from my seat companions on countless aircraft. Thank you again, my dear, for your everlasting kindness.

I *was* depressed about the reaction to the Fresno speech when I saw you in Los Angeles. I thought it was good, philosophical, forward looking, and the kind of thing that the eager young liberals would like to hear instead of a sterile recitation of traditional Democratic positions. I was wrong, I guess, but there were plenty of good reactions from the audience around the country, which comforted me. One morsel of ecstasy is enclosed, from a Republican so prominent that the author must be nameless.

But you are quite right, and I really do try to "play the game," as you put it. Certainly I have no rigid hostility to saying something people want to hear once in a while. Indeed, I thought I did.

Bless you, my dear friend, for your heartening words and confidence.

Yours,

P.S. I go East the end of the week, and on and on and on. Pretty soon I will write an essay on "How *Not* to Select a President"!

A.E.S.

Mrs. Robert Kintner, the wife of the president of the American Broadcasting Company, sent a telegram concerning Stevenson's position on civil rights.

---

[123] A copy is in A.E.S., I.S.H.L.

To Mrs. Robert Kintner[124]

February 20, 1956

Dear Jean:

Thank you, dear Jean, for your wire which reached me in Salt Lake. I hope I can remember that wonderful phrase: "Feel passionately, act reasonably, pray fervently, that we see this through wisely."

But I am alarmed that you have evidently not seen these statements issued on the West Coast a week or more before your wire reached me.

Affectionately,

P.S. If you have any ideas as to responsible Negro leaders who would express preference for integration by persuasion rather than force, I wish you would pass them along to Lloyd Garrison. Certainly there must be many, if they can be induced to say anything in view of the clamor of the NAACP.

A.E.S.

Robert Dowling, the chairman of City Investing Company in New York and a dilettante in theater production, who was active in Democratic party affairs, wrote that there was something lacking in Stevenson's recent speeches. He felt that there was an "evasiveness" in Stevenson's appearance and a hint of "equivocation" in his words. Mr. Dowling concluded his letter: "To thine own self be true!"

To Mr. Robert W. Dowling[125]

February 20, 1956

Dear Mr. Dowling:

Ever so many thanks for your letter. I am distressed, and I wish so much you could give me some indication of the "evasiveness" and "equivocation" to which you refer. I had not been conscious of either, or of any faltering in what you are good enough to call my "steadfastness to the principles of the Adlai Stevenson of 1952."

Because I have long valued your friendship, and also your candor and good will, I am curious to know to which you refer. Mostly I am being abused because I have *not* altered my principles!

With all good wishes,

Cordially yours,

[124] A copy is in A.E.S., I.S.H.L.
[125] A copy is in A.E.S., I.S.H.L.

Mr. and Mrs. Archibald MacLeish, who were spending the winter in the British West Indies, suggested that Stevenson spend a vacation with them.

To Mr. and Mrs. Archibald MacLeish

February 21, 1956

My dear Ada and Archie:

Your wire arrived just as I returned from a long and weary journey in the western provinces, rewarding on the whole, and wholly exhausting. I rather wish you hadn't wired me. It gave me an uncomfortable moment that must afflict every prisoner when he sees a chance to make a break.

I just can't come. Senator Kefauver seems to have contrived to spend my time, my energy and my patience for the whole of the spring. If there is any possible escape it will be in late March and early April, but I wonder if I dare leave the country. Assuming you will be there I will take the liberty of letting you know if by any chance I can make it, for your approval or disapproval according to your situation at that time.

I used something you did for me in part in California and enclose a copy of the speech. The reaction around the country was good, but the audience reaction at Fresno was not — they wanted raw meat.

Much, much love — and keep the ideas coming if they sprout in the sands.

Affectionately,

To James A. Finnegan

February 22, 1956

Following our shakedown period here in my long absence I want to clarify some organizational responsibilities:

Henceforth I should like you to be in charge of the whole range of our political activities, including correspondence, public relations, press relations, relationships with the Stevenson for President Committee, etc., but excepting editorial work and research. By the latter I mean the preparation of material for me for speeches, major correspondence, public policy, etc. I should like to keep personal direction of this through Bill Wirtz, and this will mean that Mr. [Harry] Ashmore, Mr. Martin,[126]

---

[126] John Bartlow Martin, a freelance writer who had worked in Stevenson's 1952 campaign and who was the author of *Adlai Stevenson* (New York: Harper, 1952) and a coeditor of Stevenson's *The New America*. Both Mr. Martin and his wife had been supporters of Stevenson since his campaign for governor in 1948.

Mr. Brademas[127] and Mr. Hechler[128] will be primarily responsible to me. Of course Bill Blair will continue to handle my personal management so far as political activities are concerned.

I have talked with Newton Minow and he has agreed to undertake at least for the present to act as your administrative assistant in carrying out these assignments.

Any organization such as this is bound to require a great deal of team work and mutual cooperation and I don't mean to suggest any rigidities by this memorandum. Moreover, things are bound to change, but I hope this coincides with the understanding I think I have all around since my return from the West.

Gilbert Harrison, publisher of the New Republic, *wrote Stevenson a lengthy letter about the Fresno speech. He felt that Stevenson's statement of the issues was bold and accurate but that he should have developed one of these in detail in order that his listeners would know what the proper approach for the Democrats was and how the Republicans had failed.*

To Gilbert A. Harrison

February 23, 1956

Dear Gil:

I have had your letter in my pocket for weeks of weary travelling and endless battering in the West. About all I am sure of now is that I will soon be ready to write an essay on "How *Not* to Choose a President."

You were, of course, quite right about Fresno. Someone had told me that warmed-over New Deal and another detailed recitation of the virtues of Democrats and sins of Republicans, and thumping the traditional drums, was not enough and that I should try to do something "good, uplifting, forward looking" with these young, visionary Democrats. So I did, or thought I did, but of course what they wanted was an old-fashioned campaign speech.

And now I am abused for not having discussed the issues, which I have been discussing *seriatim* and *ad nauseum* for years. Indeed, I had been discussing them and thumping our friends and my bosom for the previous three or four days in Sacramento, Oakland and San Mateo before I even got to Fresno.

---

[127] John Brademas, Stevenson's executive assistant and later congressman from Indiana.

[128] Kenneth Hechler, associate director of the American Political Science Association and later congressman from West Virginia.

So I plead guilty to your soft indictment and am reminded that one thing I need is a little advance notice as to my audiences. I am afraid the answer to that would be to make the same speech in a primary — hot partisan and warmed-over New Deal is good enough. But there are sometimes vast radio and TV audiences, such as the one in Fresno. I have to think about that, too.

As to the little words about out-of-hand rejection of the Russian proposals, of course it broke in that morning's paper and I had no time to elaborate it, let alone fly from Fresno to San Francisco and get the damn thing typewritten and ready for release.

You are not "all wet"; on the contrary, you are all-wise — almost. And I wish to hell you would send me along some textual suggestions that I could use. I am more bereft of writing talent than you suspect, and I usually end up late at night biting my pencil and trying to keep awake, with the press clamoring in the bar nearby for an advance, something some of the other candidates don't have to worry about too much.

Love to Nancy,[129] and keep the comments coming.

Yours,

P.S. California, especially Southern California, utterly bewilders me politically, philosophically, geographically, yes, and ethnologically!

A.E.S.

Mr. and Mrs. Herbert Agar were visiting Mr. and Mrs. Ronald Tree in Barbados when Mr. Agar sent a draft of a speech to Stevenson.

To Herbert Agar[130]

February 24, 1956

Dear Herbert:

Your manuscript has arrived, plus the engaging notes reporting your progress from island to island. How I wish I were progressing on the same course. Instead, I leave in a moment again — this time for the East and thence to the western rural recesses of Minnesota to work my way through the snowbound farms.

If nothing else, I should be prepared before this year is over to write an essay on "How *Not* To Choose A President!"

This morning, driving in from the country, I hastily read your script. I think it will be very helpful, and I am everlastingly grateful. I had thought to point it a little more to specific failures to put our best foot

---

[129] Mrs. Harrison.
[130] A copy is in A.E.S., I.S.H.L.

forward, and perhaps the failure of the press also to exercise some restraint in reporting our violent dialogue to a world that hears everything we say. Or must the circulation department always take preference over the national interest!

If any further ideas occur to you, send them along — and give my love to Barbie, the dear Trees, and that soft Caribbean.

Yours,

P.S. Need I say that I shall hope for even more of your advice and help as the 1956 campaign progresses!

A.E.S.

At Stevenson's request, New York attorneys Thomas K. Finletter and Lloyd Garrison; Stuart Gerry Brown, professor of government at Syracuse University; and Arthur M. Schlesinger, Jr., professor of history at Harvard University, met in New York City for two days and discussed Stevenson's civil rights position in order to clarify it and develop its constructive points for national leadership, hopefully from the White House. Their draft statements were important for the following speech, given at the Jefferson-Jackson Day dinner in Hartford, Connecticut, on February 25[131] and the press conference on February 27.[132]

. . . As for the Democratic Party, it stands today exactly where it has through a century and a half — on the rock of principle that Jefferson put in the imperishable phrase; "Equal rights for all; special privilege for none."

We sometimes forget, when phrases become familiar, all that they mean. And their real meaning must be in terms of the problems each generation faces.

They mean, in terms of the most crucial issue within this beloved land of ours today, equal rights for all — regardless of race and color.

America is nothing unless it stands for equal treatment for all citizens under the law. And freedom is unfinished business until all citizens may vote and live and go to school and work without encountering in their daily lives barriers which we reject in our law, our conscience and our religion.

The Supreme Court has reaffirmed this essential doctrine of democracy in the school desegregation cases. These decisions speak clearly the law and the conscience of this land, but they also do violence to ancient

[131] The text is taken from a mimeograph copy prepared for the press.
[132] Interview, Walter Johnson with Stuart Gerry Brown, September 24, 1970.

practices and prejudices. So they recognize that a time for transition and compliance is necessary, time for the adjustments that have to be made. But they do not recognize or permit repudiation or rejection of these decisions of the Court and of the people.

And I would say a word directly tonight about the re-emergence in a few states of the doctrine called interposition — the doctrine that a state has a right to interpose its power against the decision of the properly constituted authority as to the law of the land.

I recall here in all gravity what one of the men we honor — Andrew Jackson — said in his Proclamation of December 10, 1832: "I consider then," Jackson wrote, "the power to annul a law of the United States, assumed by one state, incompatible with the existence of the Union, contradicted expressly by the letter of the Constitution, unauthorized by its spirit, inconsistent with every principle on which it was founded, and destructive of the great object for which it was formed." That was essential Democratic doctrine — and American doctrine — one hundred and twenty years ago. It is essential Democratic — and American — doctrine today.

We are, as a people, at the very dawn of one of our brightest days — the day of full democracy in our public schools. This may well be one of the greatest accomplishments of our generation. Not as Democrat but as American, not as candidate but as citizen, I pray to God that this day may not be marred nor this achievement poisoned by the bitterness of any who would assert views, no matter how deeply felt, against the laws of the land and of humanity.

"Equal rights for all" must mean just that, the right of everybody to live according to the laws and freedoms which are the meaning of American and of modern Christian civilization. . . .

The following excerpts were taken from statements at a press conference held at the headquarters of the New York Stevenson for President Committee in New York City on February 27, 1956.[133]

. . . MR. KRUMPELBECK (NBC): Governor, what is your stand on the segregation program in the South? You said that you were for gradual desegregation at one time and then I think in Hartford it seems you changed your stand. Could you clarify that please?

GOV. STEVENSON: I didn't change my stand in the least that I know of, in Hartford or anywhere else.

[133] The text is taken from a mimeograph copy.

MR. KRUMPELBECK: Could you expand on what you mean by "gradual desegregation?"

GOV. STEVENSON: Just what the Supreme Court said, which means desegregation will come about with all possible speed — that was the language of the Supreme Court, and that is the law of the land.

Now, I would say this further on the subject, and that is that I for one have been very much disturbed by the mounting tensions in the South. In order to avoid any possibility of further disorder or of further damage to the nation's reputation abroad, I think that the situation merits the prompt attention of the President. The office of the President of the United States has great moral influence and great prestige and I think the time has come when that influence should be used by calling together white and Negro leaders from the areas concerned in order to explore ways and means of allaying these rising tensions.[134] This will strengthen the hands of the responsible people, the leaders of both races through whom such conspicuous progress has already been made in desegregation and in maintaining good relations between the races.

MR. PRESSMAN (NBC): You speak of a time for transition and compliance that you believed in in Hartford — how much time?

GOV. STEVENSON: You would have to ask the Supreme Court that. After all, it is the Supreme Court which has determined the schools should be desegregated, and prescribed the time in which they should be desegregated. This of course is a problem that has not yet arisen because there are no Districts in violation of the Supreme Court, nor any local District Court or Federal Circuit Court of Appeals, that I know of.

MR. KRUMPELBECK (NBC): Do you think there is any justification at all on the part of the Southern people feeling and acting as they have been doing?

GOV. STEVENSON: I don't know what you refer to, sir. You mean the violence?

MR. KRUMPELBECK: The violence and the anti-desegregation.

[134] Many leaders of both races endorsed Stevenson's proposal. On March 14, 1956, President Eisenhower gave qualified support to the idea but said he preferred to have Congress authorize a bipartisan joint commission with power to subpoena and compel testimony. Governor LeRoy Collins, of Florida, recommended that the President hold a conference with Southern governors and attorneys general. On May 23, Eisenhower announced that he would hold no conference with Southern governors for fear of "inflaming racial feelings." Not until after Governor Orval Faubus provoked the intervention of federal troops to protect the right of Negro children to attend school in Little Rock in 1957 did the President call such a conference.

GOV. STEVENSON: Well, of course there can never be justification — no justification for illegal acts.

MR. KRUMPELBECK: But the Negro has not enjoyed privileges and rights for a long time in the South.

GOV. STEVENSON: There can be no positive justification for mob violence, if that is what you are referring to. . . .

Author and lecturer Barbara Ward had been sending Stevenson material. He received a wire from her husband, Robert Jackson, that she had just given birth to a baby boy.

To Mrs. Robert Jackson

February 28, 1956

My dear dear Barbara:

Robert's wire has arrived just as I arrived in New York and just as I am leaving for Minnesota. I have cabled you, but the cold words don't begin to report our feelings, and also our anxiety to know if "mother and son are doing well." Last night shortly after my arrival I had to attend a large soiree of supporters, and the word of your remarkable achievement was spreading rapidly with hosannahs from all sides, sprinkled with rebel yells and other democratic exclamations of approval.

I wish I could take the time this very moment for a proper letter, reviewing yours and thanking you for the magnificent essay on New Tasks, which I read en route in the back of an automobile from Hartford to Boston the other day. It gives me splendid and useful material, and in it are imbedded many speeches. In abbreviated form it is what I should say to the editors on April 21, but I may well conclude on more careful rereading and reflection that some of these points could best be made directly to the editors. I was thinking of using this opportunity to talk a little about the image of America abroad, in view of the fact that the image is created in part, in spite of [John Foster] Dulles, by our newspapers.

I am, as you have observed, not thinking at all and just mumbling. And now I must run. The politicians from New Jersey are waiting to have luncheon with me, or I am waiting to have luncheon with them! Bless you, dear Barbara, and my heartfelt good wishes to you both. I yearn to see the young man, and if he has started speaking eloquently already, please urge him not to announce that he is planning a political career until I have had an opportunity to talk with him.

Robert was more than good to send Carol [Evans] the prompt wire, which has just been passed on to the [Edison] Dicks of Chicago. I am relieved to hear that your crisis is past and I will pray that all is well and that the father is also mending rapidly!

Affectionately,

Stevenson flew from New York to Minnesota on March 1, where he campaigned in St. Paul, Minneapolis, and other parts of the state for five days. On March 2, he observed in a speech that Governor Orville Freeman, in introducing him to about the eighth meeting that day, had said that Stevenson was "just getting warmed up." Stevenson added: "I was about to correct him and say, 'I was just getting worn out.'"

To Hubert H. Humphrey

March 7, 1956

Dear Hubert:

I am back in Chicago after my memorable invasion of the Western provinces of Minnesota, and feel no worse for the wear — somewhat to my surprise!

While the memory is fresh, let me thank you once more for your heroism on my behalf. How you sustain that pace baffles and also disturbs me a little, for you, too, must grow older and mend your rugged ways.

The journey was all good and all reassuring. The crowds never slacked off, and the reports of Mrs. Roosevelt's invasion of the Iron Range[135] were all ecstatic.

Hastily and gratefully,

To Mrs. Eugene Meyer[136]

March 7, 1956

My dear Agnes:

I am back after five days of cruel and relentless campaigning through the snowbound western countries of Minnesota. I made as many as eight or ten stops and speeches a day after wild rides over icy roads between the towns. The crowds were enormous and attentive. The politicians were delighted and astonished. The consensus seemed to be that it was a combination of the farm issue, which is acute there, and the

---

[135] Eleanor Roosevelt spoke in northern Minnesota on Stevenson's behalf.
[136] The original is in the Agnes Meyer files, Princeton University Library.

curiosity about me, and a vague anxiety that seems to be everywhere apparent. Now on my return I find your good letter about the President's announcement.[137] I have made statements on the matter, trying to bring out the fact that it was not his health, which is a private matter, but the conduct of the office of the Presidency, which is a public matter, which is the issue. The press, of course, ends up by condensing the reasoning process and says that I have made his health an issue.

Be that as it may, I think the problem that must be developed and discussed is the alteration in the character of the office which is contemplated by the President's announcement that he can do it on a part time basis only but evidently considers this enough for the greatest office on earth. Frankly, it frightens me a little too, and in a way I wish he had made no excuses about his health but said he thought he was as good as ever, if he saw fit to undertake it at all.

The jokes are beginning to appear — "The Republicans are so eager for Ike they are willing to pay him time and a half for undertime;" "Ike proposes to change a half-time job to a part-time job."

I have, personally, little doubt that they will dump [Vice President Richard] Nixon with no protest from the President, even as he didn't protest the embrace of [Senator Joseph] McCarthy or the silence with respect to George Marshall.[138] I am sure the Republican top politicians are just as perceptive as the Democrats and will not hazard Nixon again. All of which will make the problem more difficult for me, I suppose, although what I have witnessed in these weeks of primary traveling certainly suggests that something is cooking in spite of the President's apparent popularity. I wonder if the people don't in fact see through the superficial talk about peace and prosperity to the seething world and the shaky economy that lies behind.

I also have no doubt that we are shortly to witness the greatest organized newspaper and communications smokescreen of all time, which will gather in intensity under skillful management, while the gentlemen in the background keep their fingers crossed that the yokelry don't catch on too soon. . . .

Hastily and affectionately,

ADLAI

[137] President Eisenhower had announced on March 1 that he would be a candidate for reelection.

[138] During the 1952 campaign, Mr. Eisenhower spoke in Milwaukee on October 3. He deleted from his prepared speech a paragraph praising General George C. Marshall because he felt it inappropriate in the home state of Senator Joseph McCarthy, who had bitterly attacked the general's patriotism. However, in a press conference on August 22, 1952, Mr. Eisenhower had made remarks in support of General Marshall. See *The Papers of Adlai E. Stevenson*, Vol. IV, pp. 52, 93n.

To Ann McDougal[139]

March 7, 1956

Dear Ann:

I was lying on my bed of pain late one night in a snowbound village on the western frontier of Minnesota, fingering through a mass of clippings that had caught up with me on my travels, and lo and behold, there was an announcement of Ann McDougal's engagement in the newspapers.[140]

Congratulations, while tardy, are no less earnest; and what an engaging guy he is! I hope now that I shall see much more of him, as well as you, dear Ann.

Affectionately,

To Mrs. Franklin D. Roosevelt[141]

March 7, 1956

My dear Mrs. Roosevelt:

I returned from Western Minnesota to Minneapolis this morning after a most successful and encouraging journey through the districts in which Kefauver was said to have his largest strength. Senator Humphrey and Governor Freeman, who traveled with me, are the source of my reassurance because they tell me they found conditions far better than they had foreseen and have little apprehension any longer.

Arriving in Minneapolis I had ecstatic reports about your conquest of the city and of the Iron Range. The exclamations that stick in my mind about you and your reception there are "adored" and "terrific." Jane Dick says you are the best campaigner she has seen and that the speeches you made on my behalf were the most successful she has heard. Need I say that I am grateful beyond words.

Affectionately,

ADLAI

To Mr. and Mrs. Orville L. Freeman

March 7, 1956

My dear, dear Freemans:

Politics aside, I must tell you while the memory is still on the very top of my head, how much I enjoyed our travels together during the memo-

[139] Daughter of Mr. and Mrs. Edward D. McDougal, Jr., Stevenson's old friends and neighbors. A copy is in A.E.S., I.S.H.L.

[140] She was engaged to Dr. William B. Carey, a pediatrician. They were married on July 27, 1956.

[141] The original is in the Franklin D. Roosevelt Library, Hyde Park, New York.

rable days last past. I think you are the best political *pair* that I have yet met, and I see nothing but usefulness, honor and happiness for you both — *if* you will never let health and physical well-being get crowded out of your busy, animated lives.

I shall not even bother to thank you for all of your kindnesses to me. I hope I have made that clear.

Hastily and gratefully,

To John F. Kennedy[142]

March 12, 1956

HAVE BEEN TRAVELING ALMOST CONSTANTLY AND THIS IS THE FIRST OPPORTUNITY I HAVE HAD TO TELL YOU THAT YOUR ENDORSE-MENT GAVE ME MUCH ENCOURAGEMENT. I AM VERY GRATEFUL AND LOOK FORWARD TO SEEING YOU HERE IN CHICAGO THIS COMING WEEK-END. WARMEST REGARDS.

To Frank E. Karelsen[143]

March 13, 1956

Dear Frank:

I should have written to you long before this to thank you for your very thoughtful and helpful letter of February 20. Your suggestion about using the term "direct and reasonable speed" in connection with the segregation issue is a good one and I have been doing just that during the past few weeks.

I think you know how grateful I am for all your encouragement and good will — and particularly for giving me such wide distribution to Eric Sevareid's statement.[144]

Cordially,

ADLAI

[142] U.S. senator from Massachusetts. A telegram.

[143] A New York attorney who was an ardent supporter of Stevenson, beginning with the Draft Stevenson Committee at the 1952 Democratic Convention. The original is in the possession of Mr. Karelsen.

[144] Mr. Karelsen had printed and distributed a transcript of Eric Sevareid's broadcast of February 14, 1956, analyzing the civil rights question and praising Stevenson's position.

To Thomas K. Finletter

March 14, 1956

Dear Tom:

I wish you would read this letter from Chester Bowles.[145] I am more and more conscious of the imperative necessity of having some people who can be in more or less constant contact to digest the foreign affairs news and suggest to me by telephone, or wire, or document, what I could or should say that would be useful, both nationally and politically. It is in this field that the stature and image which we have talked about so often can be best demonstrated, I think, to the sort of people who make policy. I would have to add that foreign affairs, to my distress, does not provoke the interest at the grass roots level that I would like to be able to breathe into it. In addition to the spot news reaction, thinking constantly ahead with a view to providing me with foreign affairs materials for insertion in speeches, when circumstances permit, could be enormously helpful, and is something I have no equivalent for in my organization here. Whatever is done in this field I have to do myself, usually under trying circumstances of travel and "other work." With conditions deteriorating as they are abroad, I think it is frightfully important to come up with something sensible from time to time, in addition to the criticism of [John Foster] Dulles and the deprecation of Republican complacency, incompetence, etc. [Walter] Lippmann's column today on the way we separately treat our separate problems in the Moslem world is another reminder of the importance of some positive proposals.

It has troubled me for a long time that we have in our party many competent people in this field but we have never really exploited their value by distilling their opinions. I don't know that it is possible, but I should like to start trying as soon as possible along the line that Chester suggests, mainly himself, George Kennan,[146] Dean Rusk,[147] Paul Nitze, Ben Cohen,[148] and possibly Bob Tufts,[149] who has been doing work in disarmament in Washington on a sabbatical leave this year.

I am not including you on the theory that you already have more than

---

[145] Former governor of Connecticut and U.S. ambassador to India and Nepal, 1951–1953.

[146] Career diplomat, author, and authority on the Soviet Union.

[147] President of the Rockefeller Foundation and former Assistant Secretary of State.

[148] Benjamin V. Cohen, former New Deal "Brain Truster," member of the U.S. delegation to the United Nations, and counselor in the Department of State.

[149] Robert Tufts, professor at Oberlin College and a speechwriter for Stevenson in 1952.

you can handle and that if they want to talk with you from time to time they can readily do so.

I am sending a copy of this letter to Chester just as I leave for Minnesota with the hope that without further intervention on my part he can take it up with you and proceed at the earliest possible date to set up an experimental meeting. I hope to heaven that this can work because almost daily now there is something that needs saying, and instead of saying it I get more oppressed with the multitude of things I have to do. I am confident this will not in any way conflict with the "Finletter Group,"[150] and that if it does you can make it known to Chester, who can be reached until the first of April in care of William Benton,[151] 5520 East Camelback Road, Phoenix, Arizona.

Forgive this hasty and rather peremptory letter. I am sure you and Chester will let me know if you wish me to write letters to anyone asking them to participate.

Yours,

P.S. New Hampshire does not trouble me much, although I suppose the press will make quite a defeat out of it. Actually, to get more than a third of the vote when they have painted me as too proud to fight and disdainful of New Hampshire seemed to me not too bad.[152]

P.P.S. I can't overemphasize the importance of being able to issue brief statements that made sense in reaction to spot news. My long, carefully considered, painfully prepared speeches have a mighty meager audience in fact and get into the back country not at all. Even the speech at the University of Minnesota the other day had no press that I could discover on the basic foreign policy points. I frankly get discouraged during this primary period. But it also offers opportunities to get to the national reporters who are constantly on my tail.

New York banker and author James P. Warburg wrote after Stevenson's speech of March 10, 1956, in Detroit, which concentrated on domestic issues, that the Democratic party could not win in a year of smug complacency by placing primary emphasis on domestic issues.

[150] See *The Papers of Adlai E. Stevenson,* Vol. IV, especially pp. 267, 462.

[151] Chairman of the board of the *Encyclopaedia Britannica,* former U.S. senator from Connecticut, and longtime friend of Stevenson.

[152] Senator Estes Kefauver won all twelve Democratic delegates (eight convention votes), defeating a slate running as favorable to Stevenson. Under New Hampshire law, delegates pledged to a candidate required the candidate's consent. Stevenson had refused that consent. But delegates only favorable to a candidate required no consent. In the presidential preference vote, Kefauver, who had campaigned diligently in New Hampshire, received just over 21,000 votes. Stevenson, who neither entered the primary nor campaigned there, received just over 4,000 write-in votes.

To James P. Warburg

March 14, 1956

Dear Jim:

I admit all you say, except that I have repeatedly made it a point that Eisenhower has brought neither real peace nor real prosperity. What I should like now is what you suggest: "a clearly presented alternative to the disastrous bi-partisan policy." Can you send it to me in the sort of form that is usable in a few minutes in the sort of speech one has to make even in a place like Moorhead, Minnesota or Podunk, Florida? I hope you understand what I mean. And it has to be mighty simple to demonstrate what I suspect is true, that the people *are* interested in foreign policy.

Hastily,

To George F. Kennan

March 14, 1956

Dear George:

The enclosure from the Wall Street Journal is but one of multitudes of the same kind. Having said what I would do about virtually all of these things over and over again, I am still denounced by the Republican press and speakers repeatedly for offering no constructive alternatives and being content with negative criticism only.

I wonder if it lies within the possible for you to attempt a summary answer to this chorus. I think of myself making a speech one of these days in which I do a little denouncing of Dulles, et al, followed by a sentence in which I say something like this: "Now, if any Republican spokesman happens to see the foregoing he will almost immediately say, if in a mellow mood: 'But what does Stevenson propose?' To which I will reply, 'Well, this is what I propose and have for some three years while the Republicans evidently were not listening.'" And then I shall add a sharp digest of our situation which I hope won't sound more like Kennan than Stevenson along the lines of something you might send me. Left to my own devices, I should probably say, and too bitterly, that Congress should pass a resolution that Foster Dulles leave the country no more.

I am not asking for a ponderous study, I am sure you understand, but some sharp way of capsuling and dealing with this constant charge of negativism.

Hastily and gratefully,

[87]

Clement Davies, leader of the Liberal party in the British Parliament, wrote Stevenson that the military pacts (probably referring to the South East Asia Treaty Organization and the Baghdad pact) Britain and the United States had formed did more harm than good. He also wrote that the economic situation in Britain was discouraging in the light of poor productivity. He mentioned that in a debate in the House of Commons on the Middle East, the Prime Minister forgot to state that he would never allow Israel to be overrun. Had he said it, Mr. Davies added, it would be a sufficient warning to Egypt and her allies.

To Clement Davies[153]

March 20, 1956

Dear Mr. Davies:

Your most interesting letter of March 8 has come to hand at last. I am extremely troubled about the deteriorating situation in Britain. It is no better here, I fear.

I emphatically agree with you about the over-emphasis on military defense. Only now do we begin to detect here any disposition on Dulles' part to redirect the emphasis and there is much opposition from both parties to long term economic commitments.

I fail to understand why Britain and the United States could not have long since joined in some much more positive utterance, with France if possible, about Israel. We all know this is the case, but I wonder if the Arabs know it. And what other step is indicated now to further the realization that Israel is here to stay. Or don't the Arabs ever take anything as settled? Perhaps not.

It is always good to hear from you, and I hope you will thank Lord Boyd Orr[154] for his notes which I shall take home to read tonight.

Cordially,

To Wilson W. Wyatt[155]

March 20, 1956

Dear Wilson:

Thanks for your letter which I find on my return from the frozen North.[156] It has been a long ordeal there and I only hope for the best.

---

[153] A copy is in A.E.S., I.S.H.L.

[154] Former director of the UN Food and Agriculture Organization.

[155] Manager of Stevenson's 1952 campaign. See *The Papers of Adlai E. Stevenson*, Vol. IV.

[156] Stevenson campaigned in Minnesota from March 14 to 19. The primary election was held on March 20, the day this letter was written.

But there are many internal difficulties in the party and much evidence of Republicans coming over to embarrass me — and Humphrey and Freeman. I hope now to get away to the South for a bit in order to do some writing, get some health, and be with John Fell for a bit, but I shall probably not get off until the end of the week or the first of next week.

. . . As you know, the schedule is appalling until after the completion of the California primary June 5, or should I say my completion![157]

I enjoyed my little visit with Marriner Eccles[158] — about one o'clock in the morning when I was too tired to function — and found him stimulating as always.

I hardly know what to do about Billy Graham, and if you have any specific suggestion let me have it. [Governor] Frank Clement has spoken to me about meeting with him too.

How are you getting along with the list of people of all kinds? As I travel it becomes more and more important, it seems to me, to be keeping records on people who pop up in the path and then I promptly forget. I am afraid I am not being helpful in contributing names, but in Minnesota I have been profoundly impressed with the sobriety, good sense and vigor of Governor Freeman, and his wife is a political triple threat if I ever saw one. Be sure to put David Bruce[159] on your list. I hear he is favorable, but so far no evidence of work or money.

Yours,

p.s. I have just caught on to the fact that you wrote the review of my last book for the Courier.[160] What a man you are! — speaking of triple threats.

Blessings and thanks.

A.E.S.

On the evening of March 20, Stevenson dined at his Libertyville home with George W. Ball. Later they were joined among others by Mr. and Mrs. Willard Wirtz, Mr. and Mrs. Edison Dick, and Archibald Alex-

---

[157] On March 20, 1956, Stevenson also wrote to Lady Mary Spears: "I sometimes reach a state of total exhaustion that is more mental than physical. The repetition on a circuit like Minnesota of eight or ten [speeches] a day nauseates me."

[158] Financier and business executive and former member and chairman of the board of governors of the Federal Reserve System in the Roosevelt and Truman administrations.

[159] David K. E. Bruce, U.S. ambassador to France from 1949 to 1952 and later ambassador to the Federal Republic of Germany and to Great Britain.

[160] The editors have been unable to locate this review of *What I Think* in the Louisville *Courier-Journal.*

ander. As they listened to the Minnesota returns, it was obvious that Stevenson was suffering a crushing defeat. Kefauver won twenty-six of the thirty delegates and ran ahead of Stevenson by some sixty thousand votes in a total of over three hundred thousand votes cast.

News reporters observed that among the reasons for the Kefauver victory were that he made effective use of the charge that Senator Humphrey, Governor Freeman and other "bosses" of the Democratic Farm Labor party were dictating to voters and had tried to freeze him out of the primary; that by advocating 100 per cent of parity for the farmers he had outpromised Stevenson; that some Republicans crossed party lines to vote in the Democratic primary to weaken Stevenson nationally; and that he had great talent for handshaking and appealing to the man in the street.[161]

While editorial writers stated no matter what the reason it was a "severe setback" and "might prove fatal," Stevenson announced at a press conference on March 21:[162]

While I was personally disappointed by the Minnesota results, I hope no one will miss the real point in yesterday's primary. It was a smashing repudiation of the present administration and a two-to-one endorsement of Democratic principles by the people of Minnesota.

I do not propose to conjecture about the possibility that thousands of loyal Republicans may have voted in the Democratic primary for the cynical purpose of damaging the Democratic Party in Minnesota or me.

I consider the results full notice that the great swing back to Democratic principles which started in 1954 is even stronger in 1956.

Sen. Kefauver has won the first round and I congratulate him. As for myself, I will now work harder than ever, and I ask my kind friends everywhere to redouble their efforts, too.

As I said last night, my plans are not changed, and neither are my ideas. I have tried to tell the people the truth. I always will. I'll not promise them the moon, and I never will. This may not be the way to win elections, but it is, in my opinion, the way to conduct a political campaign in a democracy.

So I will try even harder, as a result of yesterday's primary, to state the Democratic principles as I understand them, to get the people's best judgment about America's problems and our prospects, and to help

[161] See, for instance, the Chicago *Daily News*, March 21, 24, 1956; the New York *Times*, March 25, 1956, E5.

[162] The text is taken from the Chicago *Daily News* and the Chicago *Sun-Times*, March 22, 1956.

build a firmer peace, a truer prosperity and a fuller brotherhood for our nation.

When asked at the press conference if he planned to shake more hands, Stevenson answered with a grin that apparently "a certain identity is established between shaker and shakee" when a hand was shaken. After the Minnesota primaries, he traveled relentlessly giving hundreds of talks, shaking hands by the thousands; he donned cowboy boots in Arizona and carried a stuffed alligator that had been thrust into his hands down a street, fumbling with it and laughing at the absurdity of the situation.

Looking back on his entire primary struggle from the vantage point of four years, Stevenson wrote:

> I've worn silly hats and eaten indigestible food; I've bitterly denounced the Japanese beetle and fearlessly attacked the Mediterranean fruit fly. This last, if you didn't know, attacks citrus fruits, a matter of no small importance to Florida citrus growers — and to politicians campaigning in the Florida primary.
>
> No one would pretend that cranberry chemicals and citrus diseases do not deserve attention; of course they do. But so much attention from candidates for the highest temporal office on earth? Isn't it time we grew up?[163]

To Mrs. Robert Jackson

March 21, 1956

My dear, dear Barbara:

I returned from the snows of Minnesota to find your letter of the 16th awaiting me. The news of your illness shocked and distressed me, and I pray as seldom before that the recovery *has* been as good and certain as you indicate. If you are misleading me, I shall be very wroth and probably as nasty as a rich Republican the next time we meet. So come clean, fair lady, or suffer the consequences.

And speaking of consequences, I have just suffered a few myself in Minnesota. Tens of thousands of Republicans moved into the Democratic primary into the cities to discredit the DFL party, which won for the first time in 1954, and incidentally to knock me off if possible. It appears that Mr. Stassen's[164] fine and disarming hand guided the adroit maneuver skillfully.

[163] Adlai E. Stevenson, "Choice by Hullabaloo," *This Week,* February 28, 1960.
[164] Harold E. Stassen, former governor of Minnesota; special assistant to President Eisenhower to direct studies of U.S. and world disarmament.

In view of the fact that the press is pretty well acquainted with the story of what happened, how and why, we are not as discouraged as perhaps we should be. At all events, I just returned from a monstrous press conference behind a forest of microphones and cameras where I uttered the enclosure and responded gaily and brightly, I hope, to massive and murderous questions. And now I must move on again, this time southward, to do some of that long delayed thinking and writing and also to entertain my wounded son John Fell for a few days during his spring holiday. Then I return to Illinois for a couple of days, thence back to Florida for the dreadful grind — and on and on.

I shall much miss B.W. J. [Barbara Ward Jackson] on "The Image of America," but her image I miss even more.

I pray — and use the word more than casually — that you are behaving properly and that the "king of infinite space" is flourishing. What a pity that Robert[165] had to be in Africa, and I hope there is somebody seeing to it that you take your anticoagulants if you are out of the hospital.

Should ideas creep onto paper without strain, by all means send them along. My needs are insatiable, even if the results don't indicate it.[166]

Paul Ziffren wired Stevenson, March 21, 1956, a statement he had released to the press: ". . . Many of us who believe Governor Stevenson is the best qualified candidate have been lulled into a false sense of security or misled in other ways. . . . The fight has just begun."

To Paul Ziffren[167]

March 21, 1956

Dear Paul:

The telegram from you and Mickey[168] gave me a lift. Actually, after some analysis we are not as depressed about the Minnesota results as we might be. The Republicans did quite a job on us and on the D.F.L. up there. And of course Estes' 100% of parity and no production controls wasn't exactly unpopular among the suffering small farmers. A call from Pat Brown indicated some hope that this misfortune might be

---

165 Mr. Jackson.

166 Carol Evans added to the letter: "At this point Governor Stevenson was removed again. He has been leading a dreadful life of unremitting pressure and toil and I am sure he would want this sent along, even unfinished, together with his warmest wishes and affection."

167 The original is in the possession of Mr. Ziffren.

168 Mrs. Ziffren.

converted into advantage for the very reason you suggest — our forces would get to work with redoubled effort. I hope so. For my part, I will.

Cordially,

ADLAI

To Mrs. Robbins Milbank[169]

March 22, 1956

Dear Helen:

Bless you for that heartening wire. I have had a great stack of them and it is to the same import, and if I were not a little more realistic I might think I had won in Minnesota! There are many explanations of what happened, and I was by no means the only loser. It was a bad blow for Humphrey and Freeman and the new organization they are attempting to develop there. About a hundred thousand Republicans crossed the line.

I have had reassuring telephone calls from Pat Brown, et al, in California. I hope that the work can pick up with redoubled vigor because we shall certainly need it. Kefauver will do the same man against the gods, poor boy against the bosses stuff there, I have no doubt. Moreover, the promise to the farmers will outpoint me by far along with miscellaneous other promises. Likewise, he can undoubtedly outwalk and outhandshake me.

With affectionate regards to you and Robbins.

Yours,

ADLAI

Professor Stuart Gerry Brown sent Stevenson a memorandum of conversation between himself and Morris Berinstein, influential in the American Jewish Committee, in support of Israel. Mr. Berinstein said that Israeli leaders had "no clear impression" of his views regarding Israel and Middle Eastern problems in general. Mr. Berinstein felt Stevenson should support the immediate shipment of defensive arms and pledge support for the boundaries of Israel except for minor border rectifications.

---

[169] The original is in the possession of Mrs. Milbank.

To Stuart Gerry Brown[170]

March 26, 1956

Dear Stuart:

I've just seen the attached memo. It surprises me a little in view of the fact that I would have thought that a man as obviously well informed as Mr. Berinstein would know more about my views. After all, I've spoken and written more on the Middle East in the past few years and talked with more leaders of Israel and the Jewish community about it than Harriman and Kefauver combined. And I suppose it is precisely because there are no easy answers that he says they have "no clear impression" of my views. As to maintaining the arms balance, I advocated that in a nationwide broadcast last fall. As to territory concessions, I've made it clear — to the Arabs! — that little could be expected because they started the war.

Frankly, I am perplexed by the recent almost deliberate effort I sense either *not* to understand my views or not to ascertain them, in some segments of the American Jewish community. It also discourages me.

Hastily, and with best wishes, I am

Sincerely yours,

ADLAI

To Mr and Mrs. Ronald Tree[171]

March 26, 1956

My dear Trees:

Thanks for your wire. I am not as downhearted as perhaps I should be, but the indefatigable Estes is certainly going to knock me out if he can, and exhaust me in any event. In Minnesota the Republicans organized a mass movement into the Democratic primary very subtly and adroitly, with the same people and techniques that the Eisenhower write-in was organized by in 1952. Their objective was, first to discredit the Democratic-Farmer-Labor Party leadership and, second, to injure me.

But of course it's hard to overcome the statistics in the public mind, and now Kefauver is burning up California. I shall take my armor off the kitchen door and rouse my sleeping charger and take after him.

Yours,

---

[170] The original is in the archives of Syracuse University Library.
[171] A copy is in A.E.S., I.S.H.L.

To Chester Bowles

March 26, 1956

Dear Chet:

I shall not belabor you with a long, thoughtful recitation of my experiences in Minnesota or the usual "explanations" about the skillful Republican invasion of the Democratic primary in the cities, to discredit the DFL and myself.

Rather, let me pass along some questions that were put together for me by Jim Warburg. They are the hard ones, and whether and how I could answer them during the campaign is a question. But I feel more and more that I may want at some stage to take some bold, advanced, realistic position in the foreign affairs area.

Hastily,

Professor Arthur M. Schlesinger, Jr., wrote Stevenson suggesting that Thomas Finletter join the Chicago campaign staff. On speeches, Schlesinger wrote, "You should become more concrete, programmatic and down-to-earth and less rhetorical . . . [and be] positive."

To Arthur M. Schlesinger, Jr.

March 26, 1956

Dear Arthur:

Thanks for your good letter. As to what the Young Democrats could do, I am informed by Jack Kennedy[172] that he is in communication with Dever[173] about organizing a write-in.[174] I should certainly think that they might help with this most effectively. I suppose for the present it must be considered highly confidential, however.

Tom [Finletter] and George Ball were here on Sunday, and while I should of course welcome Tom in Chicago, I have to bear in mind that

[172] Senator John F. Kennedy.
[173] Paul Dever, governor of Massachusetts.
[174] The Massachusetts presidential primary was to be held on April 24, 1956. In fact, the primary was entirely a write-in election, as no candidates' names were printed on the ballots, and preference votes were cast by the voter's writing a name on the party ballot of his or her choice. Stevenson received 19,024 votes on the Democratic ballot and 604 on the Republican, while Representative John W. McCormack of Massachusetts led the Democratic vote with 26,128, Senator Kefauver received 4,547, Senator John F. Kennedy received 949, and Governor Harriman received 394. President Eisenhower led the Republican balloting with 51,951 votes, plus 1,850 on the Democratic ballot. See Richard M. Scammon, ed., *America Votes: A Handbook of Election Statistics, 1956–57* (New York: Government Affairs Institute/Macmillan, 1958), p. 178.

Finnegan is the top man here and I also have a strong feeling that the operation which Tom and Jack Shea[175] are developing in New York can be exceedingly valuable. They did a research analysis on the Minnesota primary which we could not have done here. I shall bear your suggestion in mind, however, though I should hate to rob New York to pay Chicago.

I'm sure you must be right about the speech format, as I hear it from other sources, too. I confess that I am perplexed about the complaint that I have not been positive and concrete enough on issues. I am sometimes put to it to think of one I haven't taken a position on in speeches, articles, etc. Perhaps the explanation is that my language has been too complicated.

I communicated some views about the content of the April 21st and April 25th speeches to Tom and George. The former may be in touch with you. I am not insistent on my views as to what I should say at that time, but the suggestion seemed to me to have merit. I shall have a couple of days to work on them, and a lot more besides, between the 16th and 18th of April. I will be at my sister's place at Southern Pines. I should certainly welcome your help.

The news about the book[176] is good, and it must be a relief to you to have it off to the printer's at last. If your time now permits, I shall invade it mercilessly!

Hastily and gratefully,

To Alicia Patterson

March 26, 1956

My dear Alicia:

My plan now is to arrive in Jacksonville probably on the evening of April 3rd with John Fell and come to your house to stay until the morning of April 6. Then I must be back in Jacksonville for a day of speeching and politicking, returning to Chicago that night. I should like to leave John Fell there for a few more days until he has to return to college.

Now I hope you will be entirely candid about whether this is convenient, and if not, let Miss Carol Evans know by wire to my office as promptly as possible.

You are an angel to take us in and this turns out to be my only "holiday" — and I shall have to work most of it!

Affectionately,

[175] John B. Shea, attorney, head of the Lexington Democratic Club and executive chairman of the New York State Stevenson for President Committee.
[176] *The Crisis of the Old Order: 1919–1933* (Boston: Houghton Mifflin, 1957).

To Harry Golden[177]

March 27, 1956

Dear Harry:

Thank you, my friend, for that reminder that "westward, look, the land is bright." I am going out to find out!

Cordially,

ADLAI

Mr. Schlesinger wrote Stevenson on March 26 that he had time available to help in the last days of the California primary.

To Arthur M. Schlesinger, Jr.

March 28, 1956

Dear Arthur:

I am off in ten minutes for the airport, California and points up, down or who knows where or which way. But I must just say to you before I leave how much your note means to me coming at this time.

The Washington and New York appearances are uppermost in my mind right now, and I know how you are throwing your limitless and selfless self into those drafts. As for late May and early June, I'll be in touch with you as soon as I can get a minute to do a little planning.

God bless you!

Yours,

Stevenson delivered the following television speech in Los Angeles, California, on March 28, 1956.[178]

I have come back to California and to Los Angeles for a brief visit because there are some things I want to say and say promptly to the Democratic voters in this state.

What I have in mind is prompted, very frankly, by my experience last week in the Minnesota primary — and by my determination to win the Presidential primary contest in my native state of California.

I am not going to make any excuses for my defeat in Minnesota or talk about the massive Republican invasion of the Democratic primary there. I have no alibis.

---

[177] Publisher of the *Carolina Israelite* and author of several books. The original is in the possession of Mr. Golden.
[178] The text is taken from a mimeograph copy of a press release.

But something happened in Minnesota that I must speak about because it has also happened here in California. And other people beside myself are being unfairly hurt by it.

My candidacy in Minnesota was sponsored by United States Senator Hubert Humphrey, by Governor Orville Freeman and many of the leaders of the Democratic party. I was honored to have their unsolicited support and confidence for they are among the most devoted servants of the Democratic party and the liberal cause in America.

Yet Senator Kefauver and his supporters denounced those who supported me in Minnesota as "political bosses," and as a "machine" trying to exclude him and to deny the people a choice.

And the same thing has been done in California. Again my supporters are being described as sinister political bosses who are trying to dictate the people's choice.

Senator Kefauver knows this is not so. I want to be sure you do too.

The Californians on my slate of delegates include many leaders of the Democratic party — men and women who have won public office or who have been selected for positions of trust and responsibility in the party. They include seven of the eleven Congressmen from this state. They are headed by the only elected Democratic state official, your Attorney General, Pat Brown. They include Paul Ziffren, Democratic National Committeeman, Elizabeth Snyder, State Chairman; they include Alan Cranston, the President of the Council of Democratic Clubs, Byron Rumford and Gus Hawkins, the two Negro members of the State Assembly; they include Councilmen Ed Roybal and Rosalind Weiner of Los Angeles; they include some 15 members of Senator Kefauver's 1952 delegation, including John Anson Ford, the honored County Supervisor of Los Angeles County, and many respected leaders of labor, business, agriculture and the professions.

I have been flattered by the confidence and support of such citizens — and I am proud that it came to me voluntarily and without any strings attached.

And now I am advised that Senator Kefauver personally sought the support of many of these very same people — of Attorney General Pat Brown, of John Anson Ford, of Elizabeth Snyder, of Paul Ziffren, and a score of others.

Here in California, as in New Hampshire and Minnesota, the endorsement of the leaders of our party evidently becomes reprehensible only when the Senator doesn't get it.

But more important even than this effort to injure me and win support by confusing endorsement with dictation is that by discrediting the leaders of the Democratic party here in California the Senator and his spokesmen can only weaken and divide the party and thereby help the Republicans.

For four years I've done my level best to unite the Democratic party, not to tear it apart. And I propose to keep on thinking that the party's welfare is just as important as my own candidacy.

So much for this false and divisive boss nonsense. Now let's get down to business — and the things that count.

I shall conduct as vigorous a campaign as time permits here in California. I will tell you what I think about the tough questions of our time honestly, in plain words, and with no attempt to fool any of the people, any of the time. I will not attempt to outbid any other contender for the most responsible office on earth, Democrat or Republican; I will not promise anything I don't believe in or that I don't think is reasonable or possible. I know what another candidate for President said to the farmers in 1952, and I know what happened to those promises and also what has happened to the farmers. There is such a thing as wanting to be President too badly.

Another thing: I said in 1952 that my position would be the same in all parts of the country. It was then. And it will be this time, too. And that position will not be changed to meet the opposition of a candidate who makes it sound in Illinois as though he opposed Federal aid to segregated schools, in Florida as though he favors it, and in Minnesota as though he had not made up his mind.

I think it imperative that the Democrats recover the Executive branch of the government next November, as they recovered the Congress in 1954 — in order to arrest this deadly drift of the past three years, this leakage of our influence and power in the world, this creeping complacency, this single-interest domination of our government, this indifference to the farmer, this erosion of our liberties, this huckstering and merchandising, this selling us instead of telling us, and now this new and serious proposal to revise the role of the Presidency by turning its essential duties over to non-elected officers.[179]

I think it's time for Americans to get up and go about their country's business, and if I didn't feel this way I wouldn't be here asking for your vote at the primary. I have said who wins an election is less important than what wins, and I still believe it.

And when I read in the papers, as I have all of a sudden, that I am

[179] President Eisenhower pursued a general policy of delegating executive authority after the manner of the military chain of command. The editors have been unable to discover what specific proposal Stevenson refers to.

spending too much time discussing the issues and not enough time shaking hands, when I even read that I'm more concerned about issues than about people — well, frankly, it makes me disgusted, and then it makes me just plain mad.

There's only one reason I'm here tonight working for the Democratic nomination for President, and that's to be able to fight for the things I want and believe in for my fellow Americans. Only one who has been through a Presidential campaign can conceive of the physical and emotional ordeal it involves, and nothing but deep concern — yes, love — for this Republic and its people, could, I think, induce anyone to do it a second time.

I can't tell you tonight everything I want for all of us, for our children, our country and the world. But I can suggest some of the reasons which have been — and will continue to be — my reasons for asking for your support for my nomination.

I believe in an America whose children can grow up in decent homes and playgrounds and parks, or on thriving farms, and can go to school to good teachers in uncrowded classrooms.

I believe in an America where older people and the disabled are protected through social security adequate to their needs.

I want to see an America whose farm families are healthy and secure and share in our economy on an equal basis — buttressed by a government which will deal boldly, imaginatively and generously with this new problem of over-abundance, which seems to me more of a blessing than a disaster.

I want to live in an America where the terms and conditions of employment are constantly being improved, and where industrial progress means an ever better living for the families of working men and women.

I want this to be a place where men and women and children of every race, creed and color share alike the opportunities that this great country has to offer.

And that reminds us that eliminating segregation in the schools of some of our sister states presents us today with a national challenge to our maturity as a people. For my part, like most Northerners, I feel that the Supreme Court has decreed what our reason told us was inevitable and our conscience told us was right. I feel equally strongly that whether you agree with that decision or not, it is the law and should be obeyed.

It isn't enough, though, for any responsible public official, or for any candidate for public office, just to say which side of this issue he is on, or how strongly he feels about it. The job that has to be done now is to find even in the conflicting counsel of those who disagree so violently the best course by which the Court's decision can be carried out.

The Supreme Court has said what is to be done. The courts will determine when compliance will be expected. The question of how we will effect this transition in an orderly, peaceful way remains to be settled. This question is not going to settle itself. And the longer we drift the greater the danger — the danger from those who would violate the spirit of the Court decision by either lawless resistance or by undue provocation.

I have suggested that the President should promptly bring together white and Negro leaders to search out the way to meet this problem as a united people.

The fate of the world depends today on unity among Americans. To have that unity we must settle this problem peaceably, honorably and according to our law, our conscience and our religion. I believe deeply that there is this unity in America's heart; and I believe that no man, North or South, has any greater present duty than to help find the way to unite this nation behind the right answer to this problem.

And, to move on, I want to use what understanding I may have to restore dignity and consistency — without boasts, bluffs, or brinks — to the conduct of our foreign affairs, to regain our leadership in the free world, and the initiative in the struggle for the minds and hearts of the uncommitted third of the world, and to build up our defenses, material and spiritual, against the ever-shifting, unrelenting pressure of world Communism.

Our so-called prosperity depends on $35 or $40 billion that we spend every year for peace and security, and there is none. Asia is looking more and more toward our enemies while we talk of guns and military pacts and they talk of bread and better lives. North Africa is burning, and in the Middle East the guns are loaded in Egypt and Israel, but we are silent. I had assumed that long before this our government would make it unmistakably clear that Israel was here to stay and that it would not tolerate any alteration in the status quo in the Middle East by force, and that if her neighbors persisted in arming aggressively Israel should be armed defensively to protect herself.

I don't believe that anyone can spell out solutions during the course of a campaign to all our stubborn problems. Because there are few simple problems, I won't be able to offer easy answers. But I shall try to adhere to my resolve to talk sense — to talk honestly — and never mislead. If, as I express my views, you see fit to give me your confidence and support, I shall be a grateful and proud native son of California.

If not, I shall be disappointed, of course, but I shall have nothing to regret, because this is the only way I can campaign — and the only way I could live with myself, and with you, thereafter — win or lose.

Thank you — and God bless you all.

To Mrs. Eugene Meyer[180]

March 31, 1956

My dear Agnes:

I am home after two successful and exhausting days in California, where I found my supporters in Los Angeles and San Francisco more determined than ever, but little improvement in the organizational set-up. I sometimes despair of ever seeing what we could reasonably call an organization, or a facsimile of one, in California. But [James A.] Finnegan is going, confidentially, back out there for a long siege and there is hope of something effective, at least in the north.

I was disturbed by Jim Carey's[181] remarks. As you know, the professional liberals have been making a big fuss about my "moderation," and working especially on farmers and through the Farmers Union (their program is 100% of parity) and on the Negroes, on the basis of the wholly inaccurate quotations of what I said on my earlier trip to California as reported by [William] Lawrence in the New York Times.

I would be naive if I did not confess that they have made considerable progress, and we have not been too adroit about heading it off. In the Minnesota the Farmers Union, the largest farm organization, were evidently all instructed by Charlie Brannan,[182] Jim Patton,[183] et al., to vote for Kefauver. And I suppose it is this sort of thing that Carey has heard.

As to desegregation, I have said things at Hartford and Minneapolis lately which pleased the Negro leaders I saw in California on this trip mightily, but of course they had not even heard of what I said before, in view of the press barrier that I encounter more and more. It is possible that Carey himself has not seen either of these speeches, although I am astonished that he had not seen the Detroit one[184] which you showed him, and in which I said very little. I don't believe that my statements are simple enough, although that may have something to do with it.

---

[180] The original is in the Agnes Meyer files, Princeton University Library.

[181] James Carey, secretary-treasurer of the Congress of Industrial Organizations. The editors have been unable to discover the content or context of his remarks.

[182] General counsel of the National Farmers Union and former Secretary of Agriculture, 1948–1953.

[183] James G. Patton, vice president of the International Federation of Agricultural Producers, 1955–1958.

[184] March 10, 1956.

Mostly I think, as in his case with respect to the Detroit speech, that the wire services carry such meager excerpts and often, as I have noted, the least important material.

I wish I could see him, but I am off to Florida. I shall write him a note in any event and try to see him another time. It is imperative to my success in California that labor get busy. And Finnegan is, confidentially, coming to Washington this week to see some of them. Any that you can see and straighten out on my consistent support of 90% parity supports since 1952, and on desegregation, would be most helpful.

Affectionately,
ADLAI

P.S. I am off to Florida for a couple of days of work in the sun and a speech, and then back here. I am taking your speech with me and look forward to the usual tonic excitement from it.

. . . I've had a further thought. I am told that the District of Columbia will become a write-in battleground. The psychological importance attached to these things is, of course, far out of proportion. I will get probably little benefit if I should win, in the press, but I will suffer another publicity blow if I lose. The organized effort of the Republican press to get me is so apparent that I dare not lose that one. Hence anything that you can do there to help with the write-in business would be a positive gain.

A.E.S.

In a long letter to Stevenson on March 28, 1956, George F. Kennan, after analyzing many of the difficulties facing proper foreign policy formation and then the implementation of the policy, said as to what could be done about it, he would answer:

. . . First, I would try to re-enlist in the service of the Government the people needed to do a real job in the field of foreign affairs.
. . . If these people are not being used at present, it is not really for partisan reasons but because the security investigations were permitted to run wild and because the Administration is temperamentally uncomfortable in the presence of people who like to use their minds.

Secondly, I would try to restore the dignity of our governmental procedures. I should stop the wild travelling, the Madison Avenue glamorization of what should be the private processes of government. . . .

Thirdly, I would try to make the United States Government once more a partner in the world-wide discussion of international affairs — to re-establish some sort of rapport with currents of world thought and opinion. . . .

Fourthly, I would not boast. I would try to remember the sound maxim that in diplomacy successes claimed (not to mention successes boasted about) cease to be successes. . . . The deepest fault of the present Administration, aside from its amateurism of method and technique, is that it attempts to distort the image of our relationship to external environment in such a way as to make it acceptable to our domestic habits and prejudices, instead of insisting on the adjustment of our domestic life to the requirements of our world situation. . . .

To George F. Kennan[185]

March 31, 1956

My dear George:

I am just back after a reassuring visit to California, and I find your splendid letter of March 29. How I wish I could write with the facility and perception that you do! I may be uttering some of your words in a speech one of these days, and I hope you will forgive me if you detect no by-line! Meanwhile, I think you have restored my perspective on progress vs. performance in foreign policy, and I find it very helpful indeed.

I had hoped that Chester Bowles and you and possibly a couple of others might gather together in New York to advise me from day to day as to what I could say profitably on foreign policy. Traveling as I have, I find it difficult to keep up with what's going on, let alone saying anything sensibly and promptly which could be useful politically. Help! Help!

And thanks for this magnificent help!

Yours,
ADLAI

Henry A. Wallace wrote on March 23 to express his shock at the voting in Minnesota and went on to declare that Stevenson's self-possession after the defeat was "magnificent." He added that Stevenson was an "admirable and exceedingly rare phenomenon, a sincere, decent gentleman in politics with a sense of humor."

[185] The original is in the possession of Mr. Kennan.

To Henry A. Wallace[186]

March 31, 1956

Dear Mr. Wallace:

I was delighted to find your letter on my return from an encouraging visit to California. I have long since learned to distrust my superficial impressions of California, but the impressions were good and I found my supporters more sturdy than ever as a result of Minnesota. But the whining boss business and underdog role that our friend affects is effective. In addition, the extremists have embarrassed me somewhat on civil rights and agriculture. It's hard to be rational these days, as you well know.

In Minnesota, I am sure you realize that 125,000 to 150,000 Republicans invaded our primary, and in many areas seemed to prefer Kefauver, some doubtless on his 100% of parity program and others to injure the DFL and me.

The results have done me incalculable damage, which I must now overcome as best I can.

With all good wishes, and my thanks for your loyalty and encouragement,

Cordially yours,

After campaigning in Florida during the first days of April, Stevenson returned to Libertyville. There he was interviewed by the Columbia Broadcasting System on April 8.[187]

Governor, I suppose you've seen the newspaper headlines about the alleged Arab attacks on Israel, I wonder if you have anything to say about that?

I just read it a few minutes ago; these are preliminary reports; they have not been verified. If it turns out to be true, any such attack at nine points on the Israel frontier could be only a cynical and deliberate attack. I think it's shocking and a frightening reminder of the tenuous thread by which peace hangs in the Mideast. I hope our government will now take the steps I have recommended, personally, on many occasions beginning last November, to see to it that Israel has some of the means of self-defense and also that along with Britain

[186] A copy is in A.E.S., I.S.H.L.
[187] A copy of the transcript is in A.E.S., I.S.H.L. Because it is a very rough copy, evidently typed in haste by the interviewer, the editors have taken the liberty of correcting errors in spelling, omitting repetitious material (indicating the deletions with ellipses), and spelling out certain abbreviations, to make for easier reading.

and France I hope we reassert again our fundamental policy that there should be no change in the status quo in the Middle East by force.

To return to domestic politics, sir, there's been a lot of talk about the "new" Stevenson. Do you recognize him, and what's he like?

Well, I don't recognize him, but if by that they mean he's going to campaign more vigorously, that he doesn't feel he's getting his views across, and he's going to try all the harder to do that, to communicate with the people, so that they can understand what he stands for and represents, then perhaps there's a new Stevenson.

Sir, you've said that you regard the Illinois primary as a most important one to you. What, then, do you think the effect would be if there were a large, a substantial, Kefauver write-in?

Well, Illinois is very important to me sentimentally, you understand, because this is my home state and my family have lived here for well over 100 years and I've been governor of this state. Now there is a conscious effort, a deliberate and very well-organized I gather effort to stimulate a write-in — for Sen. K[efauver]. in the Illinois primary. I remember in 1952 something of that kind started when I was not a candidate and was not on the ballot and he was. At that time, I issued a public statement calling on all the Democrats not to vote for me and still I got something over 10 per cent of the vote that I believe he got, without being on the ballot. Therefore, I wouldn't count anything like that a serious concern at all, anything like on the order of 10 per cent. I don't know what he'll get but I know a deliberate effort's being made to get a large K[efauver]. write-in.

Sir, as you said, it is your home state. Would you consider it politically damaging should the Republicans, should President Eisenhower, pull considerably more votes than you?

No, that would be standard. This is basically a Republican state and I think they generally have cast larger Republican primary votes than we have, than the Democratic party does. I remind you also that I was only the fourth Democrat ever elected governor of this state in over 100 years. This is basically a Republican state and it's to be assumed that there will be a larger Republican primary vote than Democratic. I wish it weren't that way. . . .

Governor, there's been considerable speculation on Sen. Kefauver's, the reasons for his campaign successes to date. What would you say that they are?

Well, I don't know what successes you refer to. I was delighted in New Hampshire, when I did not enter the primary, when my, when I never appeared in the state, didn't campaign, and I had delegates that were not pledged to me but merely entered on their own behalf favorable to me, that they managed to get 40 per cent of the vote. This seemed to me rather surprising. As to Minnesota, there are many reasons, local reasons, I think for Senator Kefauver's victory. Certainly one of them was that he campaigned better and more effectively than I did; maybe he had a little more to offer to some of the people in the state than I had, and, uh. However, we cannot overlook the fact that something over 125,000 Republicans crossed over and voted in the Democratic primary. Why that was, reflects both, I think, a revolt among farmers to the Eisenhower farm administration program and also I think it reflected a good deal of discontent with the Democratic Farmer-Labor party and an effort to embarrass it up there in the forthcoming gubernatorial campaign and perhaps to embarrass me at the same time.

Well, then, you would not guess that the reason for his success had been due to any of his own specific, personal traits?

Yes, I said that, at the outset, that I thought probably he had campaigned more effectively than I did. I have no alibis for my defeat in Minnesota. I think there're always local reasons for votes in any state. There will be in Florida, there will be in California, [and] so on.

Sir, you probably have heard that Kefauver supporters are now saying that you're attempting to imitate their man's tactics. What would your answer be to that?

Well, I don't know what they mean by imitating his tactics. Then, I think maybe some people who are making those statements overlook the fact that I ran for governor of Illinois in 1948 and that I campaigned from every crossroads from Cairo to the Wisconsin line and I'm happy to say that I won this state by the largest majority ever recorded, in a state that has been overwhelmingly, for governor, overwhelmingly Republican.

. . . Governor, Kefauver himself, as you know, has accused you this weekend of mudslinging in an act of political desperation. What would you, what would your answer be to that?

Well, as to the desperation I'd say nonsense. I was grieved that the Senator used the phrase mudslinging. I've never used that phrase, in spite of the fact that he and his supporters have characterized many of the leaders of the Democratic party as "bosses," and as a machine trying to freeze him out, because they supported me rather than he. Nor have I even attacked his voting record. What I did say, in answer to many inquiries, was to attack his *non*-voting record, to point out that perhaps one reason that he doesn't have the support of his colleagues in the Senate . . . is due to his absenteeism. The fact of the matter is that during the 83rd, the last full Congress, the Congressional Quarterly discloses that on the roll calls in that Congress, Sen. Kefauver voted only 59 per cent of the time, whereas the average for all the Senators was 84 per cent. This was the second worst voting record in the 83rd Congress.

Governor, it looks as though your path is going to cross Kefauver's in Florida this week. What would you think of the idea of getting together with him, on the same platform, to discuss the issues.

Well, I'd be glad to join Sen. K. or any other Democratic leader on a platform. It would seem to me it would afford us a wonderful opportunity to spread the Democratic gospel perhaps at the expense of the television companies instead of our own.

Sir, Kefauver says also that he thinks it will give the people a chance to size up the rival candidates. What do you think of that idea?

Well, I think it's very good. I don't know about the proposal that's been made but certainly I'd be delighted to appear with Senator Kefauver anywhere.

Governor, some of your supporters have said that it's time now for you to discuss, in detail, the specific stands you would take should you become President, to outline what foreign policy you would espouse, for example. What have you to say to that?

Most of these statements don't come, I believe, from my supporters but from the Republican press, and they frankly irritate me if they don't bewilder me. Due to the fact that there is no one alive, unless perhaps it's Winston Churchill or Harry Truman, who has expressed his views more often, in more detail, on more subjects than I have for the past four years. Many of them have been published in written volumes and translated into many languages.

. . . Sir, whom would you say now is the most formidable contender for the Democratic nomination, the most likely to succeed in . . .

Well, the only other entrant at the moment is Senator Kefauver but I would have no doubt that there are a lot of dark horses waiting in the stable to come out on the track. . . .

Mrs. Roosevelt wrote Stevenson on April 2, 1956: "You are often in my thoughts and I know you are going through the hardest part of your struggle just now."

To Mrs. Franklin D. Roosevelt[188]

April 9, 1956

My dear Mrs. Roosevelt:

I was delighted to find your letter on my return from one of these incessant journeys. I suspect probably what Mrs. [Eugene] Meyer wanted to speak to you about was to try to get the labor leaders more active. We have detected a lethargy there which could be injurious in California where we need positive activity from labor.

The road is long and weary, as you know so well, and I am by no means sure that I am traversing it wisely or effectively, but at least I am traversing it!

Your confidence and encouragement are perhaps as meaningful to me as anything.

Affectionately,
ADLAI

On April 10, Stevenson flew to Florida to campaign for six days. After that, he campaigned in North Carolina on April 16 and 17 and in Pennsylvania on April 18 and 19, then spent five days in Washington, and on April 25 and 26 spoke in New York City.

To Mrs. Franklin D. Roosevelt[189]

April 17, 1956

My dear Mrs. Roosevelt:

A letter from Mrs. Agnes Meyer tells me that she thinks she has persuaded you to speak in California on my behalf. I am touched and grateful in the extreme but I must insist that you do not undertake this unless it is not too inconvenient or too much of a strain. I am afraid Mrs. Meyer's energies would exhaust me but I must not let her exhaust you!

Hastily and gratefully yours,
ADLAI

[188] The original is in the Franklin D. Roosevelt Library, Hyde Park, New York.
[189] The original is in the Franklin D. Roosevelt Library, Hyde Park, New York.

To Luther H. Hodges[190]

April 20, 1956

Dear Governor:

You and Mrs. Hodges cannot know how flattered and grateful I am for your visit to Southern Pines[191] and the picnic. Your confidence and encouragement mean more to me than perhaps I was able to communicate. I think we see things in this crowded, confused world much the same. The support of North Carolina has more than a practical meaning to me. Not only do I esteem the ju[d]gment of your people highly but there is the family sentiment which made my visit memorable.

Ever so many thanks, and I shall hope the resolution you suggest[192] may go through. All good wishes and my warm regards and thanks to Mrs. Hodges for accompanying you.

Cordially yours,

Stevenson delivered an address before the American Society of Newspaper Editors in Washington, D.C., on April 21, 1956.[193]

I have often confessed that I am a frustrated newspaperman. So you will understand the personal feelings that crowd in upon me as a renegade journalist turned politician rises to address this austere society.

Yet I have never thought that my transformation from newspaperman to politician involved very radical changes. After all, newspapermen — and especially editors — have much in common with politicians, though you may not perhaps be as ready to acknowledge this resemblance as we are. We all have messages to put over. We all deal in words. At our worst we all falter in the face of temptation to dissemble and deceive. At our best we all like to think that we elevate the national discourse and clarify the issues of our age.

But if we are going to rise to this high responsibility, we must have the information on which sound judgment is based. I know that you gentlemen are much concerned about improving the quantity and quality of the information the nation gets about the great issues of our time. I know something about the good work of your Freedom of Information

[190] Governor of North Carolina. A copy is in A.E.S., I.S.H.L.

[191] The winter home of Mr. and Mrs. Ernest L. Ives in North Carolina.

[192] The editors have been unable to identify the resolution to which Stevenson refers.

[193] The text is from Adlai E. Stevenson, *The New America*, edited by Seymour E. Harris, John Bartlow Martin, and Arthur Schlesinger, Jr. (New York: Harper, 1957), pp. 17–27.

Committee, and I was pleased to hear its praise from Congressman Moss[194] for helping strengthen the awareness in federal agencies of "the public's right to know." The American people are in your debt for these efforts.

But the very need for a Freedom of Information Committee points to a danger. Government secrecy, as your president, Mr. Kenneth Macdonald, has said, has become "entrenched behind a host of statutes and regulations." Indeed, one of the most serious criticisms I would make of this administration is that it has had so little respect for the public's right to know. We have to rethink the whole question of governmental secrecy, for without facts democracy dies at the roots. And we have not only been denied facts we ought to have, we have all too often been deliberately, intentionally misinformed. We have been sold rather than told. That is a long and dangerous step toward being told what we are permitted to think.

Peace and security are the nation's most important business. Yet nowhere has our government told us less and kidded us more. It has used foreign policy for political purposes at home. Unwilling to admit its failures, it has been unwilling to take us into its confidence. Reverses have been painted as victories. And if the administration has not succeeded in misleading the enemy, it has succeeded wonderfully well in misleading us.

When the Eisenhower administration first came to power, there was considerable talk about "operation candor" — they were going to tell us the facts of international life and national defense. But since then "operation candor" has been replaced by "operation bromide" — by vague and comforting assurances to allay anxiety and persuade us that we were comfortably ahead in the armaments race and had the love and esteem of our fellow men.

Was Secretary Dulles informing us or misleading us when he told a House committee on June 10, 1955, that the Soviet Union was "on the point of collapsing"? Was he giving us the facts when he said last November 29 that "we have the initiative, very distinctly" in the Middle East and in South Asia? Was he serious when he told the Senate Foreign Relations Committee as recently as February 24 that the free world is in a stronger position than it was a year ago and that the new Soviet economic and political challenge was a confession of failure? Was he the responsible Secretary of State of the greatest power in the world when he recently boasted that he and the President had conducted the nation

---

[194] John E. Moss, Jr., Democrat of California.

three times to the brink of war and then averted catastrophe by his own peerless statesmanship?[195]

We must do better than this. Underlying every other freedom, especially freedom of the press, is the freedom to know, to know the facts, especially the facts about our own prospects for life or for death.

Given the facts, Americans will not retreat in confusion or dissolve in terror, but will respond with determination to do whatever is necessary to assure the nation's safety.

And it is about some of the things which I think we must do and not do to ensure the nation's safety that I want to talk with you today.

Let me commence with a speech President Eisenhower made to this society here in Washington on "The Chance for Peace" exactly three years ago.[196] It endorsed the principles which had guided American policy since 1945 under President Truman; it placed the blame for the fears that gripped the world squarely on the Soviet government, and Stalin, who had died a few weeks earlier; and it held out to the new Soviet rulers a chance to work with us in building a hopeful future for mankind. You hailed it in your papers as the authentic voice of leadership in the new administration. Your reporters described the response as one of "universal acclaim."

What has happened? What has gone wrong since that speech?

But, first, let us try to recall hurriedly the context of that speech — what our position was three years ago when it was delivered.

You will recall how, in one act of constructive statesmanship after another, President Truman's administration met the postwar challenges and crises.

The United Nations and a new international order came into existence with tireless American encouragement.

Western Germany was forged into a strong nation, with a democratic constitution and self-supporting economy.

Japan was re-established with a humanitarian constitution dedicated to the arts of peace.

In 1947, when Russian power threatened the Eastern Mediterranean, the Truman Doctrine was proclaimed and Greece and Turkey were saved.

Berlin was saved by decisive action to break the blockade.

Then there followed in dramatic succession the Marshall Plan — a bold act of statesmanship that revived the economy, the self-esteem and defenses of Western Europe, to their benefit and ours; President Truman's Point Four Program, which gave new hope to the underdeveloped

195 See Shepley, "How Dulles Averted War."
196 See the New York *Times,* April 17, 1953.

nations and underprivileged peoples of the world; the North Atlantic Treaty Alliance, which confronted Russia in the West not only with economic strength but the military potential of the great coalition.

Those were great, creative years in American foreign policy. Years of achievement. Years of success.

Then, in 1950, war came to Korea. A psychopathic Stalin challenged world democracy and the United Nations. Under the decisive leadership of President Truman, that threat was stopped in its tracks. The United Nations was saved and a third world war was prevented.

This is a record in foreign affairs that we, as Americans, can all be proud of, regardless of party. In those years we confidently, courageously took the political and the moral leadership of the free peoples of the world. Compare that extraordinary outburst of creativity with the sterility of the past three years — a sterility which even the exuberance of Mr. Dulles' slogans cannot disguise.

We desperately need today a rebirth of ideas in the conduct of our foreign affairs. I would urge you, three years after that speech by the President, to think a little about America's position in the world today.

Is the United States more secure or less than it was three years ago?

Are our relations with our allies stronger or weaker? Is the mounting criticism of the United States, from Britain and France and Iceland and Turkey, in the West, to Japan and Formosa and Pakistan and Ceylon, in the East, really without foundation and justification?

Does our Secretary of State enjoy the trust, the respect and the confidence of the peoples and governments of the free world?

Is the moral position of the United States clear and unambiguous and worthy of us and our real aims? Is the image of the United States one that inspires confidence, respect and co-operation?

Do you think we are winning or losing ground in the competition with the Communist world?

I very much hope that the President will address himself to these vital questions when he speaks to you tonight. For these are the vital questions of our day. And the fact that such questions must be asked three years after his speech of 1953 shows, I fear, what all the world has discovered — that our admirable sentiments mean little when unsupported by positive and sustained action. Virtuous words are easy, but they are no substitute for policy.

The fact is that that speech never really served as a guide to policy. The tone it set found few echoes in what the President or the Vice-President or the Secretary of State and the Secretary of Defense did in the months that followed.

This is too bad. Our position in the world, I believe, would have been vastly different had we followed the guide lines laid down here before this society three years ago.

Now, where are we today — at this period of an extraordinary age which has witnessed the coincidence of three revolutions:

1. The technological revolution that has split the atom, devastated distance and made us all next-door neighbors.

2. The political revolutions that have liberated and subjugated more peoples more rapidly than ever before in history.

3. The ideological revolution, Communism, that has endangered the supremacy of Western ideas for the first time since Islam retreated from Europe.

It is against this background of violent, sudden change in all directions that the drama — or melodrama — of foreign policy must be played. This is a time of change in world affairs. The peoples sense it, even if the statesmen don't, for the peoples are, in a deep sense, forcing change. No one knows just where these changes will lead.

The administration has been slow to respond to this new mood. The Russians, on the other hand, have exploited it adroitly. Their objectives, we are told almost every day, have not changed. Of course they haven't. No one said they had. The Soviet rulers frankly state that their goal is a Communist world. But they have changed their approach; and we have not changed ours.

I seem to recall a slogan from 1952 — something about "It's time for a change." It is indeed time for a change — in a number of ways — especially in foreign policy. Our old policies are no longer adequate in the new situation. At least they are not if reports from all around the world are to be believed, and I think they are. From every corner of the globe your reporters are saying what has been apparent for a long time — that U.S. policy is rigid, unimaginative and fails to take advantage of new opportunities. And the realities of our situation bear little resemblance to the press releases.

I do not propose to chronicle here the whole long list of tension points in the world today. We know their names: Israel, Algeria, Formosa, Indochina, and Indonesia, Kashmir, Cyprus, and now the whole NATO area.

What is more basic and ominous and infinitely harder for us to accept is that in these last three years the United States has come dangerously close to losing, if indeed it has not lost, its leadership in the world — economically, militarily, and worst of all, morally. On all three of these fronts we have manifestly lost the initiative — and that is the prelude to the loss of leadership itself.

It is tragic irony that the people of America, who believe more firmly and fervently in peace and human freedom than anyone else, are not recognized as their sympathetic friend by the millions of mankind who are struggling out of the poverty and squalor and colonial bondage of ages. Instead it is Communist imperialism which has enslaved scores of millions in a decade which is usurping the role.

And only a few years back we seemed to those people the hope of the earth. America had gained freedom itself through revolution against European colonialism. Our great documents, from the Declaration of Independence to the Atlantic Charter, had spoken the aspirations of independence and growth. Our own colonial policies had been generous and forbearing. Our great leaders had affirmed the ideals of freedom with an eloquence that had won the allegiance of men and women everywhere. It was to us that new nations instinctively looked for sympathy, for support and for guidance.

Yet today, in the great arc from North Africa through Southeast Asia, the Russian challenge is developing rapidly and with great flexibility and force. Everywhere people seeking a short cut to raise their own standards of life are told that the Soviet Union alone has mastered the secret of converting a peasant economy into a modern industrial state in a single generation.

In the meantime, we, whose position is fundamentally decent and honorable and generous, have so mismanaged ourselves of late that we must now try to prove that we love peace as much as the Russians, and are as concerned with the problems of economic development and national independence as they are. It is fantastic but true.

Today the peoples of the proud, poor, new nations can find little in official United States policy which seems addressed to them and their problems, little which holds out promise of contributing to their social and national self-fulfillment.

Why is this?

It is compounded of many factors. One is the price we have been paying ever since the bomb was dropped on Hiroshima. The world is on edge and wants to blame somebody for not being able to sleep at night. And since America dropped the first bomb on Asians, and then the Japanese fishermen were burned,[197] America has been unfairly suspected of caring precious little about Asians and peace.

False and unfair as this is, we contribute to it in many ways.

On the one hand, we exhort the world about the virtues of the United States. On the other hand, most of our official dealings seem to be in

[197] Crew members of a Japanese fishing boat operating in the Pacific in March, 1954, were burned by radioactive ash which fell on them shortly after the Eniwetok-Bikini nuclear test of March 1, 1954. See the New York *Times*, March 16, 17, 1954.

terms of military threats, military alliances and military values. During the 1952 campaign, General Eisenhower and Mr. Dulles talked loosely about the liberation of the satellite countries. Since then the administration has noisily "unleashed" Chiang Kai-shek, huffed and puffed about Indochina, threatened massive atomic retaliation,[198] and scolded, boasted and bluffed — while at the same time presiding over the reduction of our armed strength. And all this has been more visible outside the United States than inside.

At a time when the new leadership in Russia has been very successfully playing on the universal desire of people everywhere for an end of the cold war tensions, the administration has clung stubbornly to its military emphasis on pacts, foreign aid, trade and international exchanges of all kinds. Much of the world has come to think of us as militarist, and even a menace to peace. In a survey last year in Calcutta people thought the United States more likely to start a war than Russia in the ratio 19 to 1.[199]

Also, on the question of colonialism the administration has done nothing to evolve a reasoned and sound American position, linked to our own traditions as well as to respect for our friends and a due concern for world stability. In the absence of a rational attitude, we have floundered, trying to be all things to all people and thereby antagonizing everyone.

We have persisted in construing the Communist threat to the underdeveloped world as essentially military. For people hungering after economic growth, we offer SEATO and place a defense effort ahead of the struggle against poverty. For people hungering after national independence, we offer little more than a policy of insensitive arrogance — witness the official derision of the Bandung Conference[200] and the clumsy reference to Goa.[201]

We had earlier this month, at Mr. Dulles' press conference on April 3, a pitiful summation of all this — and a revealing commentary on the cause of so much of it. Asked to comment on the present state of the reputation of the United States in the world, Secretary Dulles answered, and I quote from the *New York Times* report, that he "agreed that the United States was being criticized all over the world, but concluded

[198] Speech by John Foster Dulles to the Council on Foreign Relations, January 12, 1954. See the New York *Times*, January 13, 1954. See also his article in *Foreign Affairs*, April, 1954.

[199] The editors have been unable to locate any reference to this survey.

[200] A meeting of twenty-nine African and Asian nations held in April, 1955, in Bandung, Indonesia. Its aim was to promote economic and cultural cooperation among the participants, who were strongly opposed to Western colonialism.

[201] See note 72, p. 30.

that this was a fine 'tribute' to the United States because it proved nobody was afraid to criticize us."

This, of course, is dangerous nonsense. For what this criticism reflects is the infinitely sterner, more ominous fact that we have lost the moral initiative — and the rest of the world knows it.

Equally sobering is the realization that we are also losing the military advantage. Three years ago the United States had a clear margin of military superiority in the field of air-atomic power — in the production of the new weapons and in our capacity to deliver them. Today we have lost that margin of superiority.

It was, of course, inevitable that when the Soviet Union built its stockpiles to a certain level the fact that we retained a lead in the number of weapons would lose significance, and that an atomic stalemate might require us to develop more conventional forces. But it was not inevitable that we should fall behind in our air strength and in weapon development.

I trust I've made it clear that armed might should not stand as the symbol of our foreign policy. But military power is diplomacy's indispensable partner during this period when the ramparts of peace are still to be built and genuine arms control is still in the future.

To summarize: Three years ago this nation was looked to by all the free world as equipped by faith, history, accomplishment and authority to lead the peoples of the world to the promised land of security and peace. That is no longer the case. And we must squarely face the fact that there is no time to lose in re-examining and in redefining our policy to meet the challenge of today.

I know well the willfulness of the forces which affect the conduct of a nation's foreign policy. I make no pretense that there are one or two or three sure steps which would solve our problems. Wars may be won by secret weapons, but there are no secret weapons which will guarantee peace.

But I recognize the obligation to measure criticism by affirmative suggestion. So let me make some suggestions which are inherent, I think, in what I have said.

First of all, a decent respect for the opinions of others is still a basic requirement of a good foreign policy. Foreign policy is not only *what* we do, it is *how* we do it. The wisest policy will be poisonously self-defeating if mishandled. Smugness, arrogance, talking big are poison. Impulsive, abrupt actions create the impression that we are impulsive and abrupt. The restoration of composure, confidence and an impression of knowing-what-we-are-about is thus of first importance.

We want to be recognized not as bold, but as prudent, and that rules out boasting about brinks and the like. We want to be recognized as sensitive to the implications of modern warfare, and that rules out talk of massive retaliation. We want to be recognized as responsible, and that rules out trying to reconcile the irreconcilable wings of the Republican party. We want to be regarded as reasonable, and that rules out nonsense about the imminent collapse of the Soviet system. And we must reveal that craving for peace which is the true heart of America.

Second, I believe we should give prompt and earnest consideration to stopping further tests of the hydrogen bomb, as Commissioner Murray of the Atomic Energy Commission proposed.[202] As a layman I hope I can question the sense in multiplying and enlarging weapons of a destructive power already almost incomprehensible. I would call upon other nations, the Soviet Union, to follow our lead, and if they don't and persist in further tests we will know about it and we can reconsider our policy.

I deeply believe that if we are to make progress toward the effective reduction and control of armaments, it will probably come a step at a time. And this is a step which, it seems to me, we might now take, a step which would reflect our determination never to plunge the world into nuclear holocaust, a step which would reaffirm our purpose to act with humility and a decent concern for world opinion.

(After writing this last week down south, I read last night in Philadelphia that the Soviet Union has protested a scheduled H-bomb test. After some reflection I concluded that I would not be intimidated by the Communists and would not alter what I had written. For this suggestion is right or wrong and should be so considered regardless of the Soviet.)

Third, we should seriously consider basic revision of our method of giving aid; specifically, we should, I think, make greater use of the United Nations as the economic aid agency. We should try to remove economic development from the arena of the cold war. We believe, to be sure, that anything which strengthens economic growth, national independence, human welfare and democratic processes will improve a nation's resistance to the virus of Communism. But our first purpose is human betterment, and anything else is a by-product.

Also, if we propose to make economic aid most effective, we will have to stop demanding that recipient nations pass loyalty tests, and stop using our money to bribe feeble governments to set up rubber-check military pacts which will bounce as soon as we try to cash them. Rather

---

[202] Stevenson had discussed this question with Thomas E. Murray and others in March, 1956. On April 25, 1956, at his press conference, President Eisenhower dismissed Stevenson's suggestion. See note 221, p. 133.

we must convince the peoples of the underdeveloped world that we want no dominion over them in any form, and that we look forward to the end of colonialism in the world.

I don't believe we have explored all possible uses of our agricultural surpluses as raw materials of diplomacy. Surely there are ways of using our abundance, not as an embarrassment but creatively as part of a comprehensive plan of foreign assistance.

There is, too, the vast potential in peaceful use of atomic energy. It will be our ultimate ironical failure if the Soviet Union rather than the United States should provide the underdeveloped needful nations with atomic power. Our mastery of the atom, our willingness to make it mankind's public utility, should be one of our greatest contributions to human betterment.

I emphasize again, however, that all the bushels of wheat and the nuclear reactors and dollars in creation will do us little good if they seem only to be the bait with which a rich but uncertain nation seeks to buy protection for itself. If our attitude is wrong, no amount of money can do the job; and if our attitude is right, less money will go further.

These poor nations have discovered that poverty, oppression and disease are not the immutable destiny of man. They mean to improve their lot and quickly — by the methods of consent, our Western way, if possible. But if they can't they will turn away from us — to forced labor and forced savings, the totalitarian way — because they mean to industrialize one way or another.

If the United Nations administered economic development funds supplied by its members, it would strengthen international co-operation and the United Nations. It would remove economic development from the arena of the cold war. It would permit objective priorities on the needs of various backward sections of the world. It would stop competitive bidding. And if contributions were apportioned according to the existing formula, for each dollar contributed by the United States two dollars would be contributed by other UN members.

And, finally, it would involve the Soviet Union in responsible international co-operation all over the world. As it is now, there is nothing to prevent Russian penetration anywhere on a unilateral basis to serve its separate ends.

The Soviets refused to participate in a similar arrangement when we proposed the Marshall aid program in 1948. But that was Joseph Stalin — of now dishonored memory. And if his heirs should similarly reject multilateral economic assistance, the implications would be clear to all the world.

In this connection, a first step in this direction might well be taken in the Middle East, it seems to me. We all welcome the good news that a partial cease fire agreement has been arranged.[203]

But there are many tasks ahead, of course, before any genuine peace in that area can even be foreseen. Without reciting them here, let me just suggest that a co-ordinated attack on poverty in the Middle East might well be a profitable field for a United Nations economic program such as I have suggested.

Finally, it seems to me that any aid program we devise will be effective only as it expresses a healthy relationship between free and self-respecting peoples. We must show that we care about others in the world, not as bodies we would hurl into the military breach, but as men and women and children who we hope will live lives of dignity and fulfillment.

So long as we overmilitarize our international thought and statement, so long as we picture the differences between Russia and the West as part of a great military contest, hot or cold — for so long will our efforts prove futile and our motives suspect. For there is little about that struggle which penetrates the minds and hearts of the people of Asia or Africa.

Let us, rather, rally the nations for a world-wide war against want. And let us then — for men do not live by bread alone — identify what we do in the world with the one export which we can offer as no one else can. I mean liberty, human freedom, independence, the American idea — call it what you please — which is more precious and more potent than guns or butter.

For from the word "go" — which is to say, from our very first national statement in 1776 — America spoke for freedom in terms so inspiring, so sublime and so inexorably appealing to men's consciences that the Old World was shaken to its foundations. Tyrannies dissolved; hope sprang up like a fresh breeze; movements of liberation mushroomed. This was the greatest foreign aid program in history and no one has ever improved on it or ever will.

We have drifted and stumbled long enough. It is time to restore the true image of America, once so well known and well loved, which gave birth to the Declaration of Independence and the Four Freedoms — a nation marked, not by smugness, but by generosity; not by meanness, but by magnanimity; not by stale conservatism and a weary reliance on dollars and arms, but by broad vision and moral and social passion.

---

[203] UN Secretary-General Dag Hammarskjöld, on a mission to the Middle East, announced on April 19, 1956, that Egypt and Israel had agreed to an unconditional cease-fire along their border. On April 24, Syria agreed to respect the cease-fire. However, full-scale war broke out the following autumn.

It is time to regain the initiative; to release the warm, creative energies of this mighty land; it is time to resume the onward progress of mankind in pursuit of peace and freedom.

While in New York City, April 24–26, Stevenson spoke at a Stevenson for President Committee dinner, appeared on radio and television and met with many of his supporters. At a press conference Stevenson expressed his delight that Senator Herbert Lehman and New York City Mayor Robert Wagner had attended the dinner but observed, "My opponent — the Governor [Averell Harriman] — and Mr. [Carmine] De Sapio, leader of Tammany Hall, were not there."[204] At the dinner, held on April 25, he delivered the following speech.[205]

You will have to find even in the abruptness of my greeting the measure of its warmth. For I have become painfully aware that, if television is to be a candidate's servant, he must accept it even more as his master. Not silence, but talk, has become golden.

So I shall come directly to the point.

I have come to New York to ask support for my candidacy for the office of President of the United States.

But this is too large a thing for any man to seek or ask on a personal basis. And I do not. I come to you rather in the deep conviction that, if there is to be peace in the world and freedom in America, the reins of our government must be returned to those with the passion for progress and the dedication to the ideal of human dignity which are the qualities of the Democratic faith — of your faith and of mine.

I spoke in Washington on Saturday of peace in the world.

I want to speak tonight of freedom in America.

Yet these are not really two issues, but rather two parts of one.

There can be no lasting freedom in America unless there is peace in the world. And there will be peace in the world only when we here in America prove that freedom means what we say it means. We must show that freedom is the servant of the poor as well as the rich — for most of the world is poor; that it protects change — for most of the world is in revolution; that it is color-blind, for most of the world is nonwhite. We must prove that freedom contains that full measure of justice without which it could be freedom for the strong to oppress the weak.

204 Arthur Krock analyzed the Harriman-Stevenson situation in the New York *Times*, April 28, 1956.
205 The text is from Stevenson, *The New America*, pp. 190–195.

I see freedom in the world today as the great life-giving river of which America is the source. It will be whatever we are, not more, not less. So, if we hope to make the principles of freedom meaningful in the world, we must first make sure they have mighty meaning for ourselves. We must — in our land, in our own communities, and in our own hearts — live up to the values of individual freedom and individual right which are the basis of our American society.

Yet we must do this not just because it may exalt our leadership in the world, but above all for the sake of these values themselves — the values which give life and power to the great experiment in self-government to which we as a people have been so long committed, and to which so many others in Asia and Africa now urgently aspire. Our task is all the harder and the purity of our example all the more important because these peoples who know about *national* freedom know little about these values of individual freedom and rights which lie at the root of free society.

Let me speak first about the issue of freedom which is today causing greatest concern among us — civil rights for our minorities. The achievement of equal rights for all American citizens is the great unfinished business before the United States.

This would be just as much the case had there been no Supreme Court decision on desegregation in the public schools.

There remains, however, the abiding responsibility of the executive branch of the government to do its part in meeting this most fateful internal problem and the rising tensions that have followed in its train. The present administration, in my judgment, has failed to meet this responsibility; it has contributed nothing to the creation of an atmosphere in which this decision could be carried out in tranquillity and order.

The immense prestige and influence of the Presidency have been withheld from those who honestly seek to carry out the law in gathering storm and against rising resistance. Refusing to rise to this great moral and constitutional crisis, the administration has hardly even acknowledged its gravity.

It is the sworn responsibility of the President to carry out the law of the land. And I would point out that this office is the one office in the democracy, apart from the courts, where the man who fills it represents all the people. Those in the Congress bear particular responsibilities to the citizens of the states they represent, and on what is in some ways a regional problem their views are naturally divided. Not so of the Presidency. And where the nation is divided, there is special demand on him to unite and lead the people toward the common goal.

As president, if that were my privilege, I would work ceaselessly and with a sense of crucial urgency — with public officials, private groups, and educators — to meet this challenge in our life as a nation and this threat to our national good reputation.

I would act in the knowledge that law and order is the Executive's responsibility; and I would and will act, too, I pray, in the conviction that to play politics with the Court's decision and the basic rights of citizens and human beings is wicked.

It is, for me, another point of central principle that one of the most important guarantees of equality is the right to vote conferred on all citizens by the Fifteenth Amendment. Political freedom underlies all other freedoms. Wherever any American citizens have been denied by intimidation and violence the right to vote, then the right to vote of all American citizens is imperiled.

There are laws on the statute books giving the federal government authority to protect citizens' voting rights. These laws should be enforced. And if they are inadequate, they should be strengthened. And I believe that all responsible citizens, south and north, would go along with a determination to assure the right to vote under the law.

But again I say that the responsibility and the opportunity of the President in matters such as these go beyond the execution of the law. For his office is the repository of moral authority as well as legal, and it is from our chosen leader that there must come to our hearts, our heads and our spirits the common impulse to honor in our daily lives the principles we proclaim to all the world.

The protection of minority rights is in the forefront of all our minds. But it is only part of the larger problem of protecting the Bill of Rights from the grievous assaults that have scarred and stained this interval.

The flood stage of hate and hysteria among us, so alien to our nature, reached its crest in 1953 and 1954, the first two years of the present administration.

Those were the days when our government quaked before the Junior Senator from Wisconsin[206] and White House aides spoke of the President's "passion not to offend anybody in Congress."

Those were the days when books were banned and even burned in American libraries abroad.

Those were the days of the "numbers game" — a sleight-of-hand operation intended to make the country believe that the Eisenhower administration had ousted from government a whole horde of Communists hired by the Democrats — when in fact not a single one was a Communist and almost half of those discharged (on what were called

[206] Joseph R. McCarthy.

security grounds) had actually been hired by the present administration itself![207]

Those were the days when some American citizens demanded that the Girl Scouts rewrite their manual and denounced the tale of Robin Hood as Communist propaganda.

And those were the days when an emotional pressure toward a spurious conformity silenced tongues and shuttered minds throughout the land of the free and the home of the brave.

The 1954 rejection of the Vice-President's campaign appeal about Communists in government, the election of a Democratic Congress, and the senatorial censure of the man who described the great Democratic interval of victory over depression and Hitlerism as "twenty years of treason," marked the turning of the tide against the high point of the flood of hate, hysteria and fear.

But if the flood has receded, the evidence of the damage it did to the soul of America remains. There is much to be done today to restore respect for the foundation of freedom under law — the Bill of Rights.

Who can best clean up the wreckage? Who can best rebuild the structure of our Bill of Rights?

Is this a task to be entrusted now to the party whose leaders shouted treason and Communism for partisan advantage?

Is it a task to be entrusted to those who were indifferent to national dignity and individual freedom at home, while posing as champions of liberty in the world?

It is rather the task, I suggest, for those who tried faithfully to defend our liberties even as the flood mounted and rolled toward its crest.

Let us never forget some of the landmarks of sanity in this shameful period. There was President Truman's courageous defense of freedom of speech in his forthright veto message of the Internal Security Act, the McCarran Act, of 1950. There were the speeches of Democratic leaders against all that Senator McCarthy stood for at a time when he was still his party's hero. And I remind you that, finally, the Democratic senators voted to a man for his censure in December of 1954, while half of Senator McCarthy's own party still could not see that he had done anything wrong.

This is our job — yours and mine — a job, if you will, for Democrats.

We must first stop playing partisan politics with internal security. Political debate must once again be pitched on the great issues of our time, not on impugning the loyalty of any group of Americans. Commu-

---

[207] See *Report of the Committee on Post Office and Civil Service* (U.S. Senate, 84th Congress, 2nd Session, Senate Report 2750).

nism is not an issue, for both parties are dedicated to the struggle against it at home and abroad.

Our security system must be reconsidered. Today there are loyalty-security tests for between eight and ten million Americans. Federal employees, many state and municipal employees, servicemen, multitudes of workers in private plants, Coast Guard employees, and others have their private lives put under the microscope of investigation in the alleged interest of our national security.

We must, by all means, take the strongest possible measures to prevent espionage, and strengthen our counterintelligence activities and agencies in every useful way. But let us, too, weigh clearly and carefully the balance between these necessities and the equal necessities of protecting the rights of free speech and association guaranteed by the First Amendment.

I am glad to see that the administration itself has belatedly recognized that its security program has been actually endangering our security by holding back scientific progress, and that it is relaxing its requirements with respect to nonsecret research programs.

The time has come to restore to our security procedures the fundamental principle of the Bill of Rights, that no man shall lose his life, liberty or property without due process of law. The discharge of an employee by governmental edict without the right to face his accusers offends that principle.

The idea that a man's right to a commission in the armed forces or to an honorable discharge may be challenged because of his mother's or his sister's actions or associations denies the principle of personal responsibility and imitates the totalitarian doctrine of family guilt. I never thought we would live to see in America the day when not being good to one's mother was a sign of virtue.[208]

As we defaced the American image when we defaced the Bill of Rights, so we can restore that image only as we enshrine again the Bill of Rights.

I wish there were time tonight to talk of newer frontiers, of the tasks we face if we are to give freedom the breadth of meaning it can have in this age of abundance in this most blessed of countries.

Freedom isn't complete for families living in slums, for men out of work, for children in overcrowded classrooms, for people who are sick and can't afford help, or for men and women who have worked long and faithfully only to find old age a time of fear.

All of these must be our concern as we think forward to the enrich-

[208] For an earlier statement by Stevenson on the Eisenhower loyalty-security program, see *The Papers of Adlai E. Stevenson*, Vol. IV, p. 517.

ment of freedom and to putting it in a setting of life where it will mean the most. As Senator [Herbert H.] Lehman has said, "we must work to restore Freedom to her hallowed place in our hearts and in the practices of our country."

For "the trouble is," Senator Lehman said, "that we have lost the passion for the full right of freedom."

But have we really lost it? What we have lost, I think, but only for this moment in history, is the leadership that passion for freedom demands; leadership in the majestic, vital tradition of the great champions of the American ideal — Jefferson, Jackson, Lincoln, Wilson, Roosevelt and Truman.

Only by such a rekindling of this nation's passion for freedom can we persuade the world that America is genuinely the hope of free peoples everywhere. For, in the end, democracy will triumph or go down, and America will stand or fall, not by the power of our money or of our arms, but by the splendor of our ideals.

To Mrs. Robert Jackson

April 26, 1956

My dear, dear Barbara:

I am sitting now in a television studio in New York after a program and before jumping into a car to careen to Idlewild, thence to Miami and another speech tonight, thence on to Chicago tomorrow, Friday, to Oregon Saturday, to California Tuesday, and on and on to the end of time!

I am mortified that I have not acknowledged "The Image of America" long before this, and I pray that you can understand something of the fantastic ordeal through which I seem to be passing. I had 48 hours in North Carolina in which I had to construct the speech, on the basis of materials I had written and put together from other sources, and yours came too late. But now I have another speech! What I did I enclose lest you have not seen it. What I am saying is being reported less and less, I fear. I am also enclosing a couple of other recent efforts.

I wish there was time to give you some account of my adventures, but I must be contented with reporting the remark of the charming old lady who came down the line and gushed that she wanted to vote for me more than anything on earth — "But, Governor, I've never voted for a winner yet. Do you want my vote or not!"

I think my situation is mending since Minnesota. The primaries in Illinois, New Jersey, and now in Pennsylvania, Massachusetts and

Alaska have all been to my great advantage,[209] but Florida, Oregon and California will still, I presume, be decisive. Of course, it is unlikely that Kefauver can be nominated, but he could very well eliminate [me]. . . .[210]

To Mr. and Mrs. Herbert H. Lehman

April 27, 1956

Dear Herbert and Edith:

My endless "primary" journey (I sometimes feel as though it were my final journey) has allowed me few evenings off. But all the evenings on duty were compensated for by that dinner with you in Washington. I had a good time — a comforting time and a relaxing time — and for all of these three precious boons I have you to thank.

But I have you to thank for something more — a confidence and an encouragement that is of immeasurable value to me. What you said the other night at the dinner, Herbert, touched and pleased me more than I can tell you.

With affection and everlasting gratitude I am

Cordially yours,

To Walter Lippmann[211]

April 27, 1956

Dear Walter:

I cannot complain if you did not like my speech before the editors. But perhaps you will permit me to protest the suggestion that it was written in part by others. I feel the more strongly about it in view of the fact that I spent the two or three days I have had for myself for the last two months writing it! So both on my own behalf, let alone those nameless ghosts, permit me to at least claim the poor thing as my own and no one else's — in whole or in part!

If foreign policy is in large measure the how as well as the what I would have thought there had been very sharp changes in the past three years, which is the issue I was attempting to draw as well as to suggest the inadequacy of the policies in present light.

Sincerely yours,

---

[209] Stevenson carried these primaries, in which he was not seriously opposed by Kefauver.

[210] Stevenson apparently finished this letter in Chicago April 27, by hand.

[211] A copy is in A.E.S., I.S.H.L.

Chakravarti Rajagopalachari, powerful leader of the Indian Congress party in Madras and a close associate of Mahatma Gandhi, wrote Stevenson praising his speech before the American Society of Newspaper Editors.

To Chakravarti Rajagopalachari[212]

April 28, 1956

My dear Friend:

I was delighted and flattered by your letter. You were good to write me. I am presuming to send along a copy of this speech, which has been both criticized and applauded. The best applause has been a rather sharp change in Administration attitudes, if not on the hydrogen bomb itself.

How I wish I might have another trip to India and an opportunity to review these stirring and critical years with you and some of the gentlemen I was privileged to meet there.[213] I have a strong feeling that things are moving for the better here — but I am not referring to my prospects for the Presidency! That is another story and I am perhaps not the best story teller.

With many hopes for your very good fortune and health.

Cordially yours,

To Vincent Sheean[214]

April 28, 1956

Dear Jimmy:

I find your letter awaiting me in Chicago, where I am "resting" for ten hours en route from Florida to Oregon and the only visit here until early June.

These primaries are an invention of some gentleman who had little respect for the human body, mind, emotions, and least of all, possible Presidents!

I shall get after John Gunther and find the letter.[215] Meanwhile, in re. the Bill of Rights, Negroes, etc., I enclose a speech I made the other night to a Stevenson fund-raising dinner in New York. The dinner was

[212] A copy is in A.E.S., I.S.H.L.
[213] See *The Papers of Adlai E. Stevenson*, Vol. V, Chap. Eleven.
[214] Journalist and author. A copy is in A.E.S., I.S.H.L.
[215] Mr. Sheean had mentioned that fellow author John Gunther was supposed to forward to Stevenson a letter that Mr. Sheean had written, dealing with the civil rights question.

successful, the speech allegedly so, though that would be for others to say.

It is always good to hear from you, my old friend.

Cordially,

To Arthur M. Schlesinger, Jr.

April 28, 1956

Dear Arthur:

I don't believe I properly thanked you for the most recent help of all kinds. I somehow got through this last Eastern ordeal and I think with only minor misfortunes. I am certain I am on the right track on the hydrogen bomb, but I certainly haven't got it properly put forward yet. It is the difference between peaceful development and weapon development, I suppose, plus the public realization of the necessity for recapturing initiative among the people that are so hungry for peace in the East.

Off to Oregon — California — etc. — and always hopeful that you will pass along at any time anything that you think needs saying.

Yours,

To Richard J. Daley[216]

April 29, 1956

Dear Dick:

My fortunes seem to be prospering. At least when I can detach myself from the clamor long enough to find out what is happening the news is all good!

But I cannot be sure just what will come to pass in Oregon, although it appears to be considerably better than we anticipated a few weeks ago.

I was reminded by Bill Blair today that I should in turn remind you about the delegation to the Convention. I suppose I should be a delegate-at-large, and as I shall probably not be back there until after the Convention I take this means of reminding you about it.

From Oregon I go to California on Tuesday for a tough ten days, returning here for a few more, and then direct to Florida about the 18th and 19th. In short, I shall probably not be in Chicago more than for a few hours until after the California primary.

I trust all is well with you.

Yours,

[216] Mayor of Chicago. This letter was written from Portland, Oregon.

To Clay Tate[217]

En Route — May, 1956

Dear Clay:

I have your letter of May 11 in which you ask my confidential appraisal of Dick Stengel's[218] performance in the General Assembly during the period when I had an opportunity to observe him at close range. I am glad to have this opportunity because I feel very deeply about Dick's fine qualities, and I think it will be a great loss for all of us in this state if he is not given the chance to continue in public service with new and enlarged responsibilities.

Dick first appeared in Springfield the same time I did, namely, January, 1949. I was, thus, able to follow the first four years of his career there daily and at first hand, and I have taken careful note of it since, albeit from a more remote vantage point.

I am not going to spend any time in cataloging his positions on particular issues. His voting record is freely available to you, and if you have looked at it you know as well as I do that it is an excellent one. I am more concerned to try to tell you in more personal terms about the way he worked and conducted himself in Springfield, because I think that it has a great — indeed, a decisive — bearing on the way he would perform in the Senate and the kind of influence and stature he would come to have there. For us as citizens of Illinois that, it seems to me, is of the greatest consequence; my experience is that the issues tend to take care of themselves satisfactorily if a man has proven qualities of mind, character and temperament.

In the 1949 session he was, of course, a freshman representative, but it was apparent to all that he made his mark early and was headed for greater things. He gave me loyal (although never unquestioning or automatic) support but, of necessity, as a rank and file member rather than as a leader. In the honeymoon that followed the Democratic victory in 1948, I was able to get a large measure of effective cooperation in that session from the top Democratic leadership in the House of Representatives.

By the time the 1951 session came around, the situation had altered markedly. The Republicans had won control of the House. I distributed responsibility for my legislative program around and much of the burden fell on Stengel. A key measure in that session, you may recall,

---

[217] An editor of the Bloomington *Daily Pantagraph*. The text is based on a draft corrected by hand by Stevenson.

[218] Richard Stengel was running for the U.S. Senate against Republican incumbent Everett M. Dirksen.

was the highway program, including the all-important increase in the gas tax and truck license fees. This was an issue upon which powerful forces were marshalled against us; and the measure itself was highly technical and difficult to get over in terms of popular understanding. Dick, at my request, assumed the responsibility for getting this through the House, which is where it was most likely to be defeated. Not an easy job under any circumstances, it was not made any easier by the fact that he was asserting a leadership which was not his by right of title or seniority.

One of the most significant things, however, about Dick's performance on this bill was the way he did his homework and put himself in a position whereby, when he spoke and handled the matter in debate, he was obviously in command of all the relevant facts and figures. I need hardly tell you that many politicians and legislators are not distinguished for the extent to which they are willing to withdraw from general circulation and do the hard work of mastering complicated sets of facts and theories. In connection with the truck bill, Dick spent long hours with the engineers of the Highway Division, and he worked long and hard to prepare himself for the floor discussions.

I am frank to tell you that one of the reasons why I was well pleased with his endorsement for the senatorial post, despite his relative inexperience and lack of familiarity with national and international issues, was that I was certain he would bring this same talent and industry to bear on these questions and that, given a reasonable period of time, he would show to advantage in these areas as well as he did in the frequently no less complicated issues affecting the State government in Springfield. This capacity, and his willingness to use it, can and will be transferred from the one field to the other, I have no doubt.

Dick handled several other important matters for us, including many of the Schaefer Commission recommendations for improvement of the State government, and I know that I saw the end of the 1951 session with a feeling not only of personal gratitude but of real and growing respect for the abilities of this young man who had done so much under difficult conditions to make the record of [that] session a most productive, indeed distinguished one.

Another significant factor is that, although legislators, like other groups, tend to resent bright young men who move too fast, Dick was able to keep on excellent personal terms with the great majority of his colleagues in both parties, and his personal standing and influence among them are high. Legislative assemblies being what they are, this again you will identify as an important element in measuring effectiveness.

His only difficulties in this area have arisen from the fact that he has been the focus of resentment of a few against a lot of things, including the steady rise of a legislative star interested in different objectives from theirs.

I am sure you know something of what he has done since. He was one of the strong backers for judicial reform, even though the position was a highly unpopular one in his district. He also made a great contribution to the ultimate success of legislative reapportionment.

It is true that his experience in public life has been limited to eight years in the Illinois General Assembly, and I would be the last to say that he does not have a great deal to learn about the kind of issues with which he will be dealing in the Senate. I also believe, however, that the rough and tumble of the Illinois lower house is a wonderful testing ground for any individual aspirant for legislative advancement; and one who can do what Dick has done in his few years there, and who has handled himself both personally and publicly the way he has, cannot fail to be equally successful in the United States Senate.

Sincerely,

To Mrs. Franklin D. Roosevelt[219]

May 1, 1956

My dear Mrs. Roosevelt:

I've just been told of your speech on my behalf in Washington on Saturday. I have been informed, too, of the great personal inconvenience to which you went in rearranging your plans in order to do this. As if this weren't enough, your letter of endorsement in the District of Columbia is much too generous.

How can I ever thank you properly?

With warm regards,

Affectionately,

ADLAI

P.S. This was dictated several days ago — and several states! — ago, before the District results came in.[220] And I eagerly join even Kefauver in attributing the happy result to you. Thanks again!! ADLAI

---

[219] The original is in the Franklin D. Roosevelt Library, Hyde Park, New York. This letter was written from Portland, Oregon.

[220] By the time Stevenson added this handwritten postscript, he had carried the District of Columbia primary against Kefauver.

Stevenson issued the following statement on thermonuclear weapons development at San Bernardino, California, on May 4, 1956.

At his press conference on April 25th the President said with reference to guided missiles and the hydrogen bomb that "one without the other is rather useless."[221]

I am perplexed by the President's statement because the H-bomb and the guided missile are entirely different. The missile is a carrier like an airplane or a torpedo. The H bomb is an explosive, like an atomic bomb or TNT. The guided missile can and should be developed. But I understand it can be tested without carrying a hydrogen warhead and without danger.

But, as Pope Pius and others have suggested, I would like to see the United States press toward complete control of thermonuclear power and its use for peaceful purposes only.

If I am mistaken and the intercontinental guided missile is useless except with a hydrogen bomb warhead, then there is all the more reason for trying to control thermonuclear weapon development at once.

To Benjamin V. Cohen[222]

May 6, 1956

Dear Ben:

I have been badgered about the H-bomb business and finally released the enclosed. If you have any suggestions for me or advice on what I can or should say I wish you would send them along via air mail as promptly as you can to Newton Minow in my office in Chicago. He will have my itinerary and can get them to me by wire or telephone.

There is much confusion, evidently, about the missile and the bomb and most people don't seem to distinguish one from the other.

Also, if there is anything new that needs saying on the Middle East as a result of Hammarskjold's visit and the truce,[223] I should certainly like to have it.

At this distance one feels a little isolated from foreign developments.

My apologies for burdening you with this impetuous message.

Cordially,

---

221 Eisenhower had commented on Stevenson's speech to the American Society of Newspaper Editors: "It is a little bit of a paradox to urge that we work just as hard as we know how on the guided missile and that we stop all research on the hydrogen bomb, because one without the other is rather useless."

222 This letter was written from Santa Barbara, California.

223 See note 203, p. 120.

To Harry S. Truman[224]

May 7, 1956

A HAPPY BIRTHDAY TO YOU, WARRIOR EXTRAORDINARY, AND MAY YOU AND MRS. TRUMAN HAVE A THOROUGHLY INTERESTING AND ENJOYABLE TIME IN EUROPE. YOU WILL CARRY WITH YOU THE RESPECT AND AFFECTION OF MILLIONS OF YOUR FELLOW CITIZENS.

Author John Hersey sent Stevenson the draft of a speech and in his covering letter wrote: "You have, as Eleanor Roosevelt said, the courage to say things that are hard to say. I am one of the many who think that giving your courage free rein is far more important than shaking hands — and in this world more important even than winning." Stevenson replied from Los Angeles.

To John Hersey[225]

May 10, 1956

Dear John:

Ever so many thanks for your kind words — and for that splendid draft.

I've already made some use of the latter, and I hope to do it full justice a little later on, when I can catch my breath for a major effort on education.

I'm deeply grateful.

Sincerely,

Adlai Stevenson III wrote his father asking if he and his wife Nancy, who was pregnant, could live in the barn at Libertyville for the summer. He mentioned that his Harvard friend Kerry Lyne had gotten engaged to a wonderful girl — and a Democrat — and remarked that his grandmother was discouraged because his mother was evicting the English Speaking Union from the building she owned.

---

[224] This telegram was sent from San Jose, California.
[225] A copy is in A.E.S., I.S.H.L. This letter was written from Los Angeles, California.

To Adlai E. Stevenson III[226]

May 14, 1956

Dear Bear:

I wish I could write you a proper letter, but I am living in a state bordering on insanity, and I must be quick. I spoke to Mary Lou[227] and it is understood that her father will vacate before you come. You should tell her directly what you will need in the way of furniture and utensils.

I am so glad you have found an apartment that is so inexpensive and also one for Borden. Give Kerry my congratulations and tell him I look forward eagerly to meeting "that wonderful girl." Thank god she is a Democrat and we don't have to spend any time converting her!

There is incessant and repeated demand for Nancy to join me in Florida. We will be there from May 18 to 28, I believe. She evidently made a terrific hit, and I wish she could come but I am not going to press it because of her "condition" — not to mention your uxorious claims!

I can't understand why mother should be evicting the English Speaking Union. It sounds nutty. . . .

Hastily — and with love —

To Mrs. Eugene Meyer[228]

May 14, 1956

My dear Agnes:

I am mortified that I have not written you long ago. . . .

It has been an awful ordeal, day after day of incessant appearances, all of which tire me nervously and emotionally. I don't speak easily off the cuff and I have never succeeded in getting a sort of set patter that I can use over and over again that satisfies me. The result is that I still struggle and strain to say something better and end up with something worse. Sometimes I have had to speak as many as fifteen times a day, and every day is interminable agony; but curiously enough I seem to find unexpected sources of strength, and aside from a little throat and nose trouble I have no major complaint as the endless days wear on.

My greatest distress is the unsatisfied feeling of never doing anything well or useful or important in this mad interval, nor, I suppose, shall I

226 This letter was written from Portland, Oregon.
227 Stevenson's housekeeper at Libertyville.
228 The original is in the Agnes Meyer files, Princeton University Library. This was written from Portland, Oregon.

get reconciled even to that. But, nevertheless, the progress is good and the political reports are favorable.

Another disappointment is that I can never write you a proper letter!

Affectionately,

ADLAI

To Mrs. Edison Dick[229]

[no date][230]

I don't know what day it is and don't care.

. . . if anything he's[231] more tired and bruised than I am. I *really* don't see how he does it — managing, managing, thinking ahead, keeping on top of the mail, the phone calls, the schedule, the politicians, the newspapers and newspaper men, what I say, and, finally, me, myself. And thats the worst of all. You know the complaining, irritable, mean streak in me when I've had all I can take. Well, nowadays its as broad as I am —

Calif was an unmitigated, relentless horror — but I guess we're ahead, at least thats what they say. . . .

Mrs. Mary Bancroft, a novelist and daughter of the publisher of the Wall Street Journal, *was an ardent supporter of Stevenson and also a close friend of* Time-Life *publisher Henry Luce, whose staunch Republican stand she sought to mollify during 1956, urging him to switch his allegiance away from Eisenhower.*[232]

To Mary Bancroft[233]

May 14, 1956

My dear Mary Bancroft:

Your letter delighted me and relieved a weary moment here in the distant West. I wish I could hear one of your speeches — and I wish so much I didn't have to hear any more of mine. I am getting mighty sick

[229] This handwritten letter is in the possession of Mrs. Dick.

[230] Mrs. Dick has marked the date May 14, 1956, on this letter, which indicates that it was written from Portland, Oregon.

[231] Bill Blair, who was traveling with Stevenson during the primary campaign.

[232] See W. A. Swanberg, *Luce and His Empire* (New York: Scribner's, 1972), especially pp. 239–240.

[233] This letter was written from Portland, Oregon.

of them. And do write me and send along any humorous bits that occur to you. I get duller, drier and emptier!

Cordially,

P.S. A woman in the crowd said to me the other day: "Governor, you're better looking than your pictures — thank heavens!"

Joseph Keenan, secretary of the International Brotherhood of Electrical Workers, wrote Stevenson that the most important issue in the election was foreign affairs. The other main issues, he added, were civil rights, the farm question, and reform of the Taft-Hartley Act.

To Joseph D. Keenan[234]

May 16, 1956

Dear Joe:

I have a strong suspicion that I have never acknowledged your helpful letter of April 30. I have travelled so rapidly that I can scarcely remember yesterday tomorrow. At all events, it was most helpful, and I am interested that you give foreign affairs such a priority. I certainly agree with you that it is of the utmost importance, but most people put the "gut issues" at the top.

I find much more labor activity on the West Coast this trip than the last, no doubt due in part to your intervention.

Cordially yours,

On May 18, Stevenson carried the Oregon primary, winning all sixteen delegate votes. He flew to Florida on May 19 to campaign until the election on May 29.[235] Kefauver wired him on May 19: "I feel and hope that our contest in Oregon strengthened the Democratic party there."

To Estes Kefauver[236]

May 19, 1956

SO MANY THANKS FOR YOUR VERY THOUGHTFUL WIRE. I SHARE
YOUR CONVICTION THAT OUR CAMPAIGN STRENGTHENED THE

---

[234] A copy is in A.E.S., I.S.H.L. This letter was written from Portland, Oregon.
[235] For an analysis of the Florida primary, see E. W. Kenworthy, "Shall the Best Handshaker Be Nominated?" *New York Times Magazine,* May 27, 1956.
[236] This telegram is in the possession of the University of Tennessee Library.

DEMOCRATIC PARTY IN OREGON AND I LOOK FORWARD TO OUR
JOINT APPEARANCE IN MIAMI ON MONDAY AND TO SEE YOU
AGAIN. WARMEST REGARDS.

ADLAI

*Chester Bowles wrote that Stevenson had met the challenge of the
primaries in an admirable fashion. Bowles then described a lunch meeting with British Labour Party leader Hugh Gaitskell, who discussed the
recent visit of Russian leaders Khrushchev and Bulganin to London.*

To Chester Bowles[237]

May 27, 1956

Dear Chet:

I am glad you see some virtues in this interval and I am sure there are
some, but from my jaundiced view I find little consolation in this mad
weight lifting contest. It seems to have transferred the muscular from
head to hand.

Your report on Gaitskell's comment on B and K's visit to London was
most interesting and I am grateful for it. I had read the account of the
Labor Party dinner with shock.

I haven't, I regret to say, seen much of the material you have sent
along, probably because I have been too busy to absorb or use anything
and in this mad scramble nothing seems to get through of any consequence.

I leave in the early morning for California for the last week of the
marathon and regret that I cannot be in Chicago on the 5th as that is
the primary day in California. I shall probably stay there for a few days
thereafter to rest up before returning to Libertyville. I shall hope that
we can have some talks then because there are a lot of pressing questions that cannot be resolved quickly. I had hoped to say something
thoughtful about foreign affairs as this primary has progressed but I
have said nothing yet that gives me much satisfaction since the editors'
society meeting in late April. If you have any thoughts that you could
send me to California that need prompt utterance I would certainly
welcome them — but they must come at once to be of any help. The
best way of communicating is, of course, through my Chicago office.

Hastily,

[237] This letter was written from Miami Springs, Florida.

Stevenson's daughter-in-law, despite her pregnancy, campaigned in Florida for him. Among others, Mrs. Ernest L. Ives and Mrs. Charles Tillett, National Committeewoman from North Carolina, took part in the Florida primary campaign.

To Adlai E. Stevenson III[238]

May 27, 1956

Dear Bear:

I have a delightful letter from Nancy, but tell her to relax. She need not carry her extra weight to California, although the impression she made as a campaigner is indelible and almost international. And as far as the maternity clothes are concerned, my impression is that all gals are impatient and self-conscious and I would urge her to relax and believe, if she can, that she isn't as conspicuous as she thinks.

The date in Washington on the 24th, on inquiry, appears to be some sort of a myth.[239] I don't know the details, but [Bill] Blair tells me to forget it all of which I am forthwith passing along to you. I gather from what you say that you will not get back to Libertyville until after the 20th. I leave here early in the morning — still alive and kicking vigorously — for California for the last week of this insane ordeal. After the California Primary on the 5th I think I will perhaps rest up for a few days before returning to Libertyville — just where I don't yet know. I will probably take Bill Wirtz along and try to do a little tranquil thinking for the first time in months.

I think of you and the examinations even though I may not have been as articulate as a parent should. It is always easy to tell someone to relax and yet I know how hard it is to do it. I never could myself. Yet I have no better advice than to get a good night's sleep, relax — let go and let God. There, now! Having never been able to do any of those things myself I give you that advice for what it is worth which I am told by my betters is a great deal.

I am, of course, acutely interested in John Fell's summer plans and his job and am mortified that in my ghastly predicament I haven't been able to do any more about it.

Best luck to you both.

Yours,

P.S. There may be crazier ways to select a President but I can't think of one.

238 This letter was written from Miami Springs, Florida.
239 The editors have been unable to discover the appointment to which Stevenson refers.

To Mrs. Eugene Meyer[240]

May 27, 1956

My dear Agnes:

That I haven't acknowledged your good letters long before this is no measure of their value. I have done a lot of uttering here, reflecting your choice bits, but, of course, it is not reported anywhere, even in Florida. Parenthetically, the press baffles me more and more. Eddie Folliard[241] and reporters from all over the country follow me around, but the Miami papers don't even bother to cover me in Fort Lauderdale, etc., a few miles away.

I wish I knew how to react to the change in the discount rate. It seems to me they should have cracked down long ago and I had some fun on the television the other night quoting Eisenhower's utterance in 1952 about not permitting any controversy between the Treasury and the Fed[eral Reserve System]. But I rather doubt if my audience knew what the hell I was talking about.

I was enchanted with your phrase "he has always had the future in his bones." I think it *is* an apt description of Eugene[242] and it is also aptly characteristic of the genius of my "lunatic, happy friend!"

The nose and throat situation is by no means good but it has been better in this nasty heat than in comfortable Oregon.

Well, it is futile to go on or to attempt to tell you anything about my conduct or sanity. I am off early in the morning for California for the last week of this madness and then after a few days' rest I shall return to Libertyville to try to collect my wits and the remnants of my fortune. As to my friends, they will be plentiful or negligible depending on the outcome of the primaries no doubt.

Affectionately,
ADLAI

Former Congresswoman Helen Gahagan Douglas, wife of actor Melvyn Douglas, campaigned in California for Stevenson.

---

[240] The original is in the Agnes Meyer files, Princeton University Library. This letter was written from Miami Springs, Florida.
[241] A reporter for the Washington *Post.*
[242] Mr. Meyer.

To Helen Gahagan Douglas[243]

May 28, 1956

My dear Helen:

I have had so many glowing reports of your efforts on my behalf here in California that I feel I must send you this very special note of thanks. My position would be insupportable, of course, without the help and encouragement of many people, but it is the active help of such gifted people as yourself that move a campaign forward and often make the difference between a successful and unsuccessful conclusion. That you have troubled yourself so much for me touches me deeply — and I am grateful indeed.

Needless to say, the outcome of the Oregon primary was heartening to me and I hope it will be followed by equally good results in Florida — and California! But whatever happens here it will not diminish my gratitude for your important contribution.

With my everlasting gratitude and best wishes, I am

Cordially yours,

ADLAI

Stevenson defeated Kefauver in the Florida primary but only narrowly. On June 5 he scored an overwhelming victory in California, polling 1,139,964 votes to Kefauver's 680,722 votes.[244] *Charles Lucey wrote in the Washington* Daily News, *June 1, 1956: "Adlai Stevenson's new 'common touch' campaigning may help him win California Tuesday, but there is something absurdly incongruous about this man beating the brush like a candidate for township trustee."*

To Mrs. Eugene Meyer[245]

June 7, 1956

My dear Agnes:

Bless you for the wires and the letters. To the latter I will have a response more in detail and more in appreciation than present circumstances permit. I am "hiding out" for a couple of days en route to

[243] The original is in the possession of Mrs. Douglas. This letter was written from Los Angeles, California.

[244] Election statistics cited in this volume are from *Congress and the Nation, 1945–1964: A Review of Government and Politics in the Postwar Years* (Washington, D.C.: Congressional Quarterly Service, 1965), unless otherwise noted.

[245] The original is in the Agnes Meyer files, Princeton University Library. This letter was written from Santa Barbara, California.

Chicago trying to clean up my messy brief case and work my way out of the chaotic aftermath of the California victory. The vote majority approximately doubled our wildest expectations and is a little hard to understand in view of the fact that the organization here was something less than good in Eastern terms, indeed was atrocious most everywhere except San Francisco proper. I expect to move my weary carcass back to Libertyville the end of the week and shall do some plotting and planning before I try to reach any definite conclusions about the immediate future. What I shall do during the next two months on the problems, organizational, substantive, financial, etc., etc., depress me but somehow time goes on and they seem to get resolved.

I am presuming to enclose a copy of my election eve television speech from Los Angeles which was hastily contrived and would ask you to read just the concluding portion about Eisenhower and the Russians. I was surprised that there was so little comment on his astounding sequel [sequence?] of statements on the failure of Communism and our high prestige, two of the most misleading assertions made by a President I should have imagined in a long while.[246] But perhaps there was a lot of comment in the Eastern press. There was none here in California where the press situation is almost beyond understanding. Most of my travels through the state I wasn't even covered by the local press, whereas the Eastern press covered me well, including my beloved Ed Folliard.

Please understand that every sentence of this letter is interrupted by a telephone call and that any sequence is impossible!

I think you are right that Republican money went into Kefauver's campaign in Florida. We have heard about the activities of a Mr. Bell of the DuPont Company and there is no doubt but what the Republicans, registering as Democrats, did quite a job in the big Republican areas in Palm Beach, Sarasota and Orlando — the only districts Kefauver carried. Happily, they couldn't hurt us much in California.

I look forward to *Public Relations and Political Power*[247] and am depressed at the prospect of fighting the press, all of the skills of Madi-

---

246 The President stated in a speech to the National Citizens for Eisenhower: "Certainly the prestige of the U.S. since the last World War has never been so high as it is today." In the same speech Eisenhower said the U.S. had "largely nullified" the Soviet Union's "reliance upon force and threat of force," and he added that the Soviet Union had "felt the pressure of ideas and ideals circulating in its own country and back of the Iron Curtain, because they are more concerned with development of consumer goods, more concerned with status and the frame of mind of the people."

247 Stanley Kelley, Jr., *Professional Public Relations and Political Power* (Baltimore: Johns Hopkins Press, 1956), a survey of the new power of the media in electoral politics which employs a case-study approach to the role of some political public relations firms in actual elections. It contains some information on Stevenson and the 1952 campaign.

son Avenue and torrents of money for television, radio and all the mass methods in the forthcoming campaign. I think it takes more original thinking about methods and new ideas than I am afraid we have or perhaps than we are prepared to exploit. The idea then of a speech on honest and dishonest use of communication seems to me excellent. Also, there is great potential in economic coercion. I have just been told a first-hand story of the withdrawal of $100,000 of display advertising by a drug chain because of refusal to contribute to Republican campaign funds here in California. Stories of this kind multiply almost daily and I think people would react to such unfair and coercive methods if it were possible to tell the story. Maybe it is something that the [Washington] Post or some newspaper should try to "expose" . . .

I hope Eugene[248] will keep me informed through you or somehow of his estimate of the economic situation. There is nothing very visible here in this booming West Coast, but anxiety shows through everywhere.

Affectionately,

ADLAI

Barry Bingham, cochairman of the National Stevenson for President Committee, suggested to Stevenson that he travel to the Soviet Union before the Democratic Convention met.

To Barry Bingham[249]

June 7, 1956

Dear Barry:

I have only now had a chance to read your letter now that this insane endurance contest is over!

I had simultaneously a letter from Chester Bowles urging a coast-to-coast television appearance to sum up my position in regard to the nomination, the coming campaign, future policy decisions, etc., to restore the national "image" of breadth and competence which must have been badly defaced by the primary. I enclose a copy of my reply which I just dictated to bring you up to date.

There are so many things to do and I am a little appalled by the prospect of a journey, too. And I had so much wanted to approach the Convention fully prepared this time and all staff, [speeches] ready, even "written" — and most of all rested!

Hastily,

248 Mr. Meyer.
249 This letter was written from Santa Barbara, California.

To Chester Bowles[250]

June 7, 1956

Dear Chet:

I have just read your letter about the broadcast. The idea has also been advanced by people out here and I have asked Finnegan, et al, to think about it and get an estimate of expense, etc. I think it has great merit and might serve, as you suggest, to elevate the impression again which I most sorely need. Eric Sevareid came in to see me in Los Angeles the other day and said precisely the same thing.

I hope it will be possible to finance it and that I can do it within the next couple of weeks and, of course, I would welcome most eagerly an outline in some detail of the content which would accomplish the objective you have in mind. If you could send along one promptly I would appreciate it.

The California victory was exceeded by almost double any expectations we had and is a little hard for me to understand, but its implications for the autumn are splendid.

I have much to do in terms of staff, reorganization, expense control, issue analysis and decision, speech preparation, campaign technique and emphasis and I shall need a great deal of help on a sustained and continuous basis.

In addition, there is, of course, the problem of my own physical equilibrium and the repair of the ravages of these meat grinding five months. Nor have I banished the idea of a great trip behind the Iron Curtain both for education, the "feel," publicity of the right kind and escape from what will be the mounting pressures in the delegates' search here, as well as the scrambling around as the Congressional session grinds to a close. How to do all of this in the limited time I have and what can be delegated and the priorities is also a problem.

I will hope to have soon some sort of staff conferences on this and in that connection I would like to know your availability for participation during these next two months and, of course, I will look forward to seeing you on your visit to the Mid-West the 17th. I think we have a huge "picnic" of some kind of my supporters in Northern Illinois. The day before that I think I have visitors from South Africa.

Hastily,

P.S. I have neglected to thank you in this mad travel for the fragments you sent along. I have used many of them helpfully I think although these damnable primaries do not lend themselves to important speeches.

AES

[250] This letter was written from Santa Barbara, California.

To Mrs. Edison Dick[251]

June 7, 1956

Jane dear:

I sent you a telegram yesterday as we were traveling through the make believe of M-G-M, gently shepherded by Dore Schary and Marlon Brando. Strange to say, it had to do with that indelible day — your birthday! I hope it was gay and that you were surrounded by your children enjoying a moment of serenity on the threshold of the quiet, golden years. And, madam, if you have any doubt about my position about our senior citizens, I want to refer you to my record in Illinois.

Blessings and myriad thanks for your engaging wire.

Love,

To William Benton[252]

June 7, 1956

Dear Bill:

It is the "morning after" and I am enjoying the hang over.

Among other good news, Bill [Blair] tells me that you have added my indebtedness to you with another fat contribution. I am getting a little self-conscious about my relations with William Benton, but I am also a little self-conscious about the campaign check book, so it is very welcome and I am touched and grateful in the extreme.

Hastily yours,
ADLAI

To Mrs. Franklin D. Roosevelt[253]

June 8, 1956

My dear Mrs. Roosevelt:

Now that California is over and I have caught my breath and am in my right mind — or am I — I hope so — I want first of all to get this note off to you to tell you that I am quite confident that your one day contribution to the California campaign, in spite of the inexcusable chaos, was of more value than anything else that happened. I suppose

[251] This letter was written from Santa Barbara, California.

[252] The original is in the possession of the estate of William Benton. Mr. Benton died on March 8, 1973. At the time this volume went to press, his widow and four children had indicated that they wished to deposit his papers at the University of Chicago.

[253] The original is in the Franklin D. Roosevelt Library, Hyde Park, New York. This letter was written from Santa Barbara, California.

you have seen the surprising results in the Negro districts, in spite of NAACP opposition, which I carried from four and one-half to ten to one. The pattern was true among other minorities as well. The only really weak spots were some agricultural areas and places where there had been little or no organized effort.

I have little doubt now and it has been confirmed by some of the more responsible newspapermen from the East who have been out here that the Republican press will make an effort to portray Averell [Harriman] as the only authentic successor to the New Deal–Fair Deal and, therefore, the obvious Democratic candidate, dismissing me meanwhile as a pale imitation of Eisenhower, etc. The thought seems to be almost universal that having failed to dispose of me through the primaries by means of Kefauver, the next effort will be to sow disunion and doubt among the uncommitted Democratic delegates along this line and also thereby to diminish my stature through the delegates and the voters.

I think the only effective reaction to this is the positive statement of qualifications and fitness and not a defensive attitude. But this is all easier said than done what with their control of the press and so many of the writers.

But the purpose of this was to thank you once more from the bottom of a full heart for your everlasting loyalty and utterly invaluable help. I am afriad I have become a major problem in your life and I shall try not to aggravate your burdens.

Affectionately and gratefully,
ADLAI

To Mr. and Mrs. Walter Lippmann[254]

June 8, 1956

Dear Walter and Helen:

So many thanks for your very thoughtful wire. The extent of our success in California has exceeded any expectations on our part or the party leaders and even reaches down to county committeemen and local party posts, all of which excites the Democratic leadership here with the prospect of a genuine party at long last. They will, for example, have more Democratic members of the state legislature than ever before in California history.

But as for me — well, the road I have chosen seems to be endless but there can be no looking back now.

Sincerely,

[254] A copy is in A.E.S., I.S.H.L. This letter was written from Santa Barbara, California.

To James Finnegan[255]

June 8, 1956

Bob Meyner[256] suggested that you have a talk with John W. Kenney[257] when next in the East, that "he would understand it." I think you should also at least call Meyner on the telephone.

He also has in mind for July a meeting between the delegates and the various candidates at that time. I told him I would talk it over with you and Archie [Alexander] and that I didn't go much for stock shows — when the delegates look over the livestock. I'm not quite sure just what he had in mind. But he was very friendly and intimate about everything. He still has some worry that [Carmine] de Sapio might be able to get some of his leaders, referring presumably to Kenney.

I had a talk with Lyndon Johnson who talked as though my nomination was a certainty, and that after the Convention Shivers[258] would certainly support Eisenhower and be the leader of the Republican campaign in Texas. He said he is very wroth about ADA–CIO interference with his control and management of the party in Texas. He says it will be very difficult to carry the state if the extreme liberals take conspicuous leadership now which they seem to be determined to do. He says [Sam] Rayburn puts it about right — they should be on tap, but not on top, and that the key to more restrained behavior is Walter Reuther.[259] Do you think I should talk to him about this or could someone else?

I also talked with Earl Clement[260] who was very friendly and talked about the problem of organizing the Kentucky delegation in a manner which would be satisfactory to me. He thought that probably Kefauver would try to form some sort of alliance with Harriman.

Monroney[261] and Turner[262] have organized a Committee of 100 for Stevenson "just to keep something going on." He says that the delegation is divided one-third for Stevenson, one-third for Harriman, (the Governor's followers) and one-third who would like to be for Stevenson if the Governor took off the heat. As to the Governor, he reports that he now says that Stevenson is the second choice and could easily be his first choice and that he merely knows Harriman better. Monroney also

255 This memorandum was written from Santa Barbara, California.
256 Governor Robert Meyner, of New Jersey.
257 John V. Kenny, head of the Hudson County Democratic organization and former mayor of Jersey City, New Jersey.
258 Allan Shivers, governor of Texas, who had supported Eisenhower in 1952.
259 President of the United Automobile Workers of America.
260 Senator Earle C. Clements, of Kentucky.
261 Senator A. S. Mike Monroney, of Oklahoma.
262 Probably Roy Turner, governor of Oklahoma, 1947–1951.

reports that he thinks Kerr[263] is waiting hopefully in the wings against the possibility of a compromise.

Rayburn reports that he will get the civil rights legislation out of committee and that it will probably pass the House but cannot pass the Senate. Johnson hopes it will not get on the floor in the Senate where it will divide the Democrats evenly and be defeated in a last ditch filibuster thus confusing and injuring the effects of an otherwise reasonably good session with good social security, school, farm, highways and other legislation. Johnson also told me that he was appointing a committee of Pastore[264] and Irvin[265] to draft a preliminary civil rights plank picking up the '52 plank and adding a ringing declaration of the Constitution!

AES

To Mr. and Mrs. Arthur M. Schlesinger, Jr.[266]

June 8, 1956

My dear Marian and Arthur:

So many thanks for your kind wire. It was a victory beyond any professional dreams, let alone mine, and of course the party leaders are much elated with all the vistas that now open of really effective Democratic Party organization in California for the first time. Now, I am reliably informed, the Republicans, having failed to eliminate me by the primary route, will begin to build up Harriman as the only authentic successor of the New Deal–Fair Deal and therefore the only logical Democratic candidate, in an effort to spread misgivings among the delegates and either defeat me at the Convention or subsequently by diminishing the stature and the enthusiasm.

The only response seems to be not on the defensive but positive declarations of qualifications, etc.

Ho hum, the road is long and full of obstacles. And our bank account exhausted!

And now you must let me know just what your availabilities are for we will have to get down to reorganization — or perhaps Bill Wirtz is already in touch with you.

Affectionately,

---

[263] Senator Robert S. Kerr, of Oklahoma.
[264] Senator John O. Pastore, of Rhode Island.
[265] Senator Samuel J. Ervin, Jr., of North Carolina.
[266] This letter was written from Santa Barbara, California.

Theatrical producer Roger Stevens, who was in charge of fund-raising for Stevenson's campaign, wrote that nearly a million dollars had been raised for the primary elections. He enclosed a proposal for organizing fund-raising activities for the election.

To Roger Stevens[267]

June 8, 1956

Dear Roger:

I have read hurriedly your letter and am extremely alarmed about the financial situation. I had fully realized that the primary was appallingly expensive, but I had by no means appreciated how expensive.

I think rather than attempt to reply by mail I shall wait until we can talk face to face about the future and also the problem of organization.

With respect to the latter, I have had a great deal of experience in state and federal government and I am a little loathe to be issuing charts and establishing too rigid lines of authority for situations where objectives, missions and personnel are inherently fluid.

But as to the lines of authority with respect to money and flexibility in the use of funds, I could not agree more emphatically. Also I am hopeful if not convinced that we can get any precise relationship with the National Committee established at this time. This is also something that I should perhaps talk with McCloskey[268] before trying to reach any final conclusions. But perhaps you have already done so. If not, I hope you will give some more thought to the problem. In the last campaign you will recall that I left the national finance job to Palmer[269] once I had induced him to come aboard and then acquired Beardsley Ruml[270] with Palmer's assent, and that you operated quite independently, I think, through the Volunteers.[271] I am sure it was not satisfactory, but just how to do it better and prearrange it I am not clear.

All this by way of saying I think we had better have a talk. I shall be home Sunday.

Hurriedly,

267 This letter was written from Santa Barbara, California.

268 Matthew McCloskey, of Philadelphia, treasurer of the Democratic National Committee.

269 Dwight R. G. Palmer, of New Jersey, treasurer of the Democratic National Committee in 1952.

270 Divisional representative of the Democratic National Committee, businessman and former chairman of the Federal Reserve Bank of New York, and author of the "pay-as-you-go" plan of collecting federal income taxes.

271 Volunteers for Stevenson.

To Gerald W. Johnson

June 12, 1956

Dear Gerald:

Thank you for your letter which I find on my return from California. As you doubtless know, the Republicans upset me in Minnesota and tried their level best to do the same in Florida. The only counties that Kefauver carried were those that had gone heavily for Eisenhower in 1952, with a couple of exceptions. In cases where the Republicans could not interfere, as in California, Oregon, the District of Columbia and Alaska, I had no trouble at all and won handily.

The Republicans and their press will now give Harriman a big build-up as the only authentic New Deal–Fair Deal candidate in order to keep us further divided, and Harriman will enthusiastically cooperate. . . .[272] So I shall have to meet and best another Republican obstacle. I cannot, therefore, agree with you that the nomination is in the bag.

But as to the pre-election campaign, I do agree emphatically, and I feel more and more that the root theme of the attack must be irresponsibility, misinformation, and the failure of the President to use his popularity to inform us and instead aggravate our complacency. In short — duplicity and deceit either as a result of ignorance, euphoria or calculation. It is only in the last few days before his illness[273] that the President assured us that communism was a failure and that our prestige had never been higher.

Which brings me to the proposition that political maturity is essential in a country which must act mature. But how can we mature when we are constantly misled? So I would amend your sentence to say that leadership which discourages the development of maturity is not only incompetent but irresponsible.

Well, I am afraid I don't see the methods any better than you, and I hope you will be thinking about it, and keep in touch with me.

Cordially,

P.S. As to the illness, I have no doubt the attitude will be if he can walk he can run.

P.P.S. Let me try to put what I am suggesting this way: The President has failed to use his popularity, position and prestige for constructive purposes. Instead of giving the people a better understanding of the

[272] New York Governor W. Averell Harriman had announced on June 9, 1956, his candidacy for the Democratic presidential nomination.
[273] President Eisenhower had become ill on June 8, 1956, and shortly after midnight on the morning of June 9, he underwent surgery to relieve an obstruction of the ileum, a part of the small intestine.

world and its grim realities he accentuates all the national feelings of complacency and moralizing. The "father figure" has given his family such a diet of sugar that it is suffering from fatty degeneration and a flabby America means a flabby free world.

To Mr. and Mrs. Warwick Anderson[274]

June 12, 1956

My dear Mary San and Warwick:

I have come home from where I was "bawned" and find your delightful screeds on top of the pile. Bless you both. I have laughed and laughed at that exquisite verse, which may not find its way into any permanent anthologies — except mine! It has been a hideous ordeal for four months or more and I shall unwind slowly, I fear. Actually, I had no trouble with the primaries except in Minnesota and Florida where the Republicans could interfere, and did in a big way, to help Estes dispose of me. Now they will build up Harriman and I will have to go through it all again with a new opponent with the same Republican backing. Ho hum!

I hope you are coming this way and can spare an evening for me; and of course I yearn to see the children. Nancy's letters I think have become as precious to me as I think they were to Ad. What an extraordinary girl she is. And I suppose you have heard that her brief appearance on the hustings in Florida provoked insistent demands that the "best thing about Stevenson" come back. . . .

Affectionately,

Eleanor Roosevelt wrote Stevenson: "Somehow I think understanding and sympathy for the white people in the South is important as understanding and sympathy and support for the colored people. We don't want another war between the states and so the only possible solution is to get the leaders of both sides together and try to work first steps out."

To Mrs. Franklin D. Roosevelt[275]

June 15, 1956

My dear Mrs. Roosevelt:

I have just read your letter of June 13. Somehow this sort of understanding talk about the race problem coming from the voice most re-

---

[274] The parents of Mrs. Adlai E. Stevenson III.
[275] The original is in the Franklin D. Roosevelt Library, Hyde Park, New York.

spected among Negroes — leaders and rank and file — has got to be given greater currency. I agree with you so emphatically that it excites me to read even these few sentences; perhaps the more so having read [Robert] Bendiner's article in The Reporter magazine[276] only last night, which sings the Republican song that we are losing the Negro vote in the North and that there is no place for sensible talk about the race problem among the Negro leaders. I wish, somehow, we could get you on a housetop and get the whole world to listen for a few minutes. I would gladly withdraw from this political contest if it would serve in any manner to save the party from breaking up and enthroning the white extremists in the South or losing the Northern cities and thus the election. Either alternative is sad, but the former the saddest and most injurious to the Negro and his advancement toward full participation, not to mention the effect on our already diminished stature abroad where the great decisions of the future are being made.

Perhaps you could do an article for a popular magazine like LOOK or COLLIER'S. What do you think? We could readily provide some good sensitive help with preliminary drafts.

Affectionately,

ADLAI

P.S. If I come East I most certainly will assail your refuge in the country.

To Ralph McGill[277]

June 15, 1956

Dear Ralph:

I think your two words "mighty happy" were as mighty welcome as a few pounds of more ponderous telegraphic manuscripts!

Your continual goodness to me has been a constant tonic and my gratitude is boundless. I hope very much that you will feel very free to pass along suggestions to me as to issues, themes and presentation during the campaign — which have always interested me much more, whoever the candidate, than this interminable primary ordeal or the delegate hunt.

I have felt that irresponsibility should be the theme and that we are being treated to another now in the most recent ecstasy about the Presi-

---

[276] "The Negro Vote and the Democrats," May 31, 1956.
[277] Editor of the Atlanta *Constitution* and a good friend and adviser to Stevenson. The original is in the possession of Mrs. Ralph McGill.

dent's health.[278] The sort of sad thing about it all is that health itself is treated as making all the difference when the application of the job and understanding of it has been so deficient from the beginning. I have the feeling that instead of using his leadership and popularity and prestige to inform the people about the grim realities of our world he has contributed more than any other President to our delinquency, complacency and taste for moralizing. If the "father image" feeds his people sugar they will suffer from fatty degeneration; but I am writing indiscreetly and also ponderously, and you will make allowances for both.

Hastily and cordially,

ADLAI

P.S. My secretary just said if the administration kept us as informed about the state of the world and the nation as they do about the state of the President's blood pressure and insides we would be risking little of the hazards of ignorance.

Lewis Stevens, a friend of Stevenson's since their student days at Princeton University, invited him to visit Norway and England with him.

To Lewis M. Stevens[279]

June 15, 1956

Dear Lew:

So many thanks for your letter. But I wish you hadn't told me about fishing in Norway and hiking in the lake country. How cruel can you be! But if a plump, balding, little man springs out at you from flowering bushes, well, it will be me. And thank God, Kefauver won't be right behind me!

So many many thanks for all your helpfulness and thoughtfulness and kindness — and have a good time.

Yours,

[278] On June 10, the President authorized an announcement to be made that he was still running for reelection despite his surgery of the day before, and two days after the operation, he began light work. Democratic National Chairman Paul M. Butler charged that the President's health had been "propagandized" in a "new science of politico-medicine." New York *Times,* June 13, 1956.

[279] A copy is in A.E.S., I.S.H.L.

To Mr. and Mrs. Richard L. Neuberger[280]

June 15, 1956

My dear Dick and Maurine:

So many thanks for your wire about California. It was a great day for the California Democrats as well as for me. The improvement of the party's fortunes there is significant, and has not been noted in the press as much as it deserves. I think it will inevitably be a decisive state in the autumn and hence the party improvement evidenced at the primary is heartening.

You were so good to me throughout this long, weary ordeal! I am grateful indeed, and I hope that we can have a resolute talk some time. I am afraid I continue to be more interested in our problems and opportunities than I am in politics and delegate-hunting, but the latter goes so well that I have been happily spared much discussion about it.

With all good wishes, I am

Cordially,

To J. William Fulbright

June 15, 1956

Dear Bill:

So many thanks for your wire about California. I hope very much that we can have a talk one of these days although I don't know how we can contrive it, as I dare not come to Washington, at least just yet. I know you are heavily engaged in your own campaign,[281] but I hope not at the expense of some reflection about the positions we should assert and the ideas we can advance in the campaign in the field of foreign affairs. While I reluctantly concede that the politicians are probably right, and that there are mighty few votes in it, I am also convinced that the administration is most vulnerable in that area and that it is also the most important area. We ought to be able to devise some means of exploiting it for political advantage, national benefit and voter education.

Yours,

---

[280] U.S. senator from Oregon and his wife, who was elected to fill the vacancy caused by his death in 1960.
[281] Senator Fulbright was running for reelection in Arkansas.

To Lady Mary Spears[282]

June 21, 1956

My dear Mary:

I have your note of June 15 and I am happy to hear that you are planning on coming over during the campaign. I am touched by your thought of me and anxiety to help. It is hard for me to foretell now just what might be needed. Ellen has been behaving well, relatively speaking, of late, according to the boys, but that situation changes with her nervous state and could get suddenly very bad.

I have not talked to Ellen Carpenter for a long time but she has been exceedingly cordial and friendly and is, I understand, an ardent supporter. I don't suppose she will come back to Chicago until late in September if she follows her usual routine, but it could well be that her apartment would be available for you if you were to come, as you suggest, around the first of September. I rather doubt if Jane Dick would be very reliable in view of the fact that all her children will be at home, including the new grandchild, and the inevitable visitors in her capacity as co-chairman of the Stevenson for President Committee.

As for the campaign, I cannot predict just when it will start, but I suppose I will start travelling about Labor Day week-end and be here but little until the election in November. Need I add that the foregoing assumes my nomination, which may be a gross assumption. It could be that my domestic situation would permit you to stay at my place in Libertyville, although at the moment I am in the throes of servant change, which is none too easy, let alone for a bachelor. I am a little fearful, however, that being that far from town might not interest you. So perhaps you had best write Ellen Carpenter at Beverly [Massachusetts] and ascertain her plans.

I should add that the headquarters this time will doubtless be in Washington and once the convention is over there will not be much going on here. The itinerary and my travels also cannot be determined until after the convention, so that I am somewhat at a loss as to what to suggest.

John Fell is at home with me now and almost fully recovered from his dreadful accident last December. Adlai and his bride arrive any moment and are presenting me with a grandchild just in time for the election.

So I can't lose!

Affectionately,

ADLAI

[282] This letter was in the possession of General Sir Louis Spears until his death on January 27, 1974. His correspondence is now in the possession of Churchill College, Cambridge University.

To Roger Kent[283]

June 21, 1956

Dear Roger:

I was delighted to have your letter. Somehow you have a very comforting and reassuring effect on me and I am almost persuaded that I have not shrivelled in the esteem of my 27½ million. Actually, I had little trouble with the handshaking and the main thing which the press somehow thought was a novelty for me. It was not by any means. I can't understand what made them think it was; and moreover I enjoyed it. What I don't enjoy, as I explained to you, is uttering banalities and inferior stuff.

I was delighted with your letter to the newspaper,[284] and I wonder if they have not gone too far in this recent panicked effort to persuade us that with each operation and misfortune things get better and better. I feel everyone must be increasingly conscious of the uncertainty of it and the macabre quality of propping the poor man[285] up as a facade for vote bait. I doubt if he will submit to it in the long run, although I could be unhappily mistaken!

With warmest regards to you and everlasting memories of your many kindnesses to me during that memorable campaign — and especially your garden.[286]

Yours,

William Carlebach, a New York delegate who supported the draft in 1952, wrote Stevenson that their son, who was Stevenson's godson, had an attack of asthma from rabbits. Mr. Carlebach, who was running for Congress, added that he was optimistic about his race.

To William D. Carlebach

June 21, 1956

Dear Bill:

So many thanks for your delightful letter — although I am distressed by the unhappy news about my godson. What business has he playing with rabbits anyway? Or is it a paucity of donkeys in Westchester County?

[283] Vice chairman of the California Democratic State Central Committee and an avid supporter of Stevenson.
[284] San Francisco *News*, June 14, 1956.
[285] President Eisenhower.
[286] Toward the end of the primary campaign, Mr. Kent had held a garden reception for Stevenson at his home in Kentfield, California.

I was glad to hear some time ago about your candidacy, and from all I hear about your opponent, prospects must be good. You might bear in mind a possibly ally in Mrs. Eugene Meyer, who has a summer place at Mount Kisco. I would prefer if you did not use my name, at least at this point, but if you are not in touch with her you might try. I think she has little use for Mr. Quinn[287] and is very independent minded, as you know.

Please tell Priscilla[288] how grateful we are for her contribution.

Affectionate regards to you all.

Cordially,

Professor John Kenneth Galbraith wrote Stevenson that he had nearly completed a book — The Affluent Society *— while in Switzerland and had also spent three months in India.*

To John Kenneth Galbraith

June 21, 1956

Dear Ken:

I reject it that Harvard professors can make their greatest contribution to primaries in Switzerland. I insist we can all make our greatest contributions to the American primary system — in Swaziland.

I marvel at the amount you accomplish in a year of "leisure." And now that you have found a better use for man's energies than our quest for more and more goods, I wonder if the time has not come for me to unveil your conclusions in an acceptance speech in the event I am nominated. In short, if you know what to do with the human race I should be glad to make the announcement, at least to the Democrats. Think what an excellent exercise it would be to summarize your conclusions in a reverberating speech which will have perpetuity — for at least twenty-four hours!

But if you insist on doing no writing for me until after the first of September, while you are resolving the Indians' economic problems, and now, doubtless, Britain's, well, I shall just have to wait. But I am getting impatient, and we are asking the faithful to send in contributions to the enlightenment of Man as well as the candidate.

My affectionate regards to you both.

Cordially,

287 Incumbent Republican Congressman Ralph W. Gwinn, of Pawling, New York.
288 Mrs. Carlebach.

Robert Manning, who was editing Books, Music, Religion, Medicine, and Sports for Time *magazine, congratulated Stevenson on the California primary and quoted from Thoreau: "Why must people follow and paw me with their dirty institutions?"*

To Robert Manning[289]

June 22, 1956

Dear Bob:

I was delighted to have your letter, and I am afraid I am way ahead of Thoreau even now! And the institution over which people paw me that I find dirtiest — yes, you are right — primaries! But I am told on all sides that it has been a useful if exhausting winter and spring. That there is anything left of that mysterious thing called the "Stevenson image" is a miracle but perhaps there isn't!

If you are not indispensable to Books, Music, Religion, Medicine and Sports I should like to know about it. It is conceivable that I may get into real trouble again and emerge from the convention with a job and need some help of your special and esteemed variety. But don't ask me twice why I ask for the job. I may forget my well worn lines.

Cordially,

To J. William Fulbright

June 22, 1956

Dear Bill:

The reason the President often makes excellent speeches which have little to do with what's going on is, of course, that he is not informed nor is his staff. But I think we should have something to say in the way of positive proposals for exchange of persons programs[290] in the forthcoming campaign. If some time you can put together for me your ideas they would be welcome — what we are doing, what we can do, and what we should do.

Cordially,

---

[289] A copy is in A.E.S., I.S.H.L.

[290] Senator Fulbright persuaded Congress to adopt what became known as the Fulbright Program, which provided funds for the interchange of American and foreign students and the provision of American teachers to other countries, and from its inception in 1948 he maintained interest in its development. See Walter Johnson and Francis J. Colligan, *The Fulbright Program: A History* (Chicago: University of Chicago Press, 1965).

Gilbert Harrison sent recent issues of the New Republic *and expressed the hope that Stevenson would spend a month planning the policy character of the campaign.*

To Gilbert Harrison

June 22, 1956

Dear Gil:

I was delighted to have your letter and the enclosed copies, which I shall find a moment to look at promptly.

You are right that much remains to be done about the delegates, but I am not going to do much. For the next two or three weeks I am going to try to concentrate on organization, and as you put it, blue printing the policy character of the campaign. It is no easy job; indeed what I have been groping for ever since last autumn are the basic themes. We seem to be in the midst of an incessant controversy which all concede is the fundamental deficiency of the administration and the most important national problem is our foreign affairs, but I am not sure it has any voter appeal. Certainly "peace" does, but how to relate foreign affairs to peace.

Basically the theme that seems to keep recurring to me as evidenced everywhere is irresponsibility. That too is hard to define and communicate in all cases.

What you have to say is always welcome and what I find in your journal always informative and helpful and almost always highly sympathetic.

With love to Nancy,[291]

Cordially,

To Mrs. Eugene Meyer[292]

June 24, 1956

My dear dear Agnes —

Forgive me for lecturing you about Eugene [Mr. Meyer]. One so *unsuccessful* could hardly presume to instruct one so *successful* in the arts of marriage and for so long. Yet the recitation of your many enterprises and obligations followed by the anxiety that creeped into your voice when you discussed him troubled me. But *I* know *you'll* know what you can do to help as his pace slows down, if it ever does! And I

291 Mrs. Harrison.
292 This handwritten letter is in the Agnes Meyer files, Princeton University Library.

must say that the bits of his wry humor that you occasionally pass along enchant me. This surely is the most satirical, charming and, withal, tender man in the world. And how fortunate he was to have someone who could appreciate and feed his humor.

But when you talk not just of *husband* management, but of your "calm" as generalissimo of such an army of *servants* — well then my admiration turns to reverence!

And — speaking of servants and picnicking — please know, beloved friend, that *I, me,* the *candidate,* after a fortnight of crisis indoors and out and of total political neglect, is shortly to be the proud possessor of a new staff — a black indoor job of large stature, broad smile, gentle voice & indifferent references, and a man & wife in the stable with two children, good appearance and almost *no* references!! But the wonderful thing about it all is that — I just don't care any more. I'm going to *live,* take it as it comes and quit worrying, even if the hay is *all* spoiled this very night!!

The Humphrey report[293] thru Sid Hyman[294] is most interesting. I get furtive bits and pieces from all directions now that there is growing realization that they can't prop Ike up long enough or well enough and in the end will have to look elsewhere. (Perhaps you've heard the current horror — "If, God forbid, Ike dies, 3 doctors will emerge from the room and solemnly announce that "he will be fit to run at *the end of the third day.*")

Eugene's reaction on the Russia project[295] pleases me. Actually the time situation being what it is I couldn't possibly go anyway now — but I rather doubt if I could do it — (both time & wisdom) — after the election if I won, either.

Ask him now, if you will, his reaction to a Catholic Vice Pres. Also *your* view, please. My own view is that the prejudice is still so high in the back country that it is only to be considered if the boldest steps are necessary.

And, finally, as to rest and reflection — of course you're right — and its the hardest task of all what with children about, their plans, and the agitating insistence of a thousand things that need attention and thought. Walter Reuther, by the way, has been here most of the day and we've talked of many things. So it goes — *every* day, & I never get down to work, let alone rest. (He's irate about Harriman who can't get the nomination and will destroy our chances in the process or at least make

[293] Presumably George M. Humphey, Secretary of the Treasury from 1953 to 1957. The editors have been unable to locate the report to which Stevenson refers.
[294] Sidney Hyman, a freelance writer, author of *The American President* (New York: Harper, 1954), and a speechwriter for Stevenson during the 1952 campaign.
[295] It had been suggested that Stevenson visit Russia before the campaign.

[Lyndon] Johnson the kingmaker and big influence. Williams,[296] he says, will be under complete control when the time comes. But I wonder!)

But I must *run* — or rather dine, no, *"picnic"* with my fine sons & one pregnant daughter in law! And, anyway, the purpose of this was not to talk but to thank you for my hero-eagle — the loveliest item by far in my modest collection of objects d'art. How sweet of you to give it to me — and how precious this exquisite little bronze must be. I've even gone to the Encyclopaedia to read about the Han dynasty. And I'm exhibiting it to all and sundry as the gift of a mysterious admirer. I hope you don't already regret that you parted with it, but if you do I'll *loan* him back to you! I have a couple of small pieces of *good* Chinese porcelain, one given me by Run Run Shaw[297] in Singapore, a fabulous character whom I must tell you about sometime.

And — speaking of sometime — I suddenly discover that I may have to come to N.Y. this very week for appointments Thursday & Friday. If by *any chance* I could get out to Mt. Kisco on Thursday night I'll telephone to see if you are home & free.

Hastily and devotedly —
ADLAI

Stevenson wrote letters nearly identical to the following to a number of people, asking for suggestions or drafts for an acceptance speech.

To Archibald MacLeish

June 25, 1956

Dear Archie:

I have been reflecting over my difficulties and somehow hope for something good seems to lie in your direction — as usual.

I am concerned particularly with what I will say to the Convention — if that occasion presents itself — in short, if I am nominated. Have you some thoughts? Better still, some words? I must reach for the skies, with feet on the earth but not in the mud. Two thousand words should suffice, hitting the dangers here and abroad of drift, division, negativism, hypocrisy; but emphasizing affirmatively the central ideas of a truly representative government, with "a fighting ardor for mankind" and a passion for peace and for a freedom and security that pay off in people's

---

296 G. Mennen Williams, governor of Michigan.
297 An Asian movie tycoon who was later a leader in the production of "kung fu" films, which enjoyed considerable popularity in the United States.

every day lives. The point will also be made, I expect, that the difference between the two parties, today at least, in one large part is the difference between saying the right things and doing them.

But it is your ideas I need, not any play-back of these of mine which leave me at best dissatisfied.

Apologies.

Yours,

To Norman Cousins[298]

June 25, 1956

Dear Norman:

I have been reflecting in my misery over all the last minute improvisation of four years ago and its avoidance this time. But of progress there is little and somehow I turn to you as I have before.

I am concerned particularly as to what I will say to the Convention, if that occasion presents itself — that is, if I am nominated. Have you some thoughts? Better still, have you some words? It must launch a campaign from Seattle to Miami; it must project an "image" — as those advertising boys say — and it must please the egghead as well as the no-head; it should exhilarate hearts that are high and hearts that are low; it should strike terror in the heart of the enemy. I guess that is about all it must do. Or did I forget to say that it should win a deluge of votes which even a poor campaign cannot drive away?

Ho hum! And this time I even asked for it. Well, I may be offending the gods by trying to prepare for what I have asked for but don't have. Anyway, I am sure your soaring spirit, fertile brain and eloquent pen will produce much of what I need if I can enlist it. Can't I? If not, don't hesitate to say that it is inconvenient.

Cordially,

Chester Bowles wrote that he had told Willard Wirtz, Stevenson's law partner and campaign aide in charge of speech drafting, that he was not convinced that foreign policy was unimportant as a vote getter. Bowles added that he was drafting possible speeches for Stevenson.

[298] Editor of the *Saturday Review*.

To Chester Bowles

June 25, 1956

Dear Chet:

I am afraid both the speech and the trip to Russia are out. Life is catching up with me and I can hardly get my hay in, let alone do anything important!

About the speech, I wonder a little if the summer doldrums is the proper moment for a momentous TV utterance. No matter how good it is, I doubt if it would get the nomination, and perhaps I better save my ammunition for the right time. I think it emphatically important, however, that there be in the acceptance speech (perhaps I am counting eggs!) a section on foreign policy, including a sharp indictment of the administration and a sketch in broad strokes of our attitude with respect to the major questions — the disintegration of NATO, the Baghdad Pact, SEATO, world economic development, East-West trade, disarmament, etc. On that I hope you will reflect.

I shall read the Lippmann column.[299] I have long felt, and perhaps said to you, that the rigidity of our German policy was hazardous in the extreme. How it is handled is, as you say, extremely delicate.

Frankly, I do not understand Mr. [James G.] Patton at all, although I do believe I understand his associate [Charles F.] Brannan. I shall be glad to see him, however, any time, of course.

Yours,

P.S. Somehow, I have only now seen your letter of June 20, and of course I am delighted you have undertaken all those assignments from Bill Wirtz. I think the idea of the speech at the Convention which you suggest merits prompt attention and I shall make some suggestions along that line.

A.E.S.

To Herbert Agar

June 25, 1956

Dear Herbert:

I must prepare myself for the release upon my countrymen this fall of another deluge of political oratory. This time there will be no excuse for much improvization or last minute scribbling. The job should be done in advance. Yet I fear in view of the incessant diversions that my forensic preparations may end only in stillbirth unless I ask others for help.

---

299 The editors have been unable to identify the column to which Stevenson refers.

Here endeth my apology and the explanation for addressing myself to the best quality of help I know.

I am concerned particularly about what I will say to the convention if that occasion presents itself — in short, if I am nominated. Have you some thoughts? Better, too, have you some words?

I know that this must be a personal statement, and I know too how invaluable your ideas on anything of this sort have been with me in the past. If your situation permits giving me whatever comes to your mind I will be more grateful to you than I can say.

What I use should probably not exceed 2,000 words, and I suppose hit squarely the division, drift, negativism and hypocrisy of the present administration; but it should be essentially affirmative, emphasizing the ideas of a truly representative government with a "fighting ardor for mankind" and a passion for peace and for a freedom and security that pay off in people's everyday lives.

It's your ideas I need, not mine which leave me at best dissatisfied.

If, sitting where you do, you can think of what needs saying most to launch the advance along the far flung front from Seattle to Miami — well, send it along, and count me ever your debtor. I shall have to get at it by late July, along with a host of other tasks.

My love to Barbie.[300]

Yours,

To James P. Warburg

June 25, 1956

Dear Jim:

Thank you for your letter of June 4. I am much interested in your conclusion that foreign affairs — as distinguished from "peace" — is in your judgment so important in the forthcoming campaign. All of the issues research and all of the comments of political leaders from coast to coast is to the contrary. While I deplore it, the impression seems to be that people just aren't interested in details and that they generally credit me as knowledgeable in this field. What they want is assurances that somebody can bring them peace, and Ike has done it: "Nobody is shooting, are they"! I am afraid your friends, like mine, are a mighty small minority of the voters who want a blueprint on what I would do about the disintegration of NATO, the Baghdad Pact, SEATO, the Far East, disarmament, economic development, and East-West trade, and if I had all of the answers to all of these questions I would probably be threatened with a cerebral hemorrhage any moment anyway.

[300] Mrs. Agar.

However, I do intend to talk about foreign affairs, and especially in an effort to dispel the euphoria which has been so characteristic of the present leadership and try to jog people that we are not winning, but losing, the cold war.

In your letter of April 27 you suggest that if I "raise" the German question I should bear in mind the effect on the German-American vote. I should like to be further enlightened on that and on how best to effect it favorably!

Cordially,

To Harry S. Truman

June 26, 1956

Dear Mr. President:

The closing of the primary campaign has brought me now the opportunity to complete my reading of Volume Two: *Years of Trial and Hope.*[301]

If there is a more human volume than this in American history I do not know it. What it tells on every page is that the Presidency has to be above all else a place of understanding of what is in people's minds and hearts, and a place for translating people's good sense into a nation's decisions.

May I add that one of the most gratifying experiences of this recent campaign has been the expression by every audience I spoke to of their obviously deep and heartfelt love and affection for your infinite service to them.

Most sincerely,

Barbara Ward (now Lady Jackson) sent Stevenson drafts for speeches and also a phonograph record.

To Lady Barbara Jackson

July 2, 1956

My very dear Barbara:

I am distressed to be dictating a letter to you when I should sit down and tranquilly write all that comes to me, but today's trials are undiminished and the time for reflection is never at hand.

I think I have received all of your letters and you need have no

[301] Mr. Truman's memoirs were published in hardcover book form by Doubleday & Company.

concern on that score. And now the records have come. Bless you, my beloved Barbara; and you have introduced a new violin to my life which has had my little family — John Fell, Nancy and Adlai and me — entranced for two pleasant meals together in the past few days. And then, finally, John Fell hesitantly confessed that he had one of the Russian's records himself!

"The Vacuum Of Leadership" I have barely looked at. I shall take it with me now on a journey, first to Bloomington for farmers' picnics, Fourth of July celebrations, and thence to Iowa, Missouri and Nebraska and the drouth area. How I can study agriculture at first hand and the conditions there with two carloads of reporters, news reels and TV behind me I am not sure, but I am going to try it, and conclude the week with delegate barbecues in Nebraska and Iowa, returning here for a few days for a visit with Mr. Truman before going on to Maine and New England, with similar malevolent purpose. After that I get back here for a couple of days, then go to Colorado to make a formidable speech at their State Convention followed by a gathering of delegates from the Western states in Wyoming. Then, at long last, comes a stretch of some two or three weeks when I am supposed to be incommunicado. That is an obsolete word having to do with a state of serenity once enjoyed by monks having taken a vow of silence in remote valleys in the Himalayas I understand.

I don't believe I have thought to write Robert about his knighthood in the late frenzy.[302] I shall do so at once, to Accra.[303] Meanwhile, please don't think, dear Lady Jackson, that I am insensitive to the extraordinary alterations in your status. It isn't everyone who can become a mother and a Lady all at once!

Miss [Carol] Evans is suggesting that this letter is going nowhere, and as that is obvious I shall go no further.

Devotedly,

P.S. I am so glad that you saw little merit in the trip behind the Iron Curtain. I had come to that conclusion both by conviction and by necessity, too, but Barry Bingham is quite put out about it, I fear.

---

[302] Robert Jackson had been named a Knight Bachelor in the Colonial Office List, part of the Queen's Birthday Honours List announced May 31, 1956. See *The Times* (London), May 31, 1956.

[303] Sir Robert was chairman of the Preparatory Commission for the Volta River Multi-Purpose Project in the Gold Coast, and afterward chairman of the Development Commission of Ghana, as the Gold Coast was renamed at its independence in 1957.

To Paul Samuelson[304]

July 10, 1956

Dear Paul:

I am spending these last weeks of tranquility trying to get my thoughts into some sort of order for the fall. In this connection, I would greatly appreciate any thoughts of yours, especially about pending developments in the economic situation.

I have in mind particularly the fact that I probably will speak in Detroit on Labor Day. In view of the unemployment situation in Michigan, this seemed to me to provide a reasonable opportunity to discuss economic trends. I wonder, for example, how much you agree with Adolf Berle's article in the current REPORTER.[305] It has seemed to me that I might try to outline a fairly concrete program by which a Democratic Administration would seek to meet a developing unemployment crisis. Do you think there would be any point in discussing also some of the implications of automation?

I would be most grateful if you had a moment to set down any of your ideas on this subject — and in as vivid language as you would like. I am told that I must become more concrete and less rhetorical, so I should probably aim to err on the programmatic side! If you have any further questions about this, you might call Bill Wirtz or Arthur Schlesinger, Jr., here in the Chicago headquarters (collect). In any case, I hope I will have a chance for a talk with you before too long. I still remember with great appreciation our seminar a few months back.

Cordially,

To John Hersey

July 11, 1956

My dear John:

For some reason I have only now seen your letter of April 26. Your kind comment on that "effort" in New York pleases me very much.

But please don't encourage me to sound more loudly the note of "I love truth and despise winning." I have been doing my best to rise above such principles, as the politicians say, and act as though winning were important too!

Bill Wirtz has told me about his conversation with you. I hope very much that I am not presuming upon you. When I learned that your

---

[304] Professor of economics at Massachusetts Institute of Technology.
[305] "The Recession We Should Not Have," June 28, 1956.

helping me out will interrupt your work on your novel I couldn't help feeling that this represents a very improper balancing of values. I am afraid I am becoming calloused to this business of imposing on other people. But please don't let this interfere too much.

I am not clear from what Bill has told me whether your willingness to help goes beyond the matter of the preparation of the Education draft and whether it is your feeling that you might also be able to give us a few weeks of your fuller time in September or October. No one could appreciate more fully than I do your expressed feeling that it is very hard to function under the extraordinary and inordinate pressures of a campaign editorial bullpen operation. I do have the feeling, however, that if there is any prospect of your having time available we could work out some arrangement which would permit our calling upon you in a somewhat different manner. I will in any event be grateful if you will let me know just what your situation and your inclination may be so far as this possibility is concerned.

My everlasting gratitude!

Cordially,

To Sir Robert Jackson

July 11, 1956

My dear Robert:

For weeks I have been planning to write you a note of congratulation about your Knighthood. But for weeks I have been planning to do a multitude of things! I am mortified to be so negligent, but I insist that like your other friends and admirers in this country my delinquency does not measure my delight.

Certainly few people are more conspicuously entitled to a grateful government's recognition than you, but few likewise have earned it more inconspicuously. I think it is that very quality of modesty and persistent dedication which makes this recognition seem the sweeter — at least to me!

I hear from dear Barbara often and I am even the proud possessor of a picture of mother and son, not to mention writings of extreme value in my present profession of perpetual wordmongering. She is so good to me and I only hope I have not encouraged her labors beyond the bounds of reason and her own welfare. If I have, crack down in your decisive and yet gentle way.

With warm thoughts and very best wishes, always.

Cordially yours,

Governor Abraham Ribicoff of Connecticut wrote Stevenson that many of the governors that he talked to at the annual meeting of governors would be for him on an early ballot. Ribicoff recommended that Stevenson read the speech that Senator Albert Gore had delivered to the Connecticut Democratic Convention.

To Abraham Ribicoff[306]

July 16, 1956

Dear Abe:

I have just returned from my trip through some of the New England states and find your thoughtful letter. I am heartened by your encouraging report. I am very much aware of all the help you gave my cause at the Governors' Conference, and I am immensely grateful.

I am hastening to drop Albert Gore a note asking for a copy of his speech. I'm glad you called it to my attention.

Please let me know just when you'll arrive in Chicago. I will look forward to seeing you before the Convention.

With warmest good wishes,

Cordially,

To Mrs. Franklin D. Roosevelt[307]

July 16, 1956

Dear Mrs. Roosevelt:

I am mortified that I haven't answered your letter of July 2 earlier. I have been travelling through some of the farm states and have now just returned from a trip to New England.

I am immensely grateful to you for your offer to help in the fall. If I am nominated, I should like to have you speak just as much as is humanly possible — and in your case, this means super-humanly! I know this is a monstrous request, but I should like to ask you to keep every possible date open, consistent with your taking on those commitments that you deem essential. Let me know, but I should like to have you available *all* the time. . . .

Cordially,

ADLAI

---

306 A copy is in A.E.S., I.S.H.L.
307 The original is in the Franklin D. Roosevelt Library, Hyde Park, New York.

To Mrs. Eugene Meyer[308]

July 18, 1956

Dear Agnes:

I am home from the New England journey and find your letters, which I cannot even attempt to acknowledge at this time. I am distracted and find the problem of preparing proper utterances almost too difficult what with the incessant diversions. And now I must speak in Washington, Colorado, Wyoming and Nevada — with almost nothing at hand.

Speaking of the sick President, I wonder if you saw the attached from the London News Chronicle. This is only one of several like this I have had from abroad. Evidently they are meeting the absurdity of this situation with little of the domestic indifference. The [Washington] Post is rapidly becoming our best help.

Affectionately,
ADLAI

To J. William Fulbright

July 26, 1956

Dear Bill:

I have just returned from the West to find your letter and your generous offer to have John Erickson[309] come out to help. Of course we can use him, and I hope he can come out a week early (or whatever is convenient) and get in touch with Jim Finnegan, who will be expecting him.

It does seem important to emphasize that we can't be responsible for his expenses here — as the exchequer is not too healthy at the moment. Is this all right? If not, let me know.

Many, many thanks.

Cordially,

To Mrs. Eugene Meyer[310]

July 30, 1956

Dear Agnes:

I am back from my last journey. The New England and Middle West trips wearied me, but I had a couple of days of rest at the end at the

---

[308] The original is in the Agnes Meyer files, Princeton University Library.
[309] Senator Fulbright's assistant.
[310] The original is in the Agnes Meyer files, Princeton University Library.

Edward Heller's[311] lovely place on Lake Tahoe, which was a minor blessing.

I am a little distracted in view of the fact that the time is slipping away so rapidly before the convention, and lately I have been burdened with the "threat" of a biography on which I have lavished too much time trying to correct even a small portion of the manuscript.[312] All in all, I am in a none too serene state and now I find I have to go to New York to speak at some fund-raising dinner this very week. I shall not see you as I cannot tarry there.

Bill Wirtz has sent in your letter to him about the Catholic situation.[313] The problem presents so many facets, each of which induces so many memoranda pro and con, that I am perplexed to say the least. I think you make strong points, however, of a kind which would have little publicity and much influence on election day. The counter arguments, aside from the virtues of the men themselves, of the advantages in populous states and with the minority groups, are formidable.

Hurriedly and affectionately,
ADLAI

Norman Cousins sent Stevenson a memorandum about the coming campaign.

To Norman Cousins

July 30, 1956

Dear Norman:

I think it is excellent, especially the summary on page 2. I have felt more and more that our opportunities may be the basic affirmative theme, as the failure to take advantage of them by defaults of leadership and philosophical division is the basic negative issue.

I do not, however, wholly agree with your analysis. I feel that the President is popular, if he is, as a President because he has never been for anything unpopular or against anything popular and, secondly, has used his office not to educate and inform about the grim realities but to

---

311 Friends and supporters of Stevenson since 1952, when Mr. Heller served as his California state finance chairman. Mr. Heller was Northern California finance chairman in the 1956 campaign.

312 Stevenson was reading part of the manuscript of Kenneth S. Davis's *A Prophet in His Own Country,* which was published in 1957.

313 Mrs. Meyer had written Willard Wirtz that though she regretted to say it, she felt that if Stevenson ran with a Roman Catholic candidate for Vice President, this could confuse his whole campaign. She explained that leading Protestant clergy might fear that a Catholic Vice President would use his influence to secure federal aid for parochial schools and would favor sending an ambassador to the Vatican.

reassure and moralize. The result is a sort of benign euphoria and the price deterioration abroad and drift at home. Well, perhaps we don't disagree after all. And I am grateful, now and always for what you send me.

Ever so many thanks. As my life gets more active and complicated my mind gets only more complicated.

Cordially,

On July 12, 1956, former President Truman wrote Stevenson that he had enjoyed their breakfast together in Chicago and that the two of them seemed to understand each other's problems.

To Harry S. Truman

July 30, 1956

My dear Mr. President:

We were talking the other day at breakfast about a role that you can fill beyond any other living competence. I have thought more and more of it in the context of the President's health and also his limited application even before the heart attack, to which you have called such proper attention!

It seems to me that, given the difficulties of attacking his deficiency directly, it should be possible to make vital and appealing a proper concept of the Presidency, and no one can talk about it with range and depth like yourself. Enabling the American people to see exactly how much is involved in the proper operation and concept of the office is both a service to their education and a partisan opportunity in the present circumstances. The purpose, it seems to me, is to get the people to realize, without necessarily spelling it out in capital letters, that a symbol is not enough and that over-delegation of powers, for any reason, as well as undue inaccessability of the President can be damaging and dangerous.

Please don't feel it is necessary to acknowledge this letter. Its purpose is merely to record some thoughts that had come to me since our talk and your talk here in Chicago about the [Truman] Library. What I am trying to say is that I think we badly need, regardless of the election, some public education about the Presidency. And could there be a better educator than H.S.T.?

Cordially,

P.S. I suppose you have heard that the President and Secretary Dulles are collaborating on a book entitled "The Ileum and the Odyssey."[314]

[314] Mr. Truman replied on August 1, 1956, that he appreciated the suggestion and that he would plan a speech on the presidency. He added that he liked the postscript to Stevenson's letter.

Linda Morgan, the daughter of American Broadcasting Company news commentator Edward P. Morgan, had been listed as dead after the Italian liner Andrea Doria, *on which she was a passenger, collided with the Swedish motorship* Stockholm *on July 25, 1956. But Miss Morgan was scooped up in the bow of the* Stockholm *and, although seriously injured, she survived.*

To Edward P. Morgan[315]

July 30, 1956

Dear Ed:

There is a verse in the 27th Psalm (I think it is the 27th!) which perhaps you are thinking of in this incredible and joyous moment: "I had fainted unless I had believed to see the goodness of the Lord in the land of the living."

I am so glad.

Yours,

Mrs. Mary Bancroft sent Stevenson an article from the Wall Street Journal, *saying, "It caught my eye because I wanted to see if bugs and insects were working for the Democrats or the Republicans. I can't quite decide — since I can't quite decide about the farm problem!"*

To Mary Bancroft

July 31, 1956

Dear Mary:

I have twice put your note aside so that I might manage to work my way through the whole story of ants, aphids and burrowing nematodes before writing you.

I have now done so. And I know precisely your point — whether conscious or sub-conscious — in sending this on to me. This whole piece is obviously a satire on the contemporary political scene. I wasn't sure of it until I came to the section on parasitic wasps and lady-bird beetles being introduced as the only antidote for aphids. This is Animal Farm rewritten in a minor key.

I spoke profoundly on the Mediterranean fruit fly curse in the Florida primary. I can advise you too that the vernacular reference to the blight of the burrowing nematode is "spreading decline." A local politician in Lake City told me about it. I told him he didn't need to, that I *had* it.

Many thanks for this interlude. And now back to my own buttonholes.

Affectionately,

315 A copy is in A.E.S., I.S.H.L.

Professor Seymour Harris wrote Stevenson on July 20, 1956, that he had attended a conference of the governors of the New England states and that one Democrat thought it would be better if Stevenson were nominated on the second or third ballot so he would not be beholden to the South. Another Democratic governor argued that Stevenson should get the nomination as quickly as possible, but that the civil rights issue had to be faced squarely. Harris added that according to Robert J. Donovan's new book, Eisenhower: The Inside Story, *Eisenhower was furious when Stevenson said that all the Republicans had done for education in three years "was to call a conference."*[316]

To Seymour E. Harris

July 31, 1956

Dear Seymour:

Again I have so many things at hand to thank you for that my inclination is just to murmur a "God bless him" and hope you will know how fervently I mean it.

Your July 20 notes from an amateur about New England politics square precisely with my own impressions, satisfying me that I have not lost my amateur standing.

I hadn't heard about the White House explosion over my remarks about Ike and education. Do you suppose he really feels he has been accomplishing things?

I hope we haven't troubled you too much on the Small Business affair.[317] I expect Bill [Wirtz] told you the background of all that and the unimportant things that made it so important.

And now this latest memorandum about Tax Reduction etc! I just can't tell you what a relief it is to get something like this from you and to feel, when I have read it, that now I at least know where the solid roadbed lies. I expect most of these economic issues are not going to loom very large in this Fall's discussions, but they're bound to come up, and now I shall at least have my bearings. And of course the Welfare outlay questions *will* be priority items. . . .

More thanks than I can say.

Cordially,

---

[316] See Stevenson's speech to the California Democratic Council state convention of February 4, 1956, above, p. 58.

[317] On June 7, 1956, Stevenson had written Mr. Harris for his comments on a memorandum titled "Protecting the Consumer against Defaults" intended as part of an attack on Republican economic policy, which supported legislation to aid financial institutions but none to protect consumers.

To Archibald Alexander[318]

August 1, 1956
Confidential

Mr. Alexander —

Subject to the nomination, I want to move on the campaign organization quickly and if possible even outline it to the National Committee before the convention adjourns and they all depart.

Hence, would you be good enough to suggest a simple organization chart, naming suggested names, assuming that [Paul] Butler is "campaign mgr" as Nat. Chairman, that Finnegan is his deputy and travels with me.

I agree, generally, with the attached & presume your chart would roughly follow. The principal dramatis personae are now known.

AES

On July 26, Senator Estes Kefauver announced that he was withdrawing from the campaign for the nomination and that he was for Stevenson. Mrs. Eugene Meyer wrote Stevenson on August 1 that Kefauver was now in a strong position for the vice presidency. "As he overcame his resentment toward you," she added, "so you will overcome your justifiable doubts about him if you will consider that Estes has demonstrated ability to grow — to learn from experience — one of the greatest assets a human being can possess."

To Mrs. Eugene Meyer[319]

August 6, 1956

My dear Agnes:

I have your letter about "making up" with Estes. I think he behaved well, but why shouldn't he? He had always asserted his confidence in the primaries. There is actually but little support for him for Vice President except among his own former delegations and some "practical politicians" who feel he has at least harmony value. I am sure that someone else with a fresh face and greater potential use in the Congress would be far more valuable in the long run — but who!

Hastily and affectionately,
ADLAI

P.S. This letter sounds a little ill-tempered. I have never found it in my heart to be bitter about Kefauver, and I am really not. I think he does

---

[318] The handwritten draft of this letter is in the possession of Carol Evans. It was later typed.
[319] The original is in the Agnes Meyer files, Princeton University Library.

have good instincts and I've always liked him. Indeed, I could find it in neither my heart nor head to say anything harsh about him in the primary. I only wish he had done the same. Many of my supporters find him quite intolerable in view of what happened.

To the Reverend Reinhold Niebuhr[320]

August 6, 1956

Dear Reinhold:

Bless you for that wonderful letter. Your occasional reassurances, which are always so thoughtful and wise, somehow always replenish my confidence when I need it most. The civil rights situation is very difficult, as well you know — especially for Democratic politicians!

I hope so very, very much that you are well and ever better.

Cordially yours,

Gardner Cowles, publisher of Look *magazine, wrote expressing the hope that Stevenson could get the country to discuss intelligently foreign affairs in the coming campaign.*

To Gardner Cowles[321]

August 6, 1956

Dear Mike:

Thanks for your note. I enjoyed our breakfast, too, and emphatically share your view about foreign affairs. How to do it, or rather how much to do it during the campaign, however, is something else, and perplexes me a great deal.

Even more perplexing will be the problem of reappraisal which either administration must confront, and promptly. It is going to take much in the way of public education to prepare for new emphases, and I know of no more formidable responsibility for the American press. I think we shall have to look to you and John[322] and a very few others to help, and constantly, in that direction.

Yours,

---

[320] Professor at Union Theological Seminary and a leading figure in Americans for Democratic Action. A copy is in A.E.S., I.S.H.L.

[321] A copy is in A.E.S., I.S.H.L.

[322] Mr. Cowles's brother, the president of the Minneapolis *Star and Tribune* and chairman of the board of the Des Moines *Register and Tribune*.

John Steinbeck, who had written the foreword to a collection of Stevenson speeches published during the campaign in 1952,[323] wrote Stevenson that he was covering the Democratic National Convention for a number of newspapers as "an inexpert reporter in the business." He added that he had guaranteed his papers "that I am just as confused as the average voter."

To John Steinbeck

August 8, 1956

Dear Mr. Steinbeck:

I have your letter of August 5, and of course I would be delighted to see you. You had best call me at my headquarters at the Hilton Hotel — Webster 9-4911.

With very warm regards, I am

Cordially,

P.S. You may be as confused as the average voter but I hope you are not as confused as some candidates!

During the week of August 5, Democrats began arriving in Chicago for the convention, which was to open on August 13. On Monday, August 6, as Stevenson was climbing into an automobile, he said to a television reporter: "I have had a very strong feeling that the platform should express unequivocal approval of the Court's decision, although it seems odd that you should have to express your approval of the Constitution and its institutions." When this statement was televised on John Daly's American Broadcasting Company program on August 7, revolt started among Southern delegates committed to Stevenson. James A. Finnegan and his aides redoubled their efforts to hold the front-runner's delegates in line.[324]

To Mrs. Franklin D. Roosevelt[325]

August 9, 1956

Dear Mrs. Roosevelt:

I am enclosing a copy of a letter which I wrote to Paul Butler a few days ago, together with a draft of a suggested civil rights plank. I have

[323] *Speeches of Adlai Stevenson*, with a foreword by John Steinbeck and a brief biography of Adlai Stevenson by Debs Myers and Ralph Martin (New York: Random House, 1952).
[324] Stephen A. Mitchell, "Memo of Note," August 9, 1956. A copy is in the possession of the editors.
[325] The original is in the Franklin D. Roosevelt Library, Hyde Park, New York.

not disclosed either of these publicly, but want you to be fully advised as to what I have proposed.

In addition to the draft, I made an unrehearsed, spontaneous remark to a casual interviewer a couple of days ago to the effect that I had a strong feeling "that the platform should express unequivocal approval of the Court's decision, although it seems odd that you have to express your approval of the Constitution and its institutions." You will note that the enclosed draft speaks of "support" rather than "approval."

I feel you should be informed as to the background of the statement which has evoked such a strong — temporary, I hope! — reaction among some of my supporters.

Sincerely,
ADLAI

To Paul M. Butler[326]

August 4, 1956

Dear Paul:

You sent me last week a copy of a proposed Civil Rights plank for the platform.

This draft seems to me, subject to two or three exceptions, quite good.

I hardly need tell you that I attach primary significance, as I know you do, to making this platform statement a constructive contribution to meeting the nation's No. 1 domestic problem.

My experience during the primary campaigns in all parts of the country convinced me that there is no difficulty here which cannot be met by firm but in every instance responsible statement of our united purposes as a people and a party. There must be no yielding to the temptations to play the politics of opportunism with this emotion charged issue; no resort to extremism for the sake of personal political advantage and at the price of injury to the main cause of guaranteeing full and equal freedoms for all Americans. But there must also be a firm and clear statement of what we know is right.

It does seem to me that this draft does not state clearly and plainly enough part of what I have been saying in the primary campaign and what I feel strongly is right. I accordingly suggest the changes which are reflected in the enclosed revised draft.

I would think that the statement here about the education point could well be included too, either in whole or in part, in the Education plank.

[326] A copy is in the Franklin D. Roosevelt Library, Hyde Park, New York.

I am assuming that the Platform will also include the plank on Improving Congressional Procedures which was included in the 1952 Platform.

Very sincerely,

DRAFT OF CIVIL RIGHTS PLANK, AUGUST 4, 1956[327]

The Democratic Party is dedicated to the recognition of the dignity and the protection of the rights and liberties of every American.

The basic concept of our governmental system is that all men are created free and equal, are entitled as a matter of law to equal political rights and should have without discrimination equal opportunities for education, employment and housing. A person's constitutional rights cannot depend in any way on his race or his creed or his color.

The Democratic party has provided the greatest advancement in the area of human rights and in the elimination of discrimination based on race, religion or national origin. Democratic Administrations took the first concrete actions to eliminate segregation in the Armed forces; to end discrimination in Government employment and appoint qualified persons of all races to high Government posts; to ban discrimination by Government contractors; and to eliminate segregation in the Nation's capital.

The Eisenhower Administration, on the other hand, has promised much and boasted much, but accomplished little in this area. For three and a half years, President Eisenhower presented no civil rights program for the consideration of the Congress. Even his election year civil rights program abandoned essential points in the 1952 Republican platform.

Words are no substitute for deeds. What is required is cooperative effort on the part of individual citizens as well as action by local, state and Federal governments. Americans acting individually and through governmental agencies must recognize the principles enunciated in the Declaration of Independence and government must exercise the powers vested in it by the Constitution and the laws of the land.

In this spirit, the Democratic party stands firmly in support of the Supreme Court decisions regarding desegregation in the public schools and in other facilities, including transportation, as we stand firmly in support of all Supreme Court decisions.

Every American child, irrespective of race or national origin, economic status or place of residence, has full and equal right under the law to every educational opportunity to develop his potentialities.

[327] A copy is in the Franklin D. Roosevelt Library, Hyde Park, New York.

We favor legislation:

(a) To protect all citizens in the exercise of their right to vote;

(b) To secure the right to equal opportunity for employment;

(c) To provide protection for the right to security of person;

(d) To perfect and strengthen federal civil rights laws; and

(e) To provide adequate administrative machinery for the protection of Civil Rights.

On August 9, Harry S. Truman arrived in Chicago. The next day Stevenson and Governor Averell Harriman conferred separately with him. At a press conference on August 11, Truman announced that he was backing Harriman for the nomination and asserted that Stevenson did not have the experience to be President, while Harriman had "the ability to act as President immediately upon assuming that office, without risking a period of costly and dangerous trial and error." Mrs. Franklin D. Roosevelt admonished Mr. Truman and said that Stevenson had had more experience than Governor Harriman to equip him to be President. She also remarked that older people like herself and Truman should leave the political situation to younger individuals.[328]

Over the next few days Harriman failed to gain any significant support, nor did favorite son candidates, including Senator Lyndon B. Johnson, add any appreciable strength. On August 15, Truman called another press conference and blasted Stevenson for his "moderation" and stated that the Democrats needed a "fighting candidate" who thoroughly supported the New Deal and the Fair Deal. The next day the convention nominated Stevenson on the first ballot. Only 686½ votes were needed for the nomination; and Stevenson received 905½ to 210 votes for Harriman. There was a scattering of votes for seven other candidates.[329]

The permanent chairman of the convention, Sam Rayburn, speaker of the House of Representatives, declared Stevenson to be the nominee. He then introduced Stevenson, saying: "I have the unusual privilege of recognizing a gentleman whom, I think, you will recognize when he comes on this platform. He is here, not to make his acceptance speech, but to greet you and make an announcement."[330]

[328] New York *Times*, August 13, 1956.

[329] *Official Report of the Proceedings of the Democratic National Convention, August 13–17, 1956* (Richmond, Virginia: Beacon Press, 1956), p. 418.

[330] Ibid., pp. 419–421.

Mr. Chairman, fellow delegates, fellow Democrats, and guests of the Convention:

My heart is full, and I am deeply grateful.

But I did not come here tonight to speak of the action you have just taken. That I shall do tomorrow night, after you have chosen a Vice President. (Applause)

It is in connection with that choice that I have taken the unusual step of asking to be heard here very briefly tonight.

The American people have the solemn obligation to consider with the utmost care who will be their President if the elected President is prevented by a Higher Will from serving his full term. It is a sober reminder that seven out of 34 Presidents have served as a result of such indirect selection.

The responsibility of the Presidency has grown so great that the Nation's attention has become focused as never before on the office of the Vice Presidency. The choice for that office has become almost as important as the choice for the Presidency. (Applause)

Each political party has, therefore, the solemn obligation to offer the country as its choice for the Vice Presidency a person fully equipped, first to assist in the discharge of the duties of the most exacting job in the world, and second, to himself assume, if need be, this highest responsibility.

Historically, the Presidential candidate has often designated the nominee for Vice President. Sometimes the choice has been due to personal predilection or political expediency.

But always there is the importance of mutual confidence if they are to work together with maximum effectiveness in the interests of the Nation.

I recognize these considerations.

But I respect beyond measure a Convention and a Party which has conferred upon me its highest honor without there being asked of me a single commitment except faith in the program and principles of our Party. (Applause)

In these circumstances I have concluded to depart from the precedents of the past. I have decided that the selection of the Vice Presidential nominee should be made through the free processes of this Convention — (Applause) — so that the Democratic Party's candidate for this office may join me before the Nation not as one man's selection but as one chosen by our Party even as I have been chosen. (Applause)

I add only this: In taking this step I am expressing my confidence in your choice and in the many fine men whose prominence in our Party will command your consideration. The choice will be yours. The profit will be the Nation's. (Applause)

Until tomorrow night, again my heartfelt thanks, and God bless you. (Applause)

Representative Sam Rayburn, Senator Lyndon B. Johnson, and Paul Butler had opposed Stevenson's decision to let the convention select his running mate. But Stevenson had been adamant. After his announcement, supporters of Senator Hubert Humphrey, Senator Estes Kefauver, and Senator John F. Kennedy, who had placed Stevenson's name in nomination, worked all night and the next morning to win the nomination for their candidates. Meanwhile, Stevenson and his staff remained neutral. That afternoon, as state after state cast its vote, the struggle seesawed between Kefauver and Kennedy. On the second ballot, Kefauver received 755½ votes (687 votes were necessary for the nomination) and Kennedy received 589 votes.[331]

That evening, August 17, Stevenson delivered his speech of acceptance to the convention.[332]

I come here on a solemn mission.

I accept your nomination and your program. (Applause) And I pledge to you every resource of mind and strength that I possess to make your deed today a good one for our country and for our Party. (Applause)

Four years ago I stood in this same place and uttered those same words to you. But four years ago I did not seek the honor you bestowed upon me. This time it was not entirely unsolicited. (Laughter and applause)

And there is another big difference. That time we lost. This time we will win! (Applause)

My heart is full tonight as the scenes and faces and events of these busy years in between crowd my mind.

To you here tonight, and across the country who have sustained me in this great undertaking for months and even years, I am deeply, humbly grateful; and to none more than the great lady who is also the treasurer of a legacy of greatness — Mrs. Eleanor Roosevelt (Applause) — who has reminded us so movingly that this is 1956 and not 1932, nor even 1952; that our problems alter as well as their solutions; that change is

[331] Ibid., p. 481.
[332] Ibid., pp. 504–511.

the law of life, and that political parties, no less than individuals, ignore it at their peril.

I salute also the distinguished American who has been more than equal to the hard test of disagreement and has now reaffirmed our common cause so graciously — President Harry Truman. (Applause) I am glad to have you on my side again, sir! (Applause) Your heart can feel what we cannot express — how much you and Mrs. Truman are beloved in this room and this country. (Applause)

And I want to say, too, what every Democrat has known for a generation — that your Chairman will live forever in the memories of Democrats and all who love the political institutions of this land, Mr. Sam Rayburn. (Applause)

I am sure that the country is as grateful to this Convention as I am for its action of this afternoon. It has renewed and reaffirmed our faith in free democratic processes. (Applause)

The exalted office of the Vice Presidency, which I am proud to say my grandfather once occupied, has been dignified by the manner of your selection as well as by the distinction of your choice. (Applause)

Senator Kefauver is a great Democrat and a great campaigner — (Applause) — as I have special reason to know. (Applause)

If we are elected and it is God's will that I do not serve my full four years, the people will have a new President whom they can trust. (Applause) He has dignity, he has convictions, and he will command the respect of American people and the world. (Applause)

Perhaps these are simple virtues, but there are times when simple virtues deserve comment. This is such a time. (Applause) I am grateful to you for my running mate — an honorable and able American — Senator Estes Kefauver. (Applause)

And may I add that I got as excited as any of you about that photo finish this afternoon — (Applause and laughter) — and I want to pay my sincere respects too, to that great young American statesman, Senator John Kennedy of Massachusetts. (Applause)

When I stood here before you that hot night four years ago we were at the end of an era — a great era of restless, forward movement, an era of unparalleled social reform and of glorious triumph over depression and tyranny. It was a Democratic era. (Applause)

Tonight, after an interval of marking time and of aimless drifting, we are on the threshold of another great, decisive era. History's headlong course has brought us, I devoutly believe, to the threshold of a new America — to the America of the great ideals and noble visions which are the stuff our future must be made of. (Applause)

I mean a new America where poverty is abolished and our abundance is used to enrich the lives of every family. (Applause)

I mean a new America where freedom is made real for all without regard to race or belief or economic conditions. (Applause)

I mean a new America which everlastingly attacks the ancient idea that men can solve their differences by killing each other. (Applause)

These are the things I believe in and will work for with every resource I possess. These are the things I know you believe in and will work for with everything you have. These are the terms on which I accept your nomination.

Our objectives are not for the timid. They are not for those who look backward, who are satisfied with things as they are, who think that this great Nation can ever sleep or ever stand still.

The platform, the program, you have written is something much more than a consensus of the strongly-held convictions of strong men; it is a sign-post toward that new America. It speaks of the issues of our time with passion for justice, with reverence for our history and character, with a long view of the American future, and with a sober, fervent dedication to the goal of peace on earth. (Applause)

Nor has it evaded the current problems in the relations between the races who comprise America, problems which have so often tormented our national life. Of course there is disagreement in the Democratic Party on desegregation. It could not be otherwise in the only Party that must speak responsibly and responsively in both the North and the South. (Applause) If all of us are not wholly satisfied with what we have said on this explosive subject, it is because we have spoken the only way a truly national Party can.

In substituting realism and persuasion for the extremes of force or nullification (Applause) our Party has preserved its effectiveness, it has avoided a sectional crisis, and it has contributed to our national unity as only a national Party can.

As President it would be my purpose to press on in accordance with our platform toward the fuller freedom for all of our citizens which is at once our Party's pledge and the old American promise. (Applause)

I do not propose to make political capital out of the President's illness. (Applause) His ability personally to fulfill the demands of his exacting office is a matter between him and the American people. (Applause) So far as I am concerned that is where the matter rests. As we all do, I wish deeply for the President's health and well-being. (Applause)

But if the condition of President Eisenhower is not an issue as far as I am concerned, the condition and the conduct of the President's office and of the Administration is very much an issue. (Applause)

The men who run the Eisenhower Administration evidently believe that the minds of Americans can be manipulated by shows, slogans and the arts of advertising. And that conviction will, I dare say, be backed up by the greatest torrent of money ever poured out to influence an American election, poured out by men who fear nothing so much as change and who want everything to stay as it is — only more so. (Applause)

This idea that you can merchandise candidates for high office like breakfast cereal — that you can gather votes like box tops — is, I think, the ultimate indignity to the democratic process. (Applause) We Democrats must also face the fact that no President and no Administration has ever before enjoyed such an uncritical and enthusiastic support from so much of the press as this one. (Applause)

But let us ask the people of our country: To what great purpose for the Republic has the President's popularity and this unrivaled opportunity for leadership been put? Has the Eisenhower Administration used this opportunity to elevate us? To enlighten us? To inspire us? (Cries of "no") Did it, in a time of headlong, world-wide, revolutionary change, prepare us for stern decisions and great risks? (Cries of "no") Did it, in short, give men and women a glimpse of the nobility and vision without which peoples and nations perish? (Cries of "no")

Or did it just reassure us that all is well, everything is all right, that everyone is prosperous and safe, that no great decisions are required of us, and that even the Presidency of the United States has somehow become an easy job? (Applause)

I will have to confess that the Republican Administration has performed a minor miracle — after 20 years of incessant damnation of the New Deal they not only haven't repealed it, but they have swallowed it, (Laughter and applause) — or most of it, and it looks as though they could keep it down at least until after the election. (Laughter and applause)

I suppose we should be thankful that they have caught up with the New Deal at last, but what have they done to take advantage of the great opportunities of these times — a generation after the New Deal?

Well, I say they have smothered us in smiles and complacency while our social and economic advancement has ground to a halt and while our leadership and security in the world have been imperiled.

In spite of these unparalleled opportunities to lead at home and abroad they have, I say, been wasting our opportunities and losing our world. (Applause)

I say that what this country needs is not propaganda and a personality cult. What this country needs is leadership and truth. And that's what we mean to give it. (Applause)

What is the truth?

The truth is that the Republican Party is a house divided. The truth is that President Eisenhower, cynically coveted as a candidate but ignored as a leader, is largely indebted to Democrats in Congress for what accomplishments he can claim. (Applause)

The truth is that everyone is not prosperous. The truth is that the farmer, especially the family farmer who matters most, has not had his fair share of the national income and the Republicans have done nothing to help him — until an election year.

The truth is that 30 million Americans live today in families trying to make ends meet on less than $2,000 a year. The truth is that the small farmer, the small businessman, the teacher, the white collar worker, and the retired citizen trying to pay today's prices on yesterday's pensions — all these are in serious trouble. (Applause)

The truth is that in this Government of big men — big financially — no one speaks for the little man. (Applause)

The truth is not that our policy abroad has the Communists on the run. The truth, unhappily, is not — in the Republican President's words — that our "prestige since the last world war has never been as high as it is this day." The truth is that it has probably never been lower. (Applause)

The truth is that we are losing the military advantage, the economic initiative and the moral leadership. (Applause)

The truth is not that we are winning the cold war. The truth is that we are losing the cold war. (Applause)

Don't misunderstand me. I, for one, am ready to acknowledge the sincerity of the Republican President's desire for peace and happiness for all. (Applause) But good intentions are not good enough. (Applause) Our country is stalled on dead center — stalled in the middle of the road — while the world goes whirling by. America, which has lifted man to his highest economic state, which has saved freedom in war and peace, which has saved collective security, no longer sparks and flames and gives off new ideas and initiatives. (Applause) Our lights are dimmed. We chat complacently of this and that while, in Carlyle's phrase, "Death and eternity sit glaring." And I could add that opportunity, neglected opportunity, sits glaring too! (Applause)

But you cannot surround the future with arms, you cannot dominate the racing world by standing still. And I say it is time to get up and get moving again. It is time for America to be herself again. (Applause)

And that's what this election is all about! (Applause)

Here at home we can make good the lost opportunities; we can recover the wasted years; we can cross the threshold to the New America!

What we need is a rebirth of leadership — leadership which will give us a glimpse of the nobility and vision without which peoples and nations perish. Woodrow Wilson said that "When America loses its ardor for mankind, it is time to elect a Democratic President." There doesn't appear to be much ardor for anything in America just now; and it is time to elect a Democratic Administration and a Democratic Congress, yes, and a Democratic Government in every state and local office across the land. (Applause)

In our hearts we know that the horizons of the new America are as endless, its promises as staggering in its richness as the unfolding miracle of human knowledge. America renews itself with every forward thrust of the human mind.

We live in a second industrial revolution; we live at a time when the powers of the atom are about to be harnessed for ever greater production. We live at a time when even the ancient spectre of hunger is vanishing. This is the age of abundance! Never in history has there been such an opportunity to show what we can do to improve the quality of living now that the old, terrible, grinding anxieties of daily bread, of shelter and raiment, are disappearing.

With leadership, Democratic leadership, we can do justice to our children, we can repair the ravages of time and neglect in our schools. We can and we will! (Applause)

With leadership, Democratic leadership, we can restore the vitality of the American family farm. We can preserve the position of small business without injury to the large. We can strengthen labor unions and collective bargaining as vital institutions in a free economy. (Applause) We can and our Party history proves that we will! (Applause)

With leadership, Democratic leadership, we can conserve our resources of land and forest and water and develop them for the benefit of all. We can and the record shows that we will! (Applause)

With leadership, Democratic leadership, we can rekindle the spirit of liberty emblazoned in the Bill of Rights; we can build this new America where the doors of opportunity are open equally to all — the doors of our factories and the doors of our school rooms. We can make this a land where opportunity is founded on responsibility and freedom on faith, and where nothing can smother the lonely defiant spirit of the free intelligence. We can, and by our traditions as a Party we will! (Applause)

All these things we can do and we will. But in the international field the timing is only partially our own. Here the "unrepentant minute" once missed, may be missed forever. Other forces, growing yearly in potency, dispute with us the direction of our times. Here more than anywhere guidance and illumination are needed in the terrifying century of the hydrogen bomb. Here more than anywhere we must move, and rapidly, to repair the ravages of the past four years to America's repute and influence abroad.

We must move with speed and confidence to reverse the spread of communism. We must strengthen the political and economic fabric of our alliances. We must launch new programs to meet the challenge of the vast social revolution that is sweeping the world and that has liberated more than half the human race in barely a generation. We must turn the violent forces of change to the side of freedom.

We must protect the new nations in the exercise of their full independence; and we must help other people out of Communist or colonial servitude along the hard road to freedom. (Applause)

We must place our Nation where it belongs in the eyes of the world — at the head of the struggle for peace. (Applause) For in this nuclear age peace is no longer a visionary ideal. It has become an absolute, imperative, practical necessity. (Applause) Humanity's long struggle against war has to be won and won now. (Applause) Yes, and I say it can be won!

It is time to listen again to our hearts, to speak again our ideals, to be again our own great selves.

There is a spiritual hunger in the world today and it cannot be satisfied by material things alone — by better cars on longer credit terms. Our forebears came here to worship God. We must not let our aspirations so diminish that our worship becomes rather of material achievement and bigness.

For a century and a half the Democratic Party has been the Party of respect for people, of reverence for life, of hope for each child's future, of belief that "The highest revelation is that God is in every man." (Applause)

Once we were not ashamed in this country to be idealists. Once we were proud to confess that an American is a man who wants peace and believes in a better future and loves his fellow man. (Applause) We must reclaim these great Christian and humane ideas. We must dare to say that the American cause is the cause of all mankind. (Applause)

If we are to make honest citizens of our hearts we must unite them again to the ideals in which they have always believed and give those ideals the courage of our tongues. (Applause)

Standing as we do here tonight at this great fork of history, may we never be silenced, may we never lose our faith in freedom and the better destiny of man. (Applause)

Good-bye and I hope we can meet again in every town and village of America. (Tumultuous applause and cheers)

To Alicia Patterson[333]

August 20, 1956

Alicia dear —

Distressed that I didn't see more of you here — and especially that I missed your visit with your ma. I wish there was some way I could get any ideas you have as to conduct of the campaign, themes etc., attack vs positive proposals — and on & on!

On the assumption that [Averell] Harriman will not give the "organization" much encouragement in N.Y. & that [Carmine] DeSapio hasn't much to offer on his own, N.Y. becomes more difficult. I'm told there *must* be an independant campaign (which will soak up much of the money we need for the national campaign I fear!) and also a campaign *among* independants especially in "up-state" N.Y. — outside of N.Y. city I mean. To that end we are re-organizing the Volunteers for Stevenson of 1952 and hope, I'm told, that [Bernard] Baruch will join Mrs. FDR as Honorary Co-Chairmen. Archie Alexander is going to see him & if *you* have a chance to give him a nudge in that direction it would help I'm sure.

Love from THE Guv!

To Benjamin Swig[334]

August 20, 1956

Dear Ben:

Just a note to tell you how sorry I am that I did not see more of you during the Convention. It was an unbelievably hectic time for all of us, but I had hoped to see you at breakfast on Friday morning with Roger Stevens — also I sent you a message to drop by Thursday evening after the Convention but I imagine it never reached you.

I count your support during the primaries as having been indispensable to my victory and I shall hope to have a chance to express to you in person very, very soon the infinite gratitude that I have.

Cordially yours,
ADLAI

[333] This handwritten letter is in the possession of Adlai E. Stevenson III.
[334] The original is in the possession of Mr. Swig.

To Gerald W. Johnson

August 20, 1956

My dear Gerald:

Tell your wife that I appreciated her wire and I only wish that both of you had been here by my side during this fantastic interval. It turned out better, by the way, than I had any right to expect. I was both emancipated and nominated.

I do so want to have your help in connection with what I say, and how I say it. I have wisdom about me, but little wit, and few swords and daggers. When I say about me, I am, please understand, referring to others and not to my own odors, sacred or profane.

I want to develop the new America theme, because it seems to me the root of the trouble is a total failure of vision, total dedication to the advertising arts, total indifference to man's deeper sympathies and wants, and, finally, a failure to exploit the great opportunities of this fork of history.

I have just got through dictating a note to my law partner, Bill Wirtz, who is also now going to ride herd as editorial chief on my small staff. I am enclosing a copy for what it is worth.

Some of the hardest things for me to handle will be Nixon and health. Just how to do that and your advice thereon would be immeasurably valuable. Also any speech material that you could send along on anything that you feel needs saying I would cherish. What's more, I might even use it!

Cordially and hurriedly,

To Mrs. Franklin D. Roosevelt[335]

August 20, 1956

Dear Mrs. Roosevelt:

So many thanks for your wire. How you could have remembered to do that on top of everything else mystifies me.

I am sure I failed utterly to thank you properly for all you have done during these past many months, and finally at the Convention itself. The latter came off better than I had any right to expect. The serious shadows that remain are the resentment of the South over Kefauver's nomination, and possible difficulties between Paul Butler and Jim Finnegan.

I felt for many reasons that I did not wish to replace the former with

[335] The original is in the Franklin D. Roosevelt Library, Hyde Park, New York.

the latter. But Finnegan's talents and maturity are such that I am hopeful he can work harmoniously in spite of Paul Butler's sensitivity and apparent anxiety to keep everything under his own control. I have tried to make it emphatically clear to him that in designating Finnegan as Campaign Director I expect him to have full responsibility and authority with respect to *my* campaign.

I hope so much that you have a relaxing and diverting trip abroad with the young people.[336] I can imagine the diversion, but not the relaxation.

Devotedly,

ADLAI

On August 19, 1956, Harry S. Truman sent Stevenson a handwritten letter from Independence, Missouri:

DEAR GOVERNOR:

I hope that the next time I send you a letter of congratulation I can say Dear Mr. President. I do sincerely congratulate you on your great victory in the Convention.

Something had to be done to wake up the Party and I undertook to do it. I was in deadly earnest, as a Democratic Politician, to put some life and leadership into the Party. It was the purpose in 1952 to do just that for you. I am sure that you did not understand that. The Democratic Party and the United States of America never needed a leader as badly as it does at this time. You have all the qualifications for that position if you will just let them come to the top. In California and Florida primaries it began to come out — but complete satisfaction did not come to me until the Convention fight and your victory there.

I was not putting on a show at that Convention. The principles of the Democratic Party and the welfare of the nation and the world, I felt, were at stake. The Party cannot exist as a "me too party." It must exist as a Party for all the people, rich and poor, priviledged [*sic*] and under priviledged [*sic*]. It must be ever ready to see justice done to those who cannot hire expensive representatives to look after their welfare in Washington.

Only the President can do that. He must be a fighter and one whose heart is in the General Welfare.

I have never had a desire to be a party boss or to be the No. 1 Democrat. I tried to abdicate in 1952. The happenings at Chicago

---

336 Mrs. Roosevelt was leaving on August 18, 1956, to travel in Europe with her grandchildren.

gave you the leadership *on your own*. Now I am ready to do whatever I can to help the Party and its Leader to win.

It is up to you to decide what that will be. I do hope you will have a central headquarters and someone in charge who understands leadership in politics.

I wouldn't blame you if you'd never speak to me again — but let's win this campaign and think of that afterwards if it is ever necessary to be thought about.

Sincerely, HARRY TRUMAN

To Harry S. Truman

August 23, 1956

My dear Mr. President:

I am deeply grateful for your very kind letter, which you must have written almost immediately on your return after the Chicago ceremonies. I confess, as I told you, that I was disappointed by what transpired at Chicago, but I am also much relieved that the results, as you say, were actually so satisfying to you.

I note your generous proffer of help during the campaign, and I am sure that ways will be found to take full advantage of it.

In 1952, while I was Governor of Illinois, I had to continue in my capital and discharge my state business all the time during the campaign, and therefore had no choice but to have my personal headquarters where I was. That, of course, is not the case this time, and the headquarters will be in the National Committee in Washington. The Volunteers have taken space nearby. Jim Finnegan of Philadelphia will be Campaign Director.

And, finally, together with my thanks for your kind letter, let me assure you again that I appreciate fully the high motives which prompted your course of action at the Convention.

With warmest regards to you and Mrs. Truman, I am

Sincerely yours,

P.S. And thanks so much for sending on the check from Donald Rock.[337]

AES

---

[337] The editors have been unable to identify Mr. Rock.

To John J. Sparkman

August 23, 1956

Dear John:

Somehow something went wrong at the end of the Convention. Instead of having you beside me, I didn't see you anywhere around the platform. I had thought that our old team would have a public reunion. I guess the whole thing was rather hastily improvised by [Paul] Butler or somebody, I don't yet know who.

Also I had hoped for an opportunity to bid you farewell and tell you what a comfort your counsel and calm good judgment were to me — even as it has always been.

Sometime I wish you would let me have your carefully considered views as to precisely what use should be made of Mr. Truman during the campaign. He is eager to get to work and has written me a touching letter. On the other hand, this must be my campaign and not his, as I am sure you agree.

Hastily and gratefully,

To John W. McCormack[338]

August 23, 1956

Dear John:

I don't believe I had a proper opportunity to express my gratitude to you for your extraordinary management of the acutely difficult problems you encountered in the platform committee, as well as its presentation. But I know you are an old hand at the intricate task of reconciling people and opinions. I must say I marvel at the way you do it, and the way you did it again this time.

My thanks and admiration to you, sir.

Cordially yours,

P.S. I hope this time if you have *any* counsel for me and for the campaign you will pass it along promptly. While after all these years I should have everything in mind and organized, I really haven't, and your advice is eagerly welcome.

AES

[338] Congressman from Massachusetts, who served as chairman of the Democratic Platform Committee. A copy is in A.E.S., I.S.H.L.

To Sam Rayburn[339]

August 26, 1956

Dear Mr. Sam:

Before the Convention recedes much further in my mind, I want to say again that your counsel and help over these past trying years of my unwanted "leadership" have been just about my greatest comfort. Then came the culmination in the Convention, and again you gave it to me straight when I needed it.

Bless you! A man never had a more precious and useful friend, nor a party for that matter! I thank my stars for you again and again.

Yours,

To John F. Kennedy

August 26, 1956

My dear Jack:

I had hoped to see you before you left Chicago, and left, may I say, a much bigger man than you arrived! If there was a hero, it was you, and if there has been a new gallantry on our horizon in recent years, it is yourself. I say with confidence that you couldn't have been half as disappointed about the Vice Presidency as my children were, and I *know* that they reflect the view of many.

The news about your wife's misfortune[340] has just come to me and I am heartsick. I wish there was something I could say that would help either you or her — aside from the fact that I was honored beyond measure to have you nominate me, and so beautifully, and to have had your support and encouragement in this trying task.

Yours,

To Robert F. Wagner

August 26, 1956

Dear Bob:

I have only now uncovered your very kind and thoughtful telegram after the nomination. How good of you to go to all that trouble! While I attempted to seize the phone every moment to talk to you again about the senatorship,[341] I have restrained myself with more than the usual display of self-control.

---

[339] A copy is in A.E.S., I.S.H.L.
[340] Mrs. Kennedy had just had a miscarriage.
[341] Mayor Wagner was considering running for the United States Senate.

Averell [Harriman] called this morning, full of good will and enthusiasm, and said to me he was encouraged from your direction. I hope that's the case, because it is something more than strength, it's the kind of people that are congenial to you that make this business endurable, at least to me, and I count you among the foremost of that agreeable ilk.

Hastily yours,

Part Two

The 1956 Campaign

After his nomination, Stevenson moved his campaign headquarters to Washington, D.C. James A. Finnegan continued as campaign manager and was assisted by Hyman Raskin and James Rowe, Jr. Clayton Fritchey, assisted by Roger Tubby, handled press relations, and George Ball was in charge of the mass media. Jane Dick, Barry Bingham, and Archibald Alexander headed the national headquarters of the Volunteers for Stevenson and Kefauver. Matthew McCloskey, treasurer of the Democratic National Committee, and Roger Stevens were in charge of fund-raising. Newton Minow administered the personal campaign organization, while William McCormick Blair, Jr., traveled with Stevenson and performed an invaluable service in arranging appointments and other details, and W. Willard Wirtz also traveled with the candidate and worked on drafts of speeches. The research and writing group in Washington was headed by Arthur M. Schlesinger, Jr. Among those who contributed to developing the theme of the New America were Robert Tufts, John Kenneth Galbraith, John Hersey, Chester Bowles, William V. Shannon, John Bartlow Martin, William Lee Miller, Seymour E. Harris, David Lloyd, and Charles Murphy. Kenneth Hechler and Philip Stern were in charge of research.

Stevenson and his aides agreed that unlike the approach of 1952, the essence of the 1956 campaign had to be attack. The main weakness of the Republican party, they felt, was its image as the party of big business. The strength of the Democratic party was as the party of the people against the interests. At the same time, it was recognized that the main strength of the Republicans was the widespread belief that President Eisenhower was a man of peace and that under him the Republicans were less likely than the Democrats to involve the nation in wars.

Stevenson agreed reluctantly with his advisers' recommendation that the main emphasis of the campaign was to be on domestic affairs. During the campaign Stevenson enlarged on the necessity of the New

America to improve the quality of life in America. But as the campaign ground on, Stevenson shifted the emphasis to foreign policy. He was convinced that if the public knew more about the alarming situation in the Middle East and elsewhere they would respond to his analysis. Stevenson's views on many complex international issues were over-shadowed by the Republican attacks on him for proposing the suspension of hydrogen-bomb testing and the replacement of the draft with a volunteer professional army.

By election day, Stevenson had been campaigning almost incessantly for nine months. The primaries and the convention brought him close to nervous exhaustion. Then the travel and speaking schedule worked out for him immediately after the convention was, in his own words, a "man-killer."[1] On October 8, Eric Sevareid said on his Columbia Broadcasting System news analysis: "He is not running out of gas in terms of his powers of expression — on paper. To be sure, he is not producing the ringing documents he produced in fifty-two, which so stirred millions of educated and idealistic Americans seeking a new vision for their country; apparently he did not expect to do that again; his present speeches — on paper — are still strong and frequently penetrating; but the truth is that with one audience after another, the speaker is not coming across. The failure lies with the candidate himself. In spite of all his platform and studio experiences since then, he is not even reading his speeches as well as he did four years ago. He appears distracted, hesitant, often nervous."

Stevenson wrote in 1960: "In all I made more than 300 speeches and traveled close to 75,000 miles and spent more money than I care to think about. (In 1932 Franklin D. Roosevelt made only about 107 speeches and traveled less than 15,000 miles.) I am told I set a record both for words uttered and mileage traversed — and I am not proud of it and I wish no Presidential candidate ever had to do it again."[2]

On August 27, Stevenson and Kefauver left Chicago for a four-day, five-thousand-mile trip to meet with party leaders in the Southwest, the West Coast and the South. Until election day the pressure of travel, meetings, and delivering speeches was remorseless.

[1] Kenneth S. Davis, A Prophet in His Own Country: The Triumphs and Defeats of Adlai E. Stevenson (Garden City, New York: Doubleday, 1957), p. 482.
[2] "Choice by Hullabaloo," This Week, February 28, 1960.

To Archibald MacLeish

August 23, 1956

Dear Archie:

The piece was very, very helpful, and moreover it will be used as I go along, I have no doubt. Bless you!

I find it awfully hard to write to *win*, rather than writing to say just what you feel is important. The wise men all assure me that there are many votes in peace, but no votes in foreign affairs. And I have no doubt this time I must do far more attacking of the ins than last time, when I was in a sense defending the record.

I hope you will pass along anything you have a chance to contrive that you think healthy for the people or the ballot box. Ways of deflating these self-righteous gentlemen are especially welcome.

Love to Ada.[3]

Yours,

P.S. If it hadn't been for that six months primary ordeal, I wouldn't feel so squeezed and wasted.

James Rowe, Jr., who had worked for Senator Johnson's nomination at the convention, wrote that Johnson had been pleased that Stevenson consulted him about opening the vice presidential nomination at the convention. Rowe urged Stevenson to continue to "butter him up." Rowe also observed that Senator Hubert Humphrey was extremely unhappy over his poor showing in the contest for the vice presidential nomination. Rowe added that if his work for Senator Johnson at the convention was a liability, he would understand if Stevenson did not want his active help in the campaign.

To James Rowe, Jr.

August 26, 1956

Dear Jim:

Ever so many thanks for your letter, which I have just seen. I must hear the story of the conversation between Lyndon [Johnson] and Averell [Harriman] on civil rights. Please remember to tell me about it.

I am so pleased that Lyndon feels that things worked out not too badly. Certainly I have always counted him a real and understanding friend and want to continue to do so, and in the most direct and forthright possible manner.

3 Mrs. MacLeish.

I, too, am distressed about Hubert [Humphrey]. I share completely your estimate of him. I had a talk with him after the Vice Presidential nomination and he sounded philosophical, if not happy. Certainly I detected no resentment toward me, but I understand Eugenie Anderson[4] is still bitter. I shall see Hubert this week in western Iowa and have another talk. Along with Lyndon, I know no one more valuable, indeed indispensable.

I understood perfectly about Texas, and also Lyndon's and Sam [Rayburn]'s anxiety about opening the Vice Presidential nomination. Perhaps I was lucky that it worked out without any more bloodshed. I understand fully about Estes' situation in the South. But I wonder if we can count on Lyndon and some of the really important Southern leaders to help us down there, to relieve the burden on me. I hear good things from various unexpected directions, including Senator Holland,[5] but for Lyndon to make some speeches through the South for the ticket, as well as some of the people like Senator Russell[6] with whom he has such influence, would enable me to concentrate where I can do some good, and relieve us of much anxiety.

Of all this we can talk later, as I understand Jim [Finnegan] has been or will be in touch with you about joining up promptly. The latter is my answer to your suggestion that maybe your usefulness has been impaired.

So many thanks.

Cordially,

Mrs. Eugene Meyer commended Stevenson for his boldness in opening the vice presidential nomination to the convention. She also praised him for having the courage to be a real individual in an age of "conformity and cowardice."

To Mrs. Eugene Meyer[7]

August 26, 1956

My dear Agnes:

Your letters and wire have been brought out to my home in the country just as I am leaving for the West. I shall take the speech with

---

[4] A prominent member of the Democratic-Farmer-Labor Party in Minnesota and former ambassador to Denmark, 1949–1953.

[5] Spessard Holland, of Florida.

[6] Richard Russell, of Georgia.

[7] The original is in the Agnes Meyer files, Princeton University Library.

me, and not breathe its authorship to a soul. I am sure it will be helpful, as everything you say and write is.

I am glad you like the phrase "New America" which I used in the acceptance speech. The purpose, of course, will be to put some flesh on these bones during the campaign. Of course, after Eisenhower had appropriated every known virtue for his administration and the Republicans in his acceptance [speech], I am not sure whether my New America isn't old stuff to his gallant government!

Sometimes I wake up at night startled with the thought that I am doing all this again, and I can't say I look forward to it with any bouncing eagerness at the moment. But perhaps that's the consequence of three solid days of taking movies,[8] which is hard and tiresome work.

I am much interested in what you report about Eisenhower's distaste for criticism. I think he'll be getting more and more, and I only hope areas of the objective press will expand beyond the blessed [Washington] Post and [St. Louis] Post-Dispatch.

Off to the wars, with many thoughts of you and your everlasting courage and encouragement!

Affectionately,
ADLAI

To Mrs. Humphrey Bogart[9]

August 26, 1956

My dear Betty:

Ever so many thanks for your sweet letter. I was so pleased that you thought well of the acceptance speech. The Convention, as you know, went well from every point of view, I think. The campaign will be difficult, however, and we are always confronted with the problem of breaking through the sound barrier, and I also will have an acutely difficult problem of adjusting myself to much less time for speech preparation if I am going to remedy some of the defects of last time.

The self-righteousness of our adversaries infuriates me too, but the Ike-Nixon techniques of piety and folksiness are effective, I suspect we must admit. I keep trying to persuade myself that this is the Presidency of the United States, and the competition should be on an entirely different level.

---

[8] Carol Evans writes that these "were probably a series of 'spot' movies, not more than five minutes in length, that were filmed for TV in the 1956 campaign." Letter to Eric Sears, February, 1975.

[9] A copy is in the Adlai E. Stevenson collection, Illinois State Historical Society (A.E.S., I.S.H.L.).

I do hope things are going well with you, and that Bogie is himself again. Affectionate regards to those enchanting children and to you both. I shall hope to see you when I come out there soon.

Yours,

Author and lecturer John Mason Brown sent a cable to Stevenson from France congratulating him on his nomination and added: "Hate to be here feeling lonely and exiled in France."

To John Mason Brown[10]

August 26, 1956

Dear John:

"Lonely and exiled in France" — indeed! And how I wish I were lonely and exiled in France for about 48 hours. Or maybe 72. Or maybe a couple of years! As it is, I am surrounded by motion picture cameras, script writers, television, reporters, and just plain politicians. And to think that I am doing it a second time!

Affectionate regards,

ADLAI

P.S. And come home soon and write some speeches. I have to deflate these pious stuffed shirts somehow.

Archibald Alexander tried to persuade Bernard Baruch (to no avail) to be an honorary cochairman of Volunteers for Stevenson and Kefauver.

To Archibald Alexander

August 26, 1956

Dear Archie:

I have written to Baruch as per the attached. I hope as soon as Mrs. Roosevelt returns you will urge her to get after Baruch by telephone. I think he likes to be courted and that he even then will not do it, but it may be worth the effort.

Do you think there would be any advantage in adding [Senator Herbert] Lehman to Mrs. Roosevelt's name for your honorary co-chairmen? I am skeptical.

Yours,

---

[10] The original is in the possession of Mr. Brown.

To Bernard Baruch

August 26, 1956

My dear Mr. Baruch:

Archie Alexander has told me of his meeting with you, and also delivered to me a copy of "A Philosophy for Our Time."[11] I think it's precisely what I need most just now, and perhaps I'll even have a moment to read it while I'm flying around trying to make sense.

Bless you, my dear and honored friend!

Cordially yours,

Dean Acheson wrote that he and Paul Nitze were assembling material for several speeches on foreign affairs.

To Dean Acheson

August 26, 1956

Dear Dean:

You were good to write me, and I am grateful indeed to you and Alice.[12]

I know what you and Paul are up to, and I only hope I can get this material in fairly usable form, so that my editing time requirement is at a minimum. Last time — in 1952 — I am afraid I spent far too much time on texts, at the expense of politics. It's hard to do otherwise when you have some taste for responsibility and style. Evidently neither commands much of a premium in this business!

And speaking of this business, I sometimes wonder if it's a dream or if I'm really doing it again.

Ever yours,

Dore Schary joined Stevenson at Libertyville to help prepare film material for the campaign.

---

[11] Bernard M. Baruch, *A Philosophy for Our Time* (New York: Simon & Schuster, 1954).

[12] Mrs. Acheson.

To Dore Schary[13]

August 31, 1956

Dear Dore:

"Everything is settled now except winning the election." Well, we shall see what we can do!

I too feel badly that in all that highly compressed confusion there was no further opportunity to see you, but I am sure there will be another time. As for Jack Kennedy, I have a feeling that he was the real hero of the hour and that we shall hear a great deal more from this promising young man.[14]

Well, now, to work!

Cordially,

ADLAI

Jonathan Daniels, editor of the Raleigh, North Carolina, News and Observer, wrote Stevenson that he must "avoid like the plague the impression that you are the best loved candidate of the Southern politicians. . . . Some of those who most loudly love you are heading programs in the South which are repulsive to thousands of voters in crucial areas in the nation."

To Jonathan Daniels[15]

September 1, 1956

Dear Johnny —

You *never* "weary" me! Your letter was good, timely and helpful. I know how you must feel down there & I know the pitfalls up here from too much deep south affection. I had not been aware that there was that much — unless it was in N.C. But I'm glad you warned me.

Up here the sensible negro leaders dont really expect miracles; all they really insist upon is *some* honest progress in the resistence areas, as I'm sure you know; indeed I could say that *recognition* is all they demand at this stage.

I pray that something will be forthcoming in the way of voluntary action before the courts have to start moving. As for the campaign, I'll

---

[13] The original is in the possession of the State Historical Society of Wisconsin.

[14] Mr. Schary writes that Stevenson refers both to Senator Kennedy's narration of the film *Pursuit of Happiness*, presented at the convention, and to the manner in which Kennedy conducted himself in the vice presidential contest. Letter to Carol Evans, October 15, 1970.

[15] This handwritten letter is in the Jonathan Daniels papers, University of North Carolina Library.

go on saying what I have for 8 mos. and while denying the virtues or efficacy of force, I'll proclaim the necessity of law observance — Please keep me informed — and advised!

Yrs

ADLAI

Senator Lyndon Johnson sent Stevenson a Drew Pearson column in which Pearson stated that Johnson had demanded that James Rowe be chairman of the Democratic National Committee and that Senator Stuart Symington be the vice presidential candidate. Johnson wrote Stevenson that, as he recalled, the national chairmanship was not mentioned and that he had expressed no preference for Vice President.

To Lyndon B. Johnson

September 1, 1956

Dear Lyndon:

I am back in the country[16] today after a week's journey and find your letter of August 29, enclosing a clipping from a Drew Pearson column about our talk during the Convention in Chicago at which Jim Rowe and Jim Finnegan were also present.

Your recollection is precisely accurate save one thing: you told me all about the meeting at the White House on Suez.[17] You will recall that I had talked to you and Sam Rayburn about that conference and I had given you some views of my own before you went to Washington on Sunday morning.

As to the balance of the conversation, there was no mention whatever of the National Chairman either then or at any other time. You assured me in most emphatic terms that you were not interested in the Vice Presidency on your behalf nor did you express any positive preferences.

We did talk, as you say, about the platform and the many problems that you confront as majority leader in reconciling Democratic views and maintaining a coherent and effective party position.

In spite of years of experience I still am amazed by all of the "inside" stories I read in the papers and news magazines. Your experience must be even more aggravating.

Warmest good wishes.

Cordially,

16 Stevenson's farm in Libertyville.

17 The conference, on August 13, 1956, was held to warn a bipartisan group of twenty-two senators and representatives that there was danger of war in the Middle East. See the New York *Times*, August 13, 1956, for a statement from the White House on the conference.

To Lyndon B. Johnson

September 1, 1956

Dear Lyndon:

Since dictating the previous letter I have seen yours of August 22 and 25. And all the time I thought you were raising stock on that ranch instead of children.[18]

Your offer to help is most gratifying and comforting. I just don't know how the scheduling is to be managed, but before leaving Santa Fe I asked Clint Anderson[19] to help and he agreed to do so for a few days in Washington. I shall make known your availability to him and I am sure, also, that we shall exploit it beyond endurance. The latter, by the way, must be our first consideration as well as yours.

Our regional meetings were successful beyond my expectations. In the South, aside from Texas, I had most reassuring reports, as you may have heard. Virginia seems to be the most uncertain quantity, and it might well be that you could speak there with great value. I had a most gratifying wire from Dick Russell which comforted me a lot. Naturally I should like to avoid any unnecessary campaigning in view of the importance of concentration in the doubtful areas, which enlarges my anxiety to rely on you and the others there to take care of the South. Besides, you are far more effective than I am.

Cordially,

To John Steinbeck[20]

September 1, 1956

My dear Steinbeck:

I was enchanted with your letter, and especially that engaging line about the heights of inertia to which Eisenhower may climb in his second term when he is only running for retirement.

By all means pass along your bits; but it is best to address them to W. Willard Wirtz, who is my law partner and acting as a sort of editor in chief while I am travelling almost incessantly. He is here now, but plans to move to our headquarters at 1728 L Street, N.W., Washington, D.C. within the next ten days or so.

---

[18] Mr. Johnson had written that in addition to his own two daughters, some seventeen other children were at the LBJ Ranch in Texas for the weekend.

[19] Senator Clinton Anderson, of New Mexico.

[20] The original is in the possession of Mrs. John Steinbeck.

Bless you and many thanks. I am still indignant that I had no more time with you in Chicago. I shall hope for something better.

Cordially,

P.S. I am putting "Atavism and Old Lace"[21] aside for the bed table tonight.

To Mrs. Robert F. Wagner

September 1, 1956

My dear Mrs. Wagner:

I have been travelling around the country so busily that I have only now had an opportunity to read Bob's statement, published in the New York Times on August 31. Somehow, I feel I must write to you because it is his wife and family who are making a large part of whatever sacrifice is involved in his undertaking the race for the Senate. Knowing something of the price of public office, and especially residence in Washington makes my appreciation to you and to him all the keener.

With warm good wishes, I am

Cordially,

To Stuart Symington

September 1, 1956

Dear Stuart:

Someone has just called my attention to the issue of TIME magazine of August 27th in which I read that I "vetoed" you as a possible nominee for Vice President at a meeting with party leaders during the Convention.

I am distressed by this report, but not surprised as it is but one of several inaccuracies in the piece.

Actually, as I think you know, I have not only the warmest personal regard for you for many years, but also the utmost admiration for your record in the many capacities in which you have served our country.

I am sure you have put no credence in this absurd story, but I wanted to take this means to deny that I ever said such a thing or had such an idea, and I hope to have an early opportunity to repeat this denial in person.

Cordially yours,

P.S. Perhaps I'm also a little indignant because to say such a thing in a large meeting (I think there were 12 or more present) hardly credits me with normal intelligence.

[21] The editors have been unable to identify the piece to which Stevenson refers.

Mrs. Harold Hochschild, a friend since his student days at Princeton University, wrote Stevenson that any time he needed a hideaway he. could put on a beard and visit them at Princeton or their summer home. She requested that he not answer her note.

To Mrs. Harold Hochschild

September 1, 1956

My dear Mary:

Forgive me for answering your note! You were an angel to think of me, and I am touched and more grateful to the Hochschilds for this charitable thought of me and my emotional equilibrium as well as for their generosity and kindness, for which I can make no possible restitution.

I have to pinch myself sometimes to believe that I am doing it all again. How I should like to put on that false beard and run to you this minute.

Affectionate regards to you both.

Yours,

To Mrs. Eugene Meyer[22]

September 2, 1956

Agnes dear —

I hope you thought well of the regional meeting junket. It was Wilson Wyatt's idea and, while exhausting, served the purpose of taking the initiative, stepping up local activity and confidence — and, incidentally, enlightening the candidates.

My V.P. turns out on better acquaintance to be docile and largely cooperative and, if I don't for[e]see any stimulation, I can't for[e]see many difficulties at least during the campaign.

I confess I'm tired and don't feel the old urge to say everything just right as I used to. But I like to think my present more philosophical attitude is not without advantages — even if the quality of my "utterances" won't be at the old level.

And what of you, my gallant and beloved?

AES

[22] This handwritten letter is in the Agnes Meyer files, Princeton University Library. Stevenson scrawled on the top of the letter: "Sunday Sept 2 — off tomorrow to Detroit for 5 speeches!!"

President Eisenhower suggested that the Central Intelligence Agency brief Stevenson regularly on international developments. Except that the information was secret, Eisenhower noted, "The receipt of such information would impose no obligation of any kind upon you." Stevenson replied by telegram.

To Dwight D. Eisenhower

September 5, 1956

THANK YOU FOR YOUR TELEGRAM. I SHALL BE GLAD TO ACCEPT YOUR OFFER OF SEPTEMBER FOUR WITH RESPECT TO BRIEFINGS ON THE INTERNATIONAL SCENE WITH THE UNDERSTANDING THAT THIS IMPOSES NO RESTRICTION ON FULL AND FREE DISCUSSION APART FROM THE SAFEGUARDING OF THE INFORMATION FURNISHED WHERE SECURITY DICTATES. I SHALL BE IN WASHINGTON ON SEPTEMBER FOURTEEN AND HAVE ASKED MY EXECUTIVE ASSISTANT TO GET IN TOUCH WITH GENERAL CABELL[23] AT THAT TIME.

To Tom Dammann[24]

September 7, 1956

Dear Tom:

You have asked me for an expression of attitude toward the very vital problem of soil and water conservation.

It is my deep conviction that one of the most vital problems of our present day economy is the preservation of our soil and water resources. Unless we learn to conserve our soil and water all other endeavor becomes useless. All our food, most of our clothing and the majority of the necessities of our living come from that thin skin of the earth known as top soil, nourished, and all too often ravaged, by water.

I believe wholeheartedly that we have made great strides in meeting the problems of soil and water conservation efficiently and effectively through the Soil Conservation District Movement assisted by the Soil Conservation Service. Consequently, I have been alarmed by the efforts of the present administration to curtail the whole endeavor by paring budgets, switching responsibilities and reducing the Soil Conservation Service technical staff to inadequacy.

23 Lieutenant General Charles P. Cabell, deputy director of the Central Intelligence Agency.
24 A young California rancher whose father, John F. Dammann, a Chicago lawyer, was an old friend of Stevenson.

One of the most dangerous developments of the times is the trend toward bigness at the cost of individual initiative — bigness in everything. The Soil Conservation District Movement is a fundamentally democratic approach, based on the efforts of many individuals. It therefore serves as a brake on this trend toward bigness. This is especially evident, for example, in the small watershed treatment program. What more effective, what more democratic way of solving the problems of flood control could be conceived than meeting them at the source under the leadership and execution of local Soil Conservation Districts.

I assure you that under my administration everything will be done to support and strengthen the Soil Conservation Movement.

Sincerely yours,

Carl Sandburg wired Stevenson on September 5, "Superb campaign speeches. I can hear Lloyd Lewis[25] *giving three cheers."*

To Carl Sandburg

September 7, 1956

Dear Carl:

Thanks for your wire, and for your approval. It is hard for me to believe that I am doing all this again.

I shall certainly need all the help I can get, and if you have any ideas from time to time I know you will not hesitate to send them along. How I wish Lloyd were here!

Affectionate greetings to you both.

Yours,

Mrs. Hermon Dunlap Smith wrote to Stevenson from their summer camp at Desbarats, Ontario, where he had often visited.[26]

To Mrs. Hermon D. Smith[27]

September 7, 1956

Thank you, dear Ellen, and all the beloved Smiths — and the Canadian allies! — for that blessed note. The balsam brought tears to my

[25] Newspaper editor, biographer of W. T. Sherman and U. S. Grant, and neighbor and close friend of Stevenson's until his death in 1949.

[26] See Hermon D. Smith, "Politics and R & R," in *As We Knew Adlai: The Stevenson Story by Twenty-two Friends*, edited and with preface by Edward P. Doyle, foreword by Adlai E. Stevenson III (New York: Harper & Row, 1966), pp. 28–41.

[27] This handwritten letter is in the possession of Hermon Dunlap Smith.

eyes — perfume I pine for! — and I dreamed a moment of sunset on the wee porch at Point Cottage with the *drinks* — or on the porch at the big cottage with the *children!* Early in the morning I'm *off again — for 2 months* — and the dreams of many many years of blue skies, blue waters & sounds of Desbarats will come back again & again —

Much love —
ADLAI

The Reverend Ralph Nesbitt wrote Stevenson thanking him for attending Sunday service at the Fifth Avenue Presbyterian Church in New York. He said he had made no mention from the pulpit of the candidate's presence because he felt Stevenson had come to church for the purpose of worship.

To the Reverend Ralph B. Nesbitt

September 11, 1956

Dear Mr. Nesbitt:

So many thanks for your very thoughtful letter.

I enjoyed the service immensely and am only sorry that I didn't have an opportunity to see you. I looked for you after the service and unhappily my "managers" spirited me away!

I am grateful to you particularly for not mentioning my presence from the pulpit. I get little enough privacy as it is these days and I certainly did not want any public recognition.

I shall be in New York from time to time and hope very much I shall have an opportunity to worship at your church again.

Very sincerely yours,

To Lady Barbara Jackson

September 11, 1956

Dear Barbara:

This is a very hurried note dictated from the Biltmore Hotel in New York City to tell you that while my schedule is still incomplete I can at least give you this much: I shall be in Washington, D.C., staying at the Sheraton-Park Hotel, from September 14 until the morning of September 22 (to make some forays into Virginia and to do a multitude of things including the schedule) and I leave then for Iowa. I will speak at Newton at a Farm Plowing Contest on September 22. From there I believe I go on to Denver for the night and the following day, September 23. The schedule then is somewhat as follows:

September 24 – Tulsa and Oklahoma City
September 25 – Shreveport and Miami
September 26 – Jacksonville and Tampa — overnight in Kansas City
September 27 – Kansas City and St. Louis
September 28 – Indianapolis and Milwaukee
September 29 – Minneapolis — returning to Washington, D.C. that
            night or the following morning.

This is far as we have progressed.

I don't have at hand (indeed there is nothing but chaos at hand!) your letter about your dates, but if you could get aboard for any part of this it would be wonderful for me, but I warn you that the opportunities for tranquil reflection are precious few in this ghastly ordeal. I wake up night after night and have to think for minutes on end to figure out where I am! But the campaign is going very well and the results in Maine are an indication of the people's appreciation that all is not well in Washington I am told.[28]

Your last contribution is most helpful — indeed the most helpful of all. I yearn to see you.

Affectionately,

To Anna Rosenberg[29]

September 13, 1956

Dear Anna:

Just a quick note before I get any farther away from New York to thank you for your superb management these past few days. I know that Tom [Finletter] would have been delighted, as I was, by the manner which you have taken over the New York Committee and I am particularly grateful to you for your performance at that breakfast in the

---

[28] The Maine election for state and congressional offices was held on September 10, 1956. Democratic Governor Edmund Muskie won reelection with 59.2 per cent of the vote. In congressional races, Democrat Frank Coffin won the Second District (53.4 per cent), and Republican incumbent Robert Hale, with a margin of only about thirty votes, came close to being unseated by Democrat James Oliver in the First District. *Congressional Quarterly Almanac*, Vol. XVII (1957), p. 156.

[29] Cochairman, with Thomas K. Finletter, of the New York Committee for Stevenson, Kefauver and Wagner; formerly a public relations consultant serving in the Roosevelt and Truman administrations and Assistant Secretary of Defense, 1950–1953. This letter was written from Harrisburg, Pennsylvania.

Hotel.[30] Last night, of course, was something I shall not soon forget and once again I marveled at your resourcefulness.

With warmest personal regards, I am

Cordially,

On September 13, 1956, Stevenson delivered the following speech at Harrisburg, Pennsylvania. It was televised to the nation.[31]

I come here tonight to summon you Democrats to the cause of freedom, the cause of human welfare, and the cause of peace.

And I summon all Americans who believe greatly in these things to join with us. We claim no monopoly on the ideals we assert. They are America's ideals. The victory we seek is not just for a party; it is for a people.

But we do claim that this victory will come only to the bold and the brave, to those who are willing to work to make democracy's ideals come true in the lives of every man and woman and child in America — yes, and in the world. This is our Democratic goal. This is the victory we seek in November.

And I am going to fight for it with everything I have!

Why is President Eisenhower the first President in this century to lose control of Congress in his first elected term? I think it is because the fog is rising, the fog of half-truths and amiable complacency — and people perceive that all is not well in Washington and the world.

In the few minutes I have I want to tell you a little about Washington and the world and what is at stake, as I see it, in this 1956 election.

First, our Republican friends have been suggesting in one way or another that there are no real issues between the parties. And they contrive this remarkable transformation by talking — now that it is election year again — like Democrats.

Well, when someone says to me that the two parties' programs are just about the same, I say that so are two checks, signed by different people. The question is which one can be cashed and which one will bounce.

And I say that for 150 years, a check by the Democratic party, written

---

[30] The editors have been unable to locate any information on this breakfast meeting.

[31] The text is from Adlai E. Stevenson, *The New America*, edited by Seymour E. Harris, John Bartlow Martin, and Arthur Schlesinger, Jr. (New York: Harper, 1957), pp. 9–14.

out to the American people, has been worth its face value. We say what we mean. We mean what we say. And the record proves it.

This is 1956 — the fifty-sixth year of the twentieth century. America has spent twenty-eight of these years under Democratic government, twenty-eight years under Republican.

During those Democratic years we abolished child labor, commenced unemployment compensation, old-age and survivors insurance and minimum wages, made collective bargaining work, guaranteed bank deposits, financed homeownership, started public housing, put a floor under farm prices, set up TVA and REA, protected investors through the Securities and Exchange Commission, and consumers through the Federal Trade Commission, and lifted the nation from the rubble of bankruptcy and despair to a great plateau of abundance.

And, most of all, it was under Democratic leadership that this nation met and defeated the greatest threats to individual liberty and national freedom in modern history — from the Kaiser, Hitler, Tojo, and Stalin. And in those Democratic years we pressed toward ultimate peace and security through the League of Nations, the United Nations, the Marshall Plan, NATO, the Point Four Program.

These are only a few of the things we did during our twenty-eight years — not we Democrats; but we Americans under Democratic leadership.

And what did the Republicans do in their twenty-eight years of leadership? Well, there were, to be sure, some accomplishments that must not be dismissed lightly. But they don't even compare with these I have mentioned. And that's why I say that to get things done America will once again turn to Democratic leadership.

Indeed, it is a central issue in this election — whether America wants to stay on dead center, mired in complacency and cynicism; or whether it wants once more now to move forward — to meet our human needs, to make our abundance serve all of us and to make the world safer — in short, to build a New America.

The Republicans pose the issues of this campaign in terms of slogans — "peace, prosperity, progress."

I pose these issues in terms of facts — the grim facts of America's unmet human needs, the facts of a revolutionary world in the hydrogen age.

Here are some facts:

In four years — four years of wealth and abundance — our government has let the shortage of schoolrooms and teachers get worse. It has done almost nothing to stop the slum cancer which today infects 10 million American dwellings. And juvenile delinquency, which breeds in slums and poor schools, has increased at a frightening rate.

We have done nothing to help the lot of the poor and of our older people, most of whom must now subsist in a penury that gets worse as the cost of living climbs to the highest point in our history.

We have done precious little to aid the fight against cancer, arthritis, mental disease and other crippling and killing diseases, or to make up the shortage of doctors and nurses.

We have watched higher costs and lower prices close on the hapless, helpless farmer whose only offense is that he has done his job too well.

And the small businessman is now backed to the wall.

Instead of turning our natural resources — our rivers, lands and forests — to the public good, we have seen them raided for private profit.

And the facts of our progress toward peace are even more sobering. The Soviets have advanced, while we have fallen back, not only in the competition for strength of arms, but even in the education of engineeers and scientists. Millions of people have moved more toward the false promises of Communism than the true faith in freedom. And today there is doubt in the world about whether America really believes in the freedom which is our birthright and the peace which is our greatest hope.

Why has all this happened?

It has happened because for four years now we have had a government which neither fully understands nor wholly sympathizes with our human needs or the revolution that is sweeping the world.

The Republican administration took office on the pledge to make it a businessman's government. Well, that's one pledge they kept. President Eisenhower filled two out of every three top-ranking offices in his administration with men whose lives have been spent representing business, mostly big business.

Then — partly by choice, partly by a necessity we regret — President Eisenhower turned over to these men of limited interests and experience still more of the powers of government.

Where their interests are involved — cutting taxes for the well-to-do, turning our natural resources over to private companies, chipping away at TVA with Mr. Dixon and Mr. Yates[32] — the men in the Cabinet and the White House have been highly effective.

[32] The Eisenhower Administration refused to allow the Tennessee Valley Authority to build a steam plant to supply Memphis with power. Instead the Atomic Energy Commission was authorized to sign a contract with the Dixon-Yates combine. After a Senate investigation revealed a conflict of interest, the contract was canceled.

But where human interests are concerned — the interests of the young and the old, the workman, the farmer and the little fellow — where the need is to wipe out poverty, or to build schools and hospitals, to clear slums, even to distribute the Salk vaccine[33] — there no one leads.

And when all the world read with dismay Mr. Dulles' boasts about how close he had brought us all to atomic war, the President of the United States said that he had not had time to read it!

Now, I respect Mr. Eisenhower's good intentions. I have even been accused of undue moderation toward his administration. And certainly the Democrats in Congress have constantly rescued the Republican President from his own party.

Everyone shares in sympathy for the circumstances which have created a part-time Presidency. But we cannot understand — and we will not accept — turning the government over to men who work full time for the wrong people or a limited group of people.

And the plain truth is that this situation would get worse, not better; because what influence the President has with the Republican leaders in Congress has depended on his running again.

But from here on the future of Republican leaders will depend not on Mr. Eisenhower, but on the Republican heir apparent, Mr. Nixon. And the Vice-President seems to sail downwind no matter which way the wind blows.

These are stern facts. To ignore them is perilous. They are the reasons America's human needs go today unmet. Nor will they be met so long as the President is not master in his own house.

I firmly believe that America does not want to rest on dead center, that it wants — fervently — to move forward again to meet these needs. And I firmly believe that a leadership that will ask Americans to live up to the best that is in them will carry us across the threshold of the New America that now opens before us.

I think America wants to be called on to build the schoolrooms and train the teachers our children so desperately need.

[33] The poliomyelitis vaccine developed by Dr. Jonas Salk had been extensively tested in 1954 and approved for general use in 1955. However, the great demand, coupled with suspension of production for a time following cases of polio traced to the vaccine, had led to a shortage of supply. On August 12, 1955, President Eisenhower signed a bill authorizing the U.S. Public Health Service to spend $30 million to help the states buy vaccine for free distribution. The Public Health Service supervised allocation of the available vaccine until August 11, 1956, when it was decontrolled, allowing manufacturers to sell their product on the open market. However, the National Foundation for Infantile Paralysis declared at the same time that the supply of the vaccine was more than adequate to meet current demand.

I think America wants to be called to clear away the slums and bring basic decency to millions of American families.

I think America wants to attack relentlessly the vast realm of human pain, and lift from those hit by serious accident or illness at least the added burden of grinding debt.

I think America wants to give to the lives of people when they grow old the dignity and meaning they yearn for and deserve.

As I have in the past, I will lay before you, in as full detail as a campaign permits, proposals for meeting our needs. And we will talk soberly about their cost and ways and means of approaching them in a responsible manner.

Most of all we want peace. Whatever we can do here at home will be meaningless unless the world is such that what we do can endure.

When we are spending $40 billion a year for defense, when the peace the Republicans boast about looks more fragile by the moment, when the hydrogen bombs and the guided missiles are multiplying, when Communist influence is spreading among restless millions, when we can lose the cold war without firing a shot, then I say that most of all America is anxious about peace and security.

It is not enough to pile pact on pact, weapons on weapons, and to totter dangerously from crisis to crisis. There must be a call to war against the poverty, the hunger, the nothingness in people's lives that draws them to Communism's false beacon.

We must guide the hopes of mankind away from the blind alleys of extreme nationalism or bogus Communist internationalism. We must turn them instead to an ideal of partnership between the nations in which disputes are settled by conciliation, not violence, and in which the weapons of death are limited and controlled. We Americans have never been and we will never be a nation content just to count today's blessings.

We have confidence in ourselves, confidence that we can build what we have to build, grow as we have to grow, change as we must change, and play our full part in the making of a New America and a better tomorrow for ourselves and all mankind.

Our plan for twentieth-century man is not just for his survival, but for his triumph.

If I were to attempt to put my political philosophy tonight into a single phrase, it would be this: Trust the people. Trust their good sense, their decency, their fortitude, their faith. Trust them with the facts. Trust them with the great decisions. And fix as our guiding star the passion to create a society where people can fulfill their own best selves — where no American is held down by race or color, by worldly condition or social status, from gaining what his character earns him as an American citizen, as a human being and as a child of God.

So I say let us be up and doing, probing ceaselessly for solutions of today's problems and the new ones tomorrow will find on our doorstep. And if you share my view, the Democratic view, that this election is a summons to a sleeping giant, then I hope you will join us to make that summons clear and strong on election day — and help us march forward toward the New America.

To Hale Boggs[34]

September 14, 1956

Dear Hale:

Our main job in this campaign is to carry the truth to the American people — the truth about the fateful issues that face our country and the world and about the inadequacies of the Eisenhower administration.

We must convey to the nation the position of the Democratic Party on these issues, and we must expose the repeated failures of the Eisenhower administration.

In taking our case to the people, we are competing with a Republican Party campaign financed by the largest purse in history.

To tell the Democratic story, and to tell it clearly and directly, we must buy time on radio and television. That time is expensive. To pay for it we shall need the help of every loyal Democrat.

In order to concentrate our fund raising efforts we have designated October 16 as "Dollars for Democrats Day." On that day, throughout the country, we Democrats will conduct the greatest fund raising drive in history.

A national publicity campaign will help in this drive. We are doing our utmost to tell America about "Dollars for Democrats Day" so as to make your job easier.

Next to election day, October 16 will be the most important day in the campaign. I urge you to join with me in setting your state and local plans in motion in order to make "Dollars for Democrats Day" a historic success.

With cordial best wishes,

---

[34] Congressman from Louisiana. The original is in the Boggs papers, National Archives, pending selection of a permanent repository.

To Mrs. Harry Thayer[35]

September 14, 1956

My darling Joan:

Although I have no official news of the baby's arrival, I met a gentleman at a political dinner in New York, whose name I never did get, who told me all about it. Surely we must improve our family communications!

At all events, my congratulations and love. I pray that all goes well. I tried to talk to your mother by telephone, while I was in New York, but found her out of town. Doubtless she was with you. I trust that the father has survived also!

Affectionately,

Francis Biddle, former Attorney General of the United States, wrote on August 23 that after his defeat in 1952, Stevenson had worked to make the Democratic party responsible and had warned the country against drift and complacency. Mr. Biddle added that a short campaign might add to the significance of what Stevenson wanted to say.

To Francis Biddle[36]

September 14, 1956

Dear Francis:

I have finally caught up with your letter. Your perception is perfect. Those *were* the things I started out to do after 1952, but I must add another: money. It turned out that there was a large deficit that had to be paid off and funds provided to keep a reorganized National Committee afloat.

As I think you realized after completing the Congressional campaign of 1954, I had thought to "fade away," something most unusual for politicians. But that I was a politician to begin with was most unusual!

And now I find myself at it again. I wonder sometimes why — obligation or ambition?

I wish it were possible to make a few good speeches instead of a lot of lousy ones. But the pressures for an all out campaign are intolerable and the die is cast — the wrong way — and a lot of lousy ones!

It was good of you to write me. My regards to Mrs. Biddle.

Cordially,

[35] Daughter of Ellen Stevenson's sister, Mrs. Ralph Hines, by her first husband, Robert S. Pirie. A copy is in A.E.S., I.S.H.L. This letter was written from Washington, D.C.
[36] A copy is in A.E.S., I.S.H.L.

The Japanese prime minister sent Stevenson his congratulations on being nominated and added that an outstanding candidate had been selected.

To Ichiro Hatoyama

September 15, 1956

My dear Mr. Prime Minister:

I am deeply touched by your kind note, which has only now caught up with me on my travels. It was good of you to write, and I remember with so much pleasure my delightful visit to your country[37] and the many kindnesses shown me there.

With warm regards, I am

Cordially yours,

Stevenson delivered the following speech at Walnut Hill, Virginia (a part of Petersburg, about twenty miles south of Richmond), on September 15, 1956.[38]

A basic complaint about this administration that you encounter all around the country is that it so largely represents a single interest — the big people, the rich and the powerful.

But I think our government should represent all the people and especially the ordinary people, the man in the street who has no one save his elected officials to represent him. The strong can look after themselves — they have their lobbies and captive spokesmen galore. But the weak have no one.

I say we need an administration which is interested in farmers, not just in surpluses; in the small businessman, not just in abstractions about free enterprise; in a young couple trying to get a house, not just in the rediscount rate. I recall a remark by the Chairman of the Civil Service Commission,[39] who was asked at a Senate hearing whether his commission was furnished any names of persons who are declared security risks, and he replied, "No, we don't have any names. We just deal in numbers."

Well, maybe numbers are enough for the Civil Service Commission, but they are not enough for a people's government. And I say it's time

[37] See *The Papers of Adlai E. Stevenson*, Vol. V, Chap. Two.
[38] The text is from *The New America*, pp. 199–203.
[39] Philip Young.

for this administration to stop dealing in numbers and start thinking about people.

And a good place for it to start is with its own employees.

The United States government ought to be a model employer, fair, considerate, and generous. I know from my own experience as Governor of Illinois that it is not easy to attract good men and women to government, and no wonder. When I became Governor, I found that Civil Service had become no more than a figure of speech, that the employees of the state had been exploited ruthlessly and the public payrolls loaded with political agents.

During my term we took the state police out of politics and put it under a merit system for the first time; we resumed examinations and strengthened the Civil Service in many ways; we extended the career idea to new areas of state government and we lifted salaries all along the line up to levels both of competition and of self-respect. I did everything in my power to improve the morale, the repute and security of state service so that it would be more attractive to good men and women.

And I am sure that the personnel, objectives and standards of our great federal services must be the very highest.

But what has happened in Washington in the last four years?

Although those of us who had worked in our federal government here in Washington were pained, we were not surprised when during the 1952 campaign the Republican leaders damaged callously, if unwittingly, the public reputation of the government service by their crusades against "bureaucracy" and what they like to call "government red tape."

If we winced at the wild Republican charges that the government was full of Communists and spies, we were at least used to it.

But everyone, I think, was surprised when the administration's war of nerves against its own employees continued after it took office. Secretary Weeks,[40] you will recall, called civil servants "Trojan horses left behind to try to hamper, hoodwink, and wreck the new Administration." And Attorney General [Herbert] Brownell struck a more sinister note which we were to hear often when he complained of inheriting "more than our share of odd characters, log rollers and misfits."

Since then the guerrilla warfare on the people who serve the government from our responsible officials has continued.

The administration, it is true, has increased the total number of employees covered by the Civil Service. But at the same time it has removed from Civil Service and in practical effect placed at the disposal

40 Secretary of Commerce Sinclair Weeks.

of the Republican National Committee a large number of career jobs to which employees have advanced through years of outstanding service. Time and again it has forced men out of government employment just a few months short of retirement age. Thus it has penalized precisely the ability, initiative and devotion to duty which it ought to encourage.

Worst of all, perhaps, the administration, for partisan political purposes, has pilloried innocent men and women under the pretense of conducting loyalty and security investigations.

The history of this shameless political trickery goes back, as I say, to the 1952 campaign. You remember they modestly called it a Great Crusade and the orators made so much noise about "Communists in government" that when they got into office they evidently felt obliged to find some, even at the expense of innocent government workers. So they invented and popularized the term "security risk," pretended that all security risks were "subversives," and soon were able to boast — just in time for the 1954 Congressional campaign, of course — that they had cleansed government of security risks by the bushel — or was it half a bushel?[41]

Government workers were summarily suspended without pay on the basis of vague charges of ambiguous offenses, made after inadequate sifting of unevaluated information by untrained personnel officers — and then were forced to defend themselves at great expense before prosecutor-judges without being able to confront their accusers; and often without even knowing the real nature of the charges against them.

But soon a Congressional investigation disclosed that 90 per cent of the persons the administration claimed to have fired as "security risks" were never determined to be "security risks" at all; that others were not even fired but were merely transferred from one agency to another; and that half of those who were fired as security risks had been hired by the Eisenhower administration itself.

And finally the administration admitted, after about three years of such demoralizing harassments, that not a single person was fired for being a Communist.

As the *New York Times* said a couple of months ago, "The Administration deliberately used misleading statistics about the program for political purposes. The political approach has damaged the President's asserted attempt to clear the air of 'unreasoned suspicion.'" And now the Supreme Court has ruled that the Eisenhower administration violated the intent of Congress by its application of the security law.

The abuse of the security policies under this administration during

[41] See Walter Johnson, *1600 Pennsylvania Avenue: Presidents and the People, 1929–1959* (Boston: Little, Brown, 1960), pp. 287–295.

the last four years is a shameful chapter in American history which began in consecration to individual liberty. The lives of decent and devoted government servants lie buried in the wreckage it wrought. The wider consequences are incalculable. Government always needs good men worse than good men need government jobs, and now sorely needed men have deserted a government that played fast and loose with the Bill of Rights, and government has been unable to attract young people with new ideas. Government needs men of imagination and courage, men with fresh ideas and the vigor to fight for them. We don't want to turn our public servants into a collection of weak and spineless conformists.

What shall we do?

Let me say to you that a first objective of a Democratic administration will be to restore dignity and honor and self-esteem to the public service. Those who prefer to serve the commonwealth rather than themselves deserve the respect of their fellow citizens. Under a Democratic administration they will have that respect once again.

We must, of course, vigorously oppose legislation intended to override the court decision — we must hold the line where the Court has fixed it.

We mean to reconstruct the present security system and devise a program which will safeguard the state without degrading those who serve it. Already, I am glad to say, the AEC [Atomic Energy Commission] has begun to move in that direction, and even the Army is talking about it. But it is shocking that the necessary broader reforms in the security system have been so long delayed. Recently the New York City Bar Association proposed broad changes which represent a long step in the right direction. The continued hesitation of the administration about this problem reveals all too clearly both its attitude toward the public service and its reluctance to concede the wrongs it has committed.

The way a government treats its employees, it seems to me, says a lot about that government. A democracy should not treat them as game for partisan advancement or public ridicule, but as upright, decent, conscientious citizens devoted to the high calling, the unending task, of making the government better serve its proprietors, the people.

It is in this spirit that they serve their country; it is in this spirit that the people you elect should serve them.

French writer Marcel Brun wrote Stevenson congratulating him on his nomination and said that the American people owed it to themselves to elect him President.

[225]

To Marcel Brun

September 17, 1956

My dear friend:

Owing to my constant travels, I have only now received your kind and thoughtful note of August 31. I am pleased indeed to know that you are following so closely our contest here, and am deeply moved by the expressions of confidence I receive from so many of your countrymen.

With best wishes, and warm thanks for your encouragement,

Cordially yours,

To Sam Rayburn

September 17, 1956

Dear Sam:

I have neglected to respond to your inquiry about the tidelands.

I shall not rehearse what happened before or the misunderstandings which were evidently current in Texas in 1952, both about the question and about my views.[42] Let me say now, however, that regardless of what I think should have been done and might have been done for the states involved or about the principles involved, since Congress has settled the question by legislation, and the legislation has, I understand, been sustained by the Supreme Court,[43] I have considered the matter closed.

You also asked me for the most recent of my many disavowals of the use of force and violence in connection with desegregation. Speaking in New York last week, September 11, I said in this connection:

"The things that bind us all together as Americans make us want tonight to speak our admiration for those citizens of southern communities and those governors, mayors and local officials who are upholding the rule of law, sometimes even against their own personal feelings, sometimes in the face of violence.* * *

"I stand squarely, beyond this, on the statement in the Democratic platform, adopted unanimously, that 'We reject all proposals

[42] See *The Papers of Adlai E. Stevenson*, Vol. IV, especially pp. 150–158.
[43] The Submerged Lands Act of 1953, which provided for state ownership of the lands, was upheld by the Supreme Court in its decision in *Alabama* v. *Texas* on March 15, 1954.

for the use of force to interfere with the orderly determination of these matters by the courts.' "

I hope that I shall see you soon. Meanwhile my warmest regards.

Cordially,

To Harry S. Truman[44]

September 18, 1956

I SHALL BE IN KANSAS CITY WEDNESDAY NIGHT, SEPTEMBER TWENTY-SIXTH FOR A NINE O'CLOCK RALLY AND HOPE VERY MUCH THAT YOU AND MRS. TRUMAN CAN JOIN ME AT THE HOTEL MUEHLE-BACH ABOUT EIGHT FIFTEEN AND GO ON TO THE MEETING WITH ME. LOOK FORWARD TO SEEING YOU. WARMEST PERSONAL REGARDS.

In addition to sending a campaign contribution, Mrs. Walter Lippmann wrote George Ball of the importance of electing Stevenson President.

To Mrs. Walter Lippmann[45]

September 18, 1956

My dear Helen:

I was touched by the news of your contribution. I am keeping it confidential, but I wanted you to know what a tonic effect it had on the weary candidate.

Bless you! And I pray that I shall not disappoint you — at least not *all* the time. What Walter has been writing of late has helped, encouraged and elevated none more than me.

Yours,

Congressman John W. McCormack sent Stevenson a copy of a letter from James G. Patton, president of the National Farmers Union, praising the 1956 Democratic party platform.

[44] A telegram.
[45] A copy is in A.E.S., I.S.H.L.

To John W. McCormack

September 18, 1956

Dear John:

So many thanks for your note enclosing Mr. Patton's letter. Surely when both Patton and [Senator] Clint Anderson are delighted, you have performed a miracle — a major miracle!

Personally I think it a very good thing that you got the agricultural discussion off the limited level of firm price supports and onto a broader basis of both objective and method. They ought to be pleased, and grateful to you, as I am.

Cordially,

Dr. Albert Schweitzer wrote Stevenson on August 18, 1956, from Africa expressing admiration for his courage in running again for President.

To Dr. Albert Schweitzer

September 18, 1856

My dear Doctor:

I was so glad to have your thoughtful and gracious note, along with a visit from Clara Urquhart.[46] Unhappily the visit was brief and agitated in view of the campaign surroundings in New York.

I think your felicitous phrase "belonging in a way to myself" comes close to identifying what I long for most in this exposed and relentless life. I have a feeling all the time that I am two selves; one the public self, the candidate, and a bit of an imposter; the other my own self, who leads a furtive and underground life and seldom emerges in these days of flash bulbs and trumpets.

I count your letter among my richest possessions. Thank you — and may you live long to elevate and enlighten us all.

Cordially,

To Gerald W. Johnson

September 19, 1956

Dear Gerald:

I agree that the Harrisburg speech was not very heavy. Indeed, I thought the whole thing a frightful failure.

[46] A friend of Dr. Schweitzer's who acted as interpreter when Stevenson visited the doctor in Lambaréné in June, 1957. See *The Papers of Adlai E. Stevenson*, Vol. VII, Part One.

I wish so much you would send me along some textual material some day when the spirit moves you — or even if it doesn't!

Yours,

To Samuel I. Rosenman[47]

September 19, 1956

Dear Sam:

I want to say how grateful I am for your recent letter. One thing about our party is that disagreement over party leadership need not imply disagreement over liberal principle; and I am sure that we are now more united than ever in our common purpose.

So far as I am concerned, there is nothing more important than carrying New York in the fall. I know you will be of inestimable assistance in the campaign. I hope that you will continue to give Averell [Harriman] and Carmine [de Sapio] your best assistance and advice, and that you will let me know from time to time how the campaign looks to you.

Cordially,

To Alex Rose[48]

September 19, 1956

Dear Alex:

In this first moment of tranquillity in weeks I want to write and tell you how deeply grateful I have been over these past months for your ever wise counsel and ever willing assistance. I know of so many occasions — before the Convention and during and since — when I have profited from your thoughtfulness; and I am sure there are as many more which have not come to my notice.

I particularly want to say how much I enjoyed last Tuesday's meeting. So far as I am concerned, the Liberal Party convention is about the best audience in the world. There is no group I would rather address — and I fear that my own enjoyment of the occasion was all too obvious!

I count always on your counsel, and I hope you will continue to let me know how the campaign looks to you.

With warm personal regards, I am

Cordially yours,

[47] A former justice of the New York Supreme Court, adviser and friend to Franklin D. Roosevelt, and author of *Working with Roosevelt* (New York: Harper, 1952).

[48] Head of New York's Liberal party.

To James A. Finnegan[49]

September 19, 1956

I think it would be well if Mrs. Roosevelt and I appeared together on some occasions during the campaign. October 4th at the Harlem rally would be one such occasion, and possibly the last major rally before the election.

And I hope some thought is being given to giving her one of the large nationwide hookups. I am told that her Meet the Press performance was masterful — especially the characterization of Ike as a man whose experience lay in carrying out policies, not in formulating them, and her reminder that Nixon had called Helen Gahagan Douglas a communist, although he knew it was untrue.

To William H. Kittrell[50]

September 20, 1956

Dear Bill:

Carol Evans just handed me your letter, but, unhappily, I have not yet had an opportunity to read it. It is another one of those days with appointments starting at 7 A.M. and lasting all day, but I will settle down with your letter this evening. Many thanks and I'll hope to catch a glimpse of you during the course of the campaign.

I had a good talk with Mr. Sam earlier this week and just had an awfully kind and flattering wire from him.[51]

Cordially,

Eugene Davidson, president of the Washington branch of the National Association for the Advancement of Colored People, wired Stevenson urging him to use his influence to stop the hearings of a subcommittee of the House of Representatives District of Columbia Committee since Congressman James C. Davis, of Georgia, chairman of the subcommittee, was a racist and would attack integration. Stevenson replied by telegram.

---

[49] A copy of this memorandum is in the Stuart Gerry Brown collection, Syracuse University Library.

[50] A Texas Democrat close to Sam Rayburn and Lyndon B. Johnson. See Alfred Steinberg, *Sam Johnson's Boy: A Close-Up of the President from Texas* (New York: Macmillan, 1968).

[51] Mr. Rayburn had wired Stevenson that his statement on the tidelands issue was perfect.

To Eugene Davidson

September 21, 1956

THANK YOU FOR YOUR TELEGRAM. SINCE I DO NOT HOLD ANY PUBLIC OFFICE I AM WITHOUT AUTHORITY OR POWER TO INFLUENCE THE COURSE OF THE CONGRESSIONAL HEARINGS TO WHICH YOU REFER. FROM THE PUBLISHED ACCOUNTS OF THESE HEARINGS, WHICH IS ALL I KNOW ABOUT THEM, I THINK THEY ARE SERVING NO CONSTRUCTIVE PURPOSE.

To Lady Barbara Jackson

September 21, 1956

Dearest Barbara:

I have your cable from some undisclosed source, and I am elated at the prospect of a glimpse of you in St. Louis on the 27th. I shall arrive at 3:45 P.M. at Lambert Field and proceed by motorcade arriving "at the center of St. Louis at 4:00 P.M." Just what happens then I don't know, but the schedule discloses an evening rally at 8:00 P.M. and that I stay overnight at the Park Plaza Hotel. I leave at 10 the following morning for Indianapolis and Milwaukee, thence to Minneapolis on Saturday. What a lark it would be to have you along for any part of this journey, and even thereafter. Just why I have dictated the foregoing when I could enclose the schedule I don't know.

I do hope this reaches you, and I am sending a copy in care of Mrs. Huston Kenyon, 340 E. 72nd St., New York City, in case you touch base there before you go West.

The last contribution was magnificent. I only wish I had time to do something proper with such wonderful material. But I am harrassed beyond description and futile to the point of exasperation.

Much love,

Stevenson delivered the following speech at the National Plowing Matches at Newton, Iowa, on September 22, 1956.[52]

Four years ago at the plowing match at Kasson, Minnesota, both Mr. Eisenhower and I discussed farm policy. I want to take up right where we left off that day four years ago. There were some chickens hatched that day that have been waiting a long time to come home to roost. Here they come!

[52] The text is from *The New America*, pp. 179–185.

I want to start with Candidate Eisenhower's own words at Kasson. Here is what he said:

"And here, and now, and without any ifs or buts, I say to you that I stand behind — and the Republican party stands behind — the price support laws now on the books. This includes the amendment to the Basic Farm Act, passed by votes of both parties in Congress, to continue through 1954 the price supports on basic commodities at 90 per cent of parity.

"And," Candidate Eisenhower continued, "a fair share is not merely 90 per cent of parity — it is full parity."

And Candidate Eisenhower said the same thing many times during that campaign. At Brookings, South Dakota, on October 4, 1952, he said: "The Republican party is pledged to the sustaining of the 90 per cent parity price support and it is pledged even more than that to helping the farmer obtain his full parity, 100 per cent parity, with the guarantee in the price supports of 90."

Those were not idle or casual words. They were careful, calculated words. They were meant to get farm votes. And they did! And on that I am an expert!

Yet the same man who uttered those promises to the farmer four years ago said in Washington three nights ago: "We must never in a spirit of partisan warfare treat the farmer as a kind of political prize to be fought for and captured!"

What happened to those words of four years ago — which could only have been designed to capture the farmer?

First, President Eisenhower installed as Secretary of Agriculture a man who did not believe in price supports.[53] Then Secretary Benson put in charge of that program a man who, only a few months before, had condemned price supports as "modern socialism."[54] A committee loaded with bankers, manufacturers and processors then went to work to see what should be done, or how little could be done. They paid no attention to Candidate Eisenhower's promises. Also, they paid no attention to the farmers.

[53] In a speech to the Central Livestock Association in St. Paul, Minnesota, on February 11, 1953, Secretary Ezra Taft Benson advocated a "free market" economy and said that price supports were intended to "provide insurance against disaster" and not to "encourage uneconomic production" which would result in unmanageable surpluses. In 1956, the Republican party's position was that the farm problem could be solved chiefly through more efficient farm operations and expansion of markets. The Republicans also advocated a sliding scale of price supports rather than high, rigid supports, which they viewed as a "built-in mechanism for the accumulation of price-depressing surpluses."

[54] The editors have been unable to identify the official to whom Stevenson refers.

I am not going to attack President Eisenhower's motives. I am sure they are good and sincere. I am even willing to believe that he did not fully understand what he was saying to America's farmers in 1952. He had been in the Army and living in New York and Europe at that time.

But the President of the United States must be a responsible man. Secretary Benson was the hired man, and if a farm is mismanaged the farmer is responsible, not the hired man. We know that. And so should the President.

On that day at Kasson, when Candidate Eisenhower talked about 100 per cent parity, prices actually were above 100 per cent. Today the parity index is 82 — down 18 points. Then corn was 97 per cent of parity; it now is 82 per cent — down 15 points. Wheat was then 83 per cent of parity; it is now 79 — down 4 points. Cotton was 110 per cent; it is now 87 — down 23 points. Rice was 96 per cent; it is now 77 per cent — down 19 points.

President Eisenhower has said that he will run on his record. This is his record on price supports.

But there is one success in the record. Four years ago peanuts were 82 per cent of parity; now they have gone up to 88 per cent. This administration has a fine record on peanuts! It almost made me wonder if General Motors has gone into the peanut-oil business!

And something else has gone *down* — the price of hogs!

To sum up, your prices are down, your over-all costs are as high as ever, and your credit is tighter.

Two or three weeks ago at Sioux City, a farmer said it better than I can. "Governor," he said, "I'm a dairy farmer and I know how to milk cows. But those Republicans are smarter than I am. They know how to milk farmers."

I told him they were even smarter than that — only Republicans could keep the stock market up and the farm market down at the same time. They did it the last time they were in office with Hoover at the helm and they're doing it again now.

This talk about the Republicans not treating the farmer as a political prize reminds me of the delegation of Republican congressmen who asked the administration for a floor under hogs at $15.50 a hundred-weight last January when they were selling for about $11. And a high official said: "Gentlemen, do you want higher prices now or next November?"

Why November? Well, the election is in November, of course. Do the Republican politicians want higher prices in January or at election time?

That summarized pretty well, I thought, their attitude toward the farmer. First they say nothing can be done for the farmer but cut prices and reduce production — and also reduce farmers. Then, with an election approaching, they advance the soil bank proposal which they had rejected only a few months before. They fix the support prices at the higher levels they have long denounced, and they even offer $1.25 a bushel for unlimited corn production while hollering about "Democratic surpluses."

Now, after what happened at Kasson four years ago, I don't suppose we should be surprised about such brazen political expediency. But I must object when the President at the same time says from aloft — "we must never treat the farmer as a political prize."

But let's talk about the future, not the past. Let's talk about what lies ahead.

This year we have the best farm plank in our Democratic platform that any party ever had. It is a plank designed to establish not merely price parity but income parity — a fair share of the national income for farmers. It spells out ways and means. It is one that farmers can understand.

— We propose to support basic commodities at 90 per cent of parity.

— We propose to extend protection to perishables through a combination of direct production payments, marketing agreements, and production adjustments. In this connection I would like to try production payments to encourage earlier marketing of hogs in the years when the runs are heavy. This may be a good way to help end the anxiety and the anguish of violent price movements. We must have learned that it takes more than words and stopgap purchasing programs to end these periods of bankrupt prices our livestock producers suffer so often.

— We will administer vigorously the soil bank, a good Democratic idea. Most people think the Republicans adopted it when they had to do something with an election coming on. But it used to be called soil conservation, and I've wondered if it wasn't that word "bank" that made the Republicans like it better. And I would urge consideration of what could be called a "legume bank" to change the emphasis from reducing cash-crop production to increasing acreage of soil-building crops.

Senator Kefauver and I have many times talked about a broad program with a variety of methods to balance production and income; we are for them now; and we will be for them next January.

The first step is to stop and reverse the decline in farm prices.

But that is not enough.

We must go on to assure ample credit at fair rates to the farmer who has to borrow money.

We must protect REA co-ops by safeguarding the preference clause, and by assuring them adequate funds for transmission, generation and distribution.

We must preserve the greatest asset we have inherited — the soil. I feel very strongly about this because I have seen the frightful desolation of once-fertile areas from erosion, overgrazing, deforestation and over-use in many regions of the world. We must strengthen the Conservation Program and the Soil Conservation Service, restore the role of leadership to the conservation districts; we must restore the administration of agricultural programs to farmers, and take emergency measures when needed to prevent another Dust Bowl.

And finally we must go to the root of the cause of farm distress today — the inability of people both at home and in foreign lands to buy the food that they need and that you can raise. In 1932, you remember, our grocery stores were bulging with food. Yet people were hungry. Today our warehouses are bursting, yet half the world goes to bed hungry. And in our own country, many people on social security and on public assistance don't have enough to eat. We speak of a surplus of milk — but the children who need milk are not all in Calcutta — there are plenty of them in Chicago, too.

Abundance is not a blight, but a blessing. At home, we can vastly expand our school-lunch program. Did you know that less than one-third of all school-age children participate in this program? And we can launch a new program that will put food into the mouths of the many who need it.

Abroad there is much we can do with food and fiber to the advantage of mankind and the USA. We can encourage voluntary relief agencies to distribute surplus foods, and we can create a world food bank and materials reserve to help the people of other nations. The recent agreement to furnish agricultural products to India[55] seemed to me like a step in the right direction — and I am glad the administration is moving at last.

Today we are confronted not with a breakdown of our agriculture, but with a breakdown of our imagination and leadership. What we need today is the concern and determination that wrought the agricultural revolution of the 1930's.

So much for our program. This is what I propose at Newton in 1956; this is what we will do in Washington. I am not ashamed of what I said

[55] The United States and India signed a $360 million food loan aid agreement, including wheat, rice, cotton, tobacco and dairy products, that was designed to protect India from future famine. See C. L. Sulzberger, "A Sensible Arrangement — Aid to India," New York *Times*, August 27, 1956.

at Kasson four years ago; and I will not be ashamed of what I have said at Newton today.

There is something more we can do right now, and I have done it time and again and will do it every chance I get. I mean explaining the farmer's problems to the rest of the country. And this, I think, is one of the farmer's greatest needs. Politicians tell him all too often what he wants to hear about his troubles and their remedy, but all too seldom are his troubles explained to other people — the city people.

As I have traveled around this nation, I have been deeply disturbed by the lack of understanding of the farmer's problems. The farmer's story needs telling because too many people think of farmers as selfish malcontents forever demanding handouts from the sore-pressed tax-payers.

This feeling has been aggravated by the administration's setting city against country and country against city.

For four years the administration has dinned it into the ears of city people that their high living costs are the result of high rigid farm support prices. For four years now our government has accepted the proposition that the farmer is getting too much. In fact, last year one of Mr. Benson's personal assistants said that the years of Democratic prosperity on the farm were — and I quote him — "a dream world, and no one expected it to last."

I think it's time somebody told the rest of the country the truth about farming. I think we should talk *for* the farmer as well as *to* the farmer!

I want to tell the housewife that it isn't the farmer who is getting the high prices she has to pay. She ought to know that, while her market basket has been costing more and more, your share of the food dollar has fallen from 47 cents in 1952 to 38 cents in 1956.

I don't need now to tell the man who works in the farm equipment factory — or used to, before it shut down — that without a decent farm program, his job is gone.

The man with the hardware store on Main Street knows that when the farmer can't buy a new stove for his wife, his store is in trouble. But I want to say to the businessman who distributes stoves and shoes and wallpaper, and the manufacturer in a distant city who makes them, that the same thing applies to him. Every American has a stake in farm prosperity.

I want to say to the American people that the farmer just isn't getting a fair share of our national prosperity.

Many people don't fully understand the uncertainties of farming and the necessity for price stability. They never stop to think that a farmer doesn't know what price he will get when he plants a crop, or when he harvests it, or even when he loads it on a truck and takes it to town.

General Motors has built-in price supports. Suppose General Motors' production depended on the weather; suppose it has to sell all its automobiles in three weeks; suppose it didn't have the capital to hold its products off the market. It would need protection too — and from this present administration it would get it!

There are many other facts lots more people should know about agriculture. They should know that for every $4 a farmer got in 1952 he now receives less than $3. They should be told that asking farmers to accept less than a fair parity price is like asking wage earners to accept less than a fair minimum wage. They need to know what a tight money policy really means to farmers — that when dollars are scarce, they always leave the small town first.

Our people need to understand that farmers, because of their isolation and other disadvantages, have lagged behind American standards for schools, medical care, libraries, and many other things. They need to know that the per capita income of farmers has never caught up with that of city people — a quarter of all farm families have to get by on cash income of less than $1,000 a year. The ramshackle tenant house on wornout land is a disgrace in the richest country on earth, just as is the city slum, and the time has come for an all-out attack on farm poverty.

Finally, there is another thing that our people need to be told about farming, perhaps the most important thing of all. They hear about farming as a lot of cold facts and figures about prices and surpluses. They don't realize that farming isn't just a job, it is the way many Americans live, and that the family farm is the backbone of American agriculture, as it was once the backbone of American society.

They don't realize that on a family farm the most precious thing that's raised is not corn or cattle, but children — children who go to rural schools and rural churches and who will inherit the earth they live on and work in. People don't realize that when the family farm is in trouble, more, much more, than dollars and cents is involved. What is involved is the whole fabric of American rural life.

The real tragedy of a farm depression like this one is the human tragedy of young people forced off the farm, of cherished belongings up for sale, of human heartbreak, of the end of a family's chosen way of life. It is the tragedy of mounting debts, of ill-clad children, of men and women searching the skies for rains that never come, of black dust clouds in the western sky. And all this is an American tragedy that we who travel the backroads can see too plainly.

[237]

It is high time our growing urban population understood the economics and the realities of the farmer's situation. And I'm not sure a government as preoccupied with big business as this one can tell it, or will tell it, or can even understand it. I have tried to tell it because I think it is important that Americans understand one another; and I think that is the very special responsibility of candidates for public office, especially the only office elected by all the people of our blessed land.

Let's present a true picture of America to the world: the picture of these peaceful fields; the picture of the love of peace in the schools and churches of this tranquil, friendly land; the picture of the desire of all Americans to live in harmony with every neighbor. And let's do more; let's use the resources that we have to build the true conditions of peace. In doing that, nothing we have is more important than the great abundance of the peaceful, productive fields of Iowa and of the great heartland of America.

Our God-given abundance is a strong weapon in our hands for spreading democracy and freedom at home and abroad. You who open the soil to the seed know the urge to abundance in nature's vast resources. Let us work together to spread its benefits, to build a higher and more meaningful standard of living for the generations which will follow us on this good land.

The following letter to the governor of Oklahoma was dictated on an airplane between speaking engagements.

To Raymond Gary

September 25, 1956

Dear Ray:

Just a quick note before arriving in New Orleans to thank you again for taking such good care of me yesterday. I was enormously pleased and encouraged by everything that happened and I know from experience how hard all of you must have worked. I am grateful to you beyond words, not only for your help and encouragement, but also for the infinite courtesies which you and your staff extended to me and my associates. I only hope that I didn't impose on all of you too monstrously.

With warmest good wishes to you and Mrs. Gary, I am

Cordially,

Stevenson's home in Libertyville, facing the Des Plaines River.

Stevenson declares his candidacy for the Democratic nomination
at a press conference, November, 1955. Press secretary Roger Tubby is at right.

Stevenson greets the 1956 Democratic Convention after his nomination.
At right: John Fell, Mr. Ernest L. Ives, and former President Harry S Truman.
Behind Stevenson are Nancy and Adlai III.

With vice presidential nominee Senator Estes Kefauver.

Stevenson chats with reporters during a campaign stop.
George Herman is at his right.

Left to right: Adlai III, Nancy, the candidate, Buffie Ives, John Fell,
and Ernest L. Ives. Taken at Libertyville in the summer of 1956.

On the campaign train in Michigan, 1956. Mrs. Ives is at right.

Campaign speech in Toledo, Ohio.

California motorcade.

On the campaign train in Pennsylvania.
Governor George Leader is on Stevenson's left.

Francis Pickens Miller, a longtime opponent of Senator Harry Byrd's Virginia political machine, had raised the question whether his active support would embarrass Stevenson.

To Francis Pickens Miller

September 26, 1956

Dear Francis:

Ernest Ives has just told me about your recent conversation. While I don't purport to be intimately acquainted with the political situation in Virginia, I want you to know that I would have no hesitation whatsoever about any personal steps you might take on my behalf. I can hardly believe that past political conflicts between you and others would chill the latter's ardor at this stage. And the ardor appears considerable from my superficial observation.

I just wanted you to have my personal views and to know how grateful I am for your continual help, encouragement and confidence. Any way you wish to manifest it is all right with me and will only increase my gratitude.

Cordially,

P.S. I hear that Helen[56] is at work and I am delighted.

Stevenson delivered the following speech in St. Louis, Missouri, on September 27, 1956.[57]

I've made so many speeches in the last few days that I marvel that I have anything more to say. But I have! And the text of my lecture tonight is "bread and circuses." You remember how the Romans in their declining years tried to keep the uneasy populace satisfied and their minds off their troubles with food and games, gladitorial combats and spectacles.

Well, I thought of bread and circuses not long ago when I read about the great Republican bandwagons that were going out all over the country, complete with movies, jeeps, girls and gadgets of all kinds — to sell Eisenhower and Nixon again to a docile, complacent, carefree people all happily chanting, "Peace, Prosperity and Progress — ain't it wonderful!"

The whole aim of all this ballyhoo and 30-foot balloons, those

56 Mrs. Miller.
57 The text is from *The New America*, pp. 218–224.

streamers and bands, is not to excite thought or provoke discussion. It is, in the finest advertising tradition, to get at our electoral subconscious and persuade us to vote, blissfully and blindly, for things as they are.

"Politics," as the organizer of the Republican Convention put it, "is moving closer to show business."[58] It certainly is, as they present it — balloons, not arguments; the chorus line, not the political issue. Don't think, just feel — feel it's all fine and the product is splendid. Pour out the money. Forget that mushroom cloud! Don't mention Suez. The world stops at the waterfront. And whatever the gales of change and upheaval and revolution roaring around the world, take it from us that this is no time for a change. Just vote Republican and take it easy!

How remote this all seems from the classic symbol of American political maturity — the Lincoln-Douglas debates, where, before rapt crowds, the two men hammered out, with all the rational conviction and controversial skill they possessed, the real issues facing a nation in crisis.

Well, bread and circuses didn't save Rome, and it won't save the Republicans either!

With each passing day it is more apparent that people understand what's going on better and better, and banners can't obscure realities much longer, nor slogans hide the truth. And that's why we will win in November!

Yet, of course, all this is in the Republican tradition. In the long decades of Republican dominance before the First World War, social problems at home and problems abroad grew steadily more dire while the Republican party careened along on slogans of "peace and prosperity" and "the American way of Life."

The chance of being "the party of the future" was thrown out with Teddy Roosevelt. It was the Democrats — Woodrow Wilson — who began, with the policies of the New Freedom, to bring America up to date and get the arthritis out of its political joints. But Republican arthritis is not cured so easily. The twenties saw another decade of "peace and prosperity" and "chickens in every pot," and once again it was the Democratic party, under Franklin Roosevelt, who had to bring the nation back into the broad currents of human progress after its twelve years of Republican boom and bust.

Today, in spite of the President's attempt to paint the Republicans as a young party, bursting out all over with new ideas, the pattern is not much different.

Where are the fresh, new ideas and new policies? The achievements

[58] The editors have been unable to discover the source of this quotation.

to which President Eisenhower points with such pride in the past and such hope for the future consist mostly of not repealing what the Democrats have done. The innovations were Democratic ideas, molded by a Democratic Congress, and involving the federal action which, on other occasions, the Republicans always denounce as Big Government, creeping socialism, and bureaucracy — statism, and sometimes worse!

As for the specifically Republican ideas — tax reductions which favor the well-to-do, the "partnership" approach to power projects in which the private partner gets the profits and the public foots the bill, collapsible price supports, backing away at conservation. REA and TVA — these are hardly new ideas. They are as old as the Republican party and represent its lasting principle — to help those who can also help themselves.

Yet there never was a time when new ideas were more needed. In the past, the outside world was remote, safely removed from us across the oceans. Our own society was more loosely knit, and change in one part did not affect all other sections with the same speed.

In days when we were a self-sufficient distant land surrounded by seas, the periods during which the Republicans sat still on top and everything stirred underneath could last perhaps rather longer and with less devastating effect.

But the great caldron of the world is now seething to the boil, while our Republican friends say all is well and don't bother even to look at the stove.

I say we must look at the facts — they've got to be faced. We must not let them become stale even before they have become real.

The competition the Soviets offer is not simply for today and tomorrow. We must reckon on it for decades.

Today, with only one-fifth of the Communist Bloc's population, the American economy is producing almost twice as much in such key products as steel, petroleum and electricity.

But we have to look ahead. The Soviet planners intend to pull level with America by 1965 and ahead by 1970. During that period China is to build up a steel industry comparable to that of Western Europe and probably much greater than that of its chief Asian rival, India.

We must face squarely and responsibly the prospect that twenty years from now, if present rates of development continue, the balance of productive power may well have swung away from the side of freedom.

The Communists reckon that this growth will have all the more effect on the uncommitted peoples in Asia, the Middle East, in Africa and even Latin America. They are people who detest the memory of European colonial control. They sense a rising nationalist fervor and ambition. They have envious eyes for Western wealth. With these powerful emotional forces working on their side, the Communists reckon that their resources in capital and arms can be far more effectively deployed than those of the West.

Now, none of these risks will appear in Republican electoral speeches. Or, if they do, they will be dismissed as defeatism, as lack of faith in America, its way of life, but there are solid reasons for looking our dangers straight in the face, clear of cant and slogans and streamers and balloons and ballyhoo.

Complacency is not only dangerous, it is worse. It is unworthy of a great people, above all of a people as committed as we are to the pioneering of new opportunities and the dreaming of new dreams.

The breath-taking fact about America today is that for the first time in history we have the material instruments for accomplishing virtually any goal we set ourselves. Raw materials, managerial genius, skilled labor — all these means are lavishly at America's disposal. We have begun to master the techniques of keeping our great economic machine in high gear. We are learning to even out its earlier tendency to swing from bust to boom and back.

Here, in this gloriously endowed Republic, the only limitations are those we impose upon ourselves by lack of thought or lack of generosity or lack of vision.

In the last four years, a number of essential needs, particularly in defense, have been cut back on the grounds that [they?] were more than the country could afford. Budget cutting took priority over security. Foreign aid was cut — again for budgetary considerations.

The question that has not been asked is whether the economy is expanding speedily enough to meet essential demands.

We need to know whether the projected capital expansion in the basic industries is great enough to take care not of the program we can "afford," but of the program we actually need. Of this kind of forethought we have seen no trace these last few years.

But failures of compassion and generosity are much graver than failures in forethought, for here we reach the soul and spirit of our community, the emotions that can save us from brash materialism, the feelings that redeem wealth and power by getting them to serve the humblest human needs. It could be tragic if the prosperity of some were to close their hearts to the needs of others who, even today, do not share in the general growth of wealth.

And in spite of all the Republican "pointing with pride," the sloganizing and the smug self-satisfaction, there are millions of Americans who live in privation, on budgets that barely feed them, in houses that are dirty and dangerous, in congested slums that cut out the living daylight, in debt for furniture, in debt for the doctor, in debt for any emergency that may strike. We cannot say today that their poverty is inevitable and unavoidable.

To leave people in misery in America today is a matter of policy, not of destiny.

Above all, Republican complacency blinds America to its historic vision of the broader, better life for all that our new instruments of wealth make possible. Once the mass of mankind has bread, we can really begin to learn that man does not live by bread alone. We in America are the first human community to reach this new threshold. Now that physical security has been so very largely achieved, we are reaching out for more spiritual values, for better quality in our living, for a higher purpose and a richer life.

We meet new needs as soon as we seek to open this new door.

There is the need for a greatly expanded program of education — to train mind and spirit for its wider environment and for the longer leisure which technological advance brings with it.

There is the need for better environment — homes where children can grow up in health and happiness, gardens and parks where they can play away from gang warfare in the streets, towns rebuilt and decentralized.

When new Democratic plans for better education, for improving the urban environment, for helping the millions of substandard families, are advocated, the Republicans set up a double roadblock; they protest that this means increased taxation and increased government intervention.

But this is only the obstruction of narrow vision. The way to meet new needs is to expand the economy fast enough to meet them. We've got to do this anyway, to have jobs available for the one million new members each year of our labor force. If we can secure a steady increase in our national product, there will be funds available from this increased revenue to build the schools we need and to meet these other needs.

And the Old Guard Republicans aren't really opposed to intervention by government, but only to intervention by government in the support of the general welfare.

Mr. [Herbert] Hoover may get up at the Republican Convention and talk of saving the country from the Democratic policy of "legalized socialism — twin sister of Communism." Yet there is no single greater prop to American industry than the government-imposed tariff system. And no Republican calls that "legalized socialism."

The magazines and newspapers which denounce government intervention most lustily are all subsidized by the U.S. Post Office — but that is not, it seems, "legalized" or even "creeping socialism."

Nor do airlines, for example, complain of the assistance they get as mail carriers.

The private power companies — surely among the most active critics of governmental activity — have no objection to the billions of dollars' worth of government investment available free to the private builders of atomic power plants. Nor has any private company blushingly returned its tax write-offs for accelerated plant construction on the grounds that it is robbing the citizens of their tax money.

Government intervention is not government intervention so far as the Republicans are concerned when it is in aid of industry, particularly large-scale industry. In short, "giveaway" programs are sound government, assuming the right people are the beneficiaries.

The Republicans' real distaste in the past has been reserved for "giveaway" programs directed to those who really need them — social security, federal assistance for health and education, a fair share of the national income for farmers, minimum wage legislation — this is all part of the "legalized socialism" which for twenty years the Republicans denounced as a threat to the American way of life. These are the measures they will attack again when Democrats propose new advances in educational, medical and housing standards and new horizons for the life of the nation as a whole.

To make an ogre of government, to denounce its faithful officials as half-wits or traitors, to keep up the traditional Republican tirade against a mythical evil known as "Democratic socialism" weakens our whole American system and undermines the essential instrument in the partnership of all our people for wealth and growth and progress — which is the federal government.

By our long history as a party we Democrats have shown that ideals and vision and the forward march are the center of our inspiration.

We have not, before the work starts, stultified and undermined the essential federal instrument we need for some forms of further progress.

I believe with all my heart that, under democracy, this country is going forward to an uplifting of all its citizens, not just in terms of new goods and gadgets, but even more in terms of a broadening and deepening of the mind and heart of the nation.

This uplifting will not come if we wait for the good things of life to trickle down to the people from the top of the financial pyramid. It will come only as we work to assure a fair distribution, not only of the nation's wealth and production, but of the nation's opportunities.

It will come as we start measuring prosperity, not just in terms of cars and television sets, but even more in terms of the greater goods of education, health, security and peace of mind.

When we talk about ending poverty, when we undertake to extend the education, improve the environment and raise the dignity of all American citizens, we are promising to finish business we have ourselves begun.

And when we say that we will apply forethought, compassion and vision to foreign policy, we are only promising to recapture the leadership and imagination of the world which is America's historic tradition.

When, in short, we claim to be the party of tomorrow, we are only claiming to be what we have always been — pioneers of America's forward march, architects who build the future from the blueprint of America's hopes and her ideals.

To Dorothy Schiff[59]

September 28, 1956

Dear Dolly:

I have been moving so rapidly that this is the first opportunity I have had to write to you since I saw you last in New York to thank you again for the support and encouragement I have received for so long from the Post.

I think you know how much the Post's editorial support in 1952 meant to me and, in addition, I owe your readers a vast debt of gratitude for their generous encouragement that year. The Democratic Party must, of necessity, depend on thousands of small contributors for the financing of its campaign and your recent editorial announcing that the Post readers will be given an opportunity to contribute to Estes' and my campaign means that our party will be able to take its story to many more people than would otherwise have been the case. I hope you will express to your readers my profound thanks and my earnest hope that I can continue to merit their support and good wishes.

Cordially yours,

On September 29, Stevenson delivered the following speech in Minneapolis, Minnesota.[60]

---

[59] Publisher of the New York *Post*.

[60] The text is based on the transcript of the speech published in the St. Louis *Post-Dispatch*, September 30, 1956. Typographical errors have been corrected by the editors.

Minnesota is the great over-arching bridge between the old Midwest and the new Northwest, where people breathe freer and look higher and somehow the blood is quickened in the clean north air, where men are not afraid to speak their minds or vote their deep convictions. Up here in Minnesota men are never satisfied that things can't be better than they are.

Minnesota has always led the great tradition of protest in the Upper Midwest — the protest against things that could be better.

In recent years across your eastern border the heirs of the Wisconsin Progressives have found a home in the Democratic party; today to the west in North Dakota the nonpartisan league is moving in with us too.

Here in Minnesota the heirs of that same great tradition have fused their strength in the Democratic-Farmer-Labor party.

And two men who have helped to write the Democratic-Farmer-Labor story are its great leaders today — Hubert Humphrey and Orville Freeman.

These men — and the national leaders of the Democratic party down the years — had several things in common. They were not afraid of new ideas. They were not content to leave well enough alone. They had a passion for human life — they cared and they cared deeply about people. And they tackled the people's problems with an enthusiasm that was boundless and unbeatable.

I want to talk to you tonight about the need for enthusiasm and new ideas in our national life.

Of course today the Republicans would have us feel all the problems are solved, that what we need is not enthusiasm and new ideas but caution, complacency and a passion not for the people but for things as they are.

Well, here is how things are for some of our people unfortunately.

Farmers and their wives and children are being forced to pack up and leave the farm — a good farm — and uproot their whole lives.

Men are being forced to sell the store on Main Street that for years has provided for their family and served their community well.

Too many of our older citizens are spending what ought to be the golden years in want and neglect.

Too many children are going to school in crowded ramshackle buildings with teachers that are only half-trained.

Millions of sick people can't afford to call a doctor.

Hundreds of thousands of our mental patients are consigned to disgraceful medieval institutions.

One family out of five must get by on less than $2,000 in times like these.

Millions of American citizens are still barred from schools and jobs and an equal chance merely because of their color.

In the city slums children are roaming the alleys behind the tenement buildings, and in some parts of the country poverty is converting farmland into a rural slum.

I say this is not right. And I say that only the Democratic party has the passion for human justice, the enthusiasm and determination and the new ideas, to drive want and suffering from all American homes, not just some of them.

But beyond this lies another goal — the goal of peace, and I want to say something about that tonight.

Like most Americans, I've read some of what that wise New England philosopher, Ralph Waldo Emerson, wrote. I fear I've forgotten a lot of what he said, but I've remembered this: "Nothing great," Emerson said, "was ever achieved without enthusiasm." How true that is! As we look back over the centuries, we can see that nearly all the glorious achievements of mankind, nearly all the best things that characterize our society, sprang from the uncrushable enthusiasm of those who believed in the genius of man, and who believed in the possibility of doing the seemingly impossible. To these enthusiasts, whose optimism often exposed them to scorn and ridicule, we chiefly owe all the good things of our civilization.

This thought of Emerson's — this tribute to the power of man's ability to master his destiny — came to me again only recently when I heard the President's recent expression of views on war and peace — the area above all others where we need fresh and positive thinking.

I was distressed to see that the President not only had nothing new to suggest for the future but he seemed resentful over the efforts of others — including myself — to find some new and more hopeful answers to the problems of life and death that now confront us.

To be more specific, I have said before and I'll say it again that I, for one, am not content to accept the idea that there can be no end to compulsory military service. While I, like most others who have had intimate experience with our armed forces in war and peace, have felt that it was and is necessary, at the same time I have felt, and many others likewise, that the draft is a wasteful, inefficient, and often unfair way of maintaining our armed forces, and now it is fast becoming an obsolete way.

Let me make it perfectly clear that as long as danger confronts us, I believe we should have stronger, not weaker, defenses than we have now. Ever since Mr. Eisenhower became President we Democrats have fought hard to prevent the Administration from putting dollars ahead of defense. The Democrats in Congress forced the Administration to reverse itself and restore deep cuts in the strategic air force even during this last session of Congress.

But my point is that the draft does not necessarily mean a strong defense. Conditions change, and no conditions have changed more in our time than the conditions of warfare. Nothing is more hazardous in military policy than rigid adherence to obsolete ideas. France learned this in 1939; she crouched behind the Maginot line, which was designed for an earlier war, and German Panzers overran France. The Maginot line gave France a false — and fatal — sense of security. We must not let Selective Service become our Maginot line.

What I am suggesting is that we ought to take a fresh and open-minded look at the weapons revolution and the whole problem of recruiting and training military manpower. We may very well find that in the not far distant future we can abolish the draft and at the same time have a stronger defense and at lower cost. Defense is now so complex, its demand for highly skilled and specialized manpower so great, that the old-fashioned conscript army, in which many men serve short terms of duty, is becoming less and less suited to the needs of modern arms. And it is becoming more and more expensive.

Let me say right here in all frankness that I have no special pride, no conceit, in the suggestions that I have tried to advance. No one will be happier than I if others find better solutions.

Once we start exploring this possibility seriously many new ideas will be forthcoming; that is always the case when men turn their creative energies full time upon a problem. Right now I had hoped to do no more than get this kind of creative thinking started.

I am distressed that President Eisenhower should dismiss this objective out of hand. If anyone had proposed the abolition of the draft right now, today, the President's attitude would be understandable; indeed, I would share it. But I don't see how we can ever get anywhere against the rigid, negative position that we cannot even discuss the matter, or even look forward to a time when we can do away with compulsory military service. I say it's time we stopped frowning and started thinking about them!

I am even more distressed that this attitude on the part of Mr. Eisenhower carries over into the all-important problem of controlling the hydrogen bomb, for here we are talking about the actual survival of the human race itself. The testing alone of these super bombs is considered by scientists to be dangerous to man; they speak of the danger of poisoning the atmosphere; they tell us that radioactive fallout may do genetic damage with effects on unborn children which they are unable to estimate.

I think almost everyone will agree that some measure of universal disarmament — some means of taming the nuclear weapons — is the first order of business in the world today.

It is not enough to say, well, we have tried and failed to reach agreement with the Russians. It is not enough to throw up our hands and say it's no use to try this or that new approach. This is one time we cannot take no for an answer, for life itself depends on our ultimately finding the right yes.

Again, I have no foolish pride in my own ideas on this subject. But there must be a beginning, a starting point, a way to get off the dead center of disagreement. I have proposed a moratorium on the testing of more super H-bombs. If the Russians don't go along, well then at least the world will know we tried. And we will know if they don't because we can detect H-bomb explosions without inspection.

It may be that others will come forward with other ideas; indeed, I hope they do. But I say to you that in this field, as in many others, fresh and open-minded thinking is needed as never before — and in this field we may not have unlimited time to get the answers. We'd better start thinking now!

Furthermore I do not see how we can ever hope to get the answers if fresh ideas, new proposals, new solutions, are not encouraged. I was shocked when Mr. Eisenhower the other night brushed off my suggestion as a theatrical gesture. I don't believe this was worthy of the President of the United States. I have never questioned his sincerity on a matter that I am sure means more to both of us than anything else in the world — the matter of permanent peace — and I do not think he should have questioned mine.

All decent men and women everywhere hate war. We don't want our boys to be drafted. And we don't want to live forever in the shadow of a radioactive mushroom cloud. And when I say "we," I mean Democrats and Republicans alike — I mean mankind everywhere.

Peace is not a partisan issue. Every American, Democrats and Republicans alike, wants peace. There is no war party in this country; there is no peace party.

And the way to get started on the difficult road to disarmament and peace is not, I repeat, to scorn new ideas.

Just because this Administration has not been able to make any progress toward safe disarmament or even toward controlling H-bomb development, does not mean that such agreements are forever impossible. No matter which party wins in November, another supreme effort must be undertaken, and, if that fails, then another and another, for leaders must lead, and the conquest of this scourge is a more imperative goal of mankind than the conquest of the black plague in the Middle Ages.

I shall continue to concentrate my own attention on this problem, and I shall also do everything I can to encourage others to do likewise, for, as I have said, I know in my heart that Emerson was right when he said that "nothing great was ever achieved without enthusiasm."

And we saw it proved in our own time. For many years, you will recall, the world had dreamed of splitting the atom and releasing its boundless energy.

But most men despaired of ever making this dream come true. Had it not been for Franklin D. Roosevelt and his determination, the so-called impossible might still seem impossible. Then, as now, there were the skeptics, the defeatists, the non-enthusiasts who thought Roosevelt was off on a wild goose chase, who dubbed Oak Ridge his billion dollar folly. But he was not deterred. He would not take no for an answer. Nuclear energy was finally placed at the disposal of man, and if we, who survived Franklin Roosevelt, show the will to control this energy that he showed in creating it, then it still may prove to be one of the greatest blessings of all time.

Franklin Roosevelt was not a physicist. He knew nothing about the hidden secrets of uranium. But he had to a supreme degree the first attributes of political leadership — that is, he had the enthusiastic will to act, and the genius for organizing great undertakings.

I, too, know little or nothing about the mechanics of the H-bomb. But I do know this: If man is capable of creating it, he also is capable of taming it. And nothing — including presidential frowns — can make me believe otherwise.

My friends, this is not the first time the Republicans have dismissed or scorned Democratic efforts to make this a better world.

When Woodrow Wilson had his immortal dream of a League of Nations, the Republicans called it worse names than a "theatrical gesture" — yet American participation might have prevented a second world war.

Franklin Roosevelt proposed the United Nations. Yet even today many Republican leaders, even Senator [William] Knowland, are still suspicious of it or positively hostile. The U.N. isn't perfect. Like most human institutions it probably never will be, and certainly not without the wholehearted support of America's leaders.

This negative, defeatist attitude among Republican leaders comes in an unbroken line down to the present. President Hoover's fortress America concept is familiar. Senator [Robert A.] Taft's negative, isolationist views are still shared by many of his followers. And the fact is that the Republican party has been so divided since the first war and the League of Nations fight that even to this day it cannot conduct a coherent, consistent foreign policy, and the purpose of foreign policy for the United States is peace. Time and again in the past four years we have seen allied unity abroad sacrificed to Republican unity at home.

This is not to suggest for a second that the Republican party is, therefore, the war party, or that the Democratic party is the party of peace. I have no patience with such blanket charges.

Both parties are dedicated to peace, but historically they differ on how to realize this great objective. I think it is fair to say that, generally speaking, the Republican way has been the narrow, nationalistic one of the low, limited horizon, while the Democratic way has been that of the wide horizon, dotted with the ships and sails of beckoning hope.

One way, of course, is just as patriotic as the other. But in my opinion the Democratic way has usually been more attuned to the changes, the challenge and surprise, of this ever changing world. And I think this is just as true today as it has ever been.

And I think our Democratic enthusiasm for new ideas can better solve our problems here at home too. For on the record it is the Democratic party that has always made new gains for the good of all the people.

Ours is the party that stopped child labor and started the nation on an eight-hour day, invented social security and built the TVA.

It was the Democratic party that rescued the farmer with the triple-A in the great depression, curbed the excesses of the stock promoters, built housing for the people, and wrote the G.I. Bill of Rights, and I could go on and on.

I spoke a few minutes ago of the Democratic-Farmer-Labor story written here in Minnesota. We're going to tell a larger story, too, this year. Woodrow Wilson restrained the excesses of a new industrialism and met the challenge of the Kaiser; Franklin Roosevelt lifted the people from the slough of depression and beat down totalitarianism; Harry Truman made the great decision that lifted prostrate Europe and gave our nation leadership of the free in the world — and that is our story, written in the Twentieth Century here in blessed America.

I say there is yet much to be done. Great work lies ahead. I believe with all my heart and soul that this nation is about to enter a richer age than man has ever known. The question is: Shall we use our riches for all the people, or just for some of them? And, can we master the new machines, or must we serve them? And, can we put the atom to our peaceful use, or will it destroy us?

These are great questions, they require great answers, and those answers can come only from the strength and wisdom of you, the American people. And they will not be drawn forth by leadership that fails to lead, that frowns on new ideas. They will be drawn forth only by leadership that dares to try the new, that meets the crises of our times with unbeatable enthusiasm.

"Nothing great," I repeat, "was ever achieved without enthusiasm." Let us go forward in the spirit of you of Minnesota, never satisfied with things as they are, daring always to try the new, daring nobly and doing greatly, and so building a new America.

It is in this spirit that I come to you tonight. It is in this spirit that we will win in November.

To David Dubinsky[61]

October 1, 1956

Dear Dave:

I am just back in Washington for a day between trips, but that is no excuse for not having written to you long ago to tell you that seeing you in New York last trip was one of the high points of my visit — as usual! I don't know of anyone who has been more loyal than you these past few years, and I am frank to say that there is no one whose support and encouragement I would rather have than yours.

Cordially,

Stevenson delivered the following speech in New York City on October 4, 1956.[62]

I am proud to come to Harlem tonight as a candidate for the Presidency of the United States.

I am proud because I come as the representative of the party which through history has been dedicated to the people of America — the Democratic party.

From the beginning of this republic, the Democratic party has worked, worked hard, yes, and worked successfully to improve the con-

[61] President of the International Ladies' Garment Workers' Union.
[62] The text is from *The New America*, pp. 195–199.

dition, confirm the rights, and enlarge the opportunities of the Joe Smiths[63] of our land.

In the last generation, the Democratic party has achieved social and economic and spiritual gains which have transformed American society — and it has done so under the leadership of two greathearted Americans, Franklin D. Roosevelt and Harry S. Truman.

Our party has fought valiantly for the plain people of America through its past — and I am here tonight to tell you that, so long as I am its spokesman and leader, it will fight as hard as ever for the people in the years ahead.

We have come a long way in the battle for human dignity and opportunity in America. But we still have far to go. The Democratic party has led the fight against poverty and discrimination — and it is our purpose to carry on that fight as long as those ugly specters still haunt American life.

We are the richest nation in the world — the richest nation in history. And it is an indictment of our intelligence and humanity if we cannot provide every family in the country a decent opportunity to earn a living, a decent school for their children, a decent roof over their heads, and a decent prospect of security in old age.

We have had four years of Republican rule — four years of shuffling and postponement — four years of "time out" in the battle for expanding human dignity.

The time has come to resume our onward march.

There are still miles and miles of slums in America. And every American family wants to escape from misery and squalor. We need new houses — millions of them. We need a sound and imaginative public housing program. Every American who has taken the trouble to see how other people live in our country knows that these needs exist — and must be met.

How have the Republicans met these needs?

Well, the Republican leadership has fought and licked every good public housing bill proposed in these last four years — and the bills were always brought forward by Democrats.

I doubt if there will ever be much hope for an adequate public housing program under an administration which takes its policy from the real estate lobby.

But I say to you that under the Democrats we will have public housing and urban renewal programs which will help provide every

[63]A delegate at the 1956 Republican National Convention tried to nominate "Joe Smith" for Vice President but was not recognized by the chairman of the convention.

American family with an opportunity for a decent home in a decent neighborhood.

You have already seen here in Harlem how public housing can begin to transform a community and make it a place where you can be proud to live — but then you have had Democratic mayors here in New York!

The battle for housing is only one part of our Democratic battle for a New America, but in every field Democratic proposals to help the people are met by Republican indifference, obstruction and opposition.

Take the minimum wage. Over the strenuous objections of the Eisenhower administration, the Democrats in the last session of Congress raised the minimum wage to $1. But this is not enough; and it is the Democratic platform pledge to raise the minimum wage — if you will make sure that there are enough Democrats in Washington next year to help us do it.

Over the strenuous objections of the Eisenhower administration, the Democrats in the last session of Congress lowered the age at which women and disabled persons became eligible for social security benefits.

In particular, it is our determination to carry out a program which will make the last years of life more serene and happy for our older citizens. But food and dress and shelter are not all that matter to a good life. Man's highest fulfillment comes in the realm of the spirit — in the fulfillment of his inward sense of his dignity, his responsibility, and his freedom.

America has made progress toward that fulfillment, too — and that progress has come in the main, I am proud to say, through the leadership of the Democratic party.

Yes, we have seen nothing more brazen in the entire record of Republican misrepresentation in this campaign than the Republican effort to seize partisan credit for progress in civil rights.

They have claimed credit for ending segregation in the armed forces.

Well, you know, I happen to have been in on that story right from the start — and these Johnny-come-lately Republican claims make me pretty disgusted.

In 1941 and 1942, I was assistant to the Secretary of the Navy. And it was then that we took the first and the hard steps toward removing the racial barriers in the United States Navy. My part in that was small — and we only got the job started then — but we *did* get it started.[64]

Then, on July 26, 1948, President Truman issued his Executive Order No. 9981. It was that order that sounded the death knell of segregation in the armed forces.

[64] See *The Papers of Adlai E. Stevenson*, Vol. II, especially pp. 134–135.

That order was issued despite the testimony of Chief of Staff Dwight D. Eisenhower before a Congressional committee on April 2, 1948, that complete desegregation in the armed forces would, as he put it, get us "into trouble."

But, four years later, Candidate Eisenhower admitted, in a speech at Chicago on October 31, 1952, that — and these are his words — "Now, so far as I know, there is nothing in the way of segregation in the Army, Navy, Air Force or Marines left — at least as a matter of official record."

Why, then — why — did President Eisenhower tell the American people on Monday of this week, in listing the accomplishments of his administration, that one thing the Republicans have done since 1952 is to end segregation in the armed forces?

I don't mind the President's trying to make off in broad daylight with the Democratic platform — he always returns it right after election day anyway — but he better stop trying to run on the Democratic record!

The Republicans have claimed credit for stopping discrimination in employment by government contractors — though all they did was to continue the work begun by the Fair Employment Practices Commission under President Roosevelt and by the Committee on Government Contract Compliance under President Truman. For that we are grateful.

They have even claimed credit for ending segregation in the District of Columbia — though the case which meant the end of segregation in many public places in the district was initiated at the time President Truman was in office and while Mr. Eisenhower was still a private citizen.

And, finally, when the President was presented with an opportunity for great national leadership in this field, he was virtually silent. I am referring to the Supreme Court decision on desegregation in the public schools.

Surely the gravest problem we face here at home this year is this issue of civil rights. We have faced it continuously for many years in varying forms and changing urgency. I faced it when I was Governor of Illinois. During that interval, we desegregated the National Guard; we used the National Guard to protect the safety of citizens in the Cicero riots; and we came within an ace of passing a fair employment practices act — and were prevented from doing so only by a close vote in a Republican legislature. We eliminated all racial designations in the employment service of Illinois and on drivers' licenses, and so on.[65]

Yet, despite the progress we have made, the achievement of equality of rights and opportunities for all American citizens is still the great

[65] See *The Papers of Adlai E. Stevenson*, Vol. III.

unfinished business before the United States. The Supreme Court decision on desegregation in the public schools was an expression of our steady movement toward genuine equality for all before the law: it expressed in a new field the old principle that the American heritage of liberty and opportunity is not to be confined to men, women and children of a single race, a single religion, or a single color.

I have spoken about this decision many times. Last week I spoke about it in Arkansas, and I am glad to have the opportunity to say here what I said there:

"The Supreme Court of the United States has determined unanimously that the Constitution does not permit segregation in the schools. As you know, for I have made my position clear on this from the start, I believe that decision to be right!

"Some of you feel strongly to the contrary.

"But what is most important is that we agree that, once the Supreme Court has decided this constitutional question, we accept that decision as law-abiding citizens."

And this statement, I am heartened to tell you tonight, brought applause from those who heard me in Arkansas.

I continued: "Our common goal is the orderly accomplishment of the result decreed by the Court. I said long ago, and I stand now squarely on the plain statement, adopted in the Democratic platform, that 'we reject all proposals for the use of force to interfere with the orderly determination of these matters by the courts.' The Court's decree provides for the ways and means of putting into effect the principle it sets forth. I am confident that this decision will be carried out in the manner prescribed by the courts. I have repeatedly expressed the belief, however, that the office of the Presidency should be used to bring together those of opposing views in this matter — to the end of creating a climate for peaceful acceptance of this decision."

The President of the United States recently said of the Supreme Court decision, "I think it makes no difference whether or not I endorse it."[66]

As for myself, I have said from the beginning — and say now — that I support this decision!

We have a code in this country — a design by which Americans live with one another. It is called the Bill of Rights. It should not only be

[66] President Eisenhower made this statement at a news conference in September, 1956, in reply to a reporter's question: "Do you endorse [the decision] or merely accept [it] as the Republican platform does?" The President added: "What I say is the — the Constitution is as the Supreme Court interprets it; and I must conform to that and do my very best to see that it is carried out in this country." New York *Times*, September 6, 1956.

obeyed, it should be respected. The Bill of Rights is the moral spine of our nation.

I pray that all Americans, no matter what their feelings, will collaborate in working to sustain the Bill of Rights. No other course is consistent with our constitutional equality as Americans or with our human brotherhood as children of God.

The profound questions of our time remain questions of conscience and of will.

And the answers will come, at the last, "Not by might, nor by power, but by Thy spirit."

For ours is a time like that of which the prophet Amos wrote: "Let justice roll down as waters, and righteousness as a mighty stream."

Stevenson delivered the following speech at Yale University on October 5, 1956.[67]

I am particularly glad to be here in Woolsey Hall tonight because I always enjoy my visits at colleges. Now, whenever I say this I can see most of my entourage wince — particularly those eggheads who surround me, all of whom are hardboiled now.

You know that word "egghead" is interesting. Some people think it means that you have a lot in your head and some think it means that you have nothing on your head. In the latter respect I qualify as an egghead for obvious reasons. But it is when I am deemed to qualify in the former that I am happiest. And curiously enough that is usually around universities, and especially around university faculties, which I suppose proves something about the gullibility, credulity and innocence of teachers compared to undergraduates!

But I would say to the thinkers, the eggheads, that I think their prospects are improving, that I really don't believe they are as unpopular as they suppose; nor do I think that many Americans regard association with them as a criminal offense any longer.

It has been an interesting campaign, and I welcome the opportunity Woolsey Hall provides to reflect for a moment about it.

The Republican sales managers thought that the President's endorsement would be enough to make their product go. But now they are having to reconsider their sales campaign — I think they call it "agonizing reappraisal." For they have discovered that the people aren't satisfied just to see the Republican leaders. They also want to hear what they have to say.

[67] The text is from *The New America*, pp. 224–230.

This discovery has caused a serious intellectual crisis in Republican ranks. And it is, of course, why the Republicans recently issued their Macedonian cry for intellectuals. I understand that at this very moment Republican talent scouts are beating the darkest recesses of Time, Inc., the Ivy League and the *Partisan Review.*

And I say: more power to them! I have never felt that it was fair for only one major party to know how to read and write, as well as cipher! But I say, too, that liberalism — or humanity in government, or real concern for people, or whatever you want to call it — is not something that a political party can pick up like an acquired accent.

It isn't something you can buy by the speech, or on Madison Avenue. We've been working on it in the Democratic party for 150 years now. We're not going to claim any patent infringement, for we're trying to improve the product ourselves and we're glad for any help or new ideas. But we're frankly pretty confident that we can beat any competition that relies on words as a substitute for action.

The Republican candidates can't say with much vigor and enthusiasm what they want to do — because they don't want to do anything very much.

Hans Christian Andersen has already written the story of this campaign. He called it "The Emperor's New Clothes." All that Estes Kefauver and I have been doing is to tell people what they already know: that the emperor really doesn't have any clothes on at all.

I think one of the most interesting and significant questions in the campaign will be whether the shock over this revelation will not drive our Republican friends into new excesses.

Denied his favorite device of associating Democrats with Communism, at least while traveling a higher road, Mr. Nixon has reverted to the familiar technique of associating Democrats with socialism.[68]

This is standard operating procedure in the newly self-styled "party of the future." Only the other day Ezra Benson, the Secretary of Agriculture, was calling the leaders of the northwest grain co-operatives socialists.[69] And, of course, the Republicans have opposed nearly every social advance within the memory of man as "socialistic."

I would commend to the Republican leadership — and especially to Mr. Nixon — the wise words of Mr. Nixon's fellow Californian, Chief Justice Earl Warren.

"I think a lot of Republicans have been careless and politically foolish," Chief Justice Warren has said, "in the way they have confused social progress with socialism. In my opinion it does the party harm to

[68] The editors have been unable to locate a specific instance of this tactic.
[69] The editors have been unable to locate a reference to this statement.

yell about socialism every time a government, federal, state or local, does something to serve its people in the fields of health, job security, old-age security, child care, conservation, intelligent use of water resources or in any other general fields in which government today must operate because individuals can't do what is needed for the greatest good of the greatest number."[70]

I do not think the American people are going to be much more impressed in 1956 by the Vice-President's threadbare shouts about socialism than they were two years ago by his loud shouts about Communism.[71]

I really believe we have outgrown this kind of politics.

I am not opposed to a hard fight. Indeed, there are some who seem to think I have been fighting too hard in this campaign.

I was somewhat consoled the other day, however, when an old friend, comparing the 1956 campaign with 1952, said — a bit sourly, I thought — "I am glad at last to see the declarative sentence begin to triumph over the subjunctive."

Hard-hitting, factual debate is the essence of democracy. Innuendo, smear and slander are not. They debauch the language of politics; they defile the dialogue which is the means by which free society governs itself. George Orwell once said that, if you want to corrupt a people, first corrupt the words in which they express themselves. The English language can take a lot, especially in election year, but there are limits to the burden of deceit and infamy which it should be asked to bear.

This is a point in the campaign when it seems worth recalling the ground rules of political responsibility — and I mean in terms of self-reminder as much as criticism. I can only say that in the heat of battle even the obvious sometimes becomes blurred and worth reasserting.

Perhaps there is too much of the commonplace in the old injunction that victory is, after all, not an end in itself. Yet I often think that the single greatest difficulty about running for responsible public office is how you can win without, in the process, proving yourself unworthy of winning.

Don't misunderstand me: I mean to win in November.

But the perception that you can pay too great a price for victory — that the means you use may destroy the principles you think you cherish — is fundamental to Democratic responsibility.

If the rule itself seems overobvious — that there is something more to

[70] The editors have been unable to locate this quotation.

[71] Stevenson refers to Mr. Nixon's 1954 campaign speeches in support of Republican candidates. See *The Papers of Adlai E. Stevenson*, Vol. IV, pp. 392–393.

political accomplishment than electoral victory — then let me suggest two propositions that are both its corollary and its test.

First, I don't believe any victory is worth winning in a democracy unless it can be won by placing full trust in the members of the democracy.

I mean giving people the hard facts and the hard decisions — trusting their sobriety and their judgment — regarding them not as the customers of government, to be sold, but as the owners of government, to run their own affairs.

I mean resisting today's temptations to rely on soft soap, slogans, gimmicks, bandwagons, and all the other infernal machines of modern high-pressure politics in this age of mass manipulation.

The promise of such manipulations is contempt — contempt for people's intelligence, common sense and dignity.

The second corollary is that the political party can never be considered an end in itself. It is only an agency for a larger purpose.

Again, let no one misunderstand me. I believe in party loyalty and party responsibility. I am a Democrat, a good party Democrat, a very proud Democrat. But that very pride depends upon my heartfelt conviction that this party is an instrument for carrying out certain principles for the establishment of certain values. What is of fundamental and lasting importance is the ideals a party incarnates, and the purpose of the party is to make government serve our lives as it should serve them.

It is easy and proper and very right to assert that the fortunes of our party are, in the long view, closely and integrally related to our national welfare. Our long history of public service — its many contributions to that welfare in time of crisis, domestic and foreign — can leave no doubt of this. What is more important is to be sure we keep it always in mind that the fortunes of our party even in the short run are of infinitely less importance than the national interest as it is conceived by all our citizens in and out of direct party affiliation or allegiance.

Surely it is appropriate for us to consider the issues that face us in those terms.

The most important fact about any year, including the quadrennial one of national election, is its own identity, its standing apart in its own niche in time, its own remoteness from the years that have gone before, its uniqueness as the only gateway through which we may enter into the years ahead.

At Chicago a few weeks ago we Democrats were given a most timely and eloquent reminder of this fact by a great lady who, more than most, is entitled to recall the glories of years which have dropped over the far horizon.

"The world," Mrs. Roosevelt said, "looks to us again for the meaning of democracy, and we must think of that very seriously. There are new problems. They must be met in new ways. We have heard a great deal, and we were fired with enthusiasm by the tradition of our party. Thus, the new problems we face cannot be met by traditions only, but they must be met by imagination. . . . And it is a foolish thing to say that you pledge yourself to live up to the traditions of the New Deal and the Fair Deal — of course, you are proud of those traditions — but our party must live as a young party, and it must have young leadership. It must have young people, and they must be allowed to lead . . . they must take into account the advice of the elders, but they must have the courage to look ahead, to face new problems with new solutions."

Is it not the very essence of greatness, in a person as in an institution, to face squarely the often uncomfortable fact that the world moves on with the inexorable succession of the years? New problems arise, new challenges are presented, and, most important of all, new opportunities are provided which, if not seized upon with courage and energy and imagination, are shouldered aside by the relentless cycle of time.

I do not believe that we Democrats have the answers for 1956 simply because we had them for 1932. No more do I believe that the Republicans have them for this present moment in time simply because the country turned to them in 1952. And the greatest mistake we as a people could make would be to confuse 1956 with 1952 simply because the same two individuals are carrying the party standards.

As one of those individuals, I am peculiarly exposed to the temptation of thinking that the issues are the same because the faces are the same. But I try to resist it because I know that to yield is to defy the overriding law of life, which is change. And the way I resist is by continually asking myself: What is this election really all about this year? What are the watchwords of the past which have no relevance for the present? What should we be thinking, planning, initiating, doing — now?

I think the central issue in 1956, particularly for the uncommitted voter, is that complacency contains the seeds of decay, not of growth. It is at war with our national genius. It falsifies the tradition which has taken shape in sharp and glowing outline throughout our 180 years as an independent people. In the few periods when its siren song has been heard most loudly in the land, it has been a prelude to a harsher melody in which the saddest note is one of mourning for what might have been.

We have heard a very great deal and we are going to hear much in the weeks ahead about prosperity and peace. But surely the uneven measure of prosperity we now enjoy and the restless and uneasy peace in which we now find ourselves were not achieved by standing still and admiring them. We have become the world's envy because we never stopped raising our sights, because we constantly set new goals for ourselves even as we gained the old, because pretty good was never good enough.

In our hearts we know we must be up and doing, probing ceaselessly for new breakthroughs in our endless striving for solutions for today's problems and for the new ones that tomorrow will find on our doorstep, searching always for better answers than the ones we have been able to come up with thus far. We know that the gospel of discontent is the prophet of progress.

It is our mood that is the issue in this election. From whence is to come the energy to quicken it, the vision to excite it, the courage and will to lead it — to goad it, if need be — forward toward the greater fulfillment it has always demanded?

The essence of our faith is the determination to measure today's problems, not against yesterday's fears, but against tomorrow's hopes.

To you the young among us, I say that your generation confronts a baffling and difficult world. Your problems are not those of my generation. Your task is infinitely more difficult. It is not just to find a job for yourself — it is to save a world, a world in revolution. Your task is not to recover a faith, but to give that faith reality.

There have been revolutionary intervals before. They are times of danger and of opportunity — grave danger and exhilarating opportunity.

You know that America can conquer crippling disease, can discover creative uses for the new leisure which will come in the wake of abundance, can transform our surpluses into a blessing to mankind rather than a burden to the farmers, can strike a mighty blow at the ancient curse of poverty, and can achieve for all Americans that individual freedom, that equality of opportunity, and that human dignity which belong to them as American citizens and as children of God.

You know, too, that America can restore its position in the world, that it can become once again a trusted and inspiring leader, dedicated not to keeping things as they are, but to making the promise of our own revolution a light for all mankind. You know that we can lead the peoples of the earth away from the false beacons of Communism and slavery to a new age of human abundance and human fulfillment.

Our national purpose is not just to have an election and get it out of the way. Our purpose is not to watch a horse race in which all we care about is victory and at almost any price. Our purpose is to show how a great nation rises to the responsibility of self-government — and how it emerges from the experience purified in purpose, strengthened in resolution, and united in faith.

At least, speaking for myself, this is why I am here, and — if you think hard — that is why you are here at Yale. We know our goals: education will help us find our paths.

Mr. and Mrs. John B. Currie, who had been ardent supporters of Stevenson in 1952, wrote Stevenson right after his nomination and urged him not to use Harry S. Truman in the campaign because they considered the former President to be a political liability.

To Mr. and Mrs. John B. Currie[72]

October 8, 1956

My dear Friends:

I don't know just what devious routes my mail has been taking these days, but in any event your letter has only now come to my attention. My belated thanks and apologies. You have been good friends over the years, and I shall be mindful of your advice. But I may have some difficulty, as you will understand only too well!

As for Senator Kennedy, I think he emerged as the real hero of the Convention!

With every good wish and my everlasting gratitude, I am

Cordially,

Carl Sandburg wrote Stevenson that his speeches were "the best since Lincoln."

To Carl Sandburg

October 8, 1956

My dear Carl:

You were good to send me that note, and your encouraging comment on my "utterances" lifts me a lot. But "the best since Lincoln" suggests to me that you may be more of a partisan than a historian just now!

And thanks for the enclosure about the Democratic depression defenses.

Yours, ever

[72] The original is in the possession of Mrs. Currie.

To Robert M. Hutchins[73]

October 8, 1956

Dear Bob:

Please don't feel that I have overlooked your note. I haven't; but also I haven't had time to have the moment with you I had hoped for in New York. If you have some suggestions about what I should be saying, for God's sake send them along. If you'll mail them to Miss Carol Evans at the above address she will get them to me.

How to sustain the campaign to the end at this pace and how to inject a rising tempo toward the end is difficult and perplexing — not to mention exhausting.

Cordially,

Stevenson delivered the following speech in Great Falls, Montana, on October 9, 1956.[74]

Today, I want to tell you what I think about the conservation and full development of our natural resources.

This is not a Montana issue, nor even a Northwest issue. It is a national issue of the highest importance. I talked about it at length the other day in West Virginia. And certainly it is an issue that clearly draws the line between the Democratic and Republican parties. The issue can be put very simply.

The Democratic party believes that our natural resources belong to all the people and it believes in conserving and developing them to the utmost and for the benefit of all the people.

The Republican party isn't so sure about conservation and strongly favors development for private profit.

I think Great Falls is a good place to talk about this subject. We meet today at a place where Lewis and Clark paused a century and a half ago while exploring the natural resources of the great West. We meet outdoors and in the great outdoors, where men know the value of the gifts of land and river, lakes and trees, that they have received.

When the first explorers traversed the broad face of America, they found a dense wilderness, rich and beautiful beyond imagining. In that early beginning, America was covered with a blanket of trees. The soil, not yet broken by the plow, possessed a capacity to produce that was

[73] President of the Fund for the Republic and former chancellor of the University of Chicago. A copy is in A.E.S., I.S.H.L.
[74] The text is from *The New America*, pp. 173–178.

unheard of in the older parts of the world. The earth was drained by mighty rivers, and beneath the topsoil lay mineral riches unimaginable.

All this had been put here in this blessed land for men to use as wisely as they might.

Swiftly men cut down the trees, plowed the soil, dammed the rivers, and mined the minerals.

Some of this was right and necessary, something that had to be done if we were to civilize that land and ourselves.

Some was sheer waste.

Some was ruthless exploitation by greedy men.

And all of it wrought a change in the face of America.

Congress became alarmed at the swiftness of the change and determined to preserve a part of the original loveliness and richness for our children and our children's children. Congress set aside millions of acres of national forests and national parks.

Its first watchword was conservation — we had to conserve, to save, these public lands.

More recently, we have learned how to use them wisely. The parks are to be used by the public for recreation. The forests, too, are to be used by the public for recreation but they also may be used — under supervision — for selective logging, dam building, mineral prospecting, and grazing.

And for some fifty years, ever since Theodore Roosevelt and Gifford Pinchot took the lead in establishing the policy, both political parties have worked together to hammer out a bipartisan policy for the national parks and forests that would at once conserve them and use them wisely.

That policy has been scrapped by the present administration.

It was the intent of Congress that all the people should benefit from the use of the national forests.

It was decidedly not their intent that the public lands should be invaded by, and given away to, selfish private interests.

But that's precisely what the Eisenhower administration has been doing.

They gave a private mining company the right to cut the people's timber in the Rogue River National Forest in Oregon — and under such peculiar circumstances that the assay samples got dumped into Rogue River.

A Republican congressman[75] introduced a bill which would have given the big lumber companies special privileges in the national for-

[75] Harris Ellsworth, of Oregon.

ests — a bill which your great congressman, Lee Metcalf, correctly called a bill to permit "big lumbermen to trade stumps for trees."

A Republican congressman[76] introduced a bill which would have given a few big-spread cattlemen — and no one else — what amounted to perpetual rights to graze their stock in the national forests. And though the bill was defeated, President Eisenhower nominated this same congressman to be Assistant Secretary of the Interior in charge of public lands — which sounded like setting the fox to guard the henhouse.

They gave the oil and gas interests about five times as many leases to explore and exploit the wildlife refuges as had been granted in the preceding three decades.

They got rid of the career conservation men in the Fish and Wildlife Service and replaced them with patronage appointees.

It is no wonder that Ira Gabrielson, the respected conservationist who was for years head of the service, told a congressional committee, "After spending most of my lifetime in an organization that was completely career service I see it all of a sudden turned into something political." And Mr. Gabrielson — he is a lifelong Republican — added, "I have told some of my friends sometimes that this administration and its action on conservation matters come nearer making a Democrat out of me than anything that Roosevelt and Truman could do in all the years I worked for them."

I think that not only Mr. Gabrielson feels that way. I think that the Eisenhower administration has made a lot of other new Democrats in the last three years.

Nor has the administration shown more regard for the Indians, who are its wards, than for the public domain. Their treaties have been scrapped, they have been coerced, not consulted, about their future, they are losing their lands at the rate of over 500,000 acres a year, and right here in Great Falls you have Hill 57, a miserable home for landless Indians that is a disgrace in a nation that calls itself rich. May I point out that in connection with the termination of government responsibility for the Indian's affairs, the Republican platform this year speaks only of consultation while the Democratic platform proposes to obtain their consent.

But in no other area has the Eisenhower administration shown its true colors more clearly than in its water policy.

America's water policy has and should rest firmly on first principles — the rivers belong to the people and should be developed fully for the benefit of all the people.

[76] Fred G. Aandahl, of North Dakota.

And this means developed to their utmost — for their hydroelectric power, for flood control, navigation, irrigation, and recreation. Water runs downhill. Water is just as wet and life-giving to farmers' crops after it has fallen through a turbine and twirled a hydroelectric generator as it was before. The water which flows as snow-melt out of a mountain forest can be caught behind a dam and put through generators for power, then recaptured and stored to prevent floods, then diverted to irrigate arid fields, then used to establish a navigable channel and carry off municipal wastes farther downstream — all the same water. And this is all that multiple-purpose development means.

Under Franklin Roosevelt the program of putting the people's property to the service of the people went forward as never before — and today in the great Northwest and down in the valley of the Tennessee and in other parts of this broad land you can see the results — new industries and fertile farms where once was wasteland, rows of houses standing safe where floodwaters raged, homes and factories and farms and vacationlands that make America a richer and a better place for all of us to live. And all of it a result of twenty-five years of sound river policy.

But now suddenly the Eisenhower administration has scrapped this policy.

Of course, the Republicans don't talk out loud these days the way they talked in 1935, when a Republican congressman called TVA a step toward "Russianizing the United States."[77] Nowadays, and especially in election years, the Republicans pretend they are in favor of public power programs. In fact, in an election year the Republicans pretend they are in favor of developing our resources for all the people. That's what they say this year.

But look what they've *done* for the last four years.

They have taken the Hells Canyon damsite, the last great damsite on the North American continent, and handed it over to a private power company.

They have crippled reclamation and the Southwest Power Administration.

They tried to give away Niagara's power to five private corporations, and today all along the St. Lawrence the battle is hot.

They have endangered the Central Valley development in California.

In Georgia they have refused to sell power to co-operatives — even

[77] Stevenson may refer to Representative John G. Cooper, of Ohio, who described the Tennessee Valley Authority as "the biggest piece of collectivism based on the policies of a foreign government that was ever inaugurated in this country." New York *Times,* June 28, 1935.

though the Attorney General himself has warned that such refusal is illegal.

Only Congress has saved the REA from the administration.[78]

The President himself called TVA "creeping socialism," and personally ordered the signing of the odious Dixon-Yates contract, a backdoor deal to carve up TVA.

The Department of the Interior invited the admitted lobbyist of the Pacific Gas and Electric Company into Washington to help rewrite the federal regulations for transmission lines over public lands.

The Assistant Secretary of the Interior testified before a congressional committee that TVA is "a federal socialistic monopoly."[79]

The Undersecretary of the Interior said that he was "sick and tired" of listening to the "political hogwash of socialists who want to federalize the nation's electric power industry."[80]

The chairman of the Federal Power Commission[81] is a former representative of private utility companies.

The Assistant Secretary of the Interior[82] in charge of power as a congressman voted four out of six times against public power programs.

And the Secretary of the Interior himself summed it all up frankly when he said that "we're here in the saddle as an administration representing business and industry."[83]

And all this, I suppose, is what we might have expected from an administration dominated by a single interest — big business.

The administration says it favors something called "partnership" between government and private power in waterpower development.

But it turns out that one partner — the private company — takes the profit while the other partner — you, the people — pays the bills.

Back in my home town, Chicago, some years ago, we had a city planner who, when Chicago was young, drew up the blueprints that helped make Chicago the great city it is today. That man was Dan Burnham, and his favorite saying was, "Make no little plans."

[78] The Eisenhower Administration secured the passage on March 26, 1953, of a reorganization plan that gave more administrative power over the Rural Electrification Administration to Secretary Benson, who was hostile to the program. In 1954, the House Agricultural Appropriations Subcommittee, headed by Republican Representative H. Carl Andersen, of Minnesota, accused Benson of "freezing" funds for the REA in order to destroy it. The subcommittee countered by increasing the appropriations substantially, and in the Senate, Paul Douglas, Democrat of Illinois, raised the appropriations still further.

[79] The editors have been unable to identify the source of this quotation.

[80] The editors have been unable to identify the source of this quotation.

[81] Jerome K. Kuykendall.

[82] Fred G. Aandahl.

[83] The editors have been unable to locate this statement.

I say to you we need that kind of bold planning, that kind of imagination and vision in the United States today.

A high dam at Hells Canyon built by the federal government means cheaper phosphate fertilizer for the farmers, cheaper power in the farm-house, in the factory, and in city homes; it means life-giving irrigation for arid lands; it means flood control, new industry, new homes, new towns, an expanding economy in the great Northwest.

Yet a while back former Secretary of the Interior [Douglas] McKay referred to High Hells Canyon as a "white elephant."

Well, not many years ago other Republicans referred to Grand Coulee as a "white elephant," in precisely those words. But today Grand Coulee has spread its bounty over millions of acres — has made the desert bloom, the factories arise, the cities grow, the farms light up. When Grand Coulee was proposed, a private power company wanted to dam the Columbia with little dams, and waste forever the power of the mighty river. A Republican congressman said there wasn't any sense in building Grand Coulee dam because "there was no one in the Grand Coulee area to sell power to except rattlesnakes, coyotes and rabbits. Everyone knows that. There is no market for power in the Northwest." And the press agents for the private power lobby of that day used all the arguments we hear today. They said Grand Coulee was too expensive, an unfair burden on the U.S. Treasury; but today Grand Coulee is ahead of schedule in paying back the U.S. Treasury power investment in the future of the Northwest. They said Grand Coulee was a wild dream of woolly-headed professors; but today it is one of the wonders of the world. And of course they said it was socialistic.

But thousands of veterans have settled on land Grand Coulee made fertile; it has lightened the labors and brightened the lives of thousands of farmers, and it has provided employment for thousands of men and women who work in the industries created by its power, industries that wouldn't be there if Democrats hadn't had the vision to use what God gave us to make something better out there than coyotes and rattle-snakes.

And, you know, I have a feeling that all those people just wouldn't give up what they've got to prove to the Republicans how anti-socialistic they are!

I want to stop this erosion of our resources by the Eisenhower administration. And I want to get on with the full development of our resources for the benefit of the people all over this great country.

The Eisenhower administration acts as if this generation of Americans were the last.

I want a government that will honor its obligations to generations yet unborn.

This land, these rivers, these forests and mountains — they were not put there for us to despoil.

They were put here for us to use wisely, and to leave in better estate for our children and our children's children.

This issue means a great deal to us alive today but it will mean far more to our descendants. We are shaping a federal conservation policy — or a federal giveaway policy — today that will mold our children's lives. Theodore Roosevelt said, "Of all the questions which can come before this nation, short of the actual preservation of its existence in a great war, there is none which compares in importance with the great central task of leaving this land even a better land for our descendants than it is for us."

I believe that. I think we all believe that.

But we have to do more than believe it. We have to fight for it, just as we have to fight everlastingly for every good cause.

To Joseph Pulitzer, Jr.[84]

October 10, 1956

Dear Joe:

We are moving around so fast these days, that it is hard for me to keep up with everything that is going on — even important things like the Post-Dispatch endorsement of A.E.S. But now that I've had a moment to sit back and read that editorial carefully, I want to let you know how much it means to me. It has not only gladdened me, but the whole staff as well. All of us need a little encouragement and reassurance from time to time even in the most bouyant of campaigns. The friendly words of the Post-Dispatch are deeply appreciated. Will try to justify them.

With best wishes,

Sincerely,

To Harold Shuster[85]

October 11, 1956

Dear Mr. Shuster:

As you know, I have been traveling most of the time in the last month and news of the formation of the Friends of Israel for Stevenson Com-

[84] Editor and publisher of the St. Louis *Post-Dispatch*.
[85] Unable to identify.

mittee has reached me only recently. I am, of course, delighted to know of your efforts and as we go into this last month of the campaign I know that the help of the Committee will be invaluable.

On the question of United States policy toward Israel, I have repeatedly said that the difficulties in the Middle East have been greatly compounded by the fact that our government has had no firm or consistent policy in that area.

The basis of any wise American policy, it seems to me, must recognize:

(1) That Israel is here to stay.

(2) That aggression is intolerable and must be prevented.

(3) That Israel should not be deprived of means of self-defense and that the necessary weapons and training should be supplied to Israel to restore a balance with her hostile neighbors.

I firmly believe that unless we are unequivocally committed to these three steps, it will be difficult if not impossible to remove the causes of friction, re-establish a solid peace and enable Israel to pursue in peace her objective of genuine independence.

I was a member of the American delegation to the United Nations when the State of Israel was created and I have continued to study its problems and follow its progress. I will work to promote the security and well-being of this new State because I profoundly believe that peace and security in the Middle East is not only a question of national self-interest but one of justice and moral responsibility.

Please extend my warmest greetings to the members of the Committee and express my deep appreciation of their support.

Cordially,

Stevenson delivered the following speech in San Francisco on October 11, 1956.[86]

Tonight I want to outline a new Democratic program to protect ourselves from another kind of disaster — the disaster of disease — physical disaster — let's call it a program for health security.

In my opinion we are not doing enough to win the battle against cancer, and against the other crippling and killing diseases. Our government is doing very little to bring the best medical care within the reach of all the people, not just some of them.

We are the richest nation on earth.

[86] The text is from *The New America*, pp. 135–140.

We are being told these days that all is well in America, that we are prosperous, that everything is fine.

And surely we share a great thankfulness for all the blessings of this heaven-favored land.

But we must look at both sides of our ledger: as things stand now, one out of every seven Americans will die someday of cancer — a disease whose terrible secret we know we can someday discover; one out of every twelve American children born this year will have to spend some time during his life in a mental institution; ten million Americans are suffering from crippling arthritis; millions more from agonizing bursitis.

In every state and nearly every city sick people are sleeping tonight in the corridors of overcrowded hospitals. The cost of adequate medical care has skyrocketed out of the reach of millions of Americans. We are woefully short of doctors and dentists and nurses, and of the schools where these professions can be taught.

These are shocking facts.

It is time we did something about them. There is a great deal we can do. And I think we want to do it.

I propose that we attack this problem on two fronts.

The first front is the one that most Americans today know only too well: the cost of sickness and of healing.

The second front is one that the ordinary citizen sees little of but it is there that the crucial struggle must be waged and won: and that is the front of science.

First, about the high cost of health. We know that doctors, hospitals and charities have given generously of their services and money and facilities to the sick. But in spite of all their heroic contributions, medical care is still costly. Ordinary doctor and hospital bills are a heavy burden on every family budget. Serious illness can wipe out a life's savings in a few weeks. About three million American families are today in debt for medical care.

Now, it is true that roughly two-thirds of the people in this country are covered by private health insurance of some kind. But the trouble is that this coverage is usually so incomplete that you have to get sick enough to have to go to the hospital before you are covered at all; and the insurance as a rule doesn't cover house calls by the doctor, office calls, preventive services, diagnosis, treatment, or the cost of recovery after you leave the hospital. Yet these are the very things that eat up the family cash.

Most insurance covers only the cost of the hospital bed, or of surgery, and that only within limits. If you have a long sickness, your insurance runs out when you need it most. It is like being insured for a little fire but not if the house burns down.

And some insurance, I'm sorry to say, covers very little — when the time comes, you find too many exceptions in the fine print.

The fact is that present insurance covers only about a fourth of the total medical bill of the American people. And many citizens — farm people, old people, people who live alone, the handicapped, the very poor — are generally not covered at all.

And so, every night — yes, tonight — men and women lie suffering, without care, because savings are gone and pride forbids or postpones asking for charity.

And every day children don't get the care they need — and are crippled or their health is impaired for life.

Well, what can we do about it?

The answer lies, plainly, in an extension of the insurance principle — so that everyone can be covered by it if he wants to be. And it is plain that this is going to require more help from somewhere.

I have said many times, and I repeat, that I am against any form of socialized medicine.

I am equally opposed to those who resist all progress by calling it socialistic.

The present administration in Washington pretends to accept the idea of government aid to private health insurance programs. But what did it do? It did nothing but propose a so-called reinsurance plan which, after exhaustive hearings, was rejected by everybody — including the insurance industry — as being utterly useless.[87]

There are various ways in which a Democratic administration would propose to work out effective federal aid for health. But all of these would look for the answer in an expansion of the voluntary private health insurance programs that are already going concerns — like Blue Cross and Blue Shield or HIP in New York or the Permanente and Ross-Loos plans here in California.

Federal aid might take the form of long-term loans to groups of citizens who want to get started in group health insurance programs. Senator Humphrey has proposed such a plan, and in it lies an inherently sound American principle: private citizens banding together for their mutual welfare.

[87] Stevenson may refer to the health program outlined by President Eisenhower in a special message to Congress on January 18, 1954. Hearings were held during January and February, 1954, on the proposal, the most controversial feature of which was the idea of a unified health grant system which would combine a number of single-grant programs into one unit. Many Republicans favored this approach because it would reduce federal controls over state public health programs.

And some federal aid might take the form of matching grants to the states to help low-income families and individuals buy, if they want to, voluntary health insurance in private group programs.

The family, the state and often the employer would divide the cost of the premium on the insurance; the family's share would vary, depending upon income and the size of the family. The family that can pay its own way should pay, the family that can pay a part of its way should pay that part, and the family that can pay nothing should not be deprived of medical care.

These private group insurance programs would, of course, have to be bona fide programs, measuring up to standards fixed by the state or federal government. They would cover preventive medicine, diagnosis, office or home treatment, drugs, probably all hospital costs, and so forth.

Let me make it plain that only those who wanted to would buy this insurance or become members of these prepayment groups.

A few years ago a Southern editor who became a member of the Presidential Health Commission wrote: ". . . Our democracy will never be complete until every person, rich or poor, high or low, urban or rural, white or black, has an equal right to adequate hospital and medical care whenever and wherever he makes the same grim battle against ever-menacing death which sooner or later we must all make."[88]

It is this right, this chance for life, that I propose. We must, we simply must, bring the cost of medical care down within the reach of all our people. The insurance principle seems to offer a solution both practical and consistent with our experience.

And now of the second front in this battle for health: the front of science. We have long been fascinated by the great stories of medical research. One by one, ancient scourges like smallpox have been conquered. Childbirth once took the lives of many mothers; it no longer does, and what this has meant in terms of human happiness is beyond measurement. The terrible killers of children — scarlet fever, diphtheria, typhoid fever, respiratory ailments, and others — have been eradicated or brought under quite effective control.

And now we have all been thrilled to learn that poliomyelitis, a disease that darkened every summer, is being conquered.

The list of other diseases that have been successfully attacked or controlled is long.

For this spectacular progress we are in large measure indebted to private philanthropy. The splendid work of the great foundations is well known, but there remain large needs which cannot be met by existing

[88] The editors have been unable to identify the source of this quotation.

means, and broad frontiers to be crossed in the world of medical research.

There is grim irony in the fact that last year we spent less on medical research in this country than on monuments and tombstones.

What is more startling and to the point is that last year the government spent more money for eradication of hoof-and-mouth disease in cattle than for research on mental illness — which afflicts 9 million people. The government spends as much on 25 or 30 miles of highway as on cancer research — and yet 25 million people now alive in the United States are doomed to die someday of cancer.

For three years the Eisenhower administration dragged its feet on programs to aid health research and medical education.

This year — an election year — it offered some constructive proposals, and some progress was made. And it would be utterly absurd to suggest that one party is for better health in America and the other party is against it.

Yet the fact is that in four years of this administration no real breakthrough in the battle for the people's health has been proposed. A family struggling with illness and medical bills has not had much sympathy.

I say it's time to get up and start fighting in this battle against disease.

We badly need new research laboratories. Work on vitally important research projects is being held up. Able research men are unable to join the fight against disease because they have no place to work. As a Democrat, I am proud that the Democratic Congress this year appropriated $90 million to build medical research laboratories. Yet even this will not do the job.

We need right now something like 25,000 more doctors — in your neighborhood and mine, in the hospitals, and in the research centers, where a handful of overworked men and women are fighting the great fights against cancer, heart disease, and the other major killers that still afflict us.

We will get more doctors only by educating more doctors. But our medical schools are overcrowded, understaffed, and underfinanced. And to make matters worse, a medical education today costs far more than most qualified young people can afford.

We need federal aid to the medical schools. We must build more buildings. And we must make it possible for young men and women to enter them.

I favor a federal program of loans and national merit scholarships for promising and deserving young people who want to become doctors. Let's give the gifted boy from a poorer home a chance to become a doctor. And let's give the American people the doctors they need. And we must train far more nurses, too.

In addition to all this, we must press forward with our hospital building program. We must improve our health facilities for the aged and we must learn more about the health problems of older people. We must expand greatly our community mental health clinics, which have done much to curb juvenile delinquency, solve family problems, and keep people from being consigned to overcrowded state mental hospitals.

These measures taken together are a broad outline of the Democratic program for national health security.

Disease will not vanish from the land, no matter who is elected. Mortality cannot be voted away. But inaction can be voted away; complacency can be voted away. And we can throw our hearts and will power and the resources of our government as reinforcements into an all-out attack upon disease.

Health, next to character, is a man's most precious asset. We are proud of our great free education system. And our spiritual needs and the character of our young are the constant concerns not only of family, but of our churches and our great organizations like the Boy Scouts and YMCA.

But what are we doing about our health? Well, we've tried to indicate in a few minutes what we Democrats would do about it.

Today medicine is on the threshold of great discoveries. New drugs, new therapies, new techniques, offer new hope to the American people. We have made progress, the fight is far from hopeless. All over the country tuberculosis hospitals are closing down because new drugs have sent their patients home.

It is time for an all-out drive for national health security.

Great America amazed the world with the atomic bomb. We can do the same — we can conquer the crippling and killing diseases that afflict mankind.

We are rich and we are strong; we can do what we want with our strength and our riches. Let us attack human pain as we attack human poverty.

Let us attack disease as we attack discrimination.

Let us strive for health as we strive for peace.

Let us build for ourselves and for our children a healthier and so a happier life in the New America.

Senator Lyndon B. Johnson sent Stevenson a letter of September 20, 1956, from a Fort Worth constituent, Bill McMillan, who asked if

Stevenson actually proposed ending the draft. Mr. McMillan noted that he had thought up to that point that Stevenson would make a good President, but now he was skeptical, feeling that the candidate was very foolish to have suggested such a step.

To Bill McMillan

Ocotber 13, 1956

Dear Mr. McMillan:

Your letter to my good friend Lyndon Johnson has been passed on to me, and I want to answer it.

My position has been badly distorted by the Republican orators and the Republican press, and your letter shows that you have been an innocent victim of that distortion. I did not say that if elected I intended to stop the draft, nor did I say — I would never say — I intended to prohibit research on nuclear weapons. I am as firm a believer in meeting our international responsibilities, and in a strong national defense, as your letter makes it clear you are. What I said is made plain in the speeches and statements that I enclose.

I said and I believe, that the day will come when the technology of war demands a different kind of armed force than we can raise with the draft. The air force and the navy rely wholly on volunteers because they cannot get the skilled men they need through selective service. As the army adopts new weapons this is also becoming true of the army too. It is essential, therefore, that we review our manpower and training policies with a view to making all branches of the service attractive enough as a career so that we can get the kind of professional forces we need and that a changing world demands.

I have proposed a moratorium on H-bomb tests — not on nuclear research. I have studied the matter carefully and consulted with the best-informed scientists. I am assured that if Soviet Russia will agree, as it says it will, we will be the gainers from a moratorium because our development has proceeded considerably farther than the Russians'. We would of course continue with our own research and development up to the time of testing so that if Russia violated the agreement we would promptly be able to resume our own work. Meanwhile, we would gain an incalculable political and moral advantage throughout the world.

I am convinced that it is time we sought new ways to strengthen our military position while insuring maximum protection for ourselves. All I ask is that we approach this problem fairly and with open minds for the sake of our own security and survival.

Thank you for your interest.

Cordially,

[277]

To Lyndon B. Johnson

October 13, 1956

Dear Lyndon:

As you will see from the enclosed copy of my letter to Mr. McMillan, I have answered him at considerable length because I wanted to explain my position to you. However, I will spare you copies of my speeches!

I do appreciate your sending Mr. McMillan's letter to me and your request for a carbon. I am grateful for every opportunity to restate my own position as there is no question but that it has been quite deliberately distorted.

I intend to develop it in my speeches this week.

With all good wishes,

Cordially,

To Lady Barbara Jackson

October 13, 1956

Dearest Barbara:

I am back for a couple of days from a journey through Montana, Idaho, Washington, Oregon and California. On the whole the news was good, especially so in Washington and Montana, with prospects brightening in both Oregon and California. It was a weary journey and I developed acute bursitis in my left shoulder that has me in agony and I am soaked with drugs.

I used, effectively I am sure, one of your talks about Eisenhower's leadership, — what new idea — what bold position — etc. — along the way. And now on my return I find your notes on inflation which will be helpful, I am sure, and keep the meager speech pot boiling a bit. As to the latter, I have been much troubled in view of the fact that our bank is so empty and we have to improvise from hand to mouth in this ghastly schedule. All of which is another reason why Lady Jackson should be on the campaign train instead of the Island of Jersey!

I do not know how well you have been able to follow things but the H-bomb has boiled up again and I am meeting this week-end with my advisers to map out the future content of the campaign as best we can and also to prepare a full presentation of my position for national TV Monday night. I wish you could hear it — and critically — but you will have a copy of my remarks from Miss Evans in due course. I will probably have someone on the program with me who is knowledgeable, like Senator Clinton Anderson, to brighten it up a little. I am sure I am on sound ground here and that the administration is unspeakably culpable in its failure to do anything whatever about the most terrible thing on earth.

Thank you for your sweet letter, and even more for the precious hours of your short visit. My love to all the Jacksons.

Yours,

P.S. I hope you'll keep sending along any ideas that occur to you from time to time.

To Dr. T. Bielecki[89]

October 13, 1956

Dear Mr. Bielecki:

Thank you for your kind letter of good wishes following my nomination in Chicago. I am sorry that my reply has been so long delayed but as you know I have been constantly on the move.

I recall very well our conversation in Chicago in January of last year and your report of actual conditions existing in Poland and the other countries of Central and Eastern Europe. There is no need for me to assure you how deeply I feel for the people of Poland nor to reaffirm my faith in the cause of a free Poland and the restoration of the rights and privileges of her people.

Throughout the campaign — on Labor Day in Detroit, at the Convention of the Polish Legion of American Veterans, in messages to the meeting protesting the Poznan trials and to the Assembly of Captive European Nations and most recently in my statement on Pulaski Day — I have repeatedly stated my strong feelings on the tragic plight of Poland. I was honored to take part in the Pulaski Day Parade recently in New York and at that time to pay tribute to the memory of that gallant general, to Kosciusko and to all those who joined in our fight for liberty and independence.

As you are undoubtedly aware the Democratic platform I am proud to say, was unequivocal and clear in its statement on the question of Poland and the captive nations. The Platform declared:

"Our deepest concern for the plight of the freedom-loving peoples of Central and Eastern Europe and of Asia, now under the yoke of Soviet dictatorship. The United States, under Democratic leaders, has never recognized the forcible annexation of Lithuania, Latvia and Estonia, or condoned the extension of the Kremlin's tyranny over Poland, Bulgaria, Romania, Czechoslovakia, Hungary, Albania and other countries.

[89] President of the Polish Council of National Unity, London, England.

"We look forward to the day when the liberties of all captive nations will be restored to them and they can again take their rightful place in the community of free nations.

"We shall press before the United Nations the principle that Soviet Russia withdraw its troops from the captive countries, so as to permit free, fair and unfettered elections in the subjugated areas, in compliance with the Atlantic Charter and other binding commitments."

With renewed thanks to you and to your compatriots for your greetings and good wishes and let us hope that your efforts, joined with those of all freedom loving people, will see your country restored to its rightful place among the free nations of the world.

Cordially,

In 1955, Secretary of State Dulles offered Egypt aid in building the Aswan dam. But, in July, 1956, when Colonel Gamal Abdel Nasser asked for the aid, Dulles abruptly canceled the offer. Nasser thereupon took control of the operation of the Suez Canal. The British and French favored retaking the canal by force. Dulles, however, recommended negotiations. By the time the following letter was written, the British and French were reaching the conclusion that Dulles's pronouncements would not produce a solution.[90]

To Philip Noel-Baker[91]

October 13, 1956

My dear Philip:

I was so glad to find your letter of September 25. It was thoughtful and kind of you to write me and I am most grateful. The campaign is going well, on the whole, but we are, as always, at an acute disadvantage for television time for me and this wretched mass media that costs so much. But people are more and more seeing through the thin skin of "peace, prosperity and progress" and moving our way.

The deterioration of our relations over Suez is frightening. I have been in a quandary as to how to handle foreign affairs during this campaign and I am both ill informed and reluctant to cause any embar-

[90] See Herman Finer, *Dulles over Suez: The Theory and Practice of His Diplomacy* (Chicago: Quadrangle Books, 1964).

[91] A British politician who had been a good friend of Stevenson's since their collaboration in the formation of the United Nations in 1945. A copy is in A.E.S., I.S.H.L.

rassment. But on the H-bomb tests I must stick to my position and convictions and what I am also sure is fundamentally sympathetic to our people.

As you can imagine, my esteem for Mr. Dulles has not increased, and I am tempted to do an analytical attack on the whole conduct of our relations with the Middle East which culminated so disastrously.

I shall hope for a leisurely talk some time soon.

All good wishes.

Cordially,

Dean Acheson wrote that he understood that some of Stevenson's advisers were opposed to his discussing foreign policy. Acheson instead urged Stevenson to make foreign policy a main theme for the rest of the campaign.

To Dean Acheson

October 13, 1956

Dear Dean:

Your note caught up with me somewhere on my endless travels. Confirming as it does much of my own thinking, I welcomed it, and I shall also welcome the materials you and Paul [Nitze] have prepared. I am having a meeting this week-end with some of my "advisers" and I hope they will have these materials with them. If not, I think it best to send them to Miss Carol Evans, 231 South La Salle Street, Chicago 4, Illinois, who will be able to pass them along as quickly as anyone else.

Cordially,

P.S. Tell Alice[92] I saw her very courteous and nice brother in Fresno.

Stevenson delivered the following speech on nationwide television from Chicago on October 15, 1956.[93]

Thirteen years ago this winter I was in Italy.[94] The war was on, and it was a wet, cold, ugly winter. It seems a long time ago. Our men were fighting their way up a valley whose name none of you will remember — unless you happened to be one of them. The Liri Valley it was called. It was a place of mud and blood.

---

92 Mrs. Acheson.
93 The text is from *The New America*, pp. 44–49.
94 See *The Papers of Adlai E. Stevenson*, Vol. II, pp. 163–205.

I served through the war as personal assistant to the Secretary of the Navy, Frank Knox. And what I saw and experienced there in the Liri Valley was nothing very out of the ordinary — as war goes and as I saw it in the Pacific and Europe. I mention it now only because I think it was there that I decided that after the war I would do what I could to help in mankind's eternal search for peace.

For it was painfully clear, there in the Liri Valley, that civilization could not survive another world war. And that fact became even more clear on the day the first atomic bomb exploded over Hiroshima.

So, after the war, I served for several years with the American Delegation in the early days of the United Nations, both here and abroad. And that, in turn, led me into politics and brought me here tonight.

And now, thirteen years after that decision in Italy, I come before you to talk a little about the cause which means more to all of us than anything else — the cause of peace.

We are caught up today, along with the rest of the world, in an arms race which threatens mankind with stark, merciless, bleak catastrophe.

It is no accident that the instinct of survival which is common to all men and all nations is slowly but surely compelling the most practical and hardheaded statesmen to give increasing heed to the prevention and abolition of war. In this nuclear age peace is no longer merely a visionary ideal, it has become an urgent and practical necessity.

Yet we dare not tear down and abandon armed deterrents to war before we devise and secure other and more effective guaranties of peace. Great and law-abiding nations cannot leave their security at the mercy of others. We have learned that unilateral disarmament invites rather than deters aggression.

So, until there is world-wide agreement on an effective system of arms reductions with adequate safeguards, we must maintain our national defense and the defenses of the free world.

I am not only opposed to unilateral disarmament, but I have felt that we should not put too many of our eggs in the atomic and hydrogen basket. I have felt that we should try to maintain sufficient balance, flexibility and mobility in our armed strength so that we will not be forced to choose between appeasement and massive retaliation, between too little and too much, between submission and holocaust.

Effective disarmament means universal disarmament — an open world, with no secret armies, no secret weapons, and, in effect, no military secrets. Responsible statesmen do not risk the security of their countries for hopes which may prove illusory or promises that are worthless.

But nations have become so accustomed to living in the dark that it is not easy for them to learn to live in the light. And all our efforts to work out any safe, reliable, effective system of inspection to prevent evasion of arms agreements have been blocked by the Soviet rulers. They won't agree to let us inspect them; we cannot agree to disarm unless we can inspect them. And the matter has been deadlocked there for eleven years.

Yet if we are going to make any progress we must find means of breaking out of this deadly deadlock. We must come forward with proposals which will bear witness to our desire to move toward and not away from disarmament.

It was with this hard, urgent need in mind that I proposed last spring that all countries concerned halt further tests of large-size nuclear weapons — what we usually call the H-bombs. And I proposed that the United States take the lead in establishing this world policy.

I deliberately chose to make this proposal as far removed as possible from the political arena. It was made four months before the party conventions. It was made to the American Society of Newspaper Editors. It was made without criticism of the present administration's policy for H-bomb development.

Others — and not I — have chosen to make this proposal for peace a political issue. But I think this is good. After all, the issue is mankind's survival, and man should debate it, fully, openly, and in democracy's established processes.

Because there has been only negative criticism of this proposal from the Republican candidates in this campaign, I want to return to it tonight.

These are the reasons why I think the time is ripe and there is an insistent necessity for the world to stop at least the testing of these terrifying weapons:

First, the H-bomb is already so powerful that a single bomb could destroy the largest city in the world. If every man, woman and child on earth were each carrying a 16-pound bundle of dynamite — enough to blow him to smithereens and then some — the destructive force in their arms would be equal to the force of one 20-megaton hydrogen bomb, which has already been exploded.

Second, the testing of an H-bomb anywhere can be quickly detected. You can't hide the explosion any more than you can hide an earthquake.

As the President has stated: "Tests of large weapons, by any nation, may be detected when they occur." In short, H-bomb testing requires no inspection. We will know it when it happens anywhere, and by studying the dust from that explosion we can even determine what progress the other country has made.

[283]

This means that, if any country broke its pledge, we would know it and could promptly resume our own testing.

Third, these tests themselves may cause the human race unmeasured damage.

With every explosion of a superbomb huge quantities of radioactive material are pumped into the air currents of the world at all altitudes — later to fall to earth as dust or in rain. This radioactive "fallout" carries something called strontium 90, which is the most dreadful poison in the world. Only a tablespoon shared equally by all the members of the human race would produce a dangerous level of radioactivity in the bones of every individual. In sufficient concentration it can cause bone cancer and dangerously affect the reproductive processes.

Prior to the atomic age, radioactive strontium was practically nonexistent in the world. Careful studies show that today all of us — all over the world — have some of it in our bones. It enters our bodies through the foodstuffs grown in soil on which the bomb dust has fallen.

I do not wish to be an alarmist and I am not asserting that the present levels of radioactivity are dangerous. Scientists do not know exactly how dangerous the threat is. But they know the threat will increase if we go on testing. And we should remember that less than half of the strontium created by past tests by Russia and the United States has as yet fallen to earth from the stratosphere.

So it seems clear to me that, if it is humanly possible, we should stop sending this dangerous material into the air just as soon as we can!

Fourth, the dangers of testing by three powers are ominous enough, but there is another reason why it is important to act now. Last May, Mr. [Harold] Stassen, the President's disarmament assistant, said that within a year the "secret" of making the hydrogen bomb would spread around the world. Think what would happen if a maniac, another Hitler, had the hydrogen bomb. And imagine what the consequences would be of a dozen nations conducting hydrogen bomb tests and wantonly thrusting radioactive matter into the atmosphere.

These are the reasons why it seems to me imperative that a world policy of stopping these tests be established at the very first possible moment.

I proposed last April that the United States take the initiative toward this end by announcing our willingness to stop these tests, "calling upon other nations to follow our lead," and making it clear that, unless they *did*, we would have to resume our experiments too. That was my proposal. It was simple. It was safe. It was workable.

And since that time both Russia and Great Britain have declared their willingness to join us in trying to establish the kind of policy I have suggested.

What are we waiting for?

It seems to me that we should lose no more time in starting to make the most of what appears to be a better climate for progress in this field.

Therefore, if elected President, I would count it the first order of business to follow up on the opportunity presented now by the other atomic powers. I would do this by conference or by consultation — at whatever level — in whatever place — the circumstances might suggest would be most fruitful.

In the meantime — and frankly because bitter experience has proved that we cannot rely even on the firm agreement of one bloc of world powers — we will proceed both with the production of hydrogen weapons and with further research in the field.

Now, just a word about the opposition that has developed to this proposal from the President, Mr. Nixon and others.

It is said that it does not provide for "proper international safeguards." This misses the point, for, as the scientists have long explained and the President has himself acknowledged, we can detect any large explosion anywhere.

It is said that other countries might get the jump on us. The President implied that we would stop our research while others would continue theirs. But I have made no such suggestion, and obviously we should not stop our research. We should prepare ourselves so that, if another country violated the agreement, we could promptly resume our testing program. And I am informed that we could be in a position to do so — if we have to — within not more than eight weeks.

The President even implied that the proposal would somehow reduce or curtail our power to defend ourselves. It would not. We would give up none of our stockpile. We would even add to it, as needed, for current production. We could continue to develop and test smaller nuclear weapons. We should continue our research and development work on guided missiles, for the defense of our cities and for use in the field.

I call your attention to the fact that many distinguished scientists, as well as other leading figures in this country and the world, share my views. On this matter the beginning and end of wisdom do not lie in the White House and its advisers.

But what I find most disturbing is the President's desire to end this discussion which so deeply concerns all mankind. He said at his press conference last week that he has said his "last word" on this subject. We cannot sweep the hydrogen bomb under the rug. But we can discuss it seriously and soberly, with mutual respect for the desire we all have for progress toward peace. This is one subject on which there cannot be, there must not be, any last word!

This is one matter on which the defeatist view that nothing can be done must be rejected. I say that something can be done, that the deadlock can be broken, that the world can make a new beginning toward peace.

And, finally, I say that America should take the initiative; that it will reassure millions all around the globe who are troubled by our rigidity, our reliance on nuclear weapons, and our concepts of massive retaliation, if mighty, magnanimous America spoke up for the rescue of man from the elemental fire which we have kindled.

As we all know, in the world in which we live only the strong can be free. Until we succeeded in abolishing the institution of war itself, we must have, together with our allies, the strength to deter aggression and to defeat it if it comes. That is the first condition of peace in an armed world.

One last word.

The search for peace will not end, it will begin, with the halting of these tests.

What we will accomplish is a new beginning, and the world needs nothing so much as a new beginning.

People everywhere are waiting for the United States to take once more the leadership for peace and civilization.

We must regain the moral respect we once had and which our stubborn, self-righteous rigidity has nearly lost.

Finally, I say to you that leaders must lead; that where the issue is of such magnitude, I have no right to stand silent; I owe it to you to express my views, whatever the consequences.

I repeat: This step can be taken. We can break the deadlock. We can make a fresh start. We can put the world on a new path to peace.

May He who rules us all give us the courage and patience, the vision and the humility we will need, and grant His blessing to this work.

To Arthur H. Sulzberger[95]

October 16, 1956

Dear Mr. Sulzberger:

I have just seen your editorial endorsing President Eisenhower for reelection, and while I am disappointed, of course, it reminds me to tell

[95] Publisher of the New York *Times*.

you what I have wanted to tell you for some time — that I am pro-foundly grateful for the admirable treatment the Times has accorded me and the Democratic campaign from the beginning. I have no com-plaints, indeed, nothing but gratitude and admiration for the coverage we have had in the Times.

With my thanks and regards to you and Mrs. Sulzberger, I am

Cordially,

P.S. Some day I hope to have a talk with you about clinging to the draft in its present form as a suitable base for a modern defense estab-lishment!

Stevenson delivered the following speech at Youngstown, Ohio, on October 18, 1956.[96]

The issues before the country have emerged much more clearly in these past few weeks, and so has the people's mood — clearly enough, incidentally, that the Republican managers have decided that, while they don't mind a part-time President, they can't stand a part-time candidate.[97]

I want to talk with you tonight about what I think is in some ways a startling and surely a significant thing that has developed in this cam-paign. It isn't new by any means, and yet I don't believe it has come out so clearly before. We realize more and more that the political lines in this country are now sharply drawn between those who are satisfied with things exactly as they are and those who feel, on the other hand, that there is still a tremendous lot to be done in America and in the world.

And I don't need to fill in the names of the parties, either.

There are only nineteen days left until the election. And so far the Republican candidates haven't made one single new proposal or sugges-tion for conducting the affairs of this country.

They say, smugly, that they are running on their record. What record? Or maybe I should say: whose record? For the fact is that the Republi-cans' proudest boast when they return the keys of office next January will be that they left things not too much worse than they found them — thanks, I may add, to a Democratic Congress these last two years.

[96] The text is from *The New America*, pp. 59–63.
[97] President Eisenhower had added a number of speeches in October to his pre-viously announced schedule.

It isn't just that these Republicans lack new ideas. They seem to despise new ideas. When someone makes a proposal for strengthening America, the automatic Republican response is to call the proposal irresponsible, dishonest, deceitful, theatrical and even wicked. If it has to do with farmers, it may even be immoral! And worst of all, afraid to face a new idea, they twist and distort it — until public understanding or discussion becomes almost impossible.

This isn't accident. It is the deliberate design of a political leadership which doesn't want voters to think, which knows, I suspect, its own bankruptcy of new ideas; and knows that its one forlorn hope is to wage the biggest advertising campaign in the history of American politics.

They talk of peace — but they refuse to talk — and try to keep the rest of us from talking — about how we can win the peace.

I have repeatedly said, and I am glad that the Republican candidate now agrees, that there is no difference between the two parties on the goal of a peaceful world. America has no war party, just as it has no peace party.

But there are important differences about what real peace means and about how we can achieve it.

We are all deeply grateful that the guns are stilled and we are not now engaged in a shooting war. And, Republican folklore to the contrary, it wasn't Eisenhower's election but Stalin's death that caused the Communists to end the war in Korea and turn their attention to Indochina, and you know what happened then!

But we know, too, that the uneasy condition that prevails in the world today which we call "peace" is based on a balance of terror, and that's a dangerous foundation.

The world is divided into three camps, the Communist bloc, the free bloc and the uncommitted or neutral nations. The cold war, in its larger sense, is a struggle for the allegiance of those nations which have not yet made their choice between freedom and Communism. Nations to whom economic progress, a better standard of living, is more important than proving how anti-Communist they are to please us — nations who want to know what America is for, not just what it is against. When they do choose, it will tip the scales of the world — and surely history's greatest demand upon this generation is that we throw America's full weight into this crucial balance.

We know that the world is spending something like $100 billion a year for war and defense — several times more than is being spent by government on the health, education and welfare of all the human race put together.

America alone is spending almost $1,000 a year for every family in the United States. In the last three years we have spent three times as much money on defense as in any other three-year peacetime period in our entire history. And I'm astonished that the Eisenhower administration is so proud and pleased and content with this situation.

I am not content. And neither are you. This isn't what we mean by peace. And it calls for a people's decision as to how we are to achieve that true peace which can only come if America leads the way.

I have urged in this campaign that we face up to the great issues which are presented in the great struggle of the twentieth century. They call for strength — and this strength takes many forms. They call for new answers to new problems.

In our struggle for peace we have to think of everything we do from all points of view — our own security, the effect on others — friend, foe or neutral.

It is of our security in a less universal matter that I wanted to speak particularly tonight.

It is a serious subject and I must speak seriously.

We are living in an age of complex new weapons and new military techniques.

It was in this connection that I said earlier in this campaign, before the American Legion convention in Los Angeles, that:

"Many military thinkers believe that the armies of the future, a future now upon us, will employ mobile, technically trained and highly professional units, equipped with tactical atomic weapons. Already it has become apparent that our most urgent need is to encourage trained men to re-enlist rather than to multiply the number of partly trained men as we are currently doing."

I noted in connection with this matter of meeting the increasingly urgent need for experienced and professional military personnel that this may well mean that we will need and want in the foreseeable future to turn to a method other than the draft for procuring such personnel.

This suggestion has been taken by some — and deliberately misconstrued by others — as a proposal for weakening our armed forces. It is exactly the opposite. It is a proposal for strengthening our armed forces.

The point is simply that we already need and will need more and more a type of military personnel — experienced and professional — which our present draft system does not give us. The draft means a tremendous turnover in our military personnel, and a resultant high proportion of inexperienced personnel. There is ample evidence that this inexperienced personnel is not meeting today's needs.

The Assistant Deputy Chief of Staff of Personnel for the Army, Major General Donald P. Booth, said this to a Congressional committee last May 31:

"The use of the Selective Service, with its short period of duty, causes a heavy turnover of personnel throughout the Army to the detriment of efficiency, unit spirit, economy, and battle worthiness . . . the two-year system is not conducive to economy nor stability."

A total of some 750,000 men will leave our armed forces this year. Simply to give basic training — nothing more — to their replacements will cost the American taxpayer $2.5 billion.

Air Force Chief of Staff, General Nathan F. Twining, testifying before a Congressional committee, condemned this needless personnel turnover in blunt terms — as to both its cost and its damage to our military effectiveness.

"If this trend continues," said General Twining, "there would be more than a 100 per cent turnover in the Air Force every five years. No industry could absorb this rate of personnel turnover. Nor can the Air Force. This rate of turnover would lead directly to an alarming decline in operational effectiveness."

It was such facts that persuaded Senator Mike Mansfield in March, 1955, to conclude:

"An armed service of professionals cannot be built by conscription. As in any profession, there must be a certain amount of incentive. The current situation in the branches of the service gives very little incentive to a young man to make a career out of the Army, Navy, Marines or Air Force."

It was such testimony that persuaded the Democratic Congress in 1955 to pass a career incentive act which resulted in base pay increases of from 7 to 17 per cent for enlisted men. It helped, but it was only a first step.

Every young man who has served in our armed forces knows the incredible waste of our present system of forced but short-term service. He knows the money that could be saved, the new efficiency that could result from a volunteer system which calls on young men not to endure two years of service because they have to, but to choose it — and for a longer period — because it offers advantages that seem to them appealing.

There seems to me every reason for searching out ways of making military service attractive enough that sufficient numbers of young men will choose such service voluntarily and will then remain in the services for longer periods.

By cutting down on turnover we can reduce the present enormous cost of training replacement after replacement. The money that is saved by this reduction in training costs can be used to pay our soldiers, sailors and airmen better salaries, to provide them with improved working conditions and perhaps to offer special bonus inducements for longer service. In this way we can develop a more effective defense, with higher morale, and I believe no higher cost.

Where there are needs for particularly highly trained men, as for example in radar, electronics and other specialties, I think we should consider offering university scholarships which will provide specialized training, in conjunction with a liberal education, to applicants, otherwise qualified, who will agree to spend a specific period in the armed forces.

No one could feel more strongly than I do the imperative necessity of keeping our armed forces at full strength. And I include the necessity of meeting our obligations on this score under the NATO agreements.

What I have proposed, I repeat, is a consideration — from the standpoint of military effectiveness, and from no other standpoint — of what is the best way of obtaining the military personnel we need.

I do add — and I think I speak for every person in America — that we will count it a better day when we find that these military needs can best be met by a system which does not mean the disruption of the lives of an entire generation of young men; which lets them plan their education, and get started more quickly along life's ordained course.

This is, I submit, a matter that should be seriously considered by the American people. The Republican candidates insist that it should not even be discussed, that this isn't the people's business, and that with a military man in the White House things like this can best be left up to him.

Well, I say just this: What is involved here is the security, perhaps the life or death, of this nation. What is involved here is the use that should be made of two years of our sons' lives. What is involved here is whether there should be new ways of more effectively meeting new problems. And I say that these are decisions that must be made not by one man — not by one general — not even by one man as president — but by the American people.

And I say beyond this that these decisions are not to be entrusted to an administration that has now built up a four-year record of rigid refusal to consider new ideas or new ways of doing things — and a four-year record of appalling indifference to human concerns.

Stevenson delivered the following speech at Cincinnati, Ohio, on October 19, 1956.[98]

I want to talk with you about the most serious failure of the Republican administration. I mean its failures in conducting our foreign policy. For, although its failures have been serious here at home, in serving the cause of peace they are far more serious.

I'm not going to spend much time on the Secretary of State, Mr. Dulles. Under our Constitution, the President conducts America's relations with the rest of the world, and he is responsible for them, and for his Secretary of State.

But I cannot refrain from commenting on Mr. Dulles' special contribution to our public life — you might almost call it Mr. Dulles' one new idea. I mean his habit of describing every defeat as a victory and every setback as a triumph.

We would all be better off with less fiction and more plain speaking about our foreign affairs.

The Republican candidate has a list of successes he likes to recite. And let us acknowledge such successes as we have had and be thankful for them.

But there is, unfortunately, another list.

This other list shows that Korea is still divided by an uneasy armistice line and still costs us hundreds of millions of dollars in economic and military aid.

The richest half of Indochina has become a new Communist satellite, and, after loud words and gestures, America emerged from that debacle looking like a "paper tiger."

Communism and neutralism have made great gains in Ceylon and Burma and Indonesia in the past year or so.

In India, which may be the key to a free Asia, we will have had four ambassadors in three and a half years — provided the administration gets around to filling the vacancy which has existed since last July. And that is a very poor way of showing our concern for the second largest and one of the most influential countries in the world.

In Western Europe, when the idea of a European defense community collapsed, we heard no more about Mr. Dulles' threatened "agonizing reappraisal," and meanwhile the declining influence of NATO has stirred widespread concern.

[98] The text is from *The New America*, pp. 27–34.

The Cyprus dispute has gravely disturbed the relations between three of our valued allies. Yet, so far as I can discover, we have been of no help in settling that dispute.

Iceland is insisting on the withdrawal of our forces from the key base we built there.

America's relations with its oldest and strongest allies, Britain and France, are more fragile than they have been in a generation or more.

And the Republican candidates say that "all is well," that Communism is "on the run," that "American prestige has never been higher," that peace is secure!

I do not mean to criticize the compromises that have been made. But, I severely criticize this effort to mislead the people, to describe an armed truce as peace, to gloss over serious difficulties, to obscure the grim realities, to encourage the people not to know the truth.

Now, what are the realities?

We live at a watershed of history — and no man knows in what direction the elemental forces that are loose in the world will turn.

This much is plain: the West, so long the dominant force in world affairs, has now gone on the defensive, drawing back little by little from positions long established in the rest of the world, particularly in Asia and Africa.

At the same time the Communist sphere has been growing, as it welded Communist ideology to modern technology to forge a powerful weapon for expansion.

And there is a third area or group — of peoples who have recently won or who are struggling to win independence, to gain control of their own futures, to escape from poverty, to win a place for themselves in the sun.

Though we have great influence — as much as any other power, or more — we can no more, alone, control the forces at work than we can make the seas do our bidding. For our power, like all power, is limited. We are rich, but there are only 168 million of us and we have 2.5 billion neighbors. Our power is necessarily in conflict with the power of others who do not share or only partly share our aspirations.

The end of this conflict cannot be foreseen, nor the victor. History knows no sure things! But we do know that we have not been doing well these past few years.

We need to be called to labor, not lulled with rosy and misleading assurances that all is well. Leadership which fails in this is leadership to disaster.

Yet a few nights ago the Republican candidate sought to make political capital out of a crisis that could engulf the world. Wars have begun over matters of far less moment than the Suez dispute — for the canal is a lifeline of the world.

I have refrained until now from commenting on the Suez crisis. But the Republican candidate has introduced it, in a highly misleading way, into the campaign.

A week ago he came before that so-called press conference on television arranged by advertising agents of the Republican campaign evidently more for adulation than for information. He announced that he had "good news" about Suez.[99]

But there is no "good news" about Suez. Why didn't the President tell us the truth? Why hasn't he told us frankly that what has happened in these past few months is that the Communist rulers of Soviet Russia have accomplished a Russian ambition that the czars could never accomplish? Russian power and influence have moved into the Middle East — the oil tank of Europe and Asia and the great bridge between East and West.

When the historians write of our era they may, I fear, find grim irony in the fact that when Russian power and influence were for the first time being firmly established in the Middle East, our government was loudly, proudly proclaiming our victorious conduct of the cold war and the President reported good news from Suez.

This reverse was not inevitable. I cannot remember any other series of diplomatic strokes so erratic, naïve and clumsy as the events of the past few years through which Russia gained welcome to the Near and Middle East.

The trouble is that neither there nor anywhere else has the administration shown any real capacity to adjust its policies to new conditions. Three and one-half years have passed since Stalin's death. It is now fourteen months since the Geneva Conference at the Summit. And I ask the Republican candidate to tell us of a single new idea that has emerged from Washington for meeting the new Soviet challenge.

Instead of fresh ideas and creative thinking about the great struggle of our century, our approach to world affairs has remained sterile and timid. It has remained tied to old methods, old thinking, and old slogans.

It won't work.

I believe that the President knows this. I think it was this realization that led him, three years ago, to think seriously of forming a new politi-

[99] President Eisenhower had declared on October 12 that progress in settling the dispute over the Suez Canal was "most gratifying."

cal party.[100] For the central fact is that the leader of the Republican party cannot possibly deal with the problems of today's world! Does that sound startling? If the President called now for the action which is needed in the conduct of our foreign affairs, it would split the Republican party right down the middle — with the election only three weeks away. For the Republican party has been hopelessly divided over foreign policy ever since the League of Nations battle and the triumph of the isolationists thirty-five years ago.

The right to criticize — fairly, honestly, responsibly — is deeply rooted in the American political tradition. We cannot deal intelligently with problems unless we first recognize that they exist and ask ourselves what mistakes we made. Honest self-criticism is still the not-so-secret weapon of democracy.

There goes with criticism a clear responsibility to state a constructive alternative. What will a Democratic administration do to meet the challenge of our times? How will a Democratic foreign policy differ from the Republicans?

Let me say at once that I have no slick formula, no patent medicine, to cure our problems. The difficulties which face American policy makers in all parts of the world are deep-rooted and complex. And this will continue to be so regardless of who wins in November.

But it is equally true that there is much that can and must be done.

First, our entire military establishment must be re-examined to determine how we can best build and keep the forces we need for our national security.

There is much evidence that we don't have the military establishment we need now. The problem is, I think, less one of money than adjusting our thinking and planning to the revolutionary changes in weapons and in world relationships.

Among other things, I have suggested a restudy of the Selective Service system to find, if possible, some better way of meeting our manpower requirements than the draft with its rapid turnover.

I have been surprised that the Republican candidate has reacted so violently to my suggestion that this ought to be considered. I thought that it was hardly open to debate that we need to find a better way of obtaining the mobile, expert, ready forces we need in the handling of the new weapons and the new tactics of the new military age. My suggestion, I should like to add, was aimed at stronger, not weaker, forces.

Second, I would propose — in view of the unthinkable implications of

[100] For a discussion of this, see Robert J. Donovan, *Eisenhower: The Inside Story* (New York: Harper, 1956).

modern warfare — that disarmament should be at the heart of American foreign policy.

I have suggested that we could initiate a world policy of stopping the exploding of large-size nuclear bombs — the H-bombs. This appears to be a safe, workable, reliable proposal.

I call your attention to the fact that the other powers concerned have stated that they are prepared to act.

If we bring this about, all mankind will be the gainers. And I think that we, the United States, should once more assert the moral initiative which many wait and pray for to break out of the deadly deadlock which has blocked all progress toward arresting the arms race that imperils us all.

I am not dogmatic about this or any other proposal. Honest and open debate may suggest better ways. I think the heart of the issue is a weighing of different risks. The risk of permitting the arms race to continue unchecked seems to me most serious in view of the furies that have been unleashed. The world has had the last great war that civilization can afford. We must, if it is humanly possible, make a fresh start for peace and reason.

Next, I propose that we act, and act fast, to meet the challenge of the underdeveloped countries. The choices these nations make may well determine the future of freedom in the world.

We must do better than we have been doing. And the way to begin is to understand the hopes and fears of these peoples and to work out with them new relationships based on co-operation and trust and mutual respect. I might add that, in my judgment, the spirit of these new relationships is more important than an expansion of economic aid.

I believe, too, that we must breathe new life into the Atlantic Community. NATO has served and will, in some form, continue to serve an essential need for collective security. But let us recognize clearly that co-operation in defense implies and demands co-operation in political and economic affairs as well. And in the neglect of these matters lies the explanation of the declining vigor of the alliance.

Again, I propose a fresh approach to the problems of world economics. This new approach must take account of the almost universal desire for economic development and must rest solidly on the principle of mutual advantage. I am more interested in practical measures than in global plans for solving all the world's problems by some master stroke. I am impressed, for example, by the possibilities of a world food bank as a means of aiding economic development and putting our agricultural surpluses to work.

Finally, and perhaps most important, I propose that the American government deal openly, frankly, honestly with the American people. I think that in the name of security we have been sweeping far too many things under the rug. We have drawn a paper curtain between the American people and the world in which they live.

It is easy — and when mistakes have been made or reverses suffered, it is all too inviting — to use the excuse of security for not telling the people the facts.

Some things must be kept private, but a democratic government must never forget that it is no wiser and no stronger than the people whose servant it is. The sources of information are the springs from which democracy drinks. These waters alone can nourish and sustain us in a free way of life.

This seems to me the central point, for unless the American people are given the information required to understand the needs of this tempestuous, turbulent period when the swirling waters of three revolutions are converging, they will listen to demagogues who promise quick and easy solutions. But the ideological revolution of Communism cannot be met by quick and easy solutions. Neither can the political revolution of the oppressed and the newly independent peoples, or the historic revolution of technology throughout the world.

I ask your support not because I offer promises of peace and progress, but because I do not. I promise only an unending effort to use our great power wisely in pursuing the goal of peace — in full knowledge that as soon as one problem is brought under control, another is more than likely to arise.

I ask your support not because I say that all is well, but because I say that we must work hard, with tireless dedication, to make the small gains out of which, we may hope, large gains will ultimately be fashioned.

I ask your support not in the name of complacency, but in the name of anxiety.

We must take the world as we find it and try to work in the direction of peace. We did not want a contest with world Communism, but the contest is upon us. The first and in some ways the most difficult task is to recognize this fact of contest. General George Marshall used to warn his colleagues not "to fight the problem," but to deal with it. That is good advice for us today. If we try to hide the problem from our own minds, to pretend that it does not exist, to wage our political contests here at home in terms of misleading promises, we will be fighting the problem and we will fail.

Peace is our goal. I am in politics as a result of a personal decision to do what I could to help in building a peaceful world. That decision carried with it an obligation – the obligation to talk sense, to tell the truth as I see it, to discuss the realities of our situation, never to minimize the tasks that lie ahead.

I don't know whether that is the way to win in politics, but it is the only way I want to win. For, if you entrust me with the responsibility of power, I do not want to assume that power under any false pretenses nor do I want you to labor under any misapprehensions. To do otherwise would be not only to mislead you, but to make my own task almost impossibly difficult, for I would not have won your support on the basis of an understanding between us about the needs we face and the demands they place upon us.

To achieve such an understanding seems to me to be the true function of politics.

To Stanley Woodward[101]

October 22, 1956

Dear Stanley:

I should have acknowledged your letter long before this, but I have been on the move pretty constantly – to put it mildly!

I am glad you agree about the urgent need of discussing foreign relations and I am enclosing a copy of my speech at Cincinnati which I am afraid didn't get much coverage.

I see far too little of you these days and just hope we can arrange to get together after it is over.

Cordially,

ADLAI

P.S. . . .

Hollywood actor Douglas Fairbanks, Jr., had been associated with Stevenson in liberal political causes since the early 1940's.

To Douglas Fairbanks[102]

En route, October 1956[103]

Dear Doug:

Bill Blair told me of your call in New York the other day and I am sorry that my "managers" had contrived such an appalling schedule that

[101] Treasurer of the Democratic National Committee, 1953–1955, and former ambassador to Canada. The original is in the possession of Mr. Woodward.

[102] The original is in the possession of Mr. Fairbanks.

[103] This letter was written before October 24, the Wednesday referred to in the second sentence.

I just couldn't break away. I had hoped to see you on Wednesday but I now find that I have four rallies scheduled between my arrival at noon and five o'clock when I leave for Pennsylvania, which means that I won't be able to get to the hotel at all. If the spirit moves you and you would like to ride along with the press that afternoon, I hope you will do so and perhaps we can contrive a minute together along the way. Tom Finletter or Mrs. Ronald Tree who can be reached at the headquarters would know times of arrival, etc.

I am grateful to you also for that fine speech draft which will be of great help to me in the days ahead.

With warmest regards and my profound thanks, I am

Cordially,

ADLAI

Stevenson sent the following telegram to the managing editor of the Tucson Daily Citizen *on learning of the death of his old friend Dick Jenkins, at whose Arizona ranch he had stayed several times.*

To George Rosenberg

October 22, 1956

DICK JENKINS WAS ONE OF MY OLDEST AND CLOSEST FRIENDS AND I AM HEARTSICK AT THE TRAGIC NEWS. HE DIED AS HE LIVED, ERECT, FACING FORWARD AND SAYING WHAT HE BELIEVED WITH VIGOR AND DIGNITY. ARIZONA HAS SUFFERED A GRIEVOUS LOSS AND I HAVE LOST A DEAR FRIEND.

Philip Perlman, who had been Solicitor General of the United States during the Truman Administration, wrote Stevenson on October 23: "You have already proved over and over again that you are the leader our country needs so much."

To Philip B. Perlman[104]

En Route, October 1956

Dear Phil:

I am told that I received over 2,000 letters a day during these past few weeks, but, believe me, none has pleased me more than yours. I think

---

[104] A copy is in A.E.S., I.S.H.L.

you know how highly I value your confidence and good will and that you should feel the way you do is a source of enormous encouragement to me. I am profoundly grateful.

Cordially,

To Mrs. Franklin D. Roosevelt [105]

En Route, October 25, 1956

Dear Mrs. Roosevelt:

Anna Rosenberg told me today of your additional contribution to my campaign and I think you must know how profoundly touched I am. You have done so much already — but then I have long since discovered that there is no end to your kindnesses to me.

Cordially,

ADLAI

On October 19, 1956, Wladyslaw Gomulka, the leader of the Polish National Communists, was elected First Secretary of the Polish Communist party and pro-Soviet Communists were ousted. The leaders of the Soviet Union, including Khrushchev, flew to Warsaw and tried to prevent Gomulka's election. They failed. On October 23, peaceful demonstrations demanding the withdrawal of Soviet troops occurred in Hungary. The next day national Communist Imre Nagy became premier. But many Hungarians were unwilling to accept a settlement similar to that in Poland. A general strike swept the country. Nagy made concessions to non-Communists and included some of them in his government. On November 1, Nagy renounced the Warsaw Pact and declared Hungary's neutrality. On November 4, Soviet troops assaulted Budapest. For weeks there was bloody fighting but finally the back of the revolution was broken.

In a televised speech to the nation on October 31, 1956, President Eisenhower suggested that the struggles of the Poles and Hungarians pointed to the success of his Administration's having advocated liberation of the satellite nations: "We could not, of course, carry out this policy by resort to force. . . . But we did help to keep alive the hope of these people for freedom."[106]

On October 27, 1956, Stevenson delivered the following speech in Los Angeles.[107]

[105] The original is in the Franklin D. Roosevelt Library, Hyde Park, New York.
[106] New York *Times*, November 1, 1956.
[107] The text is from *The New America*, pp. 243–250.

I have spoken often in this campaign of the evils of indifference in the management of our public affairs, of absentee administration, of political administration, of administration without heart and without heart in its work. The farmer, the small businessman, the children and teachers in ramshackle and overcrowded schools, workmen in many places, the sick and the aged, and the government employee have all had a first-hand experience with this kind of government. To them a part-time president and an indifferent administration is more than a phrase. The lives of many have been altered in these past four years; the lives of some blighted. Ask the thousands who have been kicked around as security risks in the Republican effort to prove one of the calumnies of 1952 — that our government was riddled with subversives.

Tonight I want to tell you first what this kind of leadership or lack of leadership means — both abroad and here at home.

And I want to talk about the effort made by this Administration to cover up its errors — errors that result from abdication of responsibility.

In the last week the American people have watched anxiously the heroic efforts of the Poles and Hungarians to free themselves from the hard yoke of Moscow.

And the so-called Republican "truth squad"[108] last Friday in Rock Island, Illinois, celebrated the event by announcing that the great revolts were "a clear-cut result of the new American foreign policy."[109] We have said more foolish and insulting things about other peoples during the Eisenhower-Dulles period than we like to recall and at an expense in good will and respect we can ill afford, but this was a new low even for the Republicans.

If it was true, it would be shameful stupidity to say it; but as it is false, it was a gross effort to exploit the anguish of brave people to make votes in an American election. The credit goes where it belongs — to the heroic Poles and Hungarians who face the tanks and guns of their Russian rulers; it belongs to those who were willing to risk all — their lives, their fortunes, their families — for freedom. No credit goes to men who in recent weeks have exposed themselves to nothing more dan-

108 A group formed during the 1952 campaign to respond to Democratic campaign statements, and reconstituted at the suggestion of Republican party chairman Leonard Hall in 1956. Among its members were Senator Carl T. Curtis, of Nebraska; Representative George Meader, of Michigan; and Robert L. Kunzig, an attorney employed by the Republican National Committee. See Dwight D. Eisenhower, *Waging Peace, 1956–1961* (Garden City, New York: Doubleday, 1965), p. 15.

109 Stevenson's first response to this statement was: "In my judgment, the people responsible were the Poles and the Hungarians who risked their lives, who risked their fortunes and their families' futures in their fight for freedom. I am shocked that Republican politicians should claim credit. This is not a matter of politics. It is a question of the bravery of the Poles and the Hungarians." New York *Times*, October 26, 1956.

gerous than their own campaign oratory. And, as a postscript, let me remind the Republican "truth squad" that truth might be an interesting experiment for them someday; that they could have announced more accurately that we were caught off guard, that when the fighting broke out in Poland, the American ambassador wasn't even at his post — he was visiting Berlin to see his dentist. And when the revolt broke out in Hungary, our envoy was not even in that country.

And you may gauge President Eisenhower's interest in this whole problem by another bit of history. In June of last year, by a vote of 367–0 the House of Representatives passed a resolution expressing its sympathy with the satellite nations and condemning colonialism. When asked about this resolution on June 29, President Eisenhower said: "I did not know about that. Maybe I was fishing that day. I don't know."

But this was not an isolated example. Let me give you another example where the issue of war and peace was at stake.

The winter and spring of 1954 were a time of deep trial and anxiety. Indochina was falling to the Communists. I saw that frightening war in the rice paddies and jungles with my own eyes.[110] The free world was divided, troubled and alarmed. Hasty voices — Mr. Nixon's, with characteristic volubility, was among them — were advocating armed intervention by American troops. On February 12 the *New York Times* reported that Senate leaders "alarmed by fears of possible U.S. involvement in the Indo-China war" had called high members of the administration to an urgent secret conference. On the same day the *Times* also reported that President Eisenhower had gone south for hunting with Secretary Humphrey and had bagged his limit of quail.

Two days later the alarm had deepened in Washington and the papers reported that President Eisenhower was leaving for a six-day vacation in California. On February 19, Secretary Dulles returned from the critical Four-Power Conference in Berlin. He couldn't report to the President. The *New York Times* said, "It was golf again today for President Eisenhower," at Palm Springs.

Later, on April 13, Mr. Dulles and British Foreign Secretary Anthony Eden met to explore the possibilities of joint action — joint military action — in Indochina. The *New York Times* reported that President Eisenhower had landed in the South "to begin a golfing vacation."

Next day it was announced that we would airlift aid to Indochina; and also that the President was playing golf in Georgia.

On April 17, the *New York Times* said in a headline that the United States "weighs fighting in Indochina if necessary." The President, it said, was still vacationing in Georgia.

[110] See *The Papers of Adlai E. Stevenson*, Vol. V, Chap. Seven.

The next day the country learned from the papers that Nixon had said that the United States might have to intervene with military force. Less spectacular news that day was that President Eisenhower had played golf in Augusta with Billy Joe Patton.

On April 23, it was announced that the last outposts around Dien Bien Phu, the French stronghold, had fallen. That day the President arrived in Georgia for a new golfing holiday.

The free world suffered a severe defeat in Asia and lost a rich country and more than ten million people in Indochina. And after it was all over Secretary Dulles boasted in an article in *Life* magazine that it had been a victory.

He also boasted that we had won this victory by our bold behavior and by bringing the country to the brink of war. And when President Eisenhower was asked his opinion, he replied, "I have not read the article."

I could go on. The President was away golfing when it was announced early last year that our Air Force had gone on a full war footing as a result of the Formosa crisis. He was shooting quail when we evacuated the Tachen Islands.[111] He was golfing in New Hampshire in June, 1954, when the Soviets shot down a U.S. plane off Alaska. In the *New York Times*, it said, "There was no visible evidence that the President had anything on his mind other than having a good time."

In February of this year, the President was golfing in Georgia during the on-again, off-again, on-again mixup over the shipment of tanks to Saudi Arabia which so alarmed the Israeli people.[112] Mr. Dulles, as usual, was out of the country. Mr. Herbert Hoover, Jr.,[113] was running the store.

The President was asked this year whether Russia was leading us in guided missiles. He answered, and I quote him, that he was "astonished at the amount of information that others get that I don't."

The President was asked on April 4th of this year about an urgent message on the Middle Eastern Crisis that Prime Minister Eden had sent him ten days earlier. It developed that he didn't even know the letter existed!

111 The President did not consider these islands in the Formosa Strait to be worth defending and ordered the U.S. Seventh Fleet to evacuate their Nationalist Chinese population to Formosa on February 5, 1955. See the New York *Times*, February 6, 1955.
112 The press reported on February 15, 1956, that light tanks were being readied for shipment to Saudi Arabia. President Eisenhower halted the shipment, studied the matter, and on February 18 permitted the shipment to proceed. He denied that there was a "mixup" and defended his actions as an attempt to be impartial to both sides in the Middle East. See Eisenhower, *Waging Peace*, p. 29.
113 Acting Secretary of State.

The President is an honorable man. So when he smilingly assures us that all is well and America's prestige has never been higher, he just must not know that in fact the American star is low on the world's horizon.

And even what happens here at home passes the President by.

In 1953 and 1954 we had a serious drop in employment and economic activity. On February 17, 1954 the Department of Commerce announced that unemployment had passed the three million mark. The *New York Times* said that the President would act if there was no upturn soon. It also said that he had just departed for five days' vacation at Palm Springs, California.

A year ago last May he was asked why Secretary Hobby[114] had difficulty in foreseeing the great demand for Salk vaccine. He said he didn't know anything about it, and to ask Mrs. Hobby.

Last February, when the head of the General Services Administration[115] was let out for using his job to help friends get government contracts, the President thought he had resigned for "personal reasons."

The President was asked if Republican leaders had told him why they killed an important bill to bring aid to areas suffering from unemployment. He said, "No, you are telling me something now that I didn't know."

When President Eisenhower's Secretary of Labor[116] urged extending minimum wage legislation to employees of interstate retail chain stores, the President was asked where he stood. He said, "I don't know that much about it."

This list could go on endlessly.

I have left out of the list every case where the President's absence from Washington or his ignorance of crucial facts could be traced to his illnesses.

And I want to make it clear that I realize fully that any president will inevitably be gone on some occasions when a crisis arises. I surely don't begrudge the President either the recreation, the repose or the exercise necessary for health. I think even a president is entitled to enjoy himself occasionally.

But a president must assume the full responsibilities of that high post. He is the Chief Executive. And I say bluntly that I do not agree with President Eisenhower that the United States can be run by a board of directors, with the President presiding at occasional meetings.

Nothing could be more at odds with our constitutional system. The

[114] Mrs. Oveta Culp Hobby, Secretary of Health, Education, and Welfare.
[115] Edmund F. Mansure.
[116] James P. Mitchell.

President was elected to the responsibilities of leadership by the American people. [John Foster] Dulles, Wilson,[117] [Ezra Taft] Benson, [Sinclair] Weeks, and others were not elected at all. They are the hired hands, but the President runs the store.

And we know now that the Eisenhower system just doesn't work. The price of the President's abdication has been irresponsibility in our foreign policy. This irresponsibility has brought the coalition of the free nations to a point where even its survival has been threatened. And it has brought American prestige to the lowest level in our history.

Here at home, we are in the midst of a great social transition. We have come to see with new clarity the full implications of our Bill of Rights and of our democratic faith, and we are moving forward again to assure the equal rights of man to all Americans, regardless of race or color.

Throughout the nation many citizens of both races are working quietly, working hard, risking much, daring much to solve the stubborn problems that lie in the path of any great social transformation.

Who but the President could say for the whole nation that those participating in this great effort — sometimes even though they disagree with the decision itself — deserve the gratitude, the respect, the moral support of their countrymen? But President Eisenhower, far from rising to this challenge of leadership, has not even expressed his views on the decision and the goal itself.

Nor has he acted with decision to sustain even the most elementary right for all adult Americans — the right to vote. The assurance of this right to all citizens is written in our laws and must surely be the keystone of our democratic institutions. But here again Mr. Eisenhower has seen no challenge of leadership.

Nothing can be more essential to our system of government than affirmative presidential leadership. The President was elected to these responsibilities by the American people. He is the only officer of our government who is elected by all the people.

These four years of a part-time Presidency have been bad enough. But what would another four be like?

Well, I'll tell you. But I don't really need to, because yesterday, at the Commonwealth Club in San Francisco, Republican Senator [George W.] Malone of Nevada put it squarely and bluntly. The "greatest sin" the Republican party has committed, this Republican senator said, has been "carrying on what Democrats started." Then he added, "But we'll change that in 1957 and 1958 if you elect . . . President Eisenhower."

Why? Why will re-electing the same man president mean a whole

117 Charles E. Wilson, Secretary of Defense.

new and different government policy — a policy of wrecking twenty years of Democratic building in America?

We know exactly why.

The reason is simply that, if the Republicans should be returned to office again, the powers of the directorate which has governed in the last four years will be shared and perhaps pre-empted by a man you know, and know well, too well. I refer to the heir apparent, hand-picked by President Eisenhower — Richard Nixon.

President Eisenhower will not be a more vigorous leader in the next four years than in the last four years. He will almost certainly be even less disposed to lead. He will have greater need to conserve his energies. The habit of total delegation once formed is not easily changed.

More important, he will not be allowed to lead. The Republican politicians, we now know, love their leader, the President, mostly at election time. They will follow him to the polls, but no further. For four years the Democrats in Congress have repeatedly had to rescue the President's program from his own party.

Beginning in 1957, if President Eisenhower should be re-elected, the Republican leaders in Congress will owe him exactly nothing. He cannot help them get elected again because, under the Twenty-second Amendment, he couldn't run again even if his age and health permitted.

We know from past experience that the President will not lead. We know that, if he should try, his party will not follow. And into this vacuum would come Richard Nixon — beloved by the most reactionary wing of Old Guard Republicanism.

That's why Senator Malone is so confident that a new term for Mr. Eisenhower will mean an opportunity to do a wrecking job. It's because a new term for Mr. Eisenhower will mean a new destiny for Richard Nixon.

In the last few weeks a plaintive note has entered the Republican newspaper discussion of Mr. Nixon. They say in effect: "Can't people see that this man has changed?"

Well, people prefer men who don't have to be changed. And even some mighty good Republicans don't think the Republican party ought to be in the laundry business.

A lot of people just don't believe that Richard Nixon is really at home in this role as the Little Lord Fauntleroy of the Republican party. They wonder if he doesn't yearn for his old tar bucket and his brush. And they suspect that, if the circumstances let him, he will make a fast grab for them again.

Common decency is at stake here. But more is at stake even than that.

President Eisenhower does not lead because he won't. Richard Nixon cannot lead because the American people will not follow.

This is partly because Nixon has a long record against the people. He has voted against public housing, to weaken Point Four, against extending Social Security, against middle-income housing, against increased appropriations for school lunches, against increased REA loan funds and, of course, he voted repeatedly for the Taft-Hartley Act.

People mistrust a man who votes against the people. They have an additional reason to mistrust Mr. Nixon, for on several of these issues he has taken an equally firm stand on both sides.

Mr. Nixon's advertisers call him "adaptable." Well, that's just the trouble. For what "adaptable" means here is that this man has no standard of truth but convenience and no standard of morality except what will serve his interest in an election. The plain fact is that the people of this country just can't picture Richard Nixon as the leader of the greatest of the world's nations.

They can't imagine putting Richard Nixon's hand on the trigger of the H-bomb. They just don't trust him.

Our nation stands at a fork in the political road.

In one direction lies a land of slander and scare; the land of sly innuendo, the poison pen, the anonymous phone call and hustling, pushing, shoving; the land of smash and grab and anything to win.

This is Nixonland.

But I say to you that it is not America.

America is something different. It is a land of mutual trust and confidence, not suspicion and division, a land of neighborliness, of unity of purpose, and of common faith.

America is a tranquil land, where people seek fulfillment, not by the frantic service of themselves, but by the quiet and thoughtful service of their communities.

This we must be — a free land, where people speak their minds without glancing over their shoulders, where the right to think as one chooses, write as one chooses, and worship as one chooses is safe from inquisitorial arrogance and the wolf packs of conformity.

America is a just land, where people are safe from the hit-and-run politicians who ambush the innocent passers-by; a land where fact can overtake falsehood, and where the accused and the abused can count on a fair trial in a fair environment.

Above all, America is a growing land, humble not boastful, modest not arrogant, believing deeply that life means change, and that change is the product of the free contest of ideas.

[307]

This is our America. It is the America for which the Democratic party has fought before — and it is the New America that is our goal today.

I summon you tonight to join in the march to the New America — to the banishment of smear and suspicion and to the enthronement once again of reason and responsibility.

The tide of Democratic sentiment is rising through the land. As we remain steadfast in our course, I know the rising tide will sweep us to victory.

On October 13, Mr. and Mrs. John Rodgers, of Bloomington, Illinois, sent Stevenson a new pair of shoes from his hometown neighbors and friends, explaining that they did not want him to enter the White House "with a hole in the sole of your shoe."[118]

To Mr. and Mrs. John A. Rodgers III

October 29, 1956

My dear Friends:

Word has finally caught up with me that you have sent me some shoes, and I hasten to express my belated but nevertheless sincere thanks. The shoes, alas, are a half size too small, according to what my secretary tells me. She also assures me you will not be unduly offended if I return them for size 8½C — and I hope I shall be able to tread on that good fortune you talked about!

With my warm wishes and utmost thanks for your thoughtfulness in sending this most useful gift, I am

Cordially,

Stevenson made the following telephone call from Boston, Massachusetts, to all Democratic state chairmen on October 29, 1956.[119]

This election is like 1948. It is going to be decided in the last week.

This election is close. My trip around the country this week has convinced me that we are going to win. Despite the Republican press, our own private polls show that we have convinced the farmer, the small

---

[118] This refers to the Pulitzer Prize photograph of Stevenson, taken during the 1952 campaign, which is included in the illustrations to *The Papers of Adlai E. Stevenson*, Vol. IV.

[119] The text is taken from a mimeograph copy of a transcription of the call prepared as a press release.

businessman, the working man — the great majority of Americans — that their best interests are served by the Democratic Party.

And we know beyond doubt that the people do not want a part-time President. Most of all, they do not want Nixon and the Republican Party to run the destiny of America the next four years.

Last week, we had one of the most successful rallies ever held in Madison Square Garden in New York City. I hope you saw it on television. We then had what the New York Times called the largest and most enthusiastic rallies ever put on by any Party in the New York suburbs. And my trip to Illinois, to New Mexico, to California and to Arizona was beyond my most optimistic hopes. For example, 25,000 people in Los Angeles — more than Eisenhower's audience in the same city last week — had the spirit of victory in the air.

Now this week is when the real work begins, and it depends on you!

That's why I am calling you today. This election will be won in the precincts — by better organization in getting out our vote, by telephone campaigns, by that extra effort that is the difference between winning and losing.

As State Chairmen, you are the leaders of our vast army of workers. I ask each of you to now call your County Leaders, your District Chairmen, your Ward Chairmen, your Precinct Committeemen, and Committee Women. Tell them that Estes and I are depending on them to carry the Democratic message to each home — to each voter — so that our Party will once again lead America in a time when America desperately needs leadership.

My Campaign Manager, Jim Finnegan, is here in Boston with me today. He knows something about winning elections — never having lost one in his life. Jim sometimes calls me "the tiger." Well, I can only return the compliment by introducing him as the "tiger's trainer."

On October 30 — the day after Israel invaded Egypt — Britain and France, keeping their plans secret from the United States, presented Egypt and Israel with an ultimatum demanding their withdrawal from the area of the Suez Canal and acceptance of a temporary Anglo-French occupation. Israel agreed but Egypt refused. The next day Britain and France launched attacks by air on Egyptian military installations and then landed troops.

On October 30 the United States asked the Security Council of the United Nations to call for an immediate cease-fire, withdrawal of Israeli troops, and the withholding of help to aggressors by any member of the

UN. *Russia introduced a similar resolution, but both were vetoed by Britain and France. The General Assembly met in emergency session on November 1. The United States backed resolutions, which were adopted, calling for an immediate cease-fire and for the removal of Israeli, British and French troops from Egyptian soil. An emergency United Nations force to maintain and supervise the cease-fire was approved. On November 6 the cease-fire took effect.*

On October 31, President Eisenhower spoke to the nation. He stated: "The United States was not consulted in any way about any phase of these actions. Nor were we informed of them in advance. . . . We believe these actions to have been taken in error, for we do not accept the use of force as a wise or proper instrument for the settlement of international disputes." After explaining that the United States would bring the question before the UN General Assembly the next day, Eisenhower added: "As I review the march of world events in recent years I am ever more deeply convinced that the United Nations represents the soundest hope for peace in the world."[120]

Stevenson immediately requested equal television time and he delivered the following speech on November 1, 1956.[121]

The President spoke to you about the Middle East crisis last night. The networks have been good enough to accord me time to speak tonight, and I want to tell you how this crisis came about, this crisis which is so threatening to peace and to our interests in this strategic area.

This matter should be above politics — if anything can be a few days before election — because all Americans suffer from any failure of our foreign policy, and from war anywhere in the world; for in this hydrogen age war is contagious.

I have only a few moments, so let me hastily sum up the central facts of the situation. I can find no better way to do this than to read you a sentence from a special dispatch from Washington in today's *New York Times:* "The United States has lost control of events in areas vital to its security. This is the main conclusion of serious and well-informed men here tonight concerning the United States' role in the Middle East crisis."

The condition which confronts us is stark and simple — our Middle-Eastern policy is at [an] absolute dead end. And the hostilities going on tonight in which Israel, Egypt, Britain and France are involved reflect

[120] New York *Times*, November 1, 1956.
[121] The text is from *The New America*, pp. 34–38.

the bankruptcy of our policy; and they have given the Soviet Union two great victories.

The first Communist victory is the establishment in the Middle East of Russian influence.

The second Communist victory is the breakdown of the Western alliance. This has been a supreme objective of Soviet policy since the end of the Second World War.

As the climax, the United States finds itself arrayed in the United Nations with Soviet Russia and the dictator of Egypt against the democracies of Britain, France and Israel.

A foreign policy which has brought about these results — which has benefited Communism and has cut our own country off from our democratic friends — is a foreign policy which has failed.

And, at a time when the uprisings in Poland and Hungary are opening the Soviet world to freedom, the strategic Middle East is opening to Communist penetration.

I have three points to make tonight.

The first is that this series of failures could have been averted — that they were in great part the result of ill-considered and mistaken policies of this administration.

The second is that this administration not only made mistake after mistake in its Middle Eastern policy, but has withheld the consequences from the American people.

The third is that there are many things which might have been done in the past year to avert war in the Middle East.

The Middle East is one of the most important strategic areas in the world. It has three-quarters of the world's known oil reserves, and it controls the land, sea and air communications linking three continents. All nations which have sought world domination have wanted to control the Middle East.

When President Eisenhower came to office in January, 1953, Communist influence in the Middle East was at a low ebb, and the area was more free of violence than it had been in years.

Things changed.

Secretary of State Dulles began by giving General Naguib — Colonel Nasser's predecessor — a pistol as a personal gift from President Eisenhower. The fateful symbolism of this gift was not lost upon Israel or the Arab states. It was the token of a new policy called "impartiality" between the Arab states, on the one hand, and, on the other, the new democracy of Israel whom they had vowed to destroy and whom we and the United Nations were pledged to defend.

Following this, and pursuing the new policy of trying to build up

Nasser as a bulwark of stability in the Middle East, the United States pressured the British to evacuate their great military base along the Suez Canal without making any provision for international control of the canal.

Then Mr. Dulles fanned the flames of ambition, nationalism, and rivalry in the Middle East with the so-called Baghdad Pact as a defense against Russia. But its military advantages were far outweighed by its political disadvantages. And it was particularly offensive to Nasser — the very man whom we had been trying to build up.

Then in 1955 Colonel Nasser's negotiations for some arms from the United States bogged down in everlasting haggling. And so he negotiated an arms deal with the Communists.

We not only failed to stop the introduction of Communist arms into the Middle East, but we refused to assist Israel with arms too. We also refused to give Israel a guarantee of her integrity, although we had given such guarantees to others.

And in the meantime we dangled before Colonel Nasser the prospect of financial aid for building a great dam on the Nile.

In time, the bankruptcy of the Eisenhower administration's policy began to become evident even to Mr. Dulles. It became clear that Colonel Nasser was not a bulwark of stability, but a threat to peace in the Middle East. Thereupon President Eisenhower abruptly and publicly withdrew the aid he had led Colonel Nasser to expect.

As anyone could have foreseen, Colonel Nasser promptly retaliated by seizing the Suez Canal.

Driven by our policy into isolation and desperation, Israel evidently became convinced that the only hope remaining was to attack Egypt before Egypt attacked her. So she took her tragic decision.

Here we stand today. We have alienated our chief European allies. We have alienated Israel. We have alienated Egypt and the Arab countries. And in the UN our main associate in Middle Eastern matters now appears to be Communist Russia — in the very week when the Red Army has been shooting down the brave people of Hungary and Poland. We have lost every point in the game. I doubt if ever before in our diplomatic history has any policy been such an abysmal, such a complete and such a catastrophic failure.

It is bad enough to be responsible for such a disastrous policy. I think it is almost worse in a democracy to try and conceal the truth from the people. But this is what the Eisenhower administration has done systematically with regard to the situation in the Middle East.

It was only a few days ago — on October 12 — that President Eisen-

hower himself said in a political telecast: "I've got the best announcement that I think I can possibly make to America tonight. The progress
made in the settlement of the Suez dispute this afternoon at the United
Nations is most gratifying. . . . It looks like there's a very great problem
that's behind us."

And the next day Vice-President Nixon gave his views. "We have kept
the peace," Mr. Nixon said, "and it appears that Mr. Eisenhower's
tolerance and wisdom and leadership will serve to avert armed conflict
in that part of the globe."

Either the President and the Vice-President did not know how serious
the situation was in the Middle East or they did not want the American
people to know — at least, not till after the election.

And only last Sunday — just four days ago — Mr. Dulles said in a
television interview that the United States, Britain and France "have
developed a common policy, and I think it's amazing the degree to
which we have had a common policy. . . . And the fact that there are
certain minor superficial difficulties as to details about just how you
handle tolls or how much is going to get paid to Egypt and how much
isn't doesn't detract from the fact that we have a common policy."

The "superficial difficulties" of Sunday became pretty formidable by
Tuesday, when Britain and France broke with the United States in the
UN.

This is but a brief summary of this sorry chapter, but I think it
demonstrates that the Middle Eastern policy of our government in
Washington was blundering and mistaken, and that it has compounded
its blunders by a consistent policy of misleading the American people
into believing that all was well in the world.

But the question now is what to do about it.

A year ago, on Armistice Day, 1955, I discussed the Middle Eastern
crisis in a speech at Charlottesville, Virginia.[122] I pointed out the growing dangers in the area and suggested that United Nations guards
should patrol the areas of violence and collision and keep the hostile
forces apart. I said that it would take decisive acts of statesmanship to
head off all-out war in the Middle East.

As late as the summer of 1955 at the Geneva Conference, if the
President had taken an insistent stand against the shipment of Communist arms to Egypt, I am convinced that the Communists would not
have risked arming Egypt as they have.

Had the Eisenhower administration taken a firm stand in the Middle
East, had it aided Israel with arms and territorial guarantees, we might,

122 See *The Papers of Adlai E. Stevenson*, Vol. IV, pp. 584–591.

I believe, have been able to prevent the present outbreak of hostilities. And if this government had not alternately appeased and provoked Egypt, I do think that we would command more confidence there and in the Arab world. But all this is behind us. What can we do now to deal with the crisis in front of us?

It appears that President Eisenhower is now approaching this problem by trying, very properly, to check military action. But this will only restore the situation that existed up until four days ago. I say this betrays a complete lack of understanding of the crisis. The situation of four days ago was one when events were threatening strangulation of our European allies, the destruction of Israel, and increasing control of the Middle East by Communist Russia. Just to restore that situation would be another setback for the West.

I would not condone the use of force, even by our friends and allies. But I say that we now have an opportunity to use our great potential moral authority, our own statesmanship, the weight of our economic power, to bring about solutions to the whole range of complex problems confronting the free world in the Middle East.

The time has come to wipe the slate clean and begin anew. We must, for a change, be honest with ourselves and honest with the rest of the world. The search for peace demands the best that is in us. The time is now. We can no longer escape the challenge of history.

Mrs. Suzanna Miles urged Stevenson to request that the United States government send medicine and food to the people of Hungary. She identified herself in her letter as the "niece of Ted Miles (of Navy days) and the cousin of Sam Campbell (your cousin by marriage) and the one Democrat among all the Miles."

To Suzanna Whitelaw Miles

November 4, 1956

My dear Mrs. Miles:

I am so grateful for your note and your suggestion about offering help to the Hungarians. I have spoken, as you may know, about the valor of the Hungarians and proposed that we offer aid to any country in its struggle for freedom, as we did to Tito years ago.

It was good of you to write me and I am delighted to hear that there is a Democrat among the Miles.

Cordially,

To Charles Walker[123]

November 4, 1956

My dear Mr. Walker:

Your exquisite cuff links have been travelling with me on my appalling journeys for some days, and I apologize for not having had an opportunity to thank you for them before. They have given me more than a "lift" — they have given me Socrates at my elbow, or at least my wrist. A position still closer to my head might have helped. But your thoughtfulness and kindness in sending me this beautiful gift has touched me deeply and I am so grateful.

Cordially,

Stevenson delivered the following speech in Minneapolis on November 5, 1956.[124]

Well, the campaign is drawing to a close.

Tomorrow the politicians will at last fall silent — and the people will speak.

You have had to endure quite a lot of political talk already — and not all of it has been honest talk.

There is no reason why political talk shouldn't be honest. After all, politics is the means by which a democracy solves its problems. Nothing is more essential than responsible politics to the successful working of a free state.

One thing Estes Kefauver and I have tried to do in this campaign is to practice responsible politics — to talk sense to the American people.

We have not tried to kid you, to fool you or to deceive you.

But it seems to me that the effort to kid the people, to fool the people, to deceive the people has been the essence of the Republican campaign.

I think you here in Minnesota know what I mean, since you have to suffer more than your share of Republican deceit.

I don't know whether it is a compliment or an insult that so much should have been concentrated in Minnesota.

Secretary [Ezra Taft] Benson came to Minnesota and said that farm prices would rise — and they promptly fell. They have fallen 3 per cent in Minnesota in the last month.

And President Eisenhower came to Minnesota and said that the price

---

[123] An admirer of Stevenson who was associated with Petit Musee Ltd., a New York shop specializing in antique jewelry.

[124] The text is from *The New America*, pp. 38–43.

adjustment period was over — and a few days later, the Department of Agriculture reported the fourth straight monthly decline in farm prices.

And Vice-President Nixon came to Minneapolis and said — and I quote — "There will be no war in the Middle East." And you know what happened then.

When the Republican leaders say these things, you can draw only one of two possible conclusions. Either they don't know any better — in which case they shouldn't be in responsible office. Or they do know better — and have decided not to tell you the truth — and in this case there is even less argument for them.

On the national level, of course, they are overflowing with a pretense of virtue. Even the Vice-President has put away his switchblade and now assumes the aspect of an Eagle Scout. But, down at the grassroots, the Republicans haven't changed.

The President continues to act as if he had a monopoly on all the virtue in the country.

How do you reconcile the fact that the President holds forth in the pulpit while his choirboys sneak around back alleys with sandbags?

The answer must be clear. The answer is that the President doesn't know what's going on — and doesn't care enough to find out.

The answer is that the President doesn't run the store.

When Mr. Eisenhower doesn't run the store at home, it's bad enough. You know what it has meant for the farmers. The Eisenhower policy has been to throw the American farmer onto the mercy of the market, the weather and the processors — and four more years of this kind of farm relief will relieve the farmer of everything he has.

But when he doesn't run the store in foreign affairs, it is disastrous. Presidential negligence on questions of peace and war may plunge the whole world into the horror of hydrogen war.

And negligence is precisely what we have been getting.

Let us remember President Eisenhower's role in the making of our Middle Eastern policy. In February of this year, the Eisenhower administration started to send a shipload of tanks to Saudi Arabia. This was at the time that we were declining to send arms to Israel. When protests mounted, the administration first embargoed the shipment. And while it was trying to decide what to do, where was the President of the United States? On February 17, he played golf. On February 18, he shot quail. On February 22, when the ban was finally removed, the President shot eighteen holes of golf.

If the confusion over the Saudi Arabian tanks proved anything, it proved the need for some firm direction of our Middle Eastern policy. But did we get it? Toward the end of March, as the situation grew worse, Prime Minister Eden sent the President an urgent message about the Middle East. But some days later the President, when asked about it in a press conference, said, "I can't recall how long it has been since I have had a letter from the Prime Minister."

On April 9, the White House announced: "The President and the Secretary of State regard the situation [in the Middle East] with the utmost seriousness." On the same day, the President began a golfing vacation in Georgia. When Egypt took over the Suez Canal in July, the President was at Gettysburg; on August 4, when the *New York Times* called the Suez impasse the "gravest challenge to the West since Berlin and Korea," the President played golf. On August 11, when Britain rejected the Communist proposals for a Suez conference, the President played golf. As the crisis mounted toward the end of August, the press reported that the President, now at Pebble Beach, California, "golfed happily at one of America's toughest and most beautiful courses."

Now, no one begrudges the President his recreation, but peace is a full-time job.

Obviously something has gone out of our foreign policy in these Republican years — consistency, boldness, magnanimity — some instinct for leadership in a free world that begs for rescue from anarchy and disintegration.

Even the seizure of the Suez Canal by Nasser caught us by surprise, for our Secretary of State — whose erratic treatment of Egypt had precipitated this seizure — was out of the country and the President was on holiday.

And now we hear that the President of the United States first learned of the British and French ultimatum in the Middle East from newspaper reports!

And even when we have been forewarned, we have still failed to act.

Our government knew about the impending arms deal between Egypt and the Communists a full month before President Eisenhower met with the Russian leaders at Geneva. Yet our President made no protest of this action which gave the Russians the foothold in the Middle East which the czars vainly sought for three centuries. If there had been less hearts and flowers and more firm talk at Geneva, the Communists would never have dared to arm Egypt, and the tragic war that is raging in the Middle East today could have been avoided.

The last four years have presented America and the free world great opportunities to exploit weaknesses in the Communist ranks and advance the cause of peace.

But this administration has failed to take advantage of them.

The death of Stalin caught us off guard.

The uprisings in East Berlin caught us off guard.

The uprisings in Poznan caught us off guard.

The most recent revolts in Poland and Hungary obviously caught us off guard.

When there was a danger of the Communists taking over Greece and Turkey, our government responded with the Truman Doctrine.

When the Russians threatened our position in Berlin, President Truman reacted with the dramatic Berlin Airlift.

And when Communist aggression in Korea challenged the principle of collective security, President Truman led the free world in halting Red aggression in its tracks. His response was immediate; it was decisive; and it was courageous.

President Truman knew that the United States cannot survive in the world of today without friends and allies. He treated our allies with courtesy and respect. And when the United States gave its word, that word was kept.

But in the last four years we have treated our allies and our would-be allies as junior partners. We have bullied them and threatened them. And, what is worse, we have deceived them. The result is that we have lost our closest and best friends, and what friends have we won? Russia? Egypt? Of course not.

The keystone of our American foreign policy has been our co-operation with the great Western democracies of Great Britain and France, and now that foundation of the free world strength is crumbling.

What we have had in the last four years is a rigid policy for foreign affairs and a flexible policy for farm prices!

I say it's time for a change!

This has been a critical week for America. Our foreign policy has collapsed in the Middle East. Our Western alliance with Britain and France, upon which our peace and security have largely depended, has been shaken to its foundations. With the West divided, Russian tanks are now crushing freedom in Hungary, and there is war in the world — in a very dangerous place.

This is the harvest of the errors of the Eisenhower-Dulles policy, which have been pointed out time and again, step by step.

After the war, Stalin, at the peak of his power, tried to break into the Middle East, but was stopped cold in Iran and again in Greece and Turkey by a brave and courageous President — Harry Truman. Now, thanks to our incredible backing and filling, the Egyptians have turned to Russia, and Soviet influence is spreading through the Middle East and exploiting the new Arab nationalism. Meanwhile, our democratic friend, Israel, has lashed out in desperation.

Russian influence in the Middle East is sinister enough; but more alarming is the fact that there has now opened up a fateful split between the United States, on the one hand, and England and France, our oldest and strongest allies. While we deplore the use of force by Britain and France in Egypt, we dare not overlook the fact that the preservation of our security, the preservation of NATO, indeed the preservation of the United Nations itself, will depend on re-establishing the basis of mutual confidence between us.

And America reached the summit of foolishness when Mr. Nixon hailed the collapse of our alliance as "a declaration of independence that has had an electrifying effect throughout the world."

The separation of the United States from its democratic allies may delight Mr. Nixon. And it also certainly delights the Russians, who have been trying to do just that for many years. But it is a deadly threat to our future security.

Moreover, with the Atlantic Alliance divided and incapable of firm and united action, the Red Army has rolled back into Hungary to crush the rebellion. Fumbling and uncertain, the Eisenhower administration even delayed the efforts of other nations to help the people of Hungary in the United Nations.

Early yesterday morning I sent President Eisenhower a telegram urging that we call upon the United Nations Peace Observation Commission for possible help to Hungary and other satellites struggling for their freedom.[125] The commission would send teams of United Nations observers into those parts where their presence might help the situation. I am gratified that the Eisenhower administration has embodied this suggestion in the resolution which it submitted Sunday afternoon.

It is ironical that Marshal Zhukov[126] is directing the Red Army's effort to crush freedom in Hungary — the same Marshal Zhukov of whom President Eisenhower said last year that he was "intensely devoted to the idea of promoting good relations between the United States and the Soviet Union." That was at the Geneva Conference, which Mr. Eisenhower ended by assuring us that the Russian leaders "desired" peace as much as we did.

[125] For the text of this telegram, see the New York *Times*, November 5, 1956.

[126] Marshal Georgi K. Zhukov, a high-level Soviet military commander during World War II, who defended Moscow against the Germans and broke the sieges of Stalingrad and Leningrad, and after the defeat of Germany headed the Soviet occupation forces under the four-power partition.

For years the Eisenhower administration has been assuring us periodically that all is well, that we have the Communists on the run, that America is master of the situation, that our prestige was never higher, and that there was nothing that another slogan, another brink, another trip by Mr. Dulles, or another smile by Mr. Eisenhower couldn't cure.

We have had enough of this nonsense. For three years we have been retreating, confidence in America has been declining, and now our world policy is in ruins.

While everyone respects Mr. Dulles for his heroic efforts, and everyone, especially old friends like myself, lament his illness[127] at this critical period and earnestly hope for his speedy recovery, let us face the fact that in the future we must have more candor and realism.

It is clear that the events in Eastern Europe and the Middle East are symptoms of a vast new upheaval in the balance of world power. This upheaval is a challenge both to the free world and to Communism. At this point we are losing out in this contest. We are losing because our friends and allies no longer trust our leadership. And we are losing because our foreign policy is rigid and stale.

Re-establishing the solidarity of the West is our most urgent business. The United States, as it has been said so well, is the one great power that can take the lead to save the world from this creeping anarchy and disintegration. Mr. Dulles obviously can't do it. Mr. Nixon applauds the collapse of our alliance. President Eisenhower appears to be isolated, uninformed and interested only intermittently.

But we must get on with the job before our margin of time runs out. And there may not be much left.

When we think of the Hungarians and Poles sacrificing their lives to gain their country's freedom, we must prize more than ever our own good fortune in being able to choose our government freely at the polls.

The ballot is only a scrap of paper — but it is still the most powerful weapon on earth. It is the shield and the sword of the free. It is your children's insurance policy. It is our key to the future.

The ballot, like all our other rights and liberties, was won in hard struggle. John Adams said in 1777, "Posterity! You will never know how much it cost the present generation to preserve your freedom! I hope you will make good use of it. If you do not, I shall repent in heaven that I ever took half the pains to preserve it."

I do not think we have forgotten what freedom cost those men. An

[127] Mr. Dulles underwent surgery on November 3, 1956, in which part of his large intestine was removed.

American election is a reaffirmation of our freedom. It is proof anew of our enduring trust in the wisdom of the people.

And when we vote tomorrow — and vote Democratic — it will be our vote of confidence in the wisdom — not of one man or one group of men — but in all the people.

After delivering the above speech Stevenson flew to Boston to see his grandson, Adlai Ewing Stevenson IV, who had been born the day before. Waiting for him when he arrived at the airport was a letter from Adlai III: "Please forgive me for not being at the airport to meet you, but right now is one of the few times I am permitted to be with Nancy. I am looking forward with great pride in personally introducing my son — your grandson — to you."

Stevenson went directly to the hospital for a glimpse of his new grandson and a brief visit with Adlai III and Nancy. The reporters who went with him to the hospital agreed that the baby was much better-looking than his grandfather.

That evening Stevenson delivered the following speech on a nation-wide telecast.[128]

First of all, I want to thank you, my good friends everywhere, for all that you have done for me, during so many weeks and months — for having helped me find the means and the heart to fight hard for all that we of the Democratic party hold vital in this crucial election.

As Jack Kennedy has told you, this night marks the end of a long and thrilling journey. For four years now I have gone up and down the airways and rail lines and roads of this astonishing country of ours, and what rewards I have had!

I have traveled, too, all around the world: to Asia and the Middle East and Africa and Europe, and I think I have seen with open eyes the realities of this wonderful, precarious earth.

I have needed the strength of many men to get through these travels and this hard fight for what I believe — and I have drawn deeply on hidden sources of strength. I have seen millions of American faces as I have traveled. I have spoken with Americans of all conditions of life, of all ages and kinds, and I have been deeply moved and sustained by the warmth, the reliance, the confidence, the affection that they — that you — have so generously given me.

I think of the young people, boys with banners and girls with note-

128 The text is from *The New America*, pp. 274–278.

books, college students and many kids too young to vote, who wanted to participate in the exciting process of our democracy.

And so many of you have come forward to tell me that you have gone into politics in the last four years. Volunteers, precinct captains, young women who have held coffee hours to raise money. Some of you are running for office — and you've told me this was all because of things you heard me say in the '52 campaign.

And then I've been moved by the simple, kindly phrases spoken by humble people who reach out from the crowd to say "God bless you," "I hope you win," "Don't get too tired," "We need you."

I have known — and really this knowledge has given me the greatest strength of all — that these words were spoken not so much to me personally, but because I was the Democratic candidate for President of the United States — and they trust the Democratic party which has fought the people's battle so long.

And so this simple trust and confidence was a gift to me, in a way, of their faith in themselves.

And what has given me strength has been my faith in them — in you. We are surely a good and strong people, of that I am sure. We are a people who combine generosity and idealism with a practical, down-to-earth realism that we learned the hard way, as we pushed back the harsh frontiers of nature and science and politics. Ours have been the legendary broad shoulders of Paul Bunyan and the restless seeking mind of Thomas Edison and the great heart of Abraham Lincoln. We Americans are Tom Sawyer and Justice Holmes and Jackie Robinson; in our best dreams we are carefree wanderers and noble thinkers, and men who can drive in runs when they're needed.

We in the Democratic party think there is nothing we cannot do if we want to do it.

The Democratic party believes we have not yet finished making our country, that we still have important work to do.

We of the Democratic party think of "the people" as living human beings, one by one, individuals with differing ways and talents and hopes, each worth in himself the whole weight of government.

We Democrats see in "the people" the strong young man at the loom or the press or the drill in the clatter of earning a wage, and we want for that young man fair work laws and a steady job and pride in what he does.

Or we see the grandmother with a broken hip or a heart attack or cancer, sitting in the sun on the porch in the thin workless evening of life, and for her we want security and medical care and some kind of bulwark against loneliness.

Or we see the mother pushing a wire cart in the grocery store, anxious whether she can buy enough for the children, yet not too much for the family budget, and for this mother we want prices within reach and a good life of her own and high hopes for her kids.

We Democrats see the slum dweller, the workman living in the shadow of automation, the teen-ager trying to find a moral footing — and we look for ways to help them all.

Now, I want you to listen as some of my colleagues in the Democratic party tell you very briefly about a few of the real issues of this campaign.

When they have finished, I want to come back and add a final word about the most important reason of all for casting your vote tomorrow for the Democratic ticket.[129]

In the years of this Republican administration we have made little progress on the home front. All the things my friends have talked about are urgent — your child's health, your income, your child's school and teacher — how your child learns to live in this magical, dangerous world.

I have thought of that much this afternoon, here in Boston, where I've come to see my first grandchild — which I confess must be the world's finest, fattest morsel!

But I've thought even more about what kind of world this baby will live to see.

For there is no use talking about a new and better America if we can't keep the peace, and also the freedoms we cherish even above peace.

Yet today America's foreign policy, our policy for peace, is in disarray in all parts of this world. Our alliances are unraveling; NATO is disintegrating, neutralism is spreading, we are helpless in Hungary's agony.

Our policy in Asia is rigid, militaristic and unresponsive to the great revolution where hunger is spreading and hope is rising.

Our policy in the Middle East is in ruins, and has furthered the Soviet design to penetrate this strategic area, to the great damage of the cause of freedom.

Israel, surrounded by enemies growing stronger with Russian arms, has lashed out in desperation, and, worst of all, Britain and France are going in one direction and we are going in another — in the same direction as the Communists.

[129] At this point in the telecast, a number of prominent Democrats delivered short speeches, among them Mrs. Roosevelt, Senator John F. Kennedy, Senator Hubert Humphrey, and Senator Kefauver. For an account of the broadcast, see the *Christian Science Monitor*, November 6, 1956.

And tonight we have seen the ironic culmination of the disastrous Eisenhower foreign policy in the Middle East — with the Communists now urging us to go to war with them against Britain and France!

We regret what our friends have done. We do not condone the use of force. And, as I wired the President last Wednesday, there is no reason for the involvement of America's military forces in this area. But the need for some positive American leadership is desperate everywhere.

I see no hope that the Republican party can retrieve the tragic situation abroad. It is split internally — as it has been since the fight over the League of Nations; and a divided party cannot regain the confidence of our allies or rebuild the coalition on which our strength and security depends.

Worst of all, this Republican administration has not taken the American people into its confidence. Either it hasn't known what is going on, which seems incredible, or it has misled us time and again, step by step, from President Eisenhower's early statement about unleashing Chiang Kai-shek to recapture China to his statement a few days ago that he had good news from Suez and that there was no trouble with our allies.

And now we have seen in this campaign a refusal on the part of the Republican candidates even to talk seriously about the great problems of the world. Constructive proposals have been dismissed with scorn and epithet.

So it has been when I propose that we take the lead to tame the hydrogen bomb that releases poisons, war or no war, which can permanently injure your child and destroy the whole balance of life on earth.

And so it has been when I say our economic aid system is still so tied to defense policies that it appears to Asia to be little more than a bribe to take sides.

And now one other matter.

Your choice tomorrow will not be of a president for tomorrow. It will be of the man — or men — who will serve you as president for the next four years.

And distasteful as this matter is, I must say bluntly that every piece of scientific evidence we have, every lesson of history and experience, indicates that a Republican victory tomorrow would mean that Richard M. Nixon would probably be president of this country within the next four years.

I say frankly, as a citizen more than a candidate, that I recoil at the prospect of Mr. Nixon as custodian of this nation's future, as guardian of the hydrogen bomb, as representative of America in the world, as commander in chief of the United States armed forces.

Distasteful as it is, this is the truth, the central truth, about the most fateful decision the American people have to make tomorrow. I have full confidence in that decision.

After tomorrow, in the months and years to come, we have great work to do together — to improve the lot of all Americans — in the home, the office, the factory, on the farm.

I said earlier there is nothing we cannot do if we decide we want to do it.

Man always can see further than he can reach, but let us never stop reaching. He dreams more than he can achieve, but let us never lay to rest our dreams.

I was in church yesterday, and there I read this responsive reading:

> Methought I saw a nation arise in the world
>   And the strength thereof was the strength of right.
> Her bulwarks were noble spirits and ready arms . . . :
>   All factions and parties were turned to one cause;
> The transformation of evil to good.
>   Bitter words, the utterance of hate and despair,
> And envy and conceit were no more heard in the land . . .
>   To the supreme good all the people were devoted.

Let this be our vision for America. Good night. God bless you.

After the speech Stevenson flew back home to Chicago to vote the next day.

On the evening of November 6 — election day — he had dinner with his family and close friends at the Blackstone Hotel. By nine o'clock it was clear that he was losing. He retired to a bedroom to write out a statement. (He won 26,029,752 popular votes to 35,590,472 for Eisenhower. Stevenson won only 73 electoral votes — seven states — to the President's 457.) Shortly after midnight on the morning of November 7, with Borden and John Fell Stevenson beside him and Mr. and Mrs. Ernest L. Ives close behind him, Stevenson crossed the street to speak to a large group of his supporters in the Grand Ballroom of the Conrad Hilton Hotel.

According to one writer present: "And there, for those who saw him in the room and for millions who watched him over TV, he came again sharply into focus as the Stevenson of old, the gallant, urbane, witty man, sensitive and gay, whom they had long loved. He smiled and waved to the crowd upon whose faces, for the first time that evening, broad smiles appeared."[130]

He said to the crowd:[131]

I have just sent the following telegram to President Eisenhower:
"You have won not only the election, but also an expression of the great confidence of the American people. I send you my warm congratulations.

"Tonight we are not Republicans and Democrats, but Americans.

"We appreciate the grave difficulties your administration faces, and, as Americans, join in wishing you all success in the years that lie ahead."

And now let me say a word to you, my supporters and friends, all over the country.

First, I want to express my respect and thanks to a gallant partner in this great adventure — Estes Kefauver.

I wish there was some way I could properly thank you, one by one. I wish there was some way I could make you feel my gratitude for the support, the encouragement, the confidence that have sustained me through these weeks and months and years that I have been privileged to be your leader.

Thanks to many of you, I have twice had the proud experience of being selected by the Democratic party as its nominee for the most exalted office on earth. Once again I have tried hard to express my views and make clear my party's hopes for our beloved country. To you who are disappointed tonight, let me confess that I am too! But we must not be downhearted, for "there is radiance and glory in the darkness, could we but see, and to see, we have only to look."

For here, in America, the people have made their choice in a vigorous partisan contest that has affirmed again the vitality of the democratic process. And I say God bless partisanship, for this is democracy's life-blood.

But beyond the seas, in much of the world, in Russia, in China, in Hungary, in all the trembling satellites, partisan controversy is forbidden and dissent suppressed.

So I say to you, my dear and loyal friends, take heart — there are things more precious than political victory; there is the right to political contest. And who knows better how vigorous and alive it is than you who bear the fresh, painful wounds of battle.

Let me add another thought for you who have traveled with me on this great journey:

[130] Davis, *A Prophet in His Own Country*, p. 498.
[131] The text is from *The New America*, pp. 278–280.

[326]

I have tried to chart the road to a new and better America. I want to say to all of you who have followed me that, while we have lost a battle, I am supremely confident that our cause will ultimately prevail, for America can only go forward. It cannot go backward or stand still.

But even more urgent is the hope that our leaders will recognize that America wants to face up squarely to the facts of today's world. We don't want to draw back from them. We can't. We are ready for the test that we know history has set for us.

And, finally, the will of our society is announced by the majority. And if other nations have thought in the past few weeks that we were looking the other way and too divided to act, they will learn otherwise. What unites us is deeper than what divides us — love of freedom, love of justice, love of peace.

May America continue, under God, to be the shield and spear of democracy. And let us give the administration all responsible support in the troubled times ahead.

Now I bid you good night, with a full heart and a fervent prayer that we will meet often again in the liberals' everlasting battle against ignorance, poverty, misery and war.

Be of good cheer. And remember, my dear friends, what a wise man said — "A merry heart doeth good like a medicine, but a broken spirit dryeth the bones."

As for me, let there be no tears. I lost an election but won a grand-child!

The telegrams and letters that Stevenson received after his defeat were as deeply moving as those he received after his first defeat. They revealed that to some people, at least, his challenge to apathy and drift and his call for a New America were widely understood and profoundly appreciated. Only a few of his replies are published here.

Senator Lehman wrote Stevenson, "You made a wonderful fight, and you and all your friends and admirers may well take great pride in the manner in which you conducted yourself. . . . You discussed the issues freely and frankly and constructively."

To Mr. and Mrs. Herbert H. Lehman

November 9, 1956

My dear Edith and Herbert:

I want you to know how grateful I am for both your wire and your letter. I suppose that I have had literally no greater satisfactions in my brief ascent and descent in the political firmament than your unswerving loyalty and encouragement.

Well, I have been defeated, but I am not bruised. But I am profoundly alarmed by the massive ignorance of our people about our situation abroad, and the extent to which the Administration has successfully contributed to this delinquency. To ratify failure is bad enough, but the ignorance it discloses is more serious. I hope we can be more effective in the opposition in the future than we have in the past. And I hope, too, that we can talk of both the past and the future one of these days.

Affectionately and gratefully,

Eric Sevareid wired Stevenson on election day, "It's possible, God forbid, that you will be a prophet without office, but the prophets always live longest in history. . . ." He suggested to Stevenson that they should relax together while quail hunting in Virginia.

To Eric Sevareid

November 9, 1956

Dear Eric:

Your telegram pleased me more than I can tell you. While I do not feel exactly like a "prophet" I feel very much like a quail hunter. If I can contrive that day with you I can think of nothing I would rather do. Besides, there is much I should like to say and hear from one whose views have few equal values for me.

Yours,

P.S. I had hoped thoughtful people would be commenting on the irony of the overwhelming endorsement of an administration whose errors were freshly revealed.

Senator Wayne Morse wired Stevenson on November 7, "Throughout this historic campaign you have shown the highest statesmanship. Your remarks last night should stand among the great speeches of American political history. . . ."

To Wayne Morse

November 9, 1956

My dear Wayne:

First, let me congratulate you on your great triumph.[132] Oregon was the brightest spot in a dark evening.

Your charity about my remarks at the end touches me, and I am hastening to send you a copy — hoping that you will not read it and shatter the illusion.

I hope that we can have a talk about the future as well as the past one of these days. I would count it a kindness if you could stop off for a visit in Chicago on your next journey. I am profoundly concerned with the appalling ignorance about the state of the world which the election has disclosed. The ratification of failure is ironic, but the success of ignorance is dangerous.

Cordially yours,

To Sir Louis and Lady Spears

November 9, 1956

My very dear Mary and Louis:

Thanks for your wire. It was a comfort, and also all of Mary's suggestions. I was doing not badly until the Middle East came apart and then the public was, thanks to years of conditioned ignorance, rushed into endorsing the author of our disaster. But, of course, little of this is being revealed by the press. However, there are many people extremely anxious about the state of the public understanding and to this maybe I can still make some little contribution in the future.

I pray that all is well with you and that Peti[133] has recovered by this time. I feel quite out of touch with everything thanks to these months of incessant preoccupation.[134]

Affectionately,

Stevenson's running mate wired him, ". . . You have given new leadership to the American people at a time when it was badly needed. . . ."

[132] Mr. Morse was first elected to the U.S. Senate from Oregon as a Republican in 1944. In 1955 he changed parties and in 1956 was reelected as a Democrat.
[133] Their son.
[134] Sir Louis replied from London: "You have an enormous volume of affection and admiration in this country."

To Estes Kefauver[135]

November 9, 1956

Dear Estes:

You were good to wire me, and I am grateful indeed. I shall always remember your gracious and heartening words.

Now that it is over, I want you to know that I count myself fortunate to have had you in this contest with me. I suppose our politics has disclosed few more gallant figures than yours.

We must have a talk before too long. There are problems which you are thinking of, as I am. Surely this ratification of the Administration's disastrous foreign policy springs from ignorance and not consciousness. And why the ignorance? This is the challenge I suspect our party confronts, with little help from the press.

Meanwhile, my profound thanks to a gallant companion.

Cordially,

ADLAI

To Mr. and Mrs. Dore Schary[136]

November 9, 1956

My dear Friends:

Thank you, my dears, for your wire to Grandpa. And thank you from the depths of my heart for your heroic struggles in the late contest. I seem to feel less hurt than many of my friends. But I am anxious about the state of the public mind which rushes to approve a leadership whose failures have just been dramatically exposed.

Of all this we must talk at an early date I hope.

Cordially and gratefully,

ADLAI

To Harry S. Truman

November 9, 1956

Dear Mr. President:

I want you to know how very grateful I am for the help that you gave me so generously in the campaign. I attempted to call you but had some trouble getting through, and I am taking this means of expressing my warm appreciation for all that I know you have done and wanted to do.

[135] The original is in the possession of the University of Tennessee Library.
[136] The original is in the possession of Mr. Schary.

While defeated, I don't feel particularly bruised. But I am alarmed by the numbers that switched their allegiance in the last few days to support the author of our Middle Eastern crisis. It is a curious irony and must reflect not so much design as ignorance. And that presents a formidable problem to us Democrats![137]

With warm regards to Mrs. Truman, I am

Cordially yours,

Alistair Cooke, correspondent for the Manchester Guardian, *and Mrs. Cooke wired Stevenson: "We weep for ourselves. You still have Stevenson. We don't. . . ."*

To Mr. and Mrs. Alistair Cooke

November 9, 1956

My dear friends:

I was touched by your wire. But you *do* "still have Stevenson"! Indeed, he may deliver himself almost any moment, so look out!

Cordially yours,

P.S. I am profoundly disturbed by the irony of this overwhelming endorsement of the authors of disaster abroad and the large number of votes that switched in the last few days, according to reports from our political leaders. I fear me that this may be interpreted abroad as voting not from ignorance but from design.

A.E.S.

To Mrs. Percy P. Salisbury

November 9, 1956

My dear Mrs. Salisbury:

I was touched beyond words by your thoughtfulness in sending me the bib fastener that Harrison[138] had as a baby. I am sending it along for my grandson, and he will, I pray, live to admire Harrison as I do.

Most gratefully yours,

Melvyn Douglas, the actor, and his wife, actress and former Congresswoman Helen Gahagan Douglas, wired Stevenson, "We are proud to have been among your supporters. . . . Once again the liberal faith has been illuminated. . . ."

[137] Mr. Truman in reply praised the campaign and declared that only demagoguery and glamour had defeated Stevenson.

[138] Her son Harrison Salisbury, of the New York *Times.*

To Mr. and Mrs. Melvyn Douglas

November 10, 1956

My dear Friends:

So many thanks for your kind wire. It was a comfort, and it also affords me an opportunity to tell you how grateful I am for all your help in this enterprise. I feel somehow far more upset about it as a reflection of the depth of public ignorance of our situation abroad than I do about my own defeat. Surely our party must attack the causes of this ironical result.

Cordially,

Congressman Charles Diggs of Detroit wired Stevenson, ". . . You brought the issues of the campaign to the people with imagination, force, and clarity. America and the free world cannot afford to lose the potentialities of your leadership. . . ."

To Charles C. Diggs, Jr.

November 10, 1956

Dear Congressman:

So many thanks for your kind message. It was a comfort, and it also affords me an opportunity to tell you how grateful I am for all your help in this enterprise. I feel somehow far more upset about it as a reflection of the depth of public ignorance of our situation abroad than I do about my own defeat. Surely our party must attack the causes of this ironical result.

Cordially,

Senator Thomas Hennings, of Missouri, who was reelected, wired Stevenson, "Yours was a gallant campaign. . . ." (Missouri was the most populous state that Stevenson carried.)

To Thomas Hennings

November 10, 1956

Dear Tom:

Thanks for your good wire, and even more for your everlasting help and encouragement.

Your triumph was a light in the dark and a great comfort to me.

Indeed my affection for Missouri is maudlin! I hope so much that we shall meet soon.

I am sure you agree that we must somehow get at the awful ignorance about the authorship of our misfortunes abroad which this election has revealed and not permit four more years of euphoria to endanger us further.

Cordially,

G. Mennen Williams, who won reelection as governor of Michigan, wired Stevenson, ". . . Your concept of the New America has inspired us all. We shall continue to fight for the ideals which you have so ably presented. . . ."

To G. Mennen Williams

November 10, 1956

Dear Mennen:

First, let me congratulate you on your triumph, which is hardly a supporters — and profoundly grateful to all of them, yourself among the ties."

And next let me thank you for helping me in this undertaking. While the result disappoints me, I seem to be less hurt than some of my supporters — and profoundly grateful to all of them, yourself among the foremost.

I hope we can have a talk one of these days about the party's future and what should be done to improve public understanding.

Cordially,

Senator Lyndon Johnson wired Stevenson on November 7, "Have just heard your statement on television. It was graceful, non-partisan and in keeping with the high level of your campaign statements. . . ."

To Lyndon B. Johnson

November 10, 1956

Dear Lyndon:

So many thanks for your kind wire. It was a comfort, and it also affords me an opportunity to tell you how grateful I am for all your help in this enterprise. I feel somehow far more upset about it as a reflection of the depth of public ignorance of our situation abroad than I do about my own defeat. Surely our party must attack the causes of this ironical result.

Cordially,

To Paul H. Douglas

November 13, 1956

My dear Paul:

I have only now seen the report of what you and Emily did during the campaign[139] which you sent to Paul Butler, et al. I am appalled. While I knew that you both had worked indefatigably I had no idea how extensive your effort was — nor how expensive! I only wish there was some way to thank you and Emily adequately. It would also be gratifying to talk with you about the future of the party generally and about some of the areas you indicate.

I am afraid the deluge of votes at the last moment for the administration in view of the Middle East crisis which it precipitated presents very neatly the problem of public communication and enlightenment which underlies our predicament. The readiest answer would seem to be a more active opposition role in the Congress for the Democrats.

Cordially and gratefully,

Stimson Bullitt, a Seattle lawyer, wrote Stevenson, ". . . You demonstrated virtue and illuminated and defended the truth."

To Stimson Bullitt

November 13, 1956

Dear Stimson:

I am touched by your letter. You have said some things I have not heard and I am grateful and moved. If I have done half of this I have done better than I suspect!

Anyway, I have the satisfaction of the support of some people whose esteem I value, and I count you among the foremost. Bless you, my dear friend; and you promised me long ago to stop off with me here when you passed through Chicago. I hope you will remember to do this.

Cordially,

[139] Senator Douglas and his wife, Emily Taft Douglas, had campaigned widely in Illinois for Stevenson.

Congressman Richard Bolling of Missouri wrote Stevenson, ". . . The H-bomb test issue had to be discussed, regardless of political consequences, and I am proud to be on the ticket with the man who had the courage and character to bring that and many other issues squarely before the American people."

To Richard Bolling

November 13, 1956

Dear Dick:

I have just come across your letter of November 5, and I am more grateful than I can tell you for it — and for all of your aid and encouragement.

I know I was right on the H-bomb, and the problem will recur. With the administration's dexterity in obscuring facts and misleading the people, however, I suspect they will be able to escape the penalty for the discourteous arrogance with which they dismissed it during the campaign.

I so much hope that we can profit from our past experiences and develop an effective and sustained opposition this time. To persist in pressing this issue is only one of the infinite opportunities.

Cordially,

John Steinbeck wrote Stevenson, ". . . The sadness is for us who have lost our chance for greatness when greatness is needed. . . ." He suggested they should get together and "tell sad stories of the death of kings."

To John Steinbeck

November 13, 1956

Dear Mr. Steinbeck:

Yes, I want to see you. But let us waste no time on either the death of kings or the death of candidates for king. A better agenda is the life of democracies, or even Democrats, and how to preserve them against all the advertising arts, the money and the luck. Perhaps I should add also Britain, France and Israel! It was too much.

I think I will reread Thucydides.

Cordially,

Everett Case, president of Colgate University and Stevenson's class-mate at Princeton University, wrote: "You have nevertheless rendered public service of such importance that fresh opportunities are certain to present themselves." He extended Stevenson an invitation to speak at Colgate's June commencement.

To Everett Case[140]

November 13, 1956

Dear Ev:

I was delighted to have your letter, and I am so grateful to you for your charitable thoughts.

While the election was a disappointment, of course, it was not unfore-seen, nor do I feel particularly bruised, but I am appalled by the igno-rance which this last minute voters' panic disclosed about our foreign affairs and the responsibility for the crisis in the Middle East. Surely, the problem of communication with the people is our most important one against this curtain of the press, the hucksters and an administration which has now found that half truths pay. But the problem remains of how we can successfully conduct both the popular government system and an effective foreign policy in a state of popular ignorance.

Well, I'll feel better soon! And I hope I will see you soon. Why don't you ever come for a week-end as so many others do?

Cordially,

ADLAI

P.S. I have now encountered your letter about the commencement and I am sorely tempted, but my future is so uncertain that I dare not make any fast commitment for June 10 at this time. I wonder how much more time I could have. Need I say I am flattered by it, and I wonder how much nudging you gave your "Seniors."

Robert Sklar, a student at Princeton University, sent Stevenson copies of articles that the Daily Princetonian *had published on his under-graduate years and enclosed the paper's endorsement of him for Presi-dent.*

---

[140] The original is in the possession of Mr. Case.

To Robert A. Sklar

November 13, 1956

Dear Mr. Sklar:

I was delighted to have your letter and the articles from *The Daily Princetonian,* which brought back many memories and flattered me greatly. Do tell the Chairman of *The Princetonian* and the Editors how very grateful I am for their support in the campaign.

With my admiration and best wishes, I am

Cordially,

Mr. E. W. King, of Dover, Massachusetts, sent Stevenson a letter written at 1:45 A.M., November 7, with many hearts drawn on it, and the words, "Thank you, bless you, May you live forever."

To E. W. King

November 13, 1956

My dear friend:

And at 1:45 A.M.! Bless you for staying awake, and even more for those hearts. But as for living forever — well, I have my doubts.

Sincerely,

Senator Ernest Gruening, of Alaska, wrote Stevenson, ". . . Your effort, your ideas, your presentation of issues, is not lost. Their effect will be felt increasingly, and before very long. . . ."

To Ernest Gruening

November 13, 1956

Dear Ernest:

I was much moved by your letter. It was so good and kind of you to write me, and to write me so graciously. I am also told that you called me during the campaign and I am so disappointed that I missed an opportunity of talking with you. I should like to feel that you were right about the continuing impact of what I am trying to say, but I am afraid our huckstering friends have already buried it in the loud plaudits of the administration and their words and the voters' overwhelming endorsement.

While I am disappointed about the election, I don't feel in the least bruised. But I am alarmed about the appalling ignorance which the voters' panic of the last couple of weeks disclosed with respect to our foreign affairs and the responsibility for the Middle East crisis. Surely, the problem of communication gets more serious even as the means improve.

My affectionate regards to Dorothy[141] — and how I wish I could have an evening with you both.

Cordially,

Tommy Reston, the ten-year-old son of Mr. and Mrs. James Reston, wrote Stevenson that he had made a lot of friends working for the Volunteers for Stevenson and Kefauver. He added: "I still have Adlai mobiles up in my room & I still wear my Stevenson & Kefauver umbrella on rainy days. . . ."

To Tommy Reston[142]

November 13, 1956

My dear Tommy:

I want you to know how grateful I am for all of your help during the campaign. You know the Volunteers were very precious to me because most of them really *were* volunteers, just like you. I hope you were not too upset by the election. After all, it was a difficult undertaking at best. But I am sure you will agree that it was worth while keeping up a good, vigorous contest about things we believe in, and when we don't think the people are being fully informed or understand a situation we have an obligation to tell them what we think and why as best we can. This is about all we can do. If they refuse to understand or don't agree with us, or won't listen, it is distressing, but it is still government by the people.

Some day I hope we can have a good talk about it all.

Thanks, and best of luck.

Sincerely,

Tommy Reston prepared a speech for the 1980 Democratic National Convention which opened: "Distinguished guests and fellow Democrats — I come here in this year of decision, 1980. . . ." His parents sent the speech to Stevenson.

---

[141] Mrs. Gruening.
[142] The original is in the possession of James Reston.

To Mr. and Mrs. James Reston[143]

[no date]

Fellow Americans, fellow Democrats!

In this year of decision — 1980 — Well, there's *one* Democratic candidate who will be *ready*. Tell him I love him; that I apologize; that in 1952 I didn't *want* to be ready; in 1956 I didn't have time to *get* ready — and in 1980 I'll be cheering — here or there.

Earl Mazo, New York Herald Tribune *correspondent, wrote Stevenson that their seven-year-old son was unconsolable over the defeat. Finally his mother said to him that Mr. Stevenson did not seem to mind, since he had said that "in losing an election he'd gained a grandson." "Yeh," Mark sobbed, "but what did I gain?"*

To Earl Mazo

November 14, 1956

Dear Earl:

Tell Mark that he gained his daddy home for a while. And that ought to console him a little anyway. It would console me if his daddy was [at] my home a while, too.

Thanks for your engaging letter and all of your encouragement, oral and written, during the past crowded year. Perhaps you could some time explain to me how you penetrate to the heart and mind of a nation prosperous and complacent and yet so insecure and uninformed.

Cordially,

To Matthew H. McCloskey

November 14, 1956

Dear Matt:

I have seen your letter and the November 8 copy of the Philadelphia Daily News. I agree that the editorial coincides with my thinking precisely! And so does Max Lerner's column from the New York Post[144] which I had not seen. I hope you will tell the writer how grateful I am.

And speaking of gratitude, how can I ever tell *you* how grateful I am. There are few people to whom I am more indebted and whose affection and esteem I have come to value as highly. I hope and pray that the

---

143 This handwritten postcard is in the possession of Mr. and Mrs. Reston.
144 "The Triumph of Conformity," New York *Post*, November 7, 1956.

conclusion of the campaign is not the conclusion of our collaboration. And I look forward already to a full evening of that wisdom, exuberance and energy which you transfer to me with such a mysterious chemistry.

Yours,

P.S. I wish you and Roger [Stevens] would send along sometime a list of those major contributors you feel I should now write a letter of personal thanks to. I am sending along a similar note to Roger.

AES

Reinhold Niebuhr wrote on October 31 that Stevenson had "success-fully challenged the Eisenhower myth." Later in the letter he said, "If you should fail, the failure would merely prove that it is impossible to penetrate to the heart and mind of a nation which is so prosperous and yet so insecure." On November 9, he sent Stevenson his deep regret that "you should become the victim of what is the most fantastic political myth of the century." He expressed the hope that Stevenson would continue to assert a "creative influence in our political life."

To Reinhold Niebuhr

November 14, 1956

Dear Reinhold:

I have before me your letters of October 31 and November 9. And they will be letters that I shall read again and keep always. Little do you know what your encouragement has meant to me, nor the support of the ministers that you organized during the campaign. Somehow the confidence of the enduring intellects of a period are worth much more than a lot of votes. I am sure you will understand what I mean.

I am troubled less by defeat and much more by the panic that seems to have overtaken the voters in many places from our reports during the last ten days of the Middle East crisis. The irony of this sudden rush to support the author of their anxiety will be noted more widely I hope as time goes on. But the ignorance that it discloses and the reasons there-fore will not be noted by the Republican press or many audible voices. And, to borrow your phrase, "to penetrate to the heart and mind of a nation which is prosperous and yet insecure," becomes a problem of growing importance for an opposition. People deliberately and perpetu-ally misinformed and uninterested concerns me and what to do about it perplexes me. The evolution of the Eisenhower myth many of us have observed and I think we must now think about how we can counter

Madison Avenue packaging and, what's worse, the massive duplicity and misrepresentation or, rather, non disclosure.

I hope some time we can talk of these things and again my warmest thanks for all your encouragement over these busy years.

Affectionately,

Lloyd Garrison wrote Stevenson, "This is just a word of love and gratitude from Ellen and me." He added that "it is hard not to brood on the foolish judgment of the majority which has brought the country so much closer to great peril and trouble and has made us all losers in your loss."

To Lloyd K. Garrison

November 14, 1956

Dear Lloyd:

I was touched by your kind letter. I think really what has troubled me most is moments of reflection on the vast, limitless kindness, effort and generosity of so many dear friends over a period of years which has all been in vain. I put you and Ellen at the front of that legion of people to whom I owe everything and whom I will never be able to thank adequately.

I don't really feel bruised about the election at all, but I confess to shock and concern about the appalling ignorance of responsibility for the Middle East situation which the last minute voters' panic seemed to disclose. I still have an oldfashioned notion, however, that there must be some advantage to truth even in politics, but I am a little shaken. How we can more effectively communicate with the people and act as an opposition party is a problem I hope we can talk about some time.

Much love to Ellen, and so many thanks for a myriad of things.

Yours,

T. S. Matthews, a classmate of Stevenson's at Princeton University and later Time *editor, wrote from London that he and Mrs. Matthews were "hoping for the news that will make us proud of America."*

To T. S. Matthews

November 14, 1956

Dear Tom:

I have just found your letter of October 27 and the enclosures. The latter I have not read but I am taking them home and will do so promptly. That I shall approve and be grateful is certain. Of post mortems you have perhaps read much. But you will have read little of the sort of comment of which there has been too little. I mean that vast numbers of people voted in sort of a voters' panic for psychological refuge from the threatening situation in the Middle East. It is more than a little ironic that they took refuge with the authors of the crisis. Yet this is the way it is and it reflects how effective the brainwashing and euphoria has been. There is, I suspect, even yet little appreciation of the fact that the crisis was precipitated by the Administration's Middle East policy or want of one and perhaps by the time we extricate ourselves from the emergency the occasion for the emergency will have been forgotten. And thence we will move on to another.

I don't mean to suggest that had Israel, Britain and France withheld their march for a couple of weeks that I would have won. But we were moving up and there was excitement brewing in the crowds and across the land that all detected and marveled at — myself included! At worst it would have been close we think.

But all this aside now. I shall once more, I suppose, have to present my beaten body before the Gridiron Club in early December. And that reminds me of four years ago when some wise and witty words of yours livened my pages for that occasion.[145] Could you send me some more. I am weary and must go off now and confer about the future. If you could, they would be oh so welcome. Send anything, please, to Carol Evans rather than to me because of the crushing burden of the mail which has pushed us far behind.

Love to Martha[146] and my apologies for imposing on you once more. I shall not do it again, at least not soon!

Cordially,

P.S. And I have only now seen your letter of the 9th. I wish I could come over there, and maybe I will later on in the spring. Just now I am trying to get my head above water and then I am going down to South Carolina to a luxurious plantation of a rich friend, play some tennis, shoot some quail, and sleep. I wish you and Martha were to be with me. We could talk of ilietus and Israelitis and how the British intervened in the 1956 election — I like to think on the wrong side!

Now be a good boy, sit down with a jug of port and write something imperishable for your exhausted, depleted and defeated friend.

AES

[145] See *The Papers of Adlai E. Stevenson*, Vol. IV, pp. 223–229.
[146] Mrs. Matthews, the former Martha Gellhorn.

Novelist James T. Farrell wrote Stevenson, "In the 1920's, there was some gaudiness to buncome. Now it has become sanctimonious, respectable and dull. . . ." He added, "What I want to do is to express my great admiration for you, for the campaigns you have waged, and for the honesty you brought into American politics. . . ."

To James T. Farrell

November 16, 1956

Dear Jim:

Ever so many thanks for your letter. I loved your line about the gaudiness and buncome in the 20's and now "it has become sanctimonious, respectable and dull."

You were good to help me, and I think I am more disappointed by my friends' disappointment than I am my own! But it is hard to beat a man who inspires even millions to vote for him in panic for his own mistakes. And what mistakes. We have not heard the end of this bitter irony of victory for the people who let the Russians into the Middle East for the first time in centuries.

Cordially,

To Harry Golden[147]

November 16, 1956

Dear Mr. Golden:

Thank you, my dear friend, for your wire. If it pleased you to participate in my campaign think how pleased I was to have you.

And knowing your wit, humor and also, I think, your resilience, if your reflections on the campaign are not indecent, why not send them along to me and perhaps you'll not mind if I utter them before those smug, complacent, rich publishers who have just had their way with me, at the Gridiron Club post-election banquet in early December. Now let it never be said that you can help Stevenson with impunity.

Cordially,

P.S. I would not ask for this if my own resources were not so depleted.

Chakravarti Rajagopalachari wrote from India expressing his sorrow over the election results, adding that Stevenson had lost "for a world cause."

147 The original is in the possession of Mr. Golden.

To Chakravarti Rajagopalachari

November 16, 1956

My dear Friend:

I was delighted to have your letters, which have only now emerged from the heap of correspondence that has awaited me after the election.

While the President and his party have rejected my suggestion regarding the taming of the H-bomb during the campaign, I have little doubt that we have not heard the end of this problem. I had hoped that my country might take some initiative in saving the human race from the incalculable risks of this weapon in war and peace. What I fear most is that they rejected my idea for political reasons more than on the merits, but such wondrous things can now be done with propaganda and a docile press in this country, and elsewhere I suppose, that it may be they will contrive ways of adopting my proposals without discredit.

While what I proposed during the campaign, both as a liberal program at home and some new initiatives abroad, were rejected, I feel that they are only delayed and ultimately must prevail.

The world is so much more dangerous and wicked even than it was barely four years ago when we talked, that I marvel and tremble at the rapidity of this deterioration. I wish it were possible to talk again, because India and America must find a firmer, broader understanding, and not for our sakes alone.

I shall look forward to a visit, I hope, with your Prime Minister when he comes this way. I wish you were to be with him.

With my warmest thanks for your expressions of confidence and encouragement, and all good wishes, I am

Cordially,

Professor Seymour Harris wrote that Stevenson had waged a "great campaign" and added, "I am proud of my association with you the last few years."

To Seymour E. Harris

November 16, 1956

Dear Seymour:

Ever so many thanks for your wires and letters and the heartening clipping from the Providence Journal.

That the Harvard faculty supported me two to one is reward enough! Naturally I am distressed by the irony of the rush *to* Eisenhower at the last minute for refuge *from* his disastrous mistakes in the Middle East. But I don't feel that the campaign was in vain and I am confident the ideas we discussed will come to pass. For those and their articulation I have to thank my gratitude will not diminish as long as I live, and you are among the foremost.

Bless you, my dear friend, and I look forward to a good talk before long.

Cordially,

Maury Maverick, Jr., wrote that he was proud to have been a soldier in the ranks supporting Stevenson. He explained that he had not run again for the Texas State Legislature because of financial problems. He also mentioned that he had recently reread the correspondence between Stevenson and his father in 1940–1941, when the elder Maverick was mayor of San Antonio, Texas.[148]

To Maury Maverick, Jr.

November 16, 1956

Dear Maury:

It was awfully good of you to write me and I am grateful. I can understand that service in the Texas House was more than you could afford indefinitely. But somehow I hope it does not mean any real interruption in your political interests and activity. It is in your blood, and honorably so, and you can do us all a service in the great tradition of your family.

With affectionate regards to you all, I am

Cordially,

Mrs. Harold Hochschild wrote Stevenson expressing her sorrow at his defeat and added that she hoped he would "be very vocal for the next years — saying those unpleasant truths that need saying."

To Mrs. Harold Hochschild

November 16, 1956

My dear Mary:

Bless you for that sweet letter, but the world will survive — I hope! So will you, and I yearn to see you both, and I am going to find an

[148] See *The Papers of Adlai E. Stevenson*, Vol. I.

occasion to take you up on that suggestion. And can I see that beautiful Aunt[149] too?

I am going now "to withdraw from the hot debate and walk beneath the night stars and listen" for a while; thence back to Chicago by way of New York in early December. Then the law business and a little travel and a little writing I suppose. But somehow, somewhere there will be an escape to Princeton or an evening in New York I hope.

Affectionately,

To Albert M. Greenfield[150]

November 16, 1956

Dear Albert:

Your letter has pleased me more than I can tell you. While I said much of what I felt needed saying during the campaign, I don't feel that I said it very well. So you encourage me.[151]

I think the campaign revealed two significant facts. The first was the disclosure of what a combination of the press, the government, and the money of the country, can do with a people conditioned to the arts of advertising and the influence of mass communication. The other, of course, was the irony of the people rushing by millions to take refuge *with* Eisenhower *from* Eisenhower's disastrous mistakes in the Middle East.

The problem of public enlightenment and communication is something to think about when given an uncritical press and a conformist environment.

I hope we can talk of these things and many others some day.

I am going off now for a little holiday and shall probably return to my law practice in Chicago after the first of the year and do a little writing and travelling.

I shall hope some time to have a proper opportunity to thank you for all your comfort and encouragement and support in its most effective form. . . .

With all good wishes and my thanks, I am

Cordially,

---

[149] Mrs. Hochschild's seventy-six-year-old aunt, Mrs. Cross.

[150] A Philadelphia banker and real estate and business executive who was a delegate to the Democratic National Convention from 1948 through 1960.

[151] Mr. Greenfield had written that in his lifetime, he had "not known a cause to be presented more clearly or more effectively."

Judge James Doyle, of the U.S. District Court for the Western District of Wisconsin, who had been Democratic state chairman from 1951 to 1953, wrote Stevenson: "From the moment we heard you welcome the Democratic National Convention in 1952, our lives have been enriched by you, by your words, by your bearing. If there is radiance and glory in the darkness, as you say there is, it shines from you."

To James E. Doyle

November 16, 1956

Dear Jim:

Thank you, my dear friend, for those kind and generous words. As I think you know, I have been borne along by loyalty and encouragement of others and I have counted you in the forefront of the torch bearers — or should I say pallbearers.

My best to Ruth[152] and my earnest hopes that we shall meet soon again.

Cordially,

Sir Robert Jackson wrote from Africa that Stevenson's loyal supporters there remained as loyal as ever. He expressed the hope that Stevenson would remain active, since so much needed to be done.

To Sir Robert Jackson

November 16, 1956

Dear Robert:

It was so good of you to write me. I said much of what I wanted to say, if not too well, during the campaign. So, while defeated, I don't feel bruised and will resume my private life without tears. But I am, I confess, appalled by the whole calculable consequences of the press, the government and the money of the country into the same management. What it can do to a people conditioned to the arts of advertising and the techniques of mass communication is something to concern us all.

Nor can I view with indifference the last minute rush of voters to take refuge *with* Eisenhower *from* the effects of Eisenhower's policies and performance in the Middle East.

As to basic problems there, I agree that we have not attacked them at all. Let us pray that God spares us and so long to do so.

152 Mrs. Doyle.

[347]

Your views as to precisely what we could and should do in the Middle East would interest me a great deal.

I have just read a noble letter from the sainted Barbara,[153] who contrives to send me prayers, comfort, courage and arrows for the enemy all in the same brilliant, beautiful packages.

I yearn to see you both and MacDuff![154]

Cordially,

Barry Bingham sent Stevenson a letter from an eight-year-old girl and a quotation from Daniel Webster. He also invited him to spend some time at the Binghams' home.

To Barry Bingham

November 16, 1956

Dear Barry:

I am going to make no effort to set forth the width, length or depth of my gratitude. To you there is no use.

I have your letter of the 13th and the engaging enclosures. Clark Conant will have a letter at once and Daniel Webster a thoughtful reader.

I am off now for a holiday down at the Fields[155] and will make no decisions for the present. But I suspect the immediate future is law with a little writing and a little travel.

Obviously we could not foresee the last minute rush of the voters *to* Eisenhower for refuge *from* Eisenhower's appalling mistakes in the Middle East. But we could foresee, and did, what the government, the money and the press of the country can do to a people conditioned to the arts of advertising and the influence of mass manipulation.

I hope we can talk of these things and what I have been troubled (if not very much!) by in the rapidity with which most of the press has consigned me and my influence to oblivion. I think the fact is that much of what we talked about will come to pass, and also that if we are to exercise any influence over the direction of the party, ideologically, in leadership in the forthcoming struggle, I must somehow try to keep some vestige of influence on the basis of the campaign and the contribu-

153 Lady Jackson.
154 The Jacksons' son, Robin.
155 Chelsea Plantation, the winter home of Mrs. Marshall Field III in Ridgeland, South Carolina. Mr. Field had died on November 8, 1956.

tion of the past four years. I saw a good piece of this kind in the Providence Journal.

I would love to come to Glenview for a visit with you and the lovely Mary.[156] Just when I cannot foresee.

Blessings,

To Richard L. Neuberger

November 17, 1956

Dear Dick:

I have just seen your letter and your ten reasons for supporting Stevenson. I am covered with rosy confusion, and after reading the reasons I am tempted to ask what they have to do with Stevenson.

Anyway, you have pleased me immensely, and yours and Maurine's[157] gallantry in action is something that I shall always remember — with pride quite as much as with gratitude.

Bless you, my dear friends!

Cordially,

Author and former foreign correspondent Leland Stowe wrote Stevenson, "You made a magnificent fight and campaign. . . . If there's one thing Ike's got it's a mystic kind of monopoly on political immaculate conception."

To Leland Stowe[158]

November 17, 1956

Dear Leland:

It's a wonderful phrase, and I wish I had heard it before — political immaculate conception. I'll admit that it's tough, but I had never thought to see people stampeding by millions for security *with* Eisenhower *from* Eisenhower's blunders in the Middle East. Anyway, it's a wonderful country, in spite of the hazards of a partnership between the money, the government, the press and Madison Avenue.

I am flattered by your approval of the campaign. And I only hope my party shares your view about "inestimable service in a period of great danger." I'm afraid I haven't seen much evidence of it, but the non-political mail is stimulating in the extreme, and I am touched by your

156 Mrs. Bingham.
157 Mrs. Neuberger.
158 The original is in the possession of Mr. Stowe.

expressions of approval for what I have tried so hard to do in these crowded years. I have a feeling, as you say, that much of what I have talked about will ultimately prevail, and maybe even talking about it and pointing up the administration's weaknesses and failures will help them, too. I like to think so.

Bless you, my dear friend, and so many thanks.

Cordially,

ADLAI

Rabbi Jacob Weinstein of K.A.M. Temple in Chicago wrote Stevenson, "Perhaps if we Dominies had done a better job in teaching men to trust the Lord — the eternally elect — they would not have needed so desperately to trust the Father in the White House."

To Rabbi Jacob J. Weinstein

November 17, 1956

Dear Jacob:

It could be that you dominies failed, but I suspect that the lords of Madison Avenue triumphed. I'll agree that the alchemy of transmuting failures into successes and driving millions *to* him in search of refuge *from* his own errors is something that I had not comprehended until you reminded me of the fall-out. Of course, that's it!

As for the faithful, dear Jacob, holding fast to my principles, I am fearful that you are having a happy reverie. The faithful seem to be looking for someone else's principles as fast as they can.

How I wish I could write a letter like you can! If I could, you would be the first to get one.

Cordially,

Novelist Upton Sinclair wrote that Stevenson had taught the people and Eisenhower "a lot." In addition, "You got him a Democratic Congress and that will have effect. Keep up the good fight."

To Upton Sinclair

November 17, 1956

Dear Mr. Sinclair:

Thank you so much for your letter. You flatter me. But I suspect that there are a good many Democrats who think that Ike got a Democratic Congress not because of me but in spite of me!

Cordially yours,

To Estes Kefauver[159]

November 17, 1956

Dear Estes:

I have just seen your letter of November 9. I agree that we were creeping up on them until that panicky stampede *to* Eisenhower for security *from* Eisenhower's mistakes. It was ironic, but I suppose not too surprising in view of the incredible state of euphoria and ignorance that they have managed to cultivate.

By all means let's have a talk, any time at your convenience. I shall be away until the end of the month and then in New York for a few days early in December and back here about the 5th — forever more!

With my very warm regards to Nancy[160] and my earnest hope that you have recovered some of that sleep and energy that you expended with such extravagant gallantry.

Cordially yours,

ADLAI

Herbert Emmerich, director of the Public Administration Clearing House in Chicago, wrote Stevenson, "It is easy to overlook the fact that the magnificent campaign you have just completed was in many respects a great success. It was a success in strengthening the party, in securing a Democratic majority in the House and the Senate, in raising issues that have been suppressed."

To Herbert Emmerich[161]

November 17, 1956

My dear Herbert:

Bless you for that wonderful letter. I wish it could be translated into a myriad of messages, newspaper letters, columns, etc. And I mean it not just as a consolation to me, because I don't need consoling, but as a reminder to the Democratic leadership and the Republican victors that there is work to do in both directions.

I look forward to seeing you again soon.

Cordially yours,

ADLAI

159 The original is in the possession of the University of Tennessee Library.
160 Mrs. Kefauver.
161 The original is in the possession of Mr. Emmerich.

*Frank Altschul, a New York business executive and vice president of
the Council on Foreign Relations, wrote Stevenson, "Nothing you could
have done would have served to overcome the tranquilizing effect of the
Eisenhower personality on the electorate."*

To Frank Altschul

November 17, 1956

Dear Frank:

I agree. The country had a "Don't Disturb" sign hanging on the door.
But I had not quite counted on the last-minute rush *to* Eisenhower for
security *from* Eisenhower's appalling blunders in the Middle East. I
must learn more about the mystique of demonology that transmutes
failures into virtues and errors into advantages. Do you think it's the
"fall-out"? But to be more serious, do you think I could have cut
through four years of euphoria if I had started talking foreign policy
earlier and more vigorously?

Bless you for your kindness, and I look forward to a talk.

Cordially,

*Donald Breed, publisher of the Freeport, Illinois, Journal-Standard,
praised Stevenson's position on the suspension of H-bomb testing and
expressed the hope that the Administration would take his advice on
foreign policy.*

To Donald D. Breed

November 17, 1956

My dear Mr. Breed:

Yes, I get millions of letters. But I don't get millions of letters like
yours. I don't even get enough.

As you know, Governor Dewey will say anything, and has.[162] But
you would be interested to see the comment from around the world, as
well as from thoughtful people in America, about the H-bomb issue. It
is almost uniform. I am especially irritated about the Administration's,
including the President's, effort to destroy and distort this issue, because
they have done our country a great disservice.

---

[162] Thomas E. Dewey, the unsuccessful Republican candidate for President in
1944 and 1948, called Stevenson's proposal "an invitation to national suicide." For
his and other Republicans' reactions to the proposal, see the New York *Times*,
October 17, 1956.

As you know, we must exert some initiative in the disarmament field, and here is the chance to at least concede that the matter merited thought and study. Instead, they have taken a rigid position which invites the sort of letters I have had from the top leaders of Asia, asking how long they are expected to bear America's aggressions against all mankind. This is not winning us the uncommitted countries, and there may rest our future, if it has not already been decided in the Middle East.

I agree with you about the Middle East. It was ironic and a little frightening to see that stampede *to* Eisenhower for security *from* Eisenhower. As to the future and my influence and utility, I hardly know what to say. I doubt if this Administration, which is manifestly the most political of the century, is going to be asking for help from me. As you may have read in the New York Times, Eisenhower refused to listen to even my concession speech. I suggested UN troops to separate the Israeli and neighboring forces more than a year ago. The Administration wasn't interested. Now it is in effect, after Canada proposed it and something desperate had to be done.

We have warned Dulles about the hazards in Asia, and the northern tier concept,[163] etc., etc. As for the President, his interest is opaque and irregular. I am not happy about the prospect of the Russians' influence in the Middle East for the first time in history.

Perhaps you are right about the Negro vote. It perplexes me. It improved in California, and seems to have weakened elsewhere and gone Republican in the South.

I am grateful for your letter, and I hope to see you sometime.

Cordially,

Lady Mary Spears wrote Stevenson expressing her dismay over the deterioration in British-American relations and her concern as a former American citizen that she now feared the United States.

---

163 The Northern Tier was the original name of the Baghdad Pact, an alliance formed in 1955 among Britain, Turkey, Iraq and Pakistan to prevent Soviet penetration of the area. The United States, while not a member, pledged cooperation. Most Arabs viewed the pact not primarily as a defense against Russia but as a British device to retain control in the area. As a response, a Southern Tier alliance was formed, with Egypt, Saudi Arabia, Syria and later Yemen as members.

To Lady Mary Spears

November 17, 1956

My dear Mary:

Thank you for your good letter. I shall not take the time now to recount the circumstances of the campaign, nor the last-minute stampede *to* Eisenhower for security — *from* Eisenhower's policies in the Middle East. It sounds paradoxical but isn't surprising, given the degree of ignorance and complacency that had been so shamelessly cultivated.

But what is important is the point that you raise, and the long deterioration of our understanding, let alone our alliance. This must be remedied. Indeed, I think even the Administration realizes that it is imperative and will take some steps in that direction, I trust, and promptly.

I cannot tell you whether [John Foster] Dulles is to go or stay, but I am reasonably confident that the President's attention to affairs will not last very long, and just what happens next with the Russians in the Middle East, and everyone hostile to us, I can't foretell with confidence. But I hope you, who understand us so well, will appreciate that we usually gravitate back to a sensible path and position in time. I am sure we will again, and do reassure your countrymen with more conviction. But how we will get the Russians out of the Middle East is something else.

Bless you, dear Mary!

Affectionately,

Congressman Brooks Hays of Arkansas wrote Stevenson, "Your idealism, your forthrightness, your intellectual stature and your many other qualities of mind and heart will be appreciated by increasing numbers of people."

To Brooks Hays

November 17, 1956

Dear Brooks:

I was much touched by your letter. Such confidence and charity cannot but please anyone, let alone a frail and vain — and defeated — candidate! I have been more than rewarded for the effort of the past four years by the confidence of so many thoughtful people like yourself.

Of the future I hope we *can* have a talk. I think it's bright for our party. I wish it was brighter for our country. And I pray that the administration learned something from the campaign, as well as the "opposition."

Do let me know if you can ever come to see me. I would be delighted.

Cordially yours,

W. Reading Gebhardt, a lawyer of Clinton, New Jersey, urged Stevenson to remain as titular head of the Democratic party and not allow the congressional leaders to take charge. He also declared that he did not understand how Stevenson had stood the rigors of the campaign.

To W. Reading Gebhardt

November 17, 1956

Dear Mr. Gebhardt:

Thank you for your kind and interesting letter. I confess I don't know what the source of the strength is that sustains you in such prolonged travail. Perhaps it was people like yourself, who make one feel that anything one does isn't half what you deserve.

As to the future leadership of the party, I doubt if I have much to say, but I certainly hope that I can always be helpful. And I am confident that much of what I have talked about will come to pass if we keep pressing ahead.

It was good of you to write me, and I am ever so grateful.

Cordially yours,

Robert F. Kennedy wrote Stevenson to thank him for having included him on his campaign trips. At the request of the Kennedy family, Robert was assigned to the Stevenson campaign as an internship for his future role as his brother's campaign manager. See Rose Fitzgerald Kennedy, Times to Remember (New York: Doubleday, 1974), p. 358.

To Robert F. Kennedy

November 17, 1956

Dear Bobby:

Ever so many thanks for your note, but I should have been thanking you for coming with me. It was good to have you along, and I have seldom heard sounder, more sensible and thoughtful remarks stated with better verbal conservation.

I hope we'll see more of each other as time goes on, even if my public role is sharply diminished.

And my affectionate regards to your charming wife.

Cordially,

Professor Clarence Berdahl of the University of Illinois wrote that Stevenson had won for the Democrats extraordinary success in respect to the congressmen and governors who had been elected. He added, "We still look back to the years of your Governorship as the best years in Illinois."

To Clarence A. Berdahl

November 17, 1956

Dear Mr. Berdahl:

Thank you so much for your letter. I am glad you feel that the Presidential campaign contributed to the party's success elsewhere, at least. And I emphatically agree that the sudden rush *to* Eisenhower for security *from* Eisenhower's policies in the Middle East was more than we could reasonably overcome.

Perhaps even more than the ironies of the national campaign it was the astonishing indifference in Illinois that really shocked me. . . .[164]

I am flattered by your reminder of my governorship. I have always been proud of it, too, and I am glad that there are at least some of my fellow citizens who feel as you do about it. Please tell your wife how deeply grateful I am for all of her help and encouragement in both campaigns. I shall not disturb you again, but I certainly hope to see you again.

Cordially yours,

Harry Gideonse, president of Brooklyn College, wrote Stevenson that he did not regret a minute of the work he had done as chairman of the Nassau County Democratic organization. He went on: "You gave us a chance in self-respect to stand up for values to which we are deeply committed." He added a quotation from William the Silent: "Je n'ai pas besoin d'espoir pour entreprendre, et je n'ai pas besoin de succès pour persévérer."

[164] Stevenson lost the state and the Republicans reelected Governor William Stratton and Senator Everett M. Dirksen.

To Harry D. Gideonse

November 17, 1956

Dear Harry:

Thank you, my dear friend, for that gracious letter. And thank you even more for months, yes years, of diligent service to my forlorn cause.

I think your estimate of the campaign is about right. We were making promising progress until the administration's errors in the Middle East stampeded millions *to* the administration for security. I do not know whether the explanation of the transmutation of failings into virtues and errors into advantage is to be found in the mystique of demonology or the mystique of Madison Avenue! I rather suspect it may be just the latter.

I hope, dear Harry, that you get some comfort out of what your efforts did to at least improve the organization in Nassau County. Personally, those satisfactions in so many places around the country have been sufficient compensation for me. And thanks a lot for that splendid quote from William the Silent. I feel the same way, but I've done about all the undertaking and persevering that a Presbyterian-Unitarian-Democrat can!

All good wishes.

Cordially,

Columnist Leonard Lyons wrote that he and his wife Sylvia would never concede, because Stevenson was the better man. He described how his sons distributed Stevenson literature in New York City and Syracuse. He sent, for Stevenson to autograph, a dollar bill which had Stevenson's head superimposed over the face of George Washington.

To Leonard Lyons

November 17, 1956

Dear Leonard:

I have your letter, and I am returning the bill in spite of all the criminal laws about defacing the currency of the realm!

Yet that is but a small mark of my esteem for the gallant Lyons, who are obviously afraid of nothing, including the Republicans! And as for those splendid youths on the street corner and at Syracuse, may they ever have the courage to fight darkness with a handful of Democratic literature.

[357]

Some day you must explain to me the mystique that transmutes failings into virtues and converts errors into advantage. Is it Madison Avenue; or could it be the "fall-out"?

With affectionate regards to Sylvia,

Cordially yours,

Senator A. S. Mike Monroney's son, who had been an advance man in Stevenson's campaign, wrote that the campaign had "greatly enriched a sorely lacking ingredient in American politics — courage. Many young people should have gained from the precedent you have set in sacrificing political gain for your ideals."

To Mike Monroney, Jr.

November 17, 1956

Dear Mike:

Ever so many thanks for your good letter. It affords me a welcome opportunity also to thank you for your exceptional services during the campaign. I have heard only the most ecstatic comment on "Mike Junior" and his talents as an advance man.

I hope that you will be sure to let me know whenever our paths cross, and meanwhile please give my affectionate regards to your parents.

Cordially,

Nancy Stevenson's father wired: "I can wish nothing better for this baby than that he be half as good a man as his paternal grandfather. . . ."

To Warwick Anderson

November 17, 1956

Dear Warwick:

So many thanks for your note on "the morning after." My friends seem to be far more grieved than I. I hope you're not among them. Just think what I've escaped!

But sometime I want an advertising man, and I think I know his name, to explain to me the alchemy by which failings are transmuted into virtues, errors converted into advantage, and millions rush for security to the author of their anxieties.

You fellows really have what it takes. I don't see why you don't let me in on the *mystique*.

I yearn to see you both — not to mention our grandson.

Affectionately,

Professor Leon Green, formerly dean of the Northwestern University Law School, wrote that Stevenson had conducted the "most compelling" campaign of any presidential candidate in his lifetime. He explained that he felt most people out of a sense of loyalty to their leader had voted for Eisenhower.

To Leon Green

November 17, 1956

My dear Leon:

What an interesting letter! And I suspect much of your estimate of loyalty came to pass. Truly, it is a difficult thing for the human being to confess his own error. And added to that, we had the curious spectacle of the stampede *to* Eisenhower for security *from* Eisenhower's errors in the Middle East.

I only hope that the campaign served some purpose, and both gave ideological content to the Democratic party and alerted Republicans to their failures. If it did, I am fully rewarded.

It is always good and comforting to hear from you.

Cordially,

Harrison Salisbury, of the New York Times, *wrote Stevenson that he had just visited Washington, D.C., and found the newspaper reporters in a "state of despondency" because they felt Eisenhower was not in contact with what was happening in the world. He added he did not think that Senator Lyndon B. Johnson would give any leadership on foreign policy. He urged Stevenson to continue to speak out on the issues.*

To Harrison E. Salisbury

November 17, 1956

Dear Harrison:

Your report confirms some telephone advices I have had from Washington. I am a little perplexed, however, as to what to do. With the vigorous energy of a defeated candidate in such circumstances, I shall probably do nothing! I had thought for a day or so, however, to make some sort of statement suggesting that it was time for some Churchillian tough talk about limits to toleration of Russian penetration. The President seems to be saying something of that kind now, although it seems firmly embedded in a UN initiative.

I hope you will feel quite free to pass on any suggestions to me at any time as to what you think I should do. I'll not "squeal."

Cordially,

Senator John Sparkman wrote Stevenson that he was convinced that every so often "we come to a cycle in our national life when people wish just to be left alone. They want no disturbance whatsoever."

To John Sparkman

November 17, 1956

Dear John:

Maybe you're right about the folks after all, and I am sure you are right that the people like that "Don't Disturb" sign on the door that Eisenhower and Madison Avenue hung there. But how am I to thank you, my beloved friend, for your gallantry in this futile action? Anyway, you know how I feel.

I have just read a letter, the previous one in the stack, from which I am going to ask my secretary to quote an excerpt, from Winston Churchill's indictment of the lethargy of a period in Britain when his warnings of unpleasant realities went unheeded:

"Delight in smooth-sounding platitudes, refusal to face unpleasant facts, desire for popularity and electoral success irrespective of the vital interests of the State, genuine love of peace and pathetic belief that love can be its sole foundation, obvious lack of intellectual vigour in both leaders of the British Coalition Government, marked ignorance of Europe and aversion from its problems in Mr. [Stanley] Baldwin, the strong and violent pacifism which at this time dominated the Labour-Socialist Party, the utter devotion of the Liberals to sentiment apart from reality, the failure and worse than failure of Mr. Lloyd George, the erstwhile great war-time leader, to address himself to the continuity of his work, the whole supported by overwhelming majorities in both Houses of Parliament: all these constituted a picture of British fatuity and fecklessness which though devoid of guile, was not devoid of guilt, and, though free from wickedness or evil design, played a definite part in the unleashing upon the world of horrors and miseries which, even so far as they have unfolded, are already beyond comparison in human experience."

I hope that history may be kinder to this generation than it was to that one, but I am really apprehensive now that the Russians have been invited to the Middle East by [John] Foster Dulles and our amiable President.

I want so much to talk with you about mounting a more effective opposition this time. I suspect it will be up to you and [Senator J. W.] Fulbright and a few others in the Foreign Relations Committee to keep picking at them and make them answer some questions.

I really don't believe Eisenhower would have been too hard to beat if he had been chopped up a little beforehand. Our curves were in the right direction until the stampede started for refuge with Eisenhower — from Eisenhower's mistakes.

It occurred to me that if the Democratic members, or some of them, of the Foreign Relations Committee, were meeting sometime and could tolerate an outsider, I would enjoy it. Clearly, we dare not let this administration contribute to the national delinquency much longer.

Yours,

Brooks Atkinson, drama critic of the New York Times, *wrote that Stevenson had spoken "the truth day after day with clarity and courage."*

To Brooks Atkinson

November 17, 1956

My dear Mr. Atkinson:

You could have said literally nothing that would please me more than: "You spoke the truth day after day with clarity and courage." Indeed, I would say that if there's anything this country needs more than a lot of clarity, it is a little truth. I tried hard to remove the "Don't Disturb" sign which Big Brother had hung on the nation's front door, but the occupants liked it.

Well, anyway, I enjoyed the work and I am richly rewarded by the approval of a few perceptive souls, of whom I would count Brooks Atkinson among the foremost. Thank you, sir!

Cordially yours,

Archibald Alexander wrote Stevenson that it "was an honor to work for you, and God bless you for having had the courage and devotion to do what I believe was your inescapable duty."

To Archibald Alexander

November 17, 1956

Dear Archie:

I have tried in vain to think of what to say to you. It is no use. But I am sure you realize that there are a few people who come to mean more than all the rest in a man's life. I count you as one of them, and the gallantry of the last eleven months is something that few get and fewer deserve. That I had it in such measure from you and Barry [Bingham] and a few others almost embarrasses me.

Thank you, my dear friend!

Love to Jean.[165]

Yours,

Benjamin V. Cohen wrote Stevenson that in time "much that you said and did will be recalled and will help the country meet its problems."

To Benjamin V. Cohen

November 17, 1956

Dear Ben:

Thanks for your note. And thanks again and again for all you did to help us. I agree that much of what was said will come to pass.

I hope you will keep in touch with me, and if you think of anything I can or should do in the future that you will let me know promptly.

Meanwhile, my everlasting gratitude and affectionate regards.

Yours,

To Carl Sandburg[166]

November 17, 1956

DEAR CARL: I AM DISTRESSED THAT I CANNOT BE THERE[167] TO SEE YOU, TO HEAR YOU, TO TALK TO YOU, YES, AND TO THANK YOU FOR

[165] Mrs. Alexander.
[166] A telegram.
[167] Mr. Sandburg was to speak before the Modern Poetry Association in Chicago.

YOUR GALLANTRY IN ACTION IN THE LATE BATTLE. BUT I AM FOR-
SAKING THE HOT DEBATE TO WALK BENEATH THE STARS AND LISTEN
FOR A WHILE, TO PARAPHRASE SOMEONE. AND I PRAY THAT YOUR
NEXT JOURNEY THIS WAY WILL INCLUDE AN EVENING FOR ME. BEST
WISHES AND AFFECTIONATE REGARDS.

To Irving Dilliard[168]

November 17, 1956

My dear Irving:

Bless you for that sweet letter. And bless you, too, for those wonderful editorials — which I have heard about but haven't read! I will presently, and meanwhile let me echo your anxiety to get together.

I am off for a couple of weeks in the South and East now — "to
forsake the hot debate and walk beneath the stars and listen" — and
when I return early in December I hope there'll be a message that you
are both coming for a weekend with me.

Cordially,

P.S. God bless Missouri and the Post-Dispatch — and Irving Dilliard!

*Adele Smith, daughter of Mr. and Mrs. Hermon Dunlap Smith, wrote
Stevenson that she was dejected over the election, "but now you will
have the proper time to check up on the religious education of your gay
god daughter."*

To Adele Dunlap Smith

November 18, 1956

My dear Adele:

Yes. You are right. There is more time for your religious education, if
not for the country's. But from all I hear from your parents about your
activities there at school,[169] I wonder if you are providing enough time
for religious education. Take care, or I'll come down to check up.

Much love,

*Mrs. Mary Creighton of the Galesburg, Illinois, Post wrote Stevenson,
"You battled through like a soldier and a patriot and to be with you in*

---

168 Editor of the editorial page of the St. Louis *Post-Dispatch,* one of the few
major newspapers to endorse Stevenson.
169 Miss Smith was a student at the Garrison Forest School in Garrison, Maryland.

spirit, to be a member of your compatriots, has been a privilege I shall forever treasure."

To Mary Creighton

November 18, 1956

My dear Mrs. Creighton:

I was touched by your kind letter. Thank you, my friend, for all you have done on my behalf all these years. While I was beaten, I don't feel in the least bruised, and I said many of the things I felt needed saying, if not as well as I had hoped. But I am appalled at the ignorance which the voters' last minute panic disclosed about our foreign affairs and the responsibility therefor.

My warm wishes and everlasting gratitude.

Cordially,

Mrs. Archibald MacLeish wrote Stevenson that he had left a "real and lasting mark on the history of our time." She urged him to join them in Antigua during the winter before they left for Rome.

To Mrs. Archibald MacLeish

November 18, 1956

Ada, dear:

Thanks for that blessed note. I shall hope to see you in Cambridge before you get off to Antigua, and I tremble with excitement at the thought that I might even take you up on a visit to the island. But I'm afraid that's only a tremble.

And what's all this about Rome?

Devotedly,

The son of Mr. and Mrs. Edison Dick wired Stevenson that in defeat he was "magnanimous and deserve[d] the respect of every American."

To Edison Warner Dick

November 18, 1965

My dear Eddie:

Bless you for that fine telegram. What a thoughtful boy you are, and what a loyal and gallant friend!

I pray that all goes well with you, and I hope we can have a good talk during the holidays.

Affectionately,

Laird Bell, a prominent Chicago lawyer, had been a close friend of Stevenson's since the 1930's, when they were members of the board of directors of the Chicago Council on Foreign Relations. Mr. Bell wrote Stevenson that he hoped it would be a "little comfort to you to know that your friends are feeling for you and their attitude is unchanged."

To Laird Bell

November 18, 1956

Dear Laird:

I have just come to your letter in the pile. It warms me, but I have come to expect your warmth in all my crises.

Lord! What a formidable sentence that was. Actually, I never felt better, and if I have troubled the nation's sleep a little I am satisfied. The result, as you suggest, may have been ordained from the start, but I had hardly counted on that last minute stampede *to* Eisenhower for security *from* Eisenhower's appalling errors.

I hope so much that we can have a talk after I return from a short vacation around the 5th of December. Any time will do. Just let me know.

Affectionate regards to Natalie.[170]

Yours,

Barry D. Karl, a third-year graduate student at Harvard University, wrote Stevenson that "under your leadership a great many intelligent younger people have been brought to understanding and activity within the American democratic process."

[170] Mrs. Bell.

To Barry Dean Karl

November 18, 1956

Dear Mr. Karl:

I have just read your most interesting and penetrating letter. I am indebted to you for clarifying for me some of the oft-noted timidity of the intellectual. And I hardly need say that I emphatically agree that there are no alternatives.

For myself, I am not disappointed and, indeed, if I have troubled the nation's sleep a little I am quite content. Moreover, I am elated by your further confirmation of what comes to me so often: that I have had something to do with bringing many intelligent younger people into activity within the democratic process. This is compensation enough.

I should like to help in the future, and I shall as best I can. The means are not, however, altogether clear just yet.

Some day I hope we can meet and talk of these things.

Cordially yours,

Lauren Bacall wrote Stevenson that she was proud of the way he had made his speech conceding defeat. She added, "It's not fair to ask I know, but you must not waste your extraordinary talents. You have too much to give and we all have need of it. . . . Live for yourself — be happy — but having made your voice heard, you must share it with all of us now."

To Mrs. Humphrey Bogart

November 18, 1956

My dear Betty:

What a sweet letter! I am touched and grateful, but I hasten to assure you that you needn't feel "sad for me." Actually, I never felt better and more serene. Perhaps the word is beaten, but not bruised.

If I succeeded in troubling the nation's sleep a little, I am content. But I wish I might have better fulfilled the hopes and expectations of so many devoted friends. And among those, you are striving gallantly and gaily in the front ranks.

Give my best to Humphrey, and know that I shall ever be grateful for your constant encouragement and loyalty through these trying years.

Affectionately,

P.S. Be sure to come and see me when you pass this way.

AES

Miss Ruth Robinson, of Washington, D.C., wrote that she and her fellow office workers were in deep gloom over the election. "Do you think," she wrote, "there's a chance we could go underground or something, anything? Oh, the stupidity of it all." She signed the letter, "Yours for mutiny, Ruth P. Robinson and Fellow Revolutionists."

To Ruth P. Robinson et al.

November 18, 1956

Comrades!

I am charmed! And let no one call such imperishable words "pitiful." And when you have gone underground, whistle quietly, move over, and let me know where the hole is.

Yes — "Oh, the stupidity of it all!" And, yes — and the enchantment of its sequel.

Arise, you mutineers!

To John F. Kennedy

November 18, 1956

Dear Jack:

I should have thanked you long before this. I can think of no one to whom we should all be more grateful than to you. And I am only sorry that I did not better reward you for your gallantry in action. I have confident hopes for your future leadership in our party, and I am sure you will help immeasurably to keep it pointed in a positive direction.

With my boundless gratitude, and affectionate regards,

Cordially,

To Mrs. Eugene Meyer[171]

November 18, 1956

Dear Agnes —

I'm not sure just what your Post article will cover, but I'm certainly not eager to start a public quarrel with Lyndon Johnson about the form of the "opposition" etc. What I had in mind when I talked rather impulsively to you was something along the line of the enclosed — i.e. the party was indebted to Stevenson, his ideas are good etc. — to en-

---

[171] This handwritten letter is in the Agnes Meyer files, Princeton University Library.

large my *ideological*, not political influence, which has shrunk and *been shrunken* since the election I suspect —

Hurriedly and affectionately,

ADLAI

P.S. Had nice talk with Eleanor Roosevelt & will see her again in N.Y. around Dec. 1.[172]

To Dr. Benjamin Spock[173]

November 19, 1956

Dear Dr. Spock:

One of the great disappointments of the campaign was that it never allowed me enough time to watch you extol my virtues on television.[174] However, I had a number of young mothers come up to me during the course of the campaign to tell me that you had persuaded them to vote Democratic. I only wish you had been on more often!

My warmest thanks to you for all your helpfulness. If I troubled the nation's sleep a little I am satisfied. Yet I regret that I could not better fulfill the hopes and expectations of my friends.

Cordially yours,

James P. Warburg wrote that he wished he could have argued during the past summer with Stevenson's advisers who felt that foreign policy should not be the major issue of the campaign.

To James P. Warburg

November 21, 1956

Dear Jim:

Thanks, my dear friend, for your letter of November 7. I rather wish that I had followed my own inclination and talked a little more about foreign policy earlier in the campaign. Although I suspect that the analysts were right, it was impossible to alarm people who did not want to be alarmed or dispel the euphoria in two months.

---

[172] Mrs. Roosevelt had just visited Stevenson at Libertyville.
[173] Pediatrician and author of best-selling books on child care.
[174] The Democratic party had asked Dr. Spock to do a ten-minute television talk on the danger of radioactive fallout on children.

But grandfather does not feel bruised even if he didn't say everything he wanted to say or as well as he wanted to say it.

I constantly hear of your trips to Chicago. You never let me know. How come?

Cordially,

Part Three

Titular Head of the Democratic Party—Again

After Adlai E. Stevenson died in 1965, Mary McGrory wrote: "When I think of him now, it is with gratitude. I am indebted to him for the best moments I have spent at countless political banquets and rallies. I am indebted to him for his ideas, for his language, for his courtliness and his incorruptible good breeding, for the men he brought with him to public life, for the tone he gave to politics and, like everyone who knew him, for the pleasure of his company."[1]

And James Reston wrote: "When he died in a London street today, he left a good legacy. He brought a certain chivalry to American politics. He elevated the political dialogue in America and he contributed much to the style and policies later adopted by Presidents Kennedy and Johnson."[2]

As is evident from letters Stevenson wrote after his second defeat by President Eisenhower, he was determined to continue to speak out against drift and complacency. He would, through his speeches and his writings, insist that Americans realize that equality under freedom was not faring well and that the "New America" must be realized. As he told John B. Oakes, of the New York Times, the "euphoria and public complacency so vigorously cultivated by the Administration and the press" had left the public uninformed or misinformed on the crucial issues and especially on issues of foreign policy.

In addition to trying to win an election, he explained to Mr. Oakes, his purpose "was to set forth a philosophy, a faith and even suggest a program for modern liberalism. I think that I have done that during the past four years. . . . I have no doubt at all that many of the views and ideas I have tried to express will ultimately prevail."

1 "The Perfectionist and the Press," in *As We Knew Adlai: The Stevenson Story by Twenty-two Friends*, edited and with preface by Edward P. Doyle, foreword by Adlai E. Stevenson III (New York: Harper & Row, 1966), p. 181.
2 *Sketches in the Sand* (New York: Alfred A. Knopf, 1967), p. 81.

When asked what he conceived to be the role of the Democratic party during the next four years, Stevenson replied that the opposition party should maintain "the posture of opposition — not opposition for its own sake, but opposition of the utmost vigor when we think they're wrong, and a constant attitude of inquiry and skepticism to keep them on their toes and make them prove that they are right."[3]

While he was resting in late November, 1956, at the South Carolina home of Mrs. Marshall Field III, he discussed with Thomas K. Finletter, Mrs. Field, Mrs. Ronald Tree and others how to be the leader of a responsible opposition. Stevenson felt that the Democratic Congress, led by Lyndon B. Johnson and Sam Rayburn, had failed to sharpen the issues and frequently had gone out of its way to protect Eisenhower and thus sustain the myth. It was a mistake, he knew, to allow the congressional wing of the Democratic party to be the only spokesmen for the party. What was required was a "shadow Cabinet."

Three of Stevenson's strongest supporters — Jacob M. Arvey, Paul Ziffren, and David L. Lawrence — proposed to the executive committee of the Democratic National Committee that an advisory council be established to issue policy statements during the interval between the national conventions. On November 27, 1956, Paul Butler, the National Committee chairman, announced the formation of the Democratic Advisory Council with Stevenson as well as Harry Truman, Averell Harriman, David L. Lawrence, G. Mennen Williams, Estes Kefauver, Hubert Humphrey, and John F. Kennedy among the members. Johnson and Rayburn refused an invitation to join the group.

As the Advisory Council expanded, with Charles Tyroler as director of the staff, advisory panels were appointed to develop draft statements on a range of issues. Stuart Gerry Brown wrote that "it is nevertheless clear from the Council's many statements and position papers that Stevenson was the leading intellectual force among its members. . . . The measure of Stevenson's influence in the Council is the consistency with which its statements and papers followed his expressed views. . . . Thus Stevenson's personal leadership of the party was transformed into a kind of collective leadership in which he continued to play a central role."[4]

While Stevenson was in South Carolina, he received a letter from Mrs. Eugene Meyer announcing that she had completed the final editing of her book Education for a New Morality (New York: Macmillan, 1957).

---

[3] New York Times Magazine, November 25, 1956, p. 12.
[4] Conscience in Politics: Adlai E. Stevenson in the 1950's (Syracuse, New York: Syracuse University Press, 1961), p. 226.

She mentioned that as she wrote the book she thought: "Adlai will appreciate that." She added that his defeat had been agony for her.

To Mrs. Eugene Meyer[5]

November 27, 1956

My dear dear Agnes —

Thanks for your letters and the enclosures which have kept me at least conscious that there *is* a world beyond the gates of this great plantation — and that in that world, which I rather dislike rejoining, there is, after all, all manner of good things, and among the best — you dear Agnes. Of course I'll come a-running to your birthday. And how could you have thought of such flattery — *I* helped you write your book! Well, anyway, I like it!! But I don't, my dear Agnes, like your troubled spirit. The campaign is over. I said what I thought needed saying; tried to tell the country about the contemptuous ana[e]sthesia of Ike and his advertisers; gave the Dem[ocratic]. party a program and liberalism some content; and warned the nation about the precarious state of the world. What more could I do? If the people didn't care to listen, or thinkers to agree, or writers to reflect, I cannot feel that I wholly failed in *my* duty. And it *was* duty — the urgings of the leaders thru 1955 — that made me do it. So please, my beloved friend, don't feel wounded in heart or soul; know rather that your loyalty, encouragement and wise counsel and gallant lofty spirit have been wine and iron for my spirit.

It is only that I would like it — the campaign, the forecast, the program — to have some continuing value to my party that has made me a little unhappy with the fact that so little has been written or said — post-election — to invite attention both to what I said and to my continuing ideological value and potential usefulness to the party. And unless the rank and file find expression somehow I fear me that neither I nor my expressed ideas will have any further value. . . .

I'm off for a couple of days in N.Y. — thence to Boston to see my kids & back to Chicago. I'll probably get out a statement disclaiming any future political designs soon & then try by various devices to influence the Dems. to be a genuine and effective opposition. Meanwhile, do you find the world as sorry a sight as I?

And now — look out quail here I come!!

Love —
ADLAI

P.S. — What a horrid letter. I do hope we can have a talk soon.

A

5 This handwritten letter is in the Agnes Meyer files, Princeton University Library.

Stevenson issued the following statement through the Democratic na-tional headquarters in Washington, D.C., on December 4, 1956.[6]

I have said that I would make an announcement as to my future plans. Here it is:

I intend to resume the practice of law in Chicago on January 1st with my old friends and associates, W. Willard Wirtz, William McC. Blair, Jr., and Newton N. Minow.

I will not run again for the Presidency.

But my interest in the Democratic Party, which has twice accorded me its highest honor, will continue undiminished. I want to be of help wherever I can, and I have accepted membership on the Party Advisory Committee established last week.

To all the people who sent me messages since the election, I send my heartfelt thanks. And I assure them that I hope to continue to express my views on public questions from time to time as circumstances permit.

During the campaign I did what I could to bring home to the American people the facts about our situation, and to warn them against complacency and a false sense of security. I made specific proposals for social progress at home and more effective leadership in the world.

In my opinion the greatest service the Democratic Party can now render is a strong, searching, and constructive opposition. We must know from experience that progress at home for the benefit of all will depend largely on Democratic initiative. And it is more apparent every day that a sustained and critical scrutiny of our foreign policy is vital to the restoration of Allied strength and unity, the halting of Communist expansion, and the peace and security of the war-threatened world.

For these tasks of an effective opposition and national leadership, the Democratic Party is fortunately blessed with many able men who represent the humane and liberal Democratic traditions on which I believe our country's best future depends.

To Mr. and Mrs. Barry Bingham

December 8, 1956

Dear Mary and Barry:

I am back in the mire of obligations after a fortnight of shooting in South Carolina at the Fields' and a week of frenetic New York — and, best of all, twenty-four hours in Cambridge, Mass. At the latter stop I

[6] The text is from a carbon copy.

had occasion to see once more Miss Sallie Bingham. The vision was lovely, healthy, and gay. At lunch with Archie [MacLeish], we discussed her and her book[7] at great length and concluded that both were of fairest quality. What a gal!

Should the Binghams want refuge from the oppressive season of joy, please find it with me. There is so much to talk about.

Love,

To David L. Cohn[8]

December 8, 1956

Dear David:

Only during these past few days while I have been away and have been working through an accumulation of papers have I found the draft speech which you wrote for me. I am mortified that you were put to all of this inconvenience, and in vain. Moreover, it had some very usable material which we sadly needed, I fear. I'm afraid things fell into great disorder towards the end. I like to think the people did, too!

On another visit to New York I shall look forward to that meeting you promised me.

Bless you, and thank you, my dear friend!

Cordially yours,
ADLAI

P.S. I am afraid I have also neglected your lovely letter of November 20, with the splendid quote from Santayana and your piece from the September *Atlantic*.[9] I am grateful for both, and you certainly have no occasion to change your views expressed in the *Atlantic* piece!

To Mrs. Robbins Milbank[10]

December 8, 1956

My dear Helen:

I was sorry that you got away from these parts before I saw you, and I am grateful for your wire.

I hope you don't disapprove too much of what I did, but you have

---

[7] The Binghams' daughter, while an undergraduate at Radcliffe College, published a number of short stories and submitted book manuscripts to Houghton Mifflin, which eventually published her first novel, *After Such Knowledge*, in 1960.

[8] Author of a number of books about the United States, who had prepared drafts of speeches for Stevenson in 1952. The original is in the Mississippi collection, University of Mississippi Library.

[9] "The Communist Approach to Burma," *Atlantic*, September, 1956.

[10] The original is in the possession of Mrs. Milbank.

also seen the statement I issued in full. The purpose was to disarm all of the ambitious fellows by disclaiming any Presidential intentions myself, hoping thereby to possibly be of some more welcome influence in the party councils than I would be had I continued in the equivocal position.

I also tried to make it apparent that I intended to take an active part in affairs, and speak occasionally. This is about as much of "leadership" as I could claim anyway, and I hope I can do it, and usefully.

Be sure to let me know if you travel this way, and plan to come out to Libertyville.

With affectionate regards to you and Robbins,

Yours,
ADLAI

Carlos P. Romulo, the Philippine ambassador to the United States, wrote Stevenson as cochairman of World Brotherhood that the organization was contemplating an international, nongovernmental conference of leading people from all over the world to exchange ideas on the relationships that ought to exist among peoples.

To Carlos P. Romulo

December 8, 1956

My dear friend:

I am mortified that I have not acknowledged your letter of November 10 long before this. I wish also that I felt better qualified to comment intelligently and to, as you say, "measure the chances of success" of such a conference. Certainly it will depend on effective advance preparation, the quality and level of the people who attend, and, I am bold enough to add, the simplicity and limited scope of the agenda. I am sure that you and many of your correspondents are infinitely better equipped to estimate the prospects than I am. But feeling as I do that Asia is the area of decision, I am disposed to favor all such efforts to enlarge the area of mutual understanding, confidence and respect.

With all good wishes, and happy and respectful memories of our past association, I am

Cordially yours,

Morris L. Ernst, a New York lawyer and former member of President Truman's Civil Rights Commission, suggested that Stevenson undertake

a weekly television program in which he would interview Republican members of the Cabinet and of the Congress. Mr. Ernst offered to develop the idea further.

To Morris L. Ernst

December 8, 1956

Dear Morris:

Thank you for your letter and for your thoughtful and interesting suggestion about a television show. I suspect you were right and that I would find interviewing Administration leaders not uncongenial work — at least some of the time!

However, I have reflected long and earnestly since the election over various proposals to write newspaper columns, edit magazines, and conduct programs of various kinds. Reluctantly I have concluded to decline them all. I think the reason rests in my feeling that I don't want to feel committed to an inflexible schedule. Perhaps this is a mistake, but freedom of movement and activity (or inactivity!) is what I feel that I must have, at least for the present.

I hope we can talk of these things sometime.

With all good wishes, and my thanks for your flattering suggestion,

Cordially yours,

To Alicia Patterson[11]

December 8, 1956

Dear Alicia:

For your information, I am informed in confidence by Bill Benton that the Hartford Courant can be bought for around five million dollars. Visitors in New York this week also informed me that a chain of Texas papers — Austin, Waco, Beaumont and Port Arthur (I think that was it) can also be had, or perhaps one or more of them.

It's wonderful to be a lawyer again!

Affectionately,

ADLAI

P.S. And you promised you were coming out.

---

11 This handwritten letter is in the possession of Adlai E. Stevenson III.

To Dean Acheson

December 8, 1956

Dear Dean:

I am mortified that I have not long since thanked you for the excellent speech you sent me during the campaign. Somehow the opportunity to use it, or rather use *much* of it, didn't seem to arise and I am afraid I put you to much labor which was, at least in part, in vain. For that I am sorry, but I am also everlastingly grateful for your helpfulness.

I have thought sometimes that it was a mistake that I did not talk more about foreign policy from the outset of the campaign, but it appeared from most of our advice that the people were content with "peace" and not interested in details.

I came out of this campaign more than ever convinced that it is all but impossible to make issues during the campaign. They have to be made first, and the campaign is at best an effort to persuade the voters that one alternative is better than another for their solution. In view of the classic circumstances, it seems a little incredible that at the end of this campaign the people should have flocked in panic for security to an administration which had fathered more, and worse, foreign policy mistakes than any predecessor in a long while.

I wish very much that there were a visit from you in prospect in Chicago or, preferably, Libertyville!

With my love to Alice,[12]

Yours,

To Mrs. Eugene Meyer[13]

December 9, 1956

My dear Agnes:

I am mortified that I misaddressed that letter. I think I had just written one to a Circle Drive in some other town.[14]

There is much to report and to hear, and I wish that a good long talk was in early prospect. I shall certainly come to the birthday party, but please don't count on me to stay at the house. I feel it would be best if I stayed with friends, but I hope I can take you up on the pre-luncheon visit the following morning. Paul Butler told me by telephone while I was in Carolina that he was planning on calling the first meeting of the Advisory Committee for January 4, so your birthday party comes at a very convenient time.

[12] Mrs. Acheson.
[13] The original is in the Agnes Meyer files, Princeton University Library.
[14] Mr. and Mrs. Meyer had a home in Washington, D.C., at 1624 Crescent Place.

The vacation *was* a success. At least, I got a lot of exercise hunting quail, and thoroughly exhausted, to boot! That followed by a frenetic week in New York and Boston, and I am ready for anything but the Christmas madness now. I feel a little desperate about ever getting on top of the post-election accumulation, complicated by the holidays.

So there are sundry indiscreet and beautiful letters which I never received! I protest emphatically and demand them at once!

I was delighted with your speech to the National Council of Negro Women, and I hope you will keep the needle out and busy.

Forgive this hasty dictation and think of me surrounded with neglected mail — but none more welcome than yours.

Affectionately,

ADLAI

To T. S. Matthews

December 9, 1956

Dear Tom:

I am just back from a fortnight of shooting in South Carolina and a week of being shot at in New York. On the heap is your punctual response with that exquisite stuff for the Gridiron [Club speech]. Bless you, my beloved friend! And now I find that instead of the winter dinner being in December as in the past, they have moved it to March, and I have imposed on you all unnecessarily.

But with these arrows in my quiver, I shall let the date approach with all my fingernails intact. Thanks!

And Merry Christmas and love to Martha.[15]

Yours,

P.S. Thinking of your book on the American press[16] I suppose you have noticed the rapidity with which many newspapers [that] had just endorsed Eisenhower and Dulles and their foreign policy immediately began criticizing it once the election was over. It was pointed out in a story in the Christian Science Monitor, which itself had enthusiastically endorsed the Administration. But things are turning for the better. Nixon is now advocating aid and friendship — even courtship — for Britain and France, after applauding our emancipation from these dreary old colonial allies before the election.[17]

15 Mrs. Matthews.

16 *The Sugar Pill* (New York: Simon & Schuster, 1959), which Mr. Matthews was writing at the time of this letter. Letter to Carol Evans, November 3, 1970.

17 The Vice President, in a speech at the annual National Automobile Show dinner in New York on December 6, 1956, advocated American aid to Great Britain to alleviate the "financial plight" resulting from the Suez intervention. See the New York *Times*, December 7, 1956.

It must be wonderful to have a press which sees only virtue in all such things!

Senator Kefauver sent a statement that he had issued after Steven-son's announcement on December 4, reading in part: ". . . In the course of the campaign, Governor Stevenson enunciated many princi-ples which I am sure he will want to see carried out for the benefit of the nation. He can perform great service, through the Democratic party, in working for these principles as a spokesman for the type of construc-tive, imaginative and searching opposition of which he speaks in his statement. . . ."

To Estes Kefauver[18]

December 9, 1956

Dear Estes:

Thanks for your letter and your generous comments about my future in the party. I shall look forward to seeing you at the meeting of this new Advisory Committee, which I understand will be early in January. I hope we can collaborate much in the future, and I earnestly hope that the Democrats in Congress will mount a more effective offensive and opposition than they have in the past.

Cordially yours,
ADLAI

To Letitia Dick

December 9, 1956

Dear Miss Dick:

Word comes to me from the Co-Chairman of the Volunteers for Stevenson-Kefauver[19] that you did an "absolutely outstanding job as Stan Karson's assistant in the Students for Stevenson division, and work-ing with Judy Louchheim[20] on a news sheet that got out to the various colleges several times during the campaign."

I assume that this report, which, as I say, comes on the best possible authority, explains why I carried Harvard, but lost Yale. At all events, dear Miss Dick, I have felt conscience-stricken and grossly negligent

---

[18] The original is in the possession of the University of Tennessee Library.
[19] Her mother, Mrs. Edison Dick.
[20] Daughter of Mr. and Mrs. Walter C. Louchheim, Jr. See Katie Louchheim, *By the Political Sea* (Garden City, New York: Doubleday, 1970), p. 102.

that I have not long before this expressed to you my undying gratitude
— and my deathless love!

> Yours for more leisure for ex-politicians,

To Roger Tubby

December 9, 1956

Dear Roger:

Somehow in the wake of the storm I had expected to have a leisurely
farewell with you, but it never came off, and meanwhile you got away. I
am back now after a fortnight in the South and a week in New York and
Cambridge. Uppermost in my mind is the feeling that I never properly
thanked you for your infinite loyalty, patience and tolerance during that
trying year we spent together in perpetual motion and nervousness.

Sometime, and soon, I hope, we can meet for some mirthful memories
of all those horrors. Perhaps sometime you and Ann[21] will be traveling
about and could stay a night with me in the country, or I might even
invade the Adirondacks — something I am told is worth doing at any
season.

With affectionate regards to you both,

> Yours,

To Chloe Fox[22]

December 10, 1956

Dear Chloe:

I want you to know how very grateful I am to you and to all the
members of the New York Writers' Bureau for your help during the
campaign.

I know, partly from my own knowledge and beyond that from what
Bill Wirtz has told me, about the tremendous supply of things of one
kind or another you sent on to us. I could not for a moment pretend to
any adequate appreciation or more than partial realization of the contribution of individual people. But I do know that we received from you
as a group the inspiration for many and many a campaign utterance.

I hope to be able to get in touch with a number of the members of
your group personally and to express my appreciation to them. I shall
be very grateful to you, if you can some way communicate to all of them
my feeling of deepest gratitude. For your own services, I can only say
thank you very, very much. We didn't win, but a lot of us worked very

---

21 Mrs. Tubby.
22 Head of the New York Writers' Bureau for Stevenson.

hard and did the best we could and are entitled, I think, to take full measure of satisfaction from it all.

Very sincerely,

To Frank Stanton[23]

December 11, 1956

Dear Frank:

I am mortified that I have not written you long before this. My excuses lack novelty, but not sincerity. I have been crushed with post-election work and I have also been away for several weeks. And now I find that there has been awaiting me in my office the television record-ing of the highlights of the Democratic Convention. It was very thoughtful of you to send this to me, and I am arranging for an exhibi-tion at a party for the campaign staff next week.

So you have not only provided me with a record of my moment of triumph, but also entertainment for the party! Perhaps the entertainees, however, would just as soon not be reminded of those stirring days, after their inglorious sequel!

I hope so much, now that the fever of my late life has subsided, that I will see something more of you and have an opportunity to resume an old and precious acquaintance.

You were very good to send me this recording.

Cordially and gratefully yours,

Senator J. W. Fulbright wrote to Edwin W. Pauley, chairman of the Board of Regents of the University of California, recommending Steven-son for president of the university. Mr. Pauley sent a copy of his reply — saying that there were too many Republicans on the board to accom-plish it — to Stevenson.

To J. William Fulbright

December 13, 1956

Dear Bill:

I am so grateful to you for that fine letter you wrote to Mr. Pauley. It would be a happy, useful conclusion in an area I enjoy, but I gather from Mr. Pauley's comments that the prospects are meager, and politics active thereabouts.

---

[23] President of the Columbia Broadcasting System.

I had not met Mr. Pauley until the latter days of this campaign, but I assume that, if not enthusiastic about the idea, he is well informed about the prospects.

I had hoped for a chance to talk with you a little about foreign affairs and what we might do to take more political advantage of their frightening mistakes in the future than we have in the past. I still hope to!

Cordially and gratefully,

Miss Carol Hardin, Stevenson's second cousin, wrote him that she had supported him not because he was a loved member of the family but because of his rare abilities, his insight, and his program. She added that she was writing her senior honors thesis at Smith College on the non-recognition of China.

To Carol J. Hardin

December 13, 1956

My dear Carol:

What a sweet letter, and how thoughtful and perceptive you have become! And my respect for your perception is not diminished by the fact that we seem to agree!

You didn't embarrass me in the least about calling Ellen.[24] It happens often and she was not rude.

I gather from what you say that you are taking honors, and I am delighted. And some day you must let me see your thesis on recognition of Communist China. It's a vexatious problem, with which I am just as glad I don't have to deal!

But I wish I was confident that this bunch would have the courage to deal with it boldly.

I am counting on you for a visit sometime and that quiet evening.

Affectionately,

Mrs. Edward Heller, of Atherton, California, first met Stevenson in 1951 at a meeting of the Democratic National Committee in Chicago. In the spring of 1952, Stevenson was in California and went to the Hellers' home for dinner; and thereafter he and the Hellers were fast friends. Mr. Heller was California State Finance Chairman for Stevenson in 1952, and in 1956 served as Stevenson's Northern California finance

---

24 The former Mrs. Stevenson.

[385]

chairman. Mrs. Heller was a delegate to the Democratic National Convention in 1956 and was active in the planning of the 1956 campaign.[25]

To Mr. and Mrs. Edward Heller[26]

December 15, 1956

My dear Heller:

I wish that some magic carpet could whisk me to your jolly house this very moment — and I don't mean just to escape the snow and cold of Chicago!

But I must continue to hope for an opportunity, and an early one, to thank you both, and dear Mrs. Heller, for all of your aid and comfort and confidence in the campaign. You have come to mean much to me in these crowded years, and I have never expressed my gratitude adequately. Nor will I, I fear!

Anyway, *thanks!* And best wishes to all of you for the holidays.

Affectionately,

ADLAI

P.S. Is there anything to the rumor I heard about Stevenson & the presidency of the Univ of Calif? Everything about Calif, yes, and education; — yes, and *rumors* — fascinates me!

ADLAI

To Norman Cousins[27]

December 15, 1956

Dear Norman:

I am still quite confounded by my mail and all that befell us in the last days of that fantastic campaign, when the stampede commenced *to* Eisenhower for protection *from* Eisenhower's mistakes.

I know you have never properly been thanked for your splendid contribution on the hydrogen bomb. I hope to make use of it still, but at that moment it got crushed in the debris and confusion.

And now I find that you have never been thanked for your cable from Tokyo.[28] Bless you, my dear friend, and let us have a calm and lengthy talk whenever your circumstances permit.

Yours,

ADLAI

---

[25] Letter from Mrs. Heller to Carol Evans, November 27, 1961.

[26] The original is in the possession of the Adlai E. Stevenson College, University of California, Santa Cruz. The postscript is handwritten.

[27] The original is in the possession of Mr. Cousins.

[28] Mr. Cousins had cabled: "The nation and world are forever in your debt."

Gerald W. Johnson recommended that Stevenson adopt Populist Mary "Yellin'" Lease's advice to Kansas farmers in the 1890's: "Raise less corn and more hell." He added that Stevenson was in an ideal position to do this, for he did not need the support of Southern Bourbons or Northern bosses and he had the ear of the country. Writing a regular column, Johnson believed, was the way to be effective and to assist in the rebuilding of the Democratic party.

To Gerald W. Johnson

December 15, 1956

Dear Gerald:

And there's nothing I can do better than "raise less corn." But what about the "more hell"? I don't think I'm a hell raiser by nature, yet I never felt more like it! If only it wasn't for this lassitude that seems to be the sequel of sixteen years of remorseless travail.

As to cultivating neither Bourbons nor bosses, you are quite right. I've had all that, and then some. Perhaps what I really need is you or someone to put some hell in me!

I am disturbed, however, to see your recommendation to write regularly. I have already declined all sorts of propositions for newspaper columns, television shows, editing jobs, etc., feeling that I can't well practise some law, do some traveling, perhaps write a book and an occasional magazine article, and do some neglected resting if I have to meet those damn deadlines. Maybe I was wrong.

I am sure you're right about the disintegration of the existing party structure. And you may be sure that I will find myself speaking articulately, if not often, on the subject of our lamentable foreign affairs. Likewise, I expect to be numbered among the liberals in the reconstitution and rebuilding of an old party. The trouble is that I find the liberals almost more intolerant than the illiberals, which seems to add up to the illiberalism of liberalism! I am sure you know what I mean, but it's a practical problem when you're trying to build something.

I wish there had been more large-scale writing about whatever benefit my two campaigns were to the democratic process and to the party. It might have enhanced my influence. I worry a lot about such things, and whatever shreds are left I hope to use.

And that's where you come in, or rather stay in, I pray! Please, please, my dear old friend, keep feeding me what you think needs saying. But for the immediate present, I have said I would forsake the hot dispute and walk beneath the stars and listen.

Yours,

Mrs. Goldie Kennedy, Democratic national committeewoman from California, taking the idea from the 1952 photograph of Stevenson with a hole in his shoe, had had a Los Angeles silversmith fashion a small silver pin in the form of a shoe sole, with an indentation for the hole. The pin became extremely popular nationally among Democrats and was a good fund-raiser. Mrs. Kennedy wrote Stevenson that his California supporters were still wearing the silver shoe campaign emblem and hoped it would help lead to victory in four years.

To Goldie Kennedy

December 15, 1956

My dear Goldie:

Yes — we must keep our powder dry and our shoes shined and ready! I think it *was* sort of a symbol, and I wish it had enduring properties. Indeed, there are a lot of things I wish we Democrats had, including more money, more press, and more Goldie Kennedys!

You were a gallant friend and leader, and I am so blessed by such heroism beyond the call of duty that I have no regrets whatever about the election.

I hope we can meet again before long, and somehow we must contrive a reunion. [A] large part of my heart will always be in California, and I shall have to come back and look after it now and then!

Merry Christmas, and my undying thanks!

Cordially yours,

P.S. I wonder if you saw the wonderful cartoon in a French paper, of a policeman addressing a park bench sitter, who displays a large hole in his shoe: "Pas de politique ici!"

Professor Robert Tufts wrote Stevenson that from the experience of working on the campaign he had concluded that a campaign was too late to create issues, and that the groundwork had to be laid earlier. Mr. Tufts observed that the press and the Democrats in Congress had failed to make the case against Eisenhower prior to the campaign. He urged Stevenson to continue to speak out on the vital issues.

To Robert Tufts

December 15, 1956

Dear Bob:

I am mortified that I have not long since acknowledged your letter of November 12. There has been much to do, and besides, I have had to read it a dozen times! I think you've drawn some wise conclusions and clarified some things for me, too. I emphatically agree, for example, that campaigns can't create issues effectively. It must be done first, and this time it wasn't done, at least not very well done.

I have had a little holiday and a busy week in New York, and now I am back struggling out of the morass that has accumulated here. I hope to practice law in a leisurely fashion this year and recover my equilibrium and, pray God, my figure, although the latter seems more desperate than the former!

Harper's is after me for a book, a thin one on foreign policy. What would you think of it? Perhaps we could even talk about it sometime if you could spare a weekend, against the possibility of a collaboration. For the present, I think I'll keep still and resist the temptation to utter some imprecations about the Middle East and that rapid-change artist, Mr. Nixon.

I will not attempt the banal expressions of gratitude to you for your valor in combat, as always. Those you've heard often enough. For you know what you have come to mean to me and how grateful I am, I am sure.

With affectionate regards to all of you, and a Merry Christmas!

Cordially,

New York attorney Louis Nizer, after analyzing the election, expressed the hope that Stevenson would continue to lead the opposition vigorously. Mr. Nizer remarked that a necessary reform was the allocation of equal television and radio time to the two major candidates at no cost. He then asked for an autographed picture of Stevenson, since he had one of Eisenhower and wanted "to remove" his "sense of guilt every time I look at Ike's smile." He concluded, "I, too, do not believe in beauty contests, but doesn't beauty lie in the eyes of the beholder? So, how do you know who will win?"

To Louis Nizer

December 15, 1956

Dear Louis:

Yes, beauty *does* lie in the eyes of the beholder. Perhaps that was part of the trouble! At all events, I'll send the photo and give the wall some political balance, if not some beauty!

I have read and re-read your letter of November 12. It reminded me again not only of your charity, kindness and support in the most tangible way, but also of your sensitive perception and extraordinary gift for language. I agree, although I see little in the press to confirm it, that there was an enormous stampede in the last week or fortnight of the campaign to Eisenhower for security from his Administration's mistakes. Ironic as that is, it also startlingly reflects, I think, the necessity for a sustained critique of foreign policy, which seems so hard for a happiness-hungry people to understand. And how can any criticism be effective without a press? I really wonder.

Perhaps you have heard it: "Eisenhower won on a slogan of 'Peace, Prosperity, and War' "!

I wish there was more writing, much more, nowadays, bringing out the irony of this situation. It would help a lot of people to understand what they only dimly suspect — that the Administration was the beneficiary of its own failures. And it would also help, I think, to forestall future mistakes. And how many more can we afford?

As for myself, well, you have seen my statement. I want to help if I can, and when and where I can. But if my future plans were equivocal, I was fearful that many of the ambitious would be also suspicious, and my influence would be diminished. And then there are also the considerations of earning a living, and of a long neglected serenity and repose. So, for better or for worse, I concluded to disclaim any further Presidential intentions — others would have been eager to disclaim them for me, I suspect!

I think you were quite right about the allocation of unpaid air time to the major candidates, and I hope that the legislation which I supported last time[29] will be reconsidered this time, with a little more help from our friends in the Congress.

Again my thanks for all you did for us, and I hope you will include a visit with me in any future plans you have for Chicago. I will do the same for you in New York.

Cordially yours,

[29] The editors have been unable to find any reference to this legislation. Congress had instead passed legislation requiring broadcasters to sell air time to candidates at prevailing commercial rates.

Herb Graffis, Chicago Sun-Times *columnist, wrote Stevenson that the vote reflected the "national IQ rates." He concluded, "You did all that angels could do."*

To Herb Graffis

December 18, 1956

Dear Herb:

I have only now unearthed that eloquent morsel of yours of November 8. It reminds me again that had I succeeded in running you to earth one day last winter, you might have spent some unhappy hours as a ghost and traveling companion of a to-be-defeated candidate. But then he might not have been defeated! But you were in sunny places and I hope you are now, too. Indeed, I wish I were with you, wherever you are!

Blessings!

Author and playwright Jean Kerr wrote Stevenson not merely to say how sorry she was about the election, but to tell him that temporarily she had lost faith in the democratic process. She added, however, that her husband had reminded her that "the value of great men is more important to the world than the successes of ordinary men."

To Mrs. Walter Kerr

December 18, 1956

My dear Jean Kerr:

But you are wrong! "Sympathy" *is* a help. I mean the sympathy of someone who is both civilized and sensitive. It's not that I was beaten in a political contest. This is in the nature of contests. It is *how* you are defeated or victorious. Or is that too Banal — for an old Anatole!

You could do something else for me besides that exquisite letter, and even besides a daily prayer. You could come and see me in New York; or here, if you ever come here. And just say "I *know*."

I think I have known you from afar quite long enough — and I am really bored!

Cordially,

The daughter of Mr. and Mrs. John Paul Welling (in whose Astor Street home in Chicago Stevenson always had a room waiting for him) wrote him that he had "awakened the public to things they never bothered to think about before." She said that her husband, Murray

Richards, had said, "A statesman like Stevenson occurs once every 50 years, but Eisenhowers occur more frequently."

To Harriet Welling Richards

December 18, 1956

Dear Haddie:

What a sweet letter! And this is what you say when you can't think of anything to say. What a talented and thoughtful girl you are — and what a charitable and dear friend!

But if you recount any more incidents of loyalty, I shall be tempted to follow a gnawing desire and emigrate to San Francisco Bay! Indeed, somebody suggested that the University of California was looking for a president, and I was tempted to send a wire — "Available; will travel." I hope you will thank Murray for giving me that 50-year space on Eisenhower. But more frequent Eisenhowers makes me, as a Democrat, tremble a little!

Bless you, my dear, and I shall hope for a visit with you when next you come this way. Indeed, I will even vacate your room!

Affectionately,

Laura Magnuson, wife of a well-known orthopedic surgeon and a close friend of Stevenson for many years, offered him the use of their home in Washington, D.C.

To Mrs. Paul B. Magnuson[30]

December 26, 1956

Dear Laura:

So many thanks for your letter, and hospitality *in absentia!*

I have just telephoned the house, hoping that I would catch you, but the maid tells me you are away. She assured me that it would be all right if I planned to stay there from January 3rd to January 6th, if it turns out to be more convenient than the Metropolitan Club. And I think it will!

I shall be distressed to miss you and Paul, but I'll be back!

With much love, and cheeriest wishes,

Affectionately,

ADLAI

P.S. I shall not impose upon the maid except for breakfast.

[30] The original is in the possession of Mrs. Magnuson.

Professor Stuart Gerry Brown wrote Stevenson a lengthy analysis of the election. Among other points that he made were: (1) The Roosevelt coalition of the 1930's and 1940's was an accidental grouping dependent on the conditions of the time and was not a stable base for the Democrats; (2) when enough people were dissatisfied, their strength, added to the regular Democrats', won elections; (3) when a majority were contented, the Republicans won; (4) the content of his "New America" was the genuine contribution of his campaign; and (5) despite the way Stevenson warned about errors in foreign policy, the Democrats in control of Congress had supported the Eisenhower Administration, and the public remembered this. Brown observed that if congressional leaders would not work with national Democrats in developing a real alternative in foreign policy, then the national leaders should part company with them.

To Stuart Gerry Brown[31]

December 27, 1956

Dear Stuart:

I am afraid your letter of November 26 has been buried in a mountain of mail.

As I have said before, one does not run for President just because he is ambitious or because he thinks he can win, but because when your party calls you obey if you believe in the system and in your obligation to serve it. The misfortune was, of course, the primary, which exhausted minds, bodies and resources and also wasted precious time in the wrong places and in the wrong ways. I hope when in the future the party confronts as near a unanimous selection as it did this time that the ambitions of others can be restrained in the interest of the common objective. Or is that *contra naturum?*

While speculation on figures is foolish, I find a consensus among the wise guys that the Middle East crisis was worth from three to five million votes minimum — to the principal architect of the crisis!

I quite agree with your conclusion that the so-called coalition of the 30's and 40's was no such thing but a "natural drawing together of the miserable, or rather, the less fortunate." Sometimes we have mistakenly called this historical accident "liberalism." I hope that we can develop more coherent notions of the difference between "liberals" and "conservatives" and "haves" and "have-nots." The Republicans, because they share a common idea and better understand it, in times like these, are a more effective combat force than a large "coalescence" of groups some-

---

[31] The original is in the Stuart Gerry Brown papers, Syracuse University Library.

times with little in common like the Democratic party. A few well-trained, purposeful troops are better than a rabble-in-arms. This, too, I think is one of our problems, whether we call it a "coalition," a national party, or what not. I could, and I am tempted, to write you, too, about the frailties of city organizations which are in part inherent and in part due to changing factors. But I must get at those thousands of Christmas cards and the undisposed of post-election letters. Forgive me. Or, rather, come and see me. But don't think I have overlooked your conclusion that the New America series[32] was the "genuine contribution of the campaign." I think so too!

As to foreign affairs, I agree with you entirely. We cannot downgrade a man or a performance as quickly and as effectively as the Russians after years of exaltation.

I wish I could commit myself to come to lecture to the Citizenship[33] students on May 7. But I am, for good and sufficient reasons, speaking little if any for some time. Moreover, I have to get busy at my office again. I am sure you will understand.

It was a wonderful and thoughtful letter and I shall read it again. Bless you — and a Happy and Busy New Year.

Yours,

ADLAI

Actress Ella Logan wrote Stevenson that in her speeches supporting him she would sing the song that had been written for her in Finian's Rainbow: *"Look to the Rainbow, follow the fellow who follows a dream — but the poor, poor, misguided people had their eyes closed, and so could not see the rainbow, so they settled for the Wizard of Ostrich." To ease her mind since the election, she wrote, "I have been* cooking." *If she could drink alone, she added, she would have done that. As an immigrant, she said, when she looked at Nixon's picture in the newspapers she asked herself where she could emigrate to now. Then she told Stevenson he had great talent — "as they would say in Dublin — there walks a gorgeous man."*

---

[32] Stevenson apparently refers to the lengthy policy papers issued during the campaign, which are included in his *The New America*, edited by Seymour E. Harris, John Bartlow Martin and Arthur Schlesinger, Jr. (New York: Harper, 1957).

[33] The Maxwell Graduate School of Citizenship and Public Affairs, Syracuse University.

To Ella Logan

December 27, 1956

My dear Friend:

For heaven's sake, don't emigrate. Yes, and for heaven's sake don't start drinking alone, just keep on cooking — and invite me around!

And another "don't." Please don't say "pardon the awful scribble." It is the most sincere and puncturing scribble I have ever read.

Bless you; and I hope you are singing again and will be singing to me soon.

Sincerely,

To Mrs. Edgar B. Stern[34]

December 27, 1956

My dear Mrs. Stern:

I am mortified that I have only now found your letter of November 15.[35] It is a gracious, charitable and comforting letter and I am grateful indeed.

Curiously enough, while yours was on the bottom a letter from Phil[36] from Japan was on top of the heap today. He sounds keen and happy, and I think he is sensible to have a good look about while he has the opportunity.

I pray that all is well with you and Mr. Stern and that we can have a good, lowdown, Democratic reunion soon again.

With gratitude for your confidence and great encouragement, and my prayers for a busy, happy New Year, I am

Cordially yours,

Mrs. Chloe Fox wrote Stevenson that she was so proud of the letter he had written her that she was thinking of removing her Chagall and hanging the letter in its place. She said that her ten months' work with the Writers' Bureau for Stevenson was rich and satisfying. She added that she had just met with some of the members and they wanted to volunteer their services to other liberal candidates in the future. The writers had asked her to write Stevenson to see if he could help raise the funds for an office and a secretary.

[34] The former Ethel Rosenwald, wife of the chairman of WDSU Broadcasting Corporation in New Orleans.

[35] Mrs. Stern had expressed her gratitude to a "great American."

[36] Her son Philip Stern, who had been in charge of research in Stevenson's Washington headquarters during the 1956 campaign.

To Chloe Fox

December 27, 1956

Dear Chloe:

Thank you for your letter. But please leave your Chagall right where it is!

I do indeed take at least some of the gratification you suggest from the realization that people want to go on along the lines that we have tried to mark out these last five years. I am afraid there are all too many of our tribe who are heading back now for their armchairs and their classrooms. But it won't take so very many to keep the coals at least sufficiently warm that they can be fanned up again when the next time comes.

I wish I could respond in equal measure to the inquiry about my willingness to participate in doing some of the chores which will have to be done if this project is to be kept going. My impulse is good enough; I would like to say to you to go ahead and do whatever your interest and your willingness prompts you to do and to count on me to help out wherever and whenever I can about completing the necessary arrangements. And yet I know that I am not entitled to do this, that there is really not very much I could actually do about raising the rather substantial amount of money you suggest, and that it is really much fairer for me to say to you frankly that I think you probably ought to lay some firmer foundations for this before you count on going ahead with it. Of course I will help if I can, but until I can at least see my way past the deficits that already face me I know I am not entitled to speak very encouragingly about any new project.

Thank you again, and I hope I have not discouraged you.

Cordially,

Benjamin Swig, owner of the Fairmont Hotel in San Francisco, was a dedicated supporter of Stevenson and frequently advised him on investments.

To Benjamin H. Swig[37]

December 27, 1956

Dear Ben:

Ever so many thanks for your letter of the 14th. I am distressed that I missed you in the East and I hope on another journey you will give me a little advance notice.

[37] The original is in the possession of Mr. Swig.

Although I am by no means sure, I may be coming to California in mid-February and, if circumstances permit, I hope I can have a look at that famous Arrowhead Springs[38] of yours. I note your advice to keep Canadian Eagle and I shall act accordingly.

General Dynamics has been good news, as you say. But it constantly reminds me of that stupid broker who talked me into selling my Electric Boat stock back in 1950!

The news about the Lerner Stores is comforting, and I will reassure my son, who has been behaving exactly like a man with his first speculation!

I am grateful indeed for your suggestion about some more real estate investments. At the moment my funds are meager, but when I get through with the campaign cleanup and can better see my situation I will hope to take advantage of your kindness again. So don't rule me out!

I am so pleased to hear that the Esperson Building continues so promising.

With many many thanks, my dear friend, and a happy, healthy, busy New Year to all the Swigs!

Cordially,

ADLAI

To James P. Warburg

December 27, 1956

Dear Jim:

Yes, you are doubtless right. I wish I had insisted more emphatically on laying more of the groundwork for the chickens that came home to roost in the Middle East crisis. But after four years of exaltation even by the Democrats in Congress it would have been a little hard to crack the idols or the illusions after the Convention, as you say. I thought I had been beating them up for the past few years. Certainly I never missed a chance during the primary, but they weren't listening, and the press, as you know, was hardly friendly nor were there many voices in the chorus.

And now I hope that I will have some opportunity to read some of the things you have been sending me.

I know your New Year will be busy. I hope it will be happy too!

Yours,

---

[38] A resort hotel in San Bernardino, California, owned by Mr. Swig.

Mrs. Eugenie Anderson wrote Stevenson, "Few men living have done so much to lift the level of political debate in our time." She observed that the vote for Eisenhower was a triumph for the "Age of Advertising." She added that she had never realized before the serious structural weakness in the system — that it did not provide for any continuity of leadership in the party out of power.

To Eugenie Anderson

December 27, 1956

My dear Eugenie:

Perhaps it is not for *me* to say it, but I think you are right, and that it has been more a "triumph for the age of advertising" than an expression of confidence, popularity and approval of the President and his administration, which is the usual conclusion. And it is precisely of an immunity from criticism that the temptation to feel that you "can get away with almost anything," as you put it, is a real hazard. Put another way, certainly if you can get away with as many mistakes and failures as they have and enjoy increased approbation, we can only conclude that the people don't know, and why don't they? I hope we can talk of these things some time, because somehow we must develop a synthesis of ideas among our thoughtful partisans for the future. Some of the studies of the press and their treatment of the campaign which are coming in now are very revealing, and also very disturbing. An advertiser can't do much without media, and what media they had! What with the Middle East crisis, too, I wonder sometimes how we got as many votes as we did.

I shall blushingly refrain from comment but not overlook the gracious things you have said, and continue to hope that you will come for a quiet evening with me when your travels bring you this way.

With renewed thanks for your gallantry and my prayers for a busy, happy New Year, I am

Affectionately,

John Duncan Miller, special representative in Europe for the International Bank for Reconstruction and Development, and before that Washington correspondent of The Times *(London), wrote Stevenson from Paris that he had persuaded the Democrats to rebuild themselves over the past four years and this aided their victory in both houses of Congress. The decision of the British and French to go it alone in the Middle East did not help in the election, he remarked, but they had lost all faith in the words of John Foster Dulles, who, Mr. Miller said, was thoroughly distrusted in Europe.*

To John Duncan Miller

December 27, 1956

Dear Johnnie:

Your letter of November 15 was better than good music for me. You will understand, I am sure, why I have not acknowledged it long since. Surely if kindness and courtesy from one's friends is an unsuccessful politician's best reward, I have been rewarded beyond my desserts, and indeed to the point of suffocation. But we are working our way out of the post-election deluge and should emerge from the Christmas cards by the Fourth of July!

I should like to think that you are quite right about the effect of the Presidential campaign on the Congressional campaign. This theme runs through many letters but not through many newspaper columns.

But as to the exasperation of Eden[39] and Mollet[40] and the disastrous consequences there can be no doubt. I had never anticipated that Israel, France and Great Britain would turn out to be my adversary's best political allies. The vote shift in the last ten days has been estimated by the wise guys at from three to five million upwards. But I doubt if it was decisive, although there is little doubt that we would have done better percentagewise than in 1952.

I have never been persuaded that it was the President's "over-whelming personality" that accounts for his success and his party's astonishing failures. This seems to be the common explanation. But I suspect a far better one is an immunity from criticism without precedent for four years and a triumph of the advertising techniques among a people who are comfortable, allergic to bad news, and highly suscep-tible to mass influence. And, of course, their calculation that total con-centration on Eisenhower would carry the Republican party along mis-fired badly under the impact of local concerns and a sustained attack on "the Republican party" even for a few weeks.

These reflections are interesting, however, only for future advantage. But I cannot be sure yet that my party is going to take advantage of them. We shall see.

Meanwhile, the important business is relations with our British and French allies. I will not be surprised if this takes a long time or that merely replacing Dulles can do it. Nixon will emerge more and more as

[39] British Prime Minister Sir Anthony Eden.
[40] French Prime Minister Guy Mollet.

the real influence, and of course he is capable of any gymnastics that local politics seem to require — cf. during the campaign he was applauding our emancipation from Britain and France and so was the press. Now he is demanding a restoration of the alliance, and so is the press. During the campaign the President assured us that we would not be involved in the Middle East, yet I have no doubt that he will make bold gestures there now that the election is over.

Well, I wish we could talk of these and other things, and perhaps we can. I hope there is a trip abroad in my horoscope now that I shall have more leisure — and I hope some clients! You were so good to write me and I hope you will do so from time to time and let me have some impression of attitudes there. It would be most helpful in connection with occasional "utterances."

I hope the New Year will bring you everything you want.

Cordially,

Charles Guggenheim, one of Stevenson's television advisers during the 1956 campaign, sent a photograph of Stevenson's Dalmatian, King Arthur.

To Charles Guggenheim

December 31, 1956

Dear Charlie:

After looking at the handsome picture of Artie, I've decided that he should be our candidate for President in 1960! If being photogenic is one qualification, I think Artie should win in a landslide.

You were kind to send me the picture — and Artie thanks you, too!

Cordially,

P.S. Please come in to see me when you are here. Happy New Year!

AES

Mrs. Eugene Meyer wrote Stevenson a long letter on December 13, 1956. Among other things she mentioned that she was sending him an ornamental tiger. She asked if he would be able to attend her birthday party on January 5 and see her the following morning. She also spoke of his elevation of heart and mind and that he had been "forced into greatness by the tragic demands fate made" upon him.

[400]

To Mrs. Eugene Meyer[41]

December 31, 1956

My dear, dear Agnes —

The tiger has arrived and what a splendid fellow he is! Now you must tell me his period, his history and what you know about him. From the cleat on the reverse side he must have been an ornament, perhaps on stone?? (I shall plan to see you the "morning after," dear friend; and I really *don't* change my mind often!) Bless you & I pray it has been a good & gay Christmas for all the Meyers!

ADLAI

P.S. It's a superb photo — that solitary searcher amid the tumult of rock on top of the world! Thanks.

To Mrs. Eugene Meyer[42]

January 1, 1957

Agnes dear —

I have your letter with the incredible guest list. What a feast you have prepared; what a lucky man I am to be included. And what admiration, respect — and love — for you it all betokens.

May 1957 — and 70 — be the best of your years, is the prayer this New Years day of your devoted —

ADLAI

Former Under Secretary of State Sumner Welles wrote that the election saddened him, since he felt that the Eisenhower Administration did not have the vision, historical understanding, consistency, and diplomatic resiliency to cope with the problems the United States faced.

To Sumner Welles

January 2, 1957

My dear Sumner:

I am mortified that I have not long since acknowledged your thoughtful, flattering — and important — letter of November 19. I say "important" because I strongly suspect that your estimate of this period in

[41] This handwritten letter is in the Agnes Meyer files, Princeton University Library. It is written on Stevenson's 1956 Christmas card.
[42] This handwritten letter is in the Agnes Meyer files, Princeton University Library.

our history and its significance is not exaggerated. I think, and I believe you mentioned it in Maine, that a most disturbing aspect of the past crowded year has been the cultivated ignorance of the people about the state of the world. Instead of providing perspective and encouraging a wider comprehension of our situation, the government seems to me to have done precisely the reverse, i.e., to reassure and discourage anxiety and even inquiry.

Well, let us hope that we may weather this perilous passage by wiser guidance and a kind Providence even if our people are destined to little understand what it is all about.

Your kindness has meant much to me; and I hope you and Mrs. Welles will have a healthy, happy New Year.

Ever sincerely,

On January 3, 1957, when Stevenson attended the opening session of the United States Senate, he was applauded from both sides of the Senate floor as he took a seat in the diplomatic gallery. Majority Leader Lyndon Johnson referred to Stevenson as "one of our most distinguished Senators." Then he flushed and corrected himself — "distinguished citizens."

That same day Stevenson issued a statement to the press, by implication chiding the Democratic leaders in Congress — Johnson and Sam Rayburn — for having declined to join the Democratic Advisory Council.[43]

In response to numerous inquiries, as I understand it, the purpose of the Advisory Committee is to advance Democratic programs and principles throughout the country. To be an effective opposition, the Democratic Party must have a broader base than the Democrats in Congress. There are lots of Democratic Governors, Mayors, officials, leaders and workers around the country who must be informed about Party policy at the national level.

We can't be an effective opposition party just every four years for a couple of months.

And even to be an effective majority party in Congress, I think the Democratic Congressmen and Senators should and would be the first to welcome new blood, and the views and ideas of thoughtful and influential Party leaders who are not in Congress.

The Democratic Party is not just a Congressional party, it is a Na-

[43] The text is from a carbon copy.

tional party. Opposed as it is by the great publicity resources of the government, by most of the press and the money of the country, it needs all the vitality, interest and energy it can mobilize.

Stevenson also issued a statement criticizing President Eisenhower's announced plan to request a congressional resolution (which became known as the Eisenhower Doctrine) authorizing the use of American military forces to assist any Middle Eastern nation requesting such aid against aggression from a country controlled by "International Communism." Stevenson remarked that the President "is evidently trying frantically to fill the vacuum his own policies helped create before Russia does." Stevenson warned that Eisenhower was "going to ask for another military blank check, this time the right to send our forces to fight in the Middle East." He declared, however: "If the result of the Suez disaster is to jolt us into recognition at last of the bankruptcy of our Middle East policy and the hypocrisy of the Republican campaign, it may yet do some good."

On January 4, Stevenson attended the first meeting of the Democratic Advisory Council, at which various policy questions were discussed and it was agreed that the second meeting would be held in San Francisco the next month.

After attending Mrs. Eugene Meyer's birthday party and conferring privately with her the following day, Stevenson returned to Chicago.

Miss Pat Higgins, stewardess aboard the chartered American Airlines plane during the campaign, wrote Stevenson that she was sorry she missed the Christmas party for those who had traveled on the plane. She explained that the flight she was on that day was delayed in reaching Chicago.

To Pat Higgins

January 8, 1957

Dear Pat:

I am touched by your note, and I don't find it easy to thank you as I should like. It reminds me of those frantic hops from town to town when we were always working against time, and of how often your cheerful attentions lifted our spirits.

It was too bad you missed the party, but I hope there will be more reunions. And maybe American Airlines will bring us together again before long!

Cordially and gratefully yours,

[403]

To Mrs. Franklin D. Roosevelt[44]

January 10, 1957

Dear Mrs. Roosevelt:

I had a very personal and most helpful talk with Agnes Meyer following her birthday party. She said some things that made me want very much to see you if you can spare an hour alone some time.

If you pass this way and it is convenient for you to stop off or meet me, I hope you will let me know. I shall be in New York for a few days commencing January 29 and will call you against the possibility that you will be there at that time.

Affectionately,

ADLAI

To Kermit Hunter[45]

January 10, 1957

Dear Kermit:

To think that I have only now found your letter written on election eve![46] Well, for such a fine letter as that, better late than never!

I am deeply moved, my dear friend, by your kindness to me and your perception of my feeling and purpose. That you could also suggest that the latter was accomplished pleases me immensely. I really don't think that it was, because there is nothing harder than effective political communication of thought and ideas that don't lend themselves to the simplest treatment. But that a few people like you understood and thought well of the campaign is a better reward than the frail effort merited.

Please remember me to that charming lady of yours, and I shall hope to cross your path soon again.

With all good wishes, I am

Cordially,

---

[44] The original is in the Franklin D. Roosevelt Library, Hyde Park, New York.

[45] Drama teacher at Hollins College in Virginia and writer of historical dramas. His play *Forever This Land,* depicting the life of Abraham Lincoln, was staged by the New Salem Lincoln League at Petersburg, Illinois, at the suggestion of Stevenson when he was governor of Illinois. See *The Papers of Adlai E. Stevenson,* Vol. III, pp. 333, 433–434.

[46] Mr. Hunter had written: "Never have the issues of the world and our time been so beautifully and skillfully analyzed." He added: "You have made me proud of my heritage."

Reinhold Niebuhr wrote Stevenson that it was "tragic that we do not have and cannot have a parliamentary government. If we had, such a campaign as you waged would have secured you a permanent position in the political life of our nation."

To Reinhold Niebuhr

January 10, 1957

Dear Reinhold:

Only now have I found your letter of December 27. Little do you know how comforting it is — and how like all of your letters in that regard. How I wish we could talk about the Middle East and the recent absurdities, but that would only be one of many things I should like to talk about. And the most important would be how to communicate failure to the people without a press, and when they are comfortable and complacent, and constantly reassured by all the propaganda agencies of a mighty government.

Perhaps some night when I am in New York I could come up and call on you. I may want to make a speech before "Christian Action" in London late this Spring and talk about the implications of the failures of the West since Potsdam,[47] or something calculated to shed some light on our real hazards and our failures to understand the revolution that has taken place since the atom bomb was exploded and the voiceless people heard what was going on in the 20th Century.

Is it a fit theme, and useful? Or too obvious?

You shall have my prayers for the New Year, and I hope they are of some value.

Sincerely yours,

Stevenson was a member of the board of directors of Encyclopaedia Britannica. He also served as a director of Encyclopaedia Britannica Films and as a member of its advisory board. After returning to the practice of law, he also served both companies in a legal capacity. The Britannica companies' chairman, William Benton, was considering adding Stevenson to the board of directors of the British Encyclopaedia Britannica.

---

[47] The Potsdam Conference of Stalin, Churchill (supplanted by Clement Attlee) and Truman in July and August, 1945, at which Allied plans for reestablishing European peace were discussed and a demand for unconditional Japanese surrender was issued.

To William Benton[48]

January 10, 1957

Dear Bill:

I want you to know that I have been much touched by your everlasting interest in me and my "suitable employment." Our talk in the last couple of days has interested me very much and I hope we can continue it in Arizona. Most of all, I hope to get to Arizona!

I am planning to accept the invitation to San Francisco on the 16th,[49] and will probably come down there a few days later and spend part of my time with you and part with Mary[50] if her plans work out as I understand them. And now I find I must be back in Washington for the Gridiron Dinner on March 2nd, which is an awful nuisance.

I have neglected wholly to thank you for those exquisite handkerchiefs. That you have any hopes of making me a "well groomed man" is also extremely gratifying.

Yours,

ADLAI

Congressman John Flynt of Georgia wrote Stevenson he regretted that certain suggestions he made to James A. Finnegan about the campaign were not followed. He also expressed his "profound disappointment" that no Georgian was invited to participate in the Democratic Advisory Council.

To John J. Flynt, Jr.

January 10, 1957

My dear Congressman:

I was delighted to find your letter of January 8 on my return from Washington and New York. I did attend the meeting of the so-called "Advisory Committee" in Washington and also the "swearing-in ceremonies" at the Senate for the new members. It was a memorable occasion and I was flattered by the welcome suddenly accorded me while sitting in the gallery — demurely I thought!

Your loyalty to the party and what Georgia has done for me in the past two national campaigns has not gone unnoticed. I am perhaps

48 See note 252 to Part One, p. 145.
49 Stevenson was to speak to the Democratic National Conference on February 16, 1957. His speech is included in this volume, pp. 463–473.
50 Mrs. Albert Lasker, who had a winter home in Arizona.

more grateful than you realize and I hope some time to have an opportunity to express my gratitude in person. I wish I had known about your
recommendations to Jim Finnegan. I am afraid we were getting so
much advice during the campaign that we were bewildered. Certainly,
keeping up with the appalling schedule was more than I could do, or at
least do well.

The meeting of the Advisory Committee was informative if not decisive of much. Sam Rayburn evidently does not want Members of Congress to serve on it, although I gather that he and Lyndon [B. Johnson]
and others have offered to cooperate and consult. My feeling is that its
success as a committee will depend largely on the vigor of its staff.
Personally I strongly feel that a sustained and vigorous scrutiny and
criticism of the administration, not only in Congress but throughout the
country, will be necessary if we cherish any hopes of winning in 1960.
Without a press to help us it will have to be done largely by individuals.
I am hopeful that in that regard the Committee's staff might be helpful.

Certainly I am confident that Mr. [Paul] Butler as chairman of the
committee would welcome suggestions as to what could be done from
every source. As for me, I want to help in any way I can within the
limits of my circumstances.

With all good wishes and my gratitude, I am

Cordially,

*Miss Virginia Hunt, of Washington, D.C., wrote Stevenson on
January 4 that she was concerned to read his criticism of Eisenhower's
request for a congressional resolution — the Eisenhower Doctrine. She
appealed to Stevenson to put his country's interest before that of his
political party.*

To Virginia L. Hunt

January 10, 1957

Dear Madam:

Evidently if a leader of the opposition points out even a transparent
failure of the administration it is an unpatriotic attack on the President.
Were we, dear madam, never to criticize the Republican President, even
when merited, we would always have a Republican President! That to
me is not the measure of patriotism, nor is it the role of the opposition
party, nor is it consistent with the two party system, which I believe
in.

Thank you for your letter. And I hope you will accept this reply in the spirit of a friendly anxiety to inform you as to why I said, and will continue to say, what I think about this administration from time to time.

Sincerely yours,

P.S. I must add that I am delighted that the President has discovered that there is instability and Russian penetration in the Middle East. As you know, some of us have been shouting about it for more than a year.

Senator Richard L. Neuberger wrote Stevenson on January 2 that the Democratic party needed a national voice and "you are it." Too many Democrats, and particularly Southern ones, were anchored to sectional interests, he observed.

To Richard L. Neuberger

January 10, 1957

My dear Dick:

Bless you for that splendid letter. You flatter me beyond description, but I like it!

It was good to have a glimpse of you and Maurine[51] and I wish there were more in prospect. Certainly I agree about the proper place, position and purpose of our party, and also about the embarrassments it is now suffering. But we can't remedy everything and we *can* keep after the enemy better than we have in the past. For example, when only a handful of Republicans vote for amending Rule xxii,[52] why don't we liberal Democrats denounce the Republicans for their frauds and impostures rather than one another?

We made some progress with the Advisory Committee — I think!

Come again.

Yours,

[51] Mrs. Neuberger.
[52] The Senate provision for cloture, originally adopted in 1917 and since modified. On January 3, 1957, Senator Clinton Anderson moved to ease Senate rules limiting debate in an attempt to initiate action on civil rights legislation. The motion was successfully opposed by Senator Lyndon B. Johnson, and the final vote, on January 4, was 55 to 38 against it.

To Marquis Childs[53]

January 11, 1957

Dear Mark:

Bill Blair tells me that he talked to you on the phone and relayed to you the message that I would be glad to speak to the Gridiron Dinner on March 2. It means interrupting a vacation, but I guess that can't be helped.

I know how crowded those dinners are, but if it were at all possible I would very much like to have some of my closest associates in the campaign invited — my three partners, Willard Wirtz, William McC. Blair, Jr., and Newton Minow; also James A. Finnegan, George W. Ball, Archibald Alexander and Tom Finletter. I'm afraid that is quite a list!

Cordially,

ADLAI

P.S. I suppose Clayton Fritchey and Roger Tubby will be invited in any event.

To Mrs. John Kenneth Galbraith[54]

January 11, 1957

Dear Kitty:

It now looks as though I would arrive in Cambridge on February 2 for a visit with the children (and some older folks!) of two or three days. I believe the children are planning a birthday party for myself and John Fell on Saturday night, February 2nd. If the 3rd would be better and make the attendance of Mr. and Mrs. Galbraith more likely, I wish you would communicate that simple unadorned fact to my young.

As to your guest room, I think we will spare you this tenant, at least this time, but if I get in trouble, well, look out!

Hastily and affectionately,

ADLAI

To James A. Finnegan

January 11, 1957

Dear Jim:

Before leaving Washington, I had a talk with Jim Rowe by telephone. He expressed himself as emphatically in favor of a change of the chair-

---

[53] Washington columnist for the St. Louis *Post-Dispatch*. The original is in the possession of the State Historical Society of Wisconsin.
[54] The original is in the possession of Mrs. Galbraith.

manship,[55] and felt that it could be done, if someone would take the initiative and a suitable job could be found for the incumbent. I don't know whether Dave Lawrence is in touch with him or would care to be, but I thought I would pass this along for what it's worth.

Hastily,

To William Benton[56]

January 11, 1957

Dear Bill:

I have just wired you as per the attached copy.[57] I am afraid I have been an awful nuisance, but I suddenly realized I was making two trips East, one to New York and one to see the children in Cambridge for my birthday. The two can be combined into one, so I am now to come to New York around the 29th or 30th and to Cambridge on Saturday, February 2, for a couple of days with the children. I have accepted an invitation for dinner with the [Cass] Canfields for the Hamish Hamiltons[58] of London on February 1st.

Please don't feel that a party is necessary, but if you plan something and want to include me I think either the 29th, 30th or 31st would be convenient. As to guests, I trust your judgment completely — especially ladies.

I am afraid I have been an awful nuisance.

Yours,

ADLAI

To T. S. Matthews

January 11, 1957

My dear Tom:

I have maltreated you again! This time it is neglect of your letter of November 28, which got lost in the mountain that has all but crushed me since the election.

. . . Surely you are right that Anglo-American relations should be just about our most important business. There is much about it that I should like to say, none of it very flattering to the present Administration, curiously enough! But I will withhold that against another time,

---

55 Of the Democratic National Committee.
56 See note 252 to Part One, p. 145.
57 The editors do not have a copy of this telegram.
58 The managing director of the British publishing house of Hamish Hamilton, Ltd., and his wife, the former Countess Pallavicino.

and there may be a trip abroad, including England, on my spring horizon.

Among other things, I have been importuned by a gentleman named Canon Collins[59] to speak before an organization named Christian Action — a "great speech"! Herbert Agar has joined his request, and I should welcome your views. I had not thought to speak at all, as I would be coming on business, but if I should or must it occurs to me that a club or university audience might be better, or even some function in connection with the American Bar Association meeting. The latter, however, is not until July.

Views on the foregoing will be welcome and, again, my apologies for this shocking oversight (I wish it were the only one!).

Cordially yours,

To Frank H. Canaday[60]

January 14, 1957

Dear Mr. Canaday:

My post election mail is still unfinished and in a state of progressive disorder! I have been carrying your letter of November 27, together with the enchanting note from Mrs. Gertrude Mertens,[61] around with me for weeks. Her verse, indeed, I have quoted repeatedly and with devastating success. You have asked to have it returned and I do so herewith, mortified to discover sundry notes I have scribbled on the back of it. They look suspiciously like notes for an impromptu speech at some dinner, and I hope you can forgive this thoughtless desecration of this wonderful letter from a wonderful gal. (I hope some time I can meet her.)

I was much amused by your comment that America demands that its candidates be demagogues when running for office and demi-gods after they are in. How right you are! Although I would have to say that I have some misgivings about the latter, it seems to me I have noted that nonsense and demagoguery, unless they are exposed, are not altogether distasteful even when they are in. After rereading your letter for the nth time I am tempted to think that my principal mistake was not to have you helping with my speeches.

Yours,

---

[59] Lewis John Collins, Canon of St. Paul's Cathedral in London.
[60] A New York businessman who had campaigned in Vermont for Stevenson.
[61] The editors do not have a copy of Mrs. Mertens's note.

To Elmer Davis[62]

January 14, 1957

Dear Elmer:

I was touched and delighted to have your note. I have yearned for a visit with you, but coming to Washington has hardly been a tranquil experience for me for a long time; but things will improve in that respect at least!

I send you my affectionate best wishes and the gratitude of a citizen as well as a devoted friend for all you mean and have meant to my generation.

Cordially,
ADLAI

Mrs. Daniel Caulkins, the sister of Cass Canfield and an old friend of Stevenson, invited him to come to Acapulco for a vacation.

To Mrs. Daniel Caulkins

January 14, 1957

My dear Babs:

I am mortified! Weeks ago you lifted my spirits with a telephone call in New York which almost carried me to Acapulco nonstop that very moment!

Meanwhile, my plots, or the plots against my serenity and leisure, have thickened and my visions have all but vanished. I must be in San Francisco on February 16; back in Washington on March 2nd. In that little interval I have hopes for ten days of sunshine in Arizona. In March, well, I don't know, but I have hopes of some more holiday, but where and when I cannot yet foretell.

You were an angel to think of me, and I shall remember it and what happened to it — with acute pain.

I hope you have a wonderful holiday.

Yours,

[62] News analyst for the American Broadcasting Company, whose friendship with Stevenson dated back to World War II, when Mr. Davis was director of the Office of War Information in Washington, D.C. The original is in the possession of the Library of Congress.

To William Benton[63]

January 16, 1957

Dear Bill:

You can count on me for the 29th, and I will call at your apartment at 6 or before, in street clothes. (If *you* prefer a black tie, I shall have one with me, in any event.)

I hope I am not evading my responsibilities, but, as you know, I have great respect for your judgment as to the ladies! Of course, if you would like Marietta [Tree], it would be fine with me.

As to Phoenix, why don't you plan to come out when you please, and meanwhile I will visit at the other place first.[64] I am sure it will be quite satisfactory to them.

As the complexities increase and the decisions multiply, I feel more and more like taking wing to a distant spot for at least the three months that it took you to recover in 1947.

The Britannica possibility grows daily in my imagination, and I hope to defer any final decision about the New York arrangements until I have had a more leisurely talk with you. I am apprehensive about getting too involved in too many directions, but then, perhaps the reaction to too much involvement is a stampede to too little!

Yours,

ADLAI

Dr. and Mrs. Alton Kanter, of Los Angeles, wrote that they had named their son John Stevenson Kanter because Stevenson had spoken intelligently and with foresight in a troubled world. They expressed the hope that he would continue to speak out on the problems facing the United States and the world.

To Dr. and Mrs. Alton Kanter

January 16, 1957

My dear friends:

I have been deeply moved by your letter of January 4. You couldn't have flattered me more than by adding Stevenson to that innocent young man's name, but I wonder if he will forgive you! I shall hope very much for an opportunity to see him and you on another trip to California. Your kindness touches me, and your encouragement to take a continuing part in our affairs pleases me very much.

Cordially and gratefully yours,

[63] See note 252 to Part One, p. 145.
[64] Mr. Benton had invited Stevenson to vacation at his home in Arizona.

Congressman Wayne Aspinall, of Colorado, wrote that he suspected that a larger segment of independents had supported Stevenson than was the case with members of the Democratic party. Mr. Aspinall observed that he hoped the Democrats could present a constructive program to the nation in 1960, and added, "Upon you more than any other individual the fruition of this hope depends."

To Wayne N. Aspinall

January 16, 1957

My dear Wayne:

Few letters that I have received since the election have pleased me more than yours of January 15. You both flatter and comfort me. Moreover, I suspect that you are right and that some of those "Independents," so-called, were far more helpful than a lot of people we have called Democrats in the past.

I am encouraged by your suggestion of occasional expressions of opinion in the future. I hope to do just that. And I hope, even more, that the party and its leaders, in Congress and out, can this time avoid the errors of the past four years and mount and sustain an effective and honest criticism of the Eisenhower Administration. If we don't, I am afraid we will find Mr. Nixon by no means easy in 1960.

But I don't want to evade any further responsibilities that I may have to our party. I am sure you appreciate my reluctance to assert myself too positively. I will always welcome your future suggestions as to my usefulness, even as I shall always be grateful for your encouragement and support in the past.

With warm good wishes,

Cordially yours,

To Lansdell K. Christie[65]

January 17, 1957

Dear Lansdell:

I have just been talking with a client for whom I made a trip to South Africa in 1955[66] about doing the same thing again. It caused me to wonder if by any chance you are to be in Liberia at that time or are contemplating a journey to Africa, and whether or not we could join

[65] President of Liberia Mining Company, Ltd., in Monrovia, Liberia.
[66] For an account of Stevenson's trip to Africa, see *The Papers of Adlai E. Stevenson*, Vol. IV, pp. 480–493.

forces to the enlightenment of your admiring friend, the late Governor of Illinois.

With all good wishes, I am

Cordially yours,

To Richard S. Reynolds, Jr.[67]

January 17, 1957

Dear Richard:

On Tuesday I had a long visit with Sir Robert Jackson, whom I mentioned to you some time ago, and who has been in charge of the preparation of the Volta River Aluminum Project in the Gold Coast. For a variety of reasons, including the uncertainties with respect to the stability of the Gold Coast Government and the large capital requirements, it seems likely that the project will not go forward at this time. He also told me about the recent bauxite discoveries in Queensland.

But all this is probably quite familiar to you; and the purpose of this letter is to report that I shall probably undertake another journey to Africa in May or June for the same interests that sent me there in 1955. I thought I had best tell you about this in case there are any matters there of interest or possible concern to you which I could explore. There is no hurry about all this, and I shall hope for a good visit with you somewhere before I have to take this trip.

Cordially yours,

To Harold Hochschild[68]

January 17, 1957

Dear Harold:

I have just read a speech by Harry Oppenheimer made last fall on "Racial Tensions in the Union of South Africa," and had a talk with the importer for whom I did some negotiating with the Anglo American Company when I was there in 1955.

These two incidents reminded me again of my trip at that time and the important part you played in it.

I have told this client that I might undertake another journey for him there in May or June. And this in turn causes me to wonder if by any chance those dates coincide with any contemplated trip of yours. I remember you and Mary[69] told me your plans when I saw you in New

[67] President of the Reynolds Metal Company in Richmond, Virginia.
[68] Chairman of the American Metal Company, Ltd.
[69] Mrs. Hochschild.

[415]

York, and I have an unhappy feeling that you are not planning to go back until the autumn. I was hopeful that maybe our trips might coincide. If not, do let me know if there is anything I could do for you should I be going there late this spring.

Cordially yours,

The Reverend Kenneth Walker wrote that he and others were disturbed that the Eisenhower Administration had no basic philosophy of government and no real comprehension of the social forces at work. He informed Stevenson that he was about to announce his engagement.

To the Reverend Kenneth C. Walker

January 17, 1957

Dear Kenneth:

Thanks for your letter. Of course, there's nothing more painful than thought, and nothing more distasteful than bad news. Yet, while these traits are peculiarly developed in an America conditioned to advertising, there is also the problem of the press. How much do they know about the realities? Little, I fear, and to try to tell them all about it in a few speeches, for the most part poorly reported if at all, is an impossible undertaking.

All of which is by way of saying that I agree with what you say and I am much concerned with the problem of communication and public information. If the people don't want the facts of life, it is the more reason that they *must.*

And now I have reached the last paragraph of your letter, and the really important news! I am delighted, and send my hasty and enthusiastic congratulations to you and Mrs. Parker. You must bring her with you when you come up to visit me for an evening.

With warmest good wishes, and the admiration of a bachelor!

Cordially,

J. Edward Day, who had been director of the Illinois Department of Insurance while Stevenson was governor, had just been appointed executive vice president of the Prudential Insurance Company in charge of Western operations.

To J. Edward Day[70]

January 17, 1957

Dear Ed —

I have asked Ben Swig, owner of the [Fairmont] hotel (& God knows what else!) to call on you in L.A. sometime. He is an old friend, originally from Boston, and was finance chairman for me during the late unpleasantness in Calif. He has also tried to make political life more endurable for me financially. And it may be in connection with a plot in that direction that he will want to talk to you. But mostly I wanted you to get acquainted because I'm sure you will encounter him in business or politics as time goes on anyway and I wanted you to know of my acquaintance and regard for him as well as my sense of obligation to him for his many courtesies to me on my visits here.

I yearn to see you all & wish this may be the time, but I'll let you get settled first & entrust the inspection to Bill [Blair] —

Yrs

ADLAI

To Mrs. Barbara Kerr[71]

January 17, 1957

Dear Barbara:

Thanks for that delightful letter. I agree with all of your conclusions politically. The sudden demise of Crowell-Colliers[72] was a bit of a shock, even for a distant outsider, and I have some idea what a blow it must have been to you and my friend Teddy White.[73]

I shall look forward to that talk in New York, and I hope there will be an early opportunity. Meanwhile, just remember that '57 can't be *worse*.

Affectionately,

---

[70] This handwritten letter is in the possession of Mr. Day. It was written on Fairmont Hotel stationery.

[71] Public affairs editor of *Woman's Home Companion*.

[72] The Crowell-Collier Publishing Company announced on Friday night, December 14, 1956, its decision to suspend publication of *Collier's* magazine and *Woman's Home Companion*. See the New York *Times*, December 20, 1956.

[73] Mr. White wrote Stevenson on January 8, 1957: "Death, as you may have noticed, came to all of us at *Collier's* ten days before Christmas." Mr. White was a member of an informal employees' committee to raise funds to continue publication of the magazine. See the New York *Times*, December 15, 1956.

To Brooks Hays

January 17, 1957

My dear Brooks:

It has just been brought to my attention that you put my concession speech of last November in the Congressional Record. I am extremely flattered, and am grateful to you for this gracious thought of me.

I hope very much that there will be an evening together in the not too distant future. I can think of no better place to turn for enlightenment, agreeably packaged!

Cordially yours,

John Steinbeck wrote Stevenson that his publishers were sending a copy of his new book, The Short Reign of Pippin IV, *a political satire. He added that he was engaged in rendering into present-day understandable English the Arthurian stories of Sir Thomas Malory.*

To John Steinbeck

January 17, 1957

Dear John:

So many thanks for your letter of January 7. And I am looking forward to the "Short Reign of Pippin IV." If you have done a political satire and confess it has a stinger in its tail, I would be confident that it has a sledgehammer in its tail — or perhaps an Arthurian lance! I shall cart it off with me on a forthcoming holiday and read it eagerly, gaily and approvingly, I know.

The forthcoming holiday, however, has been very slow in coming forth. But there are heartening prospects, and maybe I am now to have the happy sequel of 15 years of relentless travail — time to read again!

I am delighted that you are redoing Malory. I suspect you are quite right about the imperishable influence of these stories. Who knows, maybe even that new tyrant — TV — will be interested.

I hope so much that your "intrusions" will be more frequent, and sometime even in person!

Cordially yours,

Senator Richard Neuberger sent Stevenson a speech he had delivered on the Senate floor on January 17, 1957, pointing out that while talk by Eisenhower and Dulles about "liberation" and "rolling back the Iron

Curtain" may have been good domestic politics, it may also have helped send into action some brave Hungarians who went to their doom in expectation of American aid that never came.

To Richard Neuberger

January 21, 1957

Dear Dick:

Thank you for that kind letter and those gracious words. I hope Thomas Jefferson can forgive you!

Your speech heartened me; there have been too few of them. I made one like this to the "pols" in Detroit last fall about the empty cynicism of the liberation doctrine of 1952. And, speaking of Hungary, at the very end of the campaign I pleaded that UN observers be dispatched at once.[74] Under the Arming for Peace Resolution of 1952 they could have gone then to all the area still in rebel hands which would have caused the Soviet no little inconvenience. But did the U.S. do anything about it? Of course not. Just speeches about the gallant Hungarians.

Best to you and Maurine.

Yours,

Irving Dilliard wrote in the St. Louis Post-Dispatch, *December 30, 1956, that politically speaking the year would go into history as Dwight Eisenhower's year: "Yet . . . history will save a place for Adlai E. Stevenson, with a special citation for political valor. Here was a man who brought to politics fresh ideas, moving eloquence, boldness of spirit, and breadth of vision. Intellectually he was the best prepared presidential candidate since Wilson. . . . Whatever Adlai Stevenson's future, he has already left his mark on American politics."*

To Irving Dilliard

January 21, 1957

My dear Irving:

I have only now seen your year-end tribute to me in the Post-Dispatch, and I am touched and grateful — again! Even if they had not been such kind words they would still be the best and mean the most to me — as they did eight years ago, at the beginning of my brief and meteoric political career.

[74] See Stevenson's speech of November 5, 1956, at Minneapolis, in Part Two, pp. 315–321, and the text of his telegram to President Eisenhower of November 4, 1956, in the New York *Times*, November 5, 1956.

[*419*]

I am much disturbed about the problems of political communication in these latter days and the implications both to press and public of a press which seems to do little any longer but reflect the prejudices and preconceptions of its complacent, comfortable proprietors. If it then aids and abets concealment of fact and reality to further political ends, what will befall a government which depends on the surveillance of public opinion?

I hope some time to talk of these and other things with you, and perhaps later on there will be some leisurely opportunities. I hope there will. Meanwhile, my everlasting thanks and affectionate regards to all the Dilliards.

Yours,

P.S. You continue to be almost the only voice raised for probity in political conduct in Illinois. I am ashamed of us and have dispatched two recent editorials to the Bloomington Pantagraph — but with little more than faint hope that it will prove contagious.

Niccolo Tucci, of the New Yorker, *wrote that there were many urgent issues that Stevenson must speak about. He added, "You belong to the world and the world needs you. Take a boat, go to Europe and find out."*

To Niccolo Tucci

January 21, 1957

My dear Mr. Tucci:

Thanks for that tonic letter. I am listening beneath the stars for a bit; and the flesh is weak after that long, weary year, so much of which was spent on the fruitless primary. Indeed, there has been fifteen years of pressure and travail. But in time, along with earning a living, I will have a chance to say what I think now and then, I trust.

But what of the press? Do they want to hear; do they want the people to hear; do they want "the informed electorate," which is the condition of democratic government?

I shall go to Europe. It sounds from what you say as though it would be agreeable.

All good wishes.

Cordially,

Stanley Pargellis, librarian of the Newberry Library, wrote that while he was in England in May, 1956, a group of people wanted to know how much the United States would take for Stevenson. They said, "You don't seem to want him. We can't pay too much, but would a billion tempt you? . . . You sell ball players, why not sell statesmen? They're considerably rarer than ball players."

To Stanley Pargellis

January 21, 1957

My dear Stanley:

You wrote me a letter which I am going to guard for a long time — even from Pargellis and the Newberry Library. I should have answered it long since. But I have been floundering around and it has only now emerged from the flood.

And if you could have got such a good price for a certain American statesman, why in the hell didn't you sell him? We could have gone 50-50.

Now that I am almost at large, we shall have to have lunch, or better an evening, and see what is left to say of the 20th Century.

Yours,

Stevenson had planned to have a medical checkup in November, 1956, but it was postponed until January 20, 1957, when Stevenson entered Passavant Hospital in Chicago — "The first day," he said, "when the doctor, the hospital and I could get together since that rather busy month."[75] January 20 was also the day of President Eisenhower's inauguration, which prompted Mr. and Mrs. John Horne, Mr. and Mrs. John Erickson, and Mr. and Mrs. Bill Brawley, all of whom had worked in the 1956 campaign and were assistants to senators, to wire Stevenson: "Best wishes always to the man who was right and who should be in the nation's spotlight today."

To Mr. and Mrs. John Horne, et al.

January 21, 1957

Dear Friends:

Can you believe it! It took the Hornes, the Ericksons and the Brawleys to remind me that it was Inauguration Day. Languishing in a hospital bed while the gentlemen in white are doing their annual peer-

[75] See the New York *Times*, January 22, 1957.

ing and poking, I completely forgot that if it hadn't been for some millions of my fellow citizens I would be upright in the spotlight. Well, I missed his speech too; but I missed a day with you and all my dear and loyal friends more!

Thanks for your wire!

Affectionately,

To Murray Kempton[76]

January 21, 1957

My dear Murray:

Some friends sent me, months ago, a piece of yours published November 1st which I have read only today, between the peers and pokes of an annual checkup in the hospital. It is a most remarkable and perceptive piece — even for you, my talented friend, and I shall resist no temptation to thank you for it even belatedly. How I wish I had your facility for expressing what I think! "The Republicans ask us to trust a man; Adlai Stevenson asks us to trust ourselves." Yes, that was the whole thing, and I wish I had had it sooner!

Cordially yours,

Gerald W. Johnson sent Stevenson his article "What Can Stevenson Do?" from the New Republic *of December 24, 1956. The statement that he would not run again, the article asserted, "will release Stevenson for the job at which he should have been working for the past four years; to wit, the job of welding, not patching the Democratic party together again; or, if the old wreck is too far gone for salvage, the job of hammering together a new party to represent the people in this country whose eyes look forward, not backward, or like those of Eisenhower, sidelong." Later in the article Mr. Johnson noted that Stevenson could devote himself exclusively to the practice of law, but if he did, he could "count upon the bitter disappointment of millions who have seen in him the herald of a new kind of politics in which intelligence and candor might replace the rancid goose-grease with which a one-party press has been smearing Ike and his entourage through four noxious years. To glimpse such a vision and then lose it is worse than never to have seen it at all; so although Mr. Stevenson may be legally free, it can be plausibly argued that he is under a heavy moral obligation not to let those people down."*

---

[76] Labor columnist for the New York *Post*.

In a letter to Stevenson on December 21, Johnson wrote that senators like Harry Byrd "must not be allowed to get away with his theory that the Democratic party existed as the chattels personal of its delegation in Congress." Congressional Democrats of this type, he added, were trying to resurrect King Caucus of the early nineteenth century.

To Gerald W. Johnson

January 21, 1957

My dear Gerald:

I did not find The New Republic article "rough." I was glad that you, my dear friend, felt that there was still something for me to do and, of course, I would hardly be human if I didn't want to be wanted after all of this exertion in times of manifest adversity.

Just now, however, my flesh is weak, after sixteen years of incessant activity with hardly moments for repose and reflection. So I feel more like lying "down for an eon or two" than ever before. Moreover, there are many pols and journalists who seem to find my epitaph agreeable writing!

My! How I share your view that the time has come to make it clear to all and sundry along the Potomac that the party is more, much more, than the Democrats in Congress. I tried my hand at saying this at the somewhat confused and tentative first meeting of the so-called Advisory Committee in Washington (copy enclosed), but L. Johnson and S. Rayburn (the latter echoing the former I guess) felt it was a reflection on them and spoke to me in very unkind tones. As to my tones in reply, to the former at least, deponent further sayeth not.

So agitate, my beloved and gifted friend, and I hope I can turn aside from the diversions of earning a living now and then to raise my voice a little. And I pray someone will be listening more attentively than they did last fall.

The fact is, I must speak in San Francisco (lost by only 7,000 in 1956 vs. 22,000 in 1952) at a big Democratic clambake in mid-February. What stops shall I pull? What bells shall I ring, albeit feebly? I wish, I wish, I wish I knew how to stir the torpid hearts. If a theme sprouts in your fertile field, pluck and ship at once![77]

Thanks, always — for being alive — and well, pray God!

Cordially,

[77] Mr. Johnson replied on January 23: "Lord, man, there isn't but one theme for the San Francisco speech. That is we are not going to stand for the re-crowning of King Caucus. Read up on the campaign of 1828. Note the parallel between the attitude of Henry Clay and that of Lyndon Johnson; and remember that Clay led his party to ruin."

P.S. What I really want to talk about with you is communications. I mean the press in the larger sense. How can a system which depends on the surveillance of public opinion, on an "informed electorate," be healthy if the people don't know the score — even approximately? Yesterday I was almost a subversive for warning that things were going to hell in a hack the world round, thanks to our errors. And, of course, I was giving away our power and influence when I talked of the H-bomb and the draft. Now the President is babbling about the crisis in the Middle East, has banned H-bomb tests for a year,[78] etc., and is talking of new inducements to improve our armed forces. And of course now that it is in the proper partisan garments it is all fine.

Well, who is going to tell the people — Ike? The Republicans? The Press? Business? Who then? The New Republic? Yes. Anyone else?

P.P.S. I look forward to your essay about lunatics — and you were thoughtful to arrange to send me a copy.[79]

To Mrs. John Kenneth Galbraith[80]

January 22, 1957

My dear Kitty:

I now find that I am going to Cambridge from New York on the afternoon of February 2, to celebrate John Fell's birthday and mine. Adlai and Nancy tell me they are planning a cocktail party in their little apartment for the late afternoon and will, of course, invite you and the [Arthur] Schlesingers, et al. I think after that is over, you and Ken and anyone you suggest should join the children and me and we will all go to a suitable, expensive — and I hope good! — restaurant, where I will have a birthday party for you. But your part of the deal is to make the choice of restaurant and make the reservation and decide who the other guests are to be.

[78] This inference was premature. President Eisenhower finally, on August 21, 1957, agreed to suspend the testing of nuclear weapons for two years provided the Soviet Union would agree during this period to begin a permanent cessation of the production of fissionable materials for military purposes. Stuart Gerry Brown has observed that "by its insistence on including all nuclear tests the Eisenhower policy missed the most effective element of Stevenson's proposal, that a beginning should be made with the H-bomb." *Conscience in Politics,* p. 217. The USSR rejected Eisenhower's proposals on the grounds that too many conditions were attached to them. Not until April 20, 1959, did Eisenhower propose to the Russians a prohibition of nuclear weapon tests in the atmosphere as the first step toward exploring further controls.

[79] Mr. Johnson had written that he had just completed the manuscript of *The Lunatic Fringe* (Philadelphia: Lippincott, 1957).

[80] The original is in the possession of Mrs. Galbraith.

I hope you will inform your lengthy and distinguished husband that I must utter something headline worthy and perceptive and important in San Francisco on February 16. I hope he will be full of ideas which I can extract over the week-end.

I have just emerged from the hospital after the usual horrible indignities and they could find no excuse for the long rest that I have been looking forward to.

Yours,

ADLAI

To Harold Ober[81]

January 22, 1957

Dear Mr. Ober:

In December I hurriedly wrote a piece at the request of Look Magazine on the H-bomb. I understand it is in the current issue; and Mr. [William] Attwood reports that they would be very happy if it was reprinted in Reader's Digest. I told him I would notify you at once and that I would be very happy to because I would like to get some more money out of it if possible.

While I have not checked the text as published with the final version that I approved, which had already been somewhat cut, I have a feeling that what has been published has been further edited. Perhaps if you could get "my last draft" from Bill Attwood at Look it might possibly be better to submit than what was published. Of course I would want to rely on your judgment in that respect.

With all good wishes, I am

Cordially yours,

P.S. I shall be in New York at the Savoy-Plaza from January 30 through the morning of February 2nd if you want to get in touch with me then.

To Lady Barbara Jackson

January 22, 1957

My dear Barbara:

Alas! Robert [Jackson] escaped and yielded to the call of duty before I could get him to Madam [Maria] Callas' fete. She was rather better than I thought was humanly possible. But meeting her afterward was

---

[81] Stevenson's literary agent in New York.

moderately disillusioning; yet I suspect that is always the way with operatic stars. I guess I just prefer old ballad singers!

I am, of course, disappointed about the horrible schedule, which remains complicated in the extreme. However, I shall plan to stay in New York for lunch with you on Saturday, February 2nd, and I hope you can make it early so that I can get up to Boston on an early plane. Perhaps this is cruelty, but you haven't told me when you arrive. If you can't get to Boston even by Sunday night I shall also plan to stay over Monday and perhaps we can make a little progress even in one evening! I hope you will be thinking about what I should say at the first major Democratic foregathering since the election, and be fully prepared to comb out my tangled brain — as usual.

I will be at the Savoy Plaza, and perhaps you could call me Saturday morning, when you awake, so that we can make our plans.

Yours,

P.S. The records arrived and I am mortified that you had to inquire. I thought I had thanked you long since — or, rather, I guess I have stopped thinking.

To Hale Boggs

January 22, 1957

My dear Hale:

So many thanks for your letter of January 15. It was good to hear from you, but a visit would be better. There are, I think, some important lessons for us in the past campaign. I had been hopeful that through the proposed Advisory Committee we might begin to take advantage of some of them, but I am by no means sanguine that it will have a suitable staff or the sponsorship and encouragement that it must have if we are going to correct our deficiencies *before* the next Presidential campaign.

I am sending along the [autographed] photo, and I am sure you will let me know if you ever have a chance to come here. I look forward to seeing you. Among other things I want to tell you again how profoundly grateful I am for your everlasting encouragement, support and confidence during all these trying and crowded years.

Cordially yours,

Mrs. Edward Coleman, a widow who lived in Brookline, Massachusetts, had been a registered Republican and had voted for only two Democrats in her life — Franklin D. Roosevelt and Stevenson. She wrote to Mrs. Roosevelt that Stevenson had accomplished a "major thing. He replanted some of the hope that most of us had laid to rest with President Roosevelt." She remarked that world leadership did not consist of military power plus a balanced budget. She concluded that it was not sufficient just to vote; it was necessary to work for better government constantly.

To Mrs. Edward M. Coleman

January 22, 1957

My dear Mrs. Coleman:

Mrs. Roosevelt sent me, weeks ago, your letter to her of November 8. But it has only now come to my attention. I wish somehow I could tell you how grateful I am for your charity and kindness to me. Moreover, I must confess that I get inordinate satisfaction from the letters of people who seem to understand what I was doing and some of the difficulties I confronted.

You are most certainly right that world leadership does not consist of military might plus a balanced budget, and I think we would be better off right now if we faced the fact that we had lost confidence around the world and were asking ourselves why, instead of making more and empty gestures like the present [Eisenhower] resolution.

I am heartened that you realize that voting once every two years is not enough.

With thanks and my regards, I am

Cordially yours,

To Reinhold Niebuhr[82]

January 23, 1957

Dear Reinhold:

Would it be possible to have lunch with me at The Century Club on Thursday, January 31st? I am eager to hear about "Christian Action" and whether in your judgment I should attempt to speak at a large meeting in London at the behest of The Reverend Canon L. John Collins of St. Paul's around the first of June. I shall probably be in London anyway on business.

Critical as I am of most of what this administration has done in the foreign field, I have misgivings about speaking about foreign affairs. Yet what can I talk about that is of interest or importance now save foreign affairs? What I had in mind as a possibility — and not a very good

82 The original is in the possession of the Library of Congress.

one — was that since the explosion of the bomb nothing could ever be the same again. The old Europe was gone forever. The heir to the Western empire which had for so long disposed of the destinies of far away peoples was now starkly exposed and a center of weakness. None of the old terms of reference made sense. But, of course, we went on using words like France, Germany, Europe, as if we still knew what they meant. But they had lost their former meaning and we had little knowledge of what their new meaning would be. And our leaders didn't even know that they didn't know.

War itself at that point lost much of its immemorial meaning. If conquest is now equated with suicide it can hardly be used as a method for imposing political decisions. Therefore, new thoughts for a new world are not desirable but imperative. Why not indulge our imaginations since our armor is so inadequate?

Much of what we thought we believe in has changed since that explosion, except Christianity, which is the only thing that most of the people in the world don't believe in, and now ten years after Hiroshima comes the conference at Bandung where the "voiceless ones" found a voice and stirred the imagination of half mankind. But we here have done our best to ignore this revolution too. Dulles' reference to Bandung disdainfully as a "so-called Asian-African Conference" thereby earned a few more millions of enemies for our country. I sometimes wonder how long we of the West will even be heeded unless we lift our tired minds to originality and daring.

But what originality, what daring?

While, like many of us, I am a better diagnostician than physician, I am not without some remedies for the Western patient. But it is yours that interest me far more. And your view as to whether or not this is even a theme worthy of development or too highbrow for what I gather might be a massive London audience will be very welcome.

Cordially yours,
ADLAI

To T. S. Matthews

January 23, 1957

My dear Tom:

First, note the enclosed from the editor of the *Sun-Times*.[83]

Second, I am serving notice herewith that I have accepted, from Geoffrey Crowther[84] and Bill Benton, election to the Board of Directors

---

[83] This letter was not available to the editors.

[84] Managing director of the *Economist* and a director of the British *Encyclopaedia Britannica* company.

of the British Encyclopaedia Britannica and will be attending a meeting in London, possibly the latter part of May. I hope to have with me my oldest son, Adlai, and to stay around England for a fortnight seeing friends and changing scenes. I have been importuned repeatedly by Canon Collins of St. Paul's to speak before an organization of which he seems to be the head, called "Christian Action." His most recent requests have been strongly supported by Herbert Agar. I hesitate to speak abroad because one almost has to talk about foreign affairs and there is little I can say that isn't critical of this administration and its nonsense, as you well know.

I should welcome — and at an early date — your comments on the following:

(1) Is "Christian Action" okay and should I speak before it? Clement Attlee's reaction, *confidentially*, was negative.

(2) Should I speak at all — if some other alternatives — university groups — were available or could be made available?

(3) If the answer to either of the foregoing is yes, what would be fruitful for me to talk about, thinking of both sides of the Atlantic?

With that little assignment I consider myself compensated in full for the extreme exertion of enlisting the *Sun-Times* for Cassandra.

Yours,

P.S. If you care to consult with Crowther and Agar about "Christian Action" and the wisdom of speaking at all I would have no objection. Canon Collins says he has booked, provisionally, the Royal Festival Hall for Sunday afternoon, June 2, or Monday evening, June 3. He prefers the latter. I don't know the Hall and have no views as to dates, but he is pressing me for a prompt answer else he will lose the Hall. Help! Help!

To Geoffrey Crowther

January 23, 1957

Dear Geoffrey:

I shall promise not to bother you *every* day. It now seems likely that I could leave by the 24th of May by cancelling any June engagements. Canon Collins writes that he has tentatively engaged Royal Festival Hall for either Sunday afternoon, June 2, or Monday afternoon, June 3. He seems to prefer the latter and is eager for an answer.

My sudden change of dates springs from the fact that I would rather like to take a trip — a last trip for him — with my oldest son, who finishes Law School at Harvard on May 23 and must be back in Chicago around the first of July for his bar examination review course. While I

[429]

would love to have a sea journey over for a change, I suspect that might be difficult to contrive.

The purpose of all this is merely to let you know that a date for the meeting in late May or early June would probably be agreeable, after all, and that I would be better able to fix my schedule with more certainty after I have decided if and what to do about Canon Collins and "Christian Action" — if I should do anything. I can't say I feel I have any great "message" for the U.K. and the Western world, but doubtless you are full of them!

I am flattered and would of course be delighted to dine with your friends during my stay there. I shall be going from England to the Continent for a law job in Belgium, perhaps, and then on to South Africa for a client, with a little sightseeing, I hope, en route. All of which means I will not be back in America for the June Board meeting of Encyclopaedia Britannica. However, I think I could record my conclusions about the space allocation problems in writing, for what they may be worth.

I will see Bill Benton in New York next week and may write you further thereafter.

Cordially yours,

P.S. I suppose you have heard the Inauguration witticism: When Nixon heard taps he turned to his wife, Pat, and said: "That's our song, dear."

The New Yorker, *in its issue of November 17, 1956, published a cartoon by William O'Brian showing Stevenson campaign workers dismantling their headquarters and one person saying, "You know, nothing ever* really *rhymed with 'Adlai.'"*

To William O'Brian

January 23, 1957

My dear Mr. O'Brian:

Mr. [Newton] Minow has just proudly presented the original of that enchanting cartoon illustrating one of my major deficiencies, that nothing *really* rhymes with Adlai.

But even more precious than the cartoon is the inscription. Thank you, my dear friend, for both — the cartoon and the inscription — and, yes, both votes!

If those gentlemen in Washington did not get the point of the clipping you enclosed I would not be surprised, but I would be even more worried.

Some day I hope to meet such a blithe spirit as O'Brian.

Cordially yours,

Nancy Stevenson's mother wrote, "We [Democrats] haven't learned our lesson and keep working in selfish little entities instead of that embattled whole we used to be." She inquired whether the blue table mats she had sent him clashed with his blue china.

To Mrs. Warwick Anderson

January 23, 1957

Dear Mary San:

Your letter was more perceptive than most I get. It is the selfish little entities that have endangered the whole, precisely as you say, and I have about concluded that I must talk with you as a politician and about our real crisis — how you can inform an electorate with the resources of the press, the money, and the government mobilized on the other side.

I was quite serene while the inauguration ceremonies were going on. Indeed, I was dozing peacefully in a hospital bed between the gross indignities of my annual check-up.

I yearn to see you both, and wish you were going to be at the birthday party of Mr. and Mrs. Adlai E. Stevenson III for AES II and JFS at Cambridge, Massachusetts, Saturday, February 2.

Much love,

P.S. The blue mats match the china perfectly, and I can't see what I've been doing without them so long. Bless you!

A.E.S.

Mrs. Eugene Meyer wrote Stevenson on January 11, 1957, that without his leadership the liberal cause would die of anemia. As a result he had to be the Pericles of today. She urged him to tell the people as Herman Melville once had: "We are the pioneers of the world; the advance guard sent on through the wilderness of untried things to break a new path in a new world that is ours." She enclosed a copy of her publisher's announcement of her new book, Education for a New Morality *(New York: Macmillan, 1957), and a column about her*

*written by Mrs. Franklin D. Roosevelt. On January 19, 1957, Mrs.
Meyer thanked Stevenson for writing a letter to Elmer Davis, who was
critically ill. She enclosed a speech by Senator Herbert Lehman pointing
out that Stevenson could not during his campaign make up for the
failure of the Democratic leadership in the Senate to develop issues
upon which the Democrats could campaign effectively. Lehman further
stated that the Democratic Advisory Council was essential to hold aloft
the issues in the face of the Senate Democratic leadership's "me-too"
attitude toward Eisenhower.[85] Mrs. Meyer added, "Either you will
have to run with the ball that Lehman has thrown out or there will be
no liberal leadership left in the Dem party — or for that matter in the
country."*

To Mrs. Eugene Meyer[86]

January 24, 1957

Agnes dear —

Its very early. I've missed the first train to town and am waiting with
that awful angry impatience of the frustrated commuter for the next
one.

I've had — I've been blessed — with such a flurry of letters from you
lately I scarce know where to *begin,* and this wicked pressure that never
seems to dissolve, also never lets me *end* a letter!

The M Ds report is not yet ready. But the superficial exams I passed
— all except weight. And there I evidently face another test of disci-
pline. I doubt if I can ever pass this one!! And I'm reminded again of
one of the wittiest and wisest remarks of this generation — that all the
best things in life are either immoral or fattening.

I go to N.Y. next week and am hoping for a deliberate talk with dear
Mrs. R[oosevelt]. But my heart (and head, I hope!) are still intact —
frozen indeed in this interminable grinding cold! . . .

I was so, so glad to hear about Elmer Davis. He is one of those who
have left with me an impression and a respectful affection that can
never be erased. On another trip to Washington I *must* go to see him,
altho I confess I dread it. And how sweet of you to be cheering up an
old companion in arms to the end!

Somehow I think your hasty little letter of Jan 11 may be the *best* — if

[85] The speech, entitled "The Democratic Party Faces the Future; Functions of
an Opposition Party; Analysis of the Failure of the Recent Past," was reprinted
in *U.S. News & World Report,* February 1, 1957, pp. 82–84.

[86] This handwritten letter is in the Agnes Meyer files, Princeton University
Library. It was written from Libertyville.

there can *be* comparatives in the richness of thought and emotion with which you have endowed and blessed me. Yes, and I think that God *did* send you to me, even tho I may have some misgivings about the necessity for that present "protection"! But surely the sense of purpose, of mission and the confidence & strength you've given me in these trying years, which came so unexpectedly, was a fortification, a reinforcement, that I sorely needed and that God caused you to provide just then. Even money which helped to ease my anxiety about investing another large chunk of my fruitful life.

And now you've sent me packing off to Pericles! What a woman — and the Melville quote I'll shamelessly steal, perhaps for San Francisco. (of that I've thought not at all and don't know when I will) But I'll read your piece on equality of opportunity & Herbert Lehmans, which you were both good enough to send me, before I make up my mind about what to cover out there.

Eleanor's tribute[87] *was* nice — because she's a whole soul. Yes, & I liked the blurb for the new book which I'll read on my holiday — if I ever get one!

I'm so glad you had an opportunity to measure L[yndon]. Johnson face to face and I don't think your appraisal is far off the track. But more of that another time. Indeed more of everything — another time.

Much, much love, my good angel

ADLAI

And — as someone said — "long may you wave"!

P.S. There sits on my desk beside me a stack of my books, the last one, that I set aside almost *a full year* ago to autograph & send to people — and I haven't done it yet. And there are *thousands* — repeat *thousands* — of Xmas cards many with touching messages scribbled on them that I suppose I'll never even see. Its so damn discouraging when your heart gets so entangled in the days affairs —

Birthday party with the boys in Cambridge on Dec [February] 2 — Hooray! . . .

To Mrs. Robbins Milbank[88]

January 24, 1957

Dear Helen:

Thanks for your note. I would love to come down Sunday evening and meet the new President of Princeton[89] at your house.

---

[87] The editors do not have a copy of the column by Mrs. Roosevelt about Mrs. Meyer, to which Stevenson presumably refers.
[88] The original is in the possession of Mrs. Milbank.
[89] Robert Goheen.

My California schedule is confused, or rather doesn't exist, but roughly I had in mind coming out a little early and, if convenient, spending a night up in Marin County to see Roger [Kent], Libby Smith,[90] et al. On Thursday afternoon I understand there is a meeting of the so-called advisory committee that I'm supposed to attend. If it were possible, I would like to come down to Burlingame for Thursday night with you and Robbins.

I wanted to go to Stanford the next day to inquire about the business school, which may interest my son Borden, who seems to want to come to California to live. And who could blame even a 6th generation Illinoisian for that! Perhaps the [Edward] Hellers could take me that night, and I could return to San Francisco Saturday to meet the folks and participate in the political business.

Please comment — critically or approvingly! Actually I could come West most any time and, of course, I will end up writing my speech in the Fairmont on the afternoon of the 16th — as usual!

Sunday night or Monday morning I must go to Phoenix for my "holiday" — until the Gridiron ordeal on March 2.

Affectionately,
ADLAI

Stevenson sent Senator Fulbright a copy of James Reston's column in the New York Times, *January 24, 1957, about Eisenhower's request for a congressional resolution approving the use of military force in the Middle East provided a country threatened by "international Communism" requested it.*

To J. William Fulbright

January 24, 1957

Dear Bill:

This piece, which I have just seen, certainly presents a sad picture, which I hope will improve, with at least some general agreement among the Democrats about what's wrong or what's right about the President's (to me almost meaningless) proposal, or what to offer in its place and the reasons therefor. I had so hoped that the dissatisfactions expressed so generally at the meeting in your office that day[91] would result in a

---

[90] Elizabeth Smith, Democratic National Committeewoman from Northern California, who supported Stevenson at the 1956 convention.

[91] When Stevenson visited the Senate session on January 3, he also met with a group of Democratic senators in Mr. Fulbright's office.

positive proposal, that at least the Democratic members and some of our other leaders could agree upon in order to give us some initiative in foreign policy and invite public attention to the Administration's failures — including the fact that the world has lost confidence in Dulles.

Observing from a distance, I often think that we would be better off if we were not even talking about this proposal, but first inquiring into *why* we have lost confidence in the world. Because until that confidence is restored, no such resolution and no policy is going to have much influence or real importance. Who knows, you might even strike a bargain with the Administration and get a new Secretary of State in exchange for a resolution of some kind to satisfy the President.[92]

Having *received* so much, I had almost forgotten how easy it is to *give* advice!

Yours,

Ernest Krenek, a Vienna-born composer and musician, was a naturalized American citizen living in Los Angeles. He wrote that Stevenson's speech at Yale University on October 5, 1956, was memorable and remarked: "You were reported to have said: 'I often think that the single greatest difficulty about running for responsible public office is how you can win without, in the process, proving yourself unworthy of winning.'" Mr. Krenek added, "By refusing to pay the price of destroying your principles you put the people to the test. Not you, but we, the people, were defeated at the polls." He enclosed an English translation of his opera Pallas Athene Weint, *which was premiered at the Hamburg State Opera House. (The opera, published in 1955 jointly by Schott/Mains and Universal Edition, Vienna, deals with the downfall of the Athenian democracy at the end of the Peloponnesian war.) Mr. Krenek explained that he had intended to dedicate it to Stevenson, but "you could not have taken any chances with the witch-hunters, and I wanted to spare you — and myself — any embarrassment." He continued, "You will easily discover why I felt the strong urge to dedicate it to you."*

[92] Mr. Fulbright replied on January 28, 1957, that he was opposed to the resolution primarily because he had no confidence in Secretary of State Dulles. The greatest contribution that could be made, he agreed, was to get a new Secretary of State, but Mr. Fulbright felt that it would be difficult for him to unseat Mr. Dulles.

To Ernest Krenek

January 25, 1957

My dear Mr. Krenek:

I should have acknowledged your very good letter of December 13 long before this. But somehow it got shunted aside in the post election and holiday confusion, along with the translation of the opera, for more deliberate attention. And now, at long, long last, I have found it, and also "Pallas Athene Weint."

That you have marked some of my words so well, as your letter indicates, pleases and flatters me. Coming from you, a European with a perception and concern for the basis of democratic government that all Americans do not share, makes me all the more grateful for your charitable comments on my campaigns.

It is not, as you imply, always easy to have full faith in the public judgment — "the people" — as we are fond of saying. Yet I suppose it is just when we think *they* have failed when put to the test, that *we* are put to the test. To believe in the system you have to believe in *them*. So I do — win or lose.

But the trouble is not them, as I see it, so much as what they know, think, see, hear, and feel. When communication, through all the senses, is misleading, when it conceals facts, when it cloaks reality in euphoria, then you can hardly blame the people. It seems to me, in short, that it is not people but communication that has disappointed our classic concepts. The inability of the Democrats to tell the people the truth, the almost universal determination of the press to persuade them that all was well under a beneficent and omniscient leader, created insurmountable political obstacles, at least insurmountable in a few weeks in the last campaign.

And this problem of communication, is, I believe, the underlying crisis of democratic government — that choices are exercised not on the basis of facts and realities continuously, but on the basis of half truths and, nowadays, gentle euphoria. This can only mean that abrupt changes can come about only by violent external stimulii which cannot be obscured or smothered. But who wants depression, war, corruption, etc.?

Yet, enough of what you know better than I!

The opera is superb. I have read it with fascination, swept along on its mighty moving crest. And that you went to the trouble to translate it for me touches me deeply. I am placing the manuscript on a conspicuous table to exhibit proudly to my visitors and then it will go into my library, to be read by my children and descendants — with growing esteem, I hope, for their ancestor who was admired by a great composer! I shall hope, too, that I can hear it. If there is to be any production in this country, I would count it a further kindness if you were to let me know when and where.

Goodbye; and heartfelt thanks to my valued and gifted friend.

Sincerely and gratefully,

To Mrs. Ernest L. Ives

January 28, 1957

Dear Buff:

I keep hearing about my engagement, and I am sure I don't know what the message you had referred to but I suppose it was Drew Pearson's story about Mary Lasker.[93] Relax! I will let you know if anything is cooking.

I am off now for New York and then Boston. I will be home here from the 5th to the 12th, when I leave for the West, returning to Washington to speak at the Gridiron on March 2. After that all is vague and uncertain. The children's holidays are the first week in April. May I tell Borden he can park with you if he wants to? John Fell will probably have to come home to testify in the suit against the truck driver. I hope to get to the Caribbean or some hot place during March, or back to Arizona. All that serenity and repose that you prescribe and I need seems to be almost impossible to get. But little by little I feel as though the plans for the future were beginning to begin to take shape. At all events I am now committed to a business trip to England and Africa in June and I plan to take Adlai with me.

Much love,

Justin G. Turner, a Los Angeles businessman, wrote that thieves had stolen an autographed letter that Stevenson had written on State of Illinois Executive Mansion stationery but had ignored an autographed Lincoln letter.

To Justin G. Turner[94]

January 28, 1957

Dear Justin:

Thank you so much for your letter. This must be the ultimate flattery — when a manuscript of Stevenson is stolen and an autograph of

---

[93] The editors have been unable to locate the column to which Stevenson refers.
[94] The original is in the possession of Mr. Turner.

Lincoln is unmolested. Evidently we are not properly educating our burglars!

I enclose a rewrite of the little letter from the Executive Mansion, as you request, but I regret very much that we have no Executive Mansion stationery. How I wish I did!

Sincerely,

To Wilfred H. Hotz[95]

January 29, 1957

Dear Mr. Hotz:

My old friend Leonard Schwartz[96] has sent me your contribution toward the retirement of the campaign debt. I am so grateful to you for your thoughtfulness and your generosity. If there were a few thousand more such as you the deficit would melt quickly. I am sure you are only too well aware of the cost of a Presidential campaign nowadays — and it is enough to make the stoutest spirit shrink in horror!

With all good wishes for the New Year, I am

Sincerely yours,

Stevenson was reading the manuscript of Kenneth S. Davis's biography, A Prophet in His Own Country: The Triumphs and Defeats of Adlai E. Stevenson.

To Kenneth S. Davis[97]

January 28, 1957

Dear Ken:

I have read this much, at least, and have made some few changes as I went along noting them in writing along the margins with a red mark. While I would have to confess that I was oblivious of any "two worlds" while I was at Princeton, or the conflicts you indicate, I have no doubt they existed. But I was a little disturbed by the absence of any reference to my college work other than extracurricular.

I didn't like mathematics or the physical sciences. But I enjoyed geology so much — and not because it was easy — that I well remember regretting that I had not had more of the natural sciences. But

---

[95] A lumber dealer in Edwardsville, Illinois. The original is in the possession of Leonard Schwartz.

[96] Director of the Illinois Department of Conservation while Stevenson was governor.

[97] The original is in the possession of Mr. Davis.

certainly my tastes were largely humanist and I loved the history and English and literature courses — *all* history and all literature. I suppose, actually, it has been the same ever since. A page of mathematical equations makes me shudder and the books mounting around me make me angry that there is so little time for reading.

Also, I see no reference, and the omission may be wholly unimportant, to the fact that in the years before going off to school I used to spend a lot of time during vacations at the Pantagraph doing odd jobs in the plant and I have many happy recollections of trips in the neighborhood with reporters to county fairs, preparing lists of ribbon winners, etc. In fact, I think I knew every nook and cranny of the old Pantagraph building and sat at linotype machines before I had long pants.

I shall struggle forward with the manuscript as moments are available.

Sincerely,

ADLAI

Look published the following article by Stevenson in its February 5, 1957, issue.

WHY I RAISED THE H-BOMB QUESTION

The echoes of the 1956 campaign are dying now. But many of the issues of that campaign are still unresolved. One of these is the hydrogen-bomb issue.

As the *Bulletin of the Atomic Scientists* said last month: "The H-bomb problem is by no means disposed of by Eisenhower's re-election. Scientists, in particular, cannot cease considering the world-wide danger of the nuclear arms race as the *most important challenge to man*."

It was for precisely that reason that I spoke during the campaign about the urgency of halting test explosions of these thermonuclear superbombs. I was warned that it was unwise politics to raise such a complex question, that my position could be easily distorted and misrepresented, that it would cost votes. Probably all those things were true. Certainly, the issue was grossly distorted by my opponents. (As a result of these distortions, many Americans may be under the impression that I want to stop testing smaller nuclear weapons and other new devices — I want to stop all atomic research. This is *not* true. My proposal was for a suspension of the further testing of super H-bombs, in which, I understand, we already have a long lead.)

But the issue seemed to me so important to the survival of mankind as to demand the fullest discussion and debate. And if it isn't the responsibility of candidates for President to discuss the great issues that affect our country, then what are campaigns for?

So I think the question is not *why* I talked about the H-bomb, but why I thought it was important to talk about it, even at great political risk.

Now that I can speak as a citizen, and no longer as a candidate, let me set down some of the reasons that moved me to speak as I did. In time, these reasons will, I think, cause more and more people to agree that ways must be found to halt these explosions that poison our bodies, damage the position of America in the world and threaten our very existence.

My concern dates back ten years when I was an American delegate to the United Nations and we struggled in vain to control atom-bomb development. With the advent of the superbomb, many nuclear physicists, geneticists and others with access to the facts warned us that man now had the power to exterminate himself.

The frightening truth about the superbomb convinced me that America should take the lead in halting further test explosions. So last April, four months before the political conventions, I proposed that America take the initiative in this direction and strike a blow for humanity.

I made my proposal before the American Society of Newspaper Editors, without criticism of the Administration's policy and with no intention of making it a partisan issue. My proposal was virtually ignored by the White House then. But when I restated it before the American Legion Convention on September 5, *during* the campaign, the President chose to make this proposal a political issue, and on September 19 called it "a theatrical gesture." This was followed by a barrage of epithets and ridicule from Vice-President Nixon, Thomas E. Dewey and others. I confess I had not anticipated the curious ferocity of the Republican response. There was, indeed, reason to believe that the National Security Council itself *between September 5 and September 19* had voted "unanimously" in favor of a similar superbomb proposal; but this decision had then been set aside for obviously political reasons, and my suggestion for *strengthening* our position morally and physically in the world was grievously distorted and assailed by Republican campaign orators as a proposal to *weaken* our defenses.

I hoped that there would be time further to explain my views to meet this unconscionable attack. As it turned out, events in Hungary and the war scare in the Middle East during the last days of the campaign diverted our attention to more immediate dangers.

But we cannot forget about the super H-bomb. We can't sweep it under the rug. In fact, with politics suspended for a while, we should all take a fresh and more dispassionate look at this life-touching problem and decide what to do about it.

As I saw it last April, and as I see it today, there are at least three imperative reasons why we must take the lead in establishing a world policy of halting further test explosions of superbombs:

1. *The survival of mankind may well depend upon it.*
2. *It would increase our national security.*
3. *It would strengthen our position in the cold war.*

Thus, on humanitarian, strategic and international political grounds, I believe this is a sound proposal. Here are the compelling arguments:

1. *The survival of Mankind.*
A 20-megaton H-bomb is a thousand times more powerful than the atom bomb which obliterated Hiroshima in 1945. One such superbomb could wipe out New York or London or Paris or Moscow.

Already, it has been predicted by Lt. Gen. James M. Gavin, the Army's chief of research, that a superbomb attack on Russia would result in several hundred million deaths, including many in either Western Europe or in Japan and the Philippines, depending on which way the wind was blowing. Force has now far exceeded the bounds of reason and morality and, probably, even military utility. When more than one nation can deliver such weapons to the target, any thought of "victory" in war is an illusion.

What's more, even the testing of such H-bombs in peacetime is dangerous to the whole human race. With every explosion, huge quantities of radioactive materials are thrown up into the air currents that circle the globe at all altitudes. For many years afterward, these materials gradually sift back to earth as dust, or in rain or snow. This radioactive fall-out carries many elements, including strontium-90. This is a new radioactive isotope, created by nuclear explosions, which may cause cancer and other dread diseases, and dangerously affects the reproductive processes. One tablespoonful of it shared equally by all members of the human race would endanger the lives of every one of us.

Prior to the atomic age, strontium-90 was practically nonexistent. Careful studies show that today all of us — all over the world — have some of it in our bodies. It enters our bodies through foodstuffs grown in soil on which the bomb dust has fallen. It enters through the meat and fish we eat and the milk we drink, since animals graze on land dusted with it and fish swim in water that absorbs it. It is everywhere. Since it has some of the characteristics of calcium, it is a "bone-seeker" in the human body. Children are particularly vulnerable. Further, it tends to collect in higher concentrations in those areas of the world where the soil is low in calcium — for example, the American Midwest.

The danger to health is twofold — genetic and pathologic. All the scientists appear to agree on the genetic dangers of any radiation. The report of the National Academy of Sciences on *The Biological Effects of Atomic Radiation,* released last June, states that all radiation is genetically harmful and enough of it will ultimately deform many of our children and our children's children. Certainly, the threat to our capacity to produce normal, healthy children and the danger to our posterity for generations to come should be clearly understood and not ignored.

But scientists are even more concerned by the frightening pathological damage that may be caused by strontium-90. It seeps into the human bones, particularly children's bones, and may produce blood changes and cancer — among other dread results. It has been steadily descending on the earth from the stratosphere ever since the nuclear tests began, and, even if no further tests are held, it will continue to seep down for another generation. While there is no conflict of opinion among scientists as to the danger to health — genetic and pathologic — from the fall-out, there is much controversy as to the actual damage we have suffered or will suffer.

In defense of his position opposing any moratorium agreement on further superbomb tests, President Eisenhower issued a so-called "white paper" toward the end of the campaign which was full of reassuring assertions. While, in my opinion, there were many omissions and misstatements in this official Government paper, evidently more calculated to mislead the reader about the things I had said than to answer them, it did contain this declaration on the subject of health:

"Four: The continuance of the present rate of H-bomb testing — by the most sober and responsible scientific judgment — does not imperil the health of humanity."[98]

This is not a scientific fact. Hundreds of our most outstanding scientists vigorously disagree. They emphasize that no one knows with certainty whether the present rate of superbomb testing will or will not cause significant damage to the health of millions of people who are alive today.

[98] This is the first sentence only in Point Four of the President's "white paper."

The report of the National Academy of Sciences, mentioned above, on which the President's white paper relied, itself said: ". . . How much radiation will produce a given result, how much can be done to counter-act the deleterious effects, these are largely unresolved problems."

The International Commission on Radiological Protection and the British Medical Research Council warn that the danger level for radio-active strontium should be set, not at the optimistic level used by our Atomic Energy Commission, but at *one tenth* that level.

Dr. A. H. Sturtevant of the California Institute of Technology, one of the authors of the Academy of Sciences report, has recommended that the conclusions on fall-out danger be "revised upward."

Members of the Atomic Energy Commission Research Project at the University of Rochester Medical Center have declared they fear that, if bomb testing continues, the levels likely to be reached "may not be safe."

The Federation of Atomic Scientists, with a membership of 2,100, has urged an end to tests of large nuclear weapons. And the Federation's Radiation Hazards Committee has declared: "It may well be true that in certain areas of the world, the strontium-90 hazard has already passed the danger point, to say nothing of the additional production of this material in further tests."

Furthermore, according to an AEC publication (University of California Radiation Laboratory Report 2674), AEC Commissioner Willard F. Libby himself undertook to investigate methods for removing strontium-90 from milk and got cost estimates on large-scale milk purification.

Clearly, we don't know all the answers yet. What we do know is that the hazards to human health from superbomb testing are already considerable, and even the future of the human race itself may be imperiled.

Yet we must still ask ourselves whether these risks are not offset by advantages to our national security. That is, do we need to continue testing superbombs to maintain our freedom?

2. Our National Security

We are caught up today, along with the rest of the world, in an arms race that threatens us all with disaster.

We dare not tear down and abandon our defenses and our deterrents to war before we devise more effective safeguards to peace. Indeed, we must maintain and improve them; we must lead the race if we can.

But, likewise, we must never relax our efforts to impose progressive and effective brakes on this contest of destruction, because there can be no real security for anyone, now that the superbomb is within reach of any aggressor nation. Because we have no aggressive intentions; because we are not trying to scare anyone; because we want nothing save the peace, security and independence of everyone, the big H-bombs have no value to us except for retaliation following attack. Furthermore, we have the *most* to lose should these ultimate weapons ever be used.

So the real question is: Could we rely on a moratorium agreement with the Russians without inspection?

We could — because you can't hide a superbomb explosion any more than you can hide an earthquake. President Eisenhower said in 1955: "Tests of large weapons, of any nation, may be detected by long-range monitoring methods; universal adherence to the ban could be determined without resorting to roving international inspectors." And our own monitors could be double-checked if necessary by a United Nations monitoring system.

An agreement to end such testing would deprive us of none of the advantages we presently enjoy. We would not give up any weapons. We would not give up research and development on new and different types of weapons in the megaton range. We could go on manufacturing and stockpiling more of our present proved weapons. We would not be deprived of the power to retaliate in event of an attack.

Such an agreement would freeze the test situation of the three powers now possessing superbombs; it would go far toward preventing other nations from producing such bombs; and it would break the disarmament deadlock. Ultimately, our security — and the world's too — depends not on a balance of terror, but on effective arms controls.

Finally, in appraising the likelihood of violation, we should consider the political price Soviet Russia would have to pay. For years, the Russians have been telling the neutral nations with great success that their purposes are peaceful, that the United States is warlike, that they favor a ban on further tests of nuclear weapons — and that the U.S. opposes it.

Would they violate a ban at the risk of turning the uncommitted bloc of nations against them? And what of their own people? As most observers agree, the Soviet masses deeply dread a world conflict, and their memories of World War II are still vivid.

Soviet Russia would like to speak for or represent the majority of the world's peoples. It cannot afford to cut itself off from the majority, which is what would automatically happen the moment it lit the fuse to the big bomb in violation of an international agreement.

The Soviet leaders say they are willing to halt the testing of their super hydrogen explosives if we do. To that, I say: Thank God! I say that, not because the record of Communist promises is good, but because here is a place where we can safely begin. Only when the first step is taken, can we plan for the second step toward sanity.

I believe a moratorium on superbomb testing would endure because to violate it would represent a declaration of war against all mankind. In short, it would be a major breakthrough in the disarmament deadlock and a new beginning in our continuing search for peace.

3. Victory in the Cold War

Finally, I believe that the United States must take the initiative; that the great struggle for men's minds, which is the essence of the cold war, will be won not with bigger bombs but with better ideas. The battle for the uncommitted peoples of the world, for their friendship and respect, will go to the nation that is wise, compassionate and considerate, as well as strong.

Toward the end of the campaign, I had a letter from one of the most respected elder statesmen of Asia.[99] Speaking of the superbomb tests, he said: "America cannot justly continue this aggression on the whole world and its health and yet talk convincingly of peace."

I wish we had taken this step earlier. But if we take it now, I am sure that it will reassure millions of people all over the earth who, even though they have been outraged by Russian brutality in Hungary, still are troubled by our reliance on nuclear weapons and talk of "massive retaliation."

I believe that the security of the American people consists of many things. It begins with the people themselves — their belief in themselves, the meaning they attach to their history, their faith in the future, the value they place on their freedoms, their ability to be inspired by the things that count, their readiness to think and to act. If we have this kind of strength, then military strength can have meaning. But let us not delude ourselves about what military strength *is* and what it is *not* in the present world.

The position that America holds in the world, where we stand with respect to the good will and support of the overwhelming majority of the world's peoples — this has a direct connection with true national security. We are preparing our military defenses in order to guard against the possibility of a military showdown. We pray there will be no military showdown.

One thing, however, is certain: Whether or not there is a military showdown, a *nonmilitary* showdown is coming up in the world. It is a

[99] The editors have been unable to identify the person to whom Stevenson refers.

showdown on the battlefield of world public opinion. And the side with the best ideas will win.

Our ideas must be concerned with the common security of people everywhere. Thus, we must come up with working ideas for the control of war itself and must never be separated from our moral leadership in the world.

A ban on superbomb testing is one of these ideas. That is why I talked about it during the campaign, and why I bring it up again today.

While in Cambridge, Massachusetts, to celebrate his fifty-seventh birthday with his sons, Stevenson stayed with Professor and Mrs. John Kenneth Galbraith.

To Mrs. John Kenneth Galbraith[100]

February 5, 1957

My dear Kitty —

This is (why does that damn pen never work when I need it!) Anyway — to start again — this is inscribed "in the air" or "on the wing" en route to N.Y. — to send you *at once* my thanks for that delightful visit — that comfortable bed — that lovely room — those enchanting children — that elegant food — those charming people — and you! (I forgot my *presents!!*)

*Any*way, *all* ways, *every* way — it was a perfect visit for me and a birthday with my children I shall long remember. We will not have many more *all* together!

My only disappointment was not to see more of your remarkable husband — but I'll remedy that somehow, I know, as time goes on. And a good start would be a visit with me in Libertyville when he goes West another time — with you to send us to bed at a reasonable hour!

Thank him, thank Emily,[101] — and thank you, dear Kitty.

And now 57 what surprises have *you* in store!

Affec —

ADLAI

Stevenson sent the following telegram to his sister and her husband on their wedding anniversary.

[100] This handwritten letter is in the possession of Mrs. Galbraith.
[101] Emily G. Wilson, the Galbraiths' housekeeper.

To Mr. and Mrs. Ernest L. Ives[102]

February 5, 1957

CONGRATULATIONS ON THIRTY YEARS ITS A GOOD START LOVE

ADLAI

To Mrs. Eugene Meyer[103]

"On the Wing — N.Y. to Chicago," February 6, 1957

Thanks dear Agnes for that hilarious, "over stimulated" letter! But, pray! let us have no hovering at death's door as an inducement to endow me — and, pray too, let us not have too much of that [Lyndon B.] Johnson competition! I'm green!!

Homeward bound after satisfactory visit to N.Y. — hilarity and business — and a wonderful weekend in Cambridge with my kids — christening my grandson and a half dozen joint birthday parties with John Fell. Also good talk with Eleanor [Roosevelt]. Much love —

ADLAI

P.S. I thought the plane was landing. Eleanor admonished me to do nothing impetuous romantically, and I guess there is no likelihood anyway. But she was a dear and so very, very wise and comforting. I found my children well but Borden a little anxious and worried about his future, his self confidence etc. The grandson is incomparable!

I haven't given the Calif speech a thought and will have to start now — if and when I can get a minute in this crazy life. I wish I thought our world wasn't disintegrating! But *you're* not, thank God, my good Aspasia — Pericles!

To Edward A. Weeks[104]

February 6, 1957

Dear Ted:

I am barely able to speak! My secretary has just "unpacked" my Cambridge file on my return from the East and there I find the message that you were expecting me for supper Sunday night. I was never more mortified — and I hope I will never be more apologetic! Somehow in the incredible confusion of my weekend birthday parties, in various student

---

[102] The original is in the Elizabeth Stevenson Ives collection, Illinois State Historical Society (E.S.I., I.S.H.L.).

[103] This handwritten letter is in the Agnes Meyer files, Princeton University Library.

[104] Editor of the *Atlantic*.

rooms and Cambridge houses and the christening of my grandson, I seem to have missed the most important event of all.

I hardly know what to say, unless it is to put the food in the icebox and I'll be back! I hope you and Mrs. Weeks can forgive and forget the appalling negligence of an enthralled grandpapa of advanced age.

Sincerely yours,

At this point Stevenson was working with Lloyd K. Garrison on the formation of a partnership with the New York City law firm of Paul, Weiss, Rifkind, Wharton and Garrison. Stevenson and his partners, W. Willard Wirtz, William McC. Blair, Jr., and Newton N. Minow, were to practice as the Chicago branch of that firm under the name of Stevenson, Rifkind and Wirtz. Edward D. McDougal, Jr., was counsel and John Hunt became an associate in the Chicago firm. Stevenson was also at this time working out with William Benton and Robert M. Hutchins his future association with the Encyclopaedia Britannica companies.

To Lloyd K. Garrison

February 7, 1957

Dear Lloyd:

I think the memo states our understanding admirably. I hope they realize, as I feel you do, that my greatest personal problem is my anxiety to avoid in the future the intolerable pressures of the past. It is in this connection that I have been a little apprehensive about our "deal."

I have not seen Bill Wirtz yet, but I will soon or will talk with him on the phone. He is in the East.

I think it would be best not to make a *firm* date for luncheon for Tuesday, March 5, just yet. I think I can do my Washington and Princeton chores and get to New York by noon that day but I am by no means certain. Perhaps I could telephone you about that as the time approaches.

I spent a half a day with Svengali Benton and Circe Hutchins in regard to the Britannica and its many ramifications. I think I see the light, or rather my light, in the Film Company on some such basis as I suggested to you while continuing as a director of the British and American companies and perhaps a new international company.

Yours,

To Mrs. Harold Hochschild

February 7, 1957

My dear Mary:

I have now committed myself to attend the banquet and receive an award from the American Whig–Cliosophic Society at Princeton at 7:00 o'clock on March 4. I would be delighted to stay the night with you and Harold if that is convenient, but I am afraid the banquet precludes any hope for a dinner party. If I find I can stay over the following night perhaps we could arrange something on the spur of the moment. I am a little fearful that I may have to get back to New York. I will have to let you know later about my time of arrival as I haven't the remotest idea when I can get there. I will telephone you.

Affectionately,

To Mrs. Frederic McLaughlin[105]

February 7, 1957

My dear Kit:

I have just come from Cambridge and a joint birthday party with one John Fell Stevenson and my remarkable grandson. John Fell was burbling something almost incessantly about going to Aspen for his spring vacation.[106] I think it more likely that he will be in Goshen, Indiana testifying in the trial of a truck driver who caused him a woeful accident.

But against the possibility that his impoverished father should entertain such extravagant notions as a week in Aspen, I am presuming to write you to inquire if you really did talk with him about it. He seems to be slightly vague although extremely enthusiastic.

Please don't feel that you have any commitment to him whatever, but any light on such an adventure would be most welcome.

With warm regards to Freddie[107] —

Cordially yours,

Mrs. Daniel Caulkins renewed her invitation to Stevenson to vacation in Acapulco.

---

[105] A friend of Stevenson's from Lake Forest, Illinois.

[106] The McLaughlins had a house at Basalt, Colorado. John Fell recalls that he did not stay with them on this occasion, but drove over from Aspen, where he was skiing, to visit them. Letter to Carol Evans, November 30, 1971.

[107] Mr. McLaughlin.

To Mrs. Daniel Caulkins

February 7, 1957

My dear Babs:

Stop! Don't go on!! Another sentence, and I'll either jump into the dirty snow of Chicago or into an airplane for Acapulco.

I shall wish and wish and wish, and hope and hope and hope for another year.

So many thanks.

Yours,

P.S. The [Cass] Canfields had a rout for the Hamish Hamiltons which should have a page in the history of New York, and will certainly have a page in the history of everyone present last week. You were missed by residents and, especially, visitors — or at least *a* visitor.

A.E.S.

To Harry S. Truman

February 7, 1957

Dear Mr. President:

I almost started to dictate: "For heaven sakes, keep your head!" What I meant was "Keep your head intact."[108] We need it!

Cordially,

Mrs. Herbert Zernick, a librarian and researcher for the New York Public Library, had worked as a volunteer in the 1956 campaign, doing research for the New York State Committee for Stevenson for President. She sent Stevenson a pair of hand-carved angels for his grandson, lacquered coasters for his birthday, and a check from herself and some of her friends for fifty dollars to help pay the campaign deficit.

To Mrs. Herbert Zernik

February 7, 1957

Dear Mrs. Zernik:

I am delighted to have your letter of February 2 and profoundly touched by your thought of me. Indeed you have made a major contribution to the painless achievement of my advanced age!

The angels are enchanting and I am sending them along to my grandson — age three and a half months — in Cambridge. The coasters

---

[108] Mr. Truman had just suffered a head injury.

have gone to work in my home at Libertyville, and I have seldom seen anything more engaging, and indeed I have never seen the Alpine flowers out of their native habitat before.

You were so good to send me the check, also, and it will go at once toward the payment of the indebtedness we incurred in the last campaign. Actually, we have made excellent progress toward the payment of all the hideous accumulation of bills and should be all clear in a few more months.

Some day when I am in New York I shall hope to meet you; and I shall not neglect an opportunity to impose on you for help if I need to do so. Please thank your friends, and also your husband, for their contributions.

Cordially,

Clement Davies wrote Stevenson that throughout the Suez crisis Prime Minister Anthony Eden was an ill man. He discussed the necessity of more coordination among NATO countries and expressed his concern that the United Nations Assembly was not truly representative, and he recommended a true world assembly and an international police force.

To Clement Davies

February 7, 1957

My dear friend:

Thank you for your good letter. I am flattered by your disappointment at our election returns. But I really feel the disappointment of my friends exceeded my own! And I am honored to count you among them.

What you report about Anthony [Eden] is distressing, but I had heard elsewhere that he was hardly a well man. How fantastic it is that the affairs of mighty nations at critical moments can be thus influenced.

I couldn't agree with you more about the importance of a greater political and economic liaison among the Nato countries. I wish there was some way I could help with that. I have talked about it often in this country and will continue to. While, as you so effectively demonstrate, the UN has formidable defects, isn't that true of all human institutions? And I suppose we will always be confronted with the imbalances between the effect of public opinion on authoritarian and democratic governments. Which means that our hope rests in converting the former to the latter.

But meanwhile let us, of course, try to make the Assembly, as you say, a more truly representative body, by weighted voting if that is possible. But this letter, too, is getting too long and, moreover, it isn't interesting!

I wish very much that I could accept your invitation to the Inter-Parliamentary Union Conference in September. But I cannot. I shall be in England sometime this spring, and from there I must go on a business trip to Africa. The time involved will leave no latitude for a further journey abroad this autumn. But I shall find some consolation in a visit with you, I hope, when I am in London in late May or June, or possibly at the time of the American Bar Association meeting in July.

Cordially yours,

Mr. and Mrs. Barry Bingham sent Stevenson a telegram on his birthday and urged him to join them on a Caribbean vacation. Stevenson already had discussed with Mr. and Mrs. Ronald Tree the possibility of vacationing at their home in Barbados. Mr. Bingham was in the process of inviting leading newspaper people to meet in April with Stevenson.

To Mr. and Mrs. Barry Bingham

February 7, 1957

Dear Mary and Barry:

Thanks for your wire. It made even 57 less distasteful. I consulted the Duchess of Barbados in New York and she made a mighty good case I confess. It may be that I will ask you to roll over on the hot white sands and make way for a hot, fat body!

I also find Barry's letter on the proposed meeting. Either week-end I think would be satisfactory for me and any place that you choose to designate. As to the list, my only suggestion would be whether Dorothy Schiff . . . should be included. I rather think that both she and Alicia [Patterson], who is extremely independent, might be eliminated. I am not too confident about Bob McKinney;[109] you will know best about him. Bill Evjue[110] is very old but I suspect he should be invited. Isn't there someone from a paper in Anniston, Alabama, who is very good? I can't recall his name at the moment. Otherwise, I think the list is fine and if we have any other ideas, as we doubtless will, we can make additions as time goes on. What, by the way, about Herb Block?[111]

Yours,

[109] Publisher of the Santa Fe *New Mexican*.
[110] Editor and president of the Madison, Wisconsin, *Capital Times*.
[111] Cartoonist for the Washington *Post*.

The British African colony of the Gold Coast was to become Ghana, an independent state within the British Commonwealth, on March 6, 1957. Prime Minister Kwame Nkrumah invited Stevenson to attend the celebrations of independence.

To Kwame Nkrumah

February 7, 1957

My dear Mr. Prime Minister:

I was delighted to have your cable and the invitation to attend the independence celebrations. I can think of nothing I would rather do than to be present at this historical event, not only for Ghana but for freedom everywhere.

Unhappily, my circumstances here prevent me from coming at this time, but I have in hopeful contemplation another trip to Africa later in the spring, perhaps June, and if it comes to pass I shall most certainly contrive a brief stop in the Gold Coast. I have such happy recollections of my visit there,[112] of your courtesies, and such soaring hopes for your country, that I am eager to see it again and hear more about recent developments.

You were good to think of me and I am profoundly flattered by your thoughtfulness.

With my esteem and gratitude and warmest good wishes, I am

Respectfully yours,

Mr. and Mrs. Chester Bowles were in the Soviet Union when this letter was written.

To Chester Bowles

February 7, 1957

Dear Chet:

I have just seen your splendid letter to Bill Fulbright[113] and also your letter to me of January 10 enclosing your memorandum of last May on the Northern tier.

While I agree that arms aid begets arms aid and they both beget trouble, I suspect that there is much sympathy for Pakistan in its rela-

---

[112] See *The Papers of Adlai E. Stevenson*, Vol. IV, pp. 486–487.

[113] Mr. Bowles had written to Senator Fulbright opposing both the Eisenhower Doctrine and military aid to Pakistan.

tions with India. Certainly Nehru's intemperate behavior with respect to Kashmir of late has not improved matters either.[114]

The resolution, as you know, is rocking along in the Senate with some heroic work by Fulbright and a few others to disclose the administration's ineptness in the past and the meaninglessness of the resolution now. Meanwhile, nothing is done to resolve the real questions or even approach them.

I wish I knew better what to say about it all in San Francisco next week. And perhaps that is a way of saying I wish you were here to help me! I will count it a courtesy if you will include me on any distribution list for further reports from your journey.

With much love to Steb[115] and my prayers for her good health, I am

Yours,

The noted psychiatrist and author Dr. Karl Menninger wrote that he read in the newspapers about the ladies Stevenson was supposed to be going to marry and observed that if in truth it was Mrs. Albert Lasker it was wonderful. Dr. Menninger described the work the Menninger Foundation was doing with various state hospitals and remarked that the current governor of Illinois, William Stratton, had changed Stevenson's approach and as a result the Illinois system had a poor reputation among psychiatrists.

To Dr. Karl Menninger

February 7, 1957

Dear Karl:

So many thanks for your letter, which was dictated on my birthday — and I can think of few that I would rather have heard from on that day! The news about Mary Lasker to which you refer is flattering in the extreme but highly exaggerated.

I do hope I can come down to one of the annual meetings of the Foundation. As for your work with the states, I am sure it *will* remain as one of your most valuable contributions to the country. And that is saying a good deal.

With warmest good wishes to you and Jean,[116] I am

Cordially,

---

[114] India refused to agree to a UN plebiscite to determine the future of Kashmir, and former Chief Minister Sheikh Mohammed Abdullah was jailed by the Nehru government. For a discussion of the Kashmir question and Stevenson's controversial meeting with Sheikh Abdullah in 1953, see *The Papers of Adlai E. Stevenson*, Vol. V, Chap. Eleven.
[115] Mrs. Bowles.
[116] Mrs. Menninger.

Mrs. Eugene Meyer wrote Stevenson on January 28, 1957, "If you could free yourself of all partisanship in the narrower sense and create a philosophy for your party, whose principles would appeal to our leaderless people, you could perform a service for your nation as memorable as that of Lincoln. . . . We need a voice that is persuasive on the basis of fact and reason, one that speaks to the conscience of the people rather than their desires and prejudices."

To Mrs. Eugene Meyer[117]

February 8, 1957

Dear Agnes:

I have just read again — and again — your letter of January 28, and also my birthday letter. Somehow all of your letters have a memorable impact, but these I count among the "imperishables." I am sure you are right about the danger of our period and the opportunities for statesmanship. I only wish I felt more enthusiasm for the task and more certainty of view. Somehow the incessant harassments since the election have given me no serenity nor any opportunity to gather my wits, nor do I see any in prospect.

We shall have a talk again soon I hope.

Affectionately,

ADLAI

To Mrs. Ernest L. Ives

February 8, 1957

Dear Buff:

. . . The trip to New York and Boston was fine. John Fell and I had a good half-dozen birthday parties at various locations in Cambridge, and I found Adlai, Nancy and the baby flourishing. I think I will take Adlai and Nancy with me on my trip in June if I can swing it financially. It will probably be their last trip. . . .

I think I will probably go through with the deal with the New York law firm subject to some problems with respect to practice in New York and admission to the New York bar. Meanwhile, I leave for San Francisco next week, and thence to Phoenix to visit [William] Benton, returning to Washington March 2nd for the Gridiron, to Princeton to speak on the 4th, and to New York on the 5th. About that time I hope to see the future clearly enough to go off for a good three weeks of rest. My disposition is to go to Barbados to visit the [Ronald] Trees where I

---

[117] The original is in the Agnes Meyer files, Princeton University Library.

will be taken care of and treated with English consideration. The [Barry] Binghams will be the only other guests there at that time. There are other alternatives, of course, but few with as much certainty of escape. But any suggestions you have will be welcome.

. . . Tell Ernest I appreciated his thought of me on my birthday.

Much love,

To Mrs. Warwick Anderson

February 8, 1957

Dear Mary San:

I am back behind my groaning desk after a frenzied week in the East, of which the week-end in Cambridge was the high point. I think John Fell and I had some seven birthday parties in two days, and the incredible gift from Louisville was the apex of the entertainments. How you contrive such things is beyond me, but I hope you can enjoy happiness vicariously because we all have much to thank you for — including one automobile owner!

I found the children flourishing and Nancy incomparably competent and spirited, as ever. She seemed a little fatter and I thought she was really well, if a little tired after two days of this.

The baby is obviously the incomparable creature of all time. To this modest assertion I found no dissent.

I am going abroad on business and pleasure in June and suggested that maybe they would like taking a "last trip" with me. I am not sure just how it will all work out, but the enthusiasm was contagious and I almost began to like the prospect myself.

Affectionately,

To Lady Barbara Jackson

February 8, 1957

My dear Barbara:

An ecstatic letter from Nancy reports that she has been to a seminar with you![118] Evidently this abrupt change in the routine of a young matron is most welcome and her exhilaration about you and your performance relieves me of any misgivings that I had as to whether you were ready for that ordeal.

It is apparent now that I should have demanded a complete speech

[118] Lady Jackson was conducting a seminar on Asia and the Atlantic community at Harvard.

[456]

for San Francisco without any mercy! As to that I have not lifted a finger, let alone a pen or read a morsel. Ho hum! I seem to be weary of all such things.

I am off on Tuesday next and will be moving on to Phoenix Sunday night. I think you have my address there. If not it will be in care of William Benton, 5520 East Camelback Road.

Affectionately,

p.s. Nancy also reports that an "elderly professor for baby tending" has volunteered.

To Theodore H. White

February 9, 1957

Dear Teddy:

While in New York last week I had fully expected to have at least a telephone chat with you about the matters we previously discussed.[119] Somehow I didn't get it done. I hope you will keep me informed and let me know if there is anything I should be doing. I have made some inquiries in Texas and will have some information before long about the paper at Austin which I will let you have, in confidence of course.

There are other possibilities that I hope to be able to tell you about in due course, none of them very promising or immediate, however.

My apologies for neglecting all this. I have been harassed even beyond my troubled experience.

Cordially,

To T. S. Matthews

February 11, 1957

Dear Tom:

After all the correspondence, and a talk with Barbara Ward at Harvard last week, I have written Canon Collins as per the enclosed. I think it better this way, both for the wear and tear on me and as a matter of taste. I gather that "Christian Action" is a sort of British A.D.A. [Americans for Democratic Action] I have nothing much against the latter, but I doubt if it is a suitable forum for my major and probably only utterance in Britain. To attempt more than one or two talks would be fatal to my program of rest first!

If the Pilgrims ask me I will accept. I was invited to give the Romanes

[119] Mr. White had asked Stevenson for help in finding new financing for *Collier's* magazine. In addition, Stevenson was investigating the possibility of a liberal newspaper being founded in Texas. Mr. White recalls nothing more of their conversation. Letter to Carol Evans, November 5, 1970.

Lecture several years ago and would be tempted this time — if I wasn't so darned lazy and harassed. The idea of writing anything formidable makes me shudder. All I want is sun and peace and solitude; and all I get is cold and snow and clatter.

But I am off for a speech in San Francisco now and a fortnight in Arizona followed by the Gridiron, etc., and then, pray God, a real holiday in March — somewhere.

Thanks for your everlasting help, and affectionate regards to the lovely Martha.[120]

Yours,

To the Reverend L. John Collins

February 11, 1957

Dear Canon Collins:

I have been sorely troubled about my uncertainties and the inconvenience I have caused one who has honored me so greatly. After further reflection and consultation, I have concluded that I cannot accept your invitation to speak in London under the auspices of "Christian Action." In the first place, I am in a very "non-speaking" mood these days, a mood compounded of politics, prudence, weariness, and a necessary preoccupation with my personal affairs after many years of neglect.

In the next place, I have concluded that if I must say something in the United Kingdom it should not be before a large mass meeting. I am a little fearful of a critical note about our government that is sure to creep into what I say, and I think it would be in better taste just at this time to speak, if I must, to some traditional audience for American visitors, like the Pilgrims, or a university, if I am asked.

I must confess, too, that I had rather looked forward to this journey abroad as a *little* business and a *lot* of holiday. For me, speeches, or rather their preparation, are the ruin of holidays!

At all events, I am mortified that I have put you to such appalling inconvenience, and, politician that I am, or hope I am, I say farewell to Festival Hall with wistful reluctance! It will be a comfort to me, if little to you, to meet and talk with you when I am there. Perhaps I can better explain some of my difficulties — or eccentricities. And I am consumed with curiosity about your view of "the decline of the West" as some so darkly describe this fateful interval.

With my utmost gratitude and an esteem I find is eloquently shared by our friend Reinhold Niebuhr, I am

Cordially yours,

[120] Mrs. Matthews.

To Adele Dunlap Smith

February 12, 1957

Adele dearest:

Three B's and two A's! I am exhilarated by my beloved goddaughter. But don't work too hard. Just B's and A's without overworking. It's so easy!

Affectionately,

To Seymour Harris

February 12, 1957

Dear Seymour:

So many thanks for your letter and the economics material. I expect to use some of it, although I haven't yet written a speech for San Francisco I regret to say. Isn't it ludicrous that the Secretary of the Treasury calls upon a Democratic Congress to cut his own budget?[121]

It was so good to see you and I hope that our visits don't diminish even if the political pressures do — thank God!

Cordially,

To Clayton Fritchey

February 12, 1957

Dear Clayt:

A thousand thanks for your juicy morsels for San Francisco. I can use some there and others at the Gridiron [Club], and the balance conversationally.

I would like to talk to you some time about the real crisis of giantism and monopoly as you call it, communications as I call it. We ought to be able to get some writing going in the mags and so on on something that seems to me really serious — the difficulty of sustaining the necessary debate when the truth is everlastingly obscured.

I hope you are enjoying the Carribean — and I hope I can too![122]

Yours, ever

[121] Secretary of the Treasury George Humphrey publicly criticized the size of the budget submitted by the Administration to Congress in January, 1957, and President Eisenhower at a press conference invited Congress to suggest "sensible reductions."

[122] Mr. Fritchey was vacationing at the home of Mr. and Mrs. Ronald Tree in Barbados.

Frank Holland had left Stevenson after many years of service as a farmer to take a job as custodian of one of the schools at Libertyville. A succession of farmers to replace him (Glen Clark being the last) had not worked out well. Mr. Holland agreed to come to the farm on a part-time basis to help with the work until Stevenson found a satisfactory replacement. Since Holland missed the farm and Stevenson was not able to find anyone to his liking, he eventually expanded the living quarters next to the garage and Mr. Holland and his family returned.

To Frank Holland

February 12, 1957

Dear Frank:

I believe this is our understanding:

You will go to the place for an hour or so each day to help Glen catch up with the work that needs attention until he leaves some time before the end of the month. After he leaves I hope you can give the place enough time to keep things going until I can reach a decision about building the new room or find someone else. I would like to feel free to be away until the end of March, and I hope you can carry on until that time. A carpenter is preparing estimates, and if it proves feasible I will let you know and then, as I understand it, after notice to the school you can come full time while living at home until the room is completed.

If you ever want to get in touch with me about anything, you can always do so through Miss Evans at my office (FInancial 6-5180) or at her home (Normal 7-4752); or you could call Mr. Edward D. McDougal at his home at Libertyville (2-4107). I have told Doris, the cook, that you are going to be there off and on and if she needs help about anything to talk to you.

You will find some lumber stacked in the stable which Glen bought to build a new gate for the west side of the paddock. I don't know whether it is suitable or not. If not, it should be returned for credit to the Libertyville Lumber Company. You will notice that he has done no trimming of the shrubs, but I think he is at work getting the garage and stable cleaned up at last. Also, I have told Mike, Mrs. Hermon Smith's gardener, that he can have some sheep manure if there is any. He will probably be around looking for it, but I am not sure there is any there. I hope you and Glen will help him in every way if there is some and don't hesitate to loan him the truck.

Yours,

To Glen Clark

February 12, 1957

Dear Glen:

This is to confirm my instructions.

Frank Holland will come around to help get the work caught up. Just do what he tells you until you leave by the first of March. When you are ready to go, be sure there is no danger of the pipes freezing in your quarters. If you will notify Miss Evans she will send you your check for the month, less any deductions in payment of garnishment suits filed against me.

Ed Becker, a carpenter, will come to inspect the quarters again. He is preparing some estimates for me and it will be all right to let him in.

I am sorry that things didn't work out and I wish you and Ann well. I hope you will quickly find some suitable work. Good luck.

Sincerely yours,

To William V. Shannon[123]

February 12, 1957

Dear Bill:

Bless you for that gallant draft. I shall salvage much of it, although I haven't yet thought through just what I should say, especially about the Middle East. I would like to make a full dress speech on that, but I don't see how I can contrive it at this date and I am afraid it would be too full and too dressy for the occasion.

I marvel everlastingly at your talents ·and the celerity of your response to my SOS calls. Thanks.

Cordially yours,

To Borden Stevenson

February 12, 1957

Dear Borden:

I am off in a few minutes for California and thence to Arizona on the 19th. I will be staying with Senator Benton in Phoenix, and Miss Evans says she has sent a copy of my whereabouts and complete schedule to Nancy and Adlai. (The Phoenix address is Mr. William Benton, 5520 E. Camelback Road, telephone WHitney 5-6163.) I will be in Phoenix until about March first when I go to Washington for the Gridiron dinner, then up to Princeton for a little speech, and then to New York on

---

[123] Washington correspondent of the New York *Post*.

business. If there is any reason for my coming to Cambridge after March 5 I could do so easily. Just let Miss Evans know, or write me.

Unless you have some other plans, I had in mind sending a rather handsome silver cigarette lighter to Jean McBride[124] from you boys and I will send her one of the big Encyclopaedia Britannica Atlases which everyone likes. If this is okay please notify Miss Evans promptly and she will go ahead and have the silver piece wrapped and delivered.

I hope things are going well. Try to drop me a postcard at least once in a while.

Love,

P.S. You might check with the other boys to be sure they are not sending separate presents to Jean.

Also, could you find out and let me know if Archibald MacLeish is still in Antigua and how long he expects to be there? I may go and visit him there — lucky man!

To John Fell Stevenson

February 12, 1957

Dear John Fell:

Thanks for your excellent letter. I am enclosing $1,000 to replenish your coffers and I hope for quite a long time! Miss Evans will try to reimburse Mr. Stevens,[125] although we seem to have trouble every time with his office and I am getting embarrassed.

Anyway, I am so glad you have had a good time. I only wish I could have been with you — which would of course have given you an even better time! . . .

And you are of age too! I hope you are enjoying the feeling of and are not overwhelmed with the responsibility.

I am off today for the West Coast and then to Arizona. You can reach me until the first of March in care of William Benton, 5520 E. Camelback Road, Phoenix, telephone Whitney 5-6163. Miss Evans says she has sent my complete schedule and whereabouts to Adlai and Nancy. On March 1 I go to Washington for the Gridiron, thence to Princeton for a little speech and if you think it wise I could stop at Cambridge any time after the fifth of March.

I have written Mrs. McLaughlin and Miss Evans will let you know the answer. Mrs. [Edison] Dick says they have a ranch near Aspen and

---

[124] Daughter of Stevenson's Princeton classmate W. Paul McBride, of Lake Forest, Illinois. She was marrying John K. Greene.

[125] Theatrical producer Roger Stevens occasionally provided Stevenson with theater tickets but would never send him a bill.

they have a daughter named — or called — Kitten, whom you must know. It sounds extravagant to me, and especially if you also cherish notions of a trip to Europe. You can always go to Southern Pines and play golf. I might even join you.

Love,

Stevenson spoke to the Democratic National Conference in San Francisco on February 16, 1957.[126]

This meeting in San Francisco tonight has a special meaning to me, and I am not referring to the fact that I was born in California, or that it has now produced three Republican pretenders to the throne simultaneously — which certainly must establish California as the mother of candidates if not Presidents.

Rather I am happily reminded tonight that just a year ago this month I came to California, my birthplace, to celebrate my birthday, and to thank many of you for urging me to run for President again. It was a birthday party no man could forget.

It began in Sacramento and ended a week later in San Diego. We counted 410 birthday cakes and about 410,000 friends along the way. And I'm glad to see so many of them again tonight, together with Democratic friends from other Western states.

As some of you may have noticed, something happened on my way to the White House again but I haven't lost heart. I haven't even lost weight, as I'm sure all of you have noticed.

Horace Greeley, you know, was, like myself, the victim of a Presidential contest with a Republican general. When he said, "Go West, young man," I don't know whether he was thinking about Democrats, but this meeting here in San Francisco proves again what the election last fall has already told us — that our party has no greater source of hope for the future than in the West.

For here Democrats carried the standards of our party to success unmatched in any other corner of our nation. We would have had a little pleasanter evening that Tuesday in November if the rest of the nation had been as rational and perceptive as the West.[127]

The record of the election entitles the Democrats of the West to speak in the councils of the party with a louder voice than ever before. I trust

---

[126] The text is from the New York *Times*, February 17, 1957. Typographical errors have been corrected by the editors.

[127] See Joe Miller, "How the Republicans Lost in the West," *Reporter*, December 13, 1956.

that you will not hang back. The Democratic party of the nation needs your counsel and your leadership.

What lessons are we to draw from your record? Here in the West you had strong and attractive candidates. But there were many good candidates elsewhere, too. Clearly the moral runs deeper than personalities.

It is, I think, the story of young, aggressive state parties — parties which campaigned on issues; which made those issues clear to the public; which proclaimed our party's liberal and progressive faith with clarity and conviction, and which fought the fight, not just between Labor Day and Election Day, but the year round.

There are, I believe, two fallacies popular today about the Democratic future; and both spell trouble for our party.

The first is that the Republican Presidential victory last fall was just an Eisenhower victory, a purely personal triumph. Once the President retires, this argument goes, it will be easy in 1960 for our party to recapture the White House.

In my opinion, that is a comfortable but a false, dangerously false, notion. And I say that the Republican candidate, whoever it may be, will be hard to beat. The reason should be clear. Never before, the historians tell me, have the vast agencies of big money, big government and the big press been so concentrated and so united in politics.

Never before have the techniques of mass persuasion and mass manipulation been so completely at the service of a single political party. We would be foolish to underestimate the impact of this incessant barrage of propaganda and publicity on the American people.

It has sought, and not without success, to transform the Administration's failures into successes, our friendly President into a dynamic leader, our frightening Secretary of State into a great statesman, and an absence of policy in the Middle East into a "doctrine," and the highest living costs in our history into a stern program of checking inflation.

Look at what has even happened to Mr. Nixon. Last fall he took his one-way trip to the political laundry and emerged as a certified shining knight of progress, high-mindedness and the "New Republicanism" — whatever that may be — and I think I know; it's the New Deal at its twenty-fifth reunion.

What the newspapers and news magazines, the advertising agencies, the vast publicity resources of the Government, and big business and limitless money can do to conceal as well as reveal facts, to divert as well as attract attention, to mislead as well as lead public opinion, we would discount at our peril.

And, as the Administration's veneer of virtue wears thinner and the sawdust leaks more and more, you can be sure that they will press these

[*464*]

brainwashing techniques harder than ever during the next four years.

Complacent, prosperous and well fed, most of our people want to also feel secure. They don't want to worry, so they have been particularly vulnerable to the great lullaby which has drowned our feeble alarms and warnings in these past few years. They have averted their eyes and busied themselves with their new suburban homes and communities.

We must, I say, find ways and means of breaking through this formidable coalition of government, money and so much of the press. Nor can we afford to disregard another significant change, the flight to the suburbs. Forty-two million people now live under generally suburban conditions, and this great migration has undermined the old basis of Democratic dominance in the cities.

And, again, I think the image of the Democratic party and what it stands for has been blurred of late by the Republican pretenses of liberalism and by our own internal conflicts, mostly over civil rights.

The Democratic party must pick its issues, stand by them, fight for them, not only in the lobbies and cloakrooms of Congress, but everywhere and all the time and by all of us — Congressmen, Senators, Governors, Mayors, legislators, office holders and private citizens. You cannot win national elections against such obstacles and resources and ruthlessness as we confront in two months. It will be hard enough in four years.

So let us loudly reaffirm what we are — our liberal tradition and faith, our utter dedication to the people's needs and hopes, and our allegiance to no other masters. Let us speak loudly, clearly, constantly, to the conscience of the people rather than to their desires and their prejudices. And let us leave no doubt that our universal aim is social justice and equal opportunity.

And most of all, let us speak honestly and never pander to the common desire to escape unpleasant realities and the heavy burdens of reason, for both are the price of self-government.

I hope and pray that Congress will pass civil rights legislation in this session with overwhelming Democratic support and without a filibuster or parliamentary harassment.[128] As a national party we have a special understanding of the problems of the South, and hence a special responsibility for their solution and for law observance, which is as important in the long run to the South as to the North, because it is the basis of all civilized society.

[128] Later in 1957, without a filibuster, Congress passed a Civil Rights Act (Public Law 85–315) which created the Federal Civil Rights Commission with power to investigate discriminatory conditions in voting and other situations which denied the equal protection of the laws, and to recommend corrective measures to the President.

I said a moment ago that there were two common fallacies. The first, as I say, is that we can win in 1958 and 1960 by a base on balls. The second is that, if we undertake a policy of vigorous opposition to the party in power, that opposition must, of necessity, be sterile, negative, destructive.

We all recall the grim record of the Republican party in opposition. The ruthlessness, the vindictiveness and the savagery of spirit which characterized those days make a sad chapter in American public life. But I do not believe that the Democrats are going to accept the Republicans as models.

We can show the nation what a creative opposition really is. We can show that opposition means, not picking at wounds but healing them; not destroying private reputations but rescuing America's reputation. We can demonstrate that a truly responsible opposition party need not substitute fanaticism for faith, vehemence for vigilance, or slander for truth.

We often say, and it is well to remember, that the success of democracy as a form of government depends on an informed electorate. And one of the best means of informing the people is by continuous critical analysis of public policy and performance.

Ordinarily the party in power can confidently rely on both the minority party and the press for critical examination. This was true — and then some — when we were in power.

But, alas, it is not true now. The poor Republicans are almost wholly dependent on us. We must not fail them. There is nothing worse for governments, like children, than overindulgence, and, as far as the press is concerned Mr. Eisenhower's dead-end kids don't know what the word paddle means.

But I don't mean to be facetious about this; indeed I solemnly assert that immunity from criticism from a large segment of the press, combined with massive and skillful use of propaganda and advertising, have brought us to a crisis in the honest political communication on which an informed electorate must depend.

I am not troubled by the fact that most of our press lords are partisan Republicans; nor that the big advertisers who are their big clients are even more so. After all, as somebody said, the tycoons know what they want and know where to get it — as their campaign contributions so eloquently testify. Nor am I troubled about their wealth. Most of it comes back in taxes and philanthropy. They are our greatest benefactors.

My concern, rather, is with the deterioration of democracy, when self-criticism withers, debate dries up, and power over the mass mind is concentrated in a few hands. In such circumstances the duty of the opposition to oppose, to criticize, to disclose, to take nothing for granted, and to inform the public is multiplied.

And these days there is always plenty to talk about, too. Just now the contrasts between what President Eisenhower and the Republicans said before and after the last election illustrate my point. They are amusing, yes. But they also reveal a distressing indifference to the people's right to know.

Before the election, for example, the President boasted about how his Administration had controlled inflation.[129] Now, with the cost of living at another all-time high, he has warned us that a dangerous inflation will be the fault of business and labor.[130]

Do you remember back in 1952 when General Eisenhower and Senator Taft proposed a $60,000,000,000 budget?[131]

Well, after all the righteous talk about fiscal responsibility and Republican economy, the President and Secretary [George] Humphrey have just presented the biggest peacetime budget in history — $72,000,000,000.[132]

And then a remarkable thing happened. Instead of explaining and defending it, the Republican Secretary of the Treasury promptly denounced it and called upon a Democratic Congress to cut it, and then he went off quail hunting with President Eisenhower while the press applauded them for criticizing their own handiwork.

Perhaps I shouldn't point out even the humor in such situations, because in the present climate a defeated candidate who criticizes may be charged with poor sportsmanship. To court such a reaction is not pleasant. But isn't this my duty? Isn't it yours?

For surely we know by now that if we working Democrats don't try to clear the air of the Republican incense no one is going to do it for us.

[129] See Dwight D. Eisenhower, *Mandate for Change* (Garden City, New York: Doubleday, 1963), p. 486.

[130] The President, without stating it in the accusatory terms Stevenson uses, sounded this theme in both his State of the Union and budget messages to Congress in January, 1957, calling for restraint both in demands by business and labor and in government spending and declaring that government action alone could not prevent inflation. See the New York *Times*, January 11 and 17, 1957.

[131] The statement was issued on September 12, 1952, as part of what Stevenson labeled a "surrender," after the senator had conferred with Mr. Eisenhower at Columbia University following a bitter campaign struggle. The meeting produced a statement by Mr. Taft that their differences over foreign policy were "differences of degree," and an agreement, in Mr. Eisenhower's words, that "as soon as practicable," the budget "should be cut down to something like $60 billion, but we set no arbitrary dollar figure or time limit, and I insisted that any cuts not jeopardize the national defense." *Mandate for Change*, p. 64.

[132] The actual figure was $71.8 billion. See Robert L. Branyan and Lawrence H. Larsen, *The Eisenhower Administration, 1953–1961: A Documentary History* (New York: Random House, 1971), p. 803.

We could, as I say, complain that the press in its columns and editorial pages should do a large part of the job for us. And it would be a just complaint.

We know that most of the newspapers cast a more tolerant eye at the excesses and defects of Republicans than at those of Democrats. But this is a fact of life. We must do it ourselves — all of us, from United States Senators to private citizens in every walk of life.

To demand the truth, to get the facts, to denounce fraud, to unmask imposture; to revive the concept of a fighting opposition to its true dimensions — this is the greatest task before us. If we don't do it, if we fail in this — the supreme task of the opposition party, we face defeat not only in 1960 but in years beyond. God helps those who help themselves.

The conduct of American foreign policy illustrates our problem and affords us our greatest challenge and our greatest opportunity as a responsible opposition. For here is the nation's greatest need for truth and reality; for here half truths and lullabies have done us the greatest injury.

We don't need to rake the ashes of the past, or revisit all of Mr. Dulles' "brinks," or recall all the foolish words about "unleashing Chiang," "massive retaliation," "the immorality of neutrals."

And heroic Hungary, crushed and bleeding, is a mute witness to the hollowness of those cynical vote-catching boasts about "liberating the satellites."

We don't need to marshal the dismal record. The current scene is evidence enough that we have come perilously close to disaster in the Eisenhower years. We missed our great chance and Hungary was crushed in blood. Russian influence has penetrated the Middle East for the first time. Israel is isolated again. Britain and France have blundered and been badly hurt. Our great alliance is tottering. NATO is enfeebled. The Suez Canal is still closed, its future unsettled, our best friends are crippled by the oil shortage. And whose friendship have we won? Nasser's? I doubt it.

This is the sorry harvest of appeasing and provoking the Arabs; of misleading and exasperating our best friends. Yet it was only yesterday — just before the election — that President Eisenhower said of the Middle East: "It looks like there's a very great crisis that's behind us"; that Vice President Nixon said: "It appears that Mr. Eisenhower's tolerance and wisdom and leadership will serve to avert armed conflict in the Middle East"; that Secretary Dulles called it "amazing" the degree to which the United States, Britain and France had developed a common policy; that Secretary [Charles E.] Wilson called it "a relatively small thing," and the ineffable Mr. [Thomas E.] Dewey solemnly predicted "a lasting and secure peace."

But then — after the election — they proclaimed the Middle Eastern crisis more serious than any we have faced for ten years — more serious than the fall of China to the Communists, more serious than the threatened economic collapse of Europe, and Secretary Dulles said that even delay in passing the President's resolution would mean that "in a short time [the Middle East] would be dominated by communism."

Before the election it was sweet peace; after the election it was the imminent threat of war.

And let it not be said that anything had changed; that British influence had suddenly died. It hadn't. It died when Britain withdrew from its great Suez military base three years ago, at our insistence, by the way.

I think we have had enough of this rock-and-roll diplomacy.

This is not the place to ask how they allowed this sense of isolation and reckless despair to develop among the people of Israel — and I winced when I heard our government say it would consider sanctions to force Israel to withdraw from Sinai without any security for its borders or its shipping when no such pressure was put on Russia for its defiance of the General Assembly on Hungary, or India's defiance over Kashmir, or, indeed, Egypt's defiance of the Security Council in respect of Israel['s] shipping in the Suez Canal.

You don't have to condone Israel's defiance of the General Assembly to feel a thrill that someone is ready to risk life itself for national survival.

Nor is this the place to ask how the Eisenhower Government allowed a situation to develop which caused Britain and France, our oldest and best friends, to act secretly and desperately. Nor need we recall that melancholy spectacle when the American delegate to the United Nations lined up with Russia against our Allies to save a dictator's neck, or Mr. Nixon's shocking exultation over what he called our "declaration of independence" from Britain and France.

You don't have to condone what they did, or what Israel did, or anyone else to realize that people have lost confidence in us. The brilliant cross examination by Democrats in Congress has amply demonstrated the failure of this government to maintain, let alone advance, America's leadership in the Middle East.

Behind the ill-judged action of our friends was the pacifism of the United States, that lullaby about peace and prosperity, and the gloomy sense that America did not recognize the significance of Russian penetration, Israel's mortal danger or the utter dependence of Western Europe on oil and the Suez Canal.

It was, I suppose to correct the impression that the United States didn't care much and wouldn't do anything that President Eisenhower after the election suddenly and dramatically reversed himself and announced that the Middle East was about to be overrun by the Communists and that he must have a resolution authorizing the use of force to resist them — an authority he already possessed.

Well, I was glad the President at last admitted what we Democrats had been shouting for over a year, that we're in plenty of trouble in the Middle East. But, I thought resistance to Communist aggression had been the settled policy of the United States for a decade and that Greece and Turkey and Korea were the best evidences of it. And I trust that the President's resolution wasn't intended to limit our resistance to Communist aggression to the Middle East alone.

I was glad to see the Democrats in the Senate start to clear up this resolution. It seemed to me not only to create an unnecessary and dangerous precedent, but not to meet the real problems. The danger isn't overt Communist aggression but covert Communist penetration; the danger isn't military aggression from the outside, but from the inside. And this resolution doesn't protect Israel from the Arabs or the Arabs from Israel. We won't be on the road to stability until we face the real economic and political problems.

The resolution looks less to me like a serious approach to the real problems of that area than another example of Madison Avenue diplomacy to distract public attention from the Administration's failure.

Rhetorics and dramatics will not open the canal to the ships of all nations, or quell the strife between Arab and Jew, or "fill the vacuum" we hear so much about. Indeed, I think these past weeks have proved what some of us have been saying for a long time — that the first vacuum that should be filled is not in the Middle East but in the State Department.

But if I have misgivings about this effort to implicate every member of Congress in everything that takes place hereafter in the Middle East, I have no misgiving that we must make it perfectly clear that this is an area of vital American interest. If we do no more than restore this strategic area to the condition it was in before the trouble began with a promise of protection from aggression and some economic improvement, we will have missed a great opportunity and perhaps the last.

Our objectives, I take it, are clear and simple: to open the canal to the traffic of all nations, to establish peace between Israel and her Arab neighbors, and, while we don't propose to dominate anyone ourselves, we don't propose that Russia dominate anyone either.

I would make it perfectly clear that we propose to pursue these objectives even at the risk of war, and call on all like-minded nations who want peace, national independence and economic progress in the Middle East to join us. Obviously economic development is imperative and we should help generously, either alone, or in concert with others through the United Nations, or through a regional development agency.

If the disaster in the Middle East has jolted us into a realization of the enormity of our failures and our perils it may yet do some good, and the greatest peril of all is the collapse of our Western alliance. I applaud the steps the Administration is now taking to repair the damage and restore the Atlantic alliance which two world wars have shown is essential to our safety.

It will take time. I can imagine how we would feel if we had kept Russia out of the Middle East for 100 years and thought Britain's blunders had let her in. And I can imagine how we would feel if we had no secure oil supply for our homes and factories and thought Britain was to blame for that too. I think we must make it clear by firm deed as well as fair word that we don't propose to weaken the powers who alone have some stability in the free world, and that an expanding economy in Western Europe and the Atlantic community is still an abiding interest of America.

I have talked about the Middle East tonight not because it is the only great problem we face — there's China, Germany, the satellites and the great Afro-Asian revolutions — but to illustrate the opportunity and the obligations of our party. With the shrinkage of empire, the fateful shifts in world power in Asia yesterday — and in the Middle East today — are dumping more and more responsibility in the lap of the United States. How are we doing?

Well, not very well, obviously. It is evident everywhere you look that we have lost confidence and leadership. What we should be doing is asking ourselves why; for until we do, resolutions, threats, gestures, and dollars won't do much good.

And that's why I agree emphatically with Senator Fulbright and Senator Mansfield and other Democratic leaders that the Senate should bring the whole international situation into perspective. Certainly we can't go on tottering from brink to brink and blunder to blunder while our leaders assure us that all is well and tell us to relax and buy another car or swallow another tranquilizer.

The other day I asked one of our greatest scholars what America needed most. "Foresight," he replied.

Well, I agree. Our duty as Democrats is identical with our duty as Americans. It is to face into the future, to ask hard and searching questions about where we are going, to help provide wise answers, and to help develop policies that will restore American leadership in the world.

This will not be an easy task, because it is not easy to work constructively with the President if he pays no attention to our suggestions, seeks no counsel and closes his mind to all our utterances. Mr. Eisenhower never uttered more revealing or disheartening words than his attack on his Democratic critics at his press conference on Jan. 30: "I notice this: They don't bring out any particular project. They just talk about great blundering and lack of leadership. I have seen no proposals — no constructive proposals . . . on the contrary, we just hear these generalized attacks."

If Mr. Eisenhower has seen "no constructive proposals" from Democrats on the Middle East and on other foreign problems during these past years, then I would plead with him to enlarge his reading and his listening.

Let no one mistake the mood of the Democratic party. We believe that Statesmanship is the goal of politics, and we will do everything we can, regardless of party interest, to support this Administration in honest endeavors to meet the great challenges at home and abroad that are piling up on us. I know, you know, that patriotism must come before partisanship. I know, you know, that to do the right thing is the right thing to do.

But we resent, we cannot tolerate, slickness and hypocrisy. We resent the whole notion that the way to secure the solemn asset of a great democracy is through slogans, showmanship and half truths — through fairy tales in November and ghost stories in January. We want facts not fancy. We want truth about our affairs, the whole truth, and all the time. We want foreign policy conducted for the nation's advantage and security, not for the Republican party's advantage and security.

Our problems are great; the Republican Administration needs our help and our cooperation — in the foreign field above all. Let us give it to them with a will — on the condition of total honesty with the people.

It is time that we lifted these matters of life and death, of national security, out of the realm of petty politics and partisan interest. Our period is as dangerous as any since Lincoln. Democracy's command to think, to reason, to know gets ever more trying. But it can't be evaded. We have to shoulder our burdens, make our decisions — and lead. And we Democrats, in and out of office, have to help.

Herman Melville once reminded us Americans that: "We are the pioneers of the world, the advance guard sent on through the wilderness of untried things to break a new path in a new world that is ours."

We must help each other, Democrats and Republicans alike, to break this new path to the new world.

Stevenson visited with Mr. and Mrs. William Benton in Phoenix, Arizona, from February 18 to March 1, 1957. The following letters were written while he was there.

To Carol Evans[133]

February [no date], 1957

Dear Carol —

Do I understand:

1. There is *no* BOAC service to Barbados?

2. You can't make connections from Jaxonville to Miami to San Juan to B'dos?

On the basis of what you've sent me a visit to the [Harry] Guggenheims near Jacksonville and thence to B'dos appears all but impossible. Subject to conditions at the farm and office and Cambridge, I had thought tentatively (and must let her know soon) of going to Alicia [Patterson]'s from N.Y. on the 6th and on to B'dos on the 11th or 12th, returning in time for the childrens spring holiday which I think (I didn't bring the date) commences about March 30. But if it all wastes too much time in travel I'll have to skip the Georgia visit and go direct to B'dos.

Please send along any prospects for farm job dope that looks promising either from there or Bloomington — also estimates on house remodelling.

Will send a lot of papers back for filing by WB [Bill Blair].

Tell Russell Eddy[134] that John Fell will have "*some*" money for investment and ask what he thinks of Chrysler. If he likes it tell him to buy 300 shares for JF and ask NM [Newton Minow] when we can pay for it.

No rest here! Have finished and mailed article for Mowrer.[135]

AES

---

133 This handwritten letter is in the possession of Miss Evans.

134 Stevenson's investment broker at Brown Brothers Harriman and Company.

135 Stevenson almost certainly refers to "The Support of Nationalism Helps Combat Communist Imperialism," which appeared in *Western World*, of which Edgar Ansel Mowrer was editor in chief. This article is reprinted in this volume, pp. 536–544. Cf. Stevenson's letter to Lady Barbara Jackson of May 14, 1957, pp. 533–534.

To Mrs. Ronald Tree[136]

February 20, 1957

Dear Marietta —

Thank you for your note renewing the invitation to B'dos. I am very, very tempted, as two days in Phoenix has persuaded me that there is precious little peace and solitude to be found in this portion of the desert at least, and it is too cold to go to my old friend, Dick Jenkins'; besides he's dead!

I wonder if I could let you know by wire later — around the first of March — after I have a better idea of my situation and my crises — of which I always seem to have an assortment, usually relating to my "farm," where I am again in the throes of changing farmers — if only I had something to change to! *If* I come it might be between the 6th and 10th *circa* — and I might want to stay with you, or, if not convenient, at an Inn, till toward the end of the month — to get *really* relaxed, if possible!

My "holiday" here consists of doing an article, long promised and forgotten, for a new magazine, correcting 700 (!) pages of typescript of this ghastly biography,[137] writing a speech for the Gridiron Club, discussing *my* business future and *his* — both business and political — with Bill Benton, inspecting real estate adventures with Mary Lasker, Florence Mahoney[138] and friends — taking appalling calisthenics under the lash of Eliz. Arden Mahoney[139] and, occasionally, *sleeping!*

But enough of all this. Thanks again to you & Ronnie for your charity and thoughtfulness, & let me know if it is *in*convenient for me to defer a decision. Meanwhile I'll make a BOAC reservation — just in case.

The S.F. [San Francisco] meeting was surprisingly successful as a conference; good panel discussions, good reports, crowded halls and the Sat. night dinner at which I spoke was a sell-out. The speech, written in fits and starts (mostly the former!) had a hushed and then a tumultuous reception — and I felt like "me old self" again. But the press was cold and brief, after a familiar fashion. (copy herewith.) The advisory Council meeting which added [Senator Herbert] Lehman as a member and uttered several releases on civil rts. [rights], foreign affairs, resources etc didnot encourage me about getting staffed and out of a

---

136 This handwritten letter is in the possession of Mrs. Tree.

137 Kenneth S. Davis's *A Prophet in His Own Country.*

138 A Washington socialite who was active in Democratic party affairs and was associated with Mrs. Albert Lasker in the Lasker Foundation.

139 Mrs. Mahoney writes that she persuaded Stevenson to exercise in order to reduce his weight. Letter to Carol Evans, November 5, 1970. Elizabeth Arden, founder of the cosmetics firm of the same name, operated health and reducing resorts in Maine and Arizona.

ponderous and prolonged planning stage. But another meeting of the "steering c[ommi]ttee" will take place in N.Y. Mar 4 & finally get down to cases on staff.

Again my heartfelt thanks for offering me your elegant and secure refuge & *don't hesitate to let me know if it proves in the least inconvenient or if you must know at once!*

Affectionate regards to you & Ronnie and all your numerous household. —

ADLAI

Norman Rockwell's portrait of Stevenson appeared on the cover of the Saturday Evening Post, *October 6, 1956.*

To Norman Rockwell

February 22, 1957

Dear Mr. Rockwell:

Not long ago I mentioned to one of my associates the lively desire I have had, ever since seeing the remarkable product of our "sitting" last summer, to possess this original Rockwell. Now I find it is mine, thanks to your great courtesy and that of the *Saturday Evening Post.* I have written a note to Mr. Kenneth Stuart,[140] but I cannot adequately express to you, my dear sir, the pride and admiration which your work inspires.

I was distressed to hear of your hospital sojourn, but trust you have long since recovered fully.

With profound esteem and my heartfelt thanks, I am

Cordially yours,

To Benjamin H. Swig

February 24, 1957

Dear Ben:

I have had a week mostly of gray skies and rain which should have provided me with an opportunity to get caught up with my work but somehow, I haven't — as usual.

I am so glad that you all felt that the meeting in San Francisco was a success. It seemed to me the best one of those regional conferences I have attended and surely that the dinner was a reflection once more of your heroic services to our party. So I join the chorus of thanks, and

[140] Art editor of the *Saturday Evening Post.*

with a very special personal thanks for all of your courtesy and generosity to me — again and again!

I have hastily looked through the U.S. Leasing Co. report and I am tempted to take advantage of your offer for part of it but I shall first have to find out if I have any money and what the income tax situation will be. I find my son, John Fell, will presently have some $30,000 to invest as a result of a settlement with the insurance company for his accident. Perhaps this is something I should get for him for the long pull. Also, I wonder if you had any further talk with Ed Heller about it. I mentioned it to him briefly, but our conversation was interrupted at his house.

If you bought the "call" on Chrysler which you mentioned to me in the car, I hope you will let me know and also, how much you paid for it. And I hope some time we can talk again about a depreciation real estate investment if a possibility comes to your attention.

Speaking of real estate, some friends of mine, including George Killion[141] and Ralph Davies,[142] have an option on some land near the new industrial development north of Phoenix which has to be exercised in the next couple of months and which they are going to sell due to a shortage of cash. They have just bought another ship line! It looks like a typical Arizona miracle case of very rapid appreciation and, if you like, I will have the local agent send you all the dope. Let me know promptly, care of William Benton.

I hope very much to have an opportunity to see Mr. Ford[143] and will certainly have at least a telephone talk. Life has been too busy for comfort and there is too much work for rest, but my visit here has been a pleasing one all the same.

Cordially yours,

Everett Case wrote that travel to Alaska or South Africa held a bottom priority for him. Instead of joining Stevenson in Africa he expected to vacation on Martha's Vineyard. He suggested they visit together in the autumn to review the "predicament of man — or the Democratic party."

---

[141] President of the American President Lines.
[142] A member of the board of directors of the American President Lines.
[143] Probably John Anson Ford, chairman of the Los Angeles County Board of Supervisors and a member of the California State Democratic Central Committee.

To Everett Case

February 24, 1957

Dear Ev:

Having been both to Africa and Alaska, I can assure you you are wrong about both! Unless, of course, you are getting old and the extremities of your travel taste are satisfied by that journey to distant Martha's Vineyard.

I am journeying from Arizona to Washington, New York, and the Caribbean; to Chicago for April and May, then Europe and Africa and back on my green and neglected acres in August — forever more. Come on out and I will give you a hoe. I might even give you the Democratic Party! or loan it.

Yours,

To Mrs. Edison Dick[144]

February 25, 1957

My dear Jane:

Thanks for all that helpful detail about Port Antonio [Jamaica]. You remember my telling you about my rendezvous a couple of years ago with Princess Margaret? Well, it started at Port Antonio and ended at Frenchman's Cove* on San San Beach. You remember my account of my night at the quaint hotel. Well, it was the Tichfield! And do you remember my account of the traffic jam and the tropical downpour at the Bridge? It was the Rio Grande & the Princess was "rafting" just beneath me!

. . . I think, with a taste for the picturesque, you and Eddie[145] would really enjoy Port Antonio, a banana port of 50 years ago which has suffered acute reverses and is now slowly coming back.

I only wish I could be there to recount again my engaging adventures there, including the incident of the lost chauffeur. I had to have him "paged" over a loud speaker among the crowd of 10,000 who had come to see Margaret off on the Britannia.

But I don't think I will try to join you, for when I go back to Jamaica, I would rather like to go back for business reasons, at the instance of the Reynolds.[146] Besides, hotel life just isn't what I am looking for, as you know. I am sorry about Camel Bay. And if the travel were not so difficult, I would strongly urge you and Eddie to try Sarita's[147]

[144] The original is in the possession of Mrs. Dick. It is typewritten with handwritten interlineations by Stevenson.
[145] Mr. Dick.
[146] The Reynolds Metal Company, one of Stevenson's legal clients.
[147] Mrs. Sarita Peet, an old friend of Stevenson's.

[477]

place, Guana Island Club at Roadtown, British Virgins. Letter from her makes it sound mighty attractive and what I think you would both like — twenty-two people maximum, simple, comfortable, fish, swim, and "laze." The air, the water, the peace and quiet sound perfect.

But again, I don't think I will try it and risk all the uncertainties and hazards. Instead, I shall probably head for the Trees and the *known* luxuries of Barbados.

California was a great success but the vacation here has been a lot of work and little progress. I will go on to Washington Friday, staying with the [Paul] Magnusons until Sunday evening or Monday, thence to the Savoy Plaza (care of Bill Benton) . . .

Affectionately,

ADLAI

* After dark with full moon the loveliest place in the Western hemisphere.

A schoolboy wrote Stevenson that a project in his school was to ask prominent people the question, "What is the value of Latin?"

To Howard Keller

February 26, 1957

Dear Howard:

I hope you will forgive my delay in answering your recent letter regarding the value of the study of Latin.

I would say first that the imprint of Julius Caesar upon the world exists to this day — in West Point classroom study of military strategy, in law school where it is found that much of our legal methods were originated in Roman times, and certainly in the history books where Caesar's journal showed a regard for the early peoples of France.

We also find that approximately two-thirds of our English words have Latin derivatives — that to speak good English we must actually speak a form of Latin — transformed and amended though it has become over the centuries. And it is also the basis for the study of French, Spanish and Italian.

I would say, then, briefly — to study Latin is to study the background not only of our own history, but of our own English language. If this in any way increases our understanding of one another in ordinary day-to-day relationships — and I think it does much more — then surely such study is worthy of consideration by us all.

Sincerely yours,

[478]

A twelve-year-old girl sent Stevenson the following verse she composed during the campaign:

> *Vote for Stevenson,*
> *He's the best.*
> *Vote for Stevenson,*
> *Give him the test.*
> *He'll come through,*
> *Just wait and see.*
> *Vote for Stevenson,*
> *The man for you and me.*

To Katrina Lehman

February 28, 1957

Dear Katrina,

Thank you for your friendly letter — it warmed my heart! And I do think, immodest as it may sound, that you write very good poetry.

My only regret about the election is that I could not better fulfill the hopes of my friends such as you. But for your confidence in me, and your support, I shall be forever grateful.

Cordially yours,

To Alicia Patterson[148]

[no date]

Alicia dear —

I've been struggling with my schedule by long distance and have reluctantly concluded that I can't come to the Black River[149] as I had hoped in early March. The travel connections to Barbados are too difficult from there and I *must* be back home earlier than I expected for the wretched trial of the truck driver who hit John Fell. It is all very annoying, but it just doesn't make sense to try to do too much in the brief time I have for the long planned vacation "away from it all" — and Phoenix, Ariz. is definitely *not* away from it all!!

I hope I'll see you in Wash[ington]. or N.Y. between Mar 3–6. I'll try anyway. And perhaps April will bring you to Chicago and we can walk along another river again.

Much love —

ADLAI

[148] This handwritten letter is in the possession of Adlai E. Stevenson III. It was written from Phoenix, Arizona.

[149] The Guggenheims had a plantation on St. Mary's River (the boundary between Georgia and Florida), locally known as the Black River because of its dark color, derived from mangrove roots.

Stevenson flew from Arizona to Washington, D.C., where he visited with friends and spoke at the Gridiron Club dinner held on March 2, 1957.[150]

After that sad song about my present friendless state, I am very grateful for your friendly greeting. I feel a little like that famous cow on the cold wintry morning who looked at the farmer and said, "Thanks for the warm hand."

I only wish it had been as warm and friendly last November!

I have always believed that you should never miss a chance to make others happy — even if you have to leave them alone to do it.

So, for both your sake and mine, I hesitate to come back four months after the election to rake among the embers of my funeral pyre, a bonfire which most of you publishers fanned so vigorously, and a funeral at which so few of you mourned!

But it is not an altogether uncongenial task, I confess, what with the spring air so full of Republican chickens coming home to roost. Yet good taste prescribes that I greet you humbly, contritely, as a man who has twice been tempted, and twice suffered the consequences of his weakness.

Just what made me think I could do better the second time escapes me now. I have some recollection before the accident, of a noble desire to do what my party wanted me to do.

But it was different this time from 1952, and I guess no one had told me about primaries — and certainly no one told me what Estes Kefauver would do to me in Minnesota.

Well, anyway, since the accident, a gallant fellow sufferer in Vermont sent me a verse which neatly summarizes my story, and which I read to some of you here not long ago:

> Everyone said it couldn't be done,
> But he with a grin replied,
> "How do you know it can't be done
> Leastwise, if you haven't tried?"
> And he went right to it and at it,
> And he tackled the thing that couldn't be done,
> AND HE COULDN'T DO IT!

So I guess I was not meant to be President of the United States.

I have great sympathy for the man who occupies the Presidency,

[150] The text is from a mimeograph copy.

especially the present recumbent. He is confronted with many difficulties at home and abroad. And think of the embarrassment when even
Time, the Republican House organ, reveals that his bird dogs failed to
flush a single covey of quail.

As Jefferson said, the office of the President can be "a splendid
misery." And, from personal experience, I feel deeply for the uneasy
man in sweater and cleats who approaches a tee and finds a sign reading: "440 yards, par 4"! Then, the disillusion of it all!

Even after an heroic 225 yard drive, you still have to struggle to
replace the turf in some far off place — like London or Suez.

I won't go on. But I would recommend Milltown on the rocks. It
might diminish the pain of recent scenes including, well — would you
say for example, that Mrs. Charles Wilson ranks as the first female Ike-
onoclast? If she keeps it up she may some day be as famous as Barbara
Fritchie or Betsy Ross — or even Doris Fleeson!

However, it wasn't of the President but of the campaign and myself
that I was supposed to speak. I think of a presidential campaign, and
who has thought of it more, as a chaotic interlude of voluntary frustra-
tion sandwiched in between four years of anticipation and four weeks of
recuperation. But I didn't mind the campaign so much as the primary.
More than once during that endless travail I thought of those two
wretched drunks on the railroad tracks. Stumbling, staggering along
between the rails from one rising tie to another, one of the miserable
wretches mumbled that the steps were so high, while the other allowed
that what bothered him wasn't the high steps but the low bannisters.

But don't let me discourage any of you from running for President.
It's a wonderful way to meet a lot of people you wouldn't meet otherwise — at any price! Besides, as I have often remarked, it is fine exercise
for the hands, feet, stomach and vocal chords. And I am told that it is
not too hard on the head, if you use good judgment. You don't even
have to read or write; someone will do it for you.

And this brings me to Arthur Larson.[151] I salute you, Sir! I remember
last fall when Larson[152] pitched a no-hit game for the Yankees — I
didn't know you were doing the same to me! So it seems to me very
appropriate for you to speak here tonight. And I am happy to meet the
Republican egg-head, saving your presence Dr. Milton.[153] I hope you

[151] Director of the United States Information Agency.
[152] Don Larsen of the New York Yankees, who had pitched the first no-hit base-
ball game in the history of the World Series on October 8, 1956, defeating the
Brooklyn Dodgers, 2–0.
[153] Milton Eisenhower, president of Johns Hopkins University and brother of
President Dwight D. Eisenhower.

are enjoying your missionary work among the heathen, Mr. Larson.[154] But I know that there are those who would rather be second in Rome than first in an Iberian village. So, if you should tire of your work and crave more congenial intellectual companionship, we Democrats will welcome you, Mr. Larson.

When this memorable evening concludes, Mr. Chairman, I trust the band will play, in honor of the victor's representative, not "Hail to the Chief," but "Hail to the Ghost!"

Was it Horatio who said to Hamlet: "There needs no ghost, my Lord, come from the grave to tell us this"! Well, I disagree. And I have had some experience with the perils of writing my own speeches. The price of being yourself in American politics is ruinous — your speeches are always late, the reporters are harassed, you miss their deadlines, and these things are evidently far more important than what the candidate really thinks, writes and says. And worst of all, when I added what *I insisted* on saying to what my *staff* said *must* be said, I couldn't possibly get off the air before the television time was up.

And extravagant Democrat that I am, I could never allow for any spare time at the end of a speech because I couldn't reconcile myself to paying $5,000 a minute for an ovation from the faithful.

You know that wonderful song from My Fair Lady, "Get Me to the Church on Time." Well, it wasn't until afterward that I discovered that the theme song of my staff was "Get Him Off the Air on Time." But I did realize at once how bad my major effort with the teleprompter device had been when I read that President Eisenhower had promptly gone back to using a script.

. . . After witnessing the magic, the alchemy, by which a foreign policy failure is converted into a political success, I have concluded that we poor Democrats have a lot to learn from you Republicans. And we can't say we weren't warned. When "Town Meeting" went off the air last June after more than 20 years to make way for hillbilly music, we should have known what was coming — bread, circuses, bandwagons and ballyhoo. And, again, when we bought 5 minutes at the beginning of a popular TV program which turned out to be Lucille Ball, the first telegram I got read, "I like Ike but I love Lucy — Drop dead." Obviously it would have been better if we had bought 5 minutes after the popular programs and announced that they were being extended by courtesy of the Democratic party.

[154] Stevenson presumably refers to Mr. Larson's *A Republican Looks at His Party* (New York: Harper, 1956).

. . . As I watched even the Democratic New Deal re-emerge with an Eisenhower label, I thought of that bus driver guiding sightseers through a southern battlefield.

"Here," he intoned, "a handful of our Southern boys routed 30,000 Yanks . . . Here one fine Georgia battalion annihilated a corps of Yankee troops . . . here two brave boys from Virginia captured a whole regiment of Northerners." Finally a woman with an unmistakable New England twang asked if the North didn't win a single victory. "No, Ma'am," the driver answered, "and they won't as long as I'm driving this here bus."

Now I have learned the hard way that most of you publishers are Republicans — and how!

But you're a balanced group compared to those advertising tycoons — to borrow a word from *Time*, which I seldom do. The other day when the Senate Committee made its report of campaign contributions, I noticed that those powerful gentlemen divided up politically not 60–40, or even 80–20, or even 90–10. They went down the line for the Republican Party 100%! (I've been wondering about that firm that represented the Democratic Party!)

Well, wonders never cease down here. Ten years ago when we started in earnest to resist our enemies and assist our friends, it was called "the Truman doctrine."

Now that happy incantations and righteous moralizing will no longer suffice for a foreign policy, they've put swaddling clothes on that lusty 10-year old and announced the birth of the "Eisenhower doctrine," and the kinfolk are gurgling about the bright new baby who will bring us peace — also oil!

Why, a Republican Senator even wrote his constituents recently that the largest peace-time budget was put over on President Eisenhower when he wasn't looking. And the Republican Secretary of the Treasury, Mr. [George] Humphrey, has roundly denounced the Republican budget. The other members of "the team" are discreetly silent. And Mr. Larson had admitted nothing except that the Democrats should cut the Republican budget.

It seems to me that the $72 billion question seems to be — whose budget is it? Perhaps we ought to ask Charles Van Doren,[155] before we are told that when "the team" were all occupied with the supreme task

---

[155] An instructor in English at Columbia University who was a regular contestant on the National Broadcasting Company's *Twenty-one*, a quiz program involving large sums of money which two years later was proved to have been rigged to favor certain contestants, including Mr. Van Doren.

of world peace, Truman and Snyder[156] sneaked in and made up the Republican budget.

The 1952 campaign was marked with revelations about the financial condition of the candidates. 1956 was marked by revelations about their physical condition. What next? Spiritual revelations? Well, nothing would surprise me — even the news that Nixon is in constant communication with Abraham Lincoln, or that he tried to step aside in favor of Norman Vincent Peale.[157]

Nor, speaking of Lincoln, was I very much surprised to be criticized for using the phrase "the common people" by President Eisenhower who admires so much the Republican President who said, "God must love the common people, he made so many of them."

After all, the President has lots of company among Republicans who love Lincoln more than they read him.

But in spite of my healthy respect for what a benign press, skillful advertisers and a threat of war can do for a candidate — yes, and to a candidate — I note that the Republican Party itself was more of a problem, and that the Republic is still blessed with a Democratic Congress.

I take great comfort from this, although as the defeated leader of a victorious party and surrounded by so many more fortunate Democrats, I feel like the Lone Ranger when he was riding across the country with Tonto and was suddenly confronted with a thousand Sioux Indians. Quickly they wheeled around, and there, behind them, were 2,000 Blackfeet! They turned to the right, only to see 3,000 Arapahoes coming toward them. And on the left they were cut off by 4,000 Apaches. The Lone Ranger said to Tonto, "It looks bad for us, doesn't it?" Tonto replied, "What do you mean 'us,' white man?"

Well, it doesn't look so bad for us Democrats either. Not so bad, indeed, as it looks for the New Republicanism. Now I haven't yet had an opportunity to read your book about the Republican Party, Mr. Larson. I have been waiting for a revised edition, after you have been here a little longer.

As I have said before, I'm not quite sure just what the New Republicanism is, but from what I've observed in the past few years, especially around election time, it — the New Republicanism — looks to me a good deal like the old New Deal at its 25th reunion.

But clearly we Democrats should not complain too much. We've been asking you Republicans to adopt our liberal reforms for many years,

---

[156] John W. Snyder, Secretary of the Treasury under President Truman from 1946 to 1953.

[157] Pastor of the Marble Collegiate Church in New York City and author of *The Power of Positive Thinking* (New York: Prentice-Hall, 1952) and other inspirational works.

although we didn't ask you to steal them. And I suspect that the greatest contribution of the Eisenhower Administration to political science is the accomplishment of this theft with a fresh and wide eyed innocence which has all but ennobled larceny — even if it hasn't convinced many of the Old Guard.

But I would not imply that the present Republican administration is wholly without originality. And I don't hesitate to pay my warm respects to the Post Office — [Postmaster] General Arthur Summerfield — under Republican management. Under President Taft the historic parcel post system was started. And under President Eisenhower the historic decision was made to replace those terrible post office pens with ball points. This is certainly progress!

And if you Republicans are eager to win my good will, I would strongly recommend to you an amendment to the bill providing for pensions for former Presidents. Why not include former Presidential candidates? And, of course, if twice a candidate, twice the pension!

But I have kept you too long. Let me conclude with a final word to you of the press.

Several years ago I preached to you a little about freedom of speech and your responsibility thereto.[158]

I seem to have lost my license as a preacher, but I hope you will indulge me all the same. You see it may be my last chance.

It has been well said that we spend too much time on Presidential elections before they take place, and too little time on them after they are over. This one is now over, but our job isn't. The great imperative of press and politics remains — to serve the truth.

"The truth," as Mr. Dooley told the politicians, "is a tough boss. He don't even pay board wages and if you go to work for him you want to have a job on the side."

You gentlemen, the press, work for that tough boss — the truth — but I've suspected sometimes that some of you publishers have taken Mr. Dooley's advice and have a political job on the side!

All the same, I am grateful for the courtesy, the patience and the good will I have enjoyed from you who write and print. So you will not, I pray, charge me with unworthy thoughts if I remind you once more that your function as truthful, inquisitive reporter and honest, relentless critic is essential to our system of checks and balances.

Just 100 years ago, John Stuart Mill wrote on the pursuit of truth. He said that "there is always hope when people are forced to listen to both sides; it is when they attend only to one that errors harden into prej-

---

158 For Stevenson's speech to the Gridiron Club in 1952, see *The Papers of Adlai E. Stevenson,* Vol. IV, pp. 224–229.

udices." And I could add that you cannot forever pour molasses on this government or any other without gumming it up. The antidote for error and failure is not hidden condonation, but outspoken criticism — the kind of fearless commentary that "withers myths and lays bare the clean white bones of reality."

Your job is truthful, merciless appraisal. But it is even more, I think, in this time when moral and mental fatigue seem to be overcoming mankind, when the resourcefulness that is part of the will to survive in a meaningful way seems to be fading, when so many retreat before complexity, too tired to do more than cling to their own.

I don't know where we go from here. But it seems to me that the best place to begin is with a new mood — a mood of reverence for truth about our friends, our enemies, and above all, ourselves.

This is the toughest work in the world, this business of inspiration, but it is the most essential. And it is business for thinkers, for writers, for speakers — for the press and politicians especially.

As one of you has written, the job of the good newspaper is to say the thing that needs to be said, whether it is smart politics or good business. That, as I see it, is the job of the good politician, too.

But what needs saying most right now is that I gladly accept the people's verdict, indeed I am getting used to it! I wish President Eisenhower and his administration the best of luck. I will gladly help them in office; and, of course, I will gladly help them out of office.

And to the Gridiron I say — Thanks, and long may you wave!

From Washington, D.C., Stevenson visited Princeton, New Jersey, and New York City. While in New York he dictated the following memorandum to Professor Seymour E. Harris, who with John Bartlow Martin and Professor Arthur M. Schlesinger, Jr., was selecting and editing Stevenson's 1956 campaign speeches and program papers for publication as The New America.

To Seymour E. Harris[159]

March 5, 1957

I have had a talk in New York with Cass Canfield, Jack Fischer and Bill Blair and am recording here some of our observations regarding the book.

I understand that you and Arthur [Schlesinger] are doing an Introduction and that you will send it to me as promptly as possible. I will be

---

[159] A carbon copy is in the possession of John Fischer.

c/o Ronald Tree, St. James, Barbados, British West Indies until the end of March.

I, too, will attempt to do a rather brief Foreword expressing some views about primaries, the campaign, the successes and failures, etc.

I think the Table of Contents as you have prepared it is admirable and have few comments. The questions raised by your footnote to the letter of February 15th all merit consideration. I think perhaps the best thing to do would be for you and Arthur and my associates in Chicago to each record your views as to what additional material should be included, if any, and then submit your judgment to Cass and Jack, who will see the volume in, I suspect, a better perspective than any of us who are so much closer and personally involved in the writing, etc.

For example, I would like to include the "Business Speech" made here in New York toward the end of the campaign[160] in an effort to restore a little balance to the liberal picture that the book presents.

My office in Chicago, I think, can do the best job of reconciling the selected material with the final originals. Bill Blair, Newt Minow and Bill Wirtz are prepared to make those comparisons and also to dig out the other originals that you agree to include.

Among other things, the people in Chicago should, and will, eliminate all local references and other material which has no permanent value and interest and will also do some liberal editing to eliminate awkward passages, etc.

In our discussions we have talked about repetition of material between passages. I should think the editing both by you, by the Chicago group and also Harper's on this account should be rigorous. In saying this, I appreciate that to eliminate all but one reference to a topic would be a mistake because it would impair the emphasis of the campaign.

Let us not at this stage worry too much about the contract. You can talk with Mr. Canfield about this when I return. In general, I want to be sure that you and Arthur and, I hope, John Martin will be the principal beneficiaries of whatever revenue the book produces.

Norman Cousins, who had just returned from a trip to the Middle East and Africa, wrote Stevenson of the need to create a new mood, of the need to inspire people amidst the mental and moral fatigue of the tims. He concluded, "The fact that you are able to continue working at this job, the fact that you are what you are, this brightens my homecoming."

160 "The Democratic Party and Business" (October 24, 1956), in Stevenson, *The New America*, pp. 261–265.

To Norman Cousins[161]

March 5, 1957

Dear Norman:

Your letter of February 25 moved me deeply. Indeed, I stole from it liberally. I quite agree that there is much weariness, and the anxiety to escape the hard reality and substitute just a little worry is a prevalent phenomenon that I too have witnessed.

I hope we can talk of these things one day soon.

I am planning to go on business to Africa again in June and this time I hope to stop off to see your friend Dr. [Albert] Schweitzer, and that I should like to talk about too.

With all good wishes,

Cordially,
ADLAI

On March 5, Stevenson flew to Barbados for a three-week vacation with Mrs. and Mrs. Ronald Tree.

To Mrs. Eugene Meyer[162]

March 8, 1957

Agnes dear —

I've had a for[t]night of work & rest & exercise in Ariz[ona] where somehow I contrived this piece for the Gridiron Club dinner — which wasn't too good, I fear, but was an effort at least to faithfully reflect, humorously I hope, something of what I felt and feel about the campaign and the administration. After that glimpse I think they are certainly the most somber, heavy bunch I've yet seen. But if the audience was hardly brisk the skits were pretty good & the songs on the whole very good. The Gridiron speaking, however, is becoming more and more an exchange of pleasant, graceful non-partisan amenities. I mourn the passage of the old give and take, as this rough transcript of my "confidential" may reveal.

After a speech and award at Princeton & some business meetings in N.Y. I came down here to visit Ronald & Marietta Tree. I've been here before and it is the perfect place — luxury, sea, isolation — for a rest,

[161] The original is in the possession of Mr. Cousins.
[162] This handwritten letter is in the Agnes Meyer files, Princeton University Library.

[488]

but I've brought more work than I can ever manage & I fear me that I'll be at the desk more than the beach or tennis court.

I pray that you are well, beloved Agnes.

ADLAI

P.S. And what of Eugene? I hope sea, sand & wind are good for him too!

While Stevenson was on his vacation, he completed reading the biography by Kenneth S. Davis, A Prophet in His Own Country: The Triumphs and Defeats of Adlai E. Stevenson. *Unfortunately, the galley proofs with Stevenson's marginal comments were destroyed by the publishers, Doubleday & Company.*

To Carol Evans[163]

February [March] 11, 1957

Carol —

Here's some more. So far this is where my vacation has gone! I hope it proves to have been worthwhile. The book seems to me on the whole good except for the inevitable imbalances of one whose information is entirely second hand.

Best.

AES

Leaving today for a three day visit to Dominica — & I'll drag the mss along!

Stevenson sent the following message to the Decalogue Society of Lawyers, a group founded in Chicago in 1934 for lawyers of the Jewish faith.

To the Decalogue Society of Lawyers

March 14, 1957

I greatly regret being out of the country upon the occasion of the Society's recognition of President Sparling's[164] extraordinary contribution to democracy's cause.

To realize that democracy's roots are more important than its foliage, that men are equal only if in their youth they have equal opportunity,

---

[163] This handwritten letter is in the possession of Miss Evans.

[164] Edward J. Sparling, founder and president of Roosevelt College in Chicago.

that tomorrow will be only what our young people, *all* of them, learn today — to realize these things is to know how essential an institution is Roosevelt University. And to know the University's almost unbelievable story is to find new encouragement in the capacity of a man to build almost single-handed new mansions for democracy's soul.

This award does great honor to both Jim Sparling and the Decalogue Society.

Mrs. Eugene Meyer wrote that the Gridiron Club speech was provocative, witty, and entertaining but, she felt, there was a "note of bitterness" concealed between the lines. She urged Stevenson to plunge into law work when he returned to Chicago and observed that physically, mentally, and emotionally he was younger than most men of forty. He had to use his talents, she wrote, in such a way that he would be better understood at home and abroad. Stevenson replied on his return to the Trees' Barbados home from his visit to Dominica.

To Mrs. Eugene Meyer[165]

March 15, 1957

Agnes dear —

We returned to *this* dream world late last night after 3 incredible days in the 18th century. I didn't know it was possible so close to home, but *now* I've been to *Dominica!!*

Your letter awaited me — and this one I will post *myself* — if I have to go all the way to town to do it! — to be sure you get it promptly.

I was disturbed by the note of "bitterness" you detected in the Gridiron speech. I have heard this before & it troubles me. I was trying NOT to sound that way, and yet say something worth saying to the gentlemen of the press, instead of the usual flattering banalities. I guess it was a mistake to attempt it — at least for me.

I yearn to see your letter & wish Miss Evans had sent it to me. I believe, beloved Agnes, that *you* DO know *"who I am and will be."* But I'm not the least troubled about the "Country knowing too" — altho I am intensely eager to know MYSELF!!! Ive been trying to think about it all a little down here, but the press of other work and things to do have frustrated conclusions. I've been struggling to read & correct the interminable biography that Doubleday is determined to publish this

[165] This handwritten letter is in the Agnes Meyer files, Princeton University Library.

spring. My time has run out and I've neglected the wretched chore until I'm a little frantic. But why do I worry about *what* they say??

I should know that *you* are "bursting with health," & so am I — at least *bursting*, I fear! And I want to see you in N.Y. The planes go only 3 times a week. My plan is to fly up on the 26th [of March]. That evening I was going to meet my 3 Chicago partners and reach final conclusions about merger with a large New York law firm — a deal that has been pending since the election. We met in N.Y. on the way down and agreed to meet again, when everyone (about a dozen involved) returned from vacation, at the Century Club on the 27th. That night I *must* return to Chicago to meet John Fell. The trial of the truck driver who ran into him Christmas a year ago & killed two of his friends commences at that time. (I dread the idea that he has to relive that tragedy on a witness stand in Indiana & have tried to persuade the judge & prosecutor to drop it all!)

If you are in N.Y. at the St. Regis on the *night of the 26th* & not engaged I'll try to somehow extricate myself and come to see you. I do so hope it will be possible but I know you'll understand, too, if things get too thick for me. I'll telephone in any event — just in case you're there —

With much, much love from a brown beach comber —

ADLAI

To Carol Evans[166]

March 15, 1957

Dear Carol —

Please get this to Ken Davis promptly.

Also please send me my yellow vaccination and health certificate promptly. I suppose it is put away with my passport in your files. I got into Barbados OK without it, but might have trouble getting back into the USA. It might be in my box at the bank, tho I can hardly see why.

This is the perfect place for my "rest" — and there might even be some if it wasn't for this book etc. etc. etc!!!

I pray that everything is OK at home and at the office and in another few days of this sun and surf I may even stop worrying about everything and every body — I hope!

Yrs
AES

---

[166] This handwritten letter is in the possession of Miss Evans.

To Kenneth S. Davis[167]

March 19, 1957

Dear Ken —

Herewith the last of the mss — and with it my apologies. Somehow I have found reading about myself a harder task than I had foreseen, in spite of all your grace and charity!! Hence the long delays, the fits and starts — and also the compulsion that has grown as I progressed to alter as well as correct with shameless egoism.

You know how many interruptions there have been and how hard I have found it to meet your deadlines; for that you will forgive me. As to the "corrections" — well you will use them or not as you wish and you will note that I became more & more insensitive to the niceties as I went along and have mostly just written or suggested what I liked, for you to take or reject as you wish.

I am, frankly, amazed that you could have done as good a book with as little time with me personally — the meagre amount of that time I've tried to suggest at least in the attached correction to your admirable foreword.

You wrote me once that the process of writing about a living man is an exercise in "bad taste." After reading this — at long, long last! — I can fully perceive the difficulty of the biographer, but I suspect the "bad taste" has been more mine than yours. And having already ravaged the standards, I'll add a few general comments taken from scribbles on a pad as I went along with the reading — for what they may be worth at this late date.

1. As long as I can remember I have read, read, read — anything, everything — at every waking instant — streetcars, taxis, trains, planes — even elevators & toilets! And I have never caught up! I have not "just talked" with people very much, I fear, have never played bridge or time consuming games; for 30 years or more I have found myself restless at the movies, except in rare cases, altho I love the theatre and music — concerts & opera. The price I have paid in the sacrifice of these satisfactions — literature and music — due to the exactions of work for the past 17 years, I mourn.

2. My fascination with public affairs — at home and abroad — must date from infancy, or almost! And in a curious inverted sort of way, [I] have never found my own affairs quite as absorbing. Law, business, profit, *making* money, have never interested me as much as impersonal public affairs, or as much perhaps as they should. Maybe that's one

---

[167] This handwritten letter is in the possession of Mr. Davis.

reason why I seem to have tried to *save* money, having so little time or hope of *making* it!

3. A few days after Pearl Harbor I asked Frank Knox — orally and by letter — for a commission. I felt with everyone rushing into uniform that I didn't want to go thru the war as a civilian even tho I was not vulnerable to the draft. He agreed to do so if I insisted, but asked me not to on the ground that my utility, *to* HIM *at least*, would be limited by my rank if in uniform & he couldn't properly give me, nor would I want, an admiral or captain's grade thus violating all the rules we had ourselves established for reserve officers.

I wrote or edited most of Knox's formal speeches, articles statements etc. during the war years of his life, and remember speaking before the Town Hall in L.A.[168] in 1952 just 10 yrs. after I had been there in the *same room* in the Biltmore hotel with Knox. I said this to the audience & that his speech was better than mine and that I knew what I was talking about — because I wrote both of them!

4. In 1944 in London during the war I spent a long dinner and evening *alone* with Dr. Chaim Weitzman[169] and heard from beginning to end the story of the Jewish national home in Palestine as well as getting to know another of the significant figures of our time. In 1947 as a member of the U.S. delegation to the General Assembly of the UN that year I voted for the partition of Palestine and the creation of Israel in the U.S. delegation, a decision I have never regretted.

5. While Governor, after reorganizing and decontaminating, the State Police in 1949 and giving them the security of tenure and merit advancement, I had an instrument with which I could reliably enforce the gambling laws if the local officials wouldn't. After personal talks with the law enforcement officials of some of the worst counties and plenty of notice to clean house, I started raids by the state police in 1950 for the first time in the history of Illinois. And the first county we hit — Madison — was a Democratic county. Raids continued all over the state until commercialized gambling and slot machines had virtually been eliminated from Illinois. This attracted much press attention at the time.

We also started for the first time rigid enforcement of the laws against overweight trucks which do such damage to our highways.[170]

168 "On Political Morality," delivered in Los Angeles September 11, 1952, in *Major Campaign Speeches of Adlai E. Stevenson, 1952*, with an introduction by the author (New York: Random House, 1953), pp. 100–110.

169 Chaim Weizmann, president of Israel from its founding in 1948 until his death in 1952.

170 For Stevenson's reforms while he was governor of Illinois, see *The Papers of Adlai E. Stevenson*, Vol. III.

6. My book after the 1952 election[171] was republished in a British edition in London, a French edition in Paris and an Italian edition in Rome (Spanish in BA [Buenos Aires], I think!) something theretofore unheard of for a book of contemporary political utterances.

The Look articles of 1953 were reprinted in dozens of magazines and newspapers from India to So. Am.

Call to Greatness[172] likewise had an English edition and was republished in serial or pamphlet form in many languages. These and other writings, as well as the campaigns themselves, account for the wide acquaintance, influence and correspondence I seem to have all over — even Barbados!!

7. I was very pleased when Pres. [Harold W.] Dodds notified me that Princeton was awarding me an Honorary LLD in June 1953. But I was in Asia & couldn't be there to receive it, so I was gratified when it was reawarded in 1954.[173] It was at about that time, too, I think that I made one of the principal speeches at Columbia University's bicentennial ceremony — the theme of which was Man's Right to Knowledge and the Free Use Thereof (?).[174] I think it was a good speech and I know it was a great ovation — at Gen. Eisenhower's Univ! That autumn — just before the Congressi[on]al elections — I was awarded an honorary LLD by Columbia[175] — along with Queen Mary,[176] Chancellor Adenhauer,[177] & Chief Justice Warren in the Cathedral of St. John the Divine in the most impressive academic ceremony I've ever seen —

8. While I think the book brings it out, the essence of the campaign of '56 was *Truth* — as I saw it. We owe the people the truth about their affairs or they can't make intelligent decisions; and the Reps [Republicans] have not told them the truth, the whole truth, rather they have lulled them to sleep etc etc.

[171] *Major Campaign Speeches of Adlai E. Stevenson, 1952.*

[172] The published text of Stevenson's Godkin lectures at Harvard University (New York: Harper, 1954; Atheneum, 1962), reprinted in *The Papers of Adlai E. Stevenson*, Vol. V, pp. 433–489.

[173] Stevenson received an honorary LL.D. from Princeton in June, 1954. See the New York *Times*, June 16, 1954.

[174] Stevenson gave this address at Columbia on June 5, 1954. It is reprinted with the title "The American Vision" in Adlai E. Stevenson, *What I Think* (New York: Harper, 1956), pp. 47–55; *The Papers of Adlai E. Stevenson*, Vol. IV, pp. 369–376.

[175] Stevenson received his degree from Columbia in October, 1954, together with many other notables, including the persons he mentions here, UN Secretary-General Dag Hammarskjöld, and Archibald MacLeish. See the New York *Times*, November 1, 1954.

[176] Stevenson is in error. The degree was awarded to Queen Elizabeth, the Queen Mother. Queen Mary had died in 1953.

[177] West German Chancellor Konrad Adenauer.

With supporters in Long Beach, California.

Campaign rally in California.

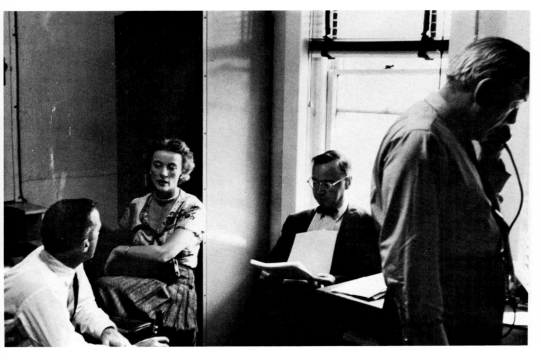

1956 campaign aides, from left to right: Bill Blair, Marietta Tree,
Arthur M. Schlesinger, Jr., and campaign manager Jim Finnegan.

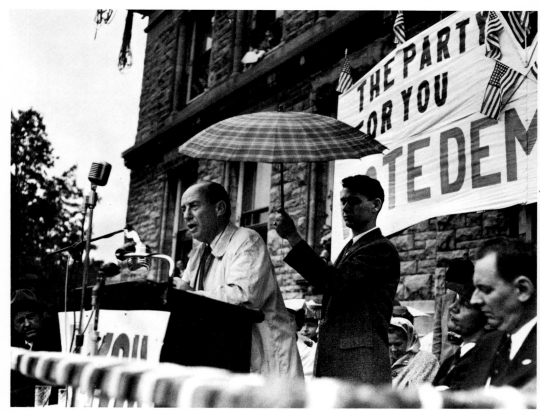

Campaigning at Fayette County Courthouse in Kentucky, October, 1956.

With Eleanor Roosevelt after his October, 1956,
speech at Madison Square Garden, New York.

Campaign motorcade in Lexington, Kentucky.

With John Fell in Providence, Rhode Island.

1956 photo that was used extensively
on campaign posters.

But the visitors are waiting — also the sea — also lunch — also in the gentle West Indian phrase — sleep is stealing me away —   .

Thank you, dear friend, for your infinite kindness, courtesy and patience — and the devotion of your extraordinary & perceptive talents to this unworthy task! I wish I had been more helpful; and I have no doubt that my vanity will be presently unendurable!

Affectionate regards to Flo[178] — and I pray that you both are well — and busy!

ADLAI E. S.

While flying from Barbados to New York City, Stevenson wrote the following letter to his hosts.

To Mr. and Mrs. Ronald Tree[179]

March 26, 1957

My dear, dear Trees —

The West Indian reverie envelops me still — even at 18,000 feet and in spite of the adjoining lady from New Caanan, Conn. (Why is it I meet so many people from New Caanan, Conn. — and why do they always start with an apology for *not* voting for me?). Reflecting comfortably, aimlessly and *very* slowly on recent events I felt something very funny and sentimental coming on about Trees, trees and God's Trees. Fortunately, it didn't *come* very far, despite yesterday's [illegible] and oratorical provocations at the community center and the close proximity of Rev. Canon Johnson.[180]

But, *un*fortunately, this lament and farewell to Barbados *did* come on, as I thought of what lay behind me, of what lies in *front* — and of Dr. Laycock[181] lying on the *floor* deriding!

> Back, back across the sunlit sea,
> Where the scented Bermanthies ride,
> — And the gay, good Trees preside!
> To the distant, chill and gloomy lea,
> Where the pale Vermanthies reside
> — and idylls sweet, with fate collide!

178 Mrs. Davis.
179 This handwritten letter is in the possession of Mrs. Tree.
180 Mrs. Tree explains that this refers to the opening of the local community center in St. James's Parish the day before Stevenson left Barbados, at which Mr. Johnson, the minister, presided and Mr. Tree made a short speech. Letter to Carol Evans, November 29, 1971.
181 A. C. Leacock, a surgeon in Barbados who was a friend of the Trees.

To lament the end of the idyll, is I suppose a way of saying how much I enjoyed it and how grateful I am for it. But more than a good time and a perfect holiday — at long last! — it was *good* for me. My woes I forgot, my work I neglected; and certainly I am brown, baked, peach-fed and rum soaked, in short, edible! — or as close to that happy state as such an unpalatable old buzzard is likely to get!

For all these blessings I thank you, my dear friends, and for more besides. You have also taught me much about another region of the world. And where else, how else, could the panorama of its personalities unfold so happily and so completely as among the subtle suburbs of Heron Beach — its lord, its lady — and its rum punch!

But most of all I loved the journeys into the past at Dominica and St. Vincent. I know few places where you can hurdle generations of time so quickly, so painlessly — by magic carpet, or, rather, magic goose! And, like all adventures that cling to the heart and head, companions are integral, for they enrich the colors, illumine the scenes, and enliven the memories of both.

So, thanks too, for good companions! I could have no better!

The dimensions of my gratitude are large — good health, good spirits, good friends — even a little learning. So if the proper purpose of man is life, liberty and the pursuit of happiness I feel ready again on all counts — even for the "happiness of pursuit"!

Thanks and blessings from your grateful debtor —

ADLAI

Stevenson returned to Chicago on March 27, 1957.

To Mrs. Eugene Meyer[182]

March 28, 1957

Agnes dear —

I thought we had a date in N.Y. for Tues. night the 26th — so picture my relief when I arrived 5 hours late, after being turned back 2 hours north of San Juan, to find that you were *not* pacing the floor at the St. Regis and pouring imprecations on my very unprotected and also innocent head — and, indeed, had "checked out."

But I was distressed that we had missed again. I wanted to see you and also show off my achie[ve]ments in my tropical trance — brown, baked corn fed, rum soaked, but hardly edible I fear!

That — my fine, healthy camouflage — was about my only achieve-

[182] This handwritten letter is in the Agnes Meyer files, Princeton University Library.

ment, however. Of writing there was none; of thinking almost *less!* But there was some editing, or rather correcting, of a rather frightening book about me that Doubleday is publishing this summer.

And now to the office — for the first time in 6 weeks! Reality has triumphed again!!

Much much love

ADLAI

Robert Yoakum, a New York businessman, sent Stevenson a pro-spectus about a new type of magazine that he was trying to launch.

To Robert H. Yoakum

March 28, 1957

Dear Mr. Yoakum:

I was very much interested in your letter which was forwarded to me in the West Indies. I hope for an early opportunity to talk with you about this interesting project. I am sure the country is in serious need of honest, objective reporting, and I applaud your effort in that direction. I have noticed with alarm so often, and again on my recent journey, the extent of the reliance on Time magazine outside of this country for information about us.

I only wish I was more optimistic about the financing possibility for a project such as you have undertaken.

Sincerely yours,

To Florence Mahoney

March 29, 1957

My beloved Florence:

I am back — brown, baked, peach-fed, and sun-soaked — but not quite edible yet!

I find your notes and I wish I were right there — even taking the after dinner treatment.[183] I am afraid it has been grossly neglected and that what I need is more Mahoney — both kinds — kind and cruel.

Blessings.

P.S. I have written a nice little blurb for Locke's book.[184] What a remarkable man!

---

[183] The reducing exercises prescribed by Mrs. Mahoney. See Stevenson's letter to Mrs. Ronald Tree of February 20, 1957, p. 474.

[184] Walter Locke, *This Is My World* (Yellow Springs, Ohio: Antioch Press, 1957).

Stevenson was a member of the board of directors of the Field Foundation. He and others had been discussing the possibility of buying the Chicago Sun-Times. *It came to naught and Field Enterprises bought John Knight's Chicago* Daily News.

To Allen Kander[185]

March 29, 1957

Dear Allen:

I am back in Chicago after a long deferred holiday and find your note. I may know more about the situation after the Field Foundation meeting in New York the end of the month. My impression is that the logic of the competitive situation seems to be pointing toward some joinder of the Field and Knight interests, although I cannot see much personal satisfaction in such a fate for the Sun-Times and Marshall [Field], Senior's ambitions for a truly liberal and good paper.[186]

We shall have a talk before too long, I hope.

Cordially,

To T. S. Matthews

March 29, 1957

Dear Tom:

I have been away and have only now reached Chicago and begun to unravel my tangled affairs. I have just dictated a series of letters after talking with Bill Blair about my horrible schedule. The net of it is that I have accepted Mr. Deakin's[187] and Mr. Waldock's[188] invitation to Oxford for Friday, May 24.[189] (Now get to work and write the greatest speech of the 20th Century that will sometime be engraved in stone over a monument to Anglo-American unity and scholarship!)

As for my beloved friend, I find it difficult to give you an evening. As to Martha,[190] I have no difficulty in suggesting Wednesday, May 22. I

---

[185] Founder and president of Allen Kander & Co., a newspaper brokerage in Washington, D.C.

[186] Actually, several years before his death in November, 1956, Marshall Field III had turned over control of the *Sun-Times*, which he had founded, to his son Marshall Field IV, who had supported Eisenhower in 1952.

[187] William Deakin, warden of St. Anthony's College, Oxford.

[188] Sir Humphrey Waldock, professor of public international law and fellow of All Souls College, Oxford.

[189] Stevenson received an honorary Doctor of Civil Law degree from Oxford University and became an honorary fellow of All Souls College on May 25, 1957. See *The Papers of Adlai E. Stevenson*, Vol. VII.

[190] Mrs. Matthews.

arrive late on Tuesday, May 21, from Brussels — I think!!! I shall hope in your drawing room to be thoroughly briefed and fully prepared for my bold invasion of Oxford.

But let me hurriedly inform you that Adlai and Nancy will not be with me. I expect to meet them later in Rome for my journey through Africa (why don't you and Martha come with us?).

As to people in after dinner, of course I have no objection; indeed I am flattered that you care to exhibit an unsuccessful American politician.

As to the Gridiron speech — yes, I think I salvaged a phrase or so. It was not a very good speech, probably because I didn't salvage more. At all events, a copy is enclosed but reading it is not compulsory.

The least I can do now is to apologize for causing everyone so much trouble. I only wish I could erase the trouble with the apology.

Yours,

P.S. And send your draft promptly; or if not a draft your suggestions.

Doris Fleeson wrote in her column that Stevenson's Gridiron Club speech, in which he indicted the press for playing along with Eisenhower's peace and prosperity campaign although it knew the actual truth, "has set Washington on its ear. . . . The rapier, they[191] protest, is an acceptable weapon, but not the surgeon's knife." She concluded by saying that Stevenson "honestly believes that unless the partisan Republican attitudes he detects in the public-opinion field can be broken up, no Democrat can again be elected President, short of a catastrophe like the last depression."[192] In a letter to Stevenson Miss Fleeson remarked that some reporters did not like the speech because "reporters notoriously can dish it out but can't take it."

To Doris Fleeson[193]

April 1, 1957

Dear Doris:

Thanks for your nice letter, which I find on my return from a journey to the 19th Century in the West Indies.

I shall look forward to seeing you in Washington on the next trip. Meanwhile, I enclose an item which I find on my desk that may be of

191 Members of the Gridiron Club.
192 Chicago *Daily News*, March 7, 1957.
193 The original is in the possession of Miss Fleeson.

interest to your sharp eye and relentless spirit. I think the accuracy can be relied upon.

I am disappointed that the Gridiron speech was unpopular with my audience. I thought it light and friendly, with only enough depth at the end to save it from froth, and sharpness to keep the torpid livers active.

That it would sound bitter disappoints me. Actually, I think that the first danger to the Gridiron is that the speaking become an exchange of benign and graceful pleasantries, *a faire* highly esteemed these days, I gather. Long may you wave!

Yours,
ADLAI

To Lady Mary Spears[194]

April 1, 1957

My dear Mary:

So many thanks for your good letter, which welcomed me home from a holiday with Ronnie and Marietta Tree in Barbados. I find some satisfaction in watching the chickens returning to roost since the election, but none in the deplorable state of our relations and the alarming indifference of most Americans including, it would sometimes appear, the President himself.

I fear that we never made the emptiness of the so-called Eisenhower doctrine apparent, but certainly the absurdity of the impetuous demand for its enactment in the special message, asking for authority to do what he was already authorized to do, and indeed what we had been doing for ten years, penetrated a few more of our receptive journalistic minds by the time the debate concluded.

I am coming to England on business for a few days, arriving about the 22nd of May and leaving the first of June or thereabouts. I suspect I shall have to make an appearance before the English Speaking Union and may have committed myself to a "lecture" at Oxford. Horrors! I will be staying at Claridge's and we shall certainly foregather for something, probably lunch, during my stay. I am afraid the week-ends are committed, what with business, politics, etc.

Adlai and Nancy are joining me in Rome and are going with me through Africa on a business trip which takes me by way of Ghana in late June.

Ellen[195] has been "quiet" of late so far as I know. John Fell is home

---

[194] This letter was in the possession of General Sir Louis Spears until his death on January 27, 1974. His correspondence is now in the possession of Churchill College, Cambridge University.

[195] The former Mrs. Stevenson.

with me now for a hasty holiday and I shall probably have a fuller report in the course of the next few days. On the whole, with the political temperature down, hers appears to be too.

With much love,

ADLAI

To Cass Canfield

April 1, 1957

Dear Cass:

I have your note of March 28, and I am sure we can do the comparison of the manuscript with the reading copies of the material to be included in the book[196] here in the office. I am asking Miss Roxane Eberlein[197] and Frances Martin (Mrs. John B. Martin) to undertake this job.

As to my introduction, well, not a word has emerged, or even an idea, and I am mortified and anxious. Somehow, my life even on an alleged holiday seems to have more in it than I could manage.

Yours,

To Roxane Eberlein and Frances Martin

April 1, 1957

I hope I can have an opportunity to talk to you both at an early date about helping me with the comparison of the material to be included in the 1956 campaign volume with the reading texts here in the files. I have promised the editors (Schlesinger and Harris at Harvard) and the publishers that we could do the work here. If we can't do it they will have to send someone out who will be quite unfamiliar with the materials.

I wonder if I can count on you two to do it with my help whenever needed.

A.E.S.

Former Vice President Alben Barkley had died on April 30, 1956. His widow sent Stevenson a letter her husband wrote him on January 23, 1956, but never mailed. She asked Stevenson if he minded if the University of Kentucky Library, where her husband's papers had been sent, released the letter.

---

196 *The New America.*
197 Secretary and researcher in Stevenson's office.

To Mrs. Alben W. Barkley

April 2, 1957

Dear Jane:

I was delighted to have your letter and the enclosure. It is, as you say, charming, gracious and also an astute letter. To beware of Senator Kefauver's campaigning capacity, and also to try to simplify my speeches and presentation, was as sound advice as I could have had at that time.

Feel quite free to give it to the University of Kentucky for any purpose as far as I am concerned. It fills me with a host of memories, all happy and thankful, that I knew and enjoyed the friendship and confidence of this remarkable man — and his beloved Jane!

I hope that we shall meet soon, and I am so grateful for your thought of me.

Affectionately,

To Claude Rice[198]

April 2, 1957

Dear Claude:

One of the burdens of being a national candidate is that it takes so long after the event to answer so many letters from people I don't know. This, together with starting up my law practice which was somewhat moribund to say the least, in 1956, together with a long delayed vacation I have just returned from this week, explains my delay in writing to you. Now at long last I am able properly to thank the people who worked the hardest for me during the campaign.

When I fly into one of our cities these days and come off the plane I half expect to see your face at the door, waiting to tell me what to do, where to go and whose hand I should shake. You would be surprised at how difficult it is for me these days to get around town like a normal American.

I am comforted in the knowledge that many of the things we fought for will ultimately prevail, as long as we can keep the Democratic Party on its liberal course.

Good luck and be sure to let me know when you come this way.

Cordially,

P.S. I am enclosing a copy of a speech I gave in San Francisco recently and also the Gridiron speech in Washington. Perhaps the most remark-

---

[198] An advance man for Stevenson during the 1956 campaign.

able thing about both of them is that they were completed 24 hours ahead of time!

AES

To Adlai E. Stevenson III

April 4, 1957

Dear Bear:

. . . While in Barbados visiting the Trees I talked about our trip to Africa and now Mr. and Mrs. Tree and her daughter Frances[199] (age 16) say they want to join us. I wish you would let me know how you feel about this promptly. Bill Blair seems to be for it, and I certainly have no objection although I am afraid it will complicate the traveling a little bit, as seven is a fairly unwieldy number. I can still call them off. . . . Their interest is serious because of their involvement in the race problem, he in the West Indies and she in New York.

It seems not unlikely that I will have to make a lecture at Oxford on May 24, and may be awarded an honorary degree (this in utmost confidence!). As this would be a most unusual recognition and the ceremony (if it takes place!) very colorful, I am wondering if perhaps you would like to fly direct to England in time to join me at Oxford and go from there to Rome after Oxford and a week-end, perhaps at Hatfield, Lord Salisbury's famous ancestral house where Queen Elizabeth I was imprisoned as a girl by Henry VIII.

But I don't want to interfere with your plans, and perhaps it would be better to defer any decision on this until I am certain about the degree. But perhaps a look at Madrid and Rome would be more worth while.

Hastily,

To Sir Ernest Oppenheimer[200]

April 4, 1957

My dear Sir Ernest:

Following a business trip to London the end of May, I expect to travel through South and West Africa with my son and daughter-in-law and some friends during the month of June. I had hoped to see you and Lady Oppenheimer during the course of my visit to Johannesburg in early June, but I understand from my friend, Maurice Tempelsman,[201]

---

[199] Frances FitzGerald, Mrs. Tree's daughter by her previous marriage.
[200] Founder and chairman of the Anglo-American Corporation of South Africa, Ltd., and other mining companies in Africa.
[201] A dealer in industrial diamonds and one of Stevenson's legal clients.

that you are going to be in England at that time. He also informs me that the Anglo-American Company is opening a new office building in London late in May.

Since I shall be there from about May 20 until I leave for Johannesburg on June 3rd, I will hope that I may interrupt your busy schedule for a moment at that time.

I was glad to hear from Tempelsman that your health is excellent.

With warm regards, I am

Cordially,

To the Reverend Alan Geyer[202]

April 4, 1957

Dear Mr. Geyer:

I was delighted to have your letter and deeply touched by your gracious expressions of confidence.[203]

Somehow your wonderful letter reminds me of the classic and irreverent remark (was it Max Beerbohm?) who said that he always liked flattery if it was fulsome enough!

But I know your flattery was intended and I am deeply grateful for not only your kindness to me but your perception of some of our current frailties which I have been able to do all too little about. Certainly one of the worst is the appalling self-righteousness and spurious religiosity of so much of our politics. Why its recent manifestations have not nauseated more of us I don't know, but I am certain that what you aptly call "our moralistic superiority complex in world affairs" has been not only transparent abroad but highly aggravating and unprofitable. I have never been wholly confident that God and virtue carry any nation's flag or are confined by any boundaries. But I like to think that realism and perception are increasing and that truth will triumph over fraud every time — given time!

It was awfully good of you to write me and I look forward to something more satisfying than a handshake.

Cordially yours,

Senator Hubert Humphrey wrote that he had placed Stevenson's "magnificent" San Francisco speech in the Congressional Record.

---

[202] A Methodist clergyman and doctoral candidate in the Boston University School of Theology; later Dag Hammarskjöld Professor of Peace Studies at Colgate University.

[203] The editors do not have a copy of Mr. Geyer's letter.

To Hubert H. Humphrey

April 4, 1957

Dear Hubert:

So many thanks for your letter which I find on my return from the blue seas, golden strands and green mountains of the Caribbean. There we talked much of you and our hope for the Democratic party. But somehow I can't recall much moaning about the fact that you were in travail in wind, rain and snow and ours was a painless, gentle languor interrupted only by rum punches.

I am glad you thought well of the Gridiron effort. I gather it was cordially disliked by some of the audience. But I wonder if good will in exchange of pleasant amenities and banalities is worth winning.

I shall be in Washington for the party affair early in May[204] and will hope for a moment with you then at least.

Affectionate regards to Muriel.[205]

Cordially yours,

To Dean Acheson

April 4, 1957

Dear Dean:

I am just back from a long journey and hear that you are going to preside at the Democratic fiesta in May. I am delighted to hear it.

Some of our mutual friends also tell me you are reluctant to do television appearances for some reason. I hope this is not the case. I can think of no one who could reinforce the attack on these characters better than yourself.

I look forward to seeing you.

Love to Alice.[206]

Yours,

Stevenson's friend and former law partner James F. Oates, Jr., was elected president and chief executive officer of the Equitable Life Assurance Society of the United States on April 1, 1957.

---

[204] Stevenson was to attend a meeting of the Democratic Advisory Council and speak at a fund-raising dinner of the Democratic National Committee on May 4, 1957.
[205] Mrs. Humphrey.
[206] Mrs. Acheson.

To James F. Oates, Jr.

April 4, 1957

Dear Jim:

Your news — which is certainly the most spectacular of the season! — fills me with memories of the many years of your "good life." I was thinking about it on the train coming back from Elkhart [Indiana] yesterday:[207] that there is no one among my acquaintances who has, I think, had any better life if it is measured by the satisfactions of children, marriage, home, and achievement. But it is not of such awkward things that I would propose to talk. Rather it is of the future and what it has in store for you and Rosalind.[208] I hope some time when you have a spare luncheon hour you will let me know.

With heartfelt wishes, I am

Yours,

Lieutenant Colonel C. J. George, aide to General George C. Marshall, wrote that he had just visited with the Marshalls at Pinehurst, North Carolina, and the general had asked him to carry his regards to Stevenson.

To Lieutenant Colonel C. J. George

April 5, 1957

My dear Colonel:

I am so grateful for your letter of March 29 with all the news about the Marshalls. You know how profound my affection and respect is for the General and Mrs. Marshall, and the news you bring me is reassuring.

I had fully expected to be with my sister in Southern Pines some time this winter or spring and had looked forward to another one of those precious evenings which I count among the most memorable incidents of late years. Unhappily, circumstances have forbidden a journey to Southern Pines, and I shall have to defer a visit with the Marshalls, but you may be sure I will seize the first opportunity.

Meanwhile, please give them my most affectionate and devoted respect.

Cordially,

---

[207] Stevenson had attended the trial resulting from the automobile accident of December, 1955, in which his son John Fell had been injured.
[208] Mrs. Oates.

[*506*]

To Sir Robert Jackson

April 5, 1957

Dear Robert:

The Edison Dicks and I had a gay evening with Barbara[209] on her way West. Having carried the light to the rim of the Pacific, she is returning East and we hope to intercept her for a few hours between planes this very day. She seemed well and gay and entirely recovered from the anxious and wan traveller I encountered on her arrival the first of February. She has told me you are in London, en route to this country, and I am taking the liberty of sending this letter to you with the hope that you may have a chance to read it and that we can confer about it, at least by telephone, while you are here.

After returning from a holiday in the West Indies the other day I talked to my diamond friends in New York about your excellent memorandum. It discloses that there are a number of companies engaged in the mining of diamonds, and also four firms licensed by the Ghana government to buy diamonds through the government diamond market in Accra. My friends tell me that the law governing the issue of these licenses provides for a total of five, and that one, therefore, is still available, for which they are most anxious to qualify in accordance with the government's regulations about paid in capital and credit facilities. They are in a position to comply with all the requirements outlined in the memorandum you were good enough to send me and are anxious to communicate to the Ghana government as promptly as possible some indication of their interest in obtaining this license. But I am at a loss as to how they should proceed in making this approach to the Ghana government. I am confident that the latter would or should be interested in the company these people would organize because it would be not only a competent purchaser, prepared to meet prices paid by other licensees, but in addition it has manufacturing operations which provide a stable and continuous demand to support a purchasing program in the Gold Coast which would be stable and immune from very rapid market fluctuations. Moreover, they are prepared to provide the necessary supervisory personnel and to commence operations promptly after the license has been granted. They also indicate an anxiety to train and employ local personnel whenever possible.

I suppose that they should be advised to employ local counsel in Accra to help them, but I don't know whom or what to suggest in this connection. And it has occurred to me that perhaps the gentleman on your staff who was good enough to prepare the most helpful memo-

---

[209] Lady Jackson.

[507]

randum would have some advice to offer in connection with all of the foregoing. I will be in Accra myself on the way back from South Africa toward the end of June and could follow through then with any steps that were indicated. You will know best whether it would be desirable to forward this letter to your staff associate in Accra who could communicate with me direct or to await your own return.

At all events, I hope when you are here you will telephone me, collect, at Financial 6-5180, or, if it is in the evening, at home, Libertyville 2-4466. It is not unlikely that I may want a moment of your time while you are here for my friends from Reynolds Metals Company. They have evidently been talking with a Dr. Stein, who produced timber in the Gold Coast, and he is confident that he could obtain mining leases from the chiefta[i]ns covering the bauxite deposits in the interior which the Prime Minister and the government would respect. In short, I think they are interested in exploring the possibilities of access to bauxite in the Gold Coast, and if my recollection serves me, the Prime Minister[210] and the other officials with whom I talked while visiting there, all indicated that more American industries and investments would be welcome in Ghana.[211]

I must not prolong this further.

Cordially,

To Herbert Agar

April 5, 1957

Dear Herbert:

I have been in California, Arizona, Washington, New York, Barbados, Dominica, St. Vincent — and Elkhart, Indiana. The foregoing erratic travel accounts for the fact that only now is my schedule beginning to take some form. I presently plan to arrive in England with my assistant, Bill Blair, from Paris or Brussels about the 22nd of May and leave for Rome and South Africa on June 3.

As best I can make out, the present *tentative* schedule contemplates a "lecture" — horrors! — at Rhodes House, Oxford, under the sponsorship of Professor Waldock on Friday, May 24, and a reception and some brief remarks at the English Speaking Union on Monday, May 27. I will have a number of business engagements in the interval and have committed myself to several evenings, one with Geoffrey Crowther, one with

210 Kwame Nkrumah.
211 Stevenson had visited the Gold Coast in 1955, before its independence and change of name to Ghana. See *The Papers of Adlai E. Stevenson,* Vol. IV, pp. 486–487.

Tom Matthews, one with Hamish Hamilton and one with Bill Benton, etc. I think I would like very much to spend the week-end of June 1 with you and Barbie[212] before my departure. I wish it could be more of a visit and another time I shall plan to stay longer in England with nothing to do but see my friends and something of England. That I have been there so many times since the age of eleven and know so little of the countryside aggravates me.

Due to an almost constant domestic crisis in my neglected bachelor home, I am almost tempted to ask Barbie to line up some British couples who might come to our country as domestic servants! But I will not impose that upon her, and surrender to the fortunes of the local market.

With affectionate regards to you both, I am

Cordially,

Adlai Stevenson III wrote to Newton Minow on April 7, 1957, "At the moment I don't look forward to the practice [of law] with much relish." Minow showed it to Stevenson, commenting, "He's beginning to sound like his father!" Stevenson scribbled on the note:

Isn't this the low period! I went to Russia!![213]

Professor Allan Nevins, in outlining the events that led to the Middle East crisis, observed that he was outraged by the lack of foresight, clumsiness, and disingenuousness on the part of Secretary of State Dulles and President Eisenhower. He concluded his letter by saying he was concentrating on writing his four volumes covering Lincoln's Administration.

To Allan Nevins

April 8, 1957

My dear Allan:

I was away in the West Indies when your letter of March 15 arrived. How I wish I had written that perfect summary of the Middle East record of the past few years! And how I wish I had used it in a speech

---

[212] Mrs. Agar.

[213] This letter is in the possession of Mr. Minow. For Stevenson's trip to Russia in 1926, shortly after he passed the Illinois bar examination, see *The Papers of Adlai E. Stevenson*, Vol. I, pp. 167–169; Davis, *A Prophet in His Own Country*, pp. 153–159. Stevenson himself referred to this trip as "one last fling" at journalism before embarking on his intermittent law career as a law clerk in the prestigious Chicago firm of Cutting, Moore and Sidley.

when it would have done some good. I must say you have condensed the sorry story beyond anything I have seen, let alone written.

And now the incredible Secretary of State (I wonder how long it will be before our people and press really realize how dangerously incredible he already is abroad!) tells us that he wisely planned a showdown with Russia by provoking Egypt into seizing the Suez Canal, with consequences that none could foretell, except that they would certainly be bad! I sometimes wonder if I am dreaming. And I listen attentively for the shocked chorus of protest to arise from the American press — in vain.

It all reminds me that I would like to talk to you about the press some time, about the past and future, and how facts and truth can be communicated and evaluated by the people who have to make the decisions in times of such complexity and such massive manipulation techniques.

But, to go back to "our leaders"; I suppose if your gloomy apprehensions are not fulfilled and Nasser falls, it will be another Eisenhower triumph, and many, with a lot of help from the press, will say that he disposed of Nasser as he did of [Senator Joseph] McCarthy, by biding his time shrewdly. I hope this idea that great things are done by doing nothing (when the cost is not counted!) is not as contagious as conformity, complacency and mental lethargy. A man's wrong strategy cannot *always* be righted by the accidents of events he did his best to prevent.

I am so, so grateful for your gallantry in action last fall, and I pray that you are exercising some restraint in the expenditure of your energies. I shall look forward to the volumes on 1861–66 and the sequel to those fine books on the "Emergence of Lincoln."[214]

Please give me an evening, at least, if you pass this way. And please, please pass along from time to time any ideas you may have for things I should say or write. I must go back to the law business now and will have fewer and fewer sources of suggestion on public affairs.

Cordially yours,

To Michael Todd[215]

April 8, 1957

Dear Mr. Todd:

I saw the incredible enchantment called "Around the World in 80 Days" the other night — thanks, I understand, to you!

---

[214] *The Emergence of Lincoln* (2 vols., New York: Scribner's, 1950).

[215] A Broadway and movie producer and codeveloper of the Cinerama and Todd-AO cinematic systems.

I have never been better entertained, and even the advance billing didn't begin to do justice to that delightful melange of nostalgia, of beauty, of gaiety and mirth on all the continents. My companions — Mr. and Mrs. Edison Dick and Barbara Ward (Lady Jackson), were as convulsed and transported as I. They share my gratitude to you.

I remember so well meeting you here with Lloyd Lewis, and then in the Navy Department long ago, and have followed your remarkable fortunes with suspense and now with great satisfaction.

As someone said, "Long may you wave"!

Cordially,

To Mr. and Mrs. Ronald Tree

April 9, 1957

Dear Marietta and Ronnie:

I found on my return from Barbados this letter from Allan Nevins. I think the first two paragraphs about the Middle East are as good a summary as I have seen and will interest you.

Do you know whether Lord Salisbury will be in England on the weekend of May 25–26? I find that I will probably have to speak at Oxford on the evening of Friday, May 24, and I had thought that I might possibly go over to Hatfield on Saturday for the night if I can arrange it conveniently and if, of course, it is entirely convenient for his household.

I hardly know why I am asking all this except that I know you are constantly in touch with him and therefore might know whether he was going to be in England, which would help me to make my plans.

Have you heard Barbara Ward on Dulles, Ike and the UN? After removing the handsome gift wrapping of their lovely prize they found it was a do-it-yourself kit with a couple of parts missing.

Yours,

To James Michael Curley[216]

April 10, 1957

My dear Mr. Curley:

Some time ago you were good enough to send me a record of excerpts from some of your speeches. It came at a time when I was leaving home for a long absence and only now have I unearthed it — and played it!

How kind of you to think of me! I am grateful indeed, and I am

[216] Former mayor of Boston, governor of Massachusetts, and U.S. representative from Massachusetts.

reminded again that seldom has there been heard in our land such eloquence as yours. I am honored to have this record and grateful indeed.

Cordially yours,

To Mrs. Ralph Hines[217]

April 10, 1957

My dear Betty:

I had breakfast the other morning with Joan[218] and found her gay and looking very well indeed — in spite of her spectacular news!

I must say that she is an extraordinarily compact, sensible and enchanting young woman and she must be a great comfort to you. To find someone who is all in one piece and knows where he is going has a contagious and healthy effect on me, and when it is someone as near and dear as Joan it makes me very happy.

She also gave me some good news about your recovery from your misfortune.[219] I pray that she didn't exaggerate.

Love,

To Robert S. Treat[220]

April 10, 1957

Dear Mr. Treat:

My very dear friends, Mr. and Mrs. John Bartlow Martin, tell me that they are entering their daughter Cindy in The Putney School. I am most happy, indeed eager, to report to you my deep affection for this charming little girl whom I have known since infancy. But more important than my affection is my respect for her industry and purposefulness. She is bright as a button and has enchanted me over many years by her devotion to my "causes."

I was for many years a law partner of Edward D. McDougal, whose children went to Putney, and heard much about the school from them. I am so happy to learn that the Martins have chosen it for their daughter too. I am confident you will be very happy with Cindy if she is admitted.

Cordially yours,

---

[217] Sister of Stevenson's former wife.
[218] Mrs. Hines's daughter, Mrs. Harry Thayer.
[219] The editors have been unable to discover what Stevenson refers to.
[220] Director of admissions of the Putney School, Putney, Vermont.

Students in the Junior Democratic Political and Science Club of Washington Heights and Inwood in New York City sent three letters from members remorseful over Stevenson's defeat. He was urged to run again because he had the foresight and vision required. The letters were replete with quotations.

To Members of the JDP&SC of WH&I

April 11, 1957

I am pleased and heartened (to say nothing of heart-warmed!) by the communications of your organization.

The future of the Democratic Party is in good hands, indeed!

Being, as I am, fresh out of Greek quotations to compare with those of your illustrious officers, I must be content with thanking you for your fine comments and pledging to do my best to be worthy of them.

For your encouragement and confidence in me (and that of your "Representative" Parents who are 21 plus), I shall be forever grateful.

Cordially yours,

To Lady Barbara Jackson

April 16, 1957

My dear Barbara:

A letter has come from Mr. Douglas Veale, of the University Registry,[221] informing me that the Hebdomadal Council (My God, what is that!) will confer the honorary degree at five o'clock on the 24th, to be followed by my lecture. So at least that much of the schedule is now clarified, and I thought I would let you know promptly — although it must be quite obvious that my motive is clear: to recover some equilibrium with the extraordinary young lady who is being honored as only one before her by Harvard![222]

Love,

To Sir Douglas Veale

April 16, 1957

My dear Mr. Veale:

I have your letter of April 13 and hope that you will advise the Hebdomadal Council that I will accept with the utmost gratitude the

---

221 Sir Douglas Veale, registrar of Oxford University.
222 Lady Jackson was to receive an honorary Litt.D. degree in June from Harvard University, which had awarded only one other honorary degree to a woman.

degree of Doctor of Civil Law, *honoris causa*, at five o'clock on May 24, prior to the speech I undertook to make at the instance of Mr. Waldock and Mr. Deakin.

The award of an honorary degree by Oxford comes to me as a surprise — a very agreeable one indeed! I hope I shall have an opportunity to express my warm thanks to the Council for this merited[223] recognition.

Cordially yours,

To Janowitz Market[224]

April 16, 1957

Gentlemen:

For some time my household has been trading at your store, and I find it impossible to understand the bills. I am here very little, but my secretary gets statements with the legend "Your account is overdrawn" and giving the amount. Please advise me if you can send me a statement itemizing the items by days instead of the present system of merely a total sum "overdrawn." I shall have to make some arrangement to enable my staff to keep track of my accounts.

Sincerely yours,

To Adlai E. Stevenson III

April 16, 1957

Dear Bear:

Dr. Raymond F. McLain, President of The American University, at Cairo, while recently here, told me he hoped very much you would let him know on your arrival and that he would have somebody help you and Nancy see the sights. I think it might be well to take advantage of his kindness, as a really informed guide can be immensely helpful, as well you know.

I had rather hoped that you might come to England with me first to see your father get an honorary degree at Oxford on the afternoon of May 24, following a lecture to the Oxonians. I can imagine that the prospect of the latter is exhilarating, but the former should certainly be interesting. I suppose I will stay the night at Oxford, and plan to go on the next morning to Cambridge University and have luncheon there with a lot of the professors who write for the Encyclopaedia Britannica. Meanwhile, you and Nancy could be looking around the University,

---

[223] Clearly a typographical error by Stevenson's secretary; he meant "unmerited."
[224] Located in Lake Forest, Illinois.

which you doubtless remember intimately. In the afternoon I had thought to go on to Hatfield, the famous Tudor Estate of the Salisburys, for the week-end, returning to London Sunday night, May 26, or Monday morning, May 27. You could go on that day to Cairo or Rome, as originally planned.

Please don't feel that I am insisting if your other plans seem better, but what a comfort it would be to have someone around on this occasion, and, who knows when you will ever see Oxford and Cambridge again, let alone the incredible Hatfield, which is so full of the memories of Elizabeth I.

Hastily,

P.S. I believe another book about Hatfield and the Salisburys has just been published called "The Queen's Mystery,"[225] or something like that.

To Kwame Nkrumah

April 16, 1957

My dear Mr. Prime Minister:

I have watched from afar and with unmeasured satisfaction the inspiring creation of the new state of Ghana, and I send you and your associates my warmest good wishes. I have already talked with Grantley Adams[226] and others who attended the ceremonies in Accra, and I hope to hear much more about your triumphs — yes, and your troubles — when I visit Ghana toward the end of June. I will hope that your crowded schedule will permit me to pay my respects in person at that time. I will have with me my son and daughter-in-law and some friends who share my admiration and high hopes for your historic achievement.

The principal reason (perhaps excuse would be more accurate!) for my journey to Africa this year is to transact some legal business for some American clients in the Union of South Africa. One of them is also applying for a license to purchase industrial diamonds in the government diamond market in Accra, which happily enables me to come there again. I plan to engage solicitors in Accra to assist me in this matter, and I very much hope that this application will merit the sympathetic consideration of the appropriate Government Departments. This company is one of the largest factors in the industrial diamond business in America and, as a large and growing consumer of industrial diamonds, it could be a useful and stabilizing influence in this industry in Ghana.

[225] The editors have been unable to identify this book.
[226] Chief minister of Barbados.

I confess a personal pleasure in the prospect of participating in some measure in the industrial life of the world's newest free country.

Respectfully yours,

To Trygve Lie[227]

April 16, 1957

My dear Trygve:

I was delighted to have your letter, and I wish I could rearrange my schedule to come to Oslo in May as you suggest. I yearn to refresh my distant recollections of Norway, but I yearn even more to renew my too distant collaboration with you!

Unhappily, there is little I can do in view of the rigidity of my schedule just now. I am assuming [resuming?] the practice of law and I have a number of fixed business engagements in England and thereafter in South and West Africa which will occupy me until mid-July. I had hoped then before returning to this country that I might have a hasty holiday visit in Scandinavia. I am afraid I will have to disappoint the students, therefore, but perhaps they would be still more disappointed if they were to meet me and listen to me! But if I get to Oslo, you may have to listen to me, and I promise to listen to you too.

With my most affectionate regards to you, my dear old friend, and to Mrs. Lie, I am

Cordially,

P.S. . . .

To Walter Reuther

April 16, 1957

Dear Walter:

I have been meaning to write you for the past several days. First, my congratulations on your reelection. That it was hardly a surprise did not diminish my satisfaction.

Next, let me say how delighted I was by your prompt and, as always, vigorous and constructive reaction to the Beck disclosures.[228] I think you did much to salvage a bad situation for labor which could and

---

[227] Former Secretary-General of the United Nations.

[228] Senator John McClellan's committee investigating racketeering in labor unions alleged that David Beck, president of the Teamsters union, had appropriated union funds for his own use. Beck was subsequently indicted and convicted on charges of income tax evasion. See Robert F. Kennedy, *The Enemy Within* (New York: Harper, 1960).

doubtless will be exploited unfairly, but, more importantly, you prescribed for the illness promptly, specifically and ethically.

All good wishes.

Cordially yours,

*Gerald W. Johnson wrote Stevenson that simply warning the country
was futile, but he thought perhaps ridicule could be effective. He complained that Postmaster General Summerfield's request for a deficiency
appropriation after spending his "allowance in the first nine months,
painting the mail-boxes red-white-and-blue" was the last straw.*

To Gerald W. Johnson

April 17, 1957

Dear Gerald:

Gee! I wish I could sit down for a long talk with you. Certainly the
eggheads are weak on ridicule and, for that matter, weak even on just
hollering like hell. And with the press as it is, the "I told you so's" are
hardly audible, and if they are, they are "bad taste" and the utterers
"poor losers." I agree that ridicule is the best weapon, but somehow our
country seems to be so deadly serious that ridicule seems to provoke an
uneasy irritation. Just what's happened to our traditional loud and
boisterous laughter I don't know, but I suspect the Madison Avenue
boys have smeared it. Then probably the ridicule strikes so many where
it hurts — intellectual pride and that sort of thing.

Anyway, whatever the afflictions that Madison Avenue and those
grinning heroes of The Unctious Age have visited upon us, I am for
ridicule and the more irreverent the better. What's more, I am not
against assault and battery, and have been egging on some of my Congressional friends and also the Democratic Advisory Council to have at
'em, let fly and keep flying.

I suppose it is quite clear that to keep the election year budget down
Summerfield, a politician first, deliberately under-budgeted last year
and hence the entirely foreseeable deficiency appropriation. This is
standard practice by Governors of Illinois — Republicans only, of
course! — and is being repeated here on an enormous and quite transparent scale.

I have not unloaded on you lately, but enclosed is my Gridiron
"effort" which I gather the comfortable pundits didn't particularly care
for. Also enclosed are some kind words from a magazine called "Fron-

tier."[229] Who was it said, "I don't mind flattery, as long as it is fulsome"? But this piece touches on what is to me the most significant aspect of any campaign for the Presidency — which candidate and which party informed the people and which misled them.

But I think I detect a rumble of discord in this happy land. Perhaps the tide is turning. Maybe the folks are catching on (see the enclosure re [Secretary of the Treasury George] Humphrey, and much more can be had).

I am going to practice law a little now, and I am off to Europe and Africa for a couple of months in mid-May. In England I must "lecture" at Oxford. God, how I wish I had your ideas about what to say to them about us Americans. As you know, the anti-U.S. feeling is running very high at all levels, but so is the pro-A.E.S. feeling, so much so indeed that Oxford is even awarding an unsuccessful American politician an honorary degree.

I repeat that I need ideas — and even more than that excellent magazine[230] you write for can give me!

Cordially,

Doris Fleeson wrote Stevenson that indeed this was "The Age of Unction."

To Doris Fleeson[231]

April 17, 1957

Dear Doris:

"The Age of Unction!" That's it; you've coined the perfect phrase. My admiration increases — which hardly seems possible.

Yours,

ADLAI

P.S. Joe Clark[232] has considerable material on the gentleman's affairs.[233]

---

[229] *Frontier,* a liberal public affairs magazine, published in Los Angeles, had devoted a number of articles and editorials to the 1956 campaign and to Stevenson in particular, and it endorsed his stand on H-bomb testing. Stevenson probably refers to William R. Allen, "Further Reflections on Stevenson's Defeat" (March, 1957, pp. 5–6, 9), which concluded: "The cost of the 1956 election was not that the Democrats lost a presidential election — there will be other elections in the future. The question is, will there be other Stevensons?"

[230] The *New Republic.*

[231] The original is in the possession of Miss Fleeson.

[232] Senator from Pennsylvania.

[233] On April 1, 1957, Stevenson had sent Miss Fleeson some material on Secretary of the Treasury George Humphrey which had been supplied by Cyrus Eaton.

Stevenson sent the following letter to the president of the American President steamship line and a similar one to the president of the Matson Line.

To George Killion

April 18, 1957

Dear George:

My extremely resourceful son, John Fell (age 21 and a Junior at Harvard, big, strong and self-reliant) has just presented me with a long brief on why he and a friend, Gilbert Butler, should get jobs, if possible, on the "President Polk" sailing from San Francisco June 12 around the world, arriving in New York September 1st. Evidently this idea was not wholly spontaneous and their imaginations have been stimulated by one David Sawyer, who did something similar a couple of years ago.

John Fell has already been around the world once, and he has also travelled abroad, but he has an insatiable urge to see the world before making up his mind what to do with himself after college, together with an active and probably romantic taste for shipping and the sea.

Given these circumstances, his father is both pleased by his enterprise and bewildered as to what to do. So I turn to you, anticipating, however, that union restrictions and other obstacles may be insurmountable. But that these boys could and would do a responsible job I have no doubt, if within their competence. At all events, I am bold enough to ask you for any counsel you can give me — and I also ask your forgiveness in advance!

I had a fine holiday in the West Indies and a good rest and a little work. Now I am on the eve of announcing my return to the law business in Chicago, New York and Washington, with a trip to Europe, South and West Africa in the immediate prospect. I hope to see you before I get off in mid-May.

Hastily,

Gilbert Harrison wrote suggesting that Stevenson write an article for the New Republic.

To Gilbert Harrison

April 18, 1957

Dear Gil:

Thanks for your nice letter. I wish there *was* something cooking in my torpid head. Mostly I confess to an unworthy satisfaction with the growing realization of the frailties of my late opponents. But I shall have to start doing some thinking before long, because I am committed to make a lecture at Oxford while in England on business at the end of May. But I doubt if it would be suitable for the N.R., which, by the way, delights me every week. What wonders you have wrought!

My love to Nancy.[234]

Cordially yours,

To Mrs. Ernest L. Ives[235]

April 18, 1957

Dear Buff:

Ed McDougal reports you are arriving May 10. I will bring my car in and you can ride out with me that evening if you like. I return from New York on the 8th and leave again on the 15th for New York en route to Europe, so any time that is agreeable to you is satisfactory with me.

The summer situation is somewhat as follows. I have released Doris[236] as of the middle of May, but she would probably be glad to stay on if I had any use for her. Borden comes back around June 5–10 and returns to summer school July 5, which lasts until August 21. Adlai and Nancy return about July 7. I assume that with a little coaching Bea's[237] mother can feed Borden in June and Adlai and Nancy in July and look after the house.[238]

My plans now are to go first to Paris, Brussels and then to England on May 22. I take my degree and make my lecture at Oxford on the afternoon of Friday, May 24. I don't know yet whether Adlai and Nancy will be there or will want to go direct to Rome. I plan to meet them for the African trip June 3 or 4. When I get back to Europe about July 7th I may go to visit Francis Plimpton[239] for a bit and then travel a little in Germany and Scandinavia with a view to law business, returning home the end of the month.

John Fell and a classmate want to get jobs on an American President Lines ship going around the world if I can arrange it. If not, he will probably go to Europe and travel with me when I am there and with classmates and an older friend from Harvard after I return.

[234] Mrs. Harrison.
[235] The original is in E.S.I., I.S.H.L.
[236] Stevenson's housekeeper in Libertyville.
[237] Beatrice Holland, wife of Frank Holland, who had been Stevenson's farmer for years.
[238] Stevenson was unable to replace his housekeeper before leaving on his trip abroad.
[239] A prominent New York lawyer who had been Stevenson's classmate and roommate at Harvard Law School.

I saw Timmy and Adrienne[240] Monday in Bloomington and also had a look at our new land. They are flourishing and so is the baby. I am elated by their apparent total satisfaction with Bloomington, the work and the prospects.[241] The new house is, I think, a good sign too. I hope to get to the christening Saturday afternoon.

Love,

AD

To Mrs. Marriner S. Eccles

April 18, 1957

My dear Sally:

I was charmed with your letter and flattered that I passed Marriner's scrutiny for the wall of the den.[242] I am sure the company is good and I shall be happy there — but would be happier still if I had an occasional glimpse of the Eccles *here*.

I am afraid I am not a "great souled American" at all, and that I have found some satisfaction, if no comfort, in the recent revelation of evident truths for all to see. I only wish the press was a little more attentive to the foresight and the warnings so that we might not suffer from the same easy credulity again.

You were so sweet to write me, and I hope you will let me know if you come my way.

Best to Marriner.

Sincerely yours,

To Mrs. Eugene Meyer[243]

April 19, 1957

Dear Agnes:

I am distressed that I can do no better than a dictated letter.

If you are at home Saturday morning, May 4, I think it may be my best chance, although Monday afternoon is a possibility too. Why don't I telephone you when I arrive early Saturday morning, probably on the night train from New York, and we will arrange a meeting. There is so much to talk about!

---

240 Mrs. Ives's son and daughter-in-law.

241 Timothy Ives managed his mother's farm property and also worked at the Bloomington radio station WJBC, in which his family had an interest.

242 Stevenson refers to a picture of himself, which Mr. Eccles had hung on his wall.

243 The original is in the Agnes Meyer files, Princeton University Library.

I think I have as heavy a schedule as I can manage,[244] and of course I have known Mendes-France[245] for many years. But I should certainly like to take advantage of some of your German friends.

Affectionately,

ADLAI

Edward E. White, Jr., of the J. B. Lippincott Company, asked Stevenson for a comment on Gerald W. Johnson's book The Lunatic Fringe, *which the company was publishing.*

To Edward E. White, Jr.

April 19, 1957

Dear Mr. White:

I am so grateful to you for sending me a copy of Gerald Johnson's book.

Some of the rogues and dreamers of the 19th century's lunatic fringe have long awaited a Gerald Johnson to do them justice. He scatters their frauds or fancies with gusts of laughter, penetrating to solid values in a wholly American tradition of reform. The Johnson blend of wisdom and shrewdness is superb equipment for handling that "most explosive of high explosives," the human mind.

Sincerely yours,

To Mrs. Franklin D. Roosevelt[246]

April 22, 1957

Dear Mrs. Roosevelt:

I am distressed that I will not be able to be with you at Hyde Park on May 30. I leave for Europe on the 16th, and after a fortnight on the continent and in England, mostly on business, I am travelling through South and West Africa for a month — with a little business and a lot of sightseeing! Adlai and Nancy are going with me on the African journey, which should make it a delight.

I will be in New York most of the week commencing Monday, April 29, and will hope for at least a telephone chat with you at that time.

Affectionately,

ADLAI

[244] Stevenson refers to his forthcoming trip abroad.

[245] Pierre Mendès-France, prime minister and minister of foreign affairs of France, 1954–1955.

[246] The original is in the Franklin D. Roosevelt Library, Hyde Park, New York.

To Mrs. Franklin D. Roosevelt[247]

April 22, 1957

Dear Mrs. Roosevelt:

So many thanks for your note about the educational movies. Certainly we must do something to try to improve primary and secondary teaching and this is one means of doing it.

Affectionately,
ADLAI

To Harold Dodds[248]

April 23, 1957

Dear Harold:

I have two letters of yours for acknowledgement, and I am embarrassed that the earlier one — about my papers — has been neglected for so long. I was in the West Indies most of March and have only now had an opportunity to examine into the situation.

You may be sure that I should like very much to take advantage of your suggestion about depositing my papers with the Princeton Library. Actually, I am flattered by the proposal. But the material is extremely voluminous in its present form, and moreover I am in some embarrassment with the Newberry Library where it has been accumulating since I left Springfield five years ago. Hence I have been obliged to write Mr. Dix[249] as per the enclosed copy, and I will follow through with him hopeful that something can be worked out to leave some remnant of me around Princeton. There is no place I would rather be in perpetuity.

As for the Stafford Little Lectures, I am going to have to decline. It is not because I don't want to or dislike the subject. I want to and I like the subject. Indeed, I would like to enlarge on my piece of a year ago in Harper's about the role of the opposition. But the trouble is that I am in transit, so to speak, and my new destination is the resumption of an active law practice. I fear that unless I can at least get it established I must assume no further burdens, and three thoughtful lectures at Princeton is more than I can easily assume. Another year it may be different.

I am afraid these are unsatisfactory answers to your letters, my dear friend, but I am sure, also, you will understand both my predicament and my gratitude.

Cordially yours,

[247] The original is in the Franklin D. Roosevelt Library, Hyde Park, New York.
[248] President of Princeton University, 1933–1957.
[249] William S. Dix, librarian of the Princeton University Library.

[523]

To John Fischer

April 23, 1957

Dear Jack:

Seymour Harris has sent me your letter of April 15. I am afraid I am going to have to forego the introduction.[250] I can't quite explain it, but I seem to have had almost less time for reflection and writing in the past three months than ever before. I suppose it is actually more inertia than pressure, but the period is totally sterile! Moreover, I think the material that Arthur [Schlesinger] and Seymour [Harris] have prepared covers most of what I could have said anyway, and doubtless better.

The manuscript is here and some girls are working on it. I am told that they should be through and ready to ship it to you by the end of the week. Perhaps I could even bring it with me, or part of it, when I come to New York on Thursday.

I have been over the Introduction and made a lot of changes and suggestions, which I am afraid are not very helpful, and whatever the editors send you as a final draft will be all right with me.

I don't know how John Martin and Arthur and Seymour have worked out their arrangements, but as they have all worked on the book I was hopeful that they might all share in the royalties — and I hope there will be some!

I will be at the Savoy-Plaza most of next week in case you want me for anything.

Yours,

To Lila Ives[251]

April 23, 1957

My dear Lila:

How sweet of you to send me that Easter card. I haven't seen my grandson for a long while but I expect to next Sunday in Cambridge. However, I *have* seen the enchanting little Alison;[252] indeed, I attended her christening only last Saturday afternoon and she hiccuped gaily through the whole performance. The Osbornes[253] gallantly took credit for the hiccups for their side of the family! She is a lovely baby, with lovely parents, as well you know.

---

[250] Stevenson eventually contributed a one-page "Author's Note" to *The New America.*

[251] Sister of Ernest L. Ives. The original is in the possession of Mrs. Ernest L. Ives.

[252] Oldest daughter of Mr. and Mrs. Timothy Ives.

[253] Mr. and Mrs. W. Irving Osborne, parents of Mrs. Timothy Ives.

Tim [Ives] has settled into Bloomington and gone to work with a will, which of course warms my heart, and I think that Adrienne finds it agreeable too. Certainly there are many advantages to life in the smaller towns.

I pray that you are well — and I was on the eve of coming down there[254] to a ship commissioning affair with the hope of a glimpse of you. Unhappily my schedule didn't permit and the glimpse will have to be deferred again.

Affectionately,
ADLAI

To Harry S. Truman

April 23, 1957

My dear Mr. President:

I have an invitation from the Trustees to the dedication ceremonies of the [Truman] Library on July 6.

I should like very much to be present at this event because I think it has historic and symbolic significance, and also because I know it is the culmination of a mighty chore which you undertook and pursued under most difficult circumstances. I don't think anyone can properly be thanked for the Truman Library but Harry S. Truman!

I shall, however, be abroad at that time. I am leaving in May for Europe on business, followed by a trip to South and West Africa, and I shall probably not be back here before the end of July. I am disappointed to miss what I am sure will be a memorable occasion.

Best wishes and my congratulations.

Cordially yours,

To Archibald S. Alexander

April 24, 1957

Dear Archie:

So many thanks for your letter. I look forward to your report,[255] although I am afraid it will only provoke once more my frustrating feeling of hopeless gratitude to many who gave me so much — and you way out in front!

I am sure my new life will mean more time in New York[256] and, I hope, more time with my beloved Alexanders.

---

[254] Norfolk, Virginia.

[255] Mr. Alexander was preparing a report on the work of the Volunteers for Stevenson.

[256] A few days earlier, Stevenson had announced the merger of his Chicago law firm with the New York firm of Paul, Weiss, Rifkind, Wharton and Garrison.

As to John Fell, I am going to Cambridge this week-end to find out precisely what that young man has in mind. Last reports were that he was trying to sign on a ship to go around the world instead of to Europe as I had assumed. Your proffer will be tempting and I am so grateful.

I leave May 16 for Europe, including some business and a lecture at Oxford. In June I go to Africa, taking Adlai and Nancy with me — and of course Bill Blair. I return to Europe early in July for a visit with Francis and Pauline Plimpton at their villa in Italy before coming back to America through Germany. I hope our paths can cross somewhere.

Affectionately,

A little girl, Amity Kaye, daughter of Mr. and Mrs. Leo Kaye, drew flowers on an Easter greeting and printed, "It is true that I love you."

To Amity Kaye

April 24, 1957

Dear Amity:

It is true that I love you, too — and I have never had a more beautiful Easter card than yours. Thank you, my dear little Amity, with all my heart!

Cordially,

Columnist May Craig wrote Stevenson that she was pleased she would be on the Meet the Press *program with him on May 5. She reminded him that she had been on the program with him on March 30, 1952, the day after President Truman announced he would not run for reelection. She asked for copies of his recent speeches.*

To May Craig

April 24, 1957

Dear May:

Thanks for your note. I shudder at the prospect of facing you again! Please be merciful!

I seem to have been becomingly silent of late — at least as far as formal speeches are concerned. So about all I can send you are the enclosed utterances before the Democrats in California in February and the Fourth Estate in March. Aren't you lucky!

Cordially,

Arthur F. Cody, of Jamaica Plain, Massachusetts, wrote Stevenson that an autographed picture of him was paired with one of Carl Sandburg. He praised Senator John F. Kennedy's book Profiles in Courage *(New York: Harper, 1955) and expressed the hope that when the time came for Stevenson to endorse a candidate for 1960 he would give great consideration to Mr. Kennedy.*

To Arthur F. Cody

April 30, 1957

Dear Mr. Cody:

Thank you for your letter. I am flattered to be "hung" with Carl Sandburg — who is an old and dear friend.

I share your regard for Senator Kennedy, whose book I have had occasion to read previously, and believe that this able young man has a promising future in our country's affairs. Indeed, the Democratic party is fortunate in having several highly capable young men who are devoted to its cause and the welfare of our country.

With every good wish, I am

Cordially,

While in Washington, Stevenson attended a meeting of the Democratic Advisory Council. On May 5 the council issued a statement labeling Administration foreign policy as one of "appeasement," "posturing," and "slogans." The New York Times, *May 6, 1957, reported: "The burden of the Democratic criticism followed the pattern already developed by Mr. Stevenson and Dean Acheson." On May 4, Stevenson, former President Truman and Governor G. Mennen Williams spoke at a Democratic National Committee fund-raising dinner.*

Stevenson appeared on Meet the Press *on May 5, 1957, where he again urged the cessation of H-bomb testing in the atmosphere. Mrs. May Craig, one of the questioners on the program, wrote him after his appearance, "Somehow I felt you were a little sad when you were here. As though a book were being closed. You have done your duty by the party. It is a wonderful wide new world opening in your travels in your new occupation. . . ." She concluded her letter, "Do give my love to Hugh Gaitskill."[257]*

---

[257] Hugh Gaitskell, leader of the Labour Party in Great Britain.

To May Craig

May 8, 1957

My dear May:

What a sweet letter! You were more than kind to me. I look forward to some lively and not altogether useless years. But not, pray heaven, as lively as in the past 15.

I hope another time we can have a talk without the inquisition. I shall share some of that love with Hugh Gaitskell, reluctantly.

Yours,

Stevenson's Princeton classmate J. Russell Forgan said that at their thirty-fifth class reunion they were planning to have Stevenson sing some special lyrics to the tune of "The Man on the Flying Trapeze."

To J. Russell Forgan

May 8, 1957

Dear Russ:

I have your letter and you have no more willing performer. Moreover, trapezes, both flying and falling, are not unfamiliar.

But unhappily I suspect while you are in bright, hot Princeton I shall be in dark, hot Africa. I am disappointed in the extreme; the more so because of the pains that I am sure you and Lou[258] have taken to entertain us — even at my expense! But I find some consolation in that my classmates will not have to be reminded of my musical voice as well as my speaking voice. I know it will be fun and I want you to send me the lyrics. I will hum them floating down the Congo — or something.

Yours,

To Joseph C. Harsch[259]

May 9, 1957

Dear Joe:

What do you mean that if we go along our present path the highest goal for our youth will be a managerial position in a vast hierarchy? Why, man, we are already there and have been there a long time. At least that is what I get from most of the young that seem to be coming out of the colleges nowadays, and especially the law schools.

[258] Louis E. Tilden, a Chicago advertising executive.
[259] Washington correspondent of the *Christian Science Monitor*.

I didn't drop this theme from the campaign consciously, but I suspect I changed it more to an inaudible wail about bigness; massiveness, and all the implications to the individual.

Anyway, I think you have been very helpful to me and I shall make some sallies in this direction if I ever recover my composure after the Oxford ceremonial. . . .

Cordially yours,

Adlai E. Stevenson III was finishing his last year at Harvard Law School and was considering seeking a position as law clerk to either Judge Walter Schaefer or Judge Harry Hershey, of the Illinois Supreme Court.

To Adlai E. Stevenson III

May 9, 1957

Dear Bear:

I talked last night to Walter Schaefer, who is only recently back from abroad. He is going to Springfield next week and will see Hershey and let me know the results. He would still be delighted to have you here in his office in Chicago, but I am tempted to think that the downstate experience for a year or so would be useful.

I will go East on Wednesday and leave for London on Thursday, the 16th, at 6:00 P.M. from Idlewild, and I have asked John Fell and Borden to come to see me off either the night before or for lunch on Thursday. They should not feel that they have to, however.

If you and Nancy arrive in London in time on Thursday, May 23, would you like to go up to Stratford in the afternoon to see a fine performance of "As You Like It" and stay the night up there under the management of Barbara Jackson? I think it might be beautiful at that season and an interesting experience. The next day we will drive over to Oxford after a look around the Cotswolds in time for the ceremony. Then you would have to dash back to London in time for your departure for Rome the next day I suppose. In other words, it would mean sacrificing your day and evening in London, which you may not care to do. Please let Carol [Evans] know what your conclusions are so that she can inform Lady Jackson. I rather like the idea.

As you may have heard Aunt Buffy and Uncle Ernest will be in England at that time. He is not a bit well, I gather, and his eyesight is failing along with his hearing. The Duke [University] hospital people

[529]

have thought the journey and change would be good for him. They are doing an inexpensive two-weeks trip to coincide with my visit there.

It looks now as though [Kwame] Nkrumah would have to leave the Gold Coast for the Prime Ministers' Conference in London before we arrive and, accordingly, I may have to change my schedule and fly there to see him direct from London, catching up with you in Johannesburg instead of Khartoum.

Love,

p.s. I think I will have plenty of pocket money along so don't worry too much about that.

The Reverend Richard Graebel wrote that Stevenson appeared in high spirits on Meet the Press *and "my heart rejoiced at your humility." He urged him to be sure and meet Marshal Tito on his European trip.*

To the Reverend Richard Paul Graebel

May 9, 1957

Dear Dick:

Thank you for that delightful letter. I am glad you thought well of "Meet the Press." For my part, I was frustrated and disappointed — as usual!

I wish I could have heard more about your trip last year. I share your view of Tito. My day with him in 1953 at Brioni I shall long remember. And I recall when he said that 1948 had been our most important post war year because of his break with Stalin I corrected him and said it was because of my election as Governor of Illinois![260]

I will be back from Europe and Africa in late July or early August and when you travel to or from your northern fastness, let me know.

Yours,

To Lady Barbara Jackson

May 9, 1957

Barbara dear:

I am back after two frenzied weeks in the East, with two "appearances" in New York and two in Washington (score: three good, one poor), and the ordeal of getting established in the new law offices, visiting the children, etc.

[260] See *The Papers of Adlai E. Stevenson*, Vol. V, pp. 340–341.

On my return I find your letter and the manuscript. The latter I have barely looked at. But I will, indeed must, at once. If it is largely about colonialism and what to do, I wonder if I shouldn't add some bits about what we must do together in the future.

I am frightened by how little I have thought about London and what's to be done there. The current demands have squeeeezed me dry and there has been no time for forethought. But anyway, blessings and heartfelt thanks.

The situation is now somewhat as follows: I arrive in London on May 21st about 8:30 P.M. from Paris, and I believe Geoffrey [Crowther] is making plans to get Bill Blair and me to Claridge's. The following evening I dine with Tom Matthews, and Thursday, the 23rd is open. I would love to go to Stratford with you for "As You Like It" but it is possible that I will feel obliged to work some more on my speech, which will be neglected — as usual! — I fear. Do you suppose we could leave it tentative? My sister and brother-in-law will be in London also. They are taking a quick two weeks trip to England for their joint morale and because it is inexpensive that way. And I suspect they would like to come too. Adlai and Nancy may be there too that day, but about that Miss Evans will inform you definitely in a day or so. All this is by way of saying that if you could *tentatively* engage tickets, lodgings, etc., at Stratford for me and the Ives and the young Stevensons I think it would be wonderful, and I will try to confirm the others as quickly as I can. As for myself, it will have to be a little uncertain I fear. I have no idea how long it takes to get there by motor from London, but I gather there will be no trouble about getting from there to Oxford the next day. I will have a car. You should by all means plan to come with us to Oxford for the ceremonies and the desecration of your mss. I have agreed to stay the night with the Vice Chancellor at Worcester College, and the Ives will stay with him or with friends in the neighborhood. I am sure you can be put up somehow easily. The young Stevensons will have to return to London after the ceremonies to catch their plane for Rome in the morning. I have told the American student group that I will meet with them in the evening if it is agreeable with the Vice Chancellor. The next day I plan to drive to Cambridge where I think I am lunching with contributors to the [*Encyclopaedia*] *Britannica*. I had thought to take Ernest and Buffie along, and you too. After a few hours in Cambridge we will go on to Albemarle — a county in the Piedmont of Virginia founded by my ancestor Colonel Joshua Fry in the mid-18th Century!

I also find imbedded in the pile a cable about the week-end for Buffie and Mrs. [Luther] Hodges. How thoughtful of you. As I have explained, Mrs. Hodges has been obliged to drop out due to her official commitments in North Carolina, and now Ernest is coming if the invitation still holds. I am sure he would love it.

A letter yesterday from Robert [Jackson] has disorganized our schedule woefully. It looks now as though I would have to change everything and fly to Accra from London on Saturday, June 1st, in order to see Nkrumah before he leaves for London. As you say, that will probably interfere with our Jackson family visit later.

MacDuff[261] excites my imagination — almost as much as his mother. I yearn to see him — and you.

P.S. And with your manuscript and letter your last book also arrived.[262] What a woman!

To Mrs. Eugene Meyer[263]

Chicago — Friday noon[264] — and what a horrible letter, again!!

Beloved Agnes —

The vision of you gallantly striding up and down the terrace in that bright spring sun will not erase — nor the memory of that relaxed visit. I've thought about it and "the letter" — and you! And — if I'm not completely clear in my mind about everything I'm not distressed — because I'll have to come back for another lesson to my beloved and most wonderful teacher. What a remarkably versatile, wise and gifted woman you are!! I marvel all over again after each visit — and each letter for that matter.

I think you are right that I've been so busy most of my life with impersonal things, and still am, that I'm not a very fit candidate for marriage and probably never was. But isn't there something to be said for the proposition that *until* I'm married to the right sort of person I won't get what you call my "ego-ambitions" (I say, *if any!*) into balance and behave, and love, etc as you have suggested I must? All of which is by way of saying that perhaps its a vicious circle?? I hope not. But its not easy to wholly dismiss the idea of marriage as you enjoin me because I would make a bad husband when my best chance of being a proper person & of fulfillment *is* by love & marriage.

261 The Jacksons' son, Robin.
262 *The Interplay of East and West: Points of Conflict and Cooperation* (New York: Norton, 1957).
263 This handwritten letter is in the Agnes Meyer files, Princeton University Library.
264 Probably May 9, 1957, or a day or two thereafter.

But enough of these contortions. It would have to be the right kind of person, and there's none in sight!! So I'll have to slow my pace without anyone's help — and that my dear friend, is not easy for me *or for you* — may I add!! The pressures from all sides go on *and* on. And to them I must now add more time for my children and lots more for making a living for the first time in many years, or almost.

As for the Oxford speech, I've not written a word and given it hardly a thought — and now, this minute, I must start, for tomorrow Ruth Field (Marshall's widow) arrives to talk about the [Field] Foundation, family problems etc! So I have no hope of writing the "great speech" — indeed I don't yet even have an *idea* about it — or even the "integration of passion and reason within my personality," as you put it. But *you* have ideas, great ones, about *everything!* And that's another reason why admiration compounds my affection, and why, as you say, I know how fortunate *we are* or *I am!*

But, madam! I protest again that "mother's boy has in self-defense never loved anyone but himself." He has, he does, love, really love, many people and very especially a great tutor, benefactor and comrade on this exciting, fearful, beautiful journey we call life —

Adlai

I'm off Thursday next and will send you an itinerary — if it ever gets straightened out. Everything went to pieces only yesterday when word came from Ghana that Nkrumah had to be in London for a Prime Ministers conf. when I had planned to be in Accra. And so it is, more or less, every day!!

And someday could we talk of *you* instead of *me!!*

To Lady Barbara Jackson

May 14, 1957

Dear Barbara:

Enclosed is a first draft of the speech — I mean "the speech"! My additions were done in the usual disorder, and show it. I also enclose an article I wrote hurriedly in Arizona on colonialism.[265] I wish you could find a moment to look them over and see if there are too obvious conflicts. Also, any editing on the speech that you have time to do would give me comfort and it distinction.

Getting off has been difficult, but it always is. I yearn to see you and will expect notice of your whereabouts immediately on arrival.

---

[265] "The Support of Nationalism Helps Combat Communist Imperialism," *Western World,* Vol. I, No. 1 (May, 1957), pp. 34–38, reprinted below, pp. 536–544.

I think you can assume that we will all come — Buffie, Ernest, the young Stevensons, Blair and myself, to Stratford on the afternoon of the 23rd. But I suppose both Blair and I will have to continue somewhat uncertain.

I understand that I must now leave for Ghana on Saturday, June 1st, in order to see Nkrumah before he leaves for England. Robert [Jackson] has been so helpful in keeping us informed, but horrors!, the diamond purchasing license I was hoping to get for my client has already been issued to someone else.

Best love,

To H. Hamilton Hackney[266]

May 15, 1957

Dear Monk:

I don't know what your postcard about bequests is all about, but I am enclosing $50.00 to Princeton — and please don't molest a poor, harassed lawyer trying desperately to earn a living and support a family any more.

I am told that you are to have the spectacular privilege of singing a song about me at the [Class] Reunion on the night of June 14. I trust you will do it with spirit and an emotion that will all but compensate for your voice. I will be in West Africa.

Blessings,

Yours,

To George Killion

May 15, 1957

Dear George:

I was distressed that we didn't have a better opportunity to talk in Washington. There was so much to talk *about* and the time was so scarce. I hope after I get back around the first of August we can find a week-end together. Your activities daze and fascinate me, and, of course, I will be looking for an audience to hear about my journey!

Yours,

P.S. John Fell called me in a great state of excitement about his pending service to the American President Lines. I hope you don't regret it, and I know he won't. I am grateful beyond words.

---

[266] A Baltimore judge and Princeton classmate of Stevenson.

Congressman Michael J. Kirwan, of Ohio, wrote of Stevenson's performance on Meet the Press: *"You handled every question hurled at you in a statesmanlike manner. You were refreshing — calm and sincere." He concluded, "Again, I say to you and to the entire country — no man who ever aspired to the Presidency was as qualified or more familiar with the details of our Government, than yourself."*

To Michael J. Kirwan

May 15, 1957

Dear Mike:

Your letter touched and pleased me immensely. I did not think well of the "Meet the Press" performance. But you have reassured me — a little!

I am off now on a law, pleasure, and educational journey in Western Europe, Britain and Africa. I hope when I get back there may be an opportunity for a leisurely talk. I will be looking for an audience and I know no more appreciative and patient one than you!

With affectionate best wishes, I am

Cordially,

To Benjamin H. Swig

May 15, 1957

Dear Ben:

My son John Fell has "shipped before the mast" and is sailing out of San Francisco with a schoolmate on the SS President Polk on June 12 I think. He has been ordered to report on board on the morning of June 10. He will be arriving in San Francisco with his friend on the evening of the 9th and I have suggested that he go to the Fairmont and that you might have someone find a couple of hammocks in the basement for him and his friend, Gilbert Butler.

Seriously, I hope the hotel can stow them away somewhere inconspicuously and inexpensively for a night. I am quite proud of his enterprise in this project.

I have the confirmation from E. F. Hutton & Company on the Chrysler call[267] and have instructed Miss [Carol] Evans to reimburse

---

[267] Stevenson purchased Chrysler Corporation stock on Mr. Swig's recommendation.

you when I get some money ahead. At the moment I am destitute and I am embarrassed to treat your kindness and thoughtfulness with such businesslike discourtesy! . . .

With warm good wishes, I am

Cordially yours,

A new magazine, Western World, *published in Brussels, Belgium, in both English and French editions (the latter under the title* Occident*), featured in its first issue articles by Stevenson and Paul Reynaud on the topic "Is American Anti-Colonialism Harmful or Helpful?" The magazine, edited by former Chicago* Daily News *correspondent Edgar Ansel Mowrer, was "dedicated to preserving and strengthening the Atlantic Community of Nations."*

THE SUPPORT OF NATIONALISM HELPS COMBAT COMMUNIST IMPERIALISM[268]

President Eisenhower's decision to vote with the USSR in the United Nations to induce Britain and France to stop their armed attack on Egypt obviously surprised and distressed many European friends of the United States. And it also caused acute distress among friends of Britain and France in the United States, myself included.

But Europe's distress is easier to understand than its surprise. For the President's action indicated nothing new. Rather, it was another expression of a policy that has become a fundamental political tenet of the American people. Even if more Americans had known about our mistakes in the Middle East and Egypt's provocations of our friends, I suspect a majority would have supported the President's action.

How could it be otherwise? We Americans are the children of a nationalist revolution against a colonial master. We had hardly achieved our own independence when we cheerfully set about "liberating" our Canadian neighbors, only to discover to our dismay that they preferred rule by Britain to self-determination with us. Nonetheless, we enthusiastically supported the Latin Americans' revolts against Spain, embodying our optimism, with British support, in the Monroe Doctrine, our first foray into world politics.

Once or twice we have, to be sure, betrayed our principles. Thus, at

268 The text is from *Western World,* Vol. I, No. 1 (May, 1957), pp. 34–38. Subheadings within the article have been omitted by the editors.

the turn of the last century, we embarked upon a brief imperial career under the slogan of our "Manifest Destiny." But the colonies we temporarily acquired were set free; Cuba immediately, the Philippines in 1946, with the single exception of Puerto Rico whose inhabitants, offered independence by us, have refused to separate from the United States.

No wonder then that during World War II President Roosevelt urged our allies to make it a war of "liberation" by establishing freer relationships with the Dutch East Indies, with Burma and India, with Indo-China and North Africa, etc.

While America's chief delegate on the Preparatory Commission of the United Nations in 1945, I myself had a hand in inducing France and Britain to withdraw from Syria and Lebanon. And a few weeks later, at the first meeting of the Security Council, we insisted on Russia's evacuation of Iran with a fervor compounded, at least in part, of anti-colonialism and the spirit of independence.

There was nothing much new in the subsequent American misgivings about France's future role in Indo-China, in American sympathy for the rebels of Indonesia, in American pressure on Britain to relinquish her vast Suez base to Egypt, or in our "neutrality" between France on the one side and rebellious Moroccans and Tunisians — or even the legally "French" Algerians — on the other.

Clearly, then, America's distasteful posture of opposition to our friends in the United Nations indicated no "preference" for Dictator Nasser. And I would also deny that it masked an official attempt to supplant our European allies economically in any of these places, whatever plans any over-selfish American companies may have made for "cashing in" on the ouster of our allies. Finally, Vice President Nixon's exultation last fall over our "declaration of independence" from Britain and France must, I hope, be dismissed as what we call "campaign oratory."

So, without implying my approval of our conduct leading up to the recent unfortunate events in the Middle East, I repeat that our behavior in the United Nations was not inconsistent with basic American policy. And the world-wide struggle against imperialist communism has, I believe, conferred a greater validity on that policy than its recent application in the Middle East suggests.

Here I see scepticism on the faces of many Europeans and I even hear amused protests.

"How do you reconcile your anti-colonialism with your treatment of your own Indians and your violent seizure of immense territories from neighboring Mexico? Who was imperialist then? How do you justify having one standard for yourselves and another for your acknowledged friends?"

All I can say is, Americans are not unmindful of what happened to the Indians a long time ago. But likewise, they are not aware of nourishing a double standard. The reason may well lie in the luck of the American colonists in settling a territory so sparsely inhabited as the North American Continent. I do not defend the treatment of our Indians in all respects, but the sparseness of the indigenous population quickly permitted the American colonists to think of themselves as the real "natives" and, after achieving their own independence, to transfer their aspirations to all peoples seeking self-determination.

Which brings me back to today's situation.

As I see it, the problem can be roughly divided into three parts. One is the rising tide of nationalism among peoples that have never previously tasted it, resulting in many cases in open revolt against dominion by, or even continued association with, their colonial masters. A second is communist encouragement of this attitude in order to create fertile ground for subversion. A third is the combination of what I like to hope is a finer moral attitude with the existence of new weapons of such horrible power that they make any appeal to war — hitherto the accepted *ultima ratio* of nations — all but unthinkable.

Let us consider these three aspects.

The explosive forces of nationalism, anti-colonialism and independence were not invented by communism. Yet they have merged in a single message which, along with Western technology, has shattered time and distance and released sources of energy beyond our comprehension and also legitimized the hope that poverty, hunger, disease and servitude are not the immutable destiny of the long-suffering two-thirds of the human race, who are largely colored.

To these multitudes nationalism, far from being anachronistic, means a chance to stand on their own feet, to govern themselves, to develop their resources for their own welfare, to prove that the color of their skins has nothing to do with their right to walk with self-respect among their fellow men in the world. It means the end of legalized inferiority.

Furthermore, it is something that the colonial peoples did not inherit from their ancestors, who were so often feudal and despotic. *Rather they took it over bodily from the West, along with some inkling of the need for the freedom and dignity of the individual.* How then can Westerners deny its validity even though they seem to have outgrown something of its original vitality? In ordinary times, and left alone in a tête-à-tête with the colonial peoples, Europeans might have been able to slow the process of emancipation, and thereby have minimized the real dangers inherent in it. Certainly they would not have felt that in relinquishing their hold upon sources of power and wealth they were not only weakening themselves but risking seeing the peoples they relinquished turn against them.

The rise of aggressive communism captained by the Kremlin both complicated and aggravated the rising national consciousness. When astute and daring communist leaders systematically promoted nationalism among the colonial peoples, Westerners naturally asked whether American support of anti-colonialism would turn out harmful or helpful to the Atlantic Community, and indeed to all mankind.

Backing independence for backward peoples was no brilliant improvisation on the part of the Soviet rulers. It goes back deep into the history of socialism. Lenin took over bodily from the Nineteenth Century Austrian socialists the doctrine that there is, or can be created, an irresistible historical development *from colonial status through nationalism to communism.* Therefore his successors have made the promotion of nationalism among such peoples a major weapon in their policy of world conquest.

To me one of the modern miracles is how the Soviets have been able to practice ruthless imperialism from the Baltic to the Black Sea and at the same time convince any one of the sincerity of their professions about independence. But there is no gainsaying the success of Moscow's anti-colonial policy. There are doubtless many reasons, including the fact that "misery loves company," as we say. While Asian and African peoples have looked upon European white conquerors with distaste and suspicion, Russia seems to be thought of as Asian. And Russia's dramatic achievement in industrializing a backward country, together with her professed lack of any color or racial prejudice, have profoundly impressed undeveloped countries with meager resources who yearn to raise themselves by their bootstraps.

These peoples know from experience a lot about feudalism, landlords, money-lenders and oppression and they have little tradition of democracy. To them, the theories of Karl Marx and the unlimited promises of Lenin-Stalin-K[h]rushchev sound pretty good since they know little to nothing about the ugly realities of communism in practice or the designs of imperialist communism. When we of the free and developed peoples think of communism, we think of what we are going to *lose.* When millions of Asians and Africans think of communism, they think of what they are going to *gain.*

So the strategy of communism in Asia and Africa is to pose as the only champion of the struggling peoples and thereby to impose its own label on these multiple revolutions. And it works. Just how well we don't yet know. It is a fateful question, for certainly many people in the West believe there is something to Lenin's dictum that "the road to Paris lies through Peiping," and that in the aspirations and grievances of the East is the communist key to world power.

Events could prove them right unless we of the West succeed in proving them wrong. Our job is to show that the evolution postulated by Lenin is anything but fatal and that it can be interrupted by appropriate action on the part of the free.

Communists start with one big advantage — the differing views of the European and American peoples concerning what should be done, a difference which they do what they can to promote. Europeans are conditioned by centuries of responsibility, by greater familiarity with the problem of backwardness and by immediate self-interest to hold back the liberation process or not let it get out of hand. Americans are pre-disposed by their history and basic beliefs to favor rapid emancipation regardless of the immediate difficulties too rapid liberation may raise. And moreover, each side of the Atlantic believes that its own method will be more effective in stopping communism and that the other's thesis will favor its development.

Many Europeans believe that the way to thwart Marx is to intervene, by force if necessary, and break the Leninist chain of colonialism-nationalism-communism at a point short of full independence. For, in their view, fully independent yet inexperienced and poor peoples will inevitably fall victim to economic disorder or communist pressure and end up in the Kremlin's bosom. These people can point to some weighty examples — communist North Viet Nam, "pink" Syria and Cambodia, wobbling Indonesia and Laos, the sorry spectacle of Egypt's Nasser welcoming communist aid — as evidence of their thesis. Why, they wonder, do not anti-communist Americans see this?

They do — I think. But they also feel that existing examples of recently liberated countries perhaps justify the thought that where nationalism is unopposed or tutored (as in Burma, Pakistan, the Gold Coast, even India) or only weakly opposed by the West (as in Morocco, Tunisia and Iraq), it stands firmly against communist wiles and pressures.

From this, Americans argue that the place to cut communist hopes short is not before independence is realized, but immediately afterwards, by friendly support, by economic aid, by security guarantees and the protection afforded by the United Nations and America's various "doctrines" of resistance to communist aggression.

In other words, the difference over the effect of American anti-colonialism is not merely one of divergent national histories, but of contrasting methods of seeking the *same end* — holding and ultimately rolling back the communist blight.

In further support of their belief that the West can best conquer communism by indulging, in most cases, rather than opposing, the drive to national independence, Americans rely upon another all-important fact: *the present unwillingness of the masters to crush rebellions, communist led or otherwise, by ruthless methods.* It is sometimes said that modern weapons make it impossible to conquer the resistance of a determined people. Yet this is precisely what the USSR has continually (and only recently in Hungary) successfully done! Against an industrial power determined to use all the technical weapons in its arsenal, modern rebels have no chance at all.

This has been publicly recognized. During the fighting in North Viet Nam, General de Linarés[269] told me that his predecessor, General Delattre de Tassigny, once remarked that he would have no difficulty breaking the Vietminh resistance in short order if allowed to evacuate whole populations from rebel infested areas, to burn villages and hide-outs, and to bomb indiscriminately. France's Foreign Minister recently told the United Nations General Assembly that France could easily crush the Algerian uprising "by waging war."[270] Surely both are right and this is precisely how the Kremlin has kept its hold over the largest "colonial" empire the modern world has seen.

It is, however, precisely what Western governments are unwilling to do — could not, in fact, set about doing without forfeiting their reputations as civilized. Whereas in the process of conquering backward peoples their ancestors sometimes indulged in both brutality and terrorism, their descendants have developed what some call a new squeamishness, and others consider a higher morality, something of which I think the West can be justly proud. Nonetheless, it complicates the situation greatly, for if rulers can hold revolting colonials only by terror, yet are unwilling to use such drastic methods, then surely it is the part of wisdom to cease opposing them half-heartedly and to seek rather to mitigate their claims and maintain the old association by persuasion

---

[269] For Stevenson's meeting with French General François de Linarès, see *The Papers of Adlai E. Stevenson,* Vol. V, Chap. Seven.

[270] For this speech by Christian Pineau on February 4, 1957, see the New York *Times,* February 5, 1957.

and the evidence of real benefits. Or, in the phrase of the American politician, "If you can't [or won't] lick 'em, join 'em."

This, I take it, is what the American government has — somewhat erratically — urged Europeans to do.

To preach this doctrine has not always been a comfortable or a confident task. Judo, or the Japanese art of yielding to win, does not come easy to Western peoples. Also, between its genuine belief in the need to accept liberation and its desire not to offend or weaken cherished allies, the United States has frequently (as in the Suez dispute) found itself poised on a tight rope between the two camps, unable to keep the confidence of either. Our European partners have accused us of destroying their political prestige and their power. The colonial peoples reproach us with betrayal of our basic political principles for the sake of maintaining our military alliances.

Our allies, furthermore, charge us with stubbornly misreading the world situation. In the first place, they argue, some of these allegedly national uprisings are nothing of the sort, but artificial and crudely synthetic. They are a mimicry of other successful rebellions fomented by small groups of disgruntled intellectuals bursting with personal resentment and unsatisfied ambitions. The people as a whole, it is argued, would ask nothing better than to be left as they are, were it not for incitement and intimidation by these leaders — and the encouragement given to any and all independence movements by the great United States! Yes, and by the Soviet Union for other reasons.

It is also argued that such peoples have more to gain in every field from close association with the colonizing peoples than from roughly breaking ancient ties, usually friendly, and exposing themselves in all their weakness and inexperience to communist intimidation and subversion.

Finally, many Europeans insist they are already recognizing the historical trend by conceding independence in degrees suited to the various developments of the respective peoples. Witness the enlightened programs of the British and the French in sub-Sahara Africa! Why then must the United States chivvy them to go faster?

Personally, I find some merit in all these objections. It is true that without foreign examples, without the presence of agitators urging immediate independence, many colonial peoples, such as the North African Berbers, might have accepted the *status quo* for many years more.

And it is certainly preferable that independence should be achieved slowly through cooperative agreements that guarantee continuing common defense. The examples of the British in some parts of Negro Africa and of the French in Togoland, Morocco and Tunisia are in every way admirable and worthy of imitation. In the case of Algeria, the United States has not encouraged separation from France.

Admittedly, too, in my judgement, the American people have not always realized that although the principle of self-determination is in general both politically sound and morally right, applying it to really underdeveloped peoples is quite another matter than supporting Polish or Hungarian patriots, either of 1848 or 1956! Our own example of liberating the Philippines from Spain could be both foolish and dangerous if taken as a reason for casting peoples barely emerging from the Stone Age adrift in a world full of predatory economics as well as predatory communists. And I would be the first to concede, and beg my impetuous fellow-countrymen to remember, that when you remove colonial paternalism you have to put something in its place besides revolutionary fervor. The elementary requirements of a viable modern state — a healthy economy, a trained civil service, trained and equipped defense forces — are not to be had for the asking or created overnight. And, most important of all, democracy must rest on a broad base of education. Government by a paper-thin educated upper crust — merely a larger oligarchy — is not genuine democracy.

I would be the first to concede, too, that we Americans have made mistakes sometimes, and that in the short run our anti-colonialism may even have weakened the Atlantic Community in important respects.

But not in others. In the long, weary competition between communism and freedom, strength cannot be measured in military power and money only. Failure to understand and sympathize with the great revolutions of rising expectations in the colonial and newly independent countries, or the use of ruthless force in defiance of our dearest principles — these could be fatal to the West. And if the United States has, in some cases, pushed its allies too fast or too far, can they deny that without such American prodding they might well have done too little and too late or nothing at all?

Therefore, on balance, I cannot but feel that American anti-colonialism is right. Certainly, as the descendants of the first revolution for political freedom, Americans cannot afford to let totalitarianism beat us in a contest of ideas among peoples either striving for, or who have recently won their freedom. Granted that anti-colonial policies are sometimes a risk, *the policy of perpetuating hated colonial dominions in defiance of popular aspiration is a greater risk and far more likely to*

[543]

lead to racial hatred or violence and communist gains. Whatever sensible anti-colonialism loses in the short run, it will recover in the long perspective. It helps more than it harms.

President Woodrow Wilson's affirmation, "our civilization cannot survive materially unless it is redeemed spiritually," is truer now than when he said it.

Acknowledgments

We are most grateful to Adlai E. Stevenson's sister, Mrs. Ernest L. Ives, for her infinite patience and considerate help at all stages in the preparation of this volume.

Professor Stuart Gerry Brown, Edward D. McDougal, Jr., Newton N. Minow, William McCormick Blair, Jr., W. Willard Wirtz, and Arthur M. Schlesinger, Jr., have read all or portions of the manuscript.

The following generously provided funds to defray the editorial expenses of this volume: Little, Brown and Company, Mrs. Eugene Meyer, Mrs. Marshall Field and the Field Foundation, Mr. and Mrs. Harold Hochschild, Arnold M. Picker, Robert S. Benjamin, Newton N. Minow, James F. Oates, Jr., Francis T. P. Plimpton, Benjamin Swig, Philip M. Klutznick, Mrs. John Paul Welling, William McCormick Blair, the late R. Keith Kane, Simon H. Rifkind, Wilson W. Wyatt, the late William Benton, Daggett Harvey, Mr. and Mrs. Edison Dick, William McCormick Blair, Jr., Lloyd K. Garrison, J. M. Kaplan, Jerrold Loebl, Hermon D. Smith, Edward D. McDougal, Jr., Glen A. Lloyd, Mr. and Mrs. Gilbert Harrison, Irving B. Harris, Edwin C. Austin, Archibald Alexander, Jacob M. Arvey, Paul Ziffren, Frank E. Karelsen, Jr., George W. Ball, C. K. McClatchy, Maurice Tempelsman, Barnet Hodes and Scott Hodes, and the J. M. Kaplan Fund, Inc.

Roger Shugg, of the University of New Mexico Press, and Ned Bradford, of Little, Brown and Company, have been constant in their encouragement.

William E. Dix, Alexander P. Clark and Mrs. Nancy Bressler, of the

Princeton University Library; Paul Edlund, of the Library of Congress; Phyllis Gustafson; John Bartlow Martin; Roxane Eberlein; Juanda Higgins; and Linda Inlay have been most helpful. Louis B. Cella, of Elmhurst, Illinois, kindly sent us his collection of newspaper clippings.

WALTER JOHNSON
CAROL EVANS
C. ERIC SEARS

Index

Aandahl, Fred G., 266n, 268n
Abdullah, Sheikh Mohammed, 454n
Acheson, Dean, 5, 205, 281, 527; letters to, 5–6, 205, 281, 380, 505
Acheson, Mrs. Dean (Alice), 205, 281
Adams, Grantley, 515
Adams, John, quoted, 320
Adenauer, Konrad, 494
advertising. See communications, mass
AFL–CIO, AES speech before convention, 11, 21, 22, 52
Africa, 47, 414, 471, 542; AES and second trip to, 228n, 414–416, 430, 437, 452, 453, 477, 488, 499–508 (passim), 515–535 passim; AES supporters in, 347; Communism in, 539–540. See also Ghana
Agar, Herbert, 76, 411, 429; The Price of Union, 12; letters to, 12–13, 41–42, 76–77, 163–164, 508–509
Agar, Mrs. Herbert ("Barbie"), 76, 509
"agonizing reappraisal," 257, 292
Agricultural Adjustment Administration (AAA), 251
Agriculture, U.S. Department of, 232, 316. See also farm issue
Alaska: primary election in, 127, 150
Alexander, Archibald, 3, 89–90, 147, 189, 199, 204, 205, 362, 409; letters to, 175, 204, 362, 525–526
Algeria, 114, 537, 541, 543
All Souls College: AES made honorary fellow of, 498n

Altschul, Frank, 352; letter to, 352
America. See United States
American Bar Association, 411, 452
American Broadcasting Company, 177
American Jewish Committee, 93
American Legion, AES speech before, 289, 440
American Municipal Association (Miami), AES speech before, 10, 20, 52
American Society of Newspaper Editors, AES speech before, 41, 71n, 110–121, 128, 133n, 138, 283, 440
American Whig-Cliosophic Society, 449
Americans for Democratic Action, ADA 147, 457
Andersen, Hans Christian, 258
Andersen, H. Carl, 268n
Anderson, Clinton, 208, 228, 278, 408n
Anderson, Mrs. Eugenie, 202, 398; letter to, 398
Anderson, Warwick, 358; letters to, 151, 358–359
Anderson, Mrs. Warwick ("Mary San"), 431; letters to, 151, 431, 456
Andrus, Rev. Robert G., 17–18; letter to, 17
Anglo-American Company, 415, 504
Arabs and Moslem world (Islam), 353n; AES on, 26, 85, 88, 94, 114, 311, 312, 314, 319, 468, 470; and tank shipment to Saudi Arabia, 303, 316. See also Egypt; Israel; Middle East
Arden, Elizabeth, 474n

Arizona: AES campaign in, 42, 309; AES trip to, 406, 413, 434, 437, 455–462 passim, 473–479 passim, 488
Arkansas, 14; AES quotes from speech in, 256
arms race. See defense
Army, U.S., 225; and Selective Service, 248, 290. See also defense
Artie (dog), 400
Arvey, Jacob M., 374
Ashmore, Harry S., 3, 63, 74
Aspinall, Wayne N., 414; letter to, 414
Aswan dam, 280, 312
Atkinson, Brooks, 361; letter to, 361
Atlantic Charter, 115, 280
Atlantic Community/Alliance, 296, 319, 471, 536, 539. See also North Atlantic Treaty Organization (NATO)
Atlantic magazine, 377
atomic bomb. See nuclear weapons and testing
atomic energy, 119, 244
Atomic Energy Commission (AEC), 118, 217, 225, 443
Attlee, Clement, 405n, 429
Attwood, William, 425

Bacall, Lauren (Mrs. Humphrey Bogart; "Betty"), 72, 366; letters to, 72, 203–204, 366
Baghdad Pact (Northern Tier), 88, 163, 164, 312, 353n
Baldwin, Stanley, 360
Ball, George W., 11, 89, 95, 96, 199, 227, 409
Ball, Lucille, 482
Bancroft, Mary, 173; letters to, 136–137, 173
Bandung Conference, 116, 428
Barbados, 459n, 494; AES vacations in, 452, 455, 473–479 passim, 487–496 passim, 500, 503
Barkley, Alben W., 501
Barkley, Mrs. Alben W. (Jane), 501; letter to, 502
Baruch, Bernard, 189, 204; letter to, 205; A Philosophy for Our Time, 205
Basic Farm Act, 232
Beck, David, 516
Becker, Ed, 461
Beerbohm, Sir Max, 504
Bell, Laird, 365; letter to, 365
Bell, Mr. (of DuPont Company), 142
Bendiner, Robert, 152

Benson, Ezra Taft, 232–233, 236, 258, 268, 305, 315
Benton, William, 86, 379, 405, 428, 430, 448, 478, 509; letters to, 145, 406, 410, 413; AES visits in Phoenix, 455, 457, 461, 462, 473, 474, 476
Berdahl, Clarence A., 356; letter to, 356
Berinstein, Morris, 93, 94
Berle, Adolf, 167
Berlin: blockade, 112, 317, 318; Four-Power Conference, 303
BEW (Board of Economic Warfare), 34
Biddle, Francis, 221; letter to, 221
Bielecki, Dr. T.: letter to, 279–80
Bill of Rights. See Constitution, U.S.
Bingham, Barry, 3, 34, 143, 166, 199, 348, 362, 452, 456; letters to, 143, 348–349, 376–377, 452
Bingham, Mrs. Barry (Mary), 452, 456; letters to, 376–377, 452
Bingham, Sallie, 377
bipartisanship, 31, 79n, 87, 265
Blair, William McCormick, Jr., 5, 23, 75, 129, 136n, 139, 145, 199, 298, 417; as AES law partner, 3, 376, 409, 448, 473; and collection of AES campaign speeches, 486, 487; and AES trip abroad (1957), 498, 503, 508, 526, 531, 534
Block, Herbert, 452
Board of Economic Warfare (BEW), 34
Bogart, Humphrey, 72, 204, 366
Bogart, Mrs. Humphrey. See Bacall, Lauren
Boggs, Hale, letters to, 220, 426
Bolling, Richard, 335; letter to, 335
Booth, Major General Donald P., quoted, 290
Bowles, Chester, 42, 43, 85, 86, 104, 138, 143, 162, 199, 453; letters to, 95, 138, 144, 162, 453–454
Boyd Orr, Lord, 88
Boyden, William C., Jr., 27
Brademas, John, 75
Brando, Marlon, 145
Brannan, Charles F., 102, 163
Brawley, Mr. and Mrs. Bill, 421; letter to, 421
Breed, Donald D., 352; letter to, 352–353
"brinksmanship." See Dulles, John Foster
British Medical Research Council, 443

Brown, Edmund G. ("Pat"), 35, 46, 92, 93, 98

Brown, John Mason, 204; letter to, 204

Brown, Stuart Gerry, 77, 93, 393; letters to, 94, 393–394; quoted, 374, 424n

Brown, Vanessa (Mrs. Mark Sandrich), 38; letter to, 38

Brownell, Herbert, 223

Bruce, David K. E., 89

Brun, Marcel, 225; letter to, 226

Bulganin, Nikolai, 57n, 138

Bulletin of the Atomic Scientists: quoted, 439

Bullitt, Stimson, 334; letter to, 334

Bunyan, Paul, 322

Burma, 292, 537, 540

Burnham, Dan, 268

business: and the press, 12, 336, 346–349 *passim*, 403, 431, 464–465, 466, 484, 510; Republican party and, 174n, 199, 217, 222, 241, 243–244, 265–266, 268, 464; and inflation, 467; AES speech on, 487

Butler, Gilbert, 519, 520, 535

Butler, Paul M., 153n, 175, 177, 182, 190–191, 193, 334; letter to, 178–179; and Democratic Advisory Council, 374, 380, 407

Byrd, Harry, 239, 423

Byrnes, James F., 36

Cabell, Lieutenant General Charles P., 211

California: AES campaign in, 24, 42, 76, 105, 109, 129, 136–141 *passim*, 145, 156, 278, 309, 385, 417, 463; primary election in, 49, 89, 94, 97, 127, 129, 138–148 *passim*, 150, 154, 158, 518n; Democratic party in, 62, 97–99, 102, 103, 142, 146, 149, 154, 463; Republican party in, 142, 143; Negro vote in, 353. *See also individual cities*

California Democratic Clubs, 24

California Democratic Council state convention (Fresno); AES speech before, 53–61, 174n

California Institute of Technology, 443

Callas, Maria, 425

Call to Greatness (Stevenson). *See* Godkin Lectures

Cambodia, 540. *See also* Indochina

Campbell, Sam, 314

Canada, 353, 536

Canaday, Frank H., letter to, 411

Canfield, Cass, 10, 13, 410, 412, 450, 486, 487; letter to, 501

Carey, James, 102–103

Carey, Dr. William B., 83n

Carlebach, William D., 156; letter to, 156–157

Carlebach, Mrs. William D. (Priscilla), 157

Carlyle, Thomas, quoted, 186

Carpenter, Mrs. John Alden (Ellen), 5, 134, 155

Case, Everett, 336, 476; letters to, 336, 477

Cassidy, John E., letter to, 15–16

Caulkins, Mrs. Daniel, 412, 449; letters to, 412, 450

Central Intelligence Agency (CIA), 211

Central Valley Project (California), 58, 267

Century Club (New York), 427, 491

Ceylon, 113, 292

Chiang Kai-shek, "unleashing," 48, 116, 324, 468

Chicago: AES press conference in (March, 1956), 90–91, 92; Democratic National Convention in, 177–195; planning of, 268; AES speech in (October, 1956), 281–286

Chicago Council on Foreign Relations, 365

Chicago *Daily News*, 498

Chicago *Sun-Times*, 428, 429, 498

Childs, Marquis, letter to, 409

China, 241, 303n, 324, 326, 385, 469, 471. *See also* Chiang Kai-shek

"Choice by Hullabaloo" (AES article in *This Week*), 91n

Christian Action (London), AES invited to address, 405, 411, 427–430 *passim*, 457, 458

Christian Century magazine, 18n

Christianity, 428. *See also* religion

Christian Science Monitor, 381

Christie, Lansdell K., letter to, 414–415

Christmas "prayer," quoted, 29n

Chrysler Corporation, 473, 476, 535

Church House Group, 6

Churchill, Winston, 108, 360, 405n; quoted, 360–361

Cicero, Illinois, riots, 52, 255

Cincinnati, Ohio, AES speech in (October, 1956), 292–298

CIO (Congress of Industrial Organizations), 147. *See also* AFL–CIO

Citizens for Stevenson Committee, 8
civil rights, 64n, 137, 174, 176, 305, 373, 465; AES statements and speeches on, (February, 1956) 51–53, 65–67, 77–80, (April, 1956) 121–126, 128–129, (October, 1956) 252–257; Mrs. Roosevelt and AES's position on, 67; legislation, 148, 408n, 465; plank of Democratic platform, 148, 177–180; Republican party and, 152, 179, 254–256. See also segregation/desegregation
Civil Rights Act, 465n
Civil Rights Commission, U.S., 378, 465n
Civil Service Commission, U.S., 222–223
Clark, Glen, 460; letter to, 461
Clark, Joseph S., Jr., 20, 518; letter to, 20
Clay, Henry, 423n
Clement, Frank, 14, 89
Clements, Earle C., 147
Cody, Arthur F., 527; letter to, 527
Coffin, Frank, 214n
Cohen, Benjamin V., 85, 362; letters to, 133, 362
Cohn, David L., letter to, 377
cold war, AES on, 47, 59, 116, 118, 165, 186, 219, 288, 441, 445
Coleman, Mrs. Edward M., 426–427; letter to, 427
Collier's magazine, 152, 417n, 457n
Collins, LeRoy, 79
Collins, Rev. Lewis John, 411, 427, 429, 430, 457; letter to, 458
colonialism, 119, 241, 531; Eisenhower/Dulles and, 30n, 116, 302; and imperialism, 47, 115, 537–539. See also nationalism
Colorado, AES campaign in, 166, 170, 214
Columbia Broadcasting System, 200; AES interviewed by, 105–108
Columbia University, 494
Commerce, U.S. Department of, 304
Commission on Human Relations, 52
Committee of 100 for Stevenson, 147
Committee on Government Contract Compliance, 255
Commonwealth Club (San Francisco), 305
communications, mass: and advertising, 55, 103, 142–143, 185, 190, 336, 337, 341, 346–350 *passim*, 357–360 *passim*, 375, 398, 399, 416, 464,

466, 470, 483, 484, 517; misuse of, 82, 143, 436, 464, 510; problem of, 334–341 *passim*, 346–348, 416, 420, 424, 436, 459; and equal time, 389, 390. See also complacency; press, the; television
Communism and Communist bloc, 30n, 445; as 1952 issue, 37; challenge and pressure of, 55, 101, 115, 118, 219, 293, 294, 317, 538–541; competition with U.S. and West, 113–117, 188, 217, 241, 242, 262, 288, 297, 303, 320, 537, 539–544; Eisenhower Administration and, 113–114, 123–124, 142, 223–225, 288, 293, 317, 320, 403, 434, 470; in Far East, 113, 114, 116, 241, 288, 292, 302–303, 318, 469; and U.S. policy, 116, 186, 376, 470, 541; Nixon and, 230, 258, 259; in Middle East, 241, 294, 311–312, 313–314, 317, 318, 469, 470; and socialism, 243, 539 (*see also* socialism); in Poland and Hungary, 300–302, 311, 312, 319; AES discusses in article (*Western World*), 538–541; in Africa, 539–540. See also Union of Soviet Socialist Republics
complacency, 86, 186, 221, 242, 261, 373, 376, 405, 465, 510; Eisenhower/Republican party and, 85, 150, 151, 153, 215, 216, 242–243, 246; ignorance and, 339, 354 (*see also* ignorance, public, of issues)
Conant, Clark, 348
Congress, U.S., 49, 108, 158n; Democrats in, 55, 99, 124, 148, 254, 275, 287, 290, 334, 351, 374, 382, 397, 398, 402, 407, 423, 454, 459, 470, 471, 484; Democratic, and Eisenhower, 58n, 186, 215, 218, 241, 248, 254, 306, 350, 388, 393, 432, 459n, 467, 469; Eisenhower and, 79n, 123; legislation and appropriations, 148, 226, 232, 265, 275, 290, 390n, 465; House of Representatives, 148, 230–231, 302; investigates "security risks," 224; and REA, 268; and Democratic Advisory Council, 402, 407. See also Senate, U.S.
Congressional Record: AES speeches inserted in, 65n, 418, 504
Connecticut Democratic Convention, 169
conservation, 187; Republican party and, 48, 58, 264, 265–269; water

policy and flood control, 58, 211–212, 266–269; soil and water, 211–212, 234–235; AES speech on (Montana, October, 1956), 264–270
Conservation Program, 235
Constitution, U.S., 78; and civil rights, 53, 69, 123, 179, 256; Bill of Rights, 123, 124–125, 128, 187, 225, 256–257, 305
Cooke, Mr. and Mrs. Alistair, 331; letter to, 331
Cooper, John G., 267n
Cordier, Andrew W., 6; letter to, 6–7
Cousins, Norman, 171, 487; letters to, 162, 171–172, 386, 488
Cowles, Gardner ("Mike"), 176; letter to, 176
Cowles, John, 176
Craig, May, 526; letters to, 526, 528; quoted, 527
Cranston, Alan, 98
Creighton, Mrs. Mary, 363; letter to, 364
Cross, Mrs., 346n
Crowell-Collier Publishing Company, 417
Crowther, Geoffrey, 428, 429, 508, 531; letter to, 429–430
Cuba, 537
Curley, James Michael, letter to, 511–512
Currie, Mr. and Mrs. John B., 263; letter to, 263
Curtis, Carl T., 301n
Cyprus, 114, 293

Daily Pantagraph, 439
Daily Princetonian, 336, 337, 420
Daley, Richard J., letter to, 129
Daly, John, 177
Dammann, John F., 211n
Dammann, Tom, 211; letter to, 211–212
Daniels, Jonathan, 206; letter to, 206–207
Davidson, Eugene, 230; telegram to, 231
Davies, Clement, 88, 451; letters to, 88, 451–452
Davies, Ralph, 476
Davis, Elmer, 21n, 432; letter to, 412
Davis, James C., 230
Davis, Jefferson, 55
Davis, Kenneth S., 491; A Prophet in

His Own Country, 171n, 438, 474n, 489; letters to, 438–439, 492–495
Day, J. Edward, 416; letter to, 417
Deakin, William, 498, 514
Decalogue Society of Lawyers, 489, 490; AES message to, 489–490
Declaration of Independence, 115, 120, 179
defense: and "massive retaliation," 48, 56, 116, 282, 445, 468; AES speaks on, 71n, 110–121, 186, 247–250, 281–286, 292–298; and militarism/aggression, 88, 116, 353, 403, 434, 444, 470 (see also Eisenhower Doctrine); and military advantage, 111, 117, 186, 285, 443–444, 445; and disarmament, 118, 163, 164, 249, 282–283, 296, 353; and draft issue (Selective Service), 200, 247–248, 277, 287, 289–291, 295, 424; spending, 219, 288–289, 467n; and economic aid, 324. See also foreign policy; nuclear weapons and testing
Defense, U.S. Department of, 113, 305n, 469
de Lattre de Tassigny, General Jean, 541
de Linarès, General François, 541
democracy: AES on, 77–78, 225, 297, 315, 326, 327, 335, 436, 466, 472, 489–490, 543; Mrs. Roosevelt quoted on, 261
Democratic Advisory Council, 426, 432, 435, 474–475, 517; AES joins, 374, 376, 380, 382, 403, 406–408; AES issues statement on, 402–403; foreign policy statement of, 527. See also Democratic National Conference (1957)
Democratic Clubs, 24, 96n
Democratic Digest, 13n
Democratic-Farmer-Labor (DFL) party, 90–95 passim, 105, 107, 202n, 246, 251. See also farm issue
Democratic National Advisory Council. See Democratic Advisory Council
Democratic National Committee, 3, 12, 175, 192, 385; and criticisms of AES speech before, 8–9, 28; chairmanship, 36, 207, 409–410; and Advisory Council, 374 (see also Democratic Advisory Council); fund-raising dinner for, 505n, 527. See also Democratic party
Democratic National Conference (1957), AES speech before, 406n,

463–473, (discussed), 406n, 423, 425, 426, 433, 434, 454, 456–457, 502, 505n, 526
Democratic National Convention (1952), 84n, 347
Democratic National Convention (1956), 129, 143, 148, 177–195, 203, 386; AES nomination at discussed, 7n, 8, 9, 23, 147, 150, 155, 157, 160–164, 169, 174, 175, 194; AES acceptance speech discussed, 161–164; the South and, 174, 177, 190; AES nominated and accepts, 180, 182–189; and choice of Vice President, 181–182, 183, 201–202; Truman letter about, 191–192; TV recording of, 384
Democratic party: task, philosophy and principles of, 3, 49, 77–78, 183, 188, 225, 247, 259–260, 308, 359, 465, 472, 502; platform, 8, 148, 177–180, 184, 193, 207, 226, 227, 228, 234, 243, 254, 255, 266, 279, 375; financing, 35, 149, 199, 220, 221, 245, 396, 505n, 527 (see also Stevenson, Adlai E.: CAMPAIGN FOR PRESIDENCY, 1956); and Minnesota primary, 44, 90–99 passim; policies adopted by Republicans, 48–49, 57, 58, 185–186, 203, 241, 253–255, 287, 305–306, 464, 483, 484–485; AES on extremism in, 62, 105, 147; in California, 62, 97–99, 102, 103, 142, 146, 149, 154, 463; and Young Democrats, 95; AES on unity/disunity of, 99, 146, 184, 431, 434–435, 465; in Illinois, 106, 130; and civil rights, 148, 176, 179–180, 465; leadership of and by, (AES on) 161, 187, 367, 376, 464, 472, (Mrs. Roosevelt on) 180, 261, (Truman on) 191–192 (see also AES as leader of, below); Lyndon Johnson and, 161, 202, 367, 374, 402, 407, 423; strength of, 199; in South, 202, 408, 465; accomplishments, 216, 246, 250–251, 252–255; AES as leader of, 229, 348, 351, 355, 356 (see also Stevenson, Adlai E.: AND LEADERSHIP OF DEMOCRATIC PARTY); and "socialism," 243–244, 258; AES's pride in, 260, 322–323; future role of and challenge to, 261, 276, 295, 330–334 passim, 348–349, 374, 402–403, 414, 463–473, 499; and conservation issue, 264, 269; AES joins

Advisory Council of, 374, 376, 380, 382, 403, 406–408 (see also Democratic Advisory Council); AES and duty to, 375, 393, 527; structure, 387, 422, 423; liberal cause and, 387, 393–394, 431–432, 502; and election analysis, 393–394; and failure of communications, 406, 436, 499 (see also press, the); or formation of new party by AES, 422; migration from cities and, 465. See also Congress, U.S.
Democratic state committees: AES telephones chairmen (October, 1956), 308–309
Democratic state conventions: California, 53, 174n, 385; Colorado and Wyoming, 166; Connecticut, 169
De Sapio, Carmine, 62, 121, 147, 189, 229
Detroit, AES speeches in, (March, 1956) 86, 102–103, (Labor Day, 1956) 167, 210n, 279, 419
Dever, Paul, 95
Dewey, Thomas E., 352, 440, 469
Dick, Edison, 81, 89, 364, 477, 507, 511
Dick, Edison Warner, 364; letter to, 365
Dick, Mrs. Edison (Jane Warner), 81, 83, 89, 199, 364, 462, 507, 511; and National Stevenson for President Committee, 3, 14, 155; letters to, 136, 145, 477–478; and Volunteers for Stevenson and Kefauver, 199, 382n
Dick, Letitia, letter to, 382–383
Dien Bien Phu, fall of, 303
Diggs, Charles C., Jr., 332; letter to, 332
Dilliard, Irving, 419; letters to, 363, 419–420
Dirksen, Everett M., 130n, 356n
disarmament. See defense
Disraeli, Benjamin: quoted, 38
District of Columbia. See Washington, D.C.
Dix, William S., 523
Dixon, Edgar H., 217; and Dixon-Yates contract, 217n, 268
Dodds, Harold W., 494; letter to, 523
"Dollars for Democrats Day," 220
Donovan, Robert J., Eisenhower: The Inside Story, 174
"Dooley, Mr." (Finley Peter Dunne), quoted, 485

Doris (cook at Libertyville), 460, 520
Doubleday & Company, 489, 490, 497
Douglas, Emily Taft (Mrs. Paul H.), 334
Douglas, Helen Gahagan (Mrs. Melvyn), 140, 230, 331; letters to, 141, 332
Douglas, Melvyn, 140, 331; letter to, 332
Douglas, Paul H., 268n; letter to, 334
Douglas, Stephen, 240
Dowling, Robert W., 73; letter to, 73
Doyle, James E., 347; letter to, 347
draft issue, *see* defense
Dubinsky, David, letter to, 252
Dulles, John Foster, 80, 85, 381, 418; and Goa, 30, 116; AES discusses, 41, 43, 48, 87, 88, 113, 172, 281, 292–293, 301–302, 305, 318, 320, 354, 361, 399, 428, 464, 511; and "brinksmanship," 42, 43, 44, 56, 111–112, 218, 303, 320, 468; and USSR, 57n, 111, 361; and Middle East, 111, 280, 311–313, 317, 353, 361, 469, 509–510; world distrust of, 113, 399, 428, 435; and Bandung Conference, 116, 428; calls criticism of U.S. a "tribute," 116–117; and "defeat as victory," 292, 303, 357, 464, 482; undergoes surgery, 320n. *See also* Eisenhower, Dwight D., and Eisenhower Administration
DuPont Company, 142
Dutch East Indies, 537. *See also* Indonesia

Eaton, Cyrus, 518n
Eberlein, Roxane, 501; joint memo to, 501
Eccles, Marriner S., 89, 521
Eccles, Mrs. Marriner S. ("Sally"): letter to, 521
economy, U.S. and world, 88, 157, 163, 164, 296, 469, 470; Republican party and, 82, 174, 185, 241–244, 304; and foreign aid, 112–113, 118–120, 216, 235, 242, 303, 314, 324, 471, 540; and economic coercion, 143 (*see also* communications, mass); and unemployment, 167, 304; and conservation, 211 (*see also* conservation); "free market," 232n (*see also* farm issue); and poverty as campaign issue, 242–243
Eddy, Russell, 473
Edelstein, Julius, 21

Eden, Anthony, 56, 302, 303, 317, 399, 451
Edison, Thomas, 322
education, 523; AES on Eisenhower Administration and, 57–58, 174, 323; White House Conference on, 58n, 174; federal aid to, 67; speech draft on, 168; in Democratic platform, 178, 179, 243. *See also* segregation/desegregation
"eggheads," AES on, 38, 46, 162, 257, 517
Egypt, 353n; vs. Israel, 88, 101, 120n, 309–314; U.S. and, 280, 309–314, 317, 318, 469, 510, 537, 542; British-French attack on, 309–314, 319, 536; USSR and, 311, 312, 317, 318, 540. *See also* Middle East; Suez
Eisenhower, Dwight D., and Eisenhower Administration, 8–9, 34, 159, 220, 230, 278, 373, 392, 401, 416, 511; AES letters and telegrams to, 27, 211, 319, 324, 326, 419n; health and illnesses of, 27n, 38, 82, 150, 152–153, 156, 160, 170, 172, 184, 190, 218, 304, 306, 324, 484; and colonialism, 30n, 116, 302; statement on Dulles, 44, 218; foreign policy, 48, 56, 103–104, 116, 292, 301–303, 318, 319, 320, 324, 410, 418, 427, 467n, 468 (*see also* and Middle East, *below*); State of the Union messages, 53, 467n; and deception/nondisclosure, 55, 111–112, 150, 311, 312–313, 315–316, 324, 328, 340–341, 351, 352, 373, 402, 420, 436, 442, 464–465, 494 (*see also* complacency); and "peace and prosperity," 56, 82, 87, 164, 186, 199, 216, 219, 239–240, 249, 280, 293, 390, 469; and Geneva Conference, 56n, 294, 313, 317, 319; and education, 57–58, 174, 393; and USSR, 57n, 142, 319, 360, 361, 408, 536 (*see also* and Communism, *below*); and Democratic policies, 58, 203, 241, 305–306 (*see also* Democratic party); and Congress, 58n, 79n, 123, 186, 215, 218, 241, 248, 254, 306, 350, 388, 393, 432, 459n, 467, 469; and Nixon, 69, 82; and racism, segregation, civil rights, 79n, 122–123, 152, 179, 255, 256; and reelection campaign, 82, 95n, 106, 147, 199, 203, 239, 287, 309, 325, 359, 388, 419, 484; AES on popularity of, 82, 150, 153, 171–172,

185–186, 398, 399; 1952 campaign, 94, 99, 114, 116, 140, 147n, 223–224, 231–234, 419; farm policy, 99, 107, 186, 231–234, 236, 315–316, 318; and delegation of authority, 99, 172, 304–307; "operation candor," 111–112; and Communism, 113–114, 123–124, 125n, 142, 223–225, 288, 293, 317, 320, 403, 434, 470; and nuclear weapons, 118n, 133 (*see also* nuclear weapons and testing); and U.S. prestige, 142, 150, 186, 293, 304, 305, 320; AES as "imitation" of, 146; as "father figure," 151, 153; AES on speeches of, 158, 247, 482; the press and, 185, 359, 381, 422, 464, 466, 500; and criticism, 202, 247, 381, 390, 398, 399, 407, 414, 466, 472, 527; indifference and lethargy of, 208, 301, 302–306, 320, 353, 500, 510; offers CIA information to AES, 211; and conservation, 211, 265–269; and business, 217, 222 (*see also* business); and TVA, REA, 217n, 268n; public health program, 218n, 273, 275, 304; and budget, 219, 288–289, 467, 483–484; and security "risks," 223–225; and draft issue, 247–248, 291, 295; endorsed by New York *Times,* 287; and "defeat as victory," 292, 303, 357, 358, 464, 482, 510; and Middle East (Eisenhower Doctrine), 294, 303, 310–314, 316–320, 323–324, 400, 403, 407, 424, 427, 434–435, 453n, 454, 464, 468–472, 483, 500, 509–510, 536; and formation of new party, 294–295; quoted on Polish and Hungarian struggles, 300, 302, 418 (*see also* foreign policy, *above*); AES speeches on shortcomings of, 315–321, 323–324, 463–473, 480–486; electoral votes for, 325; AES telegram of congratulations to, 326; AES on "stampede" to, 329–365 *passim,* 380, 386, 390; as "political myth," 340, 349, 374; "tranquilizing effect" of, 352, 360, 361, 373, 375; and AES's concession speech, 353; loyalty to, 359; second inauguration of, 421, 431; reconciliation with Taft, 467n. *See also* Dulles, John Foster; Republican party

Eisenhower, Milton, 481
Eisenhower Doctrine, 403, 407, 427, 434–435, 453n, 454, 464, 470, 483, 500
election analysis (1956), 393–394, 399. *See also* primary elections; Stevenson, Adlai E.: CAMPAIGN FOR PRESIDENCY, 1956
Eliot, Rev. Frederick May, 19; letter to, 18
Elizabeth, queen mother of England, 494n
Elizabeth I, queen of England, 503, 515
Ellsworth, Harris, 265n
Emancipation Proclamation, 64
Emerson, Ralph Waldo: quoted, 247, 250, 252
Emmerich, Herbert, 351; letter to, 351
Encyclopaedia Britannica, 514, 531; AES on board of directors of, 405, 413, 428–429, 430, 448
England. *See* Great Britain
English-Speaking Union, 134, 135, 500, 508
equality, AES on, 52, 66, 67, 77–80, 122–123, 255–257, 305, 373, 489. *See also* civil rights; segregation/desegregation
Erickson, John, 170, 421; letter to, 421
Erickson, Mrs. John, 421; letter to, 421
Ernst, Morris L., 378–379; letter to, 379
Ervin, Samuel J., Jr., 148
Evans, Carol, 3, 9, 41, 81, 97, 166, 230, 264, 279, 281, 342, 460, 461, 462, 490, 529, 531, 535; quoted, 92n, 203n; letters to, 473, 489, 491
Evjue, Bill, 452

Fairbanks, Douglas, Jr., 298; letter to, 298–299
Fair Deal, 180, 261; and New Deal, 146, 149, 150
Fair Employment Practices Commission (FEPC), 51, 255
fallout. *See* nuclear weapons and testing
Farmers Union, 102
farm issue, 81, 137, 173; and parity, 90, 92, 102, 103, 105, 232–234, 237; Eisenhower Administration and, 99, 107, 186, 231–234, 236, 315–316, 318; Democratic platform and, 227, 228, 234; AES speech on, at National Plowing Matches, 231–238. *See also* Democratic-Farmer-Labor (DFL) party
Farrell, James T., 342; letter to, 342

Faubus, Orval, 21n, 79n
Federal Aid to Education Bill, 67
Federal Power Commission, 268
Federal Reserve System, 140
Federal Trade Commission (FTC), 216
Federation of Atomic Scientists, 443
Field, Marshall, III, 348, 498
Field, Mrs. Marshall, III (Ruth), 348, 374, 376, 533
Field, Marshall, IV, 498n
Field Foundation, 498, 533
films: "spot" for TV, 203n; *Pursuit of Happiness*, 206n
Finian's Rainbow (musical comedy), 394
Finletter, Thomas K., 77, 95–96, 214, 299, 374, 409; letter to, 85–86
Finletter Group, 86, 96
Finnegan, James A., 3, 23, 96, 102, 103, 144, 170, 175, 177, 190–202 *passim*, 207, 309, 406, 407, 409; memos and letter to, 74–75, 147–148, 230, 409–410
Fischer, John ("Jack"), 13, 486, 487; letters to, 10–11, 524
Fish and Wildlife Service, U.S., 266
FitzGerald, Frances, 503
Fleeson, Doris, 481, 499, 518; letters to, 499–500, 518
flood control. *See* conservation
Florida: AES campaign in, 14, 96, 103–109 *passim*, 128, 129, 135, 139, 140, 214; primary election in, 127, 137–138, 141, 150, 151, 173; Republican party in, 142
Flynt, John J., Jr., 406; letter to, 406–407
Folliard, Eddie, 140, 142
Ford, John Anson, 98, 476
foreign policy: in Middle East, 26 (*see also* Middle East); in Far East, 30, 48, 112–116, 288, 292, 302–303, 318, 323, 324, 344, 468–471, 537, 540, 541, 543; and "brinksmanship," 42, 43, 44, 46, 111–112 (*see also* Dulles, John Foster); AES on, in speeches, 48, 56–57, 71n, 251, 301–305, 323–324, 468–472 (*see also* AES speeches on, *below*); Republican party and, 48, 251, 292–295, 301–302, 317, 324 (*see also* Eisenhower, Dwight D., and Eisenhower Administration); Nixon and, 48, 113, 302, 303, 320, 321, 381, 399–400, 537; in Europe, 57, 112–114, 163, 279, 292–293, 296, 301–302, 311, 312,

318, 319, 323, 419, 468–471, 536, 537, 542–543 (*see also* North Atlantic Treaty Organization); as campaign issue, 85–87, 95, 103–104, 108, 127, 137, 138, 154, 159, 162–165, 176, 200, 201, 280–281, 298, 352, 368, 380, 393, 397; AES speeches on, (April, 1956) 110–121, (October, 1956) 292–298, (November, 1956) 310–314, 315–321; and foreign aid, 112–113, 118–120, 216, 235, 242, 280, 303, 307, 314, 324, 381n, 453, 471, 540; Truman and, 112–113, 318; and Communism, 116, 186, 376, 470, 541 (*see also* Communism and Communist bloc); public ignorance of, 200, 328–336 *passim*, 338–342 *passim*, 351, 354, 364, 398, 402, 536; and "defeat as victory," 292, 303, 464, 482; LBJ and, 359; AES discusses book/speeches on, 389, 427–428; Democratic Advisory Council statement on, 527; AES article on, in *Western World* magazine, 536–544. *See also* colonialism; defense; Union of Soviet Socialist Republics; United States
Foreign Relations Committee. *See* Senate, U.S.: Foreign Relations Committee
Forgan, J. Russell, 528; letter to, 528
Formosa, 113, 114, 303
Four Freedoms, 120
Fox, Mrs. Chloe, 395; letters to, 383–384, 396
France, 248, 335; and Middle East, 26n, 88, 106, 280, 309–317 *passim*, 342, 398–400, 468, 469, 536, 537, 541; and USSR, 56n, 57n; relations with U.S., 113, 293, 311, 313, 318–324 *passim*, 381, 468, 469, 536, 537, 542, 543
freedom: AES on, 65, 77, 112, 115, 120, 320, 321, 543; AES speech on, 121–126; Eisenhower quoted on satellites and, 300. *See also* civil rights
Freedom of Information Committee (American Society of Newspaper Editors), 110–111
Freeman, Orville L., 44, 81, 83, 89, 90, 93, 98, 246; letter to, 83–84
Freeman, Mrs. Orville L., 89; letter to, 83–84
Fresno, California: AES birthday celebration in, 14, 24; AES speech in

(February, 1956), 53–61, (discussion of) 24, 62–63, 71–76 passim
Friends of Israel for Stevenson Committee, 270–271
Fritchey, Clayton, 12, 199, 409; letters to, 12, 459
Frontier magazine, 517–518
Fry, Colonel Joshua, 531
Fulbright, J. William, 21n, 361, 384, 434, 453, 454, 471; letters to, 154, 158, 170, 384–385, 434–435
Fulbright Program, 158n

Gabrielson, Ira, quoted, 266
Gaitskell, Hugh, 138, 527, 528
Galbraith, John Kenneth, 199, 409, 424, 425, 446; The Affluent Society, 157; letter to, 157
Galbraith, Mrs. John Kenneth ("Kitty"), 409, 446; letters to, 409, 424–425, 446
Gandhi, Mohandas K., 128
Garrison, Lloyd K., 15, 73, 77, 341, 448; letters to, 15, 341, 448
Garrison, Mrs. Lloyd K. (Ellen), 15, 341; letter to, 15
Gary, Raymond, letter to, 238
Gavin, Lieutenant General James M., 441
Gebhardt, W. Reading, 355; letter to, 355
Gellhorn, Martha. See Matthews, Martha Gellhorn (Mrs. T. S.)
General Motors, 233, 237
General Services Administration, 304
Geneva Conference, 56n, 294, 313, 317, 319
George, Lieutenant Colonel C. J., 506; letter to, 506
Georgia, 267, 406
Germany, 57, 163, 165, 248, 471. See also Berlin
Geyer, Rev. Alan: letter to, 504
Ghana (Gold Coast): renamed as independent state, 166n, 453, 515, 540; AES plans trip to, 415, 500, 507–508, 515–516, 530–534 passim. See also Africa
ghostwriting: AES discusses, 11–12, 41–44 passim, 74, 76, 87, 97, 104, 127, 134, 157, 161–168 passim, 190, 199, 228–229, 342, 343, 482
G.I. Bill of Rights, 251
Gideonse, Harry D., 356; letter to, 357
Goa, 30, 116

Godkin Lectures (Harvard), 42; published as Call to Greatness, 42n, 494
Goheen, Robert, 433n
Gold Coast. See Ghana
Golden, Harry, letters to, 97, 343
Gomulka, Wladyslaw, 300
Gore, Albert, 169
Governors' Conference (July, 1956), 169, 174
Graebel, Rev. Richard Paul, 17–18, 32, 40, 530; letters to, 40–41, 530
Graffis, Herb, 391; letter to, 391
Graham, Billy, 14, 89
Grand Coulee dam, 269
Great Britain, 157, 284, 335, 453, 542–543; and Middle East, 26n, 88, 105, 280, 309–317 passim, 342, 353n, 381n, 398, 399–400, 468, 469, 471, 536, 537; USSR and, 56n, 57n, 317, 353n; relations with U.S., 113, 293, 311–313, 318–324 passim, 353–354, 381, 410, 468, 469, 518, 536, 537; affection for AES in, 329n, 421, 518; Churchill on Coalition Government of, 360–361; AES discusses trip to and speeches in, 405, 411, 427–430 passim, 437, 452–458 passim, 477, 498–504 passim, 508–532 passim, 535
"Great Crusade," 224
Greece, 112, 318, 470
Greeley, Horace, 54, 463
Green, Leon, 359; letter to, 359
Greene, John K., 462n
Greenfield, Albert M.: letter to, 346
Gridiron Club, AES speech before, 480–486; AES discusses, 342, 343, 381, 406, 409, 434, 437, 455, 458–462 passim, 474, 488, 502, 526; reactions to, 490, 499–500, 505, 517
Gromyko, Andrei, 7
Gruening, Ernest, 337; letter to, 337–338
Guggenheim, Charles, 400; letter to, 400
Guggenheim, Mr. and Mrs. Harry, 473, 479n. See also Patterson, Alicia
Gunther, John, 128
Gwinn, Ralph W., 157n

Hackney, H. Hamilton ("Monk"; "Hacker"): letter to, 534
Hale, Robert, 214n
Hall, Leonard, 301n
Hamilton, Hamish, 410, 450, 508

Hamilton, Mrs. Hamish, 410, 450
Hammarskjöld, Dag, 120n, 133, 494n
Hardin, Carol J., 385; letter to, 385
Harlem, AES speech in (October, 1956), 230, 252–257
Harper & Brothers, 10, 389, 487, 523
Harriman, Daisy Borden, 8; letter to, 9
Harriman, W. Averell, 8, 64, 147, 195, 201, 229, 374; candidacy, 9, 95n, 160, 180; AES on, 21, 39, 94, 121, 189; Republican party and, 146, 149, 150, 151
Harris, Seymour E., 11, 12, 174, 199, 344, 501, 524; letters and memo to, 11–12, 174, 344–345, 459, 486–487
Harrisburg, Pennsylvania, AES speech in (September, 1956), 215–220, 228
Harrison, Gilbert A., 75, 159, 519; letters to, 75–76, 159, 519–520
Harsch, Joseph C.: letter to, 528–529
Hart, Jackie, 15–16
Hart-Davis, Rupert, 12–13
Hartford, Connecticut, AES speech in (February, 1956), 24, 77–78, 102
Hartford Courant, 379
Harvard University, 513; John Fell at, 11n; AES Godkin Lectures at, 42; and support of AES, 344, 382; Adlai III at Law School, 429, 529
Hatoyama, Ichiro, letter to, 222
Hauck, Janet Chase, 61
Hawkins, Gus, 98
Hayes, John, 70
Hays, Brooks, 354; letters to, 354–355, 418
H bomb. See hydrogen bomb
health. See medical care
health of President as issue, 190. See also Eisenhower, Dwight D., and Eisenhower Administration
Hebdomadal Council, 513–514. See also Oxford University
Hechler, Kenneth, 75, 199
Heller, Edward, 171, 385, 434, 476; letter to, 386
Heller, Mrs. Edward, 385–386, 424; letter to, 386
Hells Canyon, 267, 269
Hennings, Thomas, 332; letter to, 332–333
Hersey, John, 199; letters to, 134, 167–168
Hershey, Harry, 529
Higgins, Pat, 403; letter to, 403
Hines, Mrs. Ralph (Betty Borden, formerly Mrs. Robert S. Pirie), 5, 221n; letters to, 5, 512
Hiroshima, 115, 282, 428, 441. See also Japan
Hitler, Adolf, 216
Hobby, Oveta Culp, 304
Hochschild, Harold, 449; letter to, 415–416
Hochschild, Mrs. Harold (Mary Marquand), 210, 345; letters to, 210, 345–346, 449
Hodges, Luther H., letter to, 110
Hodges, Mrs. Luther H., 110, 531
Holland, Frank, 460, 461; letter to, 460
Holland, Mrs. Frank (Beatrice), 520
Holland, Spessard, 202
Holmes, Oliver Wendell, 322
Hoover, Herbert, 233, 251
Hoover, Herbert, Jr., 243, 303
Horne, Mr. and Mrs. John, 421; letter to, 421–422
Hotz, Wilfred H., letter to, 438
House of Representatives. See Congress, U.S.
housing, 307; AES on, 52, 58, 253–254
Humphrey, George M., 160n, 302, 459n, 467, 483, 518
Humphrey, Hubert H., 33, 246, 273, 323n, 374; letters to, 33–34, 44, 81, 505; and Minnesota primary, 44, 83, 89, 90, 93, 98; and vice presidency, 182, 201, 202
Hungary, 314, 323, 326; 1956 revolution in, 300–302, 311, 312, 318–320, 419, 440, 445, 468, 469, 541, 543
Hunt, John, 448
Hunt, Virginia L., 407; letter to, 407–408
Hunter, Kermit, letter to, 404
Hutchins, Robert M., 448; letter to, 264
Hutton, E. F., & Company, 535
hydrogen bomb, 128, 188, 219, 278–279, 386; AES and test ban proposal, 71n, 118, 200, 277, 281, 283–284, 296, 335, 344, 352, 424, 439–446, 527; AES comments on Eisenhower and, 133, 248–250, 283–284, 286, 344, 352, 424; AES on Nixon and, 307, 324; AES article on, in Look magazine, 425, 439–446. See also nuclear weapons and testing
Hyman, Sidney, 160

Iceland, 113, 293
Idaho: AES campaign in, 278
ignorance, public, of issues, 328–336 *passim*, 338–342 *passim*, 351, 354, 364, 373, 398, 402, 416, 424, 536; and deception/nondisclosure by Eisenhower Administration, 55, 111–112, 311, 312–313, 315–316, 324, 328, 341, 402, 442, 464–465. *See also* communications, mass; complacency; press, the
Illinois, 420, 454, 517; AES and governorship of, 4, 16, 21, 36, 37, 51–52, 67, 106, 107, 130–131, 145, 192, 223, 255, 356, 404n, 437, 493, 530; branch of National Stevenson for President Committee, 14; primary election in, 106, 126; Democratic party in, 106, 130; Republican party in, 106, 107, 130; Highways Division, 131; AES campaign in, 144, 166, 309, 356
Illinois General Assembly, 130, 132
Illinois National Guard, 52, 255
"Image of America, The," AES discusses speech on, 41–42, 71, 80, 92, 126
immigration laws, AES and hearing, 21
imperialism. *See* colonialism
"Independents," and support of AES, 414
India, 157, 241, 292, 454, 469, 540; and Goa, 30n; AES trip to, 47, 128; relations with U.S., 235, 344, 537
Indiana, AES campaign in, 214, 231
Indians, American, 266, 537–538
Indochina, 114, 116, 288, 292, 302–303, 537; and North Vietnam, 540, 541
Indonesia, 114, 292, 537, 540
inflation, 236, 278, 464, 467
integration. *See* segregation/desegregation
Interior, U.S. Department of, 266, 268
Internal Security Act. *See* McCarran Act
International Commission on Radiological Protection, 443
Interparliamentary Union Conference, 452
interposition, doctrine of, 78
Iowa: AES campaign in, 166, 202; AES speech at National Plowing Matches (September, 1956), 213, 231–238
Iran, 319, 537. *See also* Middle East
Iraq, 353n, 540. *See also* Middle East

isolationism, 251, 295
Israel, 40n, 62, 114, 335, 399; and Arab-Israeli struggle, 25–26, 33, 88, 93–94, 101, 105–106, 120n, 271, 309–314, 319, 323, 342, 353, 468–470; AES and creation of, 26, 33–34, 271, 493; Friends of, for Stevenson Committee, 270–271; and tank shipment to Saudi Arabia, 303, 316. See also Middle East
Italy, AES in, during World War II, 281–282
Ives, Alison, 524
Ives, Ernest L., 13, 14, 239, 325, 446, 456; telegram to, 447; and trip to England, 529, 531, 532, 534
Ives, Mrs. Ernest L. (Elizabeth Stevenson; "Buffie"), 6, 22, 23, 71, 325, 446; letters and telegram to, 13–14, 19–20, 437, 446, 455–456, 520–521; *My Brother Adlai*, 14n, 42, 43; and Florida campaign, 139; and trip to England, 529, 531, 534
Ives, Lila, letter to, 524–525
Ives, Mr. and Mrs. Timothy R., 13, 521, 525

Jack, Rev. Homer A., 31; letter to, 31–32
Jackson, Andrew, 126; quoted, 78
Jackson, Sir Robert, 80, 81, 92, 166, 347, 415, 425, 532, 534; knighted, 166n; letters to, 168, 347–348, 507–508
Jackson, Lady. *See* Ward, Barbara
Jackson, Robin ("MacDuff"), 348, 532
Jamaica, AES recalls trip to, 477–478
Janowitz Market, letter to, 514
Japan, 112, 113, 115, 222, 405n, 441. *See also* Hiroshima
Jefferson, Thomas, 126, 419; quoted, 77, 481
Jefferson-Jackson Day Dinner, AES speech at (Hartford, February, 1956), 24, 77–78, 102
Jenkins, Dick, 14n, 299, 474
Jews. *See* Israel
Johnson, Canon (minister in Barbados), 495
Johnson, Gerald W., 16, 387, 423, 517; letters to, 15, 150–151, 190, 228–229, 387, 423–424, 517–518; quoted by Sevareid on AES, 16; "What Can Stevenson Do?" (article in *New Republic*), 422; AES comments on book of, 522

Johnson, Lyndon B., 148, 207, 276, 277, 333, 373, 408n, 433, 447; AES visits, 7; letters to, 7, 207, 208, 278, 333–334; and Convention nominations, 147, 180, 182, 201, 202; influence and party leadership of, 161, 202, 359, 367, 374, 402, 407, 423; introduces AES in Senate, 402

Junior Democratic Political and Science Club (New York City), 513; letter to, 513

Justice, U.S. Department of, 51, 53

Kander, Allen, letter to, 498

Kantner, Dr. and Mrs. Alton, 413; letter to, 413

Kantner, John Stevenson, 413

Karelsen, Frank E., letter to, 84

Karl, Barry Dean, 365; letter to, 366

Karsh, Yousuf, 6; letter to, 6

Karson, Stan, 382

Kashmir, 114, 454, 469

Kaye, Amity, 526; letter to, 526

Kaye, Mr. and Mrs. Leo, 526

Keenan, Joseph D., 137; letter to, 137

Kefauver, Estes, 26, 153, 329, 374; and presidential candidacy, 3, 127, 147, 175; letters to, 10, 137–138, 330, 351, 382; and primaries, 44, 74, 83, 86n, 90–99 *passim*, 102, 105–108 *passim*, 132, 137, 141, 142, 146, 151, 480; and segregation, 62; Republican party and, 99, 142, 146, 151; AES discusses campaign of, 106–108, 175–176, 502; voting record of, 108; nominated for Vice President, 182, 183, 190; and joint campaign, 200, 202, 210, 234, 245, 258, 309, 315, 323n, 326; on AES, 382

Keller, Howard, letter to, 478

Kelley, Stanley, Jr., *Professional Public Relations and Political Power*, 142n

Kempton, Murray, letter to, 422

Kennan, George F., 85; letters to, 87, 104; recommends foreign policy statements, 103–104

Kennedy, Goldie, 388; letter to, 388

Kennedy, John F., 321, 323n, 355, 373, 374; telegram and letters to, 84, 194, 367; AES on, 95, 206, 263, 527; and vice presidency, 182, 183, 194, 206n; *Profiles in Courage*, 527

Kennedy, Mrs. John F., 194

Kennedy, Robert F., 355; letter to, 355–356

Kennon, Robert F., 36

Kenny, John V., 147n

Kent, Roger, 434; letter to, 156

Kentucky, 147

Kenyon, Mrs. Huston, 231

Kerr, Barbara, letter to, 417

Kerr, Jean (Mrs. Walter), 391; letter to, 391

Kerr, Robert S., 148

Khrushchev, Nikita, 138, 539

Killion, George, 476; letters to, 519, 534

Kimbell, Elmer, 22n

King, E. W., 337; letter to, 337

"King Caucus," 423

Kintner, Mrs. Robert (Jean), 72; letter to, 73

Kirkpatrick, Helen. *See* Milbank, Mrs. Robbins

Kirwan, Michael J., 535; letter to, 535

Kittrell, William H., letter to, 230

Knight, John, 498

Knowland, William, 48, 250

Knox, Frank, 34, 45n, 282; AES's writings for, 493

Korea, 113, 288, 292, 317, 318, 470

Kosciusko, Thaddeus, 279

Krenek, Ernest, *Pallas Athene Weint* (opera), 435, 436; letter to, 436–437

Krock, Arthur, 121n

Krumpelbeck, Mr. (NBC interviewer), 78, 79, 80

Kunzig, Robert L., 301n

Kuykendall, Jerome K., 268n

labor, 137, 467; and AES speech before AFL-CIO, 11, 21, 22, 52; AES on, 46, 52–53, 516–517; and minimum wage, 57, 254, 304; support of AES, 65, 103, 109. *See also* Democratic-Farmer-Labor (DFL) party

Labor, U.S. Department of, 304

Labour Party (Great Britain), 138, 360

Laos. 540. *See also* Indochina

Larsen, Don, 481

Larson, Arthur, 481–482, 483, 484

Lasker, Mary (Mrs. Albert), 406, 437, 454, 474

Latin, AES on study of, 478

Latin America, 241, 536, 538

Laughlin, Don, 14

Lawrence, David L., 374, 410

Lawrence, William, 102

Leacock, Dr. A.C., 495

League of Nations, 216, 250, 251, 295, 324
Lease, Mary "Yellin'," 387
Lebanon, 537. *See also* Middle East
Lehman, Herbert H., 39, 69, 70, 121, 204, 327, 432, 433, 474; letters to, 21, 39, 69, 127, 327–328; quoted in AES speech, 126
Lehman, Mrs. Herbert H. (Edith), 69; letters to, 127, 327–328
Lehman, Katrina, letter to, 479
Lenin, V. I., 539; quoted, 540
Lerner, Max, 339
Lewis, Lloyd, 212, 511
Lexington Democratic Club, 96n
Libby, Willard F., 443
liberal cause, 147, 373, 387, 393, 431–432, 457n, 465, 502
Liberal party (New York), 229
Lie, Trygve: letter to, 516
Life magazine, 35n, 42, 303
Lincoln, Abraham, 41, 55, 68, 126, 263, 322, 404n, 437–438, 455, 472, 484; debates with Douglas, 240; Nevins biography of, 509–510
Lincoln's Birthday speeches, Republican, 68
Lippmann, Walter, 85, 163, 227; letters to, 127, 146
Lippmann, Mrs. Walter (Helen), 227; letters to, 146, 227
Little Rock, Arkansas, federal intervention in, 79n
Lloyd, David, 199
Lloyd George, David, 360
Locke, Walter, 497
Logan, Ella, 394; letter to, 395
London *News Chronicle,* 170
Long, Russell, 21
Look magazine, 152, 176; AES articles in, 33, 425, 439–446, 494
Los Angeles, 144, 309; AES speeches in, 142, 289, 493, (March, 1956) 97–102, (October, 1956) 300–308
Louchheim, Judy, 382
Louisiana, AES campaign in, 214
Louisville *Courier-Journal,* 89n
loyalty: and security, 103; and security "risks," AES on, 124–125, 222–225, 301; to Eisenhower, 359
Luce, Henry, 136
Lucey, Charles, quoted, 141
Lyne, Kerry, 134, 135
Lyons, Leonard, 357; letter to, 357–358
Lyons, Mrs. Leonard (Sylvia), 357

McBride, Jean (Mrs. John K. Greene), 462
McBride, W. Paul, 462n
McCarran, Patrick, 36
McCarran Act (1950), 124
McCarthy, Senator Joseph R., 82, 123, 510; and "Twenty Years of Treason," 68, 124
McClatchy, C. K., 3
McClellan, John, 21n, 516n
McCloskey, Matthew H., 149, 199; letter to, 339–340
McCormack, John W., 95n, 227; letters to, 193, 228
Macdonald, Kenneth, 111
McDougal, Ann, 83n; letter to, 83
McDougal, Edward D., Jr., 448, 460, 512, 520
McDougal, Mrs. Edward D., Jr., 83n
McGill, Ralph, letter to, 152–153
McGowan, Mr. and Mrs. Carl, 20
McGrory, Mary, quoted, 373
McKay, Douglas, 269
McKinney, Robert, 452
McLain, Raymond F., 514
McLaughlin, Mrs. Frederic ("Kit"), 462; letter to, 449
MacLeish, Archibald, 11, 74, 377, 462, 494n; letters to, 11, 74, 161–162, 201
MacLeish, Mrs. Archibald (Ada), 74, 364; letters to, 74, 364
McMillan, Bill, 276, 278; letter to, 277
Madison Square Garden rally (October, 1956), 309
Maginot line, 248
Magnuson, Laura (Mrs. Paul B.), 392, 478; letter to, 392
Magnuson, Dr. Paul B., 478
Mahoney, Florence, 474; letter to, 497
Maine, 214n; AES campaign in, 166
Major Campaign Speeches of Adlai E. Stevenson, 1952, 493n, 494n
Malone, George W., 305, 306
Malory, Sir Thomas, 418
"Manifest Destiny," 537
Manning, Robert, 158; letter to, 158
Mansfield, Mike, 471; quoted, 290
Mansure, Edmund F., 304n
Margaret, Princess, 477
Marshall, General George C., 82, 506; quoted, 297
Marshall Plan, 112, 119, 216
Martin, Cindy, 512
Martin, John Bartlow, 74, 199, 487, 512, 524

Martin, Mrs. John Bartlow (Frances), 74n, 501, 512; joint memo to, 501
Marx, Karl, 539, 540
Mary Lou (housekeeper at Libertyville), 19, 135
Massachusetts, primary election in, 95n, 126
mass communications media. *See* communications, mass
"massive retaliation." *See* defense
Matthews, Martha Gellhorn (Mrs. T. S.), 341, 342, 498, 499
Matthews, T. S. ("Tom"), 341, 509, 531; letters to, 341–342, 381–382, 410–411, 498–499
Maverick, Maury, Jr., 345; letter to, 345
Maxwell Graduate School of Citizenship and Public Affairs (Syracuse University), 394
Mazo, Earl, 339; letter to, 339
Meader, George, 301n
Meadville Theological Seminary, 19
media. *See* communications, mass; television
medical care: and public health program under Eisenhower, 218n, 273, 275, 304; AES speech on (October, 1956), 271–276
Meet the Press (TV program), 230; AES appears on (May, 1957), 526, 527, 530, 535
Meir, Golda, 40n
Melton, Clinton, 22n
Melville, Herman, 433; quoted, 431, 472–473
Mendelsohn, Rev. Jack, 17–18, 32
Mendès-France, Pierre, 522
Menninger, Dr. Karl, 454; letter to, 454
Mertens, Mrs. Gertrude, 411
Metcalf, Lee, 266
Metropolitan Club (Washington), 392
Mexico, 538. *See also* Latin America
Meyer, Agnes (Mrs. Eugene), 27n, 29, 109, 157, 175, 400, 403, 404, 455, 490; *Education for a New Morality*, 374–375, 431, 433
    LETTERS TO, 23–27, 30, 39–40, 159–161, 367–368, 375, 401, 432–433, 521–522; on ghostwriting and speeches, 43–44, 71, 488, 490–491; on campaigning, 62–63, 70–71, 81–82, 102–103, 135–136, 140, 141–143, 170–171, 202–203; on Kefauver, 175–176, 210; on birthday party and

vacation, 380–381, 447; on leadership, 455; on biography, 496–497; on marriage, 532–533
Meyer, Eugene, 63, 71, 140, 143, 159–160, 489
Meyer, Dr. Karl, 14
Meyner, Robert, 147
Miami, AES speech in (November, 1955), 10, 20, 52
Middle East, 207n, 281, 389, 441, 461, 511; UN and, 26n, 309–313 *passim*, 353, 469, 536, 537; Eisenhower/Dulles and, 111, 280, 294, 303, 310–314, 316–320, 323–324, 353, 361, 400, 424, 435, 468–472, 509–510, 536 (*see also* Eisenhower Doctrine and, *below*); cease-fire in, 120, 133, 309–310; public ignorance of, 200; USSR and, 241, 294, 311–324 *passim*, 343, 353, 354, 361, 403, 407, 468–471, 510, 536, 537, 540–541; and tank shipment to Saudi Arabia, 303, 316; AES speaks on, 310–314, 316–320, 323–324; Nixon quoted on, 313, 316, 468, 469; effect on crisis on U.S. election, 329, 334, 340–342, 347, 352–359 *passim*, 393, 397, 398, 399; Eisenhower Doctrine and, 403, 407, 427, 434–435, 453n, 464, 483, 500. *See also* Arabs and Moslem world (Islam); Suez; *individual countries*
Mike (gardener at Libertyville), 460
Milbank, Robbins, 63, 434; letter to, 63–64
Milbank, Mrs. Robbins (Helen Kirkpatrick), 63; letters to, 63–64, 93, 377–378, 433–434
Miles, Suzanna Whitelaw, 314; letter to, 314
Miles, Ted, 314
militarism. *See* defense
Mill, John Stuart: quoted, 485–486
Miller, Francis Pickens, 239; letter to, 239
Miller, Joe, 463n
Miller, John Duncan, 398–399; letter to, 399–400
Miller, William Lee, 199
Mills College, 46
Minneapolis, AES speeches in, (September, 1956) 245–252, (November, 1956) 315–321, 419n
Minneapolis *Spokesman*, 53
Minnesota: primary election in, 3, 44, 88n, 90–99 *passim*, 104–105, 107,

126, 150, 151, 480; AES campaign in, 76, 81, 88, 89n, 102, 214, 231, 245, 315. *See also* Minneapolis
minority groups, 64, 122, 146, 171. *See also* civil rights; Negroes
Minow, Newton N., 75, 133, 199, 430, 473, 487; as AES law partner, 3, 376, 409, 448, 509
Missouri, 332, 333; AES campaign in, 166, 214, 227, 231; AES speech at St. Louis (September, 1956), 239–245
Mitchell, James P., 304n
Mitchell, Stephen A., 3, 36n, 177n
"moderation" as issue, 9, 65, 102, 180, 218
Mollet, Guy, 399
Monroe Doctrine, 536
Monroney, A. S. Mike, Jr., 147, 358; letter to, 358
Montana: AES speech in Great Falls (October, 1956), 264–270; campaign in, 278
Morgan, Edward P., 173; letter to, 173
Morgan, Linda, 173
Morocco, 537, 540, 543
Morse, Wayne, 328; letter to, 329
Moslem world. *See* Arabs and Moslem world (Islam)
Moss, John E., Jr., 111
Mowrer, Edgar Ansel, 473, 536
Murphy, Charles, 199
Murray, Thomas E., 118
Muskie, Edmund S., 214n
My Brother Adlai (Ives and Dolson), 14n, 42, 43
Myerson, Goldie. *See* Meir, Golda

Naguib, General Mohammed, 311
Nagy, Imre, 300
Nassau County Democratic organization, 356, 357
Nasser, Colonel Gamal Abdel, 280, 311, 312, 317, 468, 510, 537, 540
National Academy of Sciences, *The Biological Effects of Atomic Radiation*, 442, 443
National Association for the Advancement of Colored People (NAACP). *See* Negroes
National Citizens for Eisenhower, 142n
National Council of Negro Women, 381
National Education Association (NEA), AES quotes from speech before, 52–53
National Farmers Union, 227

National Foundation for Infantile Paralysis, 218n
National Guard (Illinois), 52, 255
nationalism, 219, 241, 319; AES article on, in *Western World* magazine, 473n, 533, 536–544. *See also* colonialism
national parks and forests, 265. *See also* conservation
National Plowing Matches (Iowa), AES speech at, 213, 231–238
National Press Club, 21
National Security Council, 440
National Stevenson for President Committee, 3, 14n, 21, 25, 34, 74–75, 143, 155
NATO. *See* North Atlantic Treaty Organization (NATO)
natural resources. *See* conservation
Navy Department, U.S., AES with, 34n, 45, 65, 67, 254, 281–282, 493, 511
Nebraska, AES campaign in, 166
Negroes, 128, 206, 381; and Till case, 22; and NAACP, 51, 63n, 73, 146, 230; and Powell Amendment/segregation issue, 51, 53, 58n, 63, 64, 65–67, 73, 101; Kefauver and, 62; and civil rights, 68, 69; and Southern problem, 79–80, 151–152; and support of AES, 102, 146, 353. *See also* civil rights; segregation/desegregation
Nehru, Jawaharlal, 454
Nesbitt, Rev. Ralph B., 213; letter to, 213
Neuberger, Maurine (Mrs. Richard L.), 349, 408; letter to, 154
Neuberger, Richard L., 65n, 408, 418; letters to, 154, 349, 408, 419
Nevada, AES campaign in, 170
Nevins, Allan, 509, 511; letter to, 509–510
"New America": as campaign theme, 187, 199–200, 203, 218–220, 252, 254, 276, 308, 327, 333, 393, 394; after campaign, 373
New America, The (Stevenson; edited by Harris, Martin and Schlesinger), 74n, 215n; AES discusses, 486–487, 501, 524
Newberry Library, 421, 523
New Deal, 71, 76, 261; Republican party and, 57, 185, 464, 483, 484; and Fair Deal, 146, 149, 150, 180, 261

New England, 174; AES campaign in, 24, 166, 169, 170. *See also* primary elections; *individual states*

New Freedom, 240

New Hampshire, primary election in, 86, 107

New Jersey, primary election in, 126

Newman, Cecil, AES statement on Powell Amendment to, 53

New Mexico, AES campaign in, 309

New Republic, 159, 422, 423, 424, 518n, 519, 520

"New Republicanism," 464, 484

Newsday, 61

newspapers. *See* press, the

Newsweek magazine, 17

New York City: AES speeches and press conferences in, (December, 1955) 11, 21, 22, 52, (February, 1956) 78–80, (April, 1956) 109, 121–126, 128, (July, 1956) 171, (September, 1956) 226–227, (October, 1956) 252–257; and reaction to integration statement, 70; Madison Square Garden rally, 309

New York City Bar Association, 225

New York Committee for Stevenson, Kefauver and Wagner, 214

New Yorker magazine, 430

New York *Post*, 22, 245, 339

New York Stevenson for President Committee, 96n, 450; press conference at headquarters of (February, 1956), 78–80; AES speech at dinner of, 121–126, 128

New York *Times*, 116, 209, 287, 309, 353; on Eisenhower and Administration, 224, 302, 303, 304, 527; endorses Eisenhower, 286; on Suez crisis, 310, 317

New York Writers' Bureau for Stevenson, 383, 395

Niagara Falls, 267

Niebuhr, Rev. Reinhold, 340, 405, 458; letters to, 176, 340–341, 405, 427–428

Nitze, Paul H., 5, 85, 205, 281

Nixon, Richard M., 190, 239, 285, 394, 440; and foreign policy, 48, 113, 302, 303, 320, 381, 399–400, 537; AES on statement of, re "Republican" Chief Justice, 68–69; AES on, 82, 203, 218, 306–307, 309, 324, 389, 414, 430, 464, 484; and Communism/socialism, 124, 230, 258–259; and "Nixonland," 307; on Middle East, 313, 316, 468, 469

Nizer, Louis, 389; letter to, 390

Nkrumah, Kwame, 453, 508n, 530, 532, 533, 534; letters to, 453, 515–516

Noel-Baker, Philip, letter to, 280–281

"No Peace for Israel" (AES article in *Look*), 33

North, William S., III, 27

North Africa, 537, 542, 543. *See also* Africa

North Atlantic Treaty Organization (NATO), 113, 114, 163, 164, 216, 291, 292, 296, 319, 323, 451, 468

North Carolina, 96, 206, 506; AES campaign in, 109, 110, 126

North Dakota, 246

Northern Tier. *See* Baghdad Pact

North Vietnam, 540, 541. *See also* Indochina

nuclear weapons and testing, 114, 115, 282, 405; AES and test ban proposal, 71n, 118, 200, 277, 281, 283–284, 296, 335, 344, 352, 439–446, 527; USSR and, 117, 118, 249, 277, 283, 284, 424n, 441, 444; Eisenhower Administration and, 118n, 133, 248–250, 278–279, 283, 285–286, 324, 335, 344, 424, 439–444; AES statements on, 133, 277; and fallout strontium 90), 284, 368n, 441–443. *See also* defense; hydrogen bomb

Oakes, John B., 373

Oakland, California, AES speech in, opening campaign (February, 1956), 45–51, 75

Oates, James F., Jr., 505; letter to, 506

Oates, Mrs. James F., Jr. (Rosalind), 19, 506

Ober, Harold, letter to, 425

Oberlin College, Mock Democratic Convention at, 8

O'Brian, William, 430; letter to, 430–431

Ohio, AES speeches in (October, 1956), 287–298

Oklahoma, AES campaign in, 14, 214, 238

Oliver, James, 214

Oppenheimer, Sir Ernest, letter to, 503–504

Oppenheimer, Harry, 415

Oregon, 265; AES campaign in, 24, 42,

65, 128, 129, 278; primary election in, 127, 137–138, 141, 150
Orwell, George, 259
Osborne, Mr. and Mrs. W. Irving, 524
Oxford University, 499, 515; AES plans speech before, 498, 500, 503, 508–520 *passim*, 526, 531, 533; AES receives honorary degree from, 498n, 503, 513–514, 518, 520, 529, 531

Pacific Gas and Electric Company, 268
Pakistan, 113, 353n, 453, 540
Palestine question, 26n, 493. *See also* Israel; Middle East
Palmer, Dwight R. G., 149
Pantagraph. See Daily Pantagraph
Pargellis, Stanley, 421; letter to, 421
parity. *See* farm issue
Partisan Review, 258
Pastore, John O., 148
Patterson, Alicia (Mrs. Harry Guggenheim), 61, 452, 473; AES visits, 8, 10; letters to, 61–62, 96, 189, 379, 479
Patton, Billy Joe, 303
Patton, James G., 102, 163, 227, 228
Paul, St., 65; quoted, 56
Paul, Weiss, Rifkind, Wharton and Garrison, 448, 525n
Pauley, Edwin W., 384, 385
Peale, Norman Vincent, 484
Pearson, Drew, 207, 437
Pearson, H. Talbot, 32; letter to, 33
Peel, Robert, 58
Peet, Mrs. Sarita, 477–478
Pennsylvania: AES campaign in, 109; primary election in, 126; AES speech at Harrisburg (September, 1956), 215–220, 228
Pericles, 431, 433, 447
Perlman, Philip B., 299; letter to, 299–300
Philadelphia *Daily News*, 339
Philippines, 441, 537, 543
Pinchot, Gifford, 265
Pineau, Christian, 541n
Pirie, Joan. *See* Thayer, Joan (Mrs. Harry)
Pirie, Robert S., 221n
Pius XII, Pope, 133
Plimpton, Francis, 520, 526
Plimpton, Mrs. Francis (Pauline Ames), 526
Point Four Program, 113, 216, 307
Poland: AES (letter) on, 279–280;

1956 revolt in, 300–302, 311, 312, 318, 320, 543
polio vaccine, 218n, 304
Portugal, 30n
Post Office, U.S., 244, 485
Potsdam Conference, 405
poverty as campaign issue, 242–243. *See also* economy, U.S. and world
Powell, Adam Clayton, and Powell Amendment, 51, 53, 58n, 63, 64. *See also* Negroes
power, electric. *See* conservation
Poznan trials, 279, 318
Presbyterian Church, 17–19, 25, 31, 32, 41
presidency, the: AES on qualifications for, 25, 50, 54–55, 82, 100, 121, 146; AES on "How Not to Choose a President," 70, 72, 75, 76, 91, 139, 200; AES discusses, 165, 172, 185, 203, 256, 304–305, 393, 480–481; health of president as issue, 190; AES disclaims further intentions toward, 376, 378, 390, 422
Presidential Health Commission, 274
press, the, 31, 80, 176, 243–244, 493; hostility/indifference to AES, 5, 62, 76, 77, 86, 87, 102–103, 108, 126, 140, 142, 146, 154, 156, 203, 298, 329, 330, 344, 388, 390, 397, 398, 405, 416, 420, 422, 424, 436, 474, 480, 499, 510, 517, 521; -government-money partnership, 12, 336, 346–349 *passim*, 373, 403, 420, 431, 464–465, 466, 484, 510 (*see also* Republican, *below*); AES speech before American Society of Newspaper Editors, 41, 71n, 110–121, 128, 133n, 138, 283; Republican, 87, 108, 146, 185, 277, 308, 340, 344, 373, 420, 422, 464–468 *passim*, 481, 499; AES baffled by, 108, 140, 142, 156, 207; and Eisenhower, 185, 359, 381, 422, 464, 466, 500; AES on fairness of, 287, 485–486; post-election, 359, 381–382; newspaper ownership and sale, 379; "hole in shoe" photograph, 388; and founding of liberal paper in Texas, 457n; AES speech before Gridiron Club, 480–486 (*see also* Gridiron Club). *See also* communications, mass
Pressman, Mr. (NBC interviewer), 79
price supports (parity). *See* farm issue
primary elections, 3, 24, 143, 149; Minnesota, 3, 44, 88n, 90–99 *passim*,

104–105, 107, 126, 150, 151, 480; AES on campaigning for, 41, 42, 62–64, 91, 128, 144, 157, 173, 178, 189, 201, 393, 397, 480, 481; California, 49, 89, 94, 97, 127, 129, 138–148 *passim,* 150, 154, 158, 518n; New Hampshire, 86, 107; Massachusetts, 95n, 126; District of Columbia, 103, 132, 150; Illinois, 106, 126; New Jersey, 126; Pennsylvania, 126; Alaska, 127, 150; Florida, 127, 137–138, 141, 150, 151, 173; Oregon, 127, 137–138, 141, 150. *See also* Stevenson, Adlai E.: CAMPAIGN FOR PRESIDENCY, 1956

Princeton University, 153, 210, 336, 341, 438, 462n, 486; and award to AES, 449, 488; AES speech at, 455, 461, 462, 488; and Princeton Library request for AES material, 523; and AES's 35th reunion, 528, 534

Providence *Journal,* 344, 349

Public Health Service, U.S., 218n

Puerto Rico, 537

Pulaski Day Parade, 279

Pulitzer, Joseph, Jr., letter to, 270

Pursuit of Happiness (campaign film), 206n

Putney School, 512

Rajagopalachari, Chakravarti R., 128, 343; letters to, 128, 344

Raskin, Hyman B., 3, 199

Rayburn, Sam, 7, 147, 148, 182, 183, 202, 207, 230; introduces AES at Convention, 180; letters to, 194, 226–227; and party leadership, 374, 402, 407, 423

REA. *See* Rural Electrification Administration

Reader's Digest, 425

religion: AES church affiliation controversy, 17–19, 25, 31–33, 40–41; and Catholic Vice President, 160, 171n; Christianity, 428

Reporter magazine, 152, 167

Republican National Committee, 68, 224, 301n

Republican National Convention, 240, 243, 253n

Republican party, 87, 95n, 309, 359, 393, 480; 1952 campaign, 37, 57, 301; in primaries, 44, 89–95 *passim,* 97, 105–107, 130, 142, 143, 147, 150, 151; divided, 48, 164, 186, 251, 295, 324; and conservation issue, 48,

58, 264, 265–269; and Democratic policies (New Deal), 48–49, 57, 58, 185–186, 203, 241, 253–255, 287, 305–306, 464, 483, 484–485; philosophy and principles, 49, 59, 240, 241, 244; and resistance to new ideas, 50, 241, 288; and "Republican" Chief Justice, 68–69; economic policy, 82, 174, 185, 241–244, 304; complacency, 85, 150, 151, 153, 215, 216, 242–243, 246; and press, 87, 108, 146, 185, 277, 308, 340, 344, 373, 420, 422, 464–468 *passim,* 481, 483, 499; and Kefauver, 99, 142, 146, 151; and Harriman, 146, 149, 150, 151; and civil rights, 152, 179, 254–256; AES on hypocrisy and deception of, 164, 403, 408, 466, 467, 472, 494; and big business, 174n, 199, 217, 222, 241, 243–244, 265–266, 268, 464; financing, 185, 220, 347, 348, 349, 464–466, 483, 484 (*see also* press, the); attacks AES, 200, 352n, 440; future of, 218, 351, 359, 464, 499; and "bread and circuses," 239–245; Old Guard, 243, 306; and "socialism," 243–244, 258–259, 268, 269; and League of Nations/UN, 250–251; platform, 256n, 266; and "agonizing reappraisal," 257, 292; and draft issue, 291 (*see also* defense); vs. formation by Eisenhower of new party, 294–295; "truth squad," 301–302; and election analysis, 393–394, 399; and California candidates for president, 463. *See also* Eisenhower, Dwight D., and Eisenhower Administration

Reston, James, 338, 434; letter to, 339; on AES, 373

Reston, Mrs. James, 338; letter to, 339

Reston, Tommy, 338; letter to, 338

Reuther, Walter, 147, 160–161; letter to, 516–517

Reynaud, Paul, 536

Reynolds, Richard S., Jr., letter to, 415

Reynolds Metals Company, 477, 508

Ribicoff, Abraham, 169; letter to, 169

Rice, Claude, letter to, 502–503

Richards, Harriet Welling (Mrs. Murray), 391; letter to, 392

Richards, Murray, 391–392

Robinson, Jackie, 322

Robinson, Ruth P., et al., 367; letter to, 367

Rock, Donald, 192

Rockwell, Norman, 475; letter to, 475
Rodgers, Mr. and Mrs. John A., III, 308; letter to, 308
Rogue River National Forest, 265
Romanes Lecture, 457–458
Romulo, Carlos P., 378; letter to, 378
Roosevelt, Eleanor (Mrs. Franklin D.), 27n, 109, 182, 189, 204, 230, 368, 427, 447; AES telegram honoring, 39; statement on AES's position on civil rights, 67; speaks on AES's behalf, 81, 180, 323n; quoted, 151, 261; column by, 432, 433
  LETTERS AND TELEGRAMS TO, 29, 300, 404, 522, 523; on civil rights, 67–68, 151–152, 177–178; on campaign, 83, 109, 190–191; on her speechmaking, 83, 109, 132, 145–146, 169
Roosevelt, Elliott, 29
Roosevelt, Franklin D., 31, 34, 200, 266, 426–427, 537; leadership of, 126, 240, 250, 251, 253; domestic policies of, 255, 267; coalition, 393
Roosevelt, Franklin D., Jr., 29
Roosevelt, Theodore, 240, 265; quoted, 270
Roosevelt University, 489n, 490
Rose, Alex, letter to, 229
Rosenberg, Anna, 300; letter to, 214–215
Rosenberg, George, telegram to, 299
Rosenman, Samuel I., letter to, 229
Rosenthal, A. M., quoted, 30n
Rosenwald, Ethel. See Stern, Ethel Rosenwald (Mrs. Edgar B.)
Roth, Robert, on AES campaign standards, 65
Rowe, James, Jr., 199, 201, 207, 409–410; letter to, 201–202
Roybal, Ed, 98
Rumford, Byron, 98
Ruml, Beardsley, 149
Rupert Hart-Davis, Ltd., 12, 42n
Rural Electrification Administration, 216, 234, 241, 268, 307
Rusk, Dean, 85
Russell, Richard B., 8, 202, 208; letter to, 8
Russia. See Union of Soviet Socialist Republics

Sacramento, California, 75, 463
St. Louis. See Missouri
St. Louis Post-Dispatch, 203, 363, 419; endorses AES, 270

Salisbury, Harrison E., 331, 359; letter to, 359–360
Salisbury, Mrs. Percy P., letter to, 331
Salisbury, Lord, 511, 515
Salk, Dr. Jonas, and polio vaccine, 218n, 304
Salt Lake City, 24; AES press conference in, 68–69
Samuelson, Paul, letter to, 167
Sandburg, Carl, 212, 527; letters and telegrams to, 35, 212, 263, 362–363; quoted, 55, 263
San Diego, California, 463
Sandrich, Mrs. Mark. See Brown, Vanessa
San Francisco: AES speeches in, (October, 1956) 271–276, (February, 1957) 463–473, (discussed) 423, 425, 426, 433, 434, 454–462 passim, 474, 475, 478, 502, 526
San Mateo, California, 75
Santayana, George, 377
Saturday Evening Post, 367; cover portrait of AES, 475
Saudi Arabia, 303, 316, 353n
Sawyer, David, 519
Sawyer, Tom, 322
Schaefer, Walter, 529
Schaefer Commission (Illinois), 131
Schary, Dore, 145, 205; quoted, 28; letters to, 28, 206, 330
Schiff, Dorothy, 452; letter to, 245
Schlesinger, Arthur M., Jr., 22, 77, 95, 167, 199, 424; letters to, 22–23, 95–96, 97, 129, 148; and The New America (AES speeches), 486, 487, 501, 524
Schlesinger, Mrs. Arthur M., Jr. (Marian), 424; letter to, 148
Schwartz, Leonard, 438
Schweitzer, Dr. Albert, 228, 488; letter to, 228
SEATO. See Southeast Asia Treaty Organization (SEATO)
Securities and Exchange Commission (SEC), 216
"security," AES on, 60
security risks. See loyalty
segregation/desegregation, 70, 73, 84, 103; AES statements on, 51–53, 64, 65–67, 77–80, 100–101, 102, 179, 226–227, 255–257; Supreme Court decision on, 53, 58n, 66–69, 77–79, 100–101, 122–123, 177–179, 255–256; Kefauver and, 62; Eisenhower and, 79n, 122–123, 255, 256; Demo-

cratic party and, 179, 184, 255; Truman and, 254, 255. *See also* civil rights

Selective Service, 248, 290, 295. *See also* defense

Senate, U.S., 148, 209, 217n, 408n; Foreign Relations Committee, 111, 361; AES attends opening session (1957), 402, 406, 434n; Democrats and, 432, 454, 470, 471. *See also* Congress, U.S.

Sevareid, Eric, 84, 144, 328; quoted on AES, 16, 64–65, 200; letters to, 16, 328

Seventh Fleet, U.S., 303n

Shannon, William V., 199; letter to, 461

Shaw, Run Run, 161

Shea, John B., 96

Sheean, Vincent ("Jimmy"), letter to, 128–129

Shepley, James, 42

Shivers, Allan, 36, 147

Shuster, Harold, letter to, 270–271

Sinclair, Upton, 350; letter to, 350

Singapore, 30n

Sklar, Robert, 336; letter to, 337

Smith, Adele Dunlap, 363; letters to, 363, 459

Smith, Elizabeth ("Libby"), 434

Smith, Ellen (Mrs. Hermon Dunlap), 19, 212, 363, 460; letter to, 212–213

Smith, Frank E., 22

Smith, Hermon Dunlap, 363

"Smith, Joe," 253n

Snyder, Elizabeth, 98

Snyder, John W., 484

socialism, 539; and Republican accusations, 243–244, 258–259, 268, 269

Social Security, 57, 251, 254, 307

Soil Conservation District Movement/ Service, 211–212, 235

South, the, 184, 353; tension and violence in, 69, 70, 79–80, 151; and Democratic National Convention, 174, 177, 190; and support of AES, 202, 206, 208, 387; Democratic party in, 202, 408, 465

Southeast Asia Treaty Organization (SEATO), 88, 116, 163, 164

Southern Pines, North Carolina, 96, 110, 506

Southern Tier, 353n

Southwest Power Administration, 267

Soviet Union. *See* Union of Soviet Socialist Republics

Spain, 536, 543

Sparkman, John J., 21, 360; letters to, 193, 360–361

Sparling, Edward J., 489, 490

Spears, General Sir Louis, 155n; letter to, 329

Spears, Lady (Mary Borden), 9, 353; letters to, 9, 89n, 155, 329, 354, 500–501

Speeches of Adlai Stevenson, 177n

Spencer, Richard, 4; letter to, 4

Spock, Dr. Benjamin, letter to, 368

Stafford Little Lectures, 523

Stalin, Joseph, 112, 113, 119, 216, 288, 294, 318, 405n, 530, 539

Stanton, Frank, letter to, 384

Stassen, Harold E., 91, 284

State, U.S. Department of, 470. *See also* Dulles, John Foster; foreign policy

Stein, Dr. (entrepreneur in Africa), 508

Steinbeck, John, 177, 335; letters to, 177, 208–209, 335, 418; *The Short Reign of Pippin IV,* 418

Steinberg, Alfred, 7n

Stengel, Richard, AES recommendation of, 130–132

Stern, Ethel Rosenwald (Mrs. Edgar B.), letter to, 395

Stern, Philip, 199, 395

Stevens, Lewis M., 153; letter to, 153

Stevens, Roger, 149, 189, 199, 340, 462; letter to, 149

Stevenson, Adlai E. (grandfather), 25

Stevenson, Adlai Ewing

CAMPAIGN FOR PRESIDENCY, 1952, 8n, 11, 12, 70n, 85, 143n, 160n, 171n, 263, 301, 322, 347, 385, 484, 493; discussed in letter to Truman, 35–37; headquarters for, 36, 192; and tidelands issue, 36, 226; Truman and, 37n, 191; compared to 1956, 73, 199, 259, 423, 484; "draft Stevenson" movement in, 84n, 106, 156; Eisenhower/Republican party and, 94, 99, 114, 116, 140, 147n, 223–224, 231–234, 419; platform of, 148, 179; AES speech collections from 177, 494; speech "defects" of, 203, 205; Pulitzer Prize photograph from, 308n

CAMPAIGN FOR PRESIDENCY, 1956: announces candidacy, 3; organization, 3, 95–96, 102, 175, 177, 190–193 *passim,* 199, 201–202, 207, 309,

406, 407; discusses candidacy and campaign, 4–5, 13, 23, 25, 35, 90, 152, 373, 375, 380, 386, 389, 399, 426; nomination discussed, 7n, 8, 9, 23, 147, 150, 155, 157, 160–164, 169, 174, 175, 194; itineraries, 14, 24–25, 42, 81–83, 91, 213–214, 231, 298–299; Truman and, 28, 172, 180, 183, 193, 263; finances and contributions, 35, 144, 145, 148, 149, 157, 170, 171, 199, 220, 221, 227, 245, 279, 280, 300, 340, 388, 417, 433, 438, 450–451, 483; and use of television, 38, 70, 76, 108, 143, 163, 203n, 280, 368, 482 (*see also* television); preparation for, pressures and exhaustion, 42, 62–64, 70, 74, 75, 81, 89, 92n, 102, 109, 135–136, 142, 144, 151, 158, 200, 210, 221, 264, 321, 355, 393, 407, 458, 481; opening speech (February, 1956), 45–51; and the "new" Stevenson, 54, 106, 141; compared to 1952, 73, 199, 259, 423, 484; refuses consent in New Hampshire primary, 86n; and AES "image," 143, 156, 158, 162; headquarters, 155, 192, 199; and choice of Vice President, 160, 171n, 175, 181–182, 183; Convention balloting, 180; AES accepts nomination, 182–189; shift in emphasis, 199–200; films, 203n, 206n; central issue of, 261–262; endorsements of AES, 270, 336, 337; number of letters received, 299; Madison Square Garden rally, 309; AES suggests UN intervention in Hungary, 319; closing speech, 321–325; AES telegram to Eisenhower re Middle East, 324; AES concedes election, 325–327; correspondence concerning campaign and defeat, 327–369, 375, 380, 382–383, 386–402, 404–407, 433; support by ministers in, 340; "shoe" as symbol of, 388; and election analysis, 393–394, 399; effect of, on congressional campaign, 398–399; and verse composed by twelve-year-old, 479; truth as essence of, 494. *See also* primary elections

CHARACTERISTICS, PERSONAL: Eric Sevareid on "indecisiveness" of, 16; wit and humor, 16, 55, 105, 137, 325; and "unorthodox political behavior," 21; style and delivery of speeches, 28, 62–63, 65, 73, 95, 102, 135, 156,

167, 200, 346n, 361, 373, 482; self-confidence, 39–40, 135; stamina, 62, 135; integrity, idealism, and courage, 65, 67, 72, 134, 325, 335, 343, 354, 358, 361, 362; self-possession, 104; and "common touch," 141; statesmanship and leadership, 328, 329, 332, 365, 392, 419, 535; chivalry, 373; intellect, 419; love of reading, 492; fascination with public affairs, 492–493; humility, 530

GOVERNORSHIP AND PUBLIC LIFE: and governorship of Illinois, 4, 16, 21, 36, 37, 51–52, 67, 106, 107, 130–131, 145, 192, 223, 255, 356, 404n, 437, 493, 530; proposed testimony on immigration laws, 21n; with Navy Department, 34n, 45, 65, 67, 254, 281–282, 493, 511; vs. private life, 221, 228; on Chicago Council on Foreign Relations, 365

AND LEADERSHIP OF DEMOCRATIC PARTY, 221, 356, 398; Truman on, 180, 181–182; AES discusses, 194, 229, 348, 351, 353, 355, 367–368, 375, 376, 378, 408, 414, 423, 455; friends express hopes of, 340, 345, 347, 355, 389, 408, 414, 422–423, 431, 432; and Democratic Advisory Council, 374, 376, 380, 382, 402–403; 408, 423, 464, 527 (*see also* Democratic Advisory Council); disclaims further intentions toward Presidency, 376, 378, 390, 422; Kefauver quoted on, 382; and party structure, 387, 422, 423; vs. formation of new party, 422; appears on *Meet the Press,* 526, 527, 530, 535. *See also* Democratic party

PERSONAL LIFE: on photographs and being photographed, 6, 15–16, 20, 25, 38, 71, 137, 308n, 357, 389–390, 426, 521, 527; Thanksgiving holiday (1955), 8, 10; Christmas holidays (1955–1956), 13–14, 19–20, 22, 23–24; celebrates birthday (1956), 14, 24, 463; and 1953 world trip, 15, 302, 321, 454n, 494, 530; church affiliation, 17–19, 25, 31–33, 40–41, 213; and Libertyville staff, 19, 135, 155, 160, 460–461, 473, 474, 509, 514, 520; and 1926 trip to Russia, 24, 61, 509; "holiday" in South (April, 1956), 96, 103; suffers from nose-throat ailment, 135, 140; future trip to Russia discussed, 143,

144, 160, 163, 166; and Davis biography, 171, 438–439, 474, 489, 490–495, 497; vs. public life, 221, 228; and second trip to Africa, 228n, 414–416, 430, 437, 452, 453, 477, 488, 499–508 *passim*, 515–535 *passim;* develops bursitis, 278; vacations after campaign, 342, 363, 374, 376–377, 381, 383, 389; discusses future plans, 346, 351, 353, 375, 379, 387, 389, 390, 394, 406, 412, 413, 418, 423, 437, 474; disclaims further intentions toward Presidency, 376, 378, 390, 422; and law practice and merger, 376, 389, 406, 422, 448, 455, 491, 492, 502, 509–520 *passim*, 523, 525n, 530; and Christmas holidays (1956–1957), 381; recommended for presidency of University of California, 384, 386, 392; discusses investments, 397, 473, 476, 535; attends opening of Senate (1957), 402, 406, 434n; plans trip to England and continent, 405, 411, 420, 427–430 *passim,* 437, 452–458 *passim*, 477, 498–504 *passim*, 508–532 *passim*, 535; on *Encyclopaedia Britannica* board, 405, 413, 428–429, 430, 448; plans western trip and speech, 406, 423, 425, 433, 434, 437, 447, 454–462 *passim;* and trip east for birthday party (1957), 409, 410, 424–426, 431–433, 437, 446–449, 455, 456; undergoes medical checkup, 421–422, 425, 431, 432; and Caribbean (Barbados) vacation, 437, 452, 455–456, 459, 473–479 *passim*, 487–496 *passim*, 500, 519, 523; and engagement rumors, 437, 447, 454; rewrites stolen autographed letter, 437–438; recalls boyhood, 438–439; receives Princeton awards, 449, 494; and plans for meeting with newspaper people, 452; receives Norman Rockwell portrait, 475; awarded honorary degrees, 494, 498n, 503, 513–514, 518, 520, 529, 531; on Field Foundation board, 498; discusses buying *Sun-Times*, 498; attends trial re John Fell's accident, 506n; negotiates for diamond purchasing license, Ghana, 507–508, 515–516, 534; and disposition of his papers, 523; appears on *Meet the Press*, 526, 527, 530, 535; discusses love and marriage, 532–533

QUOTED: announcing candidacy, 3; on Democratic party and platform, 3, 177, 374; on moderation vs. mediocrity, 9; on "mess in Washington," 36; on strenuousness and effectiveness of campaign, 81, 89n, 91, 200, 373; on primary struggle, 91, 121; on Poles and Hungarians, 301n; on Republican policies, 301n, 373, 403

SPEECHES, STATEMENTS, INTERVIEWS, PRESS CONFERENCES: announces candidacy (November, 1955), 3; at University of Virginia (November, 1955), 5; at University of Texas (September, 1955), 7; press conference at LBJ ranch, 7; "moderation" speech (November, 1955) criticized, 8–9, 28; in Miami (November, 1955), 10, 20, 52; before AFL–CIO convention (December, 1955), 11, 21, 22, 52; schedules of, 14, 24–25, 42, 81–83, 91, 213–214, 231, 298–299; pace of speeches criticized, 28; campaign speeches praised, 34, 212, 263, 328, 333, 346n, 361, 373; "The Image of America" discussed, 41–42, 71, 80, 92, 126; Godkin Lectures at Harvard, 42; opening 1956 campaign, 45–51; civil rights statement (February, 1956), 51–53; quotes NEA speech (of July, 1955), 52–53; at California State Convention (February, 1956), 53–61; and spontaneity, 62–63, 135; and literary allusions, 65; integration statement (February, 1956), 65–67; inserted in *Congressional Record*, 65n, 418, 504; press conference on Nixon statement (February, 1956), 68–69; "equivocation" in, 73; AES memo on preparation of, 74 (*see also* ghostwriting); *The New America*, 74n, 215n, 486–487, 501, 524; at Jefferson-Jackson Day Dinner (February, 1956), 77–78; New York press conference (February, 1956), 78–80; and need for reaction to spot news, 86, 133; at University of Minnesota (March, 1956), 86; in Detroit (March, 1956), 86, 102–103; Chicago press conference on Minnesota primary (March, 1956), 90–91, 92; "rhetoric" in, 95, 167; TV speech, Los Angeles (March, 1956), 97–102; CBS interview (April, 1956), 105–108; on foreign policy, before American Society of Newspaper Editors (April, 1956), 110–121; New York press conference (April, 1956), 121; on freedom, at New York campaign dinner (April, 1956), 121–126; statement on nuclear weapons (May, 1956), 133; and dislike of banalities, 156; at Colorado State Convention (July, 1956), 166; in Detroit (Labor Day, 1956), 167, 210n, 279, 419; of 1952, collected, 177, 494; TV statement on Supreme Court decision (August, 1956), 177; at Convention, on choosing Vice President, 181–182; accepts nomination, 182–189; delivery criticized, 200; AES on "defects" of, 203, 205, 210, 221; weariness, pressure and, 210, 221, 458; Harrisburg TV speech (September, 1956), 215–220; at Walnut Hill, Virginia (September, 1956), 222–225; New York statement on use of force in desegregation (September, 1956), 226–227; at National Plowing Matches, Iowa (September, 1956), 231–238; "bread and circuses" speech (September, 1956), 239–245; at Minneapolis (September, 1956), 245–252; at Harlem rally (October, 1956), 252–257; quotes Arkansas speech, 256; at Yale (October, 1956), 257–263; conservation speech in Montana (October, 1956), 264–270; in West Virginia, 264; medical care speech (October, 1956), 271–276; statements on Poland, 279–280; TV speech on test ban (October, 1956), 281–286; at Youngstown, Ohio (October, 1956), 287–291; refers to American Legion speech, 289, 440; foreign policy speech (October, 1956), 292–298; in Los Angeles (October, 1956), 300–308; telephone statement to state chairmen (October, 1956), 308–309; TV speech on Suez (October, 1956), 310–314; refers to 1955 speech on Middle East, 313; in Minneapolis (November, 1956), 315–321; TV speech ending campaign, 321–325; concedes election, 326–327; invited to speak at Colgate commencement, 336; announces future plans, 376; press statement

on Democratic Advisory Council, 402–403; press statement on "Eisenhower Doctrine," 403; invited to address Christian Action (London), 405, 411, 427–430 *passim*, 457, 458; and reluctance to speak on foreign affairs, 427, 429, 458; at Princeton, 455, 461, 462, 488; before Democratic National Conference, 463–473; before Gridiron Club (March, 1957), 480–486 (*see also* Gridiron Club, AES speech before); and "perils" of speech-writing, 482; "Business Speech," 487; recapitulated in letter to Kenneth Davis, 493, 494; at Columbia University (1954), 494; plans Oxford University speech, 498, 500, 503, 508–520 *passim*, 526, 531, 533; declines Stafford Little Lecture series, 523; appears on *Meet the Press* (May, 1957), 526, 527, 530, 535; speaks at fund-raising dinner (May, 1957), 527

AND UNITED NATIONS: on Preparatory Commission, 6–7, 280n, 537; and creation of Israel, 26, 33, 271, 493; as delegate to General Assembly (1946), 61, 282, 440, 493

VIEWS, SOCIOPOLITICAL: on going into politics, 23, 45, 54, 158, 297–298, 393, 435, 480–481, 482; on Presidency and presidential qualifications, 25, 50, 54–55, 82, 100, 121, 146, 165, 172, 185, 203, 256, 304–305, 393, 480–481; on "eggheads," 38, 46, 162, 257, 517; on organized labor, 46, 52–53; on cold war, 47, 59, 116, 118, 165, 186, 219, 288, 441, 445; on draft, disarmament and peace, *see* defense; on world leadership, 50, 101, 112–121, 122, 185–188 *passim*, 245, 251, 262, 283, 286, 288–289, 293–297, 309, 320, 376, 427, 446, 469, 471–472; on civil rights and segregation, 51–53, 64–67, 77–80, 100–101, 102, 122–126, 179, 184, 226–227, 252–257; on housing, 52, 58, 253–254; on equality, 52, 66, 67, 77–80, 122–123, 255–257, 305, 373, 489; on responsibility/irresponsibility, 55–56, 63, 110, 118, 122–123, 152–153, 159, 259–260, 263, 295, 298, 301–305, 440, 471; on campaign promises and "oratory," 55, 57–59, 99, 537; on truth in politics, 55, 167, 186, 220, 298, 302,

468, 472, 485–486, 494, 504, 510, 518; on "security," 60; on freedom, 65, 77, 112, 115, 120, 121–126, 320–321, 543; on Nixon, 68–69, 82, 203, 218, 306–307, 309, 324, 389, 414, 430, 464, 484; on "How Not to Choose a President," 70, 72, 75, 76, 91, 139, 200; on democracy, 77–78, 297, 315, 326, 327, 335, 436, 466, 472, 489–490, 543; on unity (party and U.S.), 99, 101, 146, 184, 431, 434–435, 465; on government secrecy, 111–112, 296–297; on "image," 143, 156, 158, 162; on trusting the people, 219–220, 260, 422, 436; on true function of politics, 298; on public ignorance of affairs, 328–336 *passim*, 338–342 *passim*, 351, 354, 364, 398, 402, 416, 424, 536 (*see also* ignorance, public, of issues); on "stampede" to Eisenhower, 329–365 *passim*, 380, 386, 390; on "government by the people," 338; on purpose, value and issues of campaign, 373, 375, 380, 389; on "creative opposition," 374, 402–403, 407, 466–468, 472; on Asia as area of decision, 378; on liberals, 387, 393; on criticizing the President, 407–408, 472; on foreign policy speeches and "new thoughts for a new world," 427–428, 429; on "highest goal for youth," 428–429; on study of Latin, 478; on flattery, 504, 518; on ridicule as weapon, 517. *See also* complacency; foreign policy

WRITINGS: *What I Think*, 9n, 10–11, 12, 89n; AES discusses, 10, 76, 379, 387, 390, 458, 459, 519–520; "No Peace for Israel" (*Look*), 33; "This I Believe," 41; *Call to Greatness* (Godkin Lectures, Harvard), 42n, 494; *The New America*, 74n, 215n, 486–487, 501, 524; on campaigning for primaries ("Choice by Hullabaloo," *This Week*), 91n; "Why I Raised the H-Bomb Question" (*Look*), 425, 439–446; "The Support of Nationalism Helps Combat Communist Imperialism" (*Western World*), 473n, 533n, 536–544; message to Decalogue Society of Lawyers, 489–490; for Secretary Knox (wartime), 493; recapitulated in letter to Kenneth Davis, 493, 494; *Look* articles of 1953, 494; *Major*

Campaign Speeches (of 1952), 494n; "blurb" for *This Is My World* (Locke), 497; comment on *The Lunatic Fringe* (Johnson), 522
Stevenson, Adlai E., III ("Bear"), 13, 14, 134, 151, 155, 166, 424, 431, 461, 462; letters to, 135, 139, 503, 514–515, 529–530; and birth of son, 321; and trip abroad, 429, 437, 455, 456, 499, 500, 515–534 *passim*; and law career, 429, 509, 529
Stevenson, Mrs. Adlai E., III (Nancy Anderson) 13, 14, 134, 155, 166, 321, 424, 431, 457, 461, 462; and 1956 campaign, 135, 139, 151; and trip abroad, 455, 456, 499, 500, 514–534 *passim*
Stevenson, Adlai E., IV, 321, 323, 327, 331, 339, 448, 450, 455, 456, 524; AES attends christening of, 447
Stevenson, Borden, 29, 135, 325, 434, 437, 447, 520, 529; letter to, 461–462
Stevenson, Ellen Borden (Mrs. Adlai E.), 5, 9, 134, 135, 155, 385, 500–501
Stevenson, John Fell, 13, 89, 96, 139, 166, 325, 473, 500, 529; at Harvard, 11; automobile accident, 26n, 27–33 *passim*, 40, 92, 155; and AES birthday celebration, 409, 424, 431, 447, 449, 455, 456; and trial resulting from accident, 437, 449, 476, 479, 491, 506; letter to, 462–463; and world trip, 463, 519, 520, 526, 534, 535
Stevenson, William E., 8
Stevenson, Rifkind and Wirtz, 448
Stevenson for President Committee. *See* National Stevenson for President Committee; New York Stevenson for President Committee
Stowe, Leland, 349; letter to, 349–350
Stratton, William, 356n, 454
strontium-90. *See* nuclear weapons and testing
Stuart, Kenneth, 475
Students for Stevenson, 382
Sturtevant, Dr. A. H., 443
Submerged Lands Act of 1953, 226n
Sudler, Mrs. Carroll (Marian), 19
Suez, 240, 280, 309, 381n, 468, 469, 470, 537, 542; White House Conference on, 207; Eisenhower/Dulles and, 294, 310, 312–313, 314, 317,

324, 403, 510; AES speech on, 310–
314. *See also* Egypt; Middle East
Sulzberger, Arthur H.: letter to, 286–
287
Summerfield, Arthur, 485, 517
Summit Conference(s): Geneva, 56n,
294, 313, 317, 319; Berlin, 303;
Potsdam, 405
"Support of Nationalism Helps Combat
Communist Imperialism, The" (AES
article in *Western World*), 473n,
533, 536–544
Supreme Court, U.S.: and school desegregation, 53, 58n, 66–69, 77–79,
100–101, 122–123, 177–179, 255–
256; and "Republican" Chief Justice,
68–69; and security law, 224, 225;
and tidelands issue, 226
Swig, Benjamin H., 396, 417; letters
to, 35, 189, 396–397, 475–476, 535–
536
Symington, Stuart, 207; letter to, 209
Syria, 120n, 353n, 537, 541. *See also*
Middle East

Tachen Islands, 303
Taft, Robert A., 251; –Eisenhower
agreement, 467
Taft, William Howard, 485
Taft-Hartley Act, 137, 307
Tate, Clay: letter to, 130–132
television, 418, 505; AES on campaign
uses of, 38, 70, 76, 108, 143, 163,
280, 482; AES and appearances on,
97, 121, 140–144 *passim*, 177, 215,
228, 278, 281, 309, 310, 321, 325;
"spot" movies for, 203n; Eisenhower
appears on, 294, 300, 313, 482; AES
supporters appear on, 323n, 368;
AES declines suggested series, 379;
and recording of Convention highlights, 384; and equal time, 389, 390.
See also communications, mass
Tempelsman, Maurice, 503–504
Tennessee Valley Authority, 216, 217,
241, 251, 267, 268
Texas, 147, 208, 226, 345, 379, 457n
Thayer, Joan (Mrs. Harry), 512; letter
to, 221
"This I Believe" (Stevenson), 41
This Week magazine: AES article in,
91n
Thoreau, Henry David: quoted, 158
Thucydides, 335
tidelands oil issue, 36, 226

Tilden, Louis E., 528
Till, Emmett, 22
Tillett, Mrs. Charles, 139
Time magazine, 158, 209, 258, 341,
481, 483, 497
Times Literary Supplement (London),
37
Tito, Marshal Josip Broz, 314, 530
Todd, Michael: letter to, 510–511
Togoland, 543
Tojo, General Hideki, 216
Toynbee, Arnold, 61, 65
Treasury Department, U.S., 140, 269,
459
Treat, Robert S.: letter to, 512
Tree, Marietta (Mrs. Ronald), 76, 299,
374, 413, 452, 455, 459n, 477, 488,
490, 500, 503; letters to, 94, 474–
475, 495–496, 511
Tree, Ronald, 76, 452, 455, 459n, 477,
487, 488, 490, 500, 503; letters to,
94, 495–496, 511
Tri Partite Declaration. *See* United Nations
Truman, Harry S, 3, 108, 166, 266,
299, 331n, 378, 405n, 484, 526, 527;
and support for AES, 28, 43, 172,
180, 183, 193, 263, 330; and overseas trip, 42; and foreign policy, 112–
113, 318; leadership of, 124, 126,
251, 253, 318; *Years of Trial and
Hope*, 165; letter of congratulation to
AES, 191–192; and segregation, 254,
255; and Democratic Advisory Council, 374
  LETTERS AND TELEGRAMS TO: 134,
172, 192, 227, 330–331, 450, 525;
on his trip abroad, 30–31, 43; on
his memoirs and 1952 campaign,
35–37, 165
Truman, Mrs. Harry S, 42, 134, 183,
227
Truman Doctrine, 112, 318, 483
Tubby, Roger, 3, 14, 199, 409; letter
to, 383
Tucci, Niccolo, 420; letter to, 420
Tufts, Robert, 85, 199, 388; letter to,
389
Tunisia, 537, 540, 543
Turkey, 112, 113, 318, 353n, 470
Turner, Justin G., 437; letter to, 437–
438
Turner, Roy, 147
TVA. *See* Tennessee Valley Authority
"Twenty Years of Treason," 68, 124